Handbook of Research on Sustainable Supply Chain Management for the Global Economy

Ulas Akkucuk
Boğaziçi University, Turkey

IGI Global
PUBLISHER of TIMELY KNOWLEDGE

A volume in the Advances in Logistics, Operations, and Management Science (ALOMS) Book Series

Published in the United States of America by
IGI Global
Business Science Reference (an imprint of IGI Global)
701 E. Chocolate Avenue
Hershey PA, USA 17033
Tel: 717-533-8845
Fax: 717-533-8661
E-mail: cust@igi-global.com
Web site: http://www.igi-global.com

Library of Congress Cataloging-in-Publication Data

Names: Akkucuk, Ulas, 1975- editor.
Title: Handbook of research on sustainable supply chain management for the global economy / Ulas Akkucuk, editor.
Description: Hershey, PA : Business Science Reference, [2020] | Includes bibliographical references and index. | Summary: "This book discusses the incorporation of sustainability in various facets of business management"-- Provided by publisher.
Identifiers: LCCN 2020000283 (print) | LCCN 2020000284 (ebook) | ISBN 9781799846017 (hardcover) | ISBN 9781799846024 (ebook)
Subjects: LCSH: Business logistics--Environmental aspects. | Industrial management--Environmental aspects.
Classification: LCC HD38.5 .H35575 2020 (print) | LCC HD38.5 (ebook) | DDC 658.7--dc23
LC record available at https://lccn.loc.gov/2020000283
LC ebook record available at https://lccn.loc.gov/2020000284

This book is published in the IGI Global book series Advances in Logistics, Operations, and Management Science (ALOMS) (ISSN: 2327-350X; eISSN: 2327-3518)

British Cataloguing in Publication Data
A Cataloguing in Publication record for this book is available from the British Library.

All work contributed to this book is new, previously-unpublished material. The views expressed in this book are those of the authors, but not necessarily of the publisher.

For electronic access to this publication, please contact: eresources@igi-global.com.

Advances in Logistics, Operations, and Management Science (ALOMS) Book Series

John Wang
Montclair State University, USA

ISSN:2327-350X
EISSN:2327-3518

Mission

Operations research and management science continue to influence business processes, administration, and management information systems, particularly in covering the application methods for decision-making processes. New case studies and applications on management science, operations management, social sciences, and other behavioral sciences have been incorporated into business and organizations real-world objectives.

The **Advances in Logistics, Operations, and Management Science** (ALOMS) Book Series provides a collection of reference publications on the current trends, applications, theories, and practices in the management science field. Providing relevant and current research, this series and its individual publications would be useful for academics, researchers, scholars, and practitioners interested in improving decision making models and business functions.

Coverage

- Risk Management
- Political Science
- Operations Management
- Networks
- Services management
- Information Management
- Decision analysis and decision support
- Organizational Behavior
- Production Management
- Marketing engineering

IGI Global is currently accepting manuscripts for publication within this series. To submit a proposal for a volume in this series, please contact our Acquisition Editors at Acquisitions@igi-global.com or visit: http://www.igi-global.com/publish/.

The Advances in Logistics, Operations, and Management Science (ALOMS) Book Series (ISSN 2327-350X) is published by IGI Global, 701 E. Chocolate Avenue, Hershey, PA 17033-1240, USA, www.igi-global.com. This series is composed of titles available for purchase individually; each title is edited to be contextually exclusive from any other title within the series. For pricing and ordering information please visit http://www.igi-global.com/book-series/advances-logistics-operations-management-science/37170. Postmaster: Send all address changes to above address.

Titles in this Series

For a list of additional titles in this series, please visit:
https://www.igi-global.com/book-series/advances-logistics-operations-management-science/37170

Managerial Issues in Digital Transformation of Global Modern Corporations
Thangasamy Esakki (Poompuhar College (Autonomous), India)
Business Science Reference • © 2020 • 270pp • H/C (ISBN: 9781799824022) • US $195.00

Contemporary Approaches to Military Operations Research
Mumtaz Karatas (National Defense University, Turkey) and Hakan Tozan (Istanbul Medipol University, Turkey)
Information Science Reference • © 2020 • 300pp • H/C (ISBN: 9781799844051) • US $195.00

Legal, Safety, and Environmental Challenges for Event Management Emerging Research and Opportunities
Vipin Nadda (University of Sunderland, London, UK) Ian Arnott (University of Westminster, London, UK) and Wendy Sealy (University of Chichester, UK)
Business Science Reference • © 2020 • 158pp • H/C (ISBN: 9781799832300) • US $195.00

Multi-Criteria Decision Analysis in Management
Abhishek Behl (Indian Institute of Technology, Bombay, India)
Business Science Reference • © 2020 • 422pp • H/C (ISBN: 9781799822165) • US $245.00

Handbook of Research on Project Management Strategies and Tools for Organizational Success
Nelson Antonio Moreno-Monsalve (Universidad EAN, Colombia) H. Mauricio Diez-Silva (Universidad EAN, Colombia) Flor Nancy Diaz-Piraquive (Universidad Catolica de Colombia, Colombia) and Rafael Ignacio Perez-Uribe (Universidad EAN, Colombia)
Business Science Reference • © 2020 • 537pp • H/C (ISBN: 9781799819349) • US $285.00

Advancing Skill Development for Business Managers in Industry 4.0 Emerging Research and Opportunities
Sara Fazzin (H-Farm College, UK)
Business Science Reference • © 2020 • 168pp • H/C (ISBN: 9781799820369) • US $185.00

Management and Inter/Intra Organizational Relationships in the Textile and Apparel Industry
Vasilica-Maria Margalina (Technical University of Ambato, Ecuador) and José M. Lavín (CESINE University Centre, Spain)
Business Science Reference • © 2020 • 427pp • H/C (ISBN: 9781799818595) • US $215.00

Neutrosophic Sets in Decision Analysis and Operations Research
Mohamed Abdel-Basset (Zagazig University, Egypt) and Florentin Smarandache (University of New Mexico, USA)
Engineering Science Reference • © 2020 • 470pp • H/C (ISBN: 9781799825555) • US $245.00

IGI Global
PUBLISHER of TIMELY KNOWLEDGE

701 East Chocolate Avenue, Hershey, PA 17033, USA
Tel: 717-533-8845 x100 • Fax: 717-533-8661
E-Mail: cust@igi-global.com • www.igi-global.com

List of Contributors

Table of Contents

Detailed Table of Contents

This chapter presents a decision support tool that can be used to evaluate the level of carbon emission and duration of delivery time for alternative distribution systems charged with just-in-time product delivery. An Excel-based transportation model is solved using linear programming to model transport truck carbon emissions and delivery time for a product landed at seaports in the United States and transported to meet customer demand at inland locations under stochastic demand conditions. The alternative network designs examined provide insights as to the viability of the optimal network design as determined by the transportation model. The model is illustrated using simulated demand scenarios and the robustness of the solution methodology is examined using a sensitivity analysis.

This study aims to understand the negative impacts of carbon emission on the foreign direct investments. For this purpose, a comparative analysis is performed for both E7 and G7 countries. In the analysis process, Pedroni panel cointegration (PPC), Kao panel cointegration (KPC), and Dumitrescu Hurlin panel causality (DHPC) analyses are taken into consideration. The findings indicate that carbon emission has a negative influence on foreign direct investments for both country groups. Nonetheless, this relationship is stronger for G7 economies. It is also identified that there is no causality relationship between these variables. It is recommended that the countries should generate appropriate policies to minimize carbon emission problem. Within this context, new tax can be implemented for the companies that lead to high carbon emission. Additionally, governments can give incentives to the projects that aim to decrease carbon emission. In this scope, decreasing tax ratio and providing a technical support can be given as examples.

Malaysia and Indonesia have been the main sources of supply for palm oil (PO), palm kernel oil (PKO), and other palm-related derivatives for most multi-national companies (MNCs). However, deforestation, new legislation in Europe, and stakeholder expectations have posed significant challenges to this industry. In response to these challenges, companies are looking at driving key sustainability initiatives in palm oil supply chains while remaining beneficial to the farmers. This chapter discusses the findings of a collaborative research project conducted through active academic-industry collaboration in South East Asia and shares an approach to identify and incorporate traceability within the supply chain. Critically, it also aims to provide a framework for both academicians and practitioners towards developing a collaborative approach of driving sustainability goals in difficult to measure parts of the supply chain. Importantly, this work also highlights the key aspects of implementing sustainability practices in the upstream palm oil supply chains, which are often ignored.

The market development and globalization requires for every organization to seek assurance in its supply chain in order to ensure that the products manufactured meet the requirements. Production quality is considered as a socio-economic category and is perceived as an aggregation of properties and features that are to satisfy the ever-growing customer needs and requirements in terms of consumption. Health insurance of all food consumers target groups is the basis of the global food safety policies. The goal of the present study is to analyze the requirements of ISO 9001:2015 and ISO 22000:2018 standards for food quality and safety management systems and thus identify the opportunities for a unified approach towards an integrated management to be implemented through risk-based thinking at all management levels. It is necessary for the assurance of food safety; it being the most important element of quality, to be perceived as an essential part of all management activities.

Millions of people in Africa require sufficient food for healthy living. However, inefficient farming practices are making a lot more people hungry and poor. Simultaneously, the population keeps on increasing. The legitimate question that this study seeks to address is how the production capacity can meet the needs of the increasing population in the future. The chapter examines the increase in population growth and its consequences on food production with the consideration of the theory of population growth by Thomas Malthus. The result of time series data analyzed shows that population growth is increasing at a high rate whereas food production growth is increasing at a decreasing rate. The trend seems to confirm that the Malthus population theory is still relevant in Africa. The study recommends that stewards and

Preface

Many fields are beginning to implement developing practices that prove to be more efficient and environmentally friendly compared to traditional practices. This holds true for the realm of business, as organizations are redesigning their operations through the incorporation of sustainable methods. Research is needed on the specific techniques companies are using to promote efficiency and improved effectiveness using sustainability.

Handbook of Research on Sustainable Supply Chain Management for the Global Economy is an essential reference source that discusses the incorporation of sustainability in various facets of business management. Featuring research on topics such as disruptive logistics, production planning, and renewable energy sources, this book is ideally designed for researchers, practitioners, students, managers, policymakers, academicians, economists, scholars, and educators seeking coverage on sustainable practices in supply chains to ensure a cleaner environment.

The many academic areas covered in this publication include:

- Carbon Emissions
- Digital Transformation
- Disruptive Logistics
- E-Commerce
- Green Supply Chains
- Life Cycle Costing
- Multi-Criteria Decision Making
- Smart Cities
- Quality Management
- Renewable Energy Sources

I am very happy to finalize the eighth book project I realized with IGI Global. I gave the first book proposal to IGI Global in the summer of 2013. This first book was finalized towards fall 2014 and published as hard copy in January 2015. This publication included 28 contributions. It has been nearly five years since the release. Later it also enjoyed Web of Science indexation. Sustainable development over the years has enjoyed ever more attention in the academic community. As a result I decided to pursue other book projects with similar titles. This last book contains 18 valuable contributions from eminent authors from different countries. The countries include Turkey, Malaysia, Russia, USA, Spain, Saudi Arabia, Republic of Serbia, Bulgaria and Czechia.

Chapter 1 starts the discussion with an excellent analytical paper entitled "Modeling Carbon Emissions of Alternative Distribution Network Designs for Seaport to Demand Center Just in Time Delivery". This paper presents a decision support tool that can be used to evaluate the level of carbon emission and duration of delivery time for alternative distribution systems charged with Just-in-Time product delivery. An Excel-based transportation model is solved using linear programming to model transport truck carbon emissions and delivery time for a product landed at seaports in the United States and transported to meet customer demand at inland locations under stochastic demand conditions. The alternative network designs examined provide insights as to the viability of the optimal network design as determined by the transportation model. The model is illustrated using simulated demand scenarios and the robustness of the solution methodology is examined using a sensitivity analysis. This paper is important as it presents a case of using software and simulation in order to minimize the greenhouse gas emissions.

Chapter 2 is about "The Negative Effects of Carbon Emission on FDI". This study aims to understand the negative impacts of carbon emission on the foreign direct investments. For this purpose, a comparative analysis is performed for both E7 and G7 countries. In the analysis process, Pedroni panel cointegration (PPC), Kao panel cointegration (KPC) and Dumitrescu Hurlin panel causality (DHPC) analyses are taken into consideration. The findings indicate that carbon emission has a negative influence on foreign direct investments for both country groups. Nonetheless, this relationship is stronger for G7 economies. It is also identified that there is no causality relationship between these variables. It is recommended that the countries should generate appropriate policies to minimize carbon emission problem. Within this context, new tax can be implemented for the companies that lead to high carbon emission. Additionally, governments can give incentives to the projects that aim to decrease carbon emission. In this scope, decreasing tax ratio and providing a technical support can be given as examples. This paper implies that by reducing carbon emissions countries will also be able to increase the level of Foreign Direct Investment.

Chapter 3 investigates "The New Concept of Logistics Platforms 4.0". This chapter aims to address a review of the new concept of logistics platform 4.0 for the improvement of global competitiveness, which is supported, within the scope of Global Sustainable Logistics, in the development of the new Omnichannel and Synchromodality Logistics 4.0, and the Global Value Networks driven by intra-industrial trade. The development of the new logistics platforms 4.0 induces public-private actions that lead to a new territorial planning and integration of routes, corridors, logistics centres and commercial areas, in which the metropolitan area stands out as a main actor, leading to the creation of chains of connected and intelligent logistics platforms worldwide. The new urban logistics, which is more effective and efficient, is analyzed as an essential vector for the development of the new logistics platforms. Likewise, the most important logistic problems and metropolitan restrictions that arise for the development of more sustainable and intelligent cities, and the applicable concept of aerotropolis are analyzed.

Chapter 4 is a discussion on "Evaluating E-Commerce-Related Distribution and Warehousing in Terms of Sustainability". In this chapter, the relationships between logistics operations and e-commerce are investigated. The logistics operations are discussed under the distribution and warehousing subjects. The effects of e-commerce on these activities are analyzed by considering the social, environmental and economic dimensions of sustainability in a broad perspective. For evaluating distribution of e-commerce products, current last-mile operations, trends and future expectations are investigated in the sustainability concept. Furthermore, the effects of e-commerce on warehouse types and operations are presented. Besides that, location and layout of warehouses, materials used in warehouse buildings and material handling equipment are discussed with a sustainability perspective.

Chapter 5 focuses on "Disruptive Logistics and Green Supply Chain Management". Today, when global warming and its negative effects are more apparent, companies and individuals have given importance to green logistics practices. At the same time, computer technologies and smart applications serve in this field, new and innovative ideas are emerging every other day. Examples of disruptive innovation can change the way we do business in an industry, such as the Uber application. These new players in the sector tend to disengage the existing players. In this article, sector-changing national and international instances of disruptive logistics will be presented and discussed. Also the effects of Industry 4.0 and smart cities on green logistics will be explained.

Chapter 6 is another look at the importance of "The Role of Technology Level and Logistics Performance on the Relationship Between Logistics Service Quality and Firm Performance". The main purpose of this study is to examine the relationship between logistics service quality, logistics performance, firm performance, and technology. Survey data, which was collected from 572 industrial consumers operating in Turkey by stratified sampling method, were analyzed and compared by factor analysis and SEM. According to the results of the analysis, the data indicate that the quality of logistic service affects logistic performance and firm performance positively and directly. Also, it is clear from the results that the mediation role of logistic performance and its indirect impact are important in the effect of logistic service quality on firm performance. In the effect of the quality of logistic performance on firm performance, it is understood that the role of technology in moderation. It is also stated that when the moderation role of technology in the logistic service quality affects firm performance, logistic performance has also the mediation role.

Chapter 7 examines "The Role of Technological Development on Renewable Energy Usage". The aim of this study is to determine the relationship between technological development and renewable energy use. Within this framework, G7 countries were included in the scope of the review. Data for the countries in question between 1990 and 2015 were used. In order to determine the relationship between these two variables, Pedroni panel cointegration analysis was utilized. As a result, it has been determined that technological development is very effective in the use of renewable energy. Therefore, countries need to improve themselves technologically in order to increase the use of renewable energy. It is very important to have technological infrastructure in renewable energy investments. Hence, technological investments should have the priority in order to increase the use of renewable energy. With the help of this issue, it can be more possible to be successful in this kind of investments

Chapter 8 focuses on "How Supply Chain Management Will Change in the Industry 4.0 Era?" Enabled by some maturated technologies in the last decades, a new industrial revolution is predicted to arise which not only affects manufacturing or industry, but many fields of life. It is named as Fourth Industrial Revolution or Industry 4.0. The triggering technologies, concepts or driving forces mentioned with Industry 4.0 are; Cyber-Physical Systems, Vertical and Horizontal Integration, Augmented Reality, Internet of Things, Internet of Services, Additive Manufacturing and 3D Printers, Big Data Analytics, Cloud Computing, Cybersecurity. Through Industry 4.0, production activities will be made by automatic machines and robot communicating each other. Supply chains will be more integrated due to information and communication technologies based on real time data sharing. The purpose of this study is to examine the effects of Industry 4.0 on supply chain management. For this purpose literature is reviewed according to effects of Industry 4.0 on procurement, production, warehousing, transportation and fulfillment functions of supply chain management.

Chapter 9 illustrates the "Recycling Technologies for Sustainability". Technology is improving every day in each aspects of daily life. This will help us to increase the sustainability rates and efficiency of recycling. In fact, waste generation is an indicator of economic activities by maintaining production output and also supplying many jobs. However, the treatment methods should also improve as the types and quantities of the wastes increase. There are many recycling technologies that are already serving to mankind, however the types of the wastes are changing everyday with composite materials. These types of "not only one origin" composite wastes make it difficult to recycle by the conventional methods. There are huge differences in the types of wastes discarded by different types of industries, that makes the situation more complicated. Conventional methods are no longer enough to treat and recycle all types of wastes. This chapter will discuss recent improvements and technologies about increasing the recycling rate without causing environmental impact.

Chapter 10 is a study on "Sustainable Supply Chain Management and Total Quality Management in the Health Sector Supply" system in health sector determines effective stock management, regular material supply, speed and quality of maintenance and service process. Elimination of all non-value-adding activities, movements and processes in the procurement process, minimizing errors, and increasing the efficiency of the process between the inputs and outputs of the hospital is possible by applying total quality in supply management. Effective supply chain management in health institutions improves the quality of health care.

Chapter 11 provides examples on "Barriers to Green Supply Chain Management Implementation". The statistical analysis of the data obtained by the survey method was performed with SPSS 22.0 program. According to the findings of the research; The most important barriers in the implementation of green supply chain management are green "projects with high investment costs in construction, changing facilities and equipment, as well as the international crisis and economic downturn. These barriers are; raw material costs are higher in "green" applications, green "projects have high operating costs, high prices in" green "applications unable to compete with lower prices of competitors, respectively. Another finding of the study; The area of activity of the company is that there is no significant difference between the implementation status of the "green" projects and the duration of the export activity on the barriers encountered in the implementation of GSCM.

Chapter 12 performs an analysis of "Ensuring the Relevance of Independent Smallholder Farmers (ISHFs) Through Sustainable Sourcing Practices". Malaysia and Indonesia have been the main source of supply for Palm Oil (PO), Palm Kernel Oil (PKO) and other palm related derivatives for most Multi-National Companies (MNCs). However, deforestation, new legislation in Europe and stakeholder expectations have posed significant challenges to this industry. In response to these challenges, companies are looking at driving key sustainability initiatives in palm oil supply chains while remaining beneficial to the farmers. This chapter discusses the findings of a collaborative research project conducted through active academic-industry collaboration in South East Asia and shares an approach to identify and incorporate traceability within the supply chain. Critically, it also aims to provide a framework for both academicians and practitioners towards developing a collaborative approach of driving sustainability goals in difficult to measure parts of the supply chain. Importantly, this work also highlights the key aspects of implementing sustainability practices in the upstream palm oil supply chains which are often ignored.

Chapter 13 explores the "Unified Approach to Integrated Food Quality and Safety Management". The market development and globalization requires for every organization to seek assurance in its supply chain in order to ensure that the products manufactured meet the requirements. Production quality is considered as a socio-economic category and is perceived as an aggregation of properties and features that are to satisfy the ever-growing customer needs and requirements in terms of consumption. Health insurance of all food consumers target groups is the basis of the global food safety policies. The goal of the present study is to analyze the requirements of ISO 9001:2015 and ISO 22000:2018 standards for food quality and safety management systems and thus identify the opportunities for a unified approach towards an integrated management to be implemented through risk-based thinking at all management levels. It is necessary for the assurance of food safety, it being the most important element of quality, to be perceived as an essential part of all management activities.

Chapter 14 explains "A Comparison of Population Growth Rate and the Rate of Increase in Food Crop Production in Africa". Millions of people in Africa require sufficient food for healthy living. However, inefficient farming practices are making a lot more people hungry and poor. Simultaneously, the population keeps on increasing. The legitimate question that this study seeks to address is how the production capacity can meet the needs of the increasing population in the future. The paper examines the increase in population growth and its consequences on food production with the consideration of the theory of population growth by Thomas Malthus. The result of time series data analyzed shows that population growth is increasing at a high rate whereas food production growth is increasing at a decreasing rate. The trend seems to confirm that the Malthus population theory is still relevant in Africa. The study recommends that stewards and policymakers invest immensely in agriculture to improve technology, skills, methods, and know-how to boost food production and invest in women in adopting family planning to decrease population growth for the solution of food deficiency.

Chapter 15 is on "Behavioral Economics". The idea of the significance of the psychological dimension of human behavior is not new and has existed in the social sciences since ancient times. Accordingly, there is an endeavor to place economic analysis on the foundations of psychological research, which takes its form of expression in economic theory through the affirmation of behavioral economics. The aim of this chapter is to critically analyze various normative research programs in behavioral economics and to consider the importance of alternative concepts, models and theories from the point of view of improving understanding of real economic and social behavior. The particular value of this chapter lies in affirming the importance of a program of behavioral economics known as new paternalism, which is based on challenging the concept of maximizing rationality and opens a new dimension of understanding the justification of state interference in the sphere of economy and society.

Chapter 16 is on "Ethics in Management: Ethical Leadership and Culture". Chapter 17 is about "Supervising System and Business Control of Local Self-Government Units in Performance Audit Function". Chapter 18 explains "Digitalization of the Development of the Fuel and Energy Balance of Russia's Northern Territories: Example of the Republic of Sakha (Yakutia)".

Ulaş Akküçük
Boğaziçi University, Turkey
March 2020

Chapter 1

Modeling Carbon Emissions of Alternative Distribution Network Designs for Seaport to Demand Center Just in Time Delivery

Alfred L. Guiffrida
Kent State University, USA

Heather L. Lincecum
Kent State University, USA

Kelly McQuade
Kent State University, USA

ABSTRACT

This chapter presents a decision support tool that can be used to evaluate the level of carbon emission and duration of delivery time for alternative distribution systems charged with just-in-time product delivery. An Excel-based transportation model is solved using linear programming to model transport truck carbon emissions and delivery time for a product landed at seaports in the United States and transported to meet customer demand at inland locations under stochastic demand conditions. The alternative network designs examined provide insights as to the viability of the optimal network design as determined by the transportation model. The model is illustrated using simulated demand scenarios and the robustness of the solution methodology is examined using a sensitivity analysis.

INTRODUCTION

In today's highly competitive marketplace, the success of many companies is highly dependent on the ability to implement a viable business strategy across a global supply chain. Managing a global supply chain is characterized by decisions involving offshoring and onshoring of manufacturing and sourcing, intermodal transportation, and intra and intercompany operations across different business cultures. A

DOI: 10.4018/978-1-7998-4601-7.ch001

global supply chain can lead to lower production and procurement costs, access to technological innovation and entry into new markets. Challenges that face supply chains such as risk, quality, and delivery timeliness are typically intensified for global supply chains (Inman & Bhaskaran, 2019; Golini, Caniato, & Kalchschmidt, 2016; Manuj & Mentzer, 2008). As a result of this enhanced risk it is essential that companies follow best practices in the management of their global supply chains.

Over the past few decades, the adoption and implementation of green and sustainable practices have become a key concern and initiative for many businesses. A major component of this concern has focused on the carbon footprint associated with acquiring raw materials, production processes which transform raw materials into finished products, and the logistics system which delivers the products to customers. In response to environmental issues and market pressures to operate green and sustainable enterprises, many businesses have embraced a triple bottom line strategic orientation whereby economic performance is interlinked with environmental stewardship and social performance (Elkington,1998). By integrating economic, environmental and social performance in overall business strategy, modern day supply chains have transitioned into green supply chains (Srivastava, 2007). Performance measurement, which is integral to the management and control of global supply chain operations, has been expanded in scope for green supply chains. Guidelines for establishing performance measurement frameworks and metrics in green supply chains are addressed by Ahi & Searcy (2015), Beske & Seuring (2014) and Hassini, Surti, & Searcy (2012).

The logistics and last mile product delivery function has been identified as being one of the most polluting segments of the overall supply chain (Ülkü, 2012; Gevaers, Van de Voorde, & Vanelslander, 2011) and is highly dependent on the effective management of fuel costs and carbon emissions (Gurtu, 2019; Bouchard, 2015; Gurtu, Jaber, & Searcy, 2015, Gourdin, 2006). The dominant mode of freight movement in the U.S. is by road and transport truck emissions, which contribute significantly to the nation's carbon footprint, are projected to increase. As a result of economic growth, transport truck vehicle miles traveled in the U.S. are predicted to increase by 52% from 397 billion miles in 2018 to 601 billion miles in 2050 (Annual Energy Outlook 2019, p. 120).

Improving logistics activities to reduce carbon emissions has become an important aspect of managing green supply chains (see for example, Ellram & Murfield, 2017; Abbasi & Nilsson, 2016; Adenso-Díaz, Lozano, & Moreno 2016). Ren, Hu, Dong, Sun, Chen, & Chen, (2020) present a comprehensive review of sustainable logistics. Transport mode specific reviews of sustainable logistics include: (i) roadways (Demir, Bektaş, & Laporte, 2014), (ii) railways (Aditjandra, Zunder, Islam, & Palacin, 2016), (iii) maritime (Davarzani, Fahimnia, Bell, & Sarkis, 2015), (iv) air (Teoh & Khoo, 2016), and (v) intermodal (Roso, 2013). Opportunities for improving the environmental impact from a given mode of transport exist and can be achieved by investigating alternative design structures of the logistic function (Kelle, Song, Jin, Schneider, & Claypool, 2019; Aronsson & Brodin, 2006).

BACKGROUND

With the value of global digital commerce sales worldwide predicted to be over $6 trillion by 2022 (McKee, 2018), the scope of product movement in global supply chains is staggering. Managing the movement of products from their point of manufacture or interim storage location to the final customer is fundamental in the operation of a global supply chain. Beginning with the pioneering work of Hitchcock (1941) who mathematically modeled the movement of goods from "origins" to "destinations", a vast amount of research has contributed decision models for designing supply chains and distribution networks for transporting products to meet customer demand. Comprehensive literature reviews on models for designing supply chains and distribution networks are found in Nasiri & Jolai (2018), Farahani, Rezapour, Drezner, & Fallah, (2014), Fahimnia, Farahani, Marian, & Luong (2013) and Meixell & Gargeya (2005). In a recent editorial, Gonzalez, Sarkis, Huisingh, Huatuco, Maculan, Montoya-Torres, & De Almeida, (2015) emphasized the need and importance of using models to help support the transition to a green supply chain. For a gateway into the use of models in green supply chain management, the reader is referred to the review papers of Barbosa-Póvoa, da Silva, & Carvalho (2017), Eskandarpour, Dejax, Miemczyk, & Péton (2015), Brandenburg, Govindan, Sarkis, & Seuring, (2014) and Dekker, Bloemhof, & Mallidis (2012).

In this chapter, we investigate and model the carbon emissions and delivery timeliness for a product landed at seaports in the U.S. and delivered to inland customer demand locations using transport trucks. The novel features of the model reported herein focus on the requirement that the product be delivered to meet customer demand on a "Just-in-Time" (JIT) basis and the use of twenty-foot equivalent unit (TEU) shipping containers as the unit measure of product demand. The amount of transport truck carbon emissions (CO_2) and the total delivery time to the final customer is modeled and evaluated for alternative designs of a supply chain distribution network that facilitates JIT product delivery from seaports to inland demand locations. Figure 1 illustrates a generic representation of the seaport to inland demand destination supply chain network design problem under study.

Figure 1. Generic illustration of seaport to inland demand city model

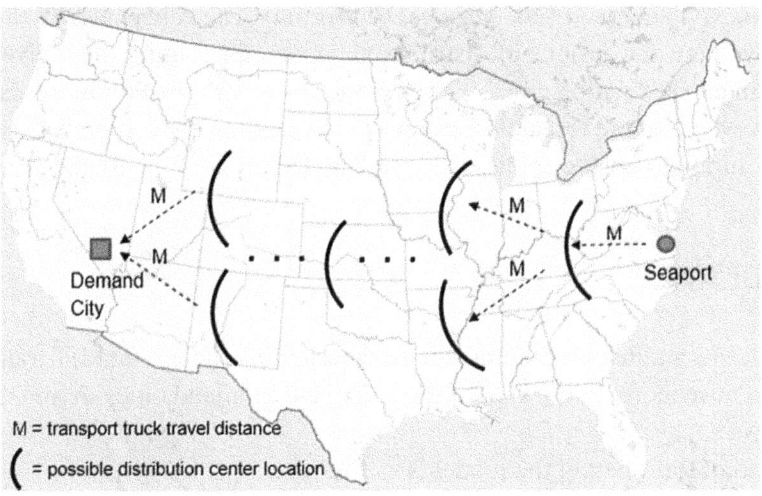

Our study of this seaport to demand city carbon emission and delivery problem aligns with two current streams of research that identify the importance of quantifying the level of carbon emissions and the timeliness of product delivery in the design of supply chain distribution networks. As a gateway into these two streams of literature the reader is referred to the following two sets of representative studies. The selected studies which are identified are not meant be exhaustive and are intended to provide the reader with a foundation for the seaport to inland demand destination model advanced in this chapter.

The importance of carbon emissions in the design of supply chain distribution networks has been addressed by Manupati, Jedidah, Gupta, Bhandari, & Ramkumar (2019), Memari, Rahim, Ahmad, & Hassan (2016), Eskandarpour, Dejax, Miemczyk, & Péton, (2015), Elhedhli & Merrick (2012) and Chaabane, Ramudhin, & Paquet (2012). The importance of delivery performance in the design of supply chain distribution networks has been addressed by Jiang, Zhou, & Xu (2019), Wu & Barnes (2018), Wang, Gunasekaran, & Ngai, (2018), Klibi, Martel, & Guitouni, (2010) and Pan & Nagi (2010).

The literature on the impact of carbon emissions and delivery timeliness in supply chain network design are each highly researched; however, modeling efforts which address and integrate both research streams are lacking in that JIT delivery is not considered. The research contributions of this chapter are as follows. First, we contribute a general modeling framework for quantifying the level of carbon emission (CO_2) resulting from product movement in terms of TEU by transport truck from seaports to inland demand locations in the United States under a JIT delivery policy. Second, a spreadsheet platform is used for implementing the modeling framework to provide the model user with the ability to evaluate the carbon footprint and delivery timeliness of alternative network designs. The model framework presented enables efficient consideration of what-if analyses on model parameters such as the stochastic nature of product demand and the available capacity levels of the product.

The rest of this chapter is organized as follows. In the Model Formulation section, the general seaport to inland demand destination model is formulated as a linear programming-based transportation model. In the Model Illustration section, numerical presentations of the model are demonstrated for a product landed at three east coast U.S. ports (Boston, Massachusetts; Norfolk, Virginia; and Charleston, South Carolina) and transported under a JIT delivery policy by transport trucks to meet demand at seven inland demand destinations (Boise, Idaho; Salt Lake City, Utah; Portland, Oregon; Reno, Nevada; Spokane, Washington; Phoenix, Arizona and Los Angeles, California). The robustness of the model is demonstrated for alternative network designs of distribution centers for routing the delivery transport trucks from seaports to demand destination cities. The chapter closes with the Future Research Directions and Conclusion sections where future research directions on expanding the comprehensiveness of the model are examined and a summary of the applicability and contribution of the model are presented.

MODEL FORMULATION

In this section, we define a transportation model for determining the optimal JIT transport truck routing for a product landed at seaports in the U.S. to meet demand in inland cities to minimize total transport truck CO_2 emissions.

The notation used in formulating the model is as follows:

i = the index of ports where the product is landed (i=1,2,..,n)
j = the index of cities where the product is demanded (j=1,2,…,m)
X_{ij} = the number of TEUs to transport from port i to city j to minimize truck CO_2 emissions
M_{ij} = the truck travel distance (in miles) from port i to city j
K_i = the capacity (as measured in number of TEUs) of port i
D_j = the demand (as measured in number of TEUs) of city j
G=0.000658 = the number of U.S. tons of truck CO_2 emissions per TEU mile (Mathers, Craft, Norsworthy, &, Wolfe, 2020, p.10)

$C_{ij}=GM_{ij}=$ U.S tons of truck CO_2 emissions resulting from transporting one TEU from port i to city j.

The optimization model stated in canonical form is:

$$Minimize \sum_{i=1}^{n}\sum_{j=1}^{m} C_{ij} X_{ij} \tag{1}$$

Subject to:

$$\sum_{j=1}^{m} X_{ij} \leq K_i \left(i = 1, 2, \cdots, n\right) \tag{2}$$

$$\sum_{i=1}^{n} X_{ij} \leq D_j \left(j = 1, 2, \cdots, m\right) \tag{3}$$

$X_{ij} \geq 0\ \forall i, \forall j$

MODEL ILLUSTRATION

We illustrate the model for a product that is imported into the U.S. at three east coast ports and is then delivered to meet customer demand at seven inland cities. The product arrives at the seaports in twenty-foot equivalent unit (TEU) shipping containers (average gross weight of 31,500 pounds, Janic, 2007) and is loaded onto transport trucks at the seaport and routed to the inland demand cities through a network of intermediary distribution centers. The TEU is the basic unit of product demand and product movement. Lot size demand for the product at each inland city is in quantities of TEUs and each transport truck has a transport capacity of one TEU. The locations of the seaports, distribution centers and demand destination cities used in the model illustration and the total travel distance from each seaport to each demand city are defined in Table 1. The routes and travel distances presented in Table 1 are specific to the seaports, distributions centers and demand cities defined in the model illustration. The model presented is clearly generalizable to different locations and numbers of seaports, distribution centers and demand cities.

Table 1 is interpreted as follows. For example, a transport truck loaded at the Boston seaport and bound for JIT delivery to Boise is routed through three distribution centers (Cleveland, Des Moines, and Laramie) and travels a total distances of 2,674 miles (639 miles from Boston to Cleveland, 668 miles from Cleveland to Des Moines, 682 miles from Des Moines to Laramie and 685 miles from Laramie to Boise). Transport truck travel distances were determined using Google Maps from the addresses of the Boston, Norfolk and Charleston seaports and existing transport truck distribution centers located in the hub cities.

The distribution centers defined in Table 1 for each seaport-demand city pair define the network routes that transport trucks follow. The cities selected for the distribution centers which serve as the intermediary hubs for each route were selected based on three criteria. First, the transport truck driver

Table 1. Seaports, distribution centers, demand cities and distances used in model illustration

Demand City	Seaport		
	Boston, MA	**Charleston, SC**	**Norfolk, VA**
Boise, ID	Cleveland, OH Des Moines, IA Laramie, WY (2,674 miles)	Paducah, KY Lincoln, NB Rock Springs, WY (2,475 miles)	Louisville, KY Lincoln, NB Rock Springs, WY (2,539 miles)
Salt Lake City, UT	Cleveland, OH Des Moines, IA Laramie, WY (2,379 miles)	Paducah, KY Lincoln, NB Rock Springs, WY (2,475 miles)	Louisville, KY Lincoln, NB Rock Springs, WY (2,539 miles)
Portland, OR	Cleveland, OH Des Moines, IA Laramie, WY Boise, ID (3,104 miles)	Paducah, KY Lincoln, NB Rock Springs, WY La Grande, OR (2,904 miles)	Louisville, KY Lincoln, NB Rock Springs, WY La Grande, OR (2,968 miles)
Reno, NV	Cleveland, OH Des Moines, IA Laramie, WY Carlin, NV (2,896 miles)	Paducah, KY Lincoln, NB Rock Springs, WY (2,695 miles)	Louisville, KY Lincoln, NB Rock Springs, WY (2,759 miles)
Spokane, WA	Cleveland, OH Rochester, MN Rapid City, SD Missoula, MT (2,765 miles)	Paducah, KY Omaha, NE Rapid City, SD Missoula, MT (2,677 miles)	Maumee, OH Rochester, MN Rapid City, SD Missoula, MT (2,663 miles)
Phoenix, AZ	Roanoke, VA Nashville, TN Oklahoma City, OK Albuquerque, NM (2,766 miles)	Memphis, TN Oklahoma City, OK Albuquerque, NM (2,119 miles)	Nashville, TN Oklahoma City, OK Albuquerque, NM (2,346 miles)
Los Angeles, CA	Roanoke, VA Nashville, TN Oklahoma City, OK Albuquerque, NM Barstow, CA (3,136 miles)	Memphis, TN Oklahoma City, OK Albuquerque, NM Barstow, CA (2,489 miles)	Nashville, TN Oklahoma City, OK Albuquerque, NM Barstow, CA (2,716 miles)

time between any two sequential locations in a given route could not exceed the federally mandated time limit of 11 hours which limits the between travel distance to a maximum of approximately 700 miles. Second, an existing distribution center capable of servicing transport trucks must exist in the city for the city to be considered. Lastly, each pair of sequential cities in a route must be linked by a highway suitable for transport truck travel.

The distance (mileage) that a transport truck can travel in the U. S. is limited by the number of federally regulated hours that a driver can drive. A driver can drive for 11 hours then must be off the road for 10 hours. During the 11 hours of driving time a transport truck typically can cover approximately 700 miles. In this study we use the 700-mile figure as the maximum mileage that a driver can cover in 11 hours and assume that the driver and transport truck are available according to a 24-hour clock. For example, a driver leaving a location can drive 11 hours (covering a maximum of 700 miles) then that driver must be idle for 10 hours after which the same driver could drive another 11 hours (covering an additional 700 miles), then must be off the road for 10 hours, etc. Assuming a 24 hour clock, a driver can move the product 700 miles every 21 hours if no change is made to the driver. We assume that there is only one driver per truck but that the transport truck can be available 24 hours per day.

Under the JIT delivery policy, we assume a new replacement driver can be assigned to a truck once the truck reaches a distribution center. For example, consider two different drivers (A and B) and one distribution center. Driver A travels 11 hours covering 700 miles and upon arriving at the distribution center that was at the 700-mile mark, driver B can replace driver A and driver B can then immediately drive another 11 hours covering another 700 miles. Thus, using one distribution center and two different drivers, the product can be moved a total of 1,400 miles in 22 hours. We assume that the time required to switch between drivers is negligible and we further assume there is no restriction on the availability of drivers and trucks. From a network perspective each pair of locations identified in Table 1 (seaport to distribution center, distribution center to distribution center and distribution center to final demand city) satisfies the federally mandated requirement of a maximum of 11 hours of drive time (which equates to a maximum of 700 miles travel distance).

As discussed in the chapter Introduction and Background sections, managing CO_2 emissions in the logistics function is a key concern of management and research has demonstrated that the design of the distribution network in a supply chain has a direct impact on the level of CO_2 emissions emitted. Using the model defined herein, we examine the level of CO_2 emissions for four alternative distribution network designs to support JIT product delivery from the seaports to the demand cities identified in Table 1. A transport truck emits 597.4 grams of CO_2 per TEU mile traveled which can be equivalently restated as 0.000658 U.S. tons of CO_2 per TEU mile traveled (Mathers, Craft, Norsworthy, & Wolfe, 2020, p.10). Given the number of TEUs demanded at each demand city (see Table 2) and the total mileage distances for the possible delivery routes (identified in Table 1), the total number of U.S. tons of transport truck CO_2 emissions emitted can be determined for a given network design. The transportation model defined by (1) – (3) can then be parameterized with this data and solved as a linear programming model using the Excel Solver to determine X_{ij}, the optimal number of TEUs to route from seaport i to demand city j to minimize the total tons of CO_2 emitted in meeting all demand.

Stochastic demand was introduced into the model under the assumption that product demand in a given city was normally distributed and independent across all cities. Under the reproductive property of the normal distribution under addition, total product demand across all cities is therefore also normally distributed. As identified in Table 2, three different levels of total product demand were investigated. Per the reproductive property of the normal distribution, the mean and variance of demand per city were equal to one-seventh of the total product demand. Using an Excel-based random number procedure, a specific demand value for each city was sampled from each level of normally distributed total demand and used in the model illustration. Seaport capacity was set to 9,000 TEUs per seaport.

Model Scenarios Investigated

The total number of tons of transport truck CO_2 emitted and the mean and standard deviation of delivery time were calculated for four alternative distribution network designs: Optimal, Boston, Charleston and Norfolk. The Optimal network design is based on the Excel Solver optimization of the transportation model defined by (1) – (3) and determines the optimal number and routing of transport trucks from the three seaports to the seven demand cities to minimize the total tons of transport truck CO_2 emissions. The remaining three network designs each utilize only one seaport to meet the total demand in the seven

Table 2. Total product demand and city demand in TEUs

Total Demand: **Mean** **Standard Deviation**	**1000** **200**	**2000** **400**	**3000** **600**
City:		**Demand Realization:**	
Boise, ID	70	277	511
Salt Lake City, UT	161	163	854
Portland, OR	59	289	495
Reno, NV	209	463	521
Spokane, WA	170	474	737
Phoenix, AZ	79	99	816
Los Angeles, CA	147	338	427

demand cities. All transport trucks routed from a given seaport to a given demand city are routed through the distribution centers identified in Table 1. Representative Excel-based solutions for the Optimal and Boston network designs are presented in Figures 4-6 in the Appendix. Table 3 summaries the total CO_2 emissions and delivery times for the four alternative network designs. Note that the last column of Table 4 identifies the percentage penalty in CO_2 emissions and mean delivery time incurred when not using the Optimal distribution network design to service total demand. Table 4 identifies the number of TEUs transported from each seaport to each demand city when total demand equaled 2,000 TEUs

Examining Table 3 we observe that the Optimal network design resulted in the lowest total number of tons of transport truck CO_2 emissions and the shortest mean delivery time across all three total demand levels. Figure 2 compares the total tons of transport truck CO_2 emissions resulting from the four distribution network designs. Across all three levels of total demand, the lowest total tons of transport truck CO_2 emissions occurred resulted from the Optimal network design which was based on the Excel Solver's linear programming solution of the transportation model. The percentage penalty in total transport truck CO_2 emissions and mean total delivery time for using a non-optimal network design is illustrated in Figure 3 when total demand was normally distributed with a mean of 2000 and a standard deviation was 400. For the set of total demand parameters used, the Optimal network design resulted in less total tons of transport truck CO_2 emissions than the Boston, Charleston and Norfolk network designs. The Optimal network design meets the total demand with the lowest mean total delivery time thus supporting the JIT policy.

As identified by Govindan, Fattahi, and, Keyvanshokooh (2017), and Caris, Macharis, and, Janssens (2013), designing supply chains networks under conditions of uncertainty and the use of decision support systems for managing intermodal transport are important concerns in the management and control of global supply chains. The seaport to demand city modeling approach and supporting spreadsheet solution platform presented in this chapter contribute to satisfying these concerns. For the parameters used, the model determined the network design that resulted in the optimal transport truck routing that minimized the total tons of transport truck CO_2 emissions under the JIT delivery policy thus meeting the environmental and delivery objectives of the decision maker. The spreadsheet modeling platform allows rapid comparisons of alternative network designs and provides the decision maker with the percentage penalties in CO_2 emissions and mean delivery time that result when not using the optimal network design.

Table 3. Summary of CO_2 emissions and delivery times for alternative distribution networks

Network Design	Total TEU Demand Mean	Std Dev	Tons of CO_2	Delivery Time in Hours Mean	Std Dev	Percentage Penalty From Optimal CO_2	Mean Delv
Optimal	1,000	200	1,499	40.0	3.1	0.0%	0.0%
	2,000	400	3,605	40.9	2.9	0.0	0.0
	3,000	600	7,173	39.2	3.8	0.0	0.0
Boston	1,000	200	1,652	44.0	3.9	10.2	10.0
	2,000	400	3,958	44.9	3.4	9.8	9.8
	3,000	600	7,953	43.5	3.8	10.9	11.0
Charleston	1,000	200	1,511	40.3	2.9	0.8	0.7
	2,000	400	3,619	41.1	2.8	0.4	0.5
	3,000	600	7,234	39.6	3.7	0.8	1.0
Norfolk	1,000	200	1,564	41.7	2.3	4.3	4.3
	2,000	400	3,730	42.3	2.3	3.5	3.4
	3,000	600	7,513	41.1	2.9	4.7	4.8

Table 4. Number of TEUs transported from seaport to demand city (total demand = 2,000)

Network Design	Port	City: Boise	Salt Lake	Portland	Reno	Spokane	Phoenix	LA
Optimal	Boston		163					
	Charleston	277		289	463		99	338
	Norfolk					474		
	CO_2 emissions = 3,605 tons Mean delivery time: = 40.9 hours							
Boston	Boston	277	163	289	463	474	99	338
	Charleston							
	Norfolk							
	CO_2 emissions = 3,958 tons Mean delivery time: = 44.9 hours							
Charleston	Boston							
	Charleston	277	163	289	463	474	99	338
	Norfolk							
	CO_2 emissions = 3,619 tons Mean delivery time: = 41.1 hours							
Norfolk	Boston							
	Charleston							
	Norfolk	277	163	289	463	474	99	338
	CO_2 emissions = 3,730 tons Mean delivery time: = 42.3 hours							

For example, in minimizing the total tons of CO_2 transport truck emissions, the Optimal network design required routing transport trucks from the Boston, Charleston and Norfolk seaports to meet demand in the seven inland cities. The nonoptimal Charleston network solution required using only the Charleston seaport and incurred a CO_2 emissions percentage penalty of under 1% across all demand levels studies. A decision maker could use this attribute of the model to assist in making the final decision as to which network design to implement since nonoptimal a single seaport network may in actuality be less risky and less costly to coordinate that an optimal network design that required three seaports.

Figure 2. CO_2 Emissions levels for alternative network designs

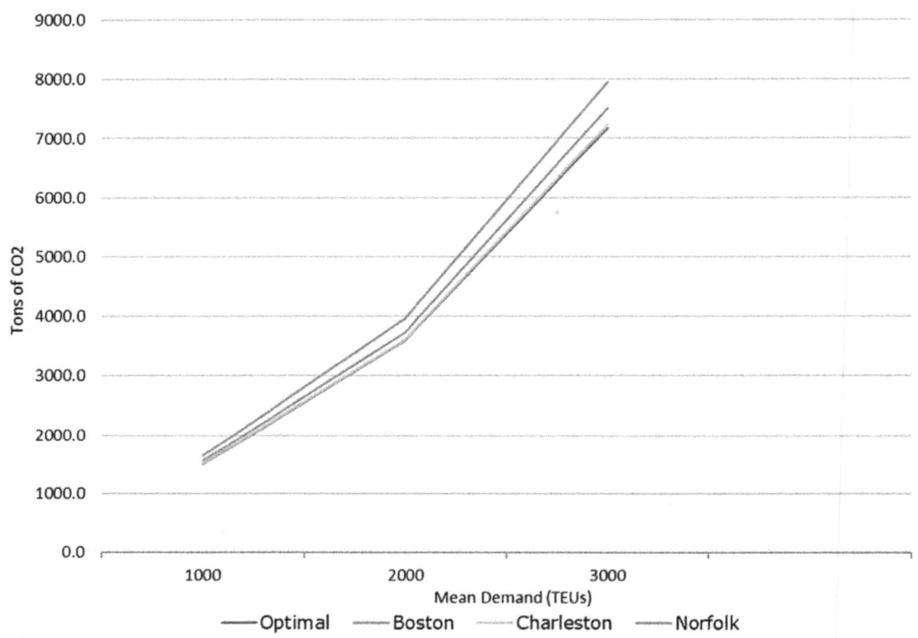

Figure 3. Percentage penalty from Optimal Network Design (total demand = 2000 TEUs)

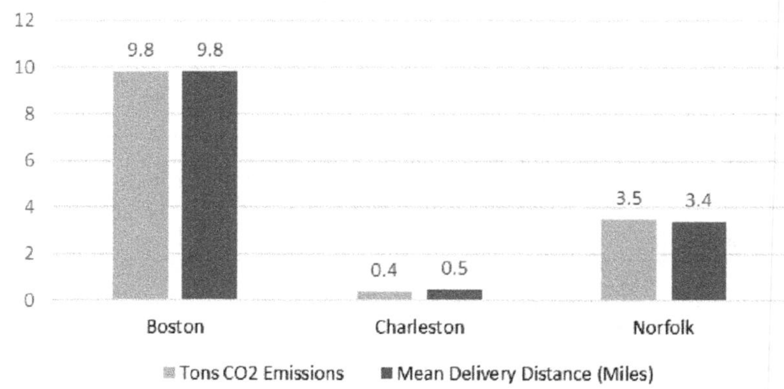

FUTURE RESEARCH DIRECTIONS

There are several aspects of this research that can be extended. First, the model as presently defined is limited to a performance objective of minimizing the total tons of transport truck CO_2 emissions generated under a JIT delivery policy. The model does not address the costs associated with the operation of an inhouse or 3PL transport truck delivery fleet nor the costs associated with importing and landing a product at a seaport. Second, the demand characteristics of the model could be generalized. Currently, demand is assumed to be the normal distribution and demand is concentrated at a single usage point in each inland city. A more robust treatment of the demand characteristics of the model would allow for stochastic demand across a wider range of distributions other than the normal and also include multiple demand locations for the product within each inland city. These considerations would support extending the model to include last mile delivery into the network design problem. Third, the model uses a volume-based measure (CO_2 tons per TEU mile) for determining total transport truck emissions. The model could be reconfigured using a weight-based CO_2 transport truck emission measure and comparisons of the model solutions across the two forms of emissions measures could be made. Lastly, the model is illustrated for U.S. seaports and demand destinations, and uses imperial measures for weight, distance and CO_2 emissions. These model attributes would have to be modified for alternative geographic locations and metric measures when using the model outside the U.S.

CONCLUSION

As worldwide commerce sales grow, market competitiveness requires firms to closely monitor the performance of their global supply chains and to adopt best practices to ensure that their global supply chain operations provide high levels of customer service. Today, concerns over the carbon footprint and the timeliness of product delivery in global supply chains have become increasingly important to stakeholders (customers, company shareholders and regulatory groups). As a result, decision makers often use quantitative models and decision support systems to assist them when making decisions on how to reduce the carbon footprint and improve delivery performance in their global supply chains.

This chapter has contributed a decision model that can be used to provide insight on the design of a distribution network for reducing the carbon footprint of a product delivered under a JIT delivery policy. An Excel-based transportation model is solved using linear programming to determine the optimal network design for routing transport trucks to deliver a product landed at seaports to meet demand at inland cities to minimize total transport truck CO_2 emissions under a JIT delivery policy. The model was numerically illustrated under conditions of stochastic product demand and demonstrated across four alternative network designs. The model is designed for spreadsheet implementation and conveniently supports what-if analyses of model parameters thereby helping to contribute to the evolution of dynamic and learning-based best practices. Considerations for model extension were also discussed which could generalize the model for application to a wider range of global supply chain decision environments.

REFERENCES

Abbasi, M., & Nilsson, F. (2016). Developing environmentally sustainable logistics: Exploring themes and challenges from a logistics service providers' perspective. *Transportation Research Part D, Transport and Environment*, *46*, 273–283. doi:10.1016/j.trd.2016.04.004

Adenso-Díaz, B., Lozano, S., & Moreno, P. (2016). How the environmental impact affects the design of logistics networks based on cost minimization. *Transportation Research Part D, Transport and Environment*, *48*, 214–224. doi:10.1016/j.trd.2016.08.022

Aditjandra, P. T., Zunder, T. H., Islam, D. M. Z., & Palacin, R. (2016). Green rail transportation: Improving rail freight to support green corridors. In H. N. Psaraftis (Ed.), *Green Transportation Logistics, the Quest for Win-Win Solutions* (pp. 413–454). Springer International Publishing. doi:10.1007/978-3-319-17175-3_12

Ahi, P., & Searcy, C. (2015). An analysis of metrics used to measure performance in green and sustainable supply chains. *Journal of Cleaner Production*, *86*, 360–377. doi:10.1016/j.jclepro.2014.08.005

Annual Energy Outlook. (2019). Retrieved from https://www.eia.gov/outlooks/aeo/pdf/aeo2019.pdf

Aronsson, H., & Brodin, M. H. (2006). The environmental impact of changing logistics structures. *International Journal of Logistics Management*, *17*(3), 394–415. doi:10.1108/09574090610717545

Barbosa-Póvoa, A. P., da Silva, C., & Carvalho, A. (2017). Opportunities and challenges in sustainable supply chain: An operations research perspective. *European Journal of Operational Research*, *268*(2), 399–431. doi:10.1016/j.ejor.2017.10.036

Beske, P., & Seuring, S. (2014). Putting sustainability into supply chain management. *Supply Chain Management*, *19*(3), 322–331. doi:10.1108/SCM-12-2013-0432

Bouchard, D. (2015). *What is globalization doing to the world of logistics*. Retrieved from https://www.inboundlogistics.com/cms/article/what-is-globalization-doing-to-the-world-of-logistics/

Brandenburg, M., Govindan, K., Sarkis, J., & Seuring, S. (2014). Quantitative models for sustainable supply chain management: Developments and directions. *European Journal of Operational Research*, *233*(2), 299–312. doi:10.1016/j.ejor.2013.09.032

Brown, J. R., & Guiffrida, A. L. (2014). Carbon emissions comparison of last mile delivery versus customer pickup. *International Journal of Logistics Research and Applications*, *17*(6), 503–521. doi:10.1080/13675567.2014.907397

Caris, A., Macharis, C., & Janssens, G. K. (2013). Decision support in intermodal transport: A new research agenda. *Computers in Industry*, *64*(2), 105–112. doi:10.1016/j.compind.2012.12.001

Chaabane, A., Ramudhin, A., & Paquet, M. (2012). Design of sustainable supply chains under the emission trading scheme. *International Journal of Production Economics*, *135*(1), 37–49. doi:10.1016/j.ijpe.2010.10.025

Davarzani, H., Fahimnia, B., Bell, M. G. H., & Sarkis, J. (2015). A Review of the literature of green ports and maritime logistics. In B. Fahimnia, M. G. H. Bell, D. A. Hensher, & J. Sarkis (Eds.), *Green Logistics and Transportation a Sustainable Supply Chain Perspective* (pp. 149–158). Springer International Publishing. doi:10.1007/978-3-319-17181-4_9

Dekker, R., Bloemhof, J., & Mallidis, I. (2012). Operations Research for green logistics–An overview of aspects, issues, contributions and challenges. *European Journal of Operational Research*, *219*(3), 671–679. doi:10.1016/j.ejor.2011.11.010

Demir, E., Bektaş, T., & Laporte, G. (2014). A review of recent research on green road freight transportation. *European Journal of Operational Research*, *237*(3), 775–793. doi:10.1016/j.ejor.2013.12.033

Elhedhli, S., & Merrick, R. (2012). Green supply chain network design to reduce carbon emissions. *Transportation Research Part D, Transport and Environment*, *17*(5), 370–379. doi:10.1016/j.trd.2012.02.002

Elkington, J. (1998). Partnerships from cannibals with forks: The triple bottom line of 21st-century business. *Environmental Quality Management*, *8*(1), 37–51. doi:10.1002/tqem.3310080106

Ellram, L. M., & Murfield, M. L. U. (2017). Environmental sustainability in freight transportation: A systematic literature review and agenda for future research. *Transportation Journal*, *56*(3), 263–298. doi:10.5325/transportationj.56.3.0263

Eskandarpour, M., Dejax, P., Miemczyk, J., & Péton, O. (2015). Sustainable supply chain network design: An optimization-oriented review. *Omega*, *54*, 11–32. doi:10.1016/j.omega.2015.01.006

Fahimnia, B., Farahani, R. Z., Marian, R., & Luong, L. (2013). A review and critique on integrated production-distribution planning models and techniques. *Journal of Manufacturing Systems*, *32*(1), 1–19. doi:10.1016/j.jmsy.2012.07.005

Farahani, R. Z., Rezapour, S., Drezner, T., & Fallah, S. (2014). Competitive supply chain network design: An overview of classifications, models, solution techniques and applications. *Omega*, *45*, 92–118. doi:10.1016/j.omega.2013.08.006

Gevaers, R., Van de Voorde, E., & Vanelslander, T. (2011). *Characteristics and Typology of Last-Mile Logistics from an Innovative Perspective in an Urban Context*. Presented at the *Transportation Research Board Annual Meeting*, Washington, DC.

Golini, R., Caniato, F., & Kalchschmidt, M. (2016). Linking global value chains and supply chain management: Evidence from the electric motors industry. *Production Planning and Control*, *27*(11), 934–951. doi:10.1080/09537287.2016.1170225

Gonzalez, E. D. R. S., Sarkis, J., Huisingh, D., Huatuco, L. H., Maculan, N., Montoya-Torres, J. R., & De Almeida, C. M. V. B. (2015). Making real progress toward more sustainable societies using decision support models and tools: Introduction to the special volume. *Journal of Cleaner Production*, *105*, 1–13. doi:10.1016/j.jclepro.2015.05.047

Gourdin, K. N. (2006). *Global logistics management: A competitive advantage for the 21st century* (2nd ed.). Wiley-Blackwell Publishing.

Govindan, K., Fattahi, M., & Keyvanshokooh, E. (2017). Supply chain network design under uncertainty: A comprehensive review and future research directions. *European Journal of Operational Research, 263*(1), 108–141. doi:10.1016/j.ejor.2017.04.009

Gurtu, A. (2019). A pioneering approach to reducing fuel cost and carbon emissions from transportation. *Transportation Journal, 58*(4), 309–322. doi:10.5325/transportationj.58.4.0309

Gurtu, A., Jaber, M. Y., & Searcy, C. (2015). Impact of fuel price and emissions on inventory policies. *Applied Mathematical Modelling, 39*(3-4), 1202–1216. doi:10.1016/j.apm.2014.08.001

Hassini, E., Surti, C., & Searcy, C. (2012). A literature review and a case study of sustainable supply chains with a focus on metrics. *International Journal of Production Economics, 140*(1), 69–82. doi:10.1016/j.ijpe.2012.01.042

Hitchcock, F. L. (1941). The distribution of a product from several sources to numerous locations. *Journal of Mathematics and Physics, 20*(1-4), 224–230. doi:10.1002apm1941201224

Inman, R. R., & Bhaskaran, S. (2019). Empirical evaluation of the delivery risk of extended supply chains. *International Journal of Production Research, 57*(11), 3466–3477. doi:10.1080/00207543.2018.1539264

Janic, M. (2007). Modelling the full costs of an intermodal and road freight transport network. *Transportation Research Part D, Transport and Environment, 12*(1), 33–44. doi:10.1016/j.trd.2006.10.004

Jiang, Y., Zhou, X., & Xu, Q. (2019). Scenario analysis-based decision and coordination in supply chain management with production and transportation scheduling. *Symmetry, 11*(2), 160. doi:10.3390ym11020160

Kelle, P., Song, J., Jin, M., Schneider, H., & Claypool, C. (2019). Evaluation of operational and environmental sustainability tradeoffs in multimodal freight transportation planning. *International Journal of Production Economics, 209*, 411–420. doi:10.1016/j.ijpe.2018.08.011

Klibi, W., Martel, A., & Guitouni, A. (2010). The design of robust value-creating supply chain networks: A critical review. *European Journal of Operational Research, 203*(2), 283–293. doi:10.1016/j.ejor.2009.06.011

Manuj, I., & Mentzer, J. T. (2008). Global supply chain risk management. *Journal of Business Logistics, 29*(1), 133–155. doi:10.1002/j.2158-1592.2008.tb00072.x

Manupati, V. K., Jedidah, S. J., Gupta, S., Bhandari, A., & Ramkumar, M. (2019). Optimization of a multi-echelon sustainable production-distribution supply chain system with lead time consideration under carbon emission policies. *Computers & Industrial Engineering, 135*, 1312–1323. doi:10.1016/j.cie.2018.10.010

Mathers, J., Craft, E., Norsworthy, M., & Wolfe, C. (2020). *The Green Freight Handbook: A Practical Guide for Developing a Sustainable Freight Transportation Strategy for Business*. Retrieved from http://business.edf.org/projects/green-freight-handbook

McKee, J. (2018). *Global Digital Commerce Sales to Near $6 Trillion By 2022*. Retrieved from https://www.forbes.com/sites/jordanmckee/2018/09/11/global-digital-commerce-sales-to-near-6-trillion-by-2022/#11f0874f4c5a

Meixell, M. J., & Gargeya, V. B. (2005). Global supply chain design: A literature review and critique. *Transportation Research Part E, Logistics and Transportation Review*, *41*(6), 531–550. doi:10.1016/j.tre.2005.06.003

Memari, A., Rahim, A. R. A., Ahmad, R., & Hassan, A. (2016). A literature review on green supply chain modelling for optimising CO2 emission. *International Journal of Operational Research*, *26*(4), 509–525. doi:10.1504/IJOR.2016.077725

Nasiri, G. R., & Jolai, F. (2018). Supply chain network design in uncertain nnvironment: A review and classification of related models. In S. L. Tilahun & J. M. T. Ngnotchouye (Eds.), *Optimization Techniques for Problem Solving in Uncertainty* (pp. 262–282). IGI Global. doi:10.4018/978-1-5225-5091-4.ch010

Pan, F., & Nagi, R. (2010). Robust supply chain design under uncertain demand in agile manufacturing. *Computers & Operations Research*, *37*(4), 668–683. doi:10.1016/j.cor.2009.06.017

Ren, R., Hu, W., Dong, J., Sun, B., Chen, Y., & Chen, Z. (2020). A systematic literature review of green and sustainable logistics: Bibliometric analysis, research trend and knowledge taxonomy. *International Journal of Environmental Research and Public Health*, *17*(1), 261. doi:10.3390/ijerph17010261 PMID:31905934

Roso, V. (2013). Sustainable intermodal transport via dry ports–importance of directional development. *World Review of Intermodal Transportation Research*, *4*(2/3), 140–156. doi:10.1504/WRITR.2013.058976

Srivastava, S. K. (2007). Green supply-chain management: A state-of-the-art literature review. *International Journal of Management Reviews*, *9*(1), 53–80. doi:10.1111/j.1468-2370.2007.00202.x

Teoh, L. E., & Khoo, H. L. (2016). Green air transport system: An overview of issues, strategies and challenges. *KSCE Journal of Civil Engineering*, *20*(3), 1040–1052. doi:10.100712205-016-1670-3

Ülkü, M. A. (2012). Dare to care: Shipment consolidation reduces not only costs, but also environmental damage. *International Journal of Production Economics*, *139*(2), 438–446. doi:10.1016/j.ijpe.2011.09.015

Wang, G., Gunasekaran, A., & Ngai, E. W. (2018). Distribution network design with big data: Model and analysis. *Annals of Operations Research*, *270*(1-2), 539–551. doi:10.100710479-016-2263-8

Wu, C., & Barnes, D. (2018). Design of agile supply chains including the trade-off between number of partners and reliability. *International Journal of Advanced Manufacturing Technology*, *97*(9-12), 3683–3700. doi:10.100700170-018-2205-5

ADDITIONAL READING

Ahi, P., & Searcy, C. (2013). A comparative literature analysis of definitions for green and sustainable supply chain management. *Journal of Cleaner Production*, *52*, 329–341. doi:10.1016/j.jclepro.2013.02.018

Arampantzi, C., & Minis, I. (2017). A new model for designing sustainable supply chain networks and its application to a global manufacturer. *Journal of Cleaner Production*, *156*, 276–292. doi:10.1016/j.jclepro.2017.03.164

Brown, J. R., & Guiffrida, A. L. (2017). Stochastic modeling of the last mile problem for delivery fleet planning. *Journal of the Transportation Research Forum*, *56*(2), 93–108.

Das, R., & Shaw, K. (2017). Uncertain supply chain network design considering carbon footprint and social factors using two-stage approach. *Clean Technologies and Environmental Policy*, *19*(10), 2491–2519. doi:10.100710098-017-1446-6

Dey, A., LaGuardia, P., & Srinivasan, M. (2011). Building sustainability in logistics operations: A research agenda. *Management Research Review*, *34*(11), 1237–1259. doi:10.1108/01409171111178774

El Saadany, A. M. A., Jaber, M. Y., & Bonney, M. (2011). Environmental performance measures for supply chains. *Management Research Review*, *34*(11), 1202–1221. doi:10.1108/01409171111178756

Gurtu, A., Searcy, C., & Jaber, M. Y. (2017). Emissions from international transport in global supply chains. *Management Research Review*, *40*(1), 53–74. doi:10.1108/MRR-09-2015-0208

Harris, I., Naim, M., Palmer, A., Potter, A., & Mumford, C. (2011). Assessing the impact of cost optimization based on infrastructure modelling on CO2 emissions. *International Journal of Production Economics*, *131*(1), 313–321. doi:10.1016/j.ijpe.2010.03.005

Isaksson, K., Evangelista, P., Huge-Brodin, M., Liimatainen, H., & Sweeney, E. (2017). The adoption of green initiatives in logistics service providers-a strategic perspective. *International Journal of Business and Systems Research*, *11*(4), 349–364. doi:10.1504/IJBSR.2017.087096

John, S. T., Sridharan, R., & Ram Kumar, P. R. (2017). Multi-period reverse logistics network design with emission cost. *International Journal of Logistics Management*, *28*(1), 127–149. doi:10.1108/IJLM-08-2015-0143

Khan, M., Hussain, M., & Saber, H. M. (2016). Information sharing in a sustainable supply chain. *International Journal of Production Economics*, *181*, 208–214. doi:10.1016/j.ijpe.2016.04.010

Piecyk, M., & McKinnon, A. (2010). Forecasting the carbon footprint of road freight transport in 2020. *International Journal of Production Economics*, *128*(1), 31–42. doi:10.1016/j.ijpe.2009.08.027

Rezaee, A., Dehghanian, F., Fahimnia, B., & Beamon, B. (2017). Green supply chain network design with stochastic demand and carbon price. *Annals of Operations Research*, *250*(2), 463–485. doi:10.100710479-015-1936-z

APPENDIX

Figures 4-6 demonstrate the model for the Optimal and Boston network solutions for a demand level of 2,000 TEUs. For a copy of the spreadsheet and screen shots of the complete set of network solutions across all seaports and demand levels please contact the lead author.

Figure 4. Transportation model solution of Optimal network design using Excel Solver (total demand = 2,000)

Transportation Model for Optimal Network Solution

US Tons (Short Tons) of CO2 to Meet All Demand	3604.5

Transport Truck Mileage from Port to City

	Demand City							
Port	Boise	Salt Lake	Portland	Reno	Spokane	Phoenix	LA	Dummy
Boston	2674	2379	3104	2896	2765	2766	3136	0
Charleston	2475	2475	2904	2695	2677	2119	2489	0
Norfolk	2539	2539	2968	2759	2663	2346	2716	0

Decision Variables (Number of TEUs Shipped From Port to City):

	Demand City							
Port	Boise	Salt Lake	Portland	Reno	Spokane	Phoenix	LA	Dummy
Boston	0	163	0	0	0	0	0	0
Charleston	277	0	289	463	0	99	338	0
Norfolk	0	0	0	0	474	0	0	0

Objective Function (TEU miles to meet all demand)	5473718

Constraints	LHS	RHS
Capacity Boston	163	9000
Capacity Charleston	1466	9000
Capacity Norfork	474	9000
Demand Boise	277	277
Demand Salt Lake	163	163
Demand Portland	289	289
Demand Reno	463	463
Demand Spokane	474	474
Demand Pheonix	99	99
Demand LA	338	338
Demand Dummy	0	0

Figure 5. Excel Solver solution for Optimal network design (total demand = 2,000)

Figure 6. Spreadsheet solution for Boston network design (total demand = 2,000)

CO2 Emissions and Delivery Time Calculator

US Tons (Short Tons) of CO2 to Meet Total Demand	**3958.2**

Transport Truck Mileage from Port to City

	Demand City						
Port	**Boise**	**Salt Lake**	**Portland**	**Reno**	**Spokane**	**Phoenix**	**LA**
Boston	2674	2379	3104	2896	2765	2766	3136
Charleston	2475	2475	2904	2695	2677	2119	2489
Norfolk	2539	2539	2968	2759	2663	2346	2716
Demand In TEUs	277	163	289	463	474	99	338

Total TEU Demand	2103	TEUs
Grams of CO2 per TEU mile	597.4	
One Metric Ton Equals	1000000	grams
Metric Tons of CO2 per TEU mile	0.000597	
Conversion Factor for Metric Ton to US Ton	1.1023	

User Based Selection of Port to City Shipments

Enter 1 for a Port to Destination Shipment
Enter 0 for no Port to Destination Shipment
For each demand city (column) enter one one and two zeros

	Demand City						
Port	**Boise**	**Salt Lake**	**Portland**	**Reno**	**Spokane**	**Phoenix**	**LA**
Boston	1	1	1	1	1	1	1
Charleston	0	0	0	0	0	0	0
Norfolk	0	0	0	0	0	0	0

Total Delivery Time

Mean	44.9	hours
Std Dev	3.4	hours

Number of TEU Shipped from Port to City

	Demand City						
Port	**Boise**	**Salt Lake**	**Portland**	**Reno**	**Spokane**	**Phoenix**	**LA**
Boston	277	163	289	463	474	99	338
Charleston	0	0	0	0	0	0	0
Norfolk	0	0	0	0	0	0	0

Chapter 2
The Negative Effects of Carbon Emission on FDI:
A Comparative Analysis Between E7 and G7 Countries

Serhat Yüksel
Istanbul Medipol University, Turkey

Hasan Dinçer
Istanbul Medipol University, Turkey

Hüsne Karakuş
https://orcid.org/0000-0003-1354-9580
Istanbul Medipol University, Turkey

Gözde Gülseven Ubay
Istanbul Medipol University, Turkey

ABSTRACT

This study aims to understand the negative impacts of carbon emission on the foreign direct investments. For this purpose, a comparative analysis is performed for both E7 and G7 countries. In the analysis process, Pedroni panel cointegration (PPC), Kao panel cointegration (KPC), and Dumitrescu Hurlin panel causality (DHPC) analyses are taken into consideration. The findings indicate that carbon emission has a negative influence on foreign direct investments for both country groups. Nonetheless, this relationship is stronger for G7 economies. It is also identified that there is no causality relationship between these variables. It is recommended that the countries should generate appropriate policies to minimize carbon emission problem. Within this context, new tax can be implemented for the companies that lead to high carbon emission. Additionally, governments can give incentives to the projects that aim to decrease carbon emission. In this scope, decreasing tax ratio and providing a technical support can be given as examples.

DOI: 10.4018/978-1-7998-4601-7.ch002

INTRODUCTION

Carbon dioxide emission means the release of carbon gas into the atmosphere. The high rate of this gas in the atmosphere causes some problems (Zheng et al., 2020). The biggest negativity created by this situation is environmental pollution. Carbon emission causes pollution of both air and water. These mentioned issues also lead to increase diseases in the country. This situation causes both loss of labor and increased treatment costs. As a result, the country's economy will be negatively affected by this situation. Another problem caused by carbon dioxide emission is the increase in the temperature of the world (Soltani et al., 2020). Many living species die as a result of the global warming problem.

It is possible to mention many factors that cause carbon dioxide emission. Fossil fuel consumption is one of the most important issues in this process. Especially, as a result of the consumption of coal, a significant amount of carbon gas is released into the atmosphere. As the consumption of coal is also cheaper compared to other energy sources, it is very difficult to prevent this problem. Another factor that causes increased carbon emissions is the uncontrolled population growth (Yao et al., 2020). In many countries around the world, the population is growing at a significant rate. As a result of this increasing population, more carbon gas is released into the atmosphere in order to meet the heating need. Increasing industrial production is another important issue in this context. Especially in recent years, industrialization has increased significantly (Wen and Wang, 2020). As the raw material of the industry, energy is also used more, and it is seen that the carbon emission problem also increases.

Due to these problems, there has been a serious increase in awareness, especially in recent years, towards reducing carbon emissions. Symposiums attended by many different countries were held and it was stated that the carbon emission problem should be reduced. In this framework, many countries have also developed strategies to reduce carbon dioxide emissions. In this context, the popularity of renewable energy use has increased significantly. A significant majority of countries aimed to prevent carbon emission problems by turning to environmentally friendly alternatives such as wind and solar energy (Qiao et al., 2020). In addition to the mentioned issue, electrically powered cars are another application that contributes to the solution of this problem. It can be easier to prevent air pollution by using such vehicles.

This issue has become an image for the countries as a result of the increase in global awareness on carbon emission. In this context, countries with high carbon emissions are criticized by many different individuals and institutions (Sesso et al., 2020). This loss of image causes countries to have some problems. In this process, one of the most prominent problems concerns the tourism sector. The reason for this is that tourists are reluctant to visit the country with high carbon emissions. This situation causes countries to experience significant loss of income. Another important issue in this process is related to financial issues. International financial institutions may be nervous about lending to companies in a country with high carbon emissions (Franco-Luesma et al., 2020; Pan et al., 2020). This can lead to a significant decrease in investments in the country.

Foreign direct investments are also thought to be affected by the carbon emission problem. As mentioned before, the country with high carbon emission has a problem of environmental pollution. As a result, the country faces both social and economic problems. As foreign investors invest in huge amounts, they take into account many different factors when entering the market in a country. In this context, the high carbon emission problem may also affect the investment decisions of foreign investors. In other words, foreign investors may be reluctant to invest in countries with emission problems. Consequently, the amount of investment in the country decreases (Buckley et al., 2020). Because of this situation, the unemployment rate in the country increases and economic growth decreases.

As can be understood from these issues, the effects of the carbon emission problem should be analyzed in detail on a country basis. In this study, the effect of the carbon emission problem on foreign direct investments is examined. In this framework, it is aimed to make a comparative evaluation by analyzing both E7 and G7 countries. On the other hand, the annual data between 1990 and 2018 is taken into consideration in the study. In addition, PPC, KPC and DHPC analyses are used in the evaluation process. As a result of the analysis obtained, the effect of the carbon emission problem on foreign direct investments can be tested on different country groups.

Compared to other similar studies, it is possible to mention many advantages of this study. Firstly, it is seen in the literature review that this study is handled by different researchers. However, it is determined that a single method, such as regression and vector error correction model, was generally used in these studies. In this study, it is aimed to provide uniqueness in methodological terms by using 3 different models. PPC and KPC analyzes question the existence of a long-term relationship between these two variables. In addition, DHPC analysis examines whether there is a very strong relationship among the items. Therefore, using these 3 different econometric methods, the strength of the possible relationship can also be measured. In addition, both E7 and G7 countries are included in the study. In this way, it will be possible to determine the situation of this relationship in different country groups.

LITERATURE REVIEW

Carbon dioxide emissions are caused by the use of non-renewable energy sources. In this context, carbon emission also affects many factors. One of them is industrial production that requires significant energy use. Therefore, using high energy means high carbon emission. This issue has been emphasized in the literature by many researchers. Kopidou and Diakoulaki (2017) conducted a study aimed at determining the influence of industrial production on carbon emissions. For this purpose, it has included four Southern European countries for examination. It has been determined that the use of industrial products emits a lot of carbon. In addition, it was determined that consumption expenditures and trade impacts on the consumption change of industrial products negatively affect carbon emissions. The presence of carbon emissions becomes important in industrial production. In their study, Álvarez and de Grado (2016) tried to determine the carbon value that occurs as a result of combustion. They determined that the importance of reducing carbon in industrial production is increasing day by day and the studies to be carried out within this framework are more and more important day by day.

Carbon emissions affect the industry sector negatively. Therefore, it is extremely important for countries and regions to set new goals and strategies. Many studies have been carried out in the literature on this subject. Yang et al. (2018) aimed to detect the presence of efforts to reduce carbon emissions from China's industrial production. For this purpose, China was included in the review. According to the results obtained, industry is an important sector in China. The non-renewable energies used in this framework emit large amounts of carbon emissions in China. Accordingly, carbon emissions affect the industry sector in China negatively in the long run. In light of this information, it is stated that the region-based sectors that use energy intensively in China should have carbon emission reduction targets and technologies aiming at saving energy should be produced within this framework. A similar study focuses on the relationship between industrial production in Japan and carbon emissions. In the analysis process of the relevant study, Granger causality analysis was performed, and similar results were obtained. It has been determined that carbon emissions in Japan negatively affect industrial production. In this context, it has been stated that the support of governments is important in the production of industrial products and the supports should be increased in this regard (Murad et al., 2019).

Energy is needed in the industrial production phase. They are energies that are mostly scarce and have the most harm to the environment. At this point, eliminating the lack of energy is an important issue. In the literature, Kumar et al. (2019) conducted a study to determine the effect of microalgae on carbon emission by obtaining biomass energy from kitchen and sewage wastewater. They found that carbon emissions are quite high in the production phase of industrial products, and in this context, the use of biomass energy, especially in industrial chimney production, significantly reduces CO2 emissions. It is also emphasized that the presence of biomass energy is very important especially in the production of microalgae. Other similar studies have been carried out, emphasizing the existence of renewable energies in industrial production. In these studies, it was emphasized that solid wastes produced as a result of combustion are processed in hydrogen biorefineries and reveal an industrial ecosystem. It has been determined that there is a high carbon emission in industrial production, and it would be beneficial for industry companies to both decrease their energy costs and reduce their carbon footprint. In this context, it has been stated that it is appropriate to prefer renewable energies (Ghayur and Verheyen, 2018).

Energy costs are high in industrial production. In this case, the resulting carbon emission level is also high. Therefore, many studies have been conducted in the literature on studies that will minimize carbon emissions. Maharloo et al. (2017) made a study aimed at determining the effect of carbon emission on sodium bicarbonate produced in an industrial reactor and determining its effects on the environment. In this study, they found that as a result of the use of industrial reactors in sodium bicarbonate production, significant carbon emission occurred. It is also underlined that for this case, the models should be generated that will minimize carbon emissions. This has been done in other similar studies. Meunier et al. (2020) also aimed to emphasize the effect of the transformation in carbon emission on the production of methanol. Consequently, they emphasized that carbon emission has negative effects on the environment and carbon emission is important in industrial production. Especially methanol production has been found to damage the environment. Within this framework, the carbon conversion process in methanol production has been determined to be important.

Various tests have been highlighted in the literature to reduce carbon emissions in industrial production. Bahmani et al. (2017) aimed to determine the effect of the change in natural gas and petroleum gas production in Iran on carbon emissions. In this context, it is stated that it will be appropriate to carry out studies that will minimize the carbon effect in industrial production. In a similar study, it was aimed to reduce carbon emission by using a different method. It has been identified that carbon emissions negatively affect industrial production (Chuang et al., 2018). Furthermore, it arises from the use of non-renewable energies. In this context, carbon emission affects many factors and is affected by many factors. One of these factors is financial developments. In the literature, this issue has been addressed by many researchers. Salahuddin et al. (2018) made also a similar study for this purpose. In this study, Granger causality analysis is considered. It is concluded that financial developments do not have a direct impact on carbon emissions in the long term. Abokyi et al. (2019) also focused on this issue and examined the relationship between fossil fuel consumption, financial developments, industrial growth and carbon emissions. During the analysis process of his study, cointegration analysis was carried out and the relationship between the related factors was established. According to the results obtained, the consumption of fossil fuels affects financial developments.

Many studies have been conducted in the literature describing the effects of financial developments on carbon emissions. Bekhet et al. (2017) investigated the causes of carbon emissions in Gulf countries.

It is stated that when there is an improvement in financial developments, energy is consumed excessively, and this situation increases carbon emission. Abbasi and Riaz (2016) did a similar study and examined the effects of Pakistan's economic and financial developments on carbon emissions. During the analysis process of the relevant study, VAR analysis was performed. It is emphasized that there is an important relationship between financial development and carbon emission in the study. Studies have also been conducted where the impact of financial developments on carbon emissions is both positive and negative. For instance, Pat (2018) and Ahmad et al. (2018) also focused on this issue in their studies and underlined the same situation.

The literature focuses on the relationship between economic growth, financial development, GDP, trade deficits and carbon emissions. İsik et al. (2017) also examined this situation for Greece. In this study, it has been determined that tourism is an important sector in Greece and therefore a lot of energy is spent. Hence, it is emphasized that the developments in the tourism sector had a high impact on carbon emissions. In this context, it was stated that policy makers should focus on this issue. Jamel and Maktouf (2017) also focused on this issue and examined 40 European countries. It is concluded that there is a bilateral relationship between financial developments and carbon emissions. Charfeddine and Kahia (2019) also conducted a study on this issue and aimed to explain the impact of renewable energy sources and financial developments on carbon emissions. As a result, it was determined that carbon emissions were not taken into consideration in financial developments. This situation is also highlighted by Khoshnevis Yazdi and Ghorchi Beygi (2018).

Especially with the acceleration of industrialization, environmental pollution problem has become one of the most important issues in the world. Environmental problems caused by overproduction and consumption leave more and more permanent damage in our world day by day. Although this negative effect is tried to be limited by agreements such as the Kyoto Protocol, carbon dioxide emission increases day by day. Besides many reasons for this increase, the main reason is the desire of the countries to achieve ideal growth rates. One of the most frequently used methods in this framework is the Environmental Kuznet Curve (EKC). According to this curve, as the income level of the countries increases, the damages of these countries to the environment go up as well. However, after a while, the relationship turns to the reverse U shape. Thus, if the income continues to increase, the damage to the environment starts to decrease (Narayan et al., 2016). Looking at the relevant literature, it is seen that different conclusions regarding the EKC hypothesis have been reached. In addition to the studies that state that the hypothesis is valid, there are many studies that do not get results in favor of the hypothesis (Alam et al., 2016).

However, in all studies conducted with many country groups, a significant relationship has been obtained in the short or long term between economic growth and environmental pollution due to carbon dioxide emission (Kais and Sami, 2016). One of the items used when examining this relationship is the decoupling effect index (Du et al., 2019). If there is a strong decoupling in a country, it argues that carbon emissions will decrease with economic growth. On the other side, if there is a weak decoupling, it argues that carbon emissions will increase with economic growth, but the increase in carbon emissions is less than the increase in economic growth (Xu and Yang, 2019). In the research, it has been observed that developing countries show a weak decoupling effect especially in China (Wang et al., 2018; Zhao et al., 2017). Furthermore, Mirza and Kanwal (2017) analyzed the presence of dynamic causality between economic growth, energy consumption and carbon emissions by using Johansen-Julius co-integration test. It is concluded that there is a relationship among these variables. In the case of India, Ahmad et al. (2016) also found a positive relationship between economic growth and carbon emission.

Due to the increasing global warming and carbon emission in the world, the quality of environmental elements is decreasing day by day. With the decrease in this quality, health expenditures also increased. The number of studies in this context is increasing day by day in the literature. Studies on both developed and developing countries have shown that high carbon emission, which is one of the main components of economic growth, directly affects health expenditures of countries (Apergis et al., 2018). The causality link between carbon emissions and health expenditures investigated in low income group, lower middle-income group and upper middle-income group within 51 countries over the period 1995 to 2013 and used dynamic simultaneous equations models. According to this research, there is a unidirectional causality from carbon emission to health expenditures except low income groups. They found that health plays an important role in GDP per capita (Chaabouni et al., 2016; Chaabouni and Saidi, 2017). On the other side, Chen et al. (2019) investigated the causal link between carbon dioxide emission and health-care expenditures over the time period 2005 to 2016 in China. Moreover, Bayesian quantile regression is taken into consideration in the analysis process. They found that carbon emissions have become one of the most important factors affecting health expenditures in most regions.

Another issue mentioned in the literature is the effect of carbon dioxide emission on foreign direct investments. In countries with high carbon dioxide emissions, both air and water resources are polluted. This situation causes people living in the country to get sick. Due to this mentioned problem, the high emission of carbon dioxide has been frequently discussed in the world public opinion, especially in recent years. Due to the increasing popularity of this subject, the image of countries with high emission rates was negatively affected. This situation is also supported by environmentally sensitive people and institutions. In this framework, international companies also expressed their reactions by not investing in countries with high emissions.

Pazienza (2019) carried out a study to determine the relationship between FDI and carbon dioxide emissions. In this study, OECD countries were included in the scope of the study. In the related study, the data between 1989 and 2016 were also examined. According to the analysis results obtained, a relationship was found between the two variables mentioned. On the other hand, Muhammad and Khan (2019) carried out a similar study for Asian countries. In this study, the relationship between foreign direct investment, carbon dioxide emission and economic growth was evaluated. In the analysis process of this study, GMM estimator method was taken into consideration. It is concluded that foreign direct investments will increase if the energy is used cleanly.

In addition to the studies mentioned, Saini and Sighania (2019) also examined the relationship between economic growth, carbon emissions and foreign direct investment. In this context, they performed bibliographic analysis on 111 articles in the literature. As a result, it was stated that there is a correlation between the variables stated in the majority of the studies. In addition, Pazienza and De Lucia (2019) examined the relationship between these variables for 30 OECD countries. In this study, panel regression analysis was performed for data between 1990 and 2015. As a result, it was concluded that these variables significantly affect each other.

On the other hand, Gong et al. (2019) also examined the effect of carbon dioxide emissions on foreign direct investments, taking into account data from 30 cities in China. Simultaneous equations model approach is also taken into consideration. Considering the results obtained, it has been determined that foreigners prefer countries that are sensitive to the environment while investing. In parallel with this study, Park et al. (2019) tried to understand whether the carbon dioxide emissions in Korea are reducing foreign direct investments. In the analysis process of this study, vector error correction method was taken into consideration. The findings show that there was a bidirectional causality relationship between the two variables.

However, some studies in the literature have argued that the carbon dioxide emission problem does not reduce foreign direct investments. It was stated in these studies that factors other than carbon dioxide emission should be taken into consideration in order to increase foreign direct investments. As an example, Xia (2019) tries to see the relationship between carbon dioxide emissions and foreign direct investment in China. In this framework, 30 different cities in this country were included in the scope of the study. On the other hand, in the related study, the data between 1995 and 2015 were used. According to the results, it has been determined that carbon dioxide emission does not affect foreign direct investments.

It can be understood that there is a wide literature related to the carbon emission. Most of these studies focused on the effects of carbon emission on the health issues. On the other side, there are also lots of studies in which the effects of carbon emission on economic growth and financial development are also underlined. In addition to these studies, the negative influences of carbon emission on foreign direct investment were also evaluated by different researchers. Hence, it is thought that a new study with different methodology contributes to the literature. Within this framework, in this study, three different approaches are considered in the analysis process. Thus, it is aimed to increase the originality of the study with respect to the methodological background.

AN APPLICATION ON G7 AND E7 COUNTRIES

A comparative evaluation is performed for E7 and G7 economies. Thus, in this section of the study, firstly, data set and variables are explained. After that, theoretical background of PPC, KPC and DHPC methods are explained. In the final stage, analysis results are shared.

Variables and Data

This study aims to evaluate the relationship between carbon emission and foreign direct investment. Therefore, with respect to the carbon emission, CO_2 intensity at constant purchasing power parities is taken into consideration. On the other side, regarding foreign direct investment, net inflows as a percentage of GDP is considered. Additionally, annual data of these variables between 1990 and 2018 is used in the analysis process. Moreover, all this data is taken from World Bank.

Pedroni and Kao Panel Cointegration Analyses

PPC analysis is aimed to evaluate whether there is a long-term relationship among the items. The variables used in the evaluation should not have unit roots. In the analysis process, 11 different test results are generated in this methodology. If at least 6 of them are significant, it gives information that there is a relationship among these factors. Moreover, in order for the result to be significant, the probability values should be lower than 0.05 (Pedroni, 1999). On the other side, KPC analysis is also preferred to see the long run relationship between the indicators. The main difference of Kao methodology is that there is only one test result and the probability value should be lower than 0.05 to have relationship. Hence, it can be said that finding relationship between the alternatives are more difficult in Kao method in comparison with PPC analysis (Nguyen and Kakinaka, 2019).

Dumitrescu Hurlin Panel Causality Analyses

DHPC analysis is considered to see the relationship between the items. Nevertheless, the main difference of this approach by comparing with cointegration analysis is that it is aimed to examine the strong relationship (Dumitrescu and Hurlin, 2012). Because of this condition, analyses are performed for three different lags. If there is a causality relationship, all probability values of these tests are lower than 0.05. There is only one precondition of DHPC analysis. The variables used in the analysis should be stationary (Dinçer et al., 2019a,b,c).

Analysis Results

In this study, analyses are performed by using three different econometric approaches for both E7 and G7 economies. With respect to the evaluation for E7 economies, first of all, stationary analysis is made by using Im Pesaran Shin (IPS) panel unit root test. The analysis results are given on Table 1.

Table 1. Unit Root Test Results of the Variables for E7 Economies

Variables	Probability (Level Value)	Probability (First Difference)	Result
Carbon Emission	0.8562	0.0036	First difference is used.
Foreign Direct Investment	0.0684	0.0000	First difference is used.

Table 1 indicates that these variables have unit root in their original forms. Due to this issue, the first differences of them are calculated and these forms are used in the analysis process. After stationary analysis, PPC test is made and the results are given on Table 2.

Table 2 explains the 11 different results of PPC test for E7 economies. It is obvious that 9 of them are significant because the probability values are lower than 0.05. Therefore, it is concluded that carbon emission has an influence on foreign direct investment for these countries. After Pedroni method, KPC analysis is also performed for E7 countries. Analysis results are summarized in Table 3.

Table 2. PPC Test Results for E7 Economies

Different Tests	Statistic	Probability	Weighted Statistic	Probability
Panel v-Statistic	-0.919343	.8210	-1.042958	.8515
Panel rho-Statistic	-9.488074	.0000	-9.033993	.0000
Panel PP-Statistic	-11.01997	.0000	-10.93702	.0000
Panel ADF-Statistic	-7.585953	.0000	-7.607831	.0000
Group rho-Statistic	-7.671026	.0000		
Group PP-Statistic	-14.03133	.0000		
Group ADF-Statistic	-8.329136	.0000		

Table 3. KPC Test Results for E7 Economies

Test Name	t-Statistic	Probability
KPC Results	-0.163832	0.4349

Table 3 indicates that probability value is higher than 0.05. It gives an information that there is no relationship between carbon emission and foreign direct investment for E7 economies. In the final stage, DHPC analysis is performed for these country groups. The results are demonstrated on Table 4.

Table 4. DHPC Test Results for E7 Economies

Null Hypothesis	Lag Number	Probability
Carbon emission does not have a causal effect on foreign direct investment	1	0.3299
	2	0.8912
	3	0.5324

According to Table 4, it is identified that there is no causal relationship among carbon emission and foreign direct investments for E7 countries. The main reason is that all probability values are greater than 0.05. This analysis process is also performed for G7 economies. Hence, in the first aspect, Im Pesaran Shin (IPS) panel unit root test is considered to see whether the variables are stationary or not. The analysis results are demonstrated on Table 5.

Table 5. Unit Root Test Results of the Variables for G7 Economies

Variables	Probability (Level Value)	Probability (First Difference)	Result
Carbon Emission	0.0212	No need to calculate	This variable is stationary with its original form.
Foreign Direct Investment	0.0259	No need to calculate	This variable is stationary with its original form.

Table 5 shows that the probability values of the original forms are lower than 0.05. This situation gives an idea that these variables do not have a unit root. Hence, these forms are used in the analysis. In the next stage, PPC test is performed for G7 economies. Analysis results are given on Table 6.

Table 6 indicates that for 9 tests, probability vales are lower than 0.05. Because more than 6 tests are significant, it can be concluded that carbon emission has a long-term effect on foreign direct investment for G7 economies. This analysis is also performed with KPC analysis for the same country groups. These results are illustrated on Table 7.

Table 7 demonstrates that probability value of the test result is lower than 0.05. This situation explains that carbon emission influences foreign direct investment for G7 economies according to KPC analysis as well. The final test for these country groups is made with DHPC analysis. The details of this evaluation are given on Table 8.

Table 6. PPC Test Results for G7 Economies

Different Tests	Statistic	Probability	Weighted Statistic	Probability
Panel v-Statistic	1.195416	0.1160	-0.092991	0.5370
Panel rho-Statistic	-5.510817	0.0000	-3.934514	0.0000
Panel PP-Statistic	-5.250097	0.0000	-4.140687	0.0000
Panel ADF-Statistic	-3.616162	0.0001	-3.652718	0.0001
Group rho-Statistic	-3.512093	0.0002		
Group PP-Statistic	-5.004189	0.0000		
Group ADF-Statistic	-3.571009	0.0002		

Table 7. KPC Test Results for G7 Economies

Test Name	t-Statistic	Probability
KPC Results	-1.882897	0.0299

Table 8 gives information that all probability values for three different lags are greater than 0.05. Thus, it is determined that carbon emission does not have a causal effect on foreign direct investment for G7 economies.

Table 8. DHPC Test Results for G7 Economies

Null Hypothesis	Lag Number	Probability
Carbon emission does not have a causal effect on foreign direct investment	1	0.6846
	2	0.9570
	3	0.7898

SOLUTIONS AND RECOMMENDATIONS

According to the results of the analysis, it is seen that carbon emissions affect foreign direct investments for both country groups. However, it has been determined that this relationship is not at the level of causality for both E7 and G7 countries. On the other hand, it is determined that this relationship is stronger for G7 countries compared to E7 countries. Considering these issues, it is recommended that countries implement policies that reduce carbon emissions. In this context, it would be a reasonable solution to bring additional tax to companies that create carbon emissions. As a result, companies with rising costs will restrict carbon emissions due to financial problems. Another important issue in this process is to monitor compliance with these legal regulations. In this context, it should be ensured that the problem can be detected on-site by making periodic inspections by the competent authorities. In addition, it is very important for the government to support carbon reduction projects. For this purpose, tax reductions and technical support will also help investors turn to these projects.

FUTURE RESEARCH DIRECTIONS

The biggest shortcoming in this study is that it only focuses on two variables. Therefore, other factors affecting foreign direct investments are ignored. Therefore, it will be appropriate to focus on carbon emissions and other variables that affect foreign direct investments in new studies. Both mentioned variables play an important role in the social and economic development of countries. For example, carbon emissions do not only affect foreign direct investments. In parallel, there are many different factors that can affect the increase of foreign direct investments. In this context, examining important concepts such as economic growth, industrial production, renewable energy use, exchange rate volatility will contribute to the development of countries. On the other hand, the use of Engle Granger cointegration analysis and Toda Yamamoto causality analysis in new studies will increase the methodological originality of these studies.

CONCLUSION

In this study, the effect of carbon dioxide emission on foreign direct investments is examined. In this framework, a comparative analysis is carried out for both E7 and G7 countries. On the other hand, PPC, KPC and DHPC approaches were used in the analysis process. In addition, the data of the mentioned variables between 1990 and 2018 were examined. As a result, according to PPC analysis, it has been determined that carbon emissions affect foreign direct investments for both country groups. However, according to KPC analysis, it has been observed that carbon emissions only reduce foreign direct investments for G7 country groups. However, it has been determined that this relationship is not meaningful for E7 countries. In addition to the mentioned issues, according to the results of DHPC analysis, it has been determined that carbon emissions are not a reason for the decrease in foreign direct investments in both countries.

One of the most important issues in this study is the need to develop a strategy to reduce the carbon dioxide emission problem. In this framework, the most duties undoubtedly fall on governments. Thanks to the new strategies to be developed, it will be possible to minimize the carbon dioxide emission problem. In this way, it will be possible to reduce environmental pollution and health problems. This will contribute to the development of the country both socially and economically. Another result found in this study is that this relationship is stronger for G7 countries compared to E7 countries. Based on this, it is possible to say that environmentally friendly firms invest more in G7 countries. Foreign direct investments play an important role in reducing the unemployment problem in a country and in the growth of the economy. Therefore, it would be appropriate for both E7 and G7 countries to contribute to the increase of foreign investments by taking measures to prevent the carbon emission problem.

REFERENCES

Abbasi, F., & Riaz, K. (2016). CO2 emissions and financial development in an emerging economy: An augmented VAR approach. *Energy Policy*, *90*, 102–114. doi:10.1016/j.enpol.2015.12.017

Abokyi, E., Appiah-Konadu, P., Abokyi, F., & Oteng-Abayie, E. F. (2019). Industrial growth and emissions of CO2 in Ghana: The role of financial development and fossil fuel consumption. *Energy Reports*, *5*, 1339–1353. doi:10.1016/j.egyr.2019.09.002

Ahmad, A., Zhao, Y., Shahbaz, M., Bano, S., Zhang, Z., Wang, S., & Liu, Y. (2016). Carbon emissions, energy consumption and economic growth: An aggregate and disaggregate analysis of the Indian economy. *Energy Policy*, *96*, 131–143. doi:10.1016/j.enpol.2016.05.032

Ahmad, M., Khan, Z., Ur Rahman, Z., & Khan, S. (2018). Does financial development asymmetrically affect CO2 emissions in China? An application of the nonlinear autoregressive distributed lag (NARDL) model. *Carbon Management*, *9*(6), 631–644. doi:10.1080/17583004.2018.1529998

Alam, M. M., Murad, M. W., Noman, A. H. M., & Ozturk, I. (2016). Relationships among carbon emissions, economic growth, energy consumption and population growth: Testing Environmental Kuznets Curve hypothesis for Brazil, China, India and Indonesia. *Ecological Indicators*, *70*, 466–479. doi:10.1016/j.ecolind.2016.06.043

Álvarez, J. F. G., & de Grado, J. G. (2016). Study of a modern industrial low pressure turbine for electricity production employed in oxy-combustion cycles with CO2 capture purposes. *Energy*, *107*, 734–747. doi:10.1016/j.energy.2016.04.038

Apergis, N., Gupta, R., Lau, C. K. M., & Mukherjee, Z. (2018). US state-level carbon dioxide emissions: Does it affect health care expenditure? *Renewable & Sustainable Energy Reviews*, *91*, 521–530. doi:10.1016/j.rser.2018.03.035

Bahmani, M., Shariati, J., & Rouzbahani, A. N. (2017). Simulation and optimization of an industrial gas condensate stabilization unit to modify LPG and NGL production with minimizing CO2 emission to the environment. *Chinese Journal of Chemical Engineering*, *25*(3), 338–346. doi:10.1016/j.cjche.2016.07.006

Bekhet, H. A., Matar, A., & Yasmin, T. (2017). CO2 emissions, energy consumption, economic growth, and financial development in GCC countries: Dynamic simultaneous equation models. *Renewable & Sustainable Energy Reviews*, *70*, 117–132. doi:10.1016/j.rser.2016.11.089

Buckley, P. J., Chen, L., Clegg, L. J., & Voss, H. (2020). The role of endogenous and exogenous risk in FDI entry choices. *Journal of World Business*, *55*(1), 101040. doi:10.1016/j.jwb.2019.101040

Chaabouni, S., & Saidi, K. (2017). The dynamic links between carbon dioxide (CO2) emissions, health spending and GDP growth: A case study for 51 countries. *Environmental Research*, *158*, 137–144. doi:10.1016/j.envres.2017.05.041 PMID:28624630

Chaabouni, S., Zghidi, N., & Mbarek, M. B. (2016). On the causal dynamics between CO2 emissions, health expenditures and economic growth. *Sustainable Cities and Society, 22*, 184-191.

Charfeddine, L., & Kahia, M. (2019). Impact of renewable energy consumption and financial development on CO2 emissions and economic growth in the MENA region: A panel vector autoregressive (PVAR) analysis. *Renewable Energy*, *139*, 198–213. doi:10.1016/j.renene.2019.01.010

Chen, L., Zhuo, Y., Xu, Z., Xu, X., & Gao, X. (2019). Is Carbon Dioxide (CO2) Emission an Important Factor Affecting Healthcare Expenditure? Evidence from China, 2005–2016. *International Journal of Environmental Research and Public Health, 16*(20), 3995. doi:10.3390/ijerph16203995 PMID:31635413

Chuang, Y. Y., Wang, J. J., Chao, P. Y., Tsai, C. T., Tsai, Y. C., Chen, W. C., & Tsai, T. C. (2018). Evaluation of on-stream industrial CO2 adsorbent in air pretreatment for cryogenic production of oxygen. *Journal of the Taiwan Institute of Chemical Engineers, 84*, 41–48. doi:10.1016/j.jtice.2017.12.030

Dinçer, H., Yüksel, S., & Adalı, Z. (2019b). Determining the Effects of Monetary Policies on Capital Markets of the Emerging Economies: An Evidence from E7 Countries. The Impacts of Monetary Policy in the 21st Century: Perspectives from Emerging Economies, 3-16.

Dinçer, H., Yüksel, S., & Canbolat, Z. N. (2019a). A strategic approach to reduce energy imports of E7 countries: use of renewable energy. In *Handbook of research on economic and political implications of green trading and energy use* (pp. 18–38). IGI Global. doi:10.4018/978-1-5225-8547-3.ch002

Dinçer, H., Yüksel, S., Pınarbaşı, F., & Çetiner, İ. T. (2019c). Measurement of economic and banking stability in emerging markets by considering income inequality and nonperforming loans. In *Maintaining financial stability in times of risk and uncertainty* (pp. 49–68). IGI Global. doi:10.4018/978-1-5225-7208-4.ch003

Du, Q., Zhou, J., Pan, T., Sun, Q., & Wu, M. (2019). Relationship of carbon emissions and economic growth in China's construction industry. *Journal of Cleaner Production, 220*, 99–109. doi:10.1016/j.jclepro.2019.02.123

Dumitrescu, E. I., & Hurlin, C. (2012). Testing for Granger non-causality in heterogeneous panels. *Economic Modelling, 29*(4), 1450–1460. doi:10.1016/j.econmod.2012.02.014

Franco-Luesma, S., Cavero, J., Plaza-Bonilla, D., Cantero-Martínez, C., Arrúe, J. L., & Álvaro-Fuentes, J. (2020). Tillage and irrigation system effects on soil carbon dioxide (CO2) and methane (CH4) emissions in a maize monoculture under Mediterranean conditions. *Soil & Tillage Research, 196*, 104488. doi:10.1016/j.still.2019.104488

Ghayur, A., & Verheyen, T. V. (2018). Technical evaluation of post-combustion CO2 capture and hydrogen production industrial symbiosis. *International Journal of Hydrogen Energy, 43*(30), 13852–13859. doi:10.1016/j.ijhydene.2018.02.069

Gong, M., Liu, H., Atif, R. M., & Jiang, X. (2019). A study on the factor market distortion and the carbon emission scale effect of two-way FDI. *Chinese Journal of Population Resources and Environment, 17*(2), 145–153. doi:10.1080/10042857.2019.1574487

Işik, C., Kasımatı, E., & Ongan, S. (2017). Analyzing the causalities between economic growth, financial development, international trade, tourism expenditure and/on the CO2 emissions in Greece. *Energy Sources. Part B, Economics, Planning, and Policy, 12*(7), 665–673. doi:10.1080/15567249.2016.1263251

Jamel, L., & Maktouf, S. (2017). The nexus between economic growth, financial development, trade openness, and CO2 emissions in European countries. *Cogent Economics & Finance, 5*(1), 1341456. doi:10.1080/23322039.2017.1341456

Kais, S., & Sami, H. (2016). An econometric study of the impact of economic growth and energy use on carbon emissions: Panel data evidence from fifty eight countries. *Renewable & Sustainable Energy Reviews, 59*, 1101–1110. doi:10.1016/j.rser.2016.01.054

Khoshnevis Yazdi, S., & Ghorchi Beygi, E. (2018). The dynamic impact of renewable energy consumption and financial development on CO2 emissions: For selected African countries. *Energy Sources. Part B, Economics, Planning, and Policy, 13*(1), 13–20. doi:10.1080/15567249.2017.1377319

Kopidou, D., & Diakoulaki, D. (2017). Decomposing industrial CO2 emissions of Southern European countries into production-and consumption-based driving factors. *Journal of Cleaner Production, 167*, 1325–1334. doi:10.1016/j.jclepro.2017.05.183

Kumar, P. K., Krishna, S. V., Naidu, S. S., Verma, K., Bhagawan, D., & Himabindu, V. (2019). Biomass production from microalgae Chlorella grown in sewage, kitchen wastewater using industrial CO2 emissions: Comparative study. *Carbon Resources Conversion, 2*(2), 126–133. doi:10.1016/j.crcon.2019.06.002

Maharloo, D. G., Darvishi, A., Davand, R., Saidi, M., & Rahimpour, M. R. (2017). Process intensification and environmental consideration of sodium bicarbonate production in an industrial soda ash bubble column reactor by CO2 recycling. *Journal of CO2 Utilization, 20*, 318-327.

Meunier, N., Chauvy, R., Mouhoubi, S., Thomas, D., & De Weireld, G. (2020). Alternative production of methanol from industrial CO2. *Renewable Energy, 146*, 1192–1203. doi:10.1016/j.renene.2019.07.010

Mirza, F. M., & Kanwal, A. (2017). Energy consumption, carbon emissions and economic growth in Pakistan: Dynamic causality analysis. *Renewable & Sustainable Energy Reviews, 72*, 1233–1240. doi:10.1016/j.rser.2016.10.081

Muhammad, B., & Khan, S. (2019). Effect of bilateral FDI, energy consumption, CO2 emission and capital on economic growth of Asia countries. *Energy Reports, 5*, 1305–1315. doi:10.1016/j.egyr.2019.09.004

Murad, M. W., Alam, M. M., & Islam, M. M. (2019). *Dynamics of Japan's Industrial Production and CO2 Emissions: Causality*. Long-Run Trend and Implication.

Narayan, P. K., Saboori, B., & Soleymani, A. (2016). Economic growth and carbon emissions. *Economic Modelling, 53*, 388–397. doi:10.1016/j.econmod.2015.10.027

Nguyen, K. H., & Kakinaka, M. (2019). Renewable energy consumption, carbon emissions, and development stages: Some evidence from panel cointegration analysis. *Renewable Energy, 132*, 1049–1057. doi:10.1016/j.renene.2018.08.069

Pan, Y., Qiao, F., Tang, K., Chen, S., & Ukkusuri, S. V. (2020). Understanding and estimating the carbon dioxide emissions for urban buses at different road locations: A comparison between new-energy buses and conventional diesel buses. *The Science of the Total Environment, 703*, 135533. doi:10.1016/j.scitotenv.2019.135533 PMID:31767339

Park, C. D., Kim, S. W., & Park, J. G. (2019). An Analysis on Causalities Among GDP, Electricity Consumption, CO 2 Emission and FDI Inflow in Korea. *Journal of Energy Engineering, 28*(2), 1–17.

Pata, U. K. (2018). Renewable energy consumption, urbanization, financial development, income and CO2 emissions in Turkey: Testing EKC hypothesis with structural breaks. *Journal of Cleaner Production, 187*, 770–779. doi:10.1016/j.jclepro.2018.03.236

Pazienza, P. (2019). The impact of FDI in the OECD manufacturing sector on CO2 emission: Evidence and policy issues. *Environmental Impact Assessment Review, 77*, 60–68. doi:10.1016/j.eiar.2019.04.002

Pazienza, P., & De Lucia, C. (2019). How does FDI in the "agricultural and fishing" sector affect methane emission? Evidence from the OECD countries. *Economics and Politics, §§§*, 1–22.

Pedroni, P. (1999). Critical values for cointegration tests in heterogeneous panels with multiple regressors. *Oxford Bulletin of Economics and Statistics, 61*(s1S1), 653–670. doi:10.1111/1468-0084.61.s1.14

Qiao, W., Lu, H., Zhou, G., Azimi, M., Yang, Q., & Tian, W. (2020). A hybrid algorithm for carbon dioxide emissions forecasting based on improved lion swarm optimizer. *Journal of Cleaner Production, 244*, 118612. doi:10.1016/j.jclepro.2019.118612

Saini, N., & Sighania, M. (2019). *Environmental impact of economic growth, emission and FDI: systematic review of reviews*. Qualitative Research in Financial Markets.

Salahuddin, M., Alam, K., Ozturk, I., & Sohag, K. (2018). The effects of electricity consumption, economic growth, financial development and foreign direct investment on CO2 emissions in Kuwait. *Renewable & Sustainable Energy Reviews, 81*, 2002–2010. doi:10.1016/j.rser.2017.06.009

Sesso, P. P., Amâncio-Vieira, S. F., Zapparoli, I. D., & Sesso Filho, U. A. (2020). Structural decomposition of variations of carbon dioxide emissions for the United States, the European Union and BRIC. *Journal of Cleaner Production, 252*, 119761. doi:10.1016/j.jclepro.2019.119761

Soltani, M., Rahmani, O., Ghasimi, D. S., Ghaderpour, Y., Pour, A. B., Misnan, S. H., & Ngah, I. (2020). Impact of household demographic characteristics on energy conservation and carbon dioxide emission: Case from Mahabad city, Iran. *Energy, 194*, 116916. doi:10.1016/j.energy.2020.116916

Wang, Q., Zhao, M., Li, R., & Su, M. (2018). Decomposition and decoupling analysis of carbon emissions from economic growth: A comparative study of China and the United States. *Journal of Cleaner Production, 197*, 178–184. doi:10.1016/j.jclepro.2018.05.285

Wen, W., & Wang, Q. (2020). Re-examining the realization of provincial carbon dioxide emission intensity reduction targets in China from a consumption-based accounting. *Journal of Cleaner Production, 244*, 118488. doi:10.1016/j.jclepro.2019.118488

Xia, X. (2019, February). FDI, Economic Growth and China's Carbon Emission Intensity: An Empirical Study Based on Spatial Panel Econometric Model. In *IOP Conference Series: Earth and Environmental Science* (Vol. 237, No. 5). IOP Publishing. 10.1088/1755-1315/237/5/052078

Xu, Q., & Yang, R. (2019). The sequential collaborative relationship between economic growth and carbon emissions in the rapid urbanization of the Pearl River Delta. *Environmental Science and Pollution Research International, 26*(29), 30130–30144. doi:10.100711356-019-06107-9 PMID:31420837

Yang, L., Yang, Y., Zhang, X., & Tang, K. (2018). Whether China's industrial sectors make efforts to reduce CO2 emissions from production?-A decomposed decoupling analysis. *Energy*, *160*, 796–809. doi:10.1016/j.energy.2018.06.186

Yao, X., Zhang, X., & Guo, Z. (2020). The tug of war between local government and enterprises in reducing China's carbon dioxide emissions intensity. *The Science of the Total Environment*, *710*, 136140. doi:10.1016/j.scitotenv.2019.136140 PMID:31923656

Zhao, X., Zhang, X., Li, N., Shao, S., & Geng, Y. (2017). Decoupling economic growth from carbon dioxide emissions in China: A sectoral factor decomposition analysis. *Journal of Cleaner Production*, *142*, 3500–3516. doi:10.1016/j.jclepro.2016.10.117

Zheng, J., Sun, X., Jia, L., & Zhou, Y. (2020). Electric passenger vehicles sales and carbon dioxide emission reduction potential in China's leading markets. *Journal of Cleaner Production*, *243*, 118607. doi:10.1016/j.jclepro.2019.118607

KEY TERMS AND DEFINITIONS

ARDL: Autoregressive distributed lag.
CO_2: Carbon dioxide.
E7 Countries: Brazil, China, India, Indonesia, Mexico, Russia, and Turkey.
EKC: Environmental Kuznets curve.
FDI: Foreign direct investment.
G7 Countries: United States, United Kingdom, Italy, France, Germany, Canada, and Japan.
GDP: Gross domestic product.
GMM: Generalized method of moments.
IPS: Im Pesaran Shin.
LMDI: Logarithmic mean divisia index.
OECD: Organization for Economic Co-Operation and Development.
Stationary Analysis: It aims to identify whether there is a unit root in the series or not.

Chapter 3
The New Concept of Logistics Platforms 4.0:
Creating Competitiveness Within the Paradigm of Global Sustainable Logistics

Manuel Antonio Fernández-Villacañas Marín
https://orcid.org/0000-0001-7397-6395
M&M Planning and Project Management, Spain & Technical University of Madrid, Spain

ABSTRACT

This chapter aims to address a review of the new concept of Logistics Platform 4.0 for the improvement of global competitiveness, which is supported, within the scope of global sustainable logistics, in the development of the new Omnichannel and Synchromodality Logistics 4.0, and the global value networks driven by intra-industrial trade. The development of the new Logistics Platforms 4.0 induces public-private actions that lead to a new territorial planning and integration of routes, corridors, logistics centres, and commercial areas, in which the metropolitan area stands out as a main actor, leading to the creation of chains of connected and intelligent logistics platforms worldwide. The new urban logistics, which is more effective and efficient, is analyzed as an essential vector for the development of the new logistics platforms. Likewise, the most important logistic problems and metropolitan restrictions that arise for the development of more sustainable and intelligent cities, and the applicable concept of aerotropolis are analyzed.

INTRODUCTION

It is well known that the phenomenon of globalization has generated radical and visible changes in the commercial structures of organizations, promoting a new global strategic mentality that tries to deal with new competitors as well as search for new markets. All this is inducing the development of logistics as an essential support to be able to respond to the increasingly demanding needs of customers worldwide. In this increasingly global, dynamic, complex and uncertain environment, logistics has experienced rapid growth and evolution in almost all industrial sectors. It has become an essential element of business

DOI: 10.4018/978-1-7998-4601-7.ch003

strategy, a true source of competitive advantage, giving rise to the polysemic and polyhedral development of the so-called New Logistics (Fernández-Villacañas, 2018).

The sustainability of global logistics and supply chain management represents a strategy of integration in a transparent way of the social, environmental and economic objectives of the organization, within the coordination system of the main inter-organizational business processes. Its purpose is to improve the long-term economic results of each company and its supply chains.

The logic of the principle of productive specialization and the processes of industrial relocation based on the labor factor, which have been raised so far in a general way, should be reviewed taking into account the increasingly significant weight of logistics costs. The concept of sustainability, which had been related by many socio-economic actors exclusively with practices of respect for the environment, evolved a few years ago to include other dimensions such as the responsibility and ethics of social behavior, the new demands of consumers or sustainable economic well-being, understood globally in terms of the analysis of international competitiveness. Increasingly, society requires industries to develop sustainable practices throughout their manufacturing, supply and distribution operations (Persdotter et al, 2019)

Consequently, many multinational companies have reviewed their manufacturing and transport processes as well as the configurations of their logistics chains based on these predicaments. However, it is still necessary to better understand the role of sustainability in the development of logistics activities as well as to still continue with a rigorous discussion of applicable multidisciplinary science and at the governmental level (Bask et al, 2018).

On the other hand, the digital transformation can conceptually be defined as the process of organizational, cultural and strategic reinvention of both companies and public entities necessary for the integral application of the technology we call digital (Fernández-Villacañas, 2018). This generates, processes, stores and uses data, information and intelligence to improve its performance as well as its ability to adapt quickly to the disruptive or radical changes generated in the environment. This new digital technological scenario, which is due to the turbulence of a strongly disruptive environment, is inducing the emergence of increasingly shorter management cycles, in which the environment changes continuously and rapidly, with a rhythm that we assume will continue to increase exponentially in the future. The main catalyst for change and the cause of this continuous acceleration is the digital revolution, motivated by the expansion of the Internet, information and communications technologies, as well as the universalization of its use, which is in turn involving the transformation of our style of life.

The response in the business field has led to the emergence of the so-called Industry 4.0 that translates into a new integrated production scenario by incorporating innovative solutions, optimizing and connecting production, logistics, commercial and management processes (Borda, 2016). The hybridization of the physical and digital world is taking place; products, machines, tools, factories, warehouses and vehicles are interconnecting with each other and working automatically, an interconnection of all the elements of the value chain that is becoming intelligent and taking place, as already envisioned by the new logistics, to the creation of authentic customer-centric networks (Navarro & Sabalza, 2016). In this way, the environment is changing, interdependent, competitive, global, hybrid and hyper-connected. The result of all this will allow us to achieve immediate responses in decision-making based on information captured in real time, through intelligent systems and processes, without variability, without errors, with full traceability in the process chains and total sustainability. This leads us to a new situation that will affect the way of producing and controlling processes, of applying logistics models, and of developing marketing and marketing strategies.

According to the above, it transcends and emerges because of the importance the concept of Logistics 4.0, which develops and assumes the concepts of the new logistics, and integrating both denominations, the New Logistics 4.0. Then it is that logistics, as a key element of global economic activity, cannot in any case stay out of the way. The intelligent factory implies that manufacturing plants, in the face of a traditional centralization derived from the search for economies of scale by volume, now consider an intelligent global relocation due to specialization factors and synergies. This leads to the creation of immense different networks and distant from interconnected production units, which will imply that the raw materials, semi-processed products and components require full mobility, perfectly synchronized and guaranteeing, participating in global intra-industrial supply and trade networks. In sum, the New Logistics 4.0 implies the optimization and full connection of all the elements and processes of the supply chain. All of this should generate improvements in the effectiveness and efficiency of the management of orders and shipments, an individual customer-oriented production that demands more and more personalized offers, the geolocation of the clients, the simultaneous multimodal omnichannel and the optimization of the global routes, a full capacity of adaptation, the total international traceability of the merchandise, the reduction of the stock and the necessary space of storage, payment automation, etc. It is about hyper-linking and making industry, logistics and markets smart, achieving a model in which innovation is collaborative, productive means are connected, supply chains are integrated, distribution and service channels are digital. Integration, holistic vision, coherence, collaboration, innovation and flexibility are key concepts to support the development of New Logistics 4.0, whose adaptation will involve the implementation of a new logistics strategy, the design of a new organization and the management of change towards a new digital culture, as well as the establishment of new methodologies and processes within the framework of the incorporation of digital tools and technologies.

The prospect of the future development of the new logistics has configured the theory of the Physical Internet (Montreuil et al, 2010), a vision that has been adopted both in the USA and in the EU as a conceptual objective of logistics by 2050. It involves achieving an open global logistics system, based on physical digital and operational interconnectivity, through encapsulation, interfaces and protocol design, in order to move, store, perform, provide and use physical objects throughout the world in an economically, environmentally and socially efficient and sustainable way. This approach is intended to eliminate existing inefficiencies in global transport and waste management of logistics networks, in a similar way to what the Internet proposed worldwide for information flows. It will be necessary to create an open market for the transport of goods, with shared, open and adaptable distribution chains, in which the products will be transported in modular, standardized and intelligent containers that allow each unit to be followed and controlled. For this, it will be necessary to achieve a full level of global collaboration, redefining the competitive space, taking it out of the logistics processes, and taking it only to the points of sale in which customers define the market shares of each product. The viability of Physical Internet will obviously require the implementation of existing digital enabling technologies. Above all, the incorporation of other technological innovations of more advanced and complex exponential evolution, which will be developed over the coming years.

As a consequence of this and in order to make the development and all the processes of permanent digital transformation within the paradigm of the Global Sustainable Logistics possible, it is necessary to design a new concept of Logistics Platforms 4.0, which allows coordination, collaboration, integration, security and synchronism of the new international corridors, logistics servers and global supply networks. In this new paradigm, the development of a new urban logistics is essential in the framework of smart and sustainable cities initiatives.

This chapter aims to study the most significant aspects of these new concepts, identifying the keys to move towards its implementation in strategic terms. In addition to the introduction section, the chapter has three more parts. In the second part, the main aspects of the sustainable global logistics paradigm are studied. In the third part, the implication of the digital transformation and the conceptual development of the new logistics 4.0 is analyzed. Finally, in the fourth part the main concepts for the design of the new logistics cargo platforms are developed, especially in the field of urban logistics of sustainable and intelligent cities.

RESEARCH METHODOLOGY

The research has been developed under an exploratory or interpretive research methodology, to have a better understanding of the problem posed without obtaining conclusive results. We have used a systemic approach with a systematized deductive process (Top-Down), guided by empirical evidence which is derived from the author's experience in the field of logistics management and international trade, and the qualitative interaction with different organizational structures, both public and private (Bottom-Up).

The literature reviewed has been used to synthesize the essential concepts and approaches on the problem investigated, reviewing it all with a level of detail that is considered sufficient and looking for its original aspects to guarantee objectivity and avoid interpretative biases.

THE PARADIGM OF THE GLOBAL SUSTAINABLE LOGISTICS

It is evident that during the last years the logistics has been assuming an increasing importance within the strategies of the companies. Today it is clear that logistics has become an essential factor for the improvement of its competitiveness in the framework of a global market, affected by a turbulent and digital environment. The great advances in the methodologies and technologies of action in the logistics field, which have been developed exponentially with the Internet, imply the obtaining of competitive advantages that are based, in addition to increasing the effectiveness and efficiency of logistics services, in the continuous increase in the value contributed to customers and, in a very prominent and socially increasingly demanded way, in their global sustainability.

To begin with, the sustainability of logistics and supply chain management in a global level represents a strategy of integration in a transparent way of the social, environmental and economic objectives of the organization, within the coordination system of the main inter-organizational business processes, with in order to improve the long-term economic results of each company and its supply chains (Carter & Rogers, 2008).

This concept is based on important background that should be remembered. To accommodate the global environmental concern, in 1983 the UN created the World Commission on Environment and Development. Within this Commission, the Brundtland Report, initially called Our Common Future, was drafted in 1987. It owes its name to the then Prime Minister of Norway, Dr. Gro Harlem Brundtland, who chaired it. In this document, in which the positions of economic development in force with those of environmental sustainability are confronted and contrasted for the first time and the concept of sustainable development is formalized. According to this report *"Sustainable development is development that meets the needs of the present without compromising the ability of future generations to meet their own*

Figure 1. Concept and Implications of Global Sustainable Logistics
Source: Fernández-Villacañas (2008), adaptation of Carter & Rogers (2008)

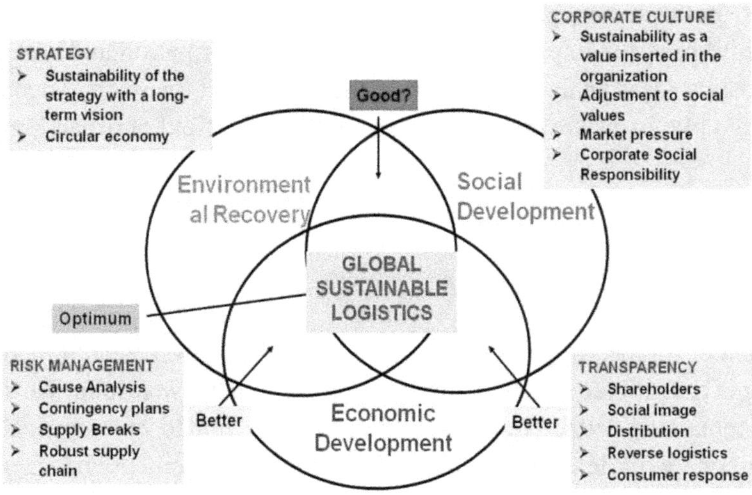

needs" (Brundtland, 1987). This definition came to question the prevailing consumerist model, calling for the transformation of the concept of development to include a triple aspect, adding to the economic dimension, the social and environmental dimensions (Fernández-Villacañas, 2008).

A few years later, the so-called Earth Summit, the United Nations Conference on Environment and Development, takes place in Rio de Janeiro (Brazil) from June 3 to 14, 1992. At that conference The Rio Declaration on Environment and Development was finalized, with twenty-seven principles that were seconded by all participating countries. The concept of sustainable development was definitively proposed as the basis for reconciling economic growth, natural resources and society, without compromising the life possibilities of future generations. Subsequently, Agenda 21 would be the germ of the Millennium Development Goals set by the UN in 2000 with 8 human development purposes whose achievement became theoretically a priority for governments around the world through international cooperation. Specifically, objective number seven sought to ensure environmental sustainability.

More recently in 2015, these objectives were revised, leading to a new UN 2030 Agenda with the so-called Sustainable Development Goals, which urge countries and all social actors to intensify their efforts to end poverty in all its forms, reduce inequality and fight against environmental deterioration. They consist of 17 objectives, of which 5 are specifically dedicated to the environment, and 169 goals of an integrated and indivisible nature that cover the economic, social and environmental spheres. Since thence, sustainability has become an important aspect of business management (Rosati & Diniz, 2019), although totally insufficient to guarantee the global sustainability of the planet (Caiado et al, 2018). In any case, this new context requires that business and logistics management implicitly carry out the critical evaluation of its activities with environmental, social and economic aspects (Yun et al, 2019).

In this way, the concept of sustainability, which had been linked by many socio-economic actors exclusively with practices of respect for the environment, has evolved to include other dimensions such as responsibility and ethics of social behavior, the new consumer requirements or sustainable economic well-being, understood globally in the analysis of international competitiveness. Indeed, the growing economic importance of the countries of Asia-Pacific and Africa, the increase in fossil fuel prices, and the search for sustainable and less polluting energy solutions for transport, are generating major changes in this model and promoting changes in the distribution of the global economic surplus. Sustainability has become an important factor in competitive advantages for industrial manufacturing companies (Le et al, 2013). As usual in the logistics field in general, the sustainability of logistics activities should be measured, as a mechanism among other issues of achieving the objectives proposed by the UN (Stindt, 2017).

One of the most significant aspects that affects environmental sustainability are the transport operations of companies that provide logistics services. It has been found that multinational companies that provide their transport services globally are the most interested in environmental issues, partly because they consider transport sustainability as a potential source of competitive advantage (Bask et al, 2018).

Research activities carried out in the field of sustainable logistics have assumed the comprehensive conceptual approach in the fields of economic, social and environmental development. Some examples emphasize the academic concern generated in this regard. The study of the relationship between sustainability innovation practices and the performance of logistics chains has shown synergistic effects between the adoption of practices and the performance of logistics chains, in particular ecological design practices, the evaluation of the cycle of life, green manufacturing, reverse logistics and waste management (Cherrafi et al, 2018). Or it has been found that among the fundamental factors that influence the success of the implementation of sustainable practices in logistics chains, the commitment of resources is cyclic (Morgan et al, 2016), and in particular the efficient use of technological resources for transformation, processing of management and transport information and operations (Watanabe et al, 2018).

Consequently, many large companies -especially multinationals- have reviewed their manufacturing processes and the configurations of their logistics chains. The words of Professor Andy Hoffman of Sustainable Enterprise at the University of Michigan written in 2006 are very guiding:

... As some work out the definition of sustainable development, the companies are dealing with its reality. They are striving for sustainability, even if they do not call it that. The reality is that the business environment is changing. New types of pressures and demands are leading to new types of business practices. And this change will only increase. We live in a shrinking world where global sourcing brings corporate interests into ever-increasing contact with peoples and issues around the world. This contact makes vivid the disparities between rich and poor, between developed and developing countries.

Information technology makes it impossible for business activities to remain hidden by geography or contractual arrangements. It also makes it possible for activists to gain the power necessary to mobilize a response to those activities. Raging issues of child labour, forced labour, hazardous work conditions, environmental contamination, public health, access to clean water, and corrupt and oppressive regimes are being forced onto the business radar screen. As companies respond to the pressure to address these issues, they are being forced to define sustainability in practical terms. Issues like transparency, social equity, and environmental protection are joining economic growth in corporate discussions.

But the real question for these corporate strategists is not whether this is happening -- it is -- but rather, what will be demanded of companies next year, in 10 years, in 50 years, and how to get ahead of it. Real sustainability requires a long view. It requires conscious attention to where the business environment is going, and what is taking it there. Sustainability is not a value projection, it is not CSR, and it is not an aspiration. It is real market pressure. And responding to that pressure means success and good management in the 21st century. (Hoffman, 2006)

In recent years, the importance of sustainability in logistics systems for business competitiveness has been confirmed, verifying that the stock market and the price of the shares react to the awarding of awards in corporate logistics sustainability, including more significant way than for the granting of other types of awards. This demonstrates that even shareholders already recognize the importance of sustainability as a strategic factor for the survival of companies (Eroglu et al, 2016).

Finally, as fundamental bases of Global Sustainable Logistics (Fernández-Villacañas, 2019), we can highlight:

- In the microeconomic field, cultural change to reconcile economic growth with responsible consumption.
- In the macroeconomic field, a long-term political vision, with the establishment of an efficient and competitive framework that allows the adequate allocation and use of resources, with an effective use and development of macro-logistic infrastructures on which productivity is supported and competitiveness
- In the environmental field, respect for the natural basis for sustainable progress.
- In the field of social policy, the consideration of citizens as "means" and as "ends" of a non-demagogic socio-economic progress.
- And finally, in the field of institutional development, structured collaboration between the public sector and the private sector.

THE LOGISTICS DIGITAL TRANSFORMATION - THE *NEW LOGISTICS 4.0*

As discussed above, the globalization phenomenon has generated a dramatic and noticeable change in the commercial structures of organizations, promoting a new global strategic mentality that tries to confront new competitors as well as the search for new markets. All these factors have led to the development of the logistics function as an essential support to meet the increasingly demanding needs of customers at an international level. In an increasingly global, dynamic, complex and uncertain environment, the logistics which started with a very limited functional definition, has experienced rapid growth and evolution in almost all industrial sectors. Therefore, it has become an essential element regarding business strategy, contributing to a main source of competitive advantage and giving rise to the polysemic and multifaceted development of the so-called new logistics.

In addition to logistics sustainability, the new logistics are based on the well-known conceptual transition from the push approach to the pull approach, from a strategic supply perspective to a demand perspective, by developing new logistics models that are more efficient, sustainable, intelligent, agile, adaptable, scalable as well as resilient.

The response to the new determining factors of the global environment has also involved changes in the relationships of the companies regarding their suppliers and clients. Both of these groups are increasingly heterogeneous and are moving from a view that was centered on the reduction of supply, storage, distribution and waste costs, towards another focused on consumers. The latter, seeks to be more flexible regarding their requirements, by systematically improving service levels, applying technology, managing

Figure 2. Conceptual transit from a push approach to a pull approach
Source: Fernández-Villacañas, 2018

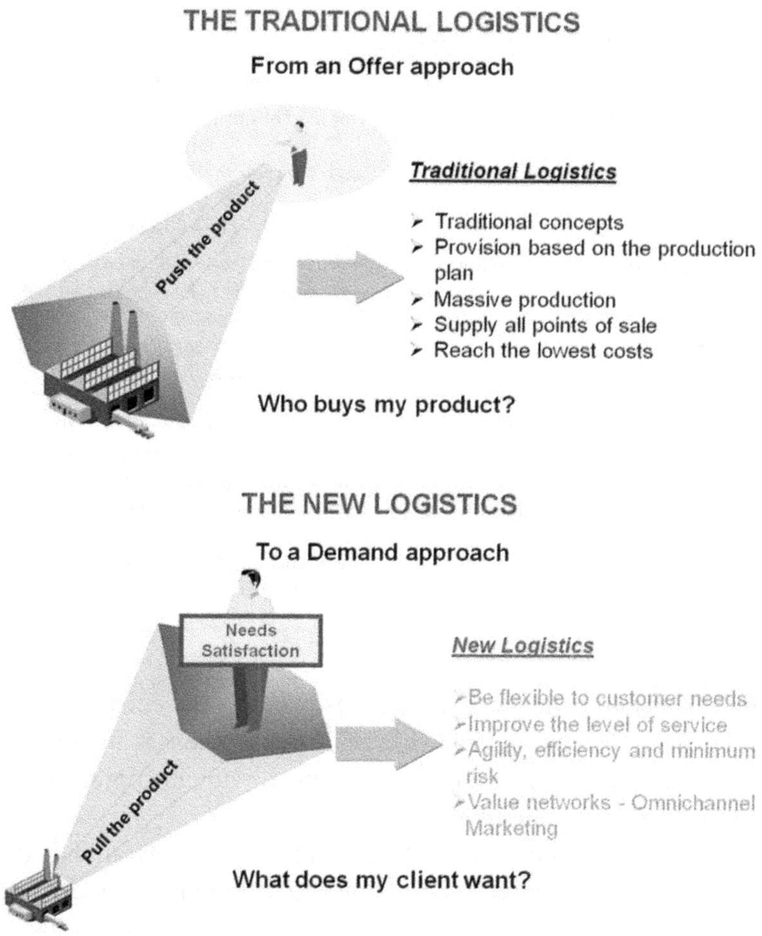

supply chains in an integrated way - not only with minimal costs but also with minimal risks - promoting competition and innovation, as well as creating and managing global value networks. In other words, beyond the supply chain in which the consumer is the last link, a complex and dense network of socio-economic "actors" can be identified, which are focused on the consumer and woven by information and communication. In this network, the consumer adopts the role of a judge who constantly evaluates the activities of all the "actors" involved thus deciding for his consumption and purchase those he considers best meet his needs (Fernández-Villacañas, 2018).

The following figure summarizes the main aspects of traditional logistics and its evolution to the new logistics.

On the other hand, the digital transformation can conceptually be defined as the process of organizational, cultural and strategic reinvention, of both companies and public entities, necessary for the integral application of the technology that we call digital, which generates, processes, stores and uses data, information and intelligence, to improve its performance as well as its ability to quickly adapt to disruptive or radical changes generated in the environment (Fernández-Villacañas, 2018). This techno-

Figure 3. The Traditional Logistics Vs the New Logistics
Source: Fernández-Villacañas, 2018

THE TRADITIONAL LOGISTICS	THE NEW LOGISTICS
Competition for price	Competition for service
Transportation of large lots, rare	Transport of smaller and more frequent lots
Supply type push, driven by the offer	Supply type pull, driven by demand
Existence of large inventories	Inventory zero (just in time)
Focus on business by contracts	Focus on the integration of processes, with the use of ICTs for coordination and control
Distribution networks organized at multiple levels with reduced areas of influence	Global networks of logistics platforms and integrated distribution centers
Producers and marketers with their own organization, including transportation	Outsourcing to logistics operators (3PL and above), focus of the entrepreneur on activities of greater added value
Provision and sales focused on the country itself	Globalization of suppliers and customers
Low environmental awareness	Greater environmental awareness, circular economy and reverse logistics

logical scenario, which is an authentic new paradigm, is inducing the emergence of shorter and shorter management cycles, in which the environment changes are continuously and increasingly faster, with a pace that we assume will continue to accelerate in the future, with an approach in exponential technological evolution as has already been highlighted.

The main catalyst for change and the cause of this continuous acceleration is the digital revolution, motivated by the expansion of the Internet, information and communication technologies, as well as the universalization of its use, which is in turn involving the transformation of our life style. In this way, we are currently fully imbricated in a process of deployment of disruptive technologies that are profoundly modifying the business reality and the society in general (Evtodieva et al, 2017). Although computer science signified a cyclopean advance in the mechanization and automation of the processes, and the later connection of the equipment between them, it also generated the beginning of a formidable process and distribution capacity of the information, the digital factor has exponentially multiplied the connectivity of all public and private actors, among which citizens are logically included as protagonists.

The inclusion of digital technologies and the transformation induced by them defines what has come to be called the Fourth Industrial Revolution. Effectively globalization, the universalization of the use of the Internet, the full automation of processes and the digitization of information, have led to an authentic Industrial Revolution, whereby the hybridization of the physical and virtual world is taking place; products, machines, tools, factories, warehouses and vehicles are interconnecting each other and work automatically, an interconnection of all the elements of the value chain that is becoming intelligent and that is leading to the creation of authentic centered networks in the clients. In this way, the environment appears to be changing, hybrid, competitive, global, connected and interdependent.

The result of all this will allow us to achieve immediate answers in decision-making based on the information captured in real time, through intelligent systems and processes, without variability or errors, with full traceability in the process chains and total sustainability. All of this leads us to a new situation that will affect the way of producing and controlling processes, applying logistic models, and developing marketing and commercialization strategies.

In this way and totally linked to the concept of Industry 4.0, the concept of Logistics 4.0, which develops and assumes the concepts of the new logistics, transcends and emerges due to its importance (Tang & Veelenturf, 2019). That is that logistics, as a key element of the industrial sector, cannot be kept aside (Winkelhaus & Grosse, 2019). The Smart Factory implicitly assumes that manufacturing plants, facing a traditional centralization derived from the search for economies of scale by volume, now consider an intelligent relocation by factors of specialization and synergies, giving rise to the creation of different and immense networks distant from interconnected production units, which will imply that the raw materials, components and semi-finished products require greater mobility, be perfectly synchronized and guaranteed, participating in global supply networks and intra-industry trade. As a result, a new economy is being formed, known as the digital economy, or Industry 4.0 (Evtodieva et al, 2019).

On the other hand, the life cycles of products in international markets tend to be continuously reduced and variations in their demands are increasingly difficult to estimate, so it is crucial to have greater connectivity and integration between the final and initial links of the global supply chains, as well as a greater capacity for the aggregation of data and automatic estimation, rigorous and real-time estimation of the different demands, with expert systems and artificial intelligence that assist in the decision-making processes (Fernández-Villacañas, 2018).

Consequently, the New Logistics 4.0 will involve the optimization and full connection of all elements and processes of the supply chain, which should generate improvements in the efficiency and effectiveness of the management of orders and shipments, a production oriented to the individual customer which increasingly demands more personalized offers, the geolocation of customers, the simultaneous multimodal omnichannel, and the optimization of global routes, a full capacity for adaptation, the total international traceability of merchandise, the reduction of stock and space necessary for storage, automation of payments, etc. (Strandhagen et al, 2019).

Intelligent logistics will not only better meet the new demands, but will also locate with greater precision and fully know the current and potential customers through the treatment and interpretation of the data collected and the optimization of the processes. Integration, holistic vision, coherence, collaboration, innovation and flexibility are key concepts to support the development of New Logistics 4.0, whose adaptation will involve the implementation of a new logistics strategy, the design of a new organization and the change management towards a new digital culture, as well as the establishment of new methodologies and processes within the framework of the incorporation of digital tools and technologies (Fernández-Villacañas A, 2019).

In relation to the deployment of enabling technologies, a wide range of applicable technologies is available (Frazzon et al, 2019), as referred to in Figure 5. The proposed logistics models must integrate these already available technologies, but most importantly, they must make the progressive integration of other technological innovations of exponential evolution, which are being developed in the future, scalable.

Regarding all these technologies, it is important to emphasize the role that Data Science within the new logistics 4.0. This concept unifies statistics, analysis and data analysis, data extraction, automatic learning and its related methods and algorithms for understanding and analyzing real phenomena with large data. It employs techniques and theories drawn from many fields within the context of mathematics, statistics, computer science and information science.

Figure 4. Dimensions of the transformation towards the new logistics 4.0
Source: Fernández-Villacañas a), 2019

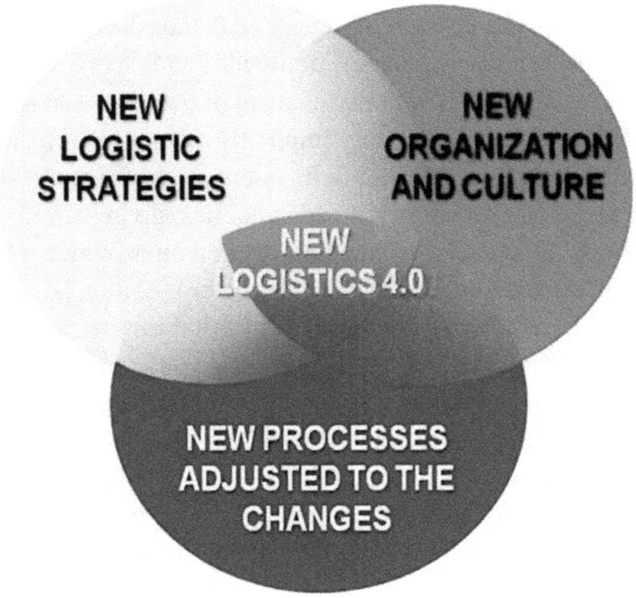

Figure 5. Enabling technologies of the new logistics 4.0
Source: Fernández-Villacañas b), 2019

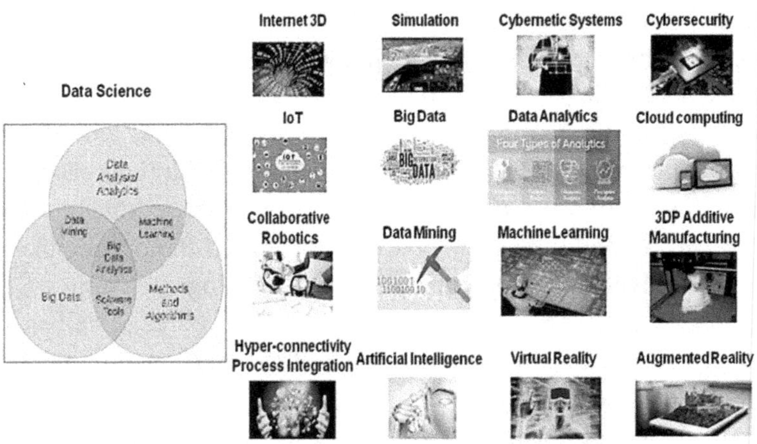

It is considered necessary to emphasize that the digital transformation and the emergence of Industry 4.0 and Logistics 4.0, beyond the technological developments and their deployment, and the reinvention of strategy, organization and corporate culture, requires, on the one hand, the development of a new holistic style of a humanitarian leadership, but also, on the other, the availability of a permanent digital leadership capacity that achieves the most critical element for the success of the analyzed evolution to be collaborate and be fully involved: this is the human factor (Borda, 2018).

The future development of the new logistics has shaped the theory of Physical Internet (Montreuil & Meller & Ballot, 2010), which has been adopted both in the United States and in the European Union as a conceptual objective of logistics for 2050. It involves achieving an open global logistics system, based on physical, digital and operational interconnectivity, through encapsulation, interfaces and protocol design, in order to move, store, perform, provide and use physical objects throughout the world in an economically, environmentally and socially efficient and sustainable manner. This approach aims to eliminate existing inefficiencies within global transport and waste management logistics networks, in a similar way to what the Internet posed globally for information flows. In order to implement this initiative, it will be necessary to create an open market for the transport of goods, with shared, open and adaptable distribution chains, whereby products will be transported in modular, standardized and intelligent containers that allow each unit to be followed and monitored. To do this, it will be necessary to reach a maximum level of global collaboration, redefining the competitive space, taking the logistics processes out of it, and taking it only to the points of sale where customers define the market shares of each product (Montreuil, 2011).

The viability of Physical Internet will obviously require the implementation of existing enabling digital technologies, but above all, the incorporation of other technological innovations of more advanced and complex exponential evolution, which will be developed over the coming years.

Figure 6. The prospective of evolution towards Physical Internet in 2050
Source: Montreuil, 2010

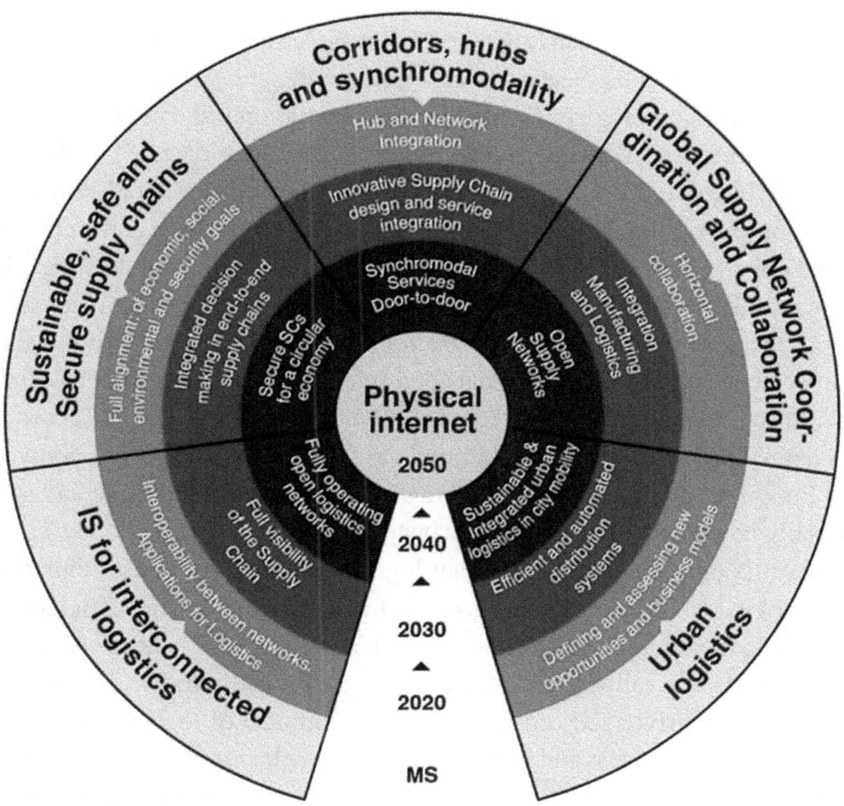

Finally, it is necessary to emphasize that this new digital culture and logistics will have to on the one hand, assume the development of a new holistic style of humanitarian leadership. On the other hand, it would need to have a permanent capacity for digital leadership that can ensure the most critical element for the success of the evolution analyzed, that it collaborates and is fully involved, in other words, the human factor (Borda, 2018).

THE CONCEPT OF LOGISTICS PLATFORMS 4.0 - THE NEW URBAN LOGISTICS PLATFORMS WITHIN THE FRAMEWORK OF THE SMART CITIES

The Logistics Platform Concept

Since the late 70s and early 80s of the previous century, the ports promoted the development of large industrial complexes around them, the so-called industrial port areas, formed mainly by large industries such as steel and petrochemicals. These large corporations were generating large movements of goods in bulk, guaranteeing the continuity of traffic and the loyalty of their international customers through their investments in large stocks of immobilized products. However, a few years later, the rapid restructuring of international production strategies and the accelerated transformation in the world of international trade, production and logistics, drove public administrations to create new nodal infrastructures: the logistics platforms. These structures represent a modern approach aimed towards fostering and facilitating logistics activities and business exchange with associated flows in a specific geographic area (Gajšek & Grzybowska, 2016).

Conceptually, following the European Logistics Platforms Association, logistics platforms are defined as delimited areas created with the objective of carrying out logistic activities of transport, storage and distribution of goods, by different logistics operators, both for national and international transport, which must be designed with intermodal criteria and can act multiple forms of transport (road, rail, sea, river, air, ...) (Gajšek & Grzybowska, 2013). They are complexes prepared to centrally assume many logistics operations, facilitating the optimization of the companies that work there and improving logistics efficiency and effectiveness. That is, the logistics platforms allow optimization of logistics management costs and the increase the speed of movement of goods, which translates into an increase in commercial margins without an increase in prices, an increase in profitability and productivity, and an increase in the quality of the service provided to intermediate and final customers (Fernandez-Villacañas a), 2019).

A logistics platform must be open to the access of all interested companies that carry out productive, logistic and commercial activities, of large, medium and small size. To ensure synergy and commercial cooperation, it is important that the logistics centre be managed under a unique and sustainable model that should preferably be raised through public-private cooperation.

The experience of its operation has shown that logistic platforms not only contribute to reduce the implicit costs of the logistics chain, but also allow a strong increase in logistics efficiency in international commercial operations, including small businesses, achieving a greater added value of logistic chains (Li et al, 2019). The ports and railway nodes, which are traditionally traffic concentration points, and now especially airports, are privileged centres for the development of logistics platforms.

These centres of logistics, business and service activities have been developed in response to a redesign of the global distribution that tends to concentrate on a limited number of areas and commercial corridors. They not only constitute nodal points of the transport chains but also territorial facilities of increasing importance such as drivers of economic-social development, fundamental pieces of the structuring of the economy of metropolitan areas and basic elements of the economic competitiveness of nations and their regions. The market is no longer satisfied with high product quality but requires high quality logistics services (deliveries in a very short time, merchandise in perfect condition, timely information, ...) that become a fundamental instrument of competitiveness. In this way, logistics platforms are essential as managers of the entire supply chain and distribution networks.

Advantages of Logistics Platforms

First, we have to consider support for economic and business development (Lyu et al, 2019). The construction of a logistics platform implies strong investments destined to the construction of the facilities, to the establishment of the companies that are going to use them and to the development of the whole network of resources and auxiliary services that arise around these companies. This implies a strong creation of both direct and indirect employment. In addition, the operation of a logistics platform generates strong business synergies and in an induced way, the revitalization of the economic activity of the region of influence, creating turnover and new opportunities for nearby companies, and increasing tax revenues for the public treasury.

On the other hand, logistics platforms reduce the logistic costs of companies by generating the benefits derived from the concentration of logistics activity and better access to global transport networks, their proximity to industrial or consumer centres and the reduction of activity dispersion. Multimodal logistics platforms also enhance coordination between different means of transport, which makes both logistics operators and their customers easier to use the best possible method for each shipment. In short, they allow the improvement of the competitiveness and efficiency of the companies located there by being able to place their products and services in their destination markets at a lower cost (Cambra-Fierro & Ruiz-Benitez, 2009).

Finally, logistics platforms contribute to urban rationalization given that they involve the concentration of logistics activities in them, generating urban land unemployment as a result of relocation of companies in the sector. In addition, various improvements are induced such as the revaluation of soils, the improvement of degraded areas or privileged conditions of accessibility, with the consequent improvement of the environmental environment and a greater degree of protection of the same (the improvement of urban traffic, the reduction of pollution by mean reduction of routes, noise reduction in urban environments, etc.). At the same time, it makes better use of the land destined for logistical purposes, due to the greater concentration of resources and needs in the same location (Boudin et al, 2014).

Typology of Logistics Platforms

When it comes to classifying the different types of logistics platforms, one of the easiest ways to do this is by attending to their relationship with intermodality, differentiating:

- *Dry Ports* that are facilities located in inland areas but that are closely linked to the surrounding ports by road and rail. Its development is essential for the extension of intermodality, by facilitating sea-rail-road connections.

- *Areas of Logistics Activities* that are located near ports or airports are those that differentiate them from the previous type. As for its functions, intermodality is again its main characteristic, being able to join three or more modes of transport.
- *Integrated Transport Centres* dedicated exclusively to road transport, without access to ports or railways. Its location no longer depends on its connection with the ports, but on optimizing its relationship with large companies and nearby urban centres.
- *Aerotropolis* born from an evolved concept of airports that today are much more than an infrastructure needed to support air operations (Kasarda, 2019). They have become multifunctional companies that generate great business development, with a great impact on economic growth and employment. As more and more companies linked to air activities are grouped around airports and along the transport corridors that emanate from them, a new urban form is emerging, which is the aerotropolis, that extends a few kilometres around airports, and their economic effects impact in quite large regions.

The aerotropolis, in addition to a new urban form, can be considered as a new type of logistics centre based on an airport and its integrated surface transport infrastructure to quickly connect urgent and high-value companies with its suppliers, customers and distant business partners. It consists of a multimodal commercial centre based at the airport and corridors and peripheral business groups linked to aviation, as well as mixed-use associated commercial developments that benefit from each other and their accessibility to the airport. We will return to them later.

The Logistics Platforms 4.0 Development: Generating a New Commercial Territorial Organization

It is evident that the new hyper-connected Industry & Logistics 4.0 generate a series of advantages of great value for the operation of logistics platforms (Barreto et al, 2017). Thus, they allow the optimization in real time and full connection of all the elements and processes of the supply chain, allowing it to be located with greater precision as well as knowing exhaustively both current and potential customers. They involve the hybridization of the physical and virtual world, facilitating the interconnection of all the elements of the value chain and the creation of customer-centered networks, in a changing, hybrid, competitive, global, connected and interdependent environment.

Since the life cycles of products in international markets tend to be continually reduced and variations in their demands increasingly difficult to estimate, it is crucial to have greater connectivity and integration between the final and initial links of the supply chains. Likewise, intelligent relocation due to factors of specialization and synergies, leading to the creation of immense networks distinct and distant from interconnected production units, which will imply that the first materials and the products in process and final have greater mobility, perfectly synchronized and guarantee. This is the functional development of Logistics 4.0 that incorporates advances and new management models as significant as *Synchromodality* (Tavasszy et al, 2015), which beyond intermodality allows efficient real-time choice of the optimal mode of transport in each case, or *Omni-channel* commercial communication (Payne et al, 2017), which, beyond multichannel, allows to unify in real time all the commercial channels in which a company or a brand is present, without the customer appreciating differences between them.

On the other hand, traditionally many goods were produced from beginning to end in a single country. Now they are produced in stages in different countries. This offers opportunities to participate in activities that were not available in the past. Participation in the so-called *global value networks* implies organizational learning for the industry and its participating companies, the permanent transfer of technology and the dissemination of knowledge, and in short the improvement of productivity. These are intra-industrial trade activities, according to which a country imports a good, adds value and then exports it to integrate it into an assembly line. Essentially, the country is importing and exporting goods within the same industry.

The performance of both factors, the omnichannel and synchromodality logistics 4.0 strongly demanded for the eCommerce processes, and the global value networks driven by intra-industry trade, both within the scope of the Global Sustainable Logistics paradigm, are generating the public-private action of a new territorial planning and integration of routes, corridors, logistics hubs and commercial areas. This action is emphasized by what we can conceptually call the logistics platforms 4.0, speaking more properly of hyper-connected and intelligent chains of logistics platforms that are being raised in all regions worldwide.

Figure 7. The logistics platforms 4.0 development
Source: Fernández-Villacañas (a), 2019

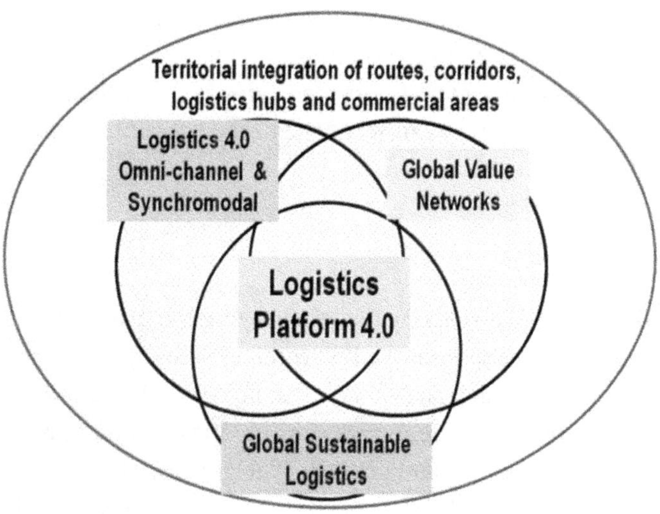

The logistics platforms 4.0 development will be driven by three strategic development vectors (Fernández-Villacañas a), 2019):

- First, the evolution of logistics strategies from a lean approach to an agile approach, through the development of global and integrated logistics operators and platforms, with a omnichannel management models based on synchromodality.
- Second, the evolution of logistics strategies based on specialization and outsourcing to other strategies based on the full integration and collaboration of logistics operators, both among themselves and with the procedures of their clients, as well as with logistics infrastructure companies and the

public sector, creating global networks of flexible and non-hierarchical value oriented integrally towards the consumer, in order to achieve, in a compatible way, the social, environmental and economic objectives.

- Third, the evolution of the logistics strategies based on talent to other strategies based on innovation, technology and knowledge, within an approach of companies aligned with consumers, efficiency, sustainability and continuous training.

Thus, the logistics platforms 4.0 represent the core of a new renewed logistics sector and a new catalyst for social-economic development, but its momentum is colliding in many developed countries with the problem of lack of land near large capitals, something that puts in check many companies, especially large ones with special space needs. The development of the sales of the companies of the sector of the electronic commerce continues unstoppable and, with it, the need of specific spaces, often of great dimensions, to manage the logistics of these companies. Large distributors are in need of continuously expanding their facilities, until they run into land shortages, especially in large capitals, where the spaces on offer are limited or do not meet the size needs of this type of companies. Multilevel logistics platforms will be one of the trends in the coming years in the development of the new logistics platforms. However, its development also faces important challenges, such as its inclusion in the new urban plans in competition with the development of the increasingly demand in urban residential housing. Another aspect to take into account is the environment in which these platforms are going to be located, in order to study the flows that they will absorb, both from vehicles and people, to determine if the areas are capable of absorbing both traffic and parking volumes.

It seems that all this leads us to reflect on the strategic concept of urban development from a logistic approach, and thus it is of interest to review in some detail the concepts of urban logistics as well as the one already presented of the aerotropolis.

Urban Logistics

Urban logistics (Lagorio et al, 2017) is responsible for studying the distribution of cargo in metropolitan areas, strategies and procedures that can improve its overall efficiency, while reducing externalities such as traffic congestion and polluting emissions (Boudin et al, 2014). It includes the provision of services that help to efficiently manage merchandise movements in cities and that provide innovative responses to the demands of commercial companies and citizens. The general objective pursued is the mobility of urban cargo through the transport of goods by or for commercial entities that take place in an urban area.

Although supply chain management and urban logistics are conceptually related, they are developed with different approaches to respond to a different set of problems (Morana, 2014). Supply chain management is concerned with the organization of supply chains to achieve the objectives, while urban logistics seeks to regulate load distribution activities that are the end result of supply chains to ensure their effectiveness in the metropolitan area. Supply chains are generally managed by private companies that work for economies of scale by concentrating their operations, and that compete and perform transactions. Urban logistics is carried out in an environment where a multitude of public and private actors participate, including the Government of the Town Halls, the Government of the Regions and the Central Governments, residents, consumers and retail activities. The relationships between these groups are often very conflictive. Supply chains operate in a network, connecting suppliers, customers and all intermediate stages, such as the performance of distribution centers. Urban logistics mainly operates in a specific space characterized by different jurisdictions, uses and densities. Finally, supply chain management focuses on efficiency through an approach that seeks to maximize profits and minimize costs. Urban logistics seeks to achieve the sustainable objective of guaranteeing permanent supply, optimizing urban circulation by reducing traffic congestion and pollution, citizens capable of guaranteeing their mobility in acceptable timeframes, residents capable of undertaking commercial and social activities without significant obstacles, and stores that can be supplied without stock breakage (Rodrigue & Dablanc, 2019).

The metropolitan area is jointly a place of production, distribution and consumption of goods and services, where material flows are constantly generated, the scope of which varies from one city to another depending on their characteristics and specialization (Rodrigue & Dablanc, 2019). Globalization has changed the functions of production, consumption and particularly distribution by generating their expansion in large supply and distribution networks, with logistics centres and areas. However, globalization has also caused many cities to specialize in financial activities and services, tourism-cultural, transport or concentration of political institutions, relegating productive activities to a secondary and even marginal role. In addition, many cities play an important intermediation role with their port and airport facilities, articulating the transfer of international trade flows from one global level to another national or regional level.

The intensity level of the urban load distribution is usually grouped around large specialized generators, which can be classified into four main types, and which act interrelated (Rodrigue & Dablanc, 2019).

- First, multimodal transport terminals, such as ports, airports and railway and highway nodes, with access points that often support high levels of traffic. The impact of a transport terminal on the logistics of the city is obviously related to the intensity of the activity of the terminal, the supply chains it serves and the extent of its area of influence.
- Second, the areas or centres of logistics activities, integral storage activities, wholesale distribution and simple manufacturing. Higher consumption levels and global supply chains have been a driving force in the establishment and expansion of logistics areas. In addition, the corresponding load terminal facilities have been a significant joint driving force, which implies more efficient interactions due to the proximity.
- Third, the zones or manufacturing areas which today, in many cases, are related to global markets and global value chains, since they can produce finished products, but more likely parts and intermediate products for subsequent assembly. They are generators of urban cargo movements related to producers that involve all possible forms of road transport. Manufacturing districts are commonly found in association with transportation terminals, and also manufacturing and logistics activities are often integrated. Therefore, the distinction between an area or centre of logistics activities and a manufacturing area tends to blur.
- Finally, the commercial areas that are the central node of the urban logistics activity, very focused on retail activities, freight movements related to consumers, and parcels related to business offices and headquarters of institutions. As cities are increasingly polycentric, several commercial districts have emerged.

A city has a spatial and functional structure in continuing transformation that impacts the organization of activities, transport infrastructures and load distribution (Valev et al, 2011). The spatial structure reflects the distribution and density of urban activities and is generally divided into areas such as the central

Figure 8. Urban logistics functions and urban distribution
Source: Rodrigue & Dablanc (2019)

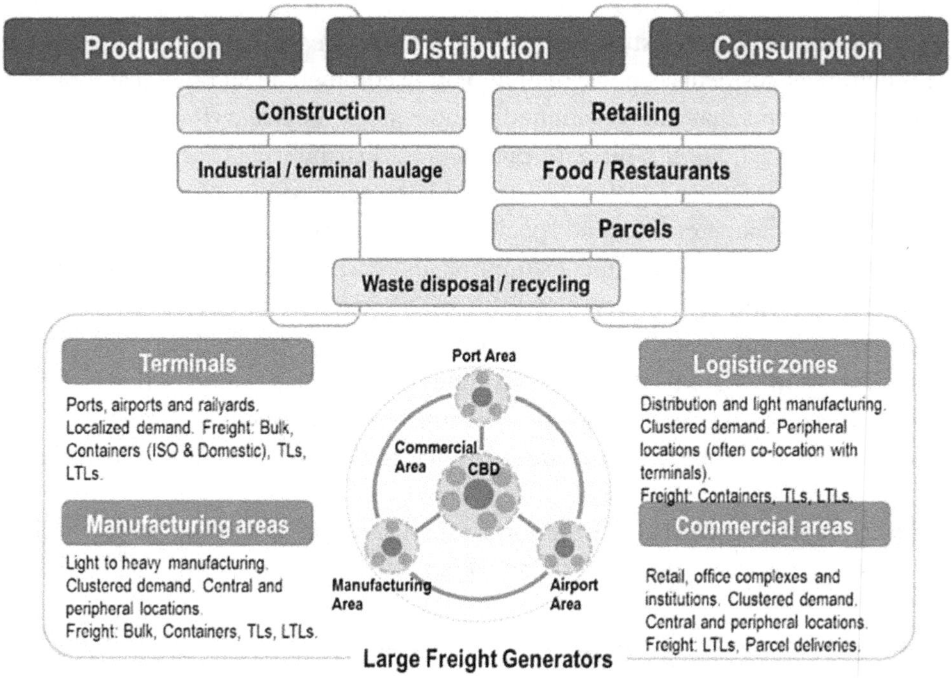

business district, the urban core, suburbs and outer peripheral neighborhoods. The functional structure consists of the infrastructure, the modes and operations that support the distribution of urban cargo.

Suburbs and outer peripheral neighbourhoods also tend to have less congestion than urban centres, which means that the last mile restrictions are less, parking difficulties are reduced, and full truck loads can circulate in most main roads The suburbs, closer to the urban core and the central business district, are therefore a highly conducive environment for logistics, as it offers market accessibility, greater land availability and lower congestion levels. Therefore, it is in the suburbs where large cargo terminals and intermodal centres tend to be located, and airports and ports are historically located, which implies that the suburbs handle most of the interface between the metropolitan area and the national and global cargo distribution areas.

Conditioning Factors of Urban Logistics

Since the mid-twentieth century, the world's urban population has grown and this growth rate up until now represents more than half of the world's population. This transition is expected to last until the second half of the 21st century, a trend that is reflected in the increasing size of cities and the growing proportion of the urbanized population. By 2050, 68% approximately of the world's population is expected to live in cities, underlining the growing importance of the urban market and the challenges of urban logistics (United Nations, 2019).

Metropolitan areas and their influence imply a variety of contexts in which urban logistics is carried out. In poorly developed countries, the large population growth and rural migration have led to very rapid urbanization, which the public supply of infrastructure and transport services has not been able to adequately address, reducing the effectiveness and efficiency of Deliveries in metropolitan areas. It is also important to analyze the evolution of certain socio-economic factors, such as the increase in income, the decrease in the relative price of goods and consumer preferences, which are generating changes in consumption patterns that create a multiplier effect on demand of cargo circulating in urban areas (United Nations, 2019). This effect drives the development of more retail facilities and support infrastructure of distribution centres. Consumption is diversifying and becoming more sophisticated, all of which generates additional volumes of cargo and logistics activity.

On the other hand, the growth of electronic commerce in advanced economies has generated a completely different marketing system, with online purchases and deliveries both at homes and in offices and lockers. Customers expect their orders to be delivered in a shorter timeframe and with a high level of reliability. This entire new paradigm is driving a new system of urban load distribution, which is also taking place in developing countries.

In addition, global procurement and manufacturing processes are imposing local forms of adaptation to ensure that the cargo is delivered in a timely and reliable manner. Outsourcing and relocation have contributed to the establishment of global supply chains where cargo distribution activities that take place within an urban area cannot be effectively explained by the urban economic structure. Supply chains go beyond a single city, a single region and even a single nation.

The actors directly involved in the distribution of urban cargo are concerned about restrictions such as traffic congestion which imposes additional costs and delays in their operations, noise, pollution and inhabitability of the city. Urban logistics management is becoming a major sustainability issue. The public authorities have responded to these concerns through temporary and partial solutions, in terms of traffic and parking regulation, imposing tolls and tariffs on vehicles, particularly trucks, and restricting deliveries during peak hours and in congested areas. All this represents partial and short-term solutions to the problems, which induces the emergence of new problems and conflicts between the actors involved. It seems that all of this must be analyzed from a public-private integral perspective, exploring new smart city models and logistics platforms 4.0 through strategic prospective and disruptive technologies that guarantee sustainable mobility and adequate levels of efficiency and efficiency of urban logistics.

Aerotropolis Concept

After the airport expansion initiated in the 60s of the previous century, with completely standardized infrastructure developments, airports built since the end of the 20th century and the beginning of the 21st in full globalization began to emerge as applied developments of advanced technologies, futuristic designs and multidisciplinary solutions.

Professor John D. Kasarda proposed in 2000 the new concept of Aerotropolis (Kasarda, 2000), which has evolved over the past two decades (Kasarda, 2000 - 2004 - a)2006 - b)2006 - 2011 - 2013 & 2019) (Kasarda & Lindsay, 2011) (Kasarda & Appold, 2014). Under this premise, airports became connecting systems between networked cities, for those global people that always is and needs to be connected and needs to move quickly from the local to the global. High tech companies, hotels, business parks, congress palaces, shopping centers and universities were concentrated around it. And it is that the airports of today have become the key to survival and momentum of the great urban economies, in the same way that the seaports and the railroad were at the time. The airport is the central element in the new concept of technological and smart city, projected outward and, therefore, developed through hyper-connectivity.

The aerotropolis are designed to support the current management of global businesses that need speed and connectivity, in which everything is absolutely connected through the internet. There are currently two types of airborne cities: those that were projected from the beginning as urban centers that have been built around an airport, considered the pulsating heart of the economy, which are the least, and those that have emerged around airports already existing that, according to the old urban conception, were located far from the urban center. In either of these types, the aerotropolis needs certain infrastructures, such as technology parks with Start-Up companies, very fast internet lines, low fiscal pressure and efficient public transport.

With the development of the aerotropolis, the airport is no longer only an integral part of the city, but also becomes the center of the city. According to Professor Kasarda, countries that do not adopt the philosophy of the aerotropolis will be left behind and their economy will not be competitive. This is what used to happen with cities without a train station: they did not develop. People outside the airfield will survive, but they will remain in the past and far from a future that is already here.

In addition to that vision of the future, what is clear is that the aerotropolis is one of the models, although not the only one, that responds to the presented development of the logistics platforms 4.0 and smart cities that can solve a large part of the problems exposed which faces a more effective and efficient global logistics management and modern urban logistics.

Figure 9. The generic aerotropolis
Source: Kasarda, 2019

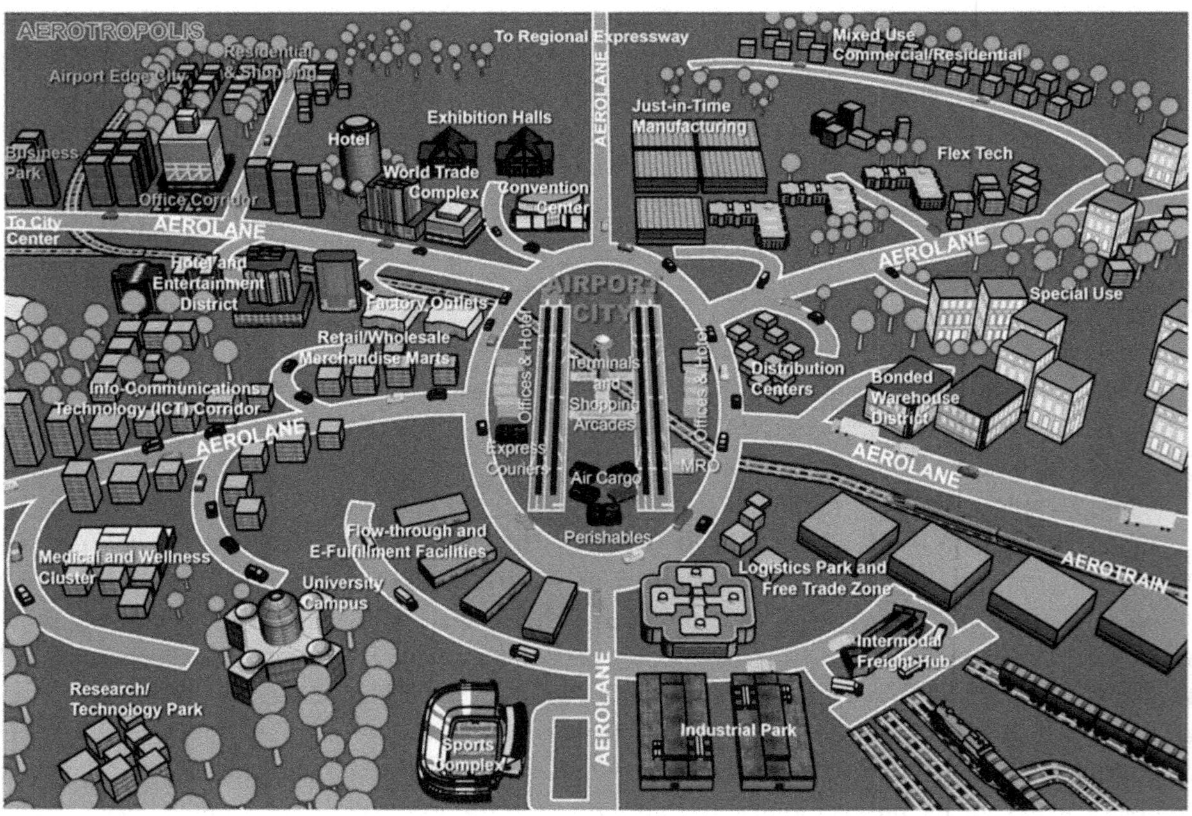

SOLUTIONS AND RECOMMENDATIONS

In an increasingly global, dynamic, complex, technological and uncertain economic and social environment, logistics has experienced rapid growth and evolution in almost all industrial sectors. It has become an essential element of business strategy, a source of competitive advantage leading to the polysemic and polyhedral development of the New Logistics 4.0.

Within this new approach, the new concept of logistics platform 4.0 arises for the improvement of logistics effectiveness and efficiency, within the Global Sustainable Logistics paradigm. These new platforms should lead to the development of measures carried by Governments and multinational companies that allow a new territorial public-private planning and the integration of routes, corridors, logistics centres and commercial areas, in which the metropolitan areas stands out as main actors, and the model of the aerotropolis as its possible conceptual support. The coordinated international measures should lead to the creation of connected and intelligent logistics platform chains worldwide.

Likewise, the promotion of a new urban logistics is essential, in addition to the achievement of more sustainable and intelligent cities, as a necessary condition for the development of the new logistics platforms.

FUTURE RESEARCH DIRECTIONS

The field that has been analyzed of logistics platforms 4.0 and the urban logistics raises interesting and leafy interdisciplinary lines of research. Among them, on the one hand, after the study of the concept it is necessary to develop the new platforms, organizationally, functionally, technologically and strategically, analyse alternative models to determine the optimal territorial location, as well as the integration models of the international platform chains. On the other hand, it is necessary to expand the applied studies of urban logistics through the analysis of real cases of metropolitan areas, as well as the closer relations between the management of urban logistics and the management of logistics platforms after their digital transformation.

CONCLUSION

A conceptual review of the most important aspects that define the new logistics platforms 4.0 has been carried out, by evolution and as an application of the digital transformation of industry and logistics, the implications of the globalization of international trade and in the field of sustainable development.

Firstly, the concepts of sustainability of logistics and supply chain management have been studied globally in the context of the paradigm of sustainability, which is also analyzed, synthesizing the fundamental bases of the concept that has been called Sustainable Global Logistics.

Secondly, the Logistics 4.0 has been studied through the analysis of the main aspects of evolution of traditional logistics towards the New Logistics concepts, the processes of digital transformation of logistics and the deployment of new enabling disruptive technologies, and all this transformation oriented towards a long-term logistics model such as the Physical Internet.

Thirdly, after reviewing the conceptual definition of traditional logistics platforms, the development of hyperconnected and intelligent logistics platforms has been studied. These new logistics platforms 4.0 will generate public-private actions that will lead to a new global territorial planning and integration of routes, corridors, logistics centres and commercial areas, in which Synchromodality and Omni-channel models are its essential characteristics. The three strategic development vectors that are considered fundamental for the promotion of logistics platforms 4.0 have also been explained.

Fourthly, the implications of the logistics of metropolitan areas in the framework of smart and sustainable cities initiatives for the development of logistics platforms 4.0 have been studied, analyzing the main problems and conditioning factors currently faced by urban logistics.

Finally, in this new approach of logistics platforms, the concept of the aerotropolis has been revised as one of the models, although it is not the only one, that responds to the presented development of logistics platforms 4.0 and smart cities, that can solve a large part of the exposed problems, facing a more effective and efficient global logistics management and modern urban logistics.

REFERENCES

Barreto, L., Amaral, A., & Pereria, T. (2017) Industry 4.0 implications in logistics: an overview. *Proceedings of the Manufacturing Engineering Society International Conference MESIC 2017*. DOI: 10.1016/j.promfg.2017.09.045

Bask, A., Rajahonka, M., Laari, S., Solakivi, T., Töyli, J., & Ojala, L. (2018). Environmental sustainability in shipper-LSP relationships. *Journal of Cleaner Production*, *172*, 20. doi:10.1016/j.jclepro.2017.11.112

Borda, J. (2016). La Fábrica del Futuro: Humana, inteligente, tecnológica y digital [The Factory of the Future: Human, intelligent, technological and digital]. Sisteplant.

Borda, J. (2018). Hombre y Tecnología: 4.0 y más [Man and Technology: 4.0 and more]. Sisteplant.

Boudoin, D., Morel, C., & Gardat, M. (2014). Supply Chains and Urban Logistics Platforms. In J. Gonzalez-Feliu, F. Semet, & J. L. Routhier (Eds.), *Sustainable Urban Logistics: Concepts, Methods and Information Systems. Environmental Issues in Logistics and Manufacturing*. Berlin, Germany: Springer; doi:10.1007/978-3-642-31788-0_1

Brundtland, G. H. (1987). *Our Common Future. Report of the World Commission on Environment and Development*. United Nations Comm.

Caiado, R. G., Filho, W. L., Quelhas, O. L. G., de Mattos, D. L., & Avila, L. V. (2018). A literature-based review on potentials and constraints in the implementation of the sustainable development goals. *Journal of Cleaner Production*, *198*, 10.

Cambra-Fierro, J., & Ruiz-Benitez, R. (2009). Advantages of intermodal logistics platforms: Insights from a Spanish platform. *Supply Chain Management*, *14*(6), 418–421. doi:10.1108/13598540910995183

Carter, C. R., & Rogers, D. S. (2008). A framework of sustainable chain management: Moving toward new theory. *International Journal of Physical Distribution & Logistics Management*, *38*(5), 360–387. doi:10.1108/09600030810882816

Cherrafi, A., Garza-Reyes, J. A., Kumar, V., Mishra, N., Ghobadian, A., & ElFezazi, S. (2018). Lean, green practices and process innovation: A model for green supply chain performance. *International Journal of Production Economics, 206*(December).

Eroglu, C., Kurt, A. C., & Elwakil, O. S. (2016). Stock Market Reaction to Quality, Safety, and Sustainability Awards in Logistics. *Journal of Business Logistics, 37*(4), 329–345. doi:10.1111/jbl.12145

Evtodieva, T. E., Chernova, D. V., Ivanova, N. V., & Kisteneva, N. S. (2019). Logistics 4.0. In S. Ashmarina & M. Vochozka (Eds.), *Sustainable Growth and Development of Economic Systems. Contributions to Economics*. Cham: Springer. doi:10.1007/978-3-030-11754-2_16

Evtodieva, T. E., Chernova, D. V., Voitkevich, N. I., Khramtsova, E. R., & Gorgodze, T. E. (2017). Transformation of logistics organization forms under the conditions of modern economy. In E. G. Popkova (Ed.), *Contributions to Economics*. Cham: Springer.

Fernández-Villacañas, M. A. (2008). *Reflexiones en torno al logro de una Logística Global Sostenible* [Reflections on the achievement of a Sustainable Global Logistics]. V Congreso Internacional ACOLOG - Asociación Colombiana de Logística, Bogotá (Colombia).

Fernández-Villacañas, M.A. (2018) *Las plataformas logística 4.0 y la mejora del comercio global: Creando ventaja competitiva logística y desarrollo sostenible* [Logistics 4.0 platforms and the improvement of global trade: Creating competitive logistics advantage and sustainable development]. VI Simposio Internacional Online de Logística y Competitividad, High Logistics Simposios, Medellín, Colombia.

Fernández-Villacañas, M. A. (2019a). Desarrollo e Implementación de Plataformas Logísticas de Carga 4.0 [Development and Implementation of Logistics Cargo Platforms 4.0]. *Proceedings of Primer Congreso Internacional de Tecnología e Innovación en Logística 4.0.*

Fernández-Villacañas, M. A. (2019b). Strategies for the Digital Transformation for the In-Service Support Phase of the Aerospace Weapon Systems. *Proceedings of the Third International Joint Conference of Logistics by EPFAC & UMNG.*

Frazzon, E., Rodriguez, C. M., Pereira, M., Pires, M., & Uhlmann, I. (2019). Towards Supply Chain Management 4.0. *Brazilian Journal of Operations & Production Management, Volume, 16*(2).

Gajšek, B., & Grzybowska, K. (2013). A cross-county contextual comparison of the understanding of the term logistics platforms in practice. Research in Logistics & Production, 3(2).

Gajšek, B., & Grzybowska, K. (2016) Supply Chain Logistics Platform as a Supply Chain Coordination Support. Highlights of Practical Applications of Scalable Multi-Agent Systems. Proceedings of Collection International Workshops of PAAMS 2016. Doi:10.1007/978-3-319-39387-2_6

Hoffman, A.J. (2006, Sept. 5). The Real Thing. Coca-Cola learns a tough lesson about corporate sustainability. *Grist Magazine: Environmental News and Commentary.*

Kasarda, J.D. (2000). Logistics & the rise of aerotropolis. *Real Estate Issues, 25*(4).

Kasarda, J. D. (2004). *Aerotropolis. The Wiley Blackwell Encyclopedia of Urban and Regional Studies.*

Kasarda, J.D. (2006a). The rise of the aerotropolis. *The Next American City, 10*(10), 35-7.

Kasarda, J.D. (2006b). Asia's emerging airport cities. *International Airport Review, 10*(2).

Kasarda, J.D. (2011). Creating an Aerotropolis. How Indianapolis Is Strategically Charting Its Airport's and Region's Future. *Global Airport Cities, 5*(1).

Kasarda, J.D. (2013). Aerotropolis: Business mobility and urban competitiveness in the 21st century. *Urban Insight, 2*(7).

Kasarda, J. D. (2019). Aerotropolis. In A. Orum (Ed.), *The Wiley Black well Encyclopedia of Urban and Regional Studies*. John Wiley & Sons Ltd.; doi:10.1002/9781118568446.eurs0436

Kasarda, J. D., & Appold, S. J. (2014). Planning a competitive Aerotropolis. In *The economics of international airline transport*. Emerald Group Publishing Limited. doi:10.1108/S2212-160920140000004010

Kasarda, J. D., & Lindsay, G. (2011). Aerotropolis: The Way We'll Live Next (A. Lane, Ed.). London, UK: Academic Press.

Lagorio, A., Pinto, R., & Golini, R. (2016). Research in urban logistics: A systematic literature review. *International Journal of Physical Distribution Management, 46*(10). doi:10.1108/IJPDLM-01-2016-0008

Le, F.; Olivier, B. & Mognol, J.H. (2013). Sustainable manufacturing: Evaluation and modeling of environmental impacts in additive manufacturing. *International Journal of Advance Manufacturing Technology, 69.*

Li, S., Wu, W., Xia, Y., Zhang, M., Wang, S., & Douglas, M. A. (2019). How do crowd logistics platforms create value? An exploratory case study from China. *International Journal of Logistics Research and Applications, 22*(5), 5. doi:10.1080/13675567.2019.1628929

Lyu, G., Chen, L., & Huo, B. (2019). The impact of logistics platforms and location on logistics resource integration and operational performance. *International Journal of Logistics Management, 30*(2), 549–568. doi:10.1108/IJLM-02-2018-0048

Mladenow, A., Bauer, C., & Strauss, C. (2016). "Crowd logistics": The contribution of social crowds in logistics activities. *International Journal of Web Information Systems, 12*(3), 379–396. doi:10.1108/IJWIS-04-2016-0020

Montreuil, B. (2011). *Toward a Physical Internet: Meeting the global logistics sustainability grand challenge. Logistics Research*, 3, 2-3.

Montreuil, B., Meller, R. D., & Ballot, E. (2010). Towards a physical internet: the impact on logistics facilities and material handling systems design and innovation. In K. Gue (Ed.), *Progress in material handling research.* Material Handling Industry of America.

Morana, J. (2014). Sustainable Supply Chain Management in Urban Logistics. In J. Gonzalez-Feliu, F. Semet, & J. L. Routhier (Eds.), *Sustainable Urban Logistics: Concepts, Methods and Information Systems. Environmental Issues in Logistics and Manufacturing*. Berlin, Germany: Springer. doi:10.1007/978-3-642-31788-0_2

Morgan, T. R., Tokman, M., Richey, R. G., & Defee, C. (2016). Resource commitment and sustainability: A reverse logistics performance process model. *International Journal of Physical Distribution & Logistics Management, 46*(3), 4.

Navarro, M., & Sabalza, X. (2016). Reflexiones sobre la Industria 4.0 desde el caso vasco [Reflections on Industry 4.0 from the Basque case]. *Ekonomiaz, 89*(1).

Payne, L. M., Peltier, J. W., & Barger, V. A. (2017). Omni-channel marketing, integrated marketing communications and consumer engagement: A research agenda. *Journal of Research in Interactive Marketing, 11*(2). doi:10.1108/JRIM-08-2016-0091

Persdotter, M., Hulthén, H., & Forslund, H. (2019). Environmentally Sustainable Logistics Performance Management Process Integration between Buyers and 3PLs. *Sustainability, 11*(11), 3061. doi:10.3390u11113061

Rodrigue, J. P., & Dablanc, L. (2020) What is City Logistics? In *City Logistics: Concepts, Policy and Practice.* MetroFreight Consortium, Dept. of Global Studies & Geography, Hofstra University. https://globalcitylogistics.org/

Rosati, F., & Diniz, L. G. (2019). Addressing the Sustainable Development Goals in sustainability reports: The relationship with institutional factors. *Journal of Cleaner Production, 215*, 1. doi:10.1016/j.jclepro.2018.12.107

Stindt, D. (2017). A generic planning approach for sustainable supply chain management—How to integrate concepts and methods to address the issues of sustainability? *Journal of Cleaner Production, 153*, 1. doi:10.1016/j.jclepro.2017.03.126

Strandhagen, J.O., Vallandingham, L.R., Fragapane, G., Strandhagen, J.W., Stangeland, A.B.H., & Sharma, N. (2019). Logistics 4.0 and emerging sustainable business models. *Advance Manufacturing, 5*(4).

Tang, C. S., & Veelenturf, L. P. (2019). The Strategic Role of Logistics in the Industry 4.0 Era. *Transportation Research Part E, Logistics and Transportation Review, 6*(June).

Tavasszy, L. A., Behdani, B., & Konings, R. (2015). *Intermodality and Synchromodality.* Available at SSRN: https://ssrn.com/abstract=2592888

United Nations. (2019). *World Urbanization Prospects. The 2018 Revision.* Department of Economic and Social Affairs: Population Division. Access https://population.un.org/wup/Publications/Files/WUP2018-Report.pdf

Valev, J.; Mitković, P. & Vasilevska, L. (2011). Spatial and functional transformation of the city center structure in the process of transition. *Facta universitatis - Series Architecture and Civil Engineering, 9*(3). Doi:10.2298/FUACE1103455V

Watanabe, E. H., Da Silva, R. M., Blos, M. F., Junqueira, F., Filho, D. J., & Miyagi, P. E. (2018). Framework to evaluate the performance and sustainability of a disperse productive system. *Journal of the Brazilian Society of Mechanical Sciences and Engineering, 40*(277).

Winkelhaus, S., & Grosse, E. (2019). Logistics 4.0: A systematic review towards a new logistics system. *International Journal of Production Research, 11*(April).

Yun, G., Yalcin, M. G., Hales, D. N., & Kwon, H. Y. (2019). Interactions in sustainable supply chain management: A framework review. *International Journal of Logistics Management, 30*(1), 140–173. doi:10.1108/IJLM-05-2017-0112

Chapter 4
Evaluating E-Commerce-Related Distribution and Warehousing in Terms of Sustainability

Yeliz Demirkıran
https://orcid.org/0000-0003-3998-7001
Yaşar University, Turkey

Ikbal Ece Dizbay
https://orcid.org/0000-0003-2431-4269
Yaşar University, Turkey

ABSTRACT

In this chapter, the relationships between logistics operations and e-commerce are investigated. The logistics operations are discussed under the distribution and warehousing subjects. The effects of e-commerce on these activities are analyzed by considering the social, environmental, and economic dimensions of sustainability in a broad perspective. For evaluating distribution of e-commerce products, current last-mile operations, trends, and future expectations are investigated in the sustainability concept. Furthermore, the effects of e-commerce on warehouse types and operations are presented. Besides that, location and layout of warehouses, materials used in warehouse buildings, and material handling equipment are discussed with a sustainability perspective.

INTRODUCTION

In the last 50 years, the population of the world increased by almost 108% and the ten-year average population growth is almost 16%. (United Nations Department of Economic and Social Affairs, 2019) Since the borders of the world have evaporated by the effect of globalization and the widespread usage of the internet, the purchasing behavior of the consumers of the growing population has been chang-

DOI: 10.4018/978-1-7998-4601-7.ch004

ing rapidly in a global environment. Customers have begun to prefer purchasing from online stores to use their time more efficiently. This change and the global economy affected many industries such as manufacturing and lead to emerge new sectors such as e-commerce.

According to Lawrence et al. (1998) e-commerce is "buying and selling information, products, and services using any of the thousands of Internet computer networks". In 2019, worldwide e-commerce sales were US$ 3.53 trillion, and e-commerce revenues are forecasted to increase to US$ 6.54 trillion in 2022 (Clement, 2019). E-commerce retailing is growing 20% while the traditional retailing is growing 6% annually. However, e-commerce is still just a small part of the total €21 trillion retailing markets in the projection of 2019 (Laudon & Traver, 2016).

In the last decade, logistics has been greatly influenced by the growth of e-commerce. Logistics and cargo companies have been forced to change their operations and facilities to keep pace with the growth of e-commerce and to adopt new delivery services, delivery points and shorter delivery times. These firms have to provide various tailor-made solutions to meet their customers' fulfillment operations and last-mile delivery requirements. In the meantime, partial shipments and cargo shipments have increased. New distribution models for last-mile-delivery, have emerged. Customer demands are more various and in smaller sizes according to the past (Boysen, Fedtke, & Weidinger, 2018). Due to changing of customer order types, warehouse operations such as receiving, storing, picking and delivering and types have also changed. Fulfillment centers (FC) are established to meet the customers' changed expectations.

By e-commerce become widespread, consumers visit and shop from brick and mortar (B&M) stores less than before. Although consumers' movement has decreased (Mokhtarian, 2004), the transportation of goods that is triggered by e-commerce has increased all around the world. Increment of transportation level caused traffic congestions. Furthermore, it produces air pollution and noise. That means a decrease in life quality especially in the center of the cities. According to the U.S. Energy Information Administration Report on energy usage (2019), in 2018, about 28% of total U.S. energy consumption was due to transporting people and goods. Besides that, transportation is the largest producer of greenhouse gas emissions (GHG) with 29% in 2017 (Environmental Protection Agency, 2019). Warehouses also play a significant role in producing GHG. By air conditioning, lighting and material handling operations, warehouses produce 13% of supply chains GHG (World Economic Forum, 2009).

The effect of transportation on energy usage and carbon emission takes the attention of the researchers and leads them to focus on the issue from a sustainability perspective. Because it is a popular subject for the last three decades, sustainability has many definitions. One of the accepted definitions is "*development that meets the needs of the present without compromising the ability of future generations to meet their own needs*" (World Commission on Environment and Development., 1987). There are three major aspects of sustainability; environmental, economic and social.

Environmental sustainability is defined as "*a condition of balance, resilience, and interconnectedness that allows human society to satisfy its needs while neither exceeding the capacity of its supporting ecosystems to continue to regenerate the services necessary to meet those needs nor by our actions diminishing biological diversity*" by Morelli (2011). Environmental sustainability issues usually include GHG, air and water pollution, biodiversity, waste management, recycling, water consumption, energy consumption, usage of neutral resources, usage of renewable energy, environmentally-conscious customers and businesses, environmentally-friendly products, environmentally-friendly packaging. Economic sustainability is defined as "*maintenance of capital, or keeping capital intact*" (Goodland et al., 2002). Economic sustainability issues usually include global e-commerce sales and the percentage of e-commerce in gross domestic products (GDP) and the cost of products. McKenzie (2004) defines social sustainability as "*a positive condition within communities, and a process within communities that can achieve that conditio*n". Social sustainability issues include unemployment, new employment areas, improved customer service level, quality of life standards, health and safety. The three aspects of sustainable logistics are given in Figure 1.

Figure 1. Three aspects of sustainable logistics
(Tambovcevs & Tambovceva, 2012)

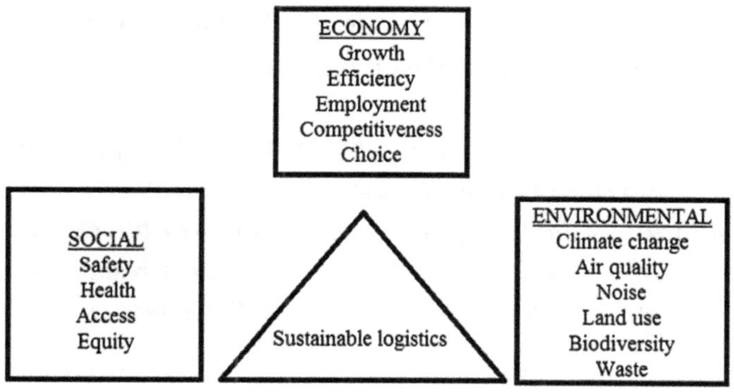

While many of the studies about e-commerce logistics emphasize just environmental or economic aspects, only a few studies and industrial reports handle the subject on three dimensions of sustainability: economic, social and environmental. Furthermore, there is no study about e-commerce related to sustainability, associated with logistic operations in a broader perspective. Therefore, this chapter aims to evaluate logistics activities related to e-commerce in terms of three dimensions of sustainability. Furthermore, recently developed innovative solutions such as drone-based deliveries, usage of automated vehicles and automated warehouses, and best practices of the companies, supporting sustainable e-commerce logistics, will be discussed. The last but not the least, future expectations in the light of current developments will be presented in the following paragraphs.

The remain part of this paper is structured as follows. The next chapter discusses the e-commerce delivery and transportation trends and gives a brief explanation about how these trends affect sustainability. In the following chapter, the issues about warehouses that are necessary for e-commerce will be discussed with the perspective of social, environmental and economic dimensions of sustainability. Lastly, this chapter ends with the conclusion section.

SUSTAINABILITY EVALUATION OF E-COMMERCE DISTRIBUTION AND TRANSPORTATION TRENDS

Sustainable transportation is a very popular and studied subject. When we write "sustainable transportation" to the Google Search Engine, there are more than 1.1 million results listed (03.01.2020). For academic papers, Google Scholar lists 49 thousand results including this term. Too many results in the search show how much people use this term; can this also indicate that a sustainable transportation system is being established today? According to Gordon (1995), people's behaviors, lifestyles, technology, and prices are changing those results in people gaining a vision of "sustainable transportation".

Sustainable transportation is a dynamic concept. While the population and human needs are growing, the meaning of "sustainable transportation" covers more issues every day. Is it impossible to reach a sustainable transportation system? Is "sustainable transportation" just a utopia? Even if the answer is "yes" for both questions, it is good to adopt the idea beyond the heading of Alberro's article, saying, "Utopia isn't just idealistic fantasy – it inspires people to change the world" (Alberro, 2019). From this point of view, it would be fitting for the very broad and widely accepted definition of sustainable transportation by the European Union Council of Ministers of Transport. According to the Council (2001), such a system

- *"allows the basic access and development needs of individuals, companies and societies to be met safely and in a manner consistent with human and ecosystem health, and promotes equity within and between successive generations;*
- *is affordable, operates fairly and efficiently, offers choice of transportation mode, and supports a competitive economy, as well as balanced regional development;*
- *limits emissions and waste within the planet's ability to absorb them, uses renewable resources at or below their rates of generation, and, uses nonrenewable resources at or below the rates of development of renewable substitutes while minimizing the impact on the use of land and the generation of noise."*

Black (2010) gives a narrower definition of sustainable transportation on purpose because the author believes that, as the definition of sustainable transportation broadens, it cannot be achieved. According to this definition, sustainable transportation is a system, which provides transportation and mobility, using renewable fuels to minimize emissions and prevents transportation-related fatalities and injuries. Although sustainable transportation, defined by Black, seems to be achievable with relevant laws and policies, it does not adequately address the needs of this era.

Litman et al. (2007) proposed sustainable transportation system indicators. According to their study for the economic aspect, a sustainable transportation system is expected to serve efficient mobility, cause local economic development and reach operational efficiency. For the social aspect, this type of system is expected to ensure social equity, affordability, human safety and health, community cohesion, and cultural preservation. Besides, a sustainable transportation system is expected to reduce air, noise and water pollution and global warming emissions. Finally yet importantly, conserving resources, preserving open-space and protecting biodiversity are important performance indicators of a sustainable transportation system. The mentioned subjects above are generally accepted sustainability goals. How can one measure these goals? There are several indexes, aiming to measure the performances of sustainable transportation systems; Framework for Measuring Sustainable Regional Development (2010), Urban Sustainability Rating Tools (2014), Green Community Checklist (Environmental Protection Agency, 2015), etc. By reviewing several reports, Litman et al. (2007) recommends a list of indicators and classifies them into three groups; most important, helpful and specialized. According to them, most important indicators are personal mobility by mode, freight mobility by mode, land use density, total transportation expenditures, average freight transportation speed and reliability, average commute travel time and reliability and per capita congestion cost.

According to WHO (2019) respiratory and cardio diseases, cancer and many other diseases are associated with air pollution. Even adverse birth outcomes and premature deaths can be seen as a result of air pollution. WHO reported that, 3.7 million premature deaths are related to air pollution. The transportation industry is a substantial contributor to air pollution, which has a 24% share among all CO_2

emissions including freight and human movements. Especially for the freight sector, it is vital to decrease the amount of transportation-related emissions by using low carbon fuels, using more energy-efficient engines and delivering products more efficiently.

Widespread use of electrical vehicles seems like an environmental friendly solution but because of the high prices of such cars, firms generally continue to use gasoline-powered vehicles. The electric car sales rate increased by more than 2.5% in 2018. However, increased e-commerce sales and increased delivery within the time limits (same-day delivery, instant delivery) also increased the use of vans (IEA, 2019), which is a less energy-efficient option than large trucks (Bonilla, 2016). More than 250 European cities have adopted Low-Emission Zones (LEZ) and few cities have adopted Zero-emission Mobility Zones (ZEZ) since the Dieselgate scandal. The entrance of some road vehicles that have high toxic emissions to these zones is restricted. LEZ or ZEZ may have an accelerating effect on the wide usage of electrical vehicles by firms. In Madrid, after applying LEZ NO_2 concentration decreased 32%. Increasing rail investments and the rail usage rate (7% in 2019) is essential since the rail is an energy-efficient mode of transportation (Transport & Environment, 2019). Besides, promoting more sustainable delivery alternatives such as bicycle and walking deliveries and using crowdsourcing options are essential.

95% of the energy consumption of the transportation sector is based on fossil fuels and the rest is a combination of natural gas, electricity, and biofuels (Kahn Riberio et al., 2012). Because of the increasing number of gasoline-powered vehicles and increasing energy consumption rate due to rapid population growth, limited petroleum resources have become an important topic. According to the forecasts of the International Energy Agency (IEA), global energy demand will increase by approximately 42% from 2009 to 2035 (Singh, Avinash, & Agarwal, 2017). Diminishing petroleum reserves affects three aspects of sustainability. The social aspect of sustainability reveals the necessity of the fair distribution of scarce resources to current and future generations. From an environmental point of view, to fulfill the necessary energy need and to lower harmful emissions, cleaner and renewable energy sources should be produced and used widely instead of fossil fuels. Besides, dependence of petroleum creates an economic problem because of increasing crude oil prices.

From an environmental point of view, another essential subject of sustainable transportation is minimizing the effects of traffic noise. To be exposed to loud or continuous noise is dangerous for human health. It may cause psychological diseases such as annoyance and physiological diseases as ischaemic heart disease (WHO, 2019). According to a report (Jones, 2010), to be exposed to chronic aircraft noise has detrimental effects on memory, sustained attention, reading ability and understanding. Among children, this may cause a high degree of helplessness, motivational decrement and a higher degree of annoyance. Not just aircraft, also vans and motorcycles are noise sources in urban areas.

Because of limited parking areas in front of urban retail locations and restricted delivery times, drivers of delivery and pick-up vehicles park to illegal areas and this increases the number of parking violations. Walkability and bikeability performance indicators of social sustainability are negatively affected by parking violations. Also, double parking, seen on narrow and busy roads, causes congestion. Han et al. (2005) conclude that parking violations increase the travel time, number of accidents and transportation costs. According to research conducted by Mobility Lab and George Mason University, 73% of freight and delivery vehicles were used unauthorized areas to park in Arlington, which results in blocking sidewalks, fire hydrants or bike lanes (Hsu, 2019).

With the rise of e-commerce sales, distribution strategies have changed. For an online shopping experiment, customers expect to reach products as soon as possible after placing an order. Delivering the right goods to the customer's place or a pre-determined place in the expected time is crucial for an online shopping experiment. Therefore, it is critical to design an efficient distribution network and to provide efficient and effective movement of goods for an e-commerce company (Huppertz, 1999). Because the success of an e-commerce company mostly depends on its delivery performance and distribution network. To meet customers' expectations regarding delivery speed same-day and instant delivery options are spread, the amount of motorcycle and bicycle deliveries are increased and new delivery options such as autonomous delivery robots were proposed.

Chopra and Meindl (2015) classifies distribution network design options into six categories, which are;

- Manufacturer stores the products and ships directly to customer (direct shipping),
- Manufacturer stores the products and ships to customer by in-transit merge,
- Retailer stores the products and customer pickups.
- Manufacturer/distributor stores the products and customer pickups,
- Distributor stores the products and sends them by package carrier,
- Distributor stores the products and uses last-mile delivery options (last-mile delivery),

Manufacturer storage with direct shipping or shipping after in-transit merge strategy is used frequently by e-commerce companies. For these options, the company sells products from its web site or application and send the products from its facility. This type of manufacturer is called a pure player (Rao, Goldsby, & Iyengar, 2009). Drop shippers may be added to this type of delivery network. In such a case, the manufacturer stores all inventory. After the drop shipper receives an order, information is relayed to the manufacturer and the manufacturer sends the product directly to the customer. If the manufacturer and the customers are distant, this distribution network results in long waiting times for the customers.

As the number of layers in a distribution network increases, customer response time decreases. If retailers and distributors participate in a distribution network then customers can reach products faster. Retailers or distributors store the products and customers can come to the stores and pick-up the products and send them to customers' places by using last-mile logistics (LML) strategies. Lim et al. (2018) classified these strategies into three groups: push, pull and hybrid. The push-centric strategy is a multilayer distribution system and requires picking up the products from the manufacturer's facility, distribution center (DC) or B&M store and delivering to the customer's houses or workplaces. Pull strategy requires the customer's involvement in the receiving stage of distribution. The customers receive physical products from local B&M stores and dematerialize products such as video games and software from information stores. The hybrid strategy combines push-centric and pull-centric strategies. In this strategy, the manufacturer or the distributor sends products to intermediate sites and customers pick-up products from these points. These delivery strategies and their effects on sustainable transportation will be discussed in the trends section.

E-Commerce Distribution Trends

Customers of an e-commerce company expect faster delivery, and this pressure forces B2C companies to chance their distribution networks. Especially the last-mile of the distribution networks, which end with customers reach their products, has to meet these expectations to stay competitive in the sector. According to Lim et al. (2018), last-mile delivery can be defined as "the last stretch of a B2C parcel delivery service, takes place from the order penetration point (factories, FCs, retail stores, etc.) to the final consignee's preferred destination point (recipients' doorsteps, collection delivery points (CDP) or pickup addresses, etc.)".

Last-mile delivery requires delivering myriad small posts to the multiple diverse locations within time limits. Due to these limitations, last-mile delivery (sometimes called final delivery) is the most expensive, inefficient and complex part of the supply chain management (Gevaers, Voorde, & Vanelslander, 2014). Especially e-commerce companies are willing to absorb last-mile delivery expenses to gain a competitive advantage even its costs exceed 50% of total shipping costs (Joerss, Schröder, Neuhaus, Klink, & Mann, 2016a).

With the rise of e-commerce, van usage for delivery operations has become widespread. Van usage has some negative effects on urban life quality. This delivery option increases the freight energy intensity, which can be interpreted as megajoules/tonne-km, and thus increase air pollution. Because of the limited capacities of vans and complex routes due to delivering small parcels to several points, this delivery method is highly cost. Vans are also effecting urban traffic congestion negatively, and this causes late deliveries, traffic violations, and accidents (Bonilla, 2016). Furthermore, human deaths or injuries due to car accidents are related to traffic congestion. According to research conducted by the U.S. Department of Transportation (2015), 94% of accidents are due to human errors and just in U.S. 4,761 people died in crashes that involve large trucks, in 2017.

To lower last mile costs and to make the delivery process more sustainable, many innovations are made by big players of the e-commerce sector (such as Amazon and Wal-Mart), academicians and startups. Some of these innovations are reception boxes (RB), click and collect points (C&C), drones, bike couriers, autonomous vehicles, crowd-sourcing logistics, anticipatory shipment, and underground delivery. Same-day, instant delivery or delivery with time windows options are becoming popular among customers. Furthermore, trucks, which can manufacture products by 3D printers, and mapping customer behavior to lower failed delivery rates by data mining are topical now.

Types of Delivery Points

If customers have to wait at home/office for their parcels to be delivered, this type of delivery is Attended Home Delivery (AHD). By using classical and most preferred (AHD) business model, costs of the last mile delivery may be up to 75% of total shipping costs (Gevaers, Voorde, & Vanelslander, 2009). In this option, courier brings the parcel to recipients' doorstep or office without a time limitation and if the recipient is not there at that time, then courier has to turn back there even two or three times by using road transportation, which causes more air pollution in urban areas, more traffic noise and more usage of transportation facilities. For the economic aspect, this kind of model leads to inefficient pricing because transportation companies do not know which product will turn back to their facility and how many visits will be conducted to the customers' home or office. Another disadvantage of this model is ringing a bell, waiting for the door to be opened and having customers' sign processes are time-consuming for both parties. Besides, setting time windows for customers results in complicated vehicle routes and more energy consumption.

Another delivery option is Unattended Delivery (UD), and this can be defined as delivering products to a specific place. According to Kamaranien et al. (2001) delivery cost can be reduced by up to 40% by using UD options in comparison with AHD. When considering the social point of view, AHD and some of the UD options are beneficial for people with disabilities, about accessibility to products. If retailers provide free shipping opportunities, these delivery options are also beneficial for people with lower incomes. By this opportunity, they can get their products without paying extra money and without using their cars.

UD options are RBs, delivery boxes and shared RBs (Hübner, Holzapfel, Kuhn, & Obermair, 2019). A reception box is a delivery point, which has generally a refrigerator and a freezer unit and provides foods to be stored at predetermined temperatures, generally used to deliver groceries. Wang et al. (2014) mention three kinds of RBs; independent reception box (IRB), delivery box (DB) and shared reception box (SRB). IRB is located at the house (home yard or garage) of the customer. DB is an insulated secured box with a locking mechanism and returns to the retailer. SRBs have separate lockers with changing opening codes and people living in apartment blocks or building complexes jointly can use them. By using RBs, parcels can be delivered even if the customer is not at home. If this box has a controlled access system, couriers may call the recipients and the customers can see the couriers from the camera and open RB by using their mobile phones. Other models of RBs generate specific codes for every delivery and the courier can open the box by using this code. Usage of RBs results with less failed deliveries (Punakivi, Yrjöla, & Holmström, 2001). Besides packages are not need to be sent twice, so energy consumption per freight ton-mile, climate change emissions, air and noise pollution are expected to be lower compared to classic AHD. However, among these alternatives, SRB is the most cost-effective, timesaving and environment-friendly option for delivering companies.

Another main type of delivery point is C&C. There are three categories of C&C points; pick-up point in store (PPS), pick-up point attached to a store (PPAS) and a solitary pick-up point at another location (SPP) (Hübner et al., 2019). A PPS is generally a temporary booth, placed inside the store. PPAS is similar to PPS but with one difference. In PPAS, the pick-up point is located outside the store and customers take their orders by drive-through opportunity. In both options, customers buy products online but they have to collect their orders by visiting the store. For customers, this will be a less time-consuming shopping experience but still, they have to go to the store and pick-up their orders. From the retailers' point of view, this option is less costly than sending the products to the customers' houses. In the SPP option, orders can be picked up by customers from a DC. This option requires a high set-up cost and increases logistics costs.

There are other delivery applications have been offered and implemented. As an example, Amazon offered in-car delivery service in 2018 that enables couriers finding customer's cars with "Key App", unlocking the trunk with keys and delivering products inside the trunk. This option also decreases the probability of failed delivery while increasing cost factors related to the delivery automation system (Reyes, Savelsbergh, & Toriello, 2017).

Delivering Within a Time Limit

Delivering products at a specific time, within a time windows, within same-day or instantly are becoming very common. Both e-commerce companies and parcel delivery services are offering these kinds of delivery options. These options are very costly but some customers are also ready to pay more for these kinds of services. According to research conducted in China, Germany, and the USA, 25% of respondents are willing to pay for same-day or instant delivery options. It is expected this share to increase due to the younger generation is keen on these options. By 2025, the share of same-day and instant delivery options of the global e-commerce parcel delivery market are expected to reach 20% to 25% and may have a larger slice of pie if these options can be extended to rural areas (Joerss, Neuhaus, & Schröder, 2016b).

While orders with time constraints increased in number and constraints became definite, solving these kinds of problems requires more time and money. The solutions are getting complicated and this results in longer freight movement times. Boyer et al. (2005) illustrated the solutions of a delivery route problem with and without time windows and showed the effects of time windows constraint on route planning. According to their study, the solution of a 1-hour time window and no window had resulted in a decrease in more than 50% miles per customer. This kind of extra tours decrease the efficiency of the delivery process, increase cost, energy consumption per freight ton-mile, climate change emissions and air and noise pollution.

Crowdsourcing Logistics

Crowdsourcing is used for last-mile delivery by giving the delivery tasks to nonprofessional individuals from a network of people on a technological platform. These individuals generally provide this service by their vehicle and if the delivery point is on their route. This may be for free (Chen & Pan, 2015) or for a fee (Wang, Zhang, Liu, Shen, & Lee, 2016). Amazon, Instacart, Postmates, Shitpt and several other startups have adapted the "Uber Model" to product delivery services, especially for meal deliveries. While generally, these companies match the orders with the proper individuals within the system, Walmart uses a different and more environmentally friendly crowdsourcing strategy than an "Uber Model". It matches orders with its employees after work routes. Also in 2018, Walmart began to use "Spark Delivery" besides its current crowdsourcing model.

Uber Model services are not always cost-efficient especially in countries with high labor costs (Starcke, 2018). However, if people use existing transportation opportunities while they are going home/work, then this kind of transportation becomes cost-efficient and environmentally friendly. If the free capacity of citizens is used to carry loads, this will lead to a reduction in idle vehicle kilometers of vans (Rai, Verlinde, Merckx, & Macharis, 2017) and related pollutants. Employment level increases in the short term (Taylor, 2015); however, in the long term, when drones and AGV's become widely used, the unemployment level for these employees is expected to increase. Also, integrating public transportation based crowdsourcing models with shared reception box and parcel locker deliveries will provide sustainability advantages (Wang et al., 2016).

Automated Delivery Vehicles (ADVs) Usage for Distribution

The usage of ADVs for e-commerce logistics is one of the topical issues of the logistics industry. There are four types of ADVs; unmanned aerial vehicles (UAVs), sidewalk delivery robots, self-driving cars and automated delivery pods (Marks, 2019). These vehicles are on progress, but only some of them are officially in service. ADVs can be used to deliver meals, groceries and other packages. According to the report of McKinsey & Company (2016b), 85% of the parcels will be delivered by ADVs, by 2025, assuming that this technology and the service will become cheaper. If they don't become cheaper, then bicycle delivery is expected to be the best instant delivery option.

According to the simulation results of Gružauskas et al. (2018), transportation costs of distribution systems, work with autonomous vehicles, are 5% less than the traditional distribution systems. Besides, they indicate that the CO_2 emission level can be lowered by 22% by using autonomous vehicles. These technologies are expected to make things easier especially for disabled and elderly people but also there are various concerns about human health. People will become immobile by using these kinds of technologies.

The smallest version of the ADVs are drones and they are already delivering in some regions of Australia (Porter, 2019), France and China. France's postal service has used this technology to deliver parcels to hard-to-reach Alpine villages (Willsher, 2019). Google's parent company Alphabet is using drones in Australia and their drone delivery system has just been approved by the US government. Amazon, Uber and other US companies are still waiting for the necessary legal permissions. By these permissions, Amazon Prime plans to deliver 80-90% of its deliveries by drones by 2030 (Spisak, 2019). They aim to carry up to 2.25 kg parcels per delivery within 30 minutes and under $1.

Especially for icy ridgeways and hard-to-reach areas, drone usage seems more reliable in comparison to delivering with vans (Boeras, Collins, & Peeling, 2019). Also by using drone deliveries, it is expected to reduce traffic and obstacles (Murray & Chu, 2015) and to lower carbon emissions using long-life rechargeable batteries. If Amazon Prime Air achieves drone usage goals by 2030, the number of trucks on the way will be reduced which also causes lower carbon emissions (Spisak, 2019). Besides the good sides of drone usage, there are many critical issues to be considered in the means of sustainability. The safety of drone usage is still an investigated research area. A small crash can be resulted by serious damages in the health of people or public infrastructures or airworthiness. According to DPD, drones have many features such as "anti-collision systems", "autonomous parachutes", flight recorders and cameras in case of emergent situations (Willsher, 2019). Another problem related to drone usage in deliveries is noise pollution. Even if the noise of trucks will be reduced by drones soon, drone-related noise pollution will be another critical issue. Another worrisome issue for the social aspect is privacy related to the usage of normal and infrared cameras, on drones. This may cause, collecting unauthorized images illegally.

Sidewalk robot usage in e-commerce deliveries will be an inescapable situation in the near future. Many models have been developed and tested by delivery companies such as Amazon and FedEx. Robots or droids are self-guided delivery vehicles, moving on a determined path (Slabinac, 2015). These are generally equipped with GPS, HD cameras and ultrasound sensors. Due to the high technology investment requirements of these robots, the costs of using robots are high. Unless they do not become more affordable, they have less chance to compete with cheaper delivery options especially in countries with cheaper labor costs.

Drones and sidewalk robots do not have negative effects on traffic congestion. However, unlike drones, these robots occupy a place in sidewalks. As the usage of sidewalk robots becomes widespread, pedestrian traffic in cities (walkability), especially with narrow sidewalks, will be affected negatively. In addition to pedestrians, wheelchair users and parents with strollers should also be taken into account while planning sidewalk robot delivery systems. While planning newly developing residential areas, sidewalk robot traffic can be considered; but for old settlements, it will be hard to adopt these robot delivery systems to existing sidewalks. For now, robots move on sidewalks slowly for safety concerns. Their speed is about 4-6 km/h and this slow movement gives robots the necessary time to think about the next steps and to move without crashing any object or people. For now, this type of delivery is available on some university campuses.

The use of vans and trucks is expected to decrease when ADVs and drones are widely used. However, in the short term, since the battery life of the current drones is short, they are expected to move with the vans. According to ADV producers, ADVs are expected to eliminate human-induced accidents by eliminating people from the transportation system. While it is expected that robots will help prevent accidents caused by trucks and vans soon, it is not yet known whether it will reveal a new source of accidents called robot accidents.

SUSTAINABILITY EVALUATION OF E-COMMERCE WAREHOUSES

E-commerce is growing at a remarkable speed. According to Statistica (2019a), in 2019, worldwide e-commerce sales were $3.53 trillion and e-commerce sales are projected to rise to $6.54 trillion in 2022. Both in the United States and Europe, the sales of business to customer (B2C) e-commerce as a percentage of gross domestic product (GDP) have an increasing trend between 2009 and 2019 (Statistica, 2019b; 2019c). The expanding e-commerce requires larger regional warehouses and smaller urban warehouses in order to facilitate the movement of goods and meet customer needs in a shorter time (Deloitte, 2014). Especially in the business-to-customer (B2C) segment, the order sizes are getting smaller while the demand variety is increasing. The expected delivery times by the customers are getting shorter. Same-day delivery or even next day delivery became obligatory for the retailers. The survey, which is conducted by Peerless report group annually on behalf of Logistics Management for Honeywell Intelligrated shows that "on-time delivery" is the most significant key performance indicator with 49% for e-commerce retailers.

Growth in e-commerce retailing caused changes in the whole supply chain. One of the most affected parts of the supply chain is the warehouses. Traditional warehouses have difficulties to meet customer requirements on time and accurately so that the traditional picking systems in warehouses need to change. Especially picking operations need to be improved. The Peerless Report Group report explains that picking is the second biggest operation in need of change with 35% (Peerless Research Group, 2019). In order to facilitate the picking operations, automation, voice-directed picking systems or robotics become interest areas of retailing companies. In addition to the operations in warehouses, the warehouse types and sizes begin to change because of the new distribution networks that appeared due to expanded e-commerce (Öztürkoğlu, 2018). Besides the big DCs, FCs to serve e-commerce orders quickly and on time, are beginning to serve. (Peerless Research Group, 2019). According to the Bureau of Labor Statistics in the U.S., the number of warehouses reached 18.500 in 2019 from 17.000 in 2016 (United States Department of Labor, 2019). The changes in the warehouse industry due to e-commerce created many consequences in the social, environmental and economic dimensions of sustainability.

Although 51 thousand jobs were lost in the retail sector due to e-commerce, 355 thousand new jobs with FCs arise in the sector (Mandel, 2017). Amazon.com which is the top e-commerce retailing company in the world according to Forbes (Angelovska, 2019) works with more than 250 thousand employees in its 104 warehouses and FCs as of 2018 (National Bureau of Economic Research, 2017). Walmart.com which is in the top 5 e-commerce retailing company has 173 DCs with 125.8 million square feet (MWPL International Inc., 2019). The second-largest e-commerce retailer in China JingDong has 166 warehouses and 7 logistics centers (Yu, Wang, Zhong, & Huang, 2016). The average warehouse area in the United States increased by 143% between 2012 and 2017 (Bartolini, Bottani, & Eric, 2019). The growth in the amount and size of the warehouses, DCs, and FCs provide an opportunity for employment. Besides the contributions of warehouses on the social dimension of sustainability, they also have an environmental impact on sustainability such as energy consumption.

According to the U.S. Green building council (USGBC), buildings use 41% of the energy and 29% are used for transportation and 30% are used in the industry in U.S. (Kaplan, 2019). The UK Green Building Council has identified construction as one of the most GHG -intensive industries in the UK with almost 50 percent (Dadhich, Genovese, Kumar, & Acquaye, 2015). UK energy policy is leading the construction industry to reduce energy usage in buildings with the target of zero-carbon (Rai, Sodagar, Fieldson, & Hu, 2011). The warehouses generate nearly 11% of the total GHG emissions, which are created by the logistics sector (Bartolini et al., 2019). The level of energy consumption and consequential emission are major indicators of environmental sustainability. Increasing social awareness about carbon and waste management forces companies to re-engineer their supply chain, especially towards sustainable warehouses. Contributions of green building practices, using green energy sources, using energy-efficient material handling equipment, operational strategies for shorter travel distances are main practices for a sustainable warehouse.

In the following sections, the issues about warehouses that are necessary for e-commerce will be discussed with the perspective of social, environmental and economic dimensions of sustainability. FCs as a new warehouse type, location of the warehouse, layout of the warehouse, building materials of the warehouse, the equipment used in the warehouses for material handling will be described in terms of sustainability by considering the relation with e-commerce. The current implications, precautions, recommendations for the warehouse industry will be explained to support sustainability.

Fulfillment Centers

The success of e-commerce depends on giving customers what they want, when and how they want with as possible as the lowest cost. This needs real-time fulfillment solutions. Fulfillment means picking and packing the products in very small quantities and shipping them by parcel carriers (Ricker and Kalakota, 2017). In e-commerce FCs as well as the main operations, attaching instruction manuals, leaflets, taking complaints, repairing returned products, gift packaging, maintenance, management of the e-shop archive, sending sales reports may be served (Kawa, 2017). The operations in a FC and a warehouse are not similar. The operations in warehouses are generally routine but in FCs are not. Since the products in a FC are various, the preparing procedure for shipment needs different processes. A FC can be used as a warehouse but a warehouse can not be used as a FC. In a warehouse, large quantity of products are stored and shipped, and especially Business to Business (B2B) transactions arise. Warehouses are proper places to store seasonal products. The products are stored in warehouses until they are required but in FCs, the inventory turnover rate is larger than warehouses and the cycle time of products is shorter than the products in warehouses. The traditional retailing companies find out it is not possible to provide home delivery service to their customers with their existing delivery network. In traditional warehouses, the picking list is fixed after the picker begins to travel. However, e-commerce demands may cause updates in picklists and routes, which is called dynamic order processing. Incoming urgent orders may be added to a current route if it is necessary and the route is updated (Boysen, De Koster, & Weidinger, 2018). One of the most important requirements of e-commerce quick response is provided by dynamic order processing in FCs. The retailing companies usually meet the customer requirements from FCs. The FCs are vital for new trends in e-commerce.

One of the newest trends in e-commerce is developing fulfillment cross border by reducing shipment costs. Another trend is same-day delivery that is provided only in selected cities. Full coverage of the country with same-day delivery service should be supported (Kawa, 2017). Warehouses do not serve an external customer while serving an external customer is the main focus of FCs. Warehouses simply store products to be used at a later date. FCs pick and pack orders and make sure they get into the hand of the customer on time. Timely replenishment is critical because customers do not tolerate out-of-stock situations. Retailing companies may provide fulfillment services themselves or other 3PL service providers may provide fulfillment services. Catalog companies or store-based retailers such as Walmart and JCPenney also have their distribution and fulfillment networks but they ship various products in large quantities in contrary to internet retailers.

Consumers spend 1.2 billion hours on unpaid work like driving to B&M stores, finding a parking lot, traveling between aisles, payment and driving back home in the U.S.. Some of these unpaid works transformed to works in FCs such as picking, packing and driving trucks for delivery. That's why e-commerce creates new jobs. Unlike traditional warehouses, in FCs orders of each customer are prepared by the products that are gathered from various suppliers so that collecting products from many different suppliers and manufacturers, consolidating them, picking and packing according to the customer order are new works emerged due to e-commerce retailing. The number of e-commerce companies and FCs increased by 400,000 from 2007 to 2017 while 140,000 B&M retailing companies closed (Progressive Policy Institute, 2017).

FCs play a critical role in employment. E-commerce FCs employ more workers than traditional warehouses (Texas A&M Transportation Institute, 2017). In Amazon's FC in Kenosha, more than 2000 permanent and 1000 seasonal workers are employed. Amazon now operates about 104 FCs around the country with a space of 80 million square feet. The company increased the number of workers from 14,000 in 2007 to 180,000 in 2016 in the United States and most of them in FCs (Progressive Policy Institute, 2017). Just growth of Amazon alone made a huge contribution to the employment. Besides that, the companies that work as both e-commerce company and retailer, operates FCs. For example, Chewy.com an online pet supplier retailer opened its fifth FC and hired 700 workers. Walmart opened an e-commerce FC in 2017 in Florida and planned to hire 1,500 workers in 2018. Between 2007 and 2017, the e-commerce industry provided 132,000 jobs and the warehouse industry provided 273,000 jobs (Progressive Policy Institute, 2017). Furthermore, as e-commerce increases product returns increase. The returned products need to be processed in the FCs. A new employment field appears due to e-commerce (Delloite, 2014). In terms of income, the average weekly earnings are 31% higher in FCs than in B&M retail jobs in the same county (Progressive Policy Institute, 2017).

Consequently, FCs that are emerged due to expanding e-commerce make a considerable contribution to the social dimension of sustainability by providing new employment fields and high income. The economic impact of those centers will be explained in the building section in detail.

Location of the Warehouses

The pressure of shorter delivery time requirement forces especially online retailers to be closer to the consumer to gain market share. This need may be met with the increased number of larger regional hubs and smaller urban warehouses. Urban warehouses like FCs play a critical role in last-mile delivery services. In the meantime, regional DCs are still required with their large volumes.

Due to transportation cause 28% of total energy consumption of U.S. in 2018 (U.S. Energy Information Administration Report on Energy Usage, 2019) and cause 29% of total GHG emissions in 2017 (United States Environmental Protection Agency, 2019), the location of the warehouses and DCs are crucial in terms of sustainability in the long run. The location of the facility is decided once and during the lifetime of the facility, the costs due to transportation are beard. The companies prefer the DCs or warehouses located near city centers and close to the highway, freeway, airport, port, and railway to minimize their distribution costs (Kaplan, 2019). Reduction distances in transportation means also a reduction in the level of GHG emission. On the other hand, getting closer to the city centers may create traffic congestion also air and noise pollution near city centers due to the vehicles that carry goods among warehouses and demand points. Therefore, the location of the warehouses, DCs, and FCs took the attention of the companies and researchers. Companies make network studies to evaluate their location of warehouses to move closer to ports or closer to customers to reduce transportation energy consumption and consequential emission (Napolitano, 2013). In facility location literature, there are many studies, which aim to select the best location alternative according to considered criteria. For example, Demirel, Demirel, & Kahraman (2010) investigated the best location of a logistics firm among four cities by considering the criteria related to costs, labor characteristics, infrastructure, and markets. Ashrafzadeh, Rafiei, Isfahani, & Zare (2015) analyzed four locations in Iran for the warehouse on behalf of the Entekhab industrial group by considering 15 criteria. These criteria are labor costs, transportation costs, handling costs, land cost, skilled labor, availability of labor force, land availability, climate, existence of transportation modes, telecommunication systems, quality and reliability of transportation modes, quality and reliability of utilities, proximity to customers, proximity to producer, lead times and responsiveness. These studies are not related to sustainability directly. They did not take into account energy consumption or GHG emissions but indirectly they contributed to the environmental dimension of sustainability because their common objective was reducing transportation and this result causes a reduction in energy consumption and emission of GHG. Besides that, there are studies that are related to sustainability directly. For example, Govindan, Garg, Gupta, & Jha (2016) assessed facility location in terms of the triple bottom line (3BTL) of sustainability. Raut, Narkhede, Gardas, & Raut (2017) aimed to select a strategic location of a sustainable warehouse in their study. They identified 11 crucial, sustainable selection criteria for the chemical industry warehouse and purposed the governmental policies and regulations, climatic conditions of the region and strategic location as the most significant three factors for sustainable warehouse location.

Besides that, many studies in literature aim to determine the optimal location of a warehouse. Gill and Ishaq Bhatti (2007) considered the product distribution cost and warehouse capital cost in selecting warehouse locations and allocating retailers. Li et al. (2008) purposed a model to determine the location of a DC by considering transport mode and carbon emission. As a conclusion, they claimed that, as the price of crude oil rises, the income of the entire supply chain and carbon emission also decline, while the number of DCs increases. Büyüksaatçi and Esnaf (2014) handled the facility location problem to minimize CO^2 emission level appeared due to the transportation between the facilities and customers. In terms of infrastructure, there are no additional costs like electricity, water pipes, and roads for the warehouses located near city centers. Furthermore, infrastructure costs reduce, as the buildings are located near city centers (Kaplan, 2019). To locate warehouses close to city centers is also important for employee perspective. The transportation of the employees gets easier to reach to work. Therefore, the selection of warehouse location is a strategic issue that has economic, environmental and social dimensions of the businesses (Tan, Ahmed, & Sundaram, 2009).

Layout of the Warehouses

In a typical warehouse, there are four major operations called, receiving, put-away, picking, and shipment (Bartholdi and Hackman, 2011). In unit load warehouses in which large amounts of goods picked up and put-away as a single object like in pallets without decomposing into small pieces (Tompkins, White, Bozer, & Tanchoco, 2003), the aforementioned four operation areas are usually seen. However, since the put-away and picking operations are done in the same area, three areas may be seen in practice. In warehouses in which piece or case picking operations are handled, there may be additional areas such as the replenishment area. The placement of the warehouse may change according to the type of products stored such as perishable, frozen foods or flammable chemicals. In such a warehouse, products may require special conditions. For instance, a product needs to be stored in a refrigerated area, or another one needs to be far away from a specific product. Therefore, placing the areas to maximize storage utilization and minimizing travel distance with the concern of providing healthy working conditions for employees is the major objective of warehouse layout problems. The layout of any facility is designed and built once so it is difficult to change but not impossible. It can be modified if necessary with additional costs.

Warehouse layout literature also includes the aisle design. Many studies investigate the number and design of aisles to decrease travel distance or increase warehouse space utilization. In traditional warehouses, the picking aisles are located parallel to each other while cross aisles are arranged perpendicular to the picking aisles. Gue and Meller (2009) proposed two new aisle layouts as an alternative to the traditional ones. They are "Flying-V" and "Fishbone designs". With these aisle designs, the researchers provide to decrease the single-command (travel between a pick-up and deposit (P&D) point and a single warehouse location that a worker store or retrieve a single product/pallet) travel distance 10% and 20% respectively according to the equivalent traditional warehouses. Gue, Ivanovic & Meller (2012) evaluated modified Flying-V and inverted Flying-V aisle designs for a warehouse with multiple P&Ds and provide less expected travel distance. Öztürkoğlu, Gue, & Meller (2012) proposed three new non-traditional aisle designs (Chevron, Leaf, and Butterfly) which have one, two and three angled cross aisles. All new designs are investigated from the perspective of both travel distance and storage utilization and among them Chevron is proposed as the most applicable one for the industry. Öztürkoğlu, Kocaman, & Gümüşoğlu (2018) examined the Chevron design in a multiple P&D point warehouse. Kocaman, Öztürkoğlu, & Gümüşoğlu (2019) searched best aisle layouts to minimize the expected single-command distance for a multiple P&D points warehouse which is used frequently in the industry. Besides that, many studies searched new aisle designs and analyzed their benefits in terms of picking time or travel distance which is indirectly affects the cost of picking operation (Öztürkoğlu, Gue and Meller, 2014; Öztürkoğlu, 2015; Öztürkoğlu and Hoşer, 2018; Öztürkoğlu and Hoşer, 2019a; Öztürkoğlu and Hoşer, 2019b). Common objectives of the mentioned studies are reducing the travel distances in a warehouse between a P&D point and any location. Reduction travel distances cause cost saving, less energy consumption, and less GHG emission. Thus, a well-designed layout of a warehouse contributes to the economic and environmental side of sustainability in long terms.

Boysen et al. (2019) explained warehousing systems that meet the four requirements of e-commerce. They are fulfilling (i) small order under (ii) large variety with (iii) a great time pressure and (iv) varying workloads. They define mixed-shelves storage systems as a good alternative for e-commerce warehouses if the warehouse space is adequate. Mixed-shelves storage is a storage system that stores the products scattered by breaking down unit loads into small units. The main goal of this storage system is reducing the distance between any point in the warehouse and the closest unit of each SKU. By this system, the non-value added travel distance of pickers reduce and shorter delivery time requirement of the customers can be met. In this kind of storage system, the picker needs Information Technology (IT) tools like barcode readers and pick by voice to find the closest product. Boysen et al. (2019) also purposed batching and zoning as a non-value added walking time reduction method. Batching is defined as picking the same units of different orders in one tour to reduce total traveling time and zoning means partitioning the warehouse into zones to make the picker's travel in smaller areas to find the product that they look for (De Koster, Le-Duc, & Roodbergen, 2007). Amazon uses batching, zoning and mixed-shelves storage systems to reduce non-value added traveling of pickers (Boysen et al., 2019).

Building of the Warehouses

The warehouse buildings are one of the major energy-consuming factors (Rai et al., 2011; Dadhich et al., 2015; Ürge-Vorsatz, Cabeza, Serrano, Barreneche, & Petrichenko, 2015) since they need energy both in the construction phase and during the lifetime of the facility. The buildings are responsible for 30% of the GHG emissions because of energy consumption (MacNaughton et al., 2017). Almost 30% of black carbon and 33% of halocarbon emissions arise from the building industry (Ürge-Vorsatz et al., 2015). The materials used for insulation, roof, walls, lighting and fan systems (which are explained in detail in the following paragraphs) in the construction phase play a critical role in energy consumption. Since it is difficult to change these systems after building is finished because of additional costs, it is very important to plan it carefully before the construction phase of the facilities. Even so, it is not impossible to transform but the additional costs affect the economies of companies negatively in the sustainability perspective.

Various green building standards lead buildings to reduce the consumption of energy, waste, and water. Leadership in Energy and Environmental Design (LEED) program which is founded by the U.S. Green Building Council (USGBC) in the United States is one of the most popular certification programs in the U.S.. The buildings certified by LEED consume 11% less water and 25% less energy and have 34% lower CO^2 emissions (Kaplan, 2019). In 2013, a new version of LEED is released specifically for construction of warehouses and DCs. LEED-certified buildings have prevented the release of 33MT of CO^2 into the atmosphere and avoided premature deaths in the United States between 172 and 405, in 2016 (MacNaughton et al., 2017). Similar to the LEED program, in Europe, the BREEAM standards (Building Research Establishment Environmental Assessment Method); in Asia, the Green Building Evaluation Label (GBEL), also known as China Three Star; In Australia, Green Star; in Japan, CASBEE (Comprehensive Assessment System for Building Environmental Efficiency), are founded. Totally, the World Green Building Council (World GBC) recognizes more than 40 rating tools for green building (MacNaughton et al., 2017). In 2017, 304 buildings in 17 different countries gained sustainable building certification (Prologis, 2017).

Green building practices reduce GHG emissions as well as other harmful air pollutants like particulate matter, sulfur dioxide and nitrogen oxides, all related to the combustion of fossil fuels for electricity and heat generation in buildings. As a conclusion, the benefits of green building practices that have not yet been quantified (MacNaughton et al., 2017) have social and environmental impacts on sustainability. In addition to green practices, there are energy-saving innovations that support sustainability.

Smart buildings are one of the last emerged developments for buildings. In smart buildings, devices are used to monitor the usage of electricity, gas, and water. The smart meters, which are replaced with gas, electric and water meters are recommended to use in buildings to analyze energy consumption and avoid unpredictable payments. The obtained data is then analyzed to identify the opportunities for energy and cost savings (Napolitano, 2013). Consumption monitoring is one of the most innovative techniques that help to manage energy consumption in the whole building and to understand their energy-related GHG emissions. Prologis reported a reduction in energy use by 8.9% and in emissions by 4% in 2017 according to the previous year. Solar panels on roofs should be set. Prologis (2017) added 10 megawatts of solar capacity (onto the roofs of medium-sized homes) to their portfolio in four countries. By the solar panels emissions-free energy is produced (Prologis, 2017).

Photovoltaic panels and wind generators are not cost-effective tools for energy generation but if they are supported by the government's incentives, they become a favorable energy source with low lifecycle emissions. To support the businesses to use renewable energy the regulations should be updated. For instance, in the UK many local authorities force the businesses to meet 10% of their requirements by renewable energy sources. According to the "Merton Rule," policy 350 tons of carbon in a year are saved (DHL, 2010). Combining innovative solutions and renewable energy usage in warehouses may cause 70% less CO^2 emission in a warehouse. (Prologis, 2017).

One of the recently emerged developments for sustainable buildings is net-zero building model which compensates every unit of consumed energy by generating a unit of energy. Pudleiner and Colton (2015) proposed a net-zero energy building design process in which external wall insulation, window properties, infiltration and natural ventilation, lighting, and equipment are considered as the parameters of the model. KSS Architect built a net-zero facility that meets the energy requirement of all campus by setting up a roof-mounted 1.2 megawatt PV panel (Napolitano, 2013).

Materials

Insulation avoids air transmission between indoor and outdoor. This provides a reduction in energy waste and thermal comfort for workers (MacNaughton et al., 2017). The paints, adhesives, wood products, sealants, and carpeting are important for air quality indoor. The material selection can save energy and reduce CO^2 emissions during the life of buildings (Rai et al., 2011). Using natural insulation materials like cork, wood fibre and sheep's wool are also preferable since they provide environmental impact. For instance, sheep's wool release almost 98% less CO^2 than polyurethane materials (European commission report on Science for environment policy, 2011). Improving the insulation of a building may cause a reduction in demanded energy for heating, ventilating and air conditioning (HVAC) by 6–15% and this reduction may lead a reduction in CO^2 emissions by 4–12% for a medium-size warehouse (Ries, Grosse, & Fichtinger, 2017).

Professionals, architects, and engineers should be encouraged to use natural materials in buildings. Using local materials such as soil, stone, and timber in buildings reduces the amount of energy used by up to 215% (Morel, Mesbah, Oggero, & Walker, 2001) so the materials used for roofs, walls, and floors of the buildings affect the sustainability in an environmental perspective. The European Commission Report on Science for Environment Policy (2011) recommends using local clays and renewable ingredients like straw in brick selection to use in walls. Timber cladding and hemcrete walling systems are suggested instead of steel wall systems. Timber cladding may save CO^2 approximately 18% according to steel. Hemcrete is a highly insulating material that can be used in roofs, walls, and floors of the buildings. Since hemcrete includes lime and cement in the binder, it can save CO^2 more than steel and timber cladding systems (Rai et al., 2011). Radhi (2010) proposed vinyl material in wall cladding systems since it reduces embodied CO^2 emissions more than stucco, masonry, aluminum.

The European Commission Report (2011) recommends using roof tiles out of concrete because it is better than the roof materials which are made of ceramic or fibre cement. Concrete tiles can save 42% energy according to ceramic roof tiles. Solar power panels can be used in the warehouse buildings as less expensive energy.

On the floor of buildings, it is better to use quarry tiles instead of ceramic tiles. It causes saving 86% in energy and 66% in emission (European commission report on Science for environment policy, 2011). Rai et al., (2011) investigated the materials such as steel, concrete, and cladding systems and recommended to use different concrete types with 50% ground granulated blast furnace slug (GGBS) to support energy saving.

Buildings made of wooden materials reduce primary energy demand and they can be carbon neutral if the wood materials are recycled at the end of its life cycle. Other materials such as steel, aluminum, copper, glass and PVC should be re-used because manufacturing secondary steel by using scrap steels reduces emissions 74%, compared to manufacturing the same amount of primary steel. The buildings should be constructed by allowing disassembly at the end of its life and the materials which are disassembled like bolts should be re-used in another building (European commission report on Science for environment policy, 2011)

Lighting

According to the US Energy Information Administration Report on Energy Usage in Commercial Buildings (2016), with 17%, lighting is a major contributor to energy consumption. Also, Dadhich et al. (2015) explain electricity consumption for lighting and diesel consumption for handling operations done by forklifts are the top two reasons for carbon emissions in the warehouses. Cook and Sproul (2011) claimed that energy consumption can be reduced up to 73% by changes in insulation, sawtooth roof, selective glazing, natural ventilation, renewal of lamps, and lighting controls in warehouse buildings. Colicchia, Marchet, Melacini, & Perotti (2013) recommended adjustments in lighting and heating systems as the primary prevention for energy saving in warehouses. Replace old mercury discharge lamps with high-pressure sodium lamps will save 15% in energy costs or replace old-style 38 m (T12) tubular triphosphorous-coated fluorescent lamps with 26 m (T8) tubes will save 8% (McKinnon et al., 2015). For example, in Deutsche Post DHL warehouse changing T5 bulbs with TS bulbs saved 40% energy consumption (DHL, 2010). The world's top retailing company Walmart provides cost-saving $200 million annually just by changing the fluorescent lighting system with the LED one in its stores and parking lots (Reagan, 2018).

Three options for warehouse lighting, high-intensity discharge (HID), fluorescent, and LED have advantages and disadvantages compared to each other. HID lamps have the lowest initial cost but need a warm-up time before reaching full illumination level. Fluorescent lighting consumes energy less than HID lamps so they are more energy-efficient but they are affected by the heat of the warehouse. If it is too cold or too hot, the lifespan of the fluorescent lighting gets shorten. The LED light is more energy-efficient than the other lighting systems and more durable than fluorescent lighting. Therefore, LED lights are the most appropriate lighting for warehouses (Davis, 2019).

In addition to the changing bulbs, using lights just when it is necessary is recommended (DHL, 2010) also using motion detectors and photo sensors should be used to turn lights on and off to avoid waste (Dadhich et al., 2015). Adding a motion sensor to the lighting design can reduce the cost of wasted energy almost 30% in large buildings like warehouses (Davis, 2019). According to Ries et al. (2017), replacing the standard incandescent lamps to fluorescents or LEDs may reduce demanded energy by 80% to 90% and consequently, emissions may decrease between 20 and 34% in the warehouses. Moreover, regular cleaning of light bulbs is recommended. Accumulated dust on bulbs in two years reduce the luminosity 50% and increase operational cost 15% (DHL, 2010).

The utilization of daylight is also an important issue for lighting. It should be considered in the construction phase of a facility (DHL, 2010). LED lighting, daylight tubes (solar tubes) are tools that reflect outside light inside. In this way, artificial lighting usage reduces. Furthermore, innovative solutions like Smart Meter, digitalSTROM or Kiwigrid should be used to monitor energy and carbon footprinting systems (DHL, 2010).

Heating, Ventilating and Air Conditioning (HVAC)

Operational energy, which is consumed for heating, cooling, ventilating, lighting and powering equipment, is the major component of building energy consumption during its life-cycle. According to the US Energy Information Administration Report on Energy Usage in Commercial Buildings (2016), ventilation and cooling consume 16 and 15% of the energy, respectively. According to the Freis, Vohlidka, & Gunthner (2016), heating and cooling system need most of the energy in a manual warehouse while the material handling equipment needs in a semi and fully automated warehouses. Dadhich et al. (2015) show that reducing the temperature of warehouse 1°C causes 10% energy saving.

There are many ways to reduce costs and emissions related to HVAC. To control the temperature of the warehouse, sensors should be used and to avoid heat loss fast-moving doors or barriers should be used. In this way, the stored goods may be kept in the required conditions. The required temperature of warehouse change according to the products stored. The products like frozen meat need to be stored -10°C, consumer goods need to be stored in 20 °C. The temperature of the indoor environment should also be set according to the working activities. In areas where hard physical activities exist like loading and unloading areas 13°C, in storage areas for dry products 10°C and in picking or inspection areas 19°C may be appropriate (McKinnon et al., 2015).

Indoor environment conditions in terms of HVAC and lighting are also crucial for workers. International WELL Building Institute gives significance to the health and wellbeing of the workers because they believe that higher conscious-workers in green buildings increase productivity. In the Harvard School of Public Health study (MacNaughton et al., 2017) 109 workers are exposed to working conditions in traditional and green buildings and a cognitive examination of higher-order decision-making ability is used to assess the workers. The results of the study show cognitive function scores of workers in green-certified buildings are better with 26.4%, according to the scores of workers in traditional buildings. Another study that investigates the effect of green buildings on the health of workers shows there are benefits providing fewer symptoms of sick building, asthma hospitalizations and lower death rates (Allen et al., 2015). In addition to the effect on health, green buildings have a positive impact on the productivity of the workers (MacNaughton et al., 2017).

The required temperature of the warehouses is maintained by the ventilation. The level of air changes means heat loss. It can be prevented by using fast-acting doors, which are opened if necessary and closed quickly, using zone-controlled thermostats. The heat source depends on the size of the warehouse. In large warehouses, the heating systems usually powered by fuel oil or gas. Heating in small warehouses is provided by warm air or radiant heaters or powered by gas or fuel oil (McKinnon et al., 2015).

Material Handling

In traditional warehouses, the products in the list of a customer order are picked by pickers by traveling between aisles and shelves. This type of picking is called picker-to-parts system. Almost 80% of the warehouses use the picker-to-parts system in Western Europe (De Koster et al., 2007). In picker-to-part system warehouses, forklifts, reach, and turret trucks are the most widely used handling equipment. They use a combustion engine that needs diesel, LPG or natural gas or powered by electricity.

According to Collom (2018), electric forklift provides less noise. This provides easier communication between employees and a good working environment for employees. Many studies compare that equipment in terms of environmental impact. Fuc et al. (2016) showed that electric forklift has a significantly smaller environmental effect than any forklift powered by an internal combustion engine (liquefied petroleum gas and diesel forklifts). On the other hand, some studies claim LPG forklifts performs better than electric forklifts in terms of environmental aspect. For example, Johnson (2008) showed that electric and LPG forklifts emit an equal amount of carbon theoretically, but in practice, LPG's have less carbon footprint than electricity. Facchini et al. (2016) show electric forklifts are environmentally preferable if the load is less than 3000 kg. While the weight of load increase the LPG forklifts become more preferable. The main disadvantage of electric forklifts is battery charging. Lead-acid batteries are used in battery-powered forklifts. The batteries may provide power for 8 hours. Changing battery takes almost 5-15 minutes in an automatic change out and it takes at least 45 minutes in a manual change out. A forklift that is charged during 8 hours needs an additional 8 hours for cooling. Therefore, an operation needs three batteries for each forklift in a 7/24 hour working environment. Since oxygen and hydrogen gasses are released in the charging duration it must be done in a temperature-controlled environment. In case of acid leakage in charging duration, the charging must be done in a reserved area and if it happens, the acid must be removed from the batteries for battery efficiency. The productivity of battery-powered forklifts may decrease while it is working. In order to reduce the decline in productivity, AC motors are recommended instead of direct current motors by EPRI (2004). As an alternative to the fossil fuel and battery-powered forklifts, fuel cell forklifts, which is designed as a hybrid system, may be used in warehouses. Fuel cell forklifts are more productive than battery-powered forklifts since they don't need time for battery changing, they can be refueled in five minutes, and it is more preferable in terms of environment since acid leakage does not arise. Although fuel cell forklifts have a high initial cost, they cause less total cost.

In addition, there are literature studies that investigate and compare efficiency of traditional equipment. For instance, Öztürkoğlu (2016) compared picking time of pallets with and without raisable turntable and showed using raisable turntable cause saving on picking time of pallets in warehouse. Since picking time reduction may cause increment in total number of picking operation in a specific period, unit cost of picking in this specific period may decrease. Therefore, it is possible that reduction in picking time can cause indirectly saving in cost of picking.

Automated Storage and Retrieval Systems (AS/RS)

The AS/RS is one of the most used material handling systems in warehouses. In AS/RS, the cranes handle unit loads by traveling vertically and horizontally at the same time. It is used for both unit loads such as pallets and totes and small units. AS/RS is usually used with equally sized rack systems. Lee, Lee, & Hur (2005) proposed an AS/RS with modular sized rack systems to meet the customer's various sized order types. As an alternative to the AS/RS, autonomous vehicle storage and retrieval systems (AVS/RSs) are proposed by considering the economic and environmental dimension of it. In AVS/RS, the unit loads are handling horizontally by vehicles and while vertical movement is provided by lifts. Many of the studies about handling systems showed that AVS/RS is much more suitable than AS/RS for unit loads in economic comparison. Tappia, Marchet, Melacini, & Perotti (2015) showed that AVS/RS is more preferable in case required handling capacity is higher than the required number of storage locations and AS/RS is more preferable in vice versa. The environmental impact of the automated warehouse is assessed by the indirect CO^2 emission resulting from energy consumption. Tappia et al. (2015) also showed that CO^2 emission arises from energy consumption due to material handling operations during one year are lower in AVS/RS than AS/RS. For each 1000 single command cycle, AVS/RS consume 1.07 kWh energy and emit 0.39 kg CO^2 while AS/RS consume 9.76 kWh energy and emit 3.54 kg CO^2. There is not much research, which considers both economic and social dimension of sustainability simultaneously but Neto, Walther, Bloemhof, Van Nunen, & Spengler (2009) claimed that decreasing environmental effect is possible with cost increment so there is a trade-off between environment and economic dimensions of sustainability.

Automated Guided Vehicles (AGV) Usage in Warehouses

AGVs have benefits on the environmental dimension of sustainability by reducing energy consumption (Acciaro and Wilmsmeier, 2015) and emissions (Geerlings and Van Duin, 2011). AGVs generate less GHGs (CO^2 and NO^2) since they minimize travel distance (Schmidt, Meyer-Barlag, Eisel, Kolbe, & Appelrath, 2015). The AGVs are evaluated according to their energy usage by Schmidt et al. (2015) and battery-powered AGVs are more beneficial compared to diesel-powered AGVs.

The social contribution of AGVs on sustainability can be evaluated by the working condition improvements and working accidents. Between 1998 and 2007, 3 million work accidents came out and most of them occurred due to forklift drivers (Sabattini et al., 2013). AGVs have the potential to improve safety (Duffy, Wu, & Ng, 2003) in the working environment so this is a big contribution to the social side of sustainability. Krüger, Lien, & Verl (2009) explain the social and economic contribution of AGVs by presenting the reducing effect of AGVs and human corporations on lower back pain, spine injuries. Furthermore, the standards and regulations about the corporation of human and robot operators to improve their safety are examined (Kabe, Tanaka, Ikeda, & Sugimoto, 2010).

Although AGVs have high initial costs (Peterson and Michalek, 2013), they eliminate the labor cost (Gosavi and Grasman, 2009) and can reduce total handling costs. The top internet-based retailing company Amazon bought the manufacturer of Kiva robots that pick and carry a shelf of goods to a picker and used 30.000 kivas in its warehouses and FCs to decrease delivery times (DHL, 2016). By the time, they provide a high level of customer satisfaction that is one of the top expectations of e-commerce customers. Ventura and Rieksts (2009) generate a model to minimize the response time of multiple vehicles by providing on-time delivery in a shift. The AGVs contribution to the operational level promotes the economic dimension of sustainability.

FUTURE RESEARCH DIRECTIONS

In this study transportation, distribution and warehousing are evaluated as logistic activities. Although transportation subject is broad in scope, we investigated road transportation in the means of sustainability. It involves maritime, air, road, rail, pipeline and inland water transportation. Each mode of transportation associate with e-commerce can be evaluated in terms of sustainability in a new chapter as a future study.

CONCLUSION

E-commerce is becoming widespread every day and this brings some challenges and benefits to the logistics world. Manufacturers, retailers and even small-scaled craftsmen can produce and sell their products using internet portals. Small parts can easily be sent to customers directly from a warehouse of a manufacturer via cargo companies. To deliver these small parts, lots of trucks and vans are on the move, which causes more CO^2 release every day. Due to e-commerce sales, last-mile distribution options are increased. While attended home delivery models increase van-miles and transport costs, unattended delivery (UD) options such as shared RBs, delivery boxes, C&C points provide environmentally and economically sustainable solutions. Instant delivery and same-day delivery options are becoming popular and time constraints make the distribution problems more complex. UD options also provide beneficial solutions for time windows constraints of customers and cause fewer van moves on the traffic. Even so, some UD options require customers to use their cars and pick up products from a specific place and this may result in more CO^2 release and traffic congestion. Crowdsourcing logistics has recently begun to use as a last-mile delivery option. These systems can be environmentally friendly and cost-effective if companies use already planned routes of workers or customers. New technologies such as sidewalk robots and drones are in use for delivering products. For now, these technologies are expensive and the effects of their common usage have not tested yet. The effects of such technologies should be evaluated in the means of environmental, economic and social aspects. Their permissions should be given locally, after evaluating the needs, the capacity and the characteristics of the related region.

Due to the changes in customer demand because of e-commerce, the FCs which provide customer orders on time and accurately are emerged in addition to the big regional warehouses. Beside the traditional equipment such as forklifts, reach trucks and turret trucks, automated systems to store and retrieve products and AGVs became widespread in the FCs. There are some advantages and disadvantages of this equipment about energy consumption, GHG emission rates, inventory cost and working environment of employees which are discussed above. Although all of these equipment have initial investment cost they provide benefit especially in terms of employees since they facilitate to lift heavy products. The equipment especially powered by electric and LPG is recommended in terms of environmental aspect. The issues such as location and layout of the facilities, materials used in wall, roof and floor systems, lighting systems, HVAC systems should be determined accurately before the facilities are built since they cause inventory costs, energy consumption and GHG emission. A brief summary of benefits emerged due to e-commerce related logistics issues that are highlighted in this chapter are shown in the Table 1.

Although there are many supply chain and logistics studies about sustainability in literature, many of them does not related to e-commerce or just one or two dimensions of sustainability has taken into account. The studies and industrial reports especially considered environmental and economic side of sustainability rather than social side. In this chapter, three dimensions of sustainability is considered while evaluating logistics activities, which are appeared due to, expanded e-commerce.

Table 1. Summary table of sustainability aspects and their benefits

Delivery and Transportation	Warehousing
Social Benefits Emerged Due to E-Commerce Related Logistic Issues	
Delivery and Transportation	**Warehousing**
· Easier reach to products with AHD and UD services (Cairns, 2007). · Reduction in idle vehicle kilometers of vans due to usage free capacity of citizens and workers as a part of crowdsourcing delivery (Rai et al., 2017). · Easier to reach products for disabled and elderly people by ADVs · More reliable deliveries to hard-to-reach areas due to drone usage (Boeras et al., 2019). · Reduction in traffic and obstacles is expected by using drones (Murray & Chu, 2015) sidewalk robots.	· Emerging of new jobs due to increased number of FCs and increase in employment (Mandel, 2017). · Reduction in unpaid work, which is transformed to work in FCs due to e-commerce (Progressive Policy Institute, 2017). · Easier reach to work for employees in warehouses/DCs/FCs, which are located closer to city centers with the aim of travel distance reduction between these facilities and e-commerce customers (Tan et al., 2009). · Reduction in sickness symptoms of workers like asthma in green buildings (Allen et al., 2015). · Better working conditions for employees in terms of air quality and noise through electric forklifts used in warehouses/DCs/FCs (Collom, 2018). · Reduction in accidents in warehouses/DCs/FCs through automated guided vehicles (Duffy et al., 2003).
Economic Benefits Emerged Due to E-Commerce Related Logistic Issues	
Delivery and Transportation	**Warehousing**
· Decrease in transportation costs due to increment in UD services (Kämäräinen et al., 2001). · Reduction in transportation cost due to usage free capacity of citizens and workers cars as a part of crowdsourcing delivery (Rai, 2017). · Reduction in transportation cost is expected in the future due to delivering with autonomous vehicles (Gružauskas et al., 2018).	· Reduction in travel distance between warehouses/DCs/FCs and e-commerce customers (Kaplan, 2019; Napolitano, 2013; Demirel et al., 2010; Raut, et al., 2017) and hence reduction in cost of transportation. · Reduction in travel distance between product locations in warehouses/DCs/FCs through new aisle layouts (Gue and Meller, 2009; Öztürkoğlu et al., 2012; Kocaman et al., 2019) and hence reduction in cost of transportation. · Reduction in travel distance through new storage systems in warehouses/DCs/FCs to pick products in an order list (Boysen et al., 2019) and hence reduction in cost of transportation. · Reduction in energy consumption by selecting appropriate light bulbs (Colicchia et al., 2013), by using them when necessary (DHL, 2010), by cleaning the bulbs regularly (DHL, 2010) and by using sensors to turn lights on and off (Dadhich et al., 2015; Davis, 2019) in the warehouse/DC/FC facilities. · Reduction in energy consumption by using sensors for HVAC and hence reduction in cost of warehousing (McKinnon et al., 2015). · Reduction in energy consumption by using AS/RS and AGVs in warehouses/DCs/FCs and hence reduction in cost of warehousing (Tappia et al., 2015; Schmidt et al., 2015). · Reduction in in energy consumption by utilizing day light more in warehouses/DCs/FCs (DHL, 2010).
Environmental Benefits Emerged Due to E-Commerce Related Logistic Issues	
Delivery and Transportation	**Warehousing**
· Reduction in GHG emissions due to increment in electrical vehicle usage (IEA, 2019). · Reduction in GHG emissions due to increment in ZEZ and LEZ (Transport & Environment, 2019). · Reduction traffic noise, air pollution and fuel-oil consumption due to usage free capacity of citizens and workers cars as a part of crowdsourcing delivery (Rai, 2017).	· Reduced energy consumption and GHG emissions due to green warehouse buildings (Kaplan, 2019). · Reduction in travel distance between warehouses/DCs/FCs and e-commerce customer and hence reduction in amount of GHG emissions (Napolitano, 2013). · Reduction in travel distance through new aisle layouts in a warehouse/DC/FC to pick products in order list (Gue and Meller, 2009; Öztürkoğlu et al., 2012; Kocaman et al., 2019) and hence reduction in amount of GHG emission. · Reduction in amount of GHG emission by using renewable energy in warehouse/DC/FC buildings (Prologis, 2017). · Reduction in energy consumption by using natural insulation materials for the wall, floor and roof of the warehouse/DC/FC buildings (MacNaughton et al., 2017; Rai et al., 2011). · Reduction in amount of GHS emissions by using electric forklifts in warehouses/DCs/FCs (Fuc et al., 2016).

REFERENCES

Acciaro, M., & Wilmsmeier, G. (2015). Energy efficiency in maritime logistics chains. *Research in Transportation Business & Management, 17*, 1–7. doi:10.1016/j.rtbm.2015.11.002

Alberro, H. (2019). *Utopia isn't just idealistic fantasy – it inspires people to change the world*. Retrieved November 20, 2019, from https://theconversation.com/utopia-isnt-just-idealistic-fantasy-it-inspires-people-to-change-the-world-118962

Allen, J. G., MacNaughton, P., Satish, U., Santanam, S., Vallarino, J., & Spengler, J. D. (2015). Associations of cognitive function scores with carbon dioxide, ventilation, and volatile organic compound exposures in office workers: A controlled exposure study of green and conventional office environments. *Environmental Health Perspectives, 124*(6), 805–812. doi:10.1289/ehp.1510037 PMID:26502459

Angelovska, N. (2019). *Top 5 online retailers*. Retrieved November 30, 2019, from https://www.forbes.com/sites/ninaangelovska/2019/05/20/top-5-online-retailers-electronics-and-media-is-the-star-of-e-commerce-worldwide/#6c9267bb1cd9

Ashrafzadeh, M., Rafiei, F. M., Isfahani, N. M., & Zare, Z. (2012). Application of fuzzy TOPSIS method for the selection of Warehouse Location: A Case Study. *Interdisciplinary Journal of Contemporary Research in Business, 3*(9), 655–671.

Bartholdi, J. J., & Hackman, S. T. (2014). *Warehouse & Distribution Science: Release 0.96*. Atlanta, GA: Supply Chain and Logistics Institute, School of Industrial and Systems Engineering, Georgia Institute of Technology.

Bartolini, M., Bottani, E., & Eric, H. (2019). Green warehousing: Systematic literature review and bibliometric analysis. *Journal of Cleaner Production, 226*, 242–258. doi:10.1016/j.jclepro.2019.04.055

Black, W. R. (2010). *Sustainable transportation: problems and solutions*. New York, NY: Guilford Press.

Boeras, D. I., Collins, B. C., & Peeling, R. W. (2019). *The Use of Drones in the Delivery of Rural Healthcare. In Revolutionizing Tropical Medicine: Point-of-Care Tests, New Imaging Technologies and Digital Health* (p. 618). John Willey and Sons.

Bonilla, D. (2016). Urban vans, e-commerce and road freight transport. *Production Planning and Control, 27*(6), 433–442. doi:10.1080/09537287.2016.1147093

Boyer, K. K., Frohlich, M. T., & Hult, G. T. M. (2005). *Extending the supply chain – How cutting-edge companies bridge the critical last mile into customers' homes*. New York: Amacom.

Boysen, N., de Koster, R., & Weidinger, F. (2019). Warehousing in the e-commerce era: A survey. *European Journal of Operational Research, 277*(2), 396–411. doi:10.1016/j.ejor.2018.08.023

Boysen, N., Fedtke, S., & Weidinger, F. (2018). Optimizing automated sorting in warehouses: The minimum order spread sequencing problem. *European Journal of Operational Research, 270*(1), 386–400. doi:10.1016/j.ejor.2018.03.026

Büyüksaatçi, S., & Esnaf, Ş. (2014). Carbon emission based optimization approach for the facility location problem. *TOJSAT, 4*(1), 9–20.

Cairns, S. (2007). Delivering supermarket shopping: More or less traffic? *Transport Reviews*, *§§§*, 51–84.

Chen, C., & Pan, S. (2015). Using the Crowd of Taxis to Last Mile Delivery in E-Commerce: a methodological research. Proceedings of SOHOMA15, 640, 61-70.

Chopra, S., & Meindl, P. (2015). *Supply Chain Management Strategy Planning, and Operation*. Edinburgh, UK: Pearson.

Clement, J. (2019). *Retail e-commerce sales worldwide from 2014 to 2023*. Retrieved 11 11, 2019 from https://www.statista.com/statistics/379046/worldwide-retail-e-commerce-sales/

Clive, M. (2015). Reducing the environmental impact of warehousing. In Green logistics: Improving the environmental sustainability of logistics (pp. 167-190). Kogan Page Publishers.

Colicchia, C., Marchet, G., Melacini, M., & Perotti, S. (2013). Building environmental sustainability: Empirical evidence from Logistics Service Providers. *Journal of Cleaner Production*, *59*, 197–209. doi:10.1016/j.jclepro.2013.06.057

Collom, L. (2018). *Electric-Powered Forklift Benefits in the Warehouse*. Retrieved (December 9, 2019) from https://www.toyotaforklift.com/blog/electric-powered-forklifts-benefits-in-the-warehouse

Cook, P., & Sproul, A. (2011). Towards low-energy retail warehouse building. *Architectural Science Review*, *54*(3), 206–214. doi:10.1080/00038628.2011.590055

Dadhich, P., Genovese, A., Kumar, N., & Acquaye, A. (2015). Developing sustainable supply chains in the UK construction industry: A case study. *International Journal of Production Economics*, *164*, 271–284. doi:10.1016/j.ijpe.2014.12.012

Davis, D. (2019). *Guide to Warehouse Lighting*. Retrieved December 5, 2019, from https://blog.1000bulbs.com/home/guide-to-warehouse-lighting

De Koster, R., Le-Duc, T., & Roodbergen, K. J. (2007). Design and control of warehouse order picking: A literature review. *European Journal of Operational Research*, *182*(2), 481–501. doi:10.1016/j.ejor.2006.07.009

Deloitte. (2014). *The shed of the future E-commerce: its impact on warehouses*. London: Deloitte LPP.

Demirel, T., Demirel, N. Ç., & Kahraman, C. (2010). Multi-criteria warehouse location selection using Choquet integral. *Expert Systems with Applications*, *37*(5), 3943–3952. doi:10.1016/j.eswa.2009.11.022

DHL. (2010). *Delivering Tomorrow: Towards Sustainable Logistics. Deutsche Post DHL*. Bonn: Christof E. Ehrhart.

DHL. (2016). *Robotic in logistics: A DPDHL perspective on implications and use cases for the logistics industry. ST. Onge Company*. Tom Bonkenburg.

Duffy, V. G., Wu, F. F., & Ng, P. P. (2003). Development of an internet virtual layout system for improving workplace safety. *Computers in Industry*, *50*(2), 207–230. doi:10.1016/S0166-3615(02)00121-5

Electric Power Research Institute (EPRI). (2004). Evaluating Opportunities for Fast Charging Application at Del Monte Foods. Electric Power Research Institute Report 1002237. Palo Alto, CA: EPRI.

Environmental Protection Agency. (2015). *2015 Green Communities Criteria*. Retrieved January 13, 2020, from https://www.enterprisecommunity.org/solutions-and-innovation/green-communities/criteria

Environmental Protection Agency. (2019). *Greenhouse Gas Emissions*. Retrieved November 12, 2019, from https://www.epa.gov/ghgemissions/sources-greenhouse-gas-emissions

European Commission. (2011). *Science for environment report*. Bristol: The University of the West of England.

European Union's Council of Ministers. (2001). *2340th Council meeting Transport/Telecommunications*. Retrieved November 26, 2019, from https://ec.europa.eu/commission/presscorner/detail/en/PRES_01_131

Facchini, F., Mummolo, G., Mossa, G., Digiesi, S., Boenzi, F., & Verriello, R. (2016). Minimizing the carbon footprint of material handling equipment: Comparison of electric and LPG forklifts. *Journal of Industrial Engineering and Management*, *9*(5), 1035–1046. doi:10.3926/jiem.2082

Freis, J., Vohlidka, P., & Gunthner, W. (2016). Low-carbon warehousing: Examining impacts of building and intra-logistics design options on energy demand and the CO^2 emissions of logistics centers. *Sustainability*, *8*(5), 448. doi:10.3390u8050448

Fuc, P., Kurczewski, P., Lewandowska, A., Nowak, E., Selech, J., & Ziolkowski, A. (2016). An environmental life cycle assessment of forklift operation: A well-to-wheel analysis. *The International Journal of Life Cycle Assessment*, *21*(10), 1438–1451. doi:10.100711367-016-1104-y

Geerlings, H., & Van Duin, R. (2011). A new method for assessing CO^2-emissions from container terminals: A promising approach applied in Rotterdam. *Journal of Cleaner Production*, *19*(6-7), 657–666. doi:10.1016/j.jclepro.2010.10.012

Gevaers, R., Voorde, E. V., & Vanelslander, T. (2009). Characteristics of Innovations in Last-Mile Logistics - Using Best Practices, Case Studies and Making the Link with Green and Sustainable Logistics. In Proceedings of the E. T. Conference. Association for t European Transport and Contibutors.

Gevaers, R., Voorde, E. V., & Vanelslander, T. (2014). Cost Modelling and Simulation of Last-mile Characteristics in an Innovative B2C Supply Chain Environment with Implications on Urban Areas and Cities. *8th International Conference on City Logistics*, *125*(2014), 398-411. 10.1016/j.sbspro.2014.01.1483

Gill, A., & Ishaq Bhatti, M. (2007). Optimal model for warehouse location and retailer allocation. *Applied Stochastic Models in Business and Industry*, *23*(3), 213–221. doi:10.1002/asmb.666

Goodland, R., & Bank, W. (2002). Sustainability: Human, Social, Economic and Environmental. *Social Science*, *6*, 220–225.

Gordon, D. (1995). Sustainable transportation: what do we mean and how do we get there. *Transportation and Energy: Strategies for a sustainable transportation system*, 1-11. doi:. doi:10.3141/1670-05

A. Gosavi, & S. E. Grasman (Eds.). (2009). Simulation-based optimization for determining AGV capacity in a manufacturing system. In *IIE Annual Conference Proceedings*. Institute of Industrial and Systems Engineers.

Govindan, K., Garg, K., Gupta, S., & Jha, P. C. (2016). Effect of product recovery and sustainability enhancing indicators on the location selection of manufacturing facility. *Ecological Indicators, 67*, 517–532. doi:10.1016/j.ecolind.2016.01.035

Gružauskas, V., Baskutis, S., & Navickas, V. (2018). Minimizing the trade-off between sustainability and cost effective performance by using autonomous vehicles. *Journal of Cleaner Production, 184*, 709–717. doi:10.1016/j.jclepro.2018.02.302

Gue, K., Ivanovi'c, G., & Meller, R. (2012). A unit-load warehouse with multiple pickup and deposit points and non-traditional aisles. *Transportation Research Part E, Logistics and Transportation Review, 48*(4), 795–806. doi:10.1016/j.tre.2012.01.002

Gue, K. R., & Meller, R. D. (2009). Aisle configurations for unit-load warehouses. *IIE Transactions, 41*(3), 171–182. doi:10.1080/07408170802112726

Han, L., Chin, S.-M., Franzese, O., & Hwang, H.-L. (2005). Estimating the impact of pickup-and delivery-related illegal parking activities on traffic. *Transportation Research Record Journal of the Transportation Research Board,* (1906), 49-55 Doi:10.3141/1906-06

Hsu, J. (2019). *Out of the Way, Human! Delivery Robots Want a Share of Your Sidewalk.* Retrieved November 22, 2019, from https://www.scientificamerican.com/article/out-of-the-way-human-delivery-robots-want-a-share-of-your-sidewalk/

Hübner, A., Holzapfel, A., Kuhn, H., & Obermair, E. (2019). Distribution in Omnichannel Groccery Retailing. In *Operations in an Omnichannel World /Springer Series in Supply Chain Management* (pp. 293–294). Cham: Springer Nature.

Huppertz, P. (1999). Market changes require new supply chain thinking. *Transportation & Distribution*, 70-4.

IEA. (2019). *Tracking Transport.* Retrieved December 16, 2019, https://www.iea.org/reports/tracking-transport-2019

Joerss, M., Neuhaus, F., & Schröder, J. (2016b). How customer demands are reshaping last-mile delivery. *The McKinsey Quarterly, 17*, 1–5.

Joerss, M., Schröder, J., Neuhaus, F., Klink, C., & Mann, F. (2016a). *Parcel delivery: The future of last mile*. McKinsey & Company.

Johnson, E. (2008). Disagreement over carbon footprints: A comparison of electric and LPG forklifts. *Energy Policy, 36*(4), 1569–1573. doi:10.1016/j.enpol.2008.01.014

Jones, K. (2010). *Aircraft Noise and Children's Learning. Civil Aviation Authority.* Norwich: The Stationery Office.

Kabe, T., Tanaka, K., Ikeda, H., & Sugimoto, N. (2010). Consideration on safety for emerging technology–Case studies of seven service robots. *Safety Science, 48*(3), 296–301. doi:10.1016/j.ssci.2009.11.008

Kahn Ribeiro, S., Figueroa, M. J., Creutzig, F., Dubeux, C., Hupe, J., & Kobayashi, S. (2012). Energy end-use: Transport. In Global Energy Assessment-Toward a Sustainable Future. Cambridge University Press.

Kämäräinen, V., Saranen, J., & Holmström, J. (2001). The reception box impact on home delivery efficiency in the e-grocery business. *International Journal of Physical Distribution & Logistics Management*, *31*(6), 414–426. doi:10.1108/09600030110399414

Kaplan, D. A. (2019). *7 elements of the sustainable warehouse.* Retrieved November 22, 2019 from https://www.supplychaindive.com/news/building-sustainable-warehouse-shippers-cost-benefits/549625/

Kawa, A. (2017). Fulfillment service in e-commerce logistics. *LogForum*, *13*(4), 429–438. doi:10.17270/J.LOG.2017.4.4

Kocaman, Y., Öztürkoğlu, Ö., & Gümüşoğlu, Ş. (2019). Aisle designs in unit-load warehouses with different flow policies of multiple pickup and deposit points. *Central European Journal of Operations Research*, *§§§*, 1–33.

Krüger, J., Lien, T. K., & Verl, A. (2009). Cooperation of human and machines in assembly lines. *CIRP Annals*, *58*(2), 628–646. doi:10.1016/j.cirp.2009.09.009

Laudon, K., & Traver, C. (2016). *E-commerce: business, technology, society*. Boston: Pearson.

Laudon, K., & Traver, C. (2016). *E-commerce: business, technology, society*. Boston: Pearson.

Lawrence, E. C. (1998). *Internet Commerce: Digital Models for Business.* Sydney, Australia: John Wiley & Sons.

Lee, Y. H., Lee, M. H., & Hur, S. (2005). Optimal design of rack structure with modular cell in AS/RS. *International Journal of Production Economics*, *98*(2), 172–178. doi:10.1016/j.ijpe.2004.05.018

F. Li, T. Liu, H. Zhang, R. Cao, W. Ding, & J. P. Fasano (Eds.). (2008). Distribution center location for green supply chain. In *Proceedings of 2008 IEEE International Conference on Service Operations and Logistics, and Informatics*. IEEE.

Lim, S. F., Jin, X., & Srai, J. S. (2018). Consumer-driven e-commerce: A literature review, design framework, and research agenda on last-mile logistics models. *International Journal of Physical Distribution & Logistics Management*, *48*(3), 308–332. doi:10.1108/IJPDLM-02-2017-0081

Litman. (2017). Developing Indicators for Comprehensive and Sustainable Transport Planning. *Transportation Research Record: Journal of the Transportation Research Board*, *2017*(1), 10–15. doi:10.3141/2017-02

MacNaughton, P., Satish, U., Laurent, J. G. C., Flanigan, S., Vallarino, J., Coull, B., ... Allen, J. G. (2017). The impact of working in a green certified building on cognitive function and health. *Building and Environment*, *114*, 178–186. doi:10.1016/j.buildenv.2016.11.041 PMID:28785124

Mandel, M. (2017). *How e-commerce is raising pay and creating jobs around the country*. Retrieved November 11, 2019, from https://www.forbes.com/sites/realspin/2017/04/03/how-e-commerce-is-raising-pay-and-creating-jobs-around-the-country/#aa393d76dff5

Marks, M. (2019). *Robots in space: Sharing our world with autonomous delivery vehicles.* SSRN 3347466.

McKenzie, S. (2004). *Social Sustainability: Towards Some Definitions*. Hawke Research Institute Working Paper Series 27.

Mokhtarian, P. L. (2004). A conceptual analysis of the transportation impacts of B2C e-commerce. *Transportation*, *31*(3), 257–284. doi:10.1023/B:PORT.0000025428.64128.d3

Morel, J. C., Mesbah, A., Oggero, M., & Walker, P. (2001). Building houses with local materials: Means to drastically reduce the environmental impact of construction. *Building and Environment*, *36*(10), 1119–1126. doi:10.1016/S0360-1323(00)00054-8

Morelli, J. (2011). Environmental Sustainability: A Definition for Environmental Professionals. *Journal of Environmental Sustainability*, *1*(1), 1–9. doi:10.14448/jes.01.0002

Murray, C. C., & Chu, A. G. (2015). The flying sidekick traveling salesman problem: Optimization of drone-assisted parcel deliveryThe flying sidekick traveling salesman problem: Optimization of drone-assisted parcel delivery. *Transportation Research Part C, Emerging Technologies*, *54*, 86–109. doi:10.1016/j.trc.2015.03.005

MWPL International Inc. (2019). *The Walmart distribution center network in the United States*. Retrieved November 11, 2019, from http://www.mwpvl.com/html/walmart.html

Napolitano, M. (2013). *7 Trends in Sustainable Warehouse Design*. Retrieved November 25, 2019, from https://www.supplychain247.com/article/7_trends_in_sustainable_warehouse_design/green

National Bureau of Economic Research. (2017). *Economies of Density in E-Commerce: A Study of Amazon's Fulfillment Center Network (No. w23361)*. Cambridge: Author.

Neto, J. Q. F., Walther, G., Bloemhof, J., Van Nunen, J. A. E. E., & Spengler, T. (2009). A methodology for assessing eco-efficiency in logistics networks. *European Journal of Operational Research*, *193*(3), 670–682. doi:10.1016/j.ejor.2007.06.056

Öztürkoğlu, Ö. (2015). *Investigating the robustness of aisles in a non-traditional unit-load warehouse design: Leverage. In 2015 IEEE congress on evolutionary computation (CEC)* (pp. 2230–2236). IEEE. doi:10.1109/CEC.2015.7257160

Öztürkoğlu, Ö. (2016). The Effects of Manual Material Handling Equipment on Loading and Unloading Time of a Case in a Pallet. *Journal of Yaşar University*, *11*(44), 278–290.

Öztürkoğlu, Ö. (2018). Lean and Sustainable Warehousing. In U. Akküçük (Ed.), *Handbook of Research on Supply Chain Management for Sustainable Development* (pp. 218–241). IGI Global. doi:10.4018/978-1-5225-5757-9.ch012

Öztürkoğlu, Ö., Gue, K. R., & Meller, R. D. (2012). Optimal unit-load warehouse designs for single-command operations. *IIE Transactions*, *44*(6), 459–475. doi:10.1080/0740817X.2011.636793

Öztürkoğlu, Ö., Gue, K. R., & Meller, R. D. (2014). A constructive aisle design model for unit-load warehouses with multiple pickup and deposit points. *European Journal of Operational Research*, *236*(1), 382–394. doi:10.1016/j.ejor.2013.12.023

Öztürkoğlu, Ö., & Hoşer, D. (2018). A new warehouse design problem and a proposed polynomial-time optimal order picking algorithm. *Journal of the Faculty of Engineering and Architecture of Gazi University*, *33*(4), 1569–1588.

Öztürkoğlu, Ö., & Hoser, D. (2019a). A discrete cross aisle design model for order-picking warehouses. *European Journal of Operational Research*, *275*(2), 411–430. doi:10.1016/j.ejor.2018.11.037

Öztürkoğlu, Ö., & Hoser, D. (2019b). An evaluation of order picking tour efficiency in two-block warehouses. *Operations and Supply Chain Management: An International Journal*, *12*(2), 74–78. doi:10.31387/oscm0370225

Öztürkoğlu, Ö., Kocaman, Y., & Gümüşoğlu, Ş. (2018). Evaluating Chevron aisle design in unit load warehouses with multiple pickup and deposit points. *Journal of the Faculty of Engineering and Architecture of Gazi University*, *33*(3), 793–807.

Peerless research group. (2019). *The Impacts of e-Commerce: Fulfillment Challenges and Improvement Priorities.* Retrieved November 30, 2019, from https://scg-peerless.s3.amazonaws.com/reseach_briefs/Honeywell-Intelligrated_RB5.pdf

Peterson, S. B., & Michalek, J. J. (2013). Cost-effectiveness of plug-in hybrid electric vehicle battery capacity and charging infrastructure investment for reducing US gasoline consumption. *Energy Policy*, *52*, 429–438. doi:10.1016/j.enpol.2012.09.059

Planners, C. (2014). A Global Survey of Urban Sustainability Rating Tools. *Global Symposium on Urban Sustainability Rating Tool.*

Porter, J. (2019). *Google's Wing drones approved to make public deliveries in Australia.* Retrieved December 11, 2019, from https://www.theverge.com/2019/4/9/18301782/wing-drone-delivery-google-alphabet-canberra-australia-public-launch

Progressive Policy Institute. (2017). *How ecommerce creates jobs and reduces income inequality.* Washington, DC: Author.

Prologis. (2017). *Sustainability Report.* San Francisco: Author.

Pudleiner, D., & Colton, J. (2015). Using sensitivity analysis to improve the efficiency of a Net-Zero Energy vaccine warehouse design. *Building and Environment*, *87*, 302–314. doi:10.1016/j.buildenv.2014.12.026

Punakivi, M., Yrjölä, H., & Holmström, J. (2001). Solving the last mile issue: Reception box or delivery box? *International Journal of Physical Distribution & Logistics Management*, *31*(6), 427–439. doi:10.1108/09600030110399423

Radhi, H. (2010). On the optimal selection of wall cladding system to reduce direct and indirect CO^2 emissions. *Energy*, *35*(3), 1412–1424. doi:10.1016/j.energy.2009.11.026

Rai, D., Sodagar, B., Fieldson, R., & Hu, X. (2011). Assessment of CO^2 emissions reduction in a distribution warehouse. *Energy*, *36*(4), 2271–2277. doi:10.1016/j.energy.2010.05.006

Rai, H. B., Verlinde, S., Merckx, J., & Macharis, C. (2017). Crowd logistics: an opportunity for more sustainableurban freight transport? *Eur. Transp. Res. Rev.*, 9-39 . doi:10.100712544-017-0256-6

Rao, S., Goldsby, T., & Iyengar, D. (2009). The marketing and logistics efficacy of online sales channels. *International Journal of Physical Distribution & Logistics Management, 39*(2), 106–130. doi:10.1108/09600030910942386

Raut, R. D., Narkhede, B. E., Gardas, B. B., & Raut, V. (2017). Multi-criteria decision making approach: A sustainable warehouse location selection problem. *International Journal of Management Concepts and Philosophy, 10*(3), 260–281. doi:10.1504/IJMCP.2017.085834

Reagan, C. (2018). *Walmart saves $200 million by changing its light bulbs and $20 million with a new floor wax.* Retrieved December 4, 2019, from https://www.cnbc.com/2018/10/16/walmart-saves-200-million-by-changing-its-light-bulbs.html

Reyes, D., Savelsbergh, M., & Toriello, A. (2017). Vehicle routing with roaming delivery locations. *Transportation Research Part C, Emerging Technologies, 80*, 71–91. doi:10.1016/j.trc.2017.04.003

Ricker, F., & Kalakota, R. (1999). Order fulfillment: the hidden key to e-commerce success. *Supply Chain Management Review, 11*(3), 60-70.

Ries, J. M., Grosse, E. H., & Fichtinger, J. (2017). Environmental impact of warehousing: A scenario analysis for the United States. *International Journal of Production Research, 55*(21), 6485–6499. doi: 10.1080/00207543.2016.1211342

Sabattini, L., Digani, V., Secchi, C., Cotena, G., Ronzoni, D., Foppoli, M., & Oleari, F. (Eds.). (2013). Technological roadmap to boost the introduction of AGVs in industrial applications. In *Proceedings* of *2013 IEEE 9th International Conference on Intelligent Computer Communication and Processing (ICCP).* IEEE. 10.1109/ICCP.2013.6646109

Schmidt, J., Meyer-Barlag, C., Eisel, M., Kolbe, L. M., & Appelrath, H. J. (2015). Using battery-electric AGVs in container terminals—Assessing the potential and optimizing the economic viability. *Research in Transportation Business & Management, 17*, 99–111. doi:10.1016/j.rtbm.2015.09.002

Singh, A. P., Avinash, A. D., & Agarwal, K. (2017). *Evolving Energy Scenario: Role and Scope for Alternative Fuels in Transport Sector. In Prospects of Alternative Transportation Fuels. Energy, Environment, and Sustainability* (pp. 7–19). Singapore: Springer.

Singh, S. (2015). Critical Reasons for Crashes Investigated in the National Motor Vehicle Crash Causation Survey. U.S. Department of Transportation. Washington, DC: NHTSA's National Center for Statistics and Analysis.

Slabinac, M. (2015). Innovative Solutions For A "Last-Mile" Delivery – A European Experience. *Proceedings of The 15th International Scientific Conference Business Logistics in Modern Management.*

Spisak, K. (2019). *How Can Drone Delivery Change E-commerce?* Retrieved December 09, 2019, from https://www.business2community.com/ecommerce/how-can-drone-delivery-change-e-commerce-02198890

Stanley Frederick, W.T., & Lim, X. J. (2018). Consumer-driven e-commerce: A literature review, design framework, and research agenda on last-mile logistics models. *International Journal of Physical Distribution & Logistics Management, 48*(3), 308-332.

Starcke, D. (2018). *Creative Crowdsourcing for Last Mile Efficiency.* Retrieved August 12, 2019, from https://firstflightsolutions.com/creative-crowdsourcing-last-mile-efficiency/

Statistica. (2019a). *Retail e-commerce sales worldwide from 2014 to 2023.* Retrieved Nov 11, 2019 from statista.com: https://www.statista.com/statistics/379046/worldwide-retail-e-commerce-sales/

Statistica. (2019b). *B2C e-commerce as percentage of GDP in Western Europe from 2009 to 2018.* Retrieved Nov 3, 2019 from https://www.statista.com/statistics/324588/b2c-e-commerce-as-percentage-of-gdp-western-europe/

Statistica. (2019c). *B2C e-commerce as percentage of GDP in the United States from 2009 to 2018.* Retrieved Nov 3, 2019 from https://www.statista.com/statistics/324582/b2c-e-commerce-as-percentage-of-gdp-usa/

Tambovcevs, A., & Tambovceva, T. (2012). Logistic system ıntegration with environmental management system: A case study of ınternational company. ISEE 2012 Conference "Ecological Economics and Rio+20": Abstracts and Full Papers.

K. S. Tan, M. D. Ahmed, & D. Sundaram (Eds.). (2009). Sustainable warehouse management. In *Proceedings of the International Workshop on Enterprises & Organizational Modeling and Simulation.* New York: Association for Computng Machinery.

Tappia, E., Marchet, G., Melacini, M., & Perotti, S. (2015). Incorporating the environmental dimension in the assessment of automated warehouses. *Production Planning and Control, 26*(10), 824–838. doi:10.1080/09537287.2014.990945

Taylor, J. (2015). Crowdsourcing IT Work: A Three-Fold Perspective from the Workers, Buyers, and Platform Providers. *Proceedings of the 2015 ACM SIGMIS conference on computers and people research.* 10.1145/2751957.2755504

Texas A&M Transportation Institute. (2017). *How will e-commerce growth impact our transportation network? Final report* (No. PRC 17-79 F). Author.

Tompkins, J. A., White, J. A., Bozer, Y. A., & Tanchoco, J. M. A. (2003). *Facilities Planning.* John Wiley & Sons.

Transport & Environment. (2019). *Low-Emission Zones are a success - but they must now move to zero-emission mobility.* Retrieved 02 07, 2020, from https://www.transportenvironment.org/sites/te/files/publications/2019_09_Briefing_LEZ-ZEZ_final.pdf

United Nations Department of Economic and Social Affairs. (2019). *Population Prospects 2019.* New York: Population Division. Retrieved from https://population.un.org/wpp2019/Publications/Files/WPP2019_Volume-I_Comprehensive-Tables.pdf

United States Department of Labor. (2019). *Industries at a glance: Warehousing and storage (NAICS 493).* Retrieved Nov 30, 2019 from https://www.bls.gov/iag/tgs/iag493.htm#workplace_trends

United States Energy Information Administration. (2019). *Use of energy explained: Energy use for transportation.* Retrieved November 11, 2019, from https://www.eia.gov/energyexplained/use-of-energy/transportation.php

United States Environmental Protection Agency. (2019). *Greenhouse Gas Emissions*. Retrieved December 12, 2019 from https://www.epa.gov/ghgemissions/sources-greenhouse-gas-emissions

University of Minnesota Center for Urban and Regional Affairs. (2010). *Framework for Measuring Sustainable Regional Development for the Twin Cities Region*. University of Minnesota Center for Transportation Studies.

Ürge-Vorsatz, D., Cabeza, L. F., Serrano, S., Barreneche, C., & Petrichenko, K. (2015). Heating and cooling energy trends and drivers in buildings. *Renewable & Sustainable Energy Reviews*, *41*, 85–98. doi:10.1016/j.rser.2014.08.039

US Energy Information Administration. (2016). *Energy use in commercial buildings*. Retrieved Dec 5, 2019 from https://www.eia.gov/energyexplained/use-of-energy/commercial-buildings.php

Ventura, J. A., & Rieksts, B. Q. (2009). Optimal location of dwell points in a single loop AGV system with time restrictions on vehicle availability. *European Journal of Operational Research*, *192*(1), 93–104. doi:10.1016/j.ejor.2007.09.014

Wang, X., Zhan, L., Ruan, J., & Zhang, J. (2014). How to choose "last mile" delivery modes for e-fulfillment. *Mathematical Problems in Engineering*.

Wang, Y., Zhang, D., Liu, Q., Shen, F., & Lee, L. (2016). Towards enhancing the last-mile delivery: An effective crowd-tasking model with scalable solutions. *Transportation Research Part E, Logistics and Transportation Review*, *93*, 279–293. doi:10.1016/j.tre.2016.06.002

WHO. (2019). *Air pollution*. Retrieved December 15, 2019, from www.who.int: https://www.who.int/sustainable-development/transport/health-risks/air-pollution/en/

WHO. (2019). *Noise*. Retrieved November 27, 2019, from https://www.who.int/sustainable-development/transport/health- www.who.int/.risks/noise/en

Willsher, K. (2019). *Drones used to deliver parcels to remote Alpine villages*. Retrieved November 23, 2019, from https://www.theguardian.com/technology/2019/dec/02/drones-used-to-deliver-parcels-to-remote-alpine-villages

World Commission on Environment and Development. (1987). *Our Common Future*. New York: Oxford University Press.

World Economic Forum. (2009). *Supply Chain Decarbonization*. Geneva: World Economic Forum.

Yu, Y., Wang, X., Zhong, R. Y., & Huang, G. Q. (2016). *E-commerce logistics in supply chain management*. Academic Press.

Chapter 5
Disruptive Logistics and Green Supply Chain Management

Yasin Galip Gencer
https://orcid.org/0000-0003-2133-351X
Yalova University, Turkey

Ulas Akkucuk
https://orcid.org/0000-0001-6731-0634
Bogazici University, Turkey

ABSTRACT

Today, when global warming and its negative effects are more apparent, companies and individuals have given importance to green logistics practices. At the same time that computer technologies and smart applications serve in this field, new and innovative ideas are emerging every other day. Examples of disruptive innovation can change the way we do business in an industry, such as the Uber application. These new players in the sector tend to disengage the existing players. In this chapter, sector-changing national and international instances of disruptive logistics will be presented and discussed. Also, the effects of Industry 4.0 and smart cities on green logistics will be explained.

INTRODUCTION

The green movement, which is among the main political movements, places more emphasis on environmental issues than ever before. One such issue is global warming. Anxiety about global warming is increasing worldwide. In this regard, the logistics sector, which is one of the sectors that contribute the most to global warming, stands out as an important player on this issue and efforts are concentrated under the green logistics framework. The logistics industry is already using technology to design and increase the leadership of innovative business models.

DOI: 10.4018/978-1-7998-4601-7.ch005

Some important concepts that have revolutionized the traditional logistics landscape are given below:

- 3PL
- DC
- LCL
- EDI
- RFID
- 4PL

In terms of green logistics the most important terms stand out as 3PL and 4PL. Third party logistics (3PL) service providers have emerged since the late 1980s, they are considered to be logistics outsourcing suppliers. 3PL has been growing rapidly as a new business since the 1990s. Continuing logistics activities with outsourcing has become a service that is frequently encountered today with the expertise and experience of 3PL service providers in helping customers. The concept of fourth party logistics started to appear in the logistics sector after 1990s due to the insufficiency of third party logistics companies. 4PL serves at the level of expertise on solutions of the complex logistics chains. The concept of 4PL was developed by the end of the 1990s. It is defined as an integrator enterprise bringing together 3PL service providers and businesses that will receive logistics services by using their own resources, technology, knowledge and skills, and providing logistics management solutions. The main policy that the 4PL service provider must follow in order to be successful is to bring together the most suitable 3PL service providers with the customers. Thus, 4PL service providers aim at the highest level of customer satisfaction by creating the best mix among 3PL service providers and aiming to highlight the advantages of each. It can be said that the contracts that companies will make with 4PL service providers should have a longer term compared to 3PL contracts. The main reason for this is that although 3PLs perform some of the logistics services, 4PL service providers aspire to perform all aspects of logistics management.

New applications using innovation and information technologies also lead to technologies that benefit green logistics. When innovative movements are evaluated, it is seen that they are generally three types. Three types of innovation can be listed as follows:

- Incremental
- Radical
- Disruptive

Incremental innovation includes all kinds of innovations that provide more benefits to consumers as a result of the improvement of a product or process that is generally released as a result of radical innovation. Incremental innovation that provides more satisfaction to consumers with less effort and includes minor improvements and changes in the final product or process to be used easily, on the one hand, increases the competitiveness of the companies, while providing better products or services to the consumers. The first mobile phone invented in 1973 weighed 850 grams. With the rapid development of technology since 1973, the quality of mobile phones has been continuously improved. First, a few additional features such as radio and flashlight were added to the mobile phone. Improvements were made with Bluetooth, color screen, sound recording feature, camera and the Internet. The memory has been expanded, Wi-Fi has been added, touch screens have been released and nowadays the iPhone stage has been started. In this way, continuous improvement of the qualities of the mobile phone with the development of existing information and technologies is an example of incremental innovation.

Radical Innovations include new product, service, process or methods that have not been used or tried before and are developed and converted into social and economic benefits as a result of major breakthroughs. With radical innovation, some changes and transformations emerge in the lives and behaviors of those who start using the new product in society. TV, mobile phones and ATMs can be provided as examples to radical innovation.

Disruptive Innovation term, which means innovation that creates a market from scratch, disrupts the established product, competition and marketing patterns of the sectors. Disruptive innovation aims to create an unprecedented reaction by breaking the rules of the business, the market and the customer. For example, "Walkman" developed by Sony company at the end of 1970s have emerged as a great invention for young people who could not buy big and expensive stereo sets. Pegasus Airlines can be given as a different example of disruptive innovation. The most striking feature of Pegasus Airlines is an airline that uses the low cost model in Turkey. Pegasus Airlines offers the opportunity to pay the bare flight fee and if anybody is interested in ancillary services like food, beverage and even extra luggage they have to pay more. This makes travel by plane possible for individuals who cannot travel by plane due to their low income. Also companies like UBER also revolutionized the taxi business.

One of such applications, Roadie (Figure 1) is one of the leading applications in logistics recently and can be seen as an example of disruptive innovation such as Uber. Finally, the application was mentioned in the Economist magazine on October 5, 2019. It is mentioned in the Economist magazine with the title that stated "Crowdshipping is the next stop for the sharing economy". Roadie is now used in sending parcels, and with the help of an application, the masses are already delivering a package sent to the destination in some cases.

One of the innovative examples is the Bukoli application implemented by Borusan Holding. In Figure 2, an example of the box collection point of this application is given. This application has not been active for a long time and was closed on June 30, 2017.

Figure 1. Roadie APP used for making deliveries
Source: https://theincomespot.com/roadie-review

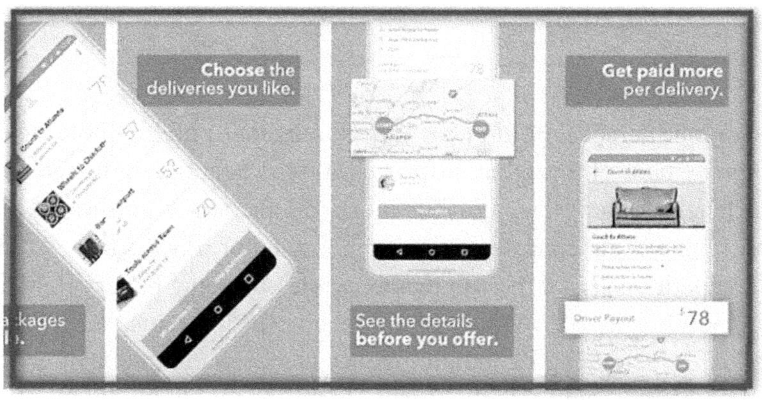

Figure 2. Bukoli delivery point
Source: https://webrazzi.com/2017/06/05/bukoli-kapandi-mi

Logistics is one of the sectors that will undergo transformations brought about by the Information Technologies and Artificial Intelligence. Driverless cars and drones are already being used by major players in the industry and are increasingly used. Also AI technologies may be used by companies like Amazon.com in order to predict consumer preferences and ship products even before the orders are given. This paper will talk about the major developments in the disruptive logistics area and will highlight the effects on green logistics.

LITERATURE RESEARCH

Many studies have previously been conducted to examine the relationship between the transport sector and carbon emissions. Some of these studies have examined one of the land, air and sea elements for the transportation sector and offered solutions. One of the most important of these studies is Sgouridis et al. (2011), which was made for air transportation and offers some important strategies. Another article written by Edwards et al (2016), aims to reduce emissions in flights by calculating the carbon index.

The relationship between disruptive innovation and logistics sector has also been examined from different perspectives in the literature. These different studies range from the impact of three-dimensional printers on the supply chain (Mohr & Kahn, 2015) to how the vehicles powered by alternative energy sources can dramatically change the logistics industry (Datta, 2008). Dhillon et al. (2001) article generally analyzes the effects of disruptive technologies on e-business for big companies. Evangelista (2012), on the other hand, talks about disruptive innovation examples in the transportation and logistics sector. Hofmann and Osterwalder (2017) examine how third-party logistics (3PL) firms are affected by digital transformation. Angeleanu (2015), on the other hand, talks about concepts that gain importance along with digital transformation such as "Omni-channel" and "anticipatory" logistics. Omni-channel is a concept that can be explained as a multi-channel fraemwork, and it involves coordinating e-commerce companies with their physical locations in terms of logistics. Anticipatory logistics, on the other hand, can be described as predictive logistics and is a more complex concept. Since the industrial revolution, the dominant business model requires predicting what customers will want in the future. Predictive Logistics is where this idea meets today's information technologies. It is a modern logistics system that uses information that "predicts" the customer's needs. Companies perform various analyses over big data in order to identify the need and send a shipment even before the customer places an order. Big data is based on customer product searches, shopping histories, wish lists and even data analysis of mouse movements.

Many logistics problems are also faced by the military. Military operations involve moving large amounts of personnel and equipment over large distances and prediction of the demand fort the materials may be tricky. Anticipatory logistics has also been suggested for the military (Lenzini, 2002). Operations research (OR) algorithms have been widely used for optimizing the transfer of loads over a shipping network. These algorithms have been widely used by world famous parcel shipping companies like UPS and FedEx. UPS even has its own software for transportation cost optimization. Some algorithms for anticipatory logistics are explained by Ghiani et. al. (2009). Other studies have also focused on the quantitative aspects of anticipatory logistics (Rivera & Mes, 2017; Lee et al., 2009.; Ulmer et al., 2015).

Also the relationship of Supply Chain Management and Anticipatory Logistics is discussed by many authors in different studies. Closs et al. (1998) provide simulation results with regards to the SCM performance under different levels of information sharing. Also Bowersox et al. (1999) have investigated the issue of response based logistics. Postponement strategies have been discussed by Pagh and Cooper (1998). Also Kaddoussi et al. (2011) have investigated the concept in relation to crisis management in disaster relief scenarios. Viet et al. (2019) have examined the idea with respect to food chains.

Another phenomenon that is surely also related to logistics is the fourth industrial revolution of Industry 4.0. Industry 4.0 poses certain opportunities and threats that the academic and professional world need to address. Industry 4.0 contains many elements involving artificial intelligence, machine learning and internet of things (particularly industrial internet of things – IIOT). Manners-Bell and Lyon (2019) discuss among other things how IOT and Big Data would influence the logistics sector. Again Blockchain is another disruptive technology that logistics companies may make use of. Pervez and Haq (2019) provide us with one of the studies about Blockchain and logistics.

CONCLUSION

New studies may involve finding the attitudes of millennials about the disruptive technologies. Also studies on millennials (the very young generation) are flourishing today with countless examples (Akkucuk & Turan, 2016). Also newer studies may focus on grouping of the new technologies by means of clustering algorithms (Akkucuk, 2011a; 2011b).

A different technique that can be used in visualizing disruptive technologies is Multidimensional Scaling. Multidimensional Scaling or MDS is the name given to a series of techniques used to create a perceptual map. In fact, the MDS technique is a broad term that is used for many algorithms, rather than a single method (Akkucuk, 2011c). This technique has been applied on universities (Akküçük & Küçükkancabaş, 2007), high court judges (Akküçük, Carroll & France, 2010) and patent data (Akküçük & Artemel, 2016).

Sustainability in all disciplines has been under investigation by different researchers for a long time. Sustainability in logistics is also a developing area of interest. Logistics, Supply Chain and Recycling are among the areas most frequently visited by sustainability researchers (Akkucuk, 2016; Gencer, 2016; Gencer & Akkucuk, 2016). In the future, innovation in IT and logistics together will pave the way for a greener future and lower carbon emissions.

It is important that every company pay close attention to monitoring carbon emissions and environmental issues caused by the industry. The future of the transportation industry in terms of carbon footprint can also be strengthened by innovation and green logistics practices. In this context, we have presented some solutions and examples in this article. Some of these questions can be summarized below.

- What awaits the logistics industry in the future?
- Will disruptive innovation create the earthquake UBER created in this sector in the taxi industry?
- The importance of green logistics
    - Reducing total carbon emission
    - Decrease in transportation with low load
    - Better customer service
- Impact on the economy
    - Effect on air land transportation
    - Impact on classic logistics companies
- New startup companies

In fact, the logistics sector carbon emissions are only one aspect of sustainability overall. Many aspects of sustainability have been discussed in the literature before. Sustainability in all disciplines has been explored by different researchers for a long time. Logistics, Supply Chain and Recycling are among the most frequently visited areas by sustainability researchers (Akkucuk, 2016; Gencer, 2016; Gencer & Akkucuk, 2016). Akkucuk and Şekercioğlu (2016) describes a case study detailing an NGO that works to promote sustainable ecotourism in Turkey. In the future, studies on the impact of transportation on global carbon emissions will be conducted and the importance of innovative solutions will become apparent.

Industry 4.0 poses many challenges for the manufacturing sector and the supporting sectors. We are now experiencing the fourth phase of the Industrial Revolution that started in the 18th century with the introduction of the Steam Engine. While the previous phases of the industrial revolution only affected the manufacturing companies and the business sector as a whole, Industry 4.0 will affect all sectors of society. The main question many people have when they see Industry 4.0 is whether humans will completely be replaced by machines. While humans will see that automation and smart computers will be able to replace many functions, still the management and maintenance will create jobs. Also research and development and intellectual property will gain an ever increasing role. We should also continue this discussion by stating that 5G telecommunication infrastructure comes to the fore in communication between devices as an essential element of Industry 4.0.

Smart cities that are already built or are planned to be built from scratch (such as Indonesia's new capital or Kanal İstanbul) also will form an integral element of green logistics and disruptive technologies. Smart cities will make use of integrated devices, IoT and AI algorithms in order to make life better for the citizens and reduce the carbon footprint as well. Smart cities can bring the following benefits.

- Time savings due to transportation
- Water savings
- Reduction in greenhouse gas emissions
- Reduction in solid waste
- Reduction in traffic accidents
- Faster emergency response time

REFERENCES

Akkucuk, U. (2011a). *Veri Madenciliği: Kümeleme ve Sınıflama Algoritmaları*. İstanbul: Yalın Yayıncılık.

Akkucuk, U. (2011b). A Study on the Competitive Positions of Countries Using Cluster Analysis and Multidimensional Scaling. *European Journal of Economics Finance and Administrative Sciences*, *37*, 17–26.

Akkucuk, U. (2011c). *Görselleştirme Teknikleri: Pazarlama ve Patent Analizi Örnek Uygulamaları İle*. İstanbul: Yalın Yayıncılık.

Akkucuk, U. (2016). SCOR Model and the Green Supply Chain. In U. Akkucuk (Ed.), *Handbook of Research on Waste Management Techniques for Sustainability* (pp. 108–124). Hershey, PA: IGI Global. doi:10.4018/978-1-4666-9723-2.ch006

Akkucuk, U., & Artemel, M. N. (2016). Patent Data Visualization: A Regional Study. *International Journal of Research in Business and Social Science*, *5*(3), 66–79.

Akkucuk, U., Carroll, J. D., & France, S. L. (2013). *Visualizing Data in Social and Behavioral Sciences: An Application of PARAMAP on Judicial Statistics. In Algorithms from and for Nature and Life* (pp. 147–154). Springer International Publishing.

Akkucuk, U., & Kucukkancabas, S. (2007). Analyzing the Perceptions of Turkish Universities Using Multidimensional Scaling (MDS) Analysis. *Bogazici Journal*, *21*(1-2), 125–141. doi:10.21773/boun.21.1.8

Akkucuk, U., & Sekercioglu, C. H. (2016). NGOs for Environmental Sustainability: The Case of Kuzey-doga Foundation. *Fresenius Environmental Bulletin*, *25*(12), 6038–6044.

Akkucuk, U., & Turan, C. (2016). Mobile use and online preferences of the millenials: A study in Yalova. *Journal of Internet Banking and Commerce*, *21*(1), 142.

Angeleanu, A. (2015). New technology trends and their transformative impact on logistics and supply chain processes. *International Journal of Economic Practices and Theories*, *5*(5), 413–419.

Bowersox, D. J., Stank, T. P., & Daugherty, P. J. (1999). Lean launch: Managing product introduction risk through response-based logistics. *Journal of Product Innovation Management*, *16*(6), 557–568. doi:10.1111/1540-5885.1660030

Closs, D. J., Roath, A. S., Goldsby, T. J., Eckert, J. A., & Swartz, S. M. (1998). An empirical comparison of anticipatory and response-based supply chain strategies. *International Journal of Logistics Management*, *9*(2), 21–34. doi:10.1108/09574099810805816

Datta, S. (2008). *WiFi meet FuFi: Disruptive innovation in logistics catalysed by energy*. Academic Press.

Dhillon, G., Coss, D., & Hackney, R. (2001). Interpreting the role of disruptive technologies in e-businesses. *Logistics Information Management*, *14*(1/2), 163–171. doi:10.1108/09576050110363167

Edwards, H. A., Dixon-Hardy, D., & Wadud, Z. (2016). Aircraft cost index and the future of carbon emissions from air travel. *Applied Energy*, *164*, 553–562. doi:10.1016/j.apenergy.2015.11.058

Evangelista, P. (2012). Disruptive innovation trends in transport and logistics. INNO-GripsWorkshop on Disruptive Innovation, Brussels, Belgium.

Gencer, Y. G. (2016). Mystery of Recycling: Glass and Aluminum Examples. In U. Akkucuk (Ed.), *Handbook of Research on Waste Management Techniques for Sustainability* (pp. 172–191). Hershey, PA: IGI Global. doi:10.4018/978-1-4666-9723-2.ch009

Gencer, Y. G., & Akkucuk, U. (2016). Reverse Logistics: Automobile Recalls and Other Conditions. In U. Akkucuk (Ed.), *Handbook of Research on Waste Management Techniques for Sustainability* (pp. 125–154). Hershey, PA: IGI Global. doi:10.4018/978-1-4666-9723-2.ch007

Ghiani, G., Manni, E., Quaranta, A., & Triki, C. (2009). Anticipatory algorithms for same-day courier dispatching. *Transportation Research Part E, Logistics and Transportation Review*, *45*(1), 96–106. doi:10.1016/j.tre.2008.08.003

Hofmann, E., & Osterwalder, F. (2017). Third-party logistics providers in the digital age: Towards a new competitive arena? *Logistics*, *1*(2), 9. doi:10.3390/logistics1020009

Kaddoussi, A., Zoghlami, N., Zgaya, H., Hammadi, S., & Bretaudeau, F. (2011, October). A preventive anticipation model for crisis management supply chain. In *2011 IEEE International Conference on Systems, Man, and Cybernetics* (pp. 109-114). IEEE. 10.1109/ICSMC.2011.6083651

Lee, K. L., Huang, W. C., & Teng, J. Y. (2009). Locating the competitive relation of global logistics hub using quantitative SWOT analytical method. *Quality & Quantity*, *43*(1), 87–107. doi:10.100711135-007-9087-1

Lenzini, J. M. (2002). Anticipatory logistics: The army's answer to supply chain management. *Army Logistician*, *34*(5), 11–13.

Manners-Bell, J., & Lyon, K. (2019). *The Logistics and Supply Chain Innovation Handbook: Disruptive Technologies and New Business Models*. Kogan Page Publishers.

Mohr, S., & Khan, O. (2015). 3D printing and its disruptive impacts on supply chains of the future. *Technology Innovation Management Review*, *5*(11), 20–25. doi:10.22215/timreview/942

Pagh, J. D., & Cooper, M. C. (1998). Supply chain postponement and speculation strategies: How to choose the right strategy. *Journal of Business Logistics*, *19*(2), 13.

Pervez, H., & Haq, I. U. (2019, March). Blockchain and IoT Based Disruption in Logistics. In *2019 2nd International Conference on Communication, Computing and Digital systems (C-CODE)* (pp. 276-281). IEEE. 10.1109/C-CODE.2019.8680971

Rivera, A. E. P., & Mes, M. R. (2017). Anticipatory freight selection in intermodal long-haul round-trips. *Transportation Research Part E, Logistics and Transportation Review*, *105*, 176–194. doi:10.1016/j.tre.2016.09.002

Sgouridis, S., Bonnefoy, P. A., & Hansman, R. J. (2011). Air transportation in a carbon constrained world: Long-term dynamics of policies and strategies for mitigating the carbon footprint of commercial aviation. *Transportation Research Part A, Policy and Practice*, *45*(10), 1077–1091. doi:10.1016/j.tra.2010.03.019

Ulmer, M. W., Brinkmann, J., & Mattfeld, D. C. (2015). Anticipatory planning for courier, express and parcel services. In *Logistics Management* (pp. 313–324). Cham: Springer. doi:10.1007/978-3-319-13177-1_25

Viet, N. Q., Behdani, B., & Bloemhof, J. (2019). Data-driven process redesign: Anticipatory shipping in agro-food supply chains. *International Journal of Production Research*, 1–17.

ADDITIONAL READINGS

Baaken, T., & Teczke, J. (2014). Managing Disruptive Change by Partnering. *Managing Disruption and Destabilisation*, 129-141.

Cheung, A., Ling, P. S., & Huang, J. (2001). Managing Knowledge Activities as Part of E-Commerce Implementation: The Next Step After the ERP Implementation. *AMCIS 2001 Proceedings*, 201.

Crofts, S., Fox, M., Retsema, A., & Williams, B. (2005). Podcasting: A new technology in search of viable business models. *First Monday*, *10*(9). doi:10.5210/fm.v10i9.1273

Cullinane, S. L., & Cullinane, K. P. (2018). The reverse logistics of cross-border e-tailing in Europe: Developing a research agenda to assess the environmental impacts. *International Journal of Applied Logistics*, *8*(1), 1–19. doi:10.4018/IJAL.2018010101

Currah, A. (2002). Behind the web store: The organisational and spatial evolution of multichannel retailing in Toronto. *Environment & Planning A*, *34*(8), 1411–1441. doi:10.1068/a3562

Doolin, B., McLeod, L., McQueen, B., & Watton, M. (2003). Internet strategies for established retailers: Four New Zealand case studies. *Journal of Information Technology Case and Application Research*, *5*(4), 3–20. doi:10.1080/15228053.2003.10856030

Doolin, B., McQueen, R., & Watton, M. (2003). Towards a Framework of Internet Strategies for Established Retailers. *PACIS 2003 Proceedings*, 1.

Gaigher, S., Le Roux, E., & Bothma, T. (2014). The predictive value of disruptive technology theory for digital publishing in the traditional publishing environment: A South African case study. *Journal of Scholarly Publishing*, *45*(3), 261–288. doi:10.3138/jsp.45.3.003

Gaigher, S. S. E. (2013). *Digital publishing in the South African trade sub-sector: lessons to learn from disruptive technology* (Doctoral dissertation, University of Pretoria).

Huesig, S., Timar, K., & Doblinger, C. (2014). The influence of regulation and disruptive potential on incumbents' submarket entry decision and success in the context of a network industry. *Journal of Product Innovation Management*, *31*(5), 1039–1056. doi:10.1111/jpim.12143

Kimble, C., & Bourdon, I. (2013). The link among information technology, business models, and strategic breakthroughs: Examples from Amazon, Dell, and eBay. *Global Business and Organizational Excellence*, *33*(1), 58–68. doi:10.1002/joe.21523

Kimble, C., Bourdon, I., & Lehmann-Ortega, L. (2009, August). Business meta-models and the saga of business-IT strategic alignment. In *Proceedings of the Fifteenth Americas Conference on Information Systems, San Francisco, California.*

Latzer, M. (2009). Information and communication technology innovations: Radical and disruptive? *New Media & Society, 11*(4), 599–619. doi:10.1177/1461444809102964

Michalak, W., & Calder, L. (2003). Integration of e-commerce as a retail channel: impact of youth: on e-commerce trends in Canada. *Progress in Planning, 1*(60), 111–126. doi:10.1016/S0305-9006(02)00094-6

Michalak, W., & Jones, K. (2003). Canadian e-commerce. *International Journal of Retail & Distribution Management, 31*(1), 5–15. doi:10.1108/09590550310457809

Miller, L., Miller, R., & Dismukes, J. (2005). The critical role of information and information technology in future accelerated radical innovation. *Information, Knowledge, Systems Management, 5*(2), 63–99.

Whitten, P., Smith, S., Munday, S., & LaPlante, C. (2008). Communication assessment of the most frequented breast cancer websites: Evaluation of design and theoretical criteria. *Journal of Computer-Mediated Communication, 13*(4), 880–911. doi:10.1111/j.1083-6101.2008.00423.x PMID:26478694

Wrigley, N., Lowe, M., & Currah, A. (2002). Retailing and e-tailing. *Urban Geography, 23*(2), 180–197. doi:10.2747/0272-3638.23.2.180

Xu, X., Zhang, W., & Li, L. (2016). The impact of technology type and life cycle on IT productivity variance: A contingency theoretical perspective. *International Journal of Information Management, 36*(6), 1193–1204. doi:10.1016/j.ijinfomgt.2016.08.007

KEY TERMS AND DEFINITIONS

3PL: Third party logistics. Logistics functions are outsourced to an entity outside the manufacturing company.

4PL: Fourth party logistics.

DC: Distribution center. Some retailers such as Walmart make use of large DCs in order to store the products prior to distribution to final retail locations. These DCs may also include value adding actitivities such as material handling and packaging.

EDI: Electronic data interchange. The sending and receiving of business documents in a standard format among companies. With EDI, information is transferred directly from the computer application in one organization to the application in another. EDI standards, which determine what information goes where in an EDI document or message, eliminate the need to re-enter information manually in order to be accepted.

FCL: Full container load. It means that the goods in a container belong to the same/single seller or to the same/single buyer.

HGV: High gravity vehicle.

LCL: Less than container load. It indicates that the cargo in a container belongs to more than one cargo owner or buyer. Whether the container is 20ft or 40ft, if the term LCL is mentioned in the bill of lading, it is understood that the goods belong to more than one cargo owner.

RFID: Radio frequency identification systems. It is a technology that continues its development in wireless communication technologies rapidly and can be applied in many sectors. This technology basically consists of the reader, tag and the connected antennas. Information is read or written from the label via the radio frequency. In this way, information storage, control and follow-up are performed in many areas thanks to the labels placed on objects or portable. RFID technology may allow to work integrated with other wireless technologies.

Smart City: In the smart city vision, the city develops by analyzing data from IoT-related connections and sensors. The main advantage of the Smart City stems from the processing of sensor data and analyzing data for making better decisions. On the way to smart cities, an essential component will be the algorithms for machine learning and predictive analysis. Today, "smart cities" are considered as the places where different stakeholders use technology to make better decisions and achieve a superior quality of life.

Chapter 6
The Role of Technology Level and Logistics Performance on the Relationship Between Logistics Service Quality and Firm Performance

Özgür Kayapınar
https://orcid.org/0000-0002-2003-5863
Trakya University, Turkey

Fatma Lorcu
https://orcid.org/0000-0003-4361-8348
Trakya University, Turkey

ABSTRACT

The main purpose of this study is to examine the relationship between logistics service quality, logistics performance, firm performance, and technology. Survey data, which was collected from 572 industrial consumers operating in Turkey by stratified sampling method, were analyzed and compared by factor analysis and SEM. According to the results of the analysis, the data indicate that the quality of logistic service affects logistic performance and firm performance positively and directly. Also, it is clear from the results that the mediation role of logistic performance and its indirect impact are important in the effect of logistic service quality on firm performance. In the effect of the quality of logistic performance on firm performance, the role of technology in moderation is understood. It is also stated that when the moderation role of technology in the logistic service quality affects firm performance, logistic performance has also the mediation role.

DOI: 10.4018/978-1-7998-4601-7.ch006

INTRODUCTION

Companies that compete for meeting the increasing needs of their customers strive to design and present the best quality products to their customers in accordance with their mission and objectives. The expectation of the customers is that the satisfaction of the products which are bought by customers is provided with quality. Two approaches are used to explore the concept of quality in the literature According to the first approach, quality means that the adaptability of the technical specifications determined by service providers. Service is shown as a physical object that can be evaluated and observed with its qualities while the second approach asserts that the quality is based on customers' evaluation and perception (Gil Saura, Servera Frances, Berenguer Contri, & Fuentes Blasco, 2008; Thai, 2013). Both approaches are based on the assessment and evaluation of customer expectations. In the first approach, the quality of the service provided to the client is based entirely on the adaptation of the service provided by the companies as if it reflects an object. In the second approach, the assumption that the expectations and perceptions of customers are influenced by quality is emphasized.

Services offered within the logistics framework fulfill the role of coordinating the capabilities needed to create customer value and satisfy customers at companies, and to provide the supply-demand boundary and scope. (Panayides & So, 2005). The quality of logistic service performance constitutes an important marketing component which helps to create customer satisfaction (Mentzer, Flint, & Hult, 2001) and the creation of customer value in terms of logistics takes place through two different mechanisms. These mechanisms are the reduction of the costs and the increasing responsiveness to customer needs (Panayides & So, 2005).

According to Gil Saura, Servera Frances, et al. (2008), companies need to invest in information communication technologies to improve the management of information flow internally throughout the supply chain. Companies that want to increase the quality of customer service have to focus on some issues, including the recovery of the order process to make it easier, and behaving in accordance with the delivery conditions created by customers.

Quality in logistics is defined as one of the capabilities of a company's logistics system for satisfying the users in terms of customer service, time, reliability, communication, and convenience (Berkowitz, Kerin, Hartley, & Rudelius, 1997). Logistics service quality is determined within the framework of the perception of the after-sale service and service quality provided to the customers, and customer service representatives and conformity of information provided by order and delivery procedures. (Micu, Aivaz, & Capatina, 2013).

Logistic service quality, which is derived from a number series of interactions in terms of the perceptions of customers and the processes businesses with the logistics service providers and (Thai, 2013), depends on the monitoring of logistics processes in order to help customers benefit from time and space. The logistics process plays an active role in how consumers can benefit most effectively from the products they buy (Gil Saura, Ruiz Molina, & Frances, 2008).

While logistics service quality focuses on the performance results of companies in the process of bringing goods and information from the stores of the firms to the customers' homes (Gil Saura & Ruiz Molina, 2011), customer expectations become the most important determinant of logistics service quality. While customers choose a firm, they prefer companies that can provide the best service to them. Firms also tend to win and keep customers by anticipating customers' expectations and improving their services. Development of customer service and improvement of other services are important to establish direct relationships with customers. Logistic services offered to customers include the staff responsible for taking orders, and ordering the products required for different products, transportation, and other procedures (Mentzer et al., 2001).

Logistics service quality consists of the characteristics of the technical and functional quality. While technical quality is expressed as a service formation and output that is technically acceptable and leads to concrete result; functional quality includes a service delivery process, is a way of bringing solutions throughout the service delivery process (Gil Saura, Servera Frances, et al., 2008; Thai, 2013).

Thai (2013), suggests that improving the logistics service quality must be a permanent focal point for logistics service providers and these companies should avoid instant customer satisfaction by providing better logistics services as their ultimate goal is to do business in the long run with the customers who buy their products or services.

Until the opportunities provided by physical and psychological qualities were presented, the products represented only a small value for customers (Mentzer, Gomes, & Krapfel, 1989). In such a case, the quality of the service provided to customers plays an active role in customer retention and acquisition, and the quality of service in the value frame presented to customers in marketing becomes prominent. Thai (2013), explains the logistics service quality as a concept called "marketing customer service" which also includes other customer service elements. Marketing. Logistics groups that work well together and develop effective relationships are prepared to guide information technology strategies and decisions to be taken in comparison to marketing and logistics groups that are less interactive and collaborative than themselves (Daugherty, Chen, Mattioda, & Grawe, 2009).

The impact of time and quality based systems introduce the need for marketing/logistics compliance as a competitive advantage (Bowersox, Mentzer, & Speh, 2008). Logistics service quality; since the customer is dependent on the follow-up process to benefit from time and space, it can be considered as an innovation source and can provide suppliers with a competitive advantage (Gil Saura & Ruiz Molina, 2011).

The logistics service quality should be conceptualized as a process rather than just a second level structure or a single concept (Mentzer et al., 2001). When the logistics service quality is regarded as a process, it can also be expressed as a way to manage the logistics service quality perceptions of suppliers and customers. Therefore, service quality should focus on bringing forward the value to customers by examining the strategic importance of quality as an element of innovation among its suppliers (Gil Saura & Ruiz Molina, 2011).

LITERATURE REVIEW

In this study, the effects of logistics service quality on firm performance are discussed. In this section of the study, logistics service quality, information technology, logistics performance and firm performance are defined.

According to Thai (2013), logistics service quality consists of dimensions, including personnel contact quality, information quality, order handling quality, physical distribution service quality, timeliness, image, and social responsibility.

- *Personal contact quality:* It refers to the customer-oriented attitude of the personnel towards logistics communication. Customers give particular importance to whether the customer service personnel have sufficient information, the extent to which they helped them to solve their problems and whether they are able to empathize with the situation customers are in. Personnel contact quality is a kind of interface between the personnel and the customers (Mentzer et al., 2001). Marketing and logistics personnel, who are faithful to the activities of the company are helpful to determine the best and most effective information systems and to transfer resources to the areas which needs them. (Daugherty et al., 2009).

- *Information quality:* Information is an important resource for companies as well as for customers. The logistics information system is an interactive structure consisting of individuals, teams, methods, and controls and it needs to be based on decision making on information management, planning, implementation, and control (Gil Saura, Servera Frances, et al., 2008). Meeting the processes such as performance expectations with the effective use of logistics information technologies can improve customer satisfaction as a logistics system capability (Bienstock, Royne, Sherrell, & Stafford, 2008). Developments in information and communication technologies and the transport sector increase retailers' sources of supplies, affects product availability, sales support and flexibility, and also influence retailers' ultimate decision-making in terms of reliability. (Giovanis, Tomaras, & Zondiros, 2013).
- *Order handling quality:* The customers are pleased when they are able to supply the desired product in desired time, from place and firm. Product status, product, and processing quality have been on the forefront as important components in terms of companies to have logistics superiority for many years (Mentzer et al., 2001). Order quality is a concept related to the operation or process of a product and deals with how convenient products are in terms of their characteristics and customer needs (Berkowitz et al., 1997; Mentzer et al., 2001).
- *Physical distribution service quality:* Distribution services, are regarded as being more important than product quality or price at the point of creating customer satisfaction (Daugherty, Stank, & Ellinger, 1998). Physical distribution service is defined as a package of interrelated activities which are provided by the supplier to guarantee the forms of benefits by creating time and place benefits for a buyer. (Perreault & Russ, 1976). Physical distribution constitutes an important part of logistics, ranging from customer services to the delivery of products to customers (Rabinovich & Bailey, 2004) and focuses on creating a balance between product delivery features and related system alternatives (Bowersox, 1969). According to Bienstock, Mentzer, and Bird (1996) physical distribution service is a type of logistics and includes activities such as transportation, facility management (warehouse location), inventory management, materials and carrying (packaging, loading). The quality of the physical distribution service purchased by the industrial buyers from the suppliers constitutes an important element in the industrial purchasing decision. Many firms have been focusing on the distribution competencies to keep in touch with their key customers by customizing the basic services they provide in line with the changing needs of the customers (Alexander E Ellinger, 2000).
- *Timeliness:* Time, can also be called order cycle time or supply time and can be more important to retailers and wholesalers than customers (Berkowitz et al., 1997). Order cycle time is defined as the variability in the expected time of the order fulfillment by customers. Expected time can also be called warranty or commitment time, average time or acceptable a long time (Perreault & Russ, 1976). Mentzer et al. (1989) define timeliness as the order cycle time performance of the whole distribution systems connected with buyers and sellers while Mentzer et al. (2001) defines it as a part of the order taking.

- *Image:* Image hold an important place in terms of retaining customers in firms, acquiring new customers and encouraging customers to purchase again and can be expressed from the perspective of the customers as a demonstration of the work done by the companies. As an attitude, while the image is defined as a kind of subjective knowledge, it is different from the physical product, but it is also discussed as a combination of product characteristics (Nguyen & LeBlanc, 1998). Corporate image is associated with all the information that individuals and companies have (such as perceptions, inferences, and beliefs) and it should influence the behavioural intentions of customers such as corporate, customer loyalty and satisfaction. (Martenson, 2007; Rahman, 2012).
- *Social responsibility;* There are three approaches used to definite corporate social responsibility. According to the first point of view, corporate social responsibility consists of special activities and dimensional sets that include topics such as charity and philanthropic donations, social issues, gender at work, race, religious diversity, security, human rights and the environment. The second point of view deals with business ethics as an important aspect of corporate social responsibility. In the last point of view, corporate social responsibility includes company behaviour and activities (Carter & Jennings, 2004). Social responsibility is divided into four basic groups that are hierarchically related and contributing to each other. Volunteer responsibility is placed at the top of these responsibilities, followed by ethical, legal and economic responsibilities. (Carroll, 1979, 1991). On the other hand, Ciliberti, Pontrandolfo, and Scozzi (2008), classified logistical social responsibility classify into five groups based on their areas, as an alternative to corporate social responsibility, which are purchasing social responsibility, sustainable transportation, sustainable storage, sustainable packaging and reverse logistics.
- *Perceived information technologies:* The ability of information technology is the ability of a firm to obtain process and information and it expresses the delivery of information to support decision-making. Because of information technology has the potential to be the main source of economic wealth, its effective use of information technology plays a critical role in achieving the success of an entrepreneurial strategy to be created (Micu et al., 2013). Information technology is one of the most important factors of success in any organization. On the other hand, the development and change in information technologies affect logistics (Gil Saura, Ruiz Molina, et al., 2008). Furthermore, information technology is one of the productivity tools used to increase capacity while reducing costs across the firm and effective use of information technology within logistics activities improve services, increase productivity, offering flexible and operational competitiveness at the same time (Lai, Zhao, & Wang, 2007). Information technology can have significant effects on logistics activities on behalf of the facilitating cooperation by automation of many activities among supply chain partners. Thus, it can be used to focus on more strategic issues in logistics management by logistics specialists (Bienstock et al., 2008). Developments such as the Internet and electronic commerce in information technology and communication capabilities allow for increased integration within the supply chain. (Stank, Keller, & Daugherty, 2001).
- *Firm performance:* Firm performance depends on a company's strategy structure and compatibility with the environment (O'Leary-Kelly & Flores, 2002). Successful relational marketing efforts improve firm performance and customer loyalty through stronger associative commitment as it impacts customer-generated expectations (Alrubaiee & Al-Nazer, 2010; Innis & La Londe, 1994). In order to maximize the performance in customer retention, sales growth, and profitability in the long-term, a firm needs to build, protect and develop long-lasting and mutually beneficial relationships with customers (Sin, Tse, Yau, Lee, & Chow, 2002). According to Zhao, Dröge, and

Stank (2001) information technology and information-based skills developed within the company have been regarded as one of the key determinants of firm performance.

- *Logistics performance:* A logistics service provider will have a positive impact on firm performance by increasing customer satisfaction and loyalty through solving problems that will arise, keeping the records accurate, providing good service and performing effective communication (Panayides, 2007). The performance of logistics, which is one of the most important tools in the supply chain, affects all of the supply chain members in general. Logistics service providers engaged in transportation business should focus on the overall performance of the supply chain as well as organizational performance (Green Jr, Whitten, & Inman, 2008). Collaboration to be established among supply chain partners will reduce the costs and improve service performance (Stank et al., 2001). The supply chain management, which is based on collaboration between partners, is designed to constitute organizational performance benefits (Sanders & Premus, 2005). Sometimes conflicts arise between the buyer and the seller in supply chain. While conflict between buyer and supplier relationships is inevitable, the constructive resolution of such conflict is unlikely to harm and may even improve supplier performance (Carter & Kaufmann, 2007).

THE PURPOSE, MODEL, AND HYPOTHESES OF THE RESEARCH

This research has three main purposes. The first one is to measure whether the logistics service quality has a direct effect on logistics performance and firm performance. The second one is to examine the mediating role of logistics performance on the impact of logistics service quality on firm performance. The third one is to investigate the moderating effect of technology on the direct and indirect effects of logistics service quality on logistics and firm performance

Figure 1. Conceptual Model

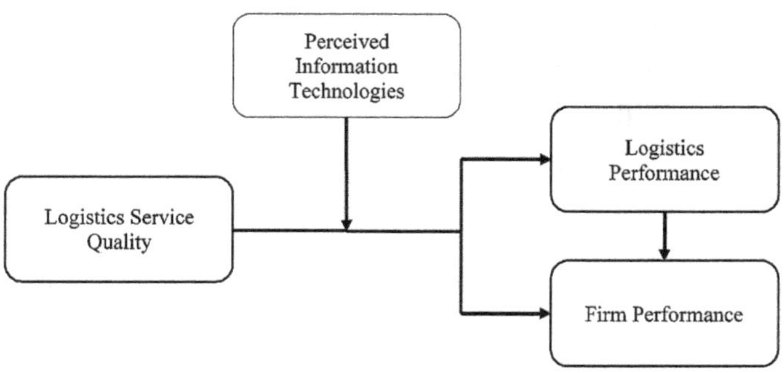

DIRECT AND INDIRECT EFFECTS OF LOGISTICS SERVICE QUALITY ON FIRM PERFORMANCE

The quality of outsourced logistics service is important in terms of competition and because of the increasing intensive firm costs. Therefore, the logistics service quality has attracted the attention of both companies and researchers and there have been many studies on the subject contributing to the current literature.

In a study conducted by Panayides and So (2005), logistics performance was examined at the operational dimension and it was found that the logistics service quality has a direct and indirect effect on the firm performance of logistics service provider companies. In the study of Wong, Soh, Sinnandavar, and Mushtaq (2018), the direct effect between service quality and national logistic performance, and indirect effect which with appear mediation effect of Hauliers' sustainable performance was analyzed. After the analysis, they found no direct relationship, but they determined the existence of the indirect relationship. Furthermore, Novack, Rinehart, and Langley Jr (1994) demonstrated the logistics efficiency has a direct and indirect relationship with quality and the quality has a direct and indirect relationship with logistics performance while the logistics managers' perceptions of logistics performance has a direct relationship with consumer's perceptions of the company. In their work focusing on the delivery service performance as operational performance, Alexander E. Ellinger, Daugherty, and Keller (2000) put forth that the relationship between marketing and logistics has a positive and direct effect on distribution service performance. Similarly, Panayides (2007) found that logistics service effectiveness has a direct and positive effect on firm performance. In their study, Stank et al. (2001) found that there are differences in overall logistics performances of firms, and about 30% of this difference can be explained by the customers as a factor and the integration of internal logistics. In addition, Alexander E. Ellinger et al. (2000), Zhao et al. (2001), Stank, Goldsby, Vickery, and Savitskie (2003), Panayides (2007), Green Jr et al. (2008), Daugherty et al. (2009), and Hoang and Nguyen (2019) demonstrated that logistics service quality, logistics service dimensions and marketing integration have positive effects on firm performance, especially on the financial performance of the firm. The hypotheses are as follows:

H_1: There is a significant relationship between logistics service quality and logistics performance.
H_2: There is a significant relationship between logistics service quality and firm performance.
H_3: Logistics performance has a mediating effect on the relationship between logistics service quality and firm performance.

DIRECT AND INDIRECT EFFECTS OF TECHNOLOGY ON FIRM PERFORMANCE

Although the need for external and internal information has always been there for companies, the access speed to information has never been so great and important, which has been a major subject of research recently. Sanders and Premus (2005) found that information technologies had a significant impact on both internal and external cooperation and had a direct impact on firm performance.

When the studies on technology suggest a relationship between the role of technology and the integration of technology with respect to competitive advantages and overall performance. Electronic commerce companies and online trading companies mainly rely on technology to rely on logistics service providers (Lai et al., 2007; Micu et al., 2013; Oláh, Karmazin, Pető, & Popp, 2018; Paulraj & Chen, 2007; Rabinovich & Bailey, 2004). Kim (2017) found that integrative information technology was positively associated with firm performance through supply chain integration. In some other studies, the effects of information technologies on logistics performance and firm performance have been observed (Bardi, Raghunathan, & Bagchi, 1994; Daugherty et al., 2009; Rodrigues, Stank, & Lynch, 2004; Tippins & Sohi, 2003).

On the other hand, companies that want to increase their performance should adapt to technology and develop the values they give to their customers by developing their customer-oriented capabilities on the basis of technology. According to Zhao et al. (2001), information technologies and the knowledge-oriented capabilities developed within the company have been seen as key determinants of firm performance. As a result, based on these studies, hypotheses were formed as follows:

H_4: There is a significant relationship between information technology and logistics performance.
H_5: There is a significant relationship between information technology quality and firm performance.
H_6: Logistics performance has a mediating effect on the relationship between information technology and firm performance.

THE MODERATING EFFECT OF INFORMATION TECHNOLOGY

Logistics creates competitive advantage for companies with factors such as distribution speed, quick response, and delivery security. Therefore, the use of information technology to improve these factors and ensure quality will have a positive affect on logistics output at firms (Zacharia & Mentzer, 2004). Online retailers focus on determining the qualification of logistics services that will contribute to the increase in the degree of customer satisfaction and their retention rate by using information technology and electronic devices. (Micu et al., 2013). Other studies show that technology has an effect on the logistics service quality and that technology and logistics service quality has significant effects on performance, and that especially information technologies play a critical role in logistics performance and firm performance. (Bardi et al., 1994; Daugherty et al., 2009; Lai et al., 2007; Rodrigues et al., 2004; Tippins & Sohi, 2003). On the other hand in their study of Sriram and Stump (2004), who explored the direct and indirect influences of the investments in information technology on performance, found an indirect relationship for only one of the performance variables.

In another study, Gil Saura, Ruiz Molina, et al. (2008) investigated the impact of technology intensity on logistical service quality through the comparison of customers and retailers and the effect of technology on the logistics service quality were observed neither in the customers nor in the retailers. In their study on bank clients, Curry and Penman (2004) suggested that the information technologies alone do not offer a competitive advantage but have a moderating effect on the determinants of logistics service quality. So, the following hypotheses were formed:

H_7: Information Technology has a moderating role on the relationship between logistics service quality and logistics performance.
H_8: Information Technology has a moderating role on the relationship between logistics service quality and firm performance.
H_9: Information Technology has a moderating role on the mediating effect of logistics performance on logistics performance and firm performance.

METHODOLOGY

Data Collection and Sample

The aim of the study is to determine the direct and indirect effects external logistics service quality on firm performance and the contributions of logistics performance and technology to these effects. The effects of purchasing logistics on the performance of industrial firms will also be observed. The valid and reliable scales that have not been used in Turkey, especially in Thrace, were preferred to form the survey questions and for the scale design based on the current literature. The Thrace region is an important industrial area as a gateway to Europe with abundant transportation opportunities as it is quite close to Istanbul, which has become a financial and industrial center. The logistics industry covers about 12% of the Gross Domestic Product of Turkey in 2014 and 2015 (Kaya, 2015). According to 10th Development Plan published by the Ministry of Development (2014a, 2014b), growth and sustainability form an important part of the logistics framework. Within the plan, the main objective is to reduce logistic cost, improve trade and increase competition power by ensuring that Turkey is a regional base in logistics.

The scale used to measure the logistics service quality was updated and improved by Thai (2013) and it is based on the scale developed by Bienstock, Mentzer, and Bird (1996). The scale consists of seven dimensions and a total of thirty-four items, including four items of personal communication quality, five items of information quality, and six items of order handling quality six items of physical distribution service quality, four items of timeliness, five items of the corporate image, and four items of corporate social responsibility. The scale, which has one dimension and nine items, was developed by Bienstock and Royne (2010) to measure the level of information technology use in firms. The scale developed by Stank et al. (2003) was used to assess logistics performance. The scale consists of three dimensions and eight items, including three items of operational performance, three items of relational performance, and two items of cost performance. A 5-point Likert type scale (1: Strongly Disagree - 5: Strongly Agree) was used for the evaluation of questionnaires. The scale including one dimension and nine items which was developed by (Sozuer, Altuntas, & Semercioz, 2017) was used to measure firm performance. At the end of the scale, participants were asked some questions related to demographics, company and personal information.

A preliminary application of the scale was carried out with unit managers in logistics employed in 58 companies operating in Tekirdağ. The missing data, outlier data and exploratory factor (EFA) analyses were employed and the results showed that there were no missing data. Based on the findings, some questions in logistics service quality scale were excluded from the question set, and logistics service quality scale as a result of factor analysis was factorized according to the sub-dimensions of personal communication quality (3 items), information quality (4 item), order handling quality-image (8 items) and corporate social responsibility (4 items). In addition, information technology (9 items), logistics performance (relational and operational performance (4 items), and cost performance (3 items)), and firm performance (9 items) have been identified with the factors. The questionnaire was rearranged and the final version also included ten items to measure the demographics of the participants.

The face-to-face survey method was adopted for the data collection in order to prevent data loss and respond to questions of the participants instantly. The questionnaire was conducted in 572 companies (Edirne: 105, Kırklareli: 75 and Tekirdağ: 392), which volunteered to participate and which were randomly selected from 2.027 medium and large-sized companies Edirne: 370, Kırklareli: 267, and Tekirdağ:1390 with the use of stratified sampling method in 2016. According to Lohr (2010), if the studied population is below different subgroups and over different mean values, it is possible to obtain more accurate estimates of the population by taking stratified random samples. Stratified sampling refers to the random selection of samples from each layer as a result of the separation of a population into subpopulations (strata) in a homogeneous and independent manner. (Rex B Kline, 2011). Having more than one subgroup, researchers have been directed to choose stratified random sampling. Demographic data are shown in Table 1.

Table 1. Demographic Characteristics of the Firms and the Managers

	f	Percentage (%)
	General Characteristics of Surveyed Firms	
Sector	59 (Textile)	10.3
Activity time in the Sector	406 (Over ten year) 221 (Over twenty-one year)	71.0 38.6
Internationalization level of companies	362 (International)	63.3

In table, the top contributors to the survey were listed

According to the demographic data, 18.7% of the interviews were conducted with employees working in the logistics department. 64.9% of the interviewed participants had a bachelor's degree while 65.7% of them were male. 85.8% of the companies participating in the analysis, mostly purchase and use logistics services for transportation activities. Most companies use logistics service quality for more than one activity. It was determined that 572 firms use electronic mail with 70.6% as their information system. It is also seen that all firms use more than one information system.

DATA ANALYSIS

Exploratory Factor Analysis

Before the proposed relationships between the factors are tested by structural equation modelling, EFA was applied separately to the scales in order to evaluate the measurement model, construction the factors, and examination of whether the scales used are structurally valid (Jöreskog & Sörbom, 1993; Rex B Kline, 2011; Tabachnick & Fidell, 2013). Considering the EFA assumptions in terms of scales, they provide all assumptions. Principal component and varimax rotation methods were applied to EFA with SPSS 24.0 Statistical Package Program.

EFA was performed twice on the logistics service quality scale. In the first analysis, four questions (5, 8, 10 and 11), which were below 0.50 according to the communalities, were subtracted from the question set and applied re-factor analysis.

It is necessary to apply the KMO and Bartlett's sphericity test to look at the total significance of the data and the correlation obtained (Alpar, 2014; Kaiser & Rice, 1974). When KMO values were examined (Table 2), it was found that all scales were between 0.868 and 0.924, which proved that they were at an adequate level. According to the results of Bartlett's sphericity test, the variables were significant at the level of significance of 0.05.

Table 2. Reliability and Validity Analysis of Scales

Scales	Factor Loadings	% of Variance	Eigen-Value
Logistics Service Quality (LSQ) ***KMO: 0.924;*** ***Bartlett's sphericity test; (χ2=5440.709; df=171; p=0.000)***			
Personal Communication Quality (PSQ)		**6.096**	**1.158**
PCQ2: The staff of the logistics company which I work with meets my needs and requirements.	0.821		
PCQ1: The attitudes and behaviors of the logistics company's staff, which I work with, are satisfactory.	0.751		
PCQ3: The staff of the logistics company which I work with can understand my needs and requirements.	0.685		
Information Quality (IQ)		**7.014**	**1.333**
IQ2: The logistics company that I work with is using the information technologies and electronic data exchange applications sufficiently in customer service.	0.734		
IQ3: The new information technology applications are used in the customer service of the logistics company that I work with.	0.714		
IQ5: The ability to track shipments at the logistics firm that I work with is satisfactory.	0.707		
OHQ5: The process that takes place from the receipt of the order to the delivery at the logistics firm that I work with is carried out in an appropriate manner.	0.625		
Order Handling Quality and Image (IM)		**42.983**	**8.167**
IM2: The logistics company that I work with is known as a reliable company on the market.	0.777		
IM5: The logistics company that I work with has a good image in terms of ethics.	0.701		
IM1: The logistics company which I work with taking into accounts of my claims, complaints, and feedbacks.	0.701		
OHQ3: The logistics company that I am working with can cope with the inconsistency problem with the orders.	0.639		
IM3: The logistics company that I work with is known as for being satisfied, professional and consistent for its customers.	0.621		
OHQ4: The logistics company's total order cycle time which I work with is sufficient.	0.605		
OHQ6: The order processing processes of the logistics company that I work with are consistent.	0.602		
IM4: The logistics company that I work with is known for fulfilling its promises.	0.600		
Social Responsibility (SR)		**7.618**	**1.447**
SR4: The logistics company I work with has a vision in fulfilling its responsibilities towards society.	0.817		
SR3: The logistics company that I work with participates in social activities such as social responsibility projects.	0.794		
SR2: The logistics company that I work with is sensitive to the environment and gives importance to environmental safety.	0.739		
SR1: The logistics company that I work with attach importance to social responsibility and human security.	0.685		

continues on following page

Table 2. Continued

Scales	Factor Loadings	% of Variance	Eigen-Value
Technology (TEC) ***KMO: 0.899;*** ***Bartlett's sphericity test; (χ2=2780.164; df=28; p=0.000***		**61.321**	**4.906**
TEC6: The technology that is used by the logistics company we work with increases our performance.	0.844		
TEC8: The technology that is used by the logistics company we work with increases our effectiveness.	0.831		
TEC7: The technology that is used by the logistics company we work with improves our productivity.	0.819		
TEC4: The technology that is used by logistics company we work with is useful.	0.782		
TEC5: The technology that is used by logistics company we work with is easy to use.	0.773		
TEC3: I can easily do what I want in the technology that is used by the logistics company we are working with.	0.766		
TEC9: I intend to continue doing business with this logistics company due to the technology that the logistics company we have worked with has.	0.752		
TEC1: I think that I will continue to use the technology which is used by the logistics company we have worked with.	0.685		
Logistics Performance (LP) ***KMO: 0.868;*** ***Bartlett's sphericity test; (χ2=2107.477; df=28; p=0.000***			
Relational and Operational Performance (LPO)		**53.983**	**4.319**
LPO3: The logistics company that I work with will bring the products we ordered correctly.	0.865		
LPO2: The logistics company that I work with is delivering the products it carries harmlessly.	0.819		
LPO1: The logistics company that I work with respects the dates that promise for my orders.	0.748		
LPR1: The logistics company that I work with cares about my needs.	0.681		
LPR2: The logistics company that we work with is in communication with us to do its job properly.	0.592		
Cost Performance (LPC)		**12.858**	**1.029**
LPC2: The logistics company that we work with operate offers competitive prices.	0.868		
LPC1: The logistics company that we work with offers the lowest cost solutions possible.	0.822		
LPR3: The logistics company that we work with is always on the recommendation to improve its logistics performance.	0.594		
Firm Performance (FP) ***KMO: 0.923;*** ***Bartlett's sphericity test; (χ2=2890.559; df=36; p=0.000***		**59.558**	**5.360**
FP4: Total sales revenue of our company on the market	0.825		
FP6: Performance of our company on the market	0.799		
FP3: Increase in sales of our company on the market	0.783		
FP7: In our company's market activities are	0.772		
FP2: Our company's market share increase	0.771		
FP1: Offer the new products of our company on market	0.756		

continues on following page

Table 2. Continued

Scales	Factor Loadings	% of Variance	Eigen-Value
FP5: The profitability of our company on the market	0.751		
FP8: The results of our company in the market .... our expectation	0.744		
FP9: Rate your company's overall performance	0.741		

Extraction Method: Principal Component (PC)
Rotation Method: Varimax with Kaiser Normalization (Rotation converged in 6 iterations)

As seen in Table 2, the factor loadings ranged range between 0.821 and 0.685 for personal communication quality, between 0.734 and 0.625 for information quality, between 0.777 and 0.600 for order handling quality and image, between 0.817 and 0.685 for social responsibility, between 0.844 and 0.685 for the technology variable, between 0.865 and 0.592 for the operational and relational performance, between 0.868 and 0.594 for cost performance, and between 0.825 and 0.741 for the firm performance variable. The four factors of logistics service quality accounted for 63.711% of the total variance, one-factor technology variable accounted for 61.321% of the total variance, the two factors of logistics performance accounted for 66.841% of total variance, and one factor of firm performance accounted for 69.558% of the total variance.

Confirmatory Factor Analysis

As a result of the EFA, the multiple iterations of the CFA for the verification and evaluation of the scale were performed using the Maximum Likelihood (ML) estimation method. (Byrne, 2010; Çelik & Yılmaz, 2013; Jöreskog & Sörbom, 1993; Schumacker & Lomax, 2010; Tabachnick & Fidell, 2013). CFA was performed for each of the scales used in the current study and the fit indices are presented in Table 3.

Table 3. The Fit Indices Results in CFA of The Scales

Scales	$\chi 2$	$\chi 2/df$	RMSEA	CFI	NFI	NNFI	GFI	AGFI	RMR	SRMR
Logistics Service Quality	423.58	2.9	0.059	0.98	0.97	0.97	0.93	0.90	0.032	0.044
Personnel Communication Quality	3.65	3,65	0.068	1.00	1.00	0.99	1.00	0.97	0.0068	0.011
Information Quality	0.94	0.94	0.0	1.00	1.00	1.00	1.00	0.99	0.0041	0.0051
Order Handling Quality and Corporate Image	37.78	1.89	0.039	1.00	0.99	0.99	0.99	0.97	0.013	0.02
Corporate Social Responsibility	0.32	0.16	0.0	1.00	1.00	1.00	1.00	1.00	0.0021	0.0026
Information Technology	26.26	2.08	0.049	1.00	0.99	0.99	0.99	0.96	0.014	0.02
Logistics performance	36.63	2.44	0.05	0.99	0.99	0.99	0.99	0.96	0.018	0.022
Relational and Operational Performance	15.75	2.25	0.047	1.00	1.00	0.99	0.99	0.97	0.012	0.016
Cost Performance	1.86	1.86	0.039	1.00	1.00	1.00	1.00	0.98	0.0094	0.01
Firm Performance	55.05	2.50	0.051	0.99	0.99	0.99	0.98	0.96	0.018	0.023

As a result of the analysis, goodness of the fit values for the scales showed that all of the factor scores explained the availability of the Structural Equation Modelling (SEM) and related factors and items. While χ^2/df values were generally within the "acceptable fit" limits, the subscales of the logistics service quality showed "good fit". It was also observed that all of the RMSEA, CFA, NFI, NNFI, GFI, AGFI, RMR, SRMR goodness of fit values were at least within "acceptable fit" limits and generally demonstrated "good fit" (Hooper, Coughlan, & Mullen, 2008; Hu & Bentler, 1999; R.B. Kline, 2005; Schermelleh-Engel, Moosbrugger, & Müller, 2003).

Table 4. Cronbach Alpha, AVE (Average Variance Extracted), Composite Reliability & Discriminant Validity

Factors		Cronbach Alfa (α)	AVE	CR	IM	SR	IQ	PSQ	LPO	LPC	TEC	FP
LSQ	IM	0.888	0.496*	0.887	**0.705***							
	SR	0.857	0.602	0.858	0.632	**0.776**						
	IQ	0.788	0.479*	0.785	0.641	0.518	**0.692**					
	PSQ	0.788	0.553	0.788	0.600	0.541	0.573	**0.744**				
LP	LPO	0.856	0.543	0.856	0.723*	0.580	0.638	0.599	**0.737**			
	LPC	0.765	0.518	0.761	0.447	0.385	0.359	0.283	0.421	**0.719**		
TEC		0,909	0.550	0.907	0.594	0.600	0.607	0.528	0.602	0.335	**0.742**	
FP		0,915	0.542	0.914	0.615	0.534	0.477	0.488	0.635	0.507	0.564	**0.736**

LSQ (α) = 0.94, LP (α) = 0.88

When the AVE values for the validity analysis were examined, it was shown that all the values were above 0.50 and for this reason, it provided convergence validity (Altunışık, Coşkun, Bayraktaroğlu, & Yıldırım, 2005; Chiang & Hsieh, 2012; Cronbach, 1951; Fornell & Larcker, 1981; Karatepe, 2006; Lorcu, 2015; Perreault & Leigh, 1989; Peter, 1981; Peterson, 1994).

Cronbach's Alpha, AVE, Composite Reliability and Discriminant Validity values were used for the reliability analysis of the factors obtained from EFA, CFA. According to the reliability and validity analysis results presented in Table 4, it is clear that Cronbach's Alpha and composite reliability values were within the required confidence limits for all scales and sub-dimensions of scales. The AVE values for validity analysis showed that all values except IM and IQ factors are greater than 0.50. Therefore, it is determined that convergent validity is ensured (Altunışık et al., 2005; Chiang & Hsieh, 2012; Cronbach, 1951; Fornell & Larcker, 1981; Karatepe, 2006; Lorcu, 2015; Perreault & Leigh, 1989; Peter, 1981; Peterson, 1994; Yürük, Akyol, & Şimşek, 2017). According to Fornell and Larcker (1981), if the AVE values are smaller than 0.5 but the combined reliability values are greater than 0.6, then the composite reliability values are examined for structural validity. As the AVE values of IM and IQ were less than 0.5, they provided structural validity because their combined reliability was greater than 0.6. For discriminant validity, factor correlations were created and used with EFA which was applied by using principal axis factoring and varimax rotation methods and the square root of the calculated AVE values was also used. When discriminant validity was examined, it is concluded that the discriminant validity is generally achieved. It was seen that the value of the single factor, which does not provide discriminant validity, but which arises with a very small difference from the square root of the AVE, is the value of the IM factor. Although it is frequently used in applied research according to Hair Jr, Hult, Ringle, and Sarstedt (2017), Fornell & Larcker criterion does not allow reliable detection of discriminant validity problems. Thus, it is also recommended to perform discriminant analysis with hetero-monotrait matrix (HTMT) method considering that each scale used in the analysis measures multifarious and different structures (Hair Jr et al., 2017; Henseler, Ringle, & Sarstedt, 2015).

According to Hair Jr et al. (2017), HTMT values of the scales should be smaller than 0,85 or 0,90 threshold values. When Table 5 is examined, it is seen that all of the values are smaller than the values of 0,85 and 0,90. Therefore, it is observed that the model consisting of the scales used in the research has provided discriminant validity at the 0.85 and 0.90 threshold values.

Table 5. Matrix of HTMT Discriminant Validity

		IM	SR	IQ	PSQ	LPO	LPC	TEC	FP
LSQ	IM								
	SR	0.712							
	IQ	0.733	0.617						
	PSQ	0.669	0.557	0.668					
LP	LPO	0.789	0.661	0.694	0.605				
	LPC	0.681	0.621	0.574	0.615	0.780			
TEC		0,732	0.674	0.744	0.577	0.719	0.634		
FP		0,672	0.581	0.561	0.509	0.743	0.736	0.632	

$HTMT_{85}$, $HTMT_{90}$

Structural Equation Modelling

In this section, structural models which were composed for the logistics service quality, technology, logistics performance and firm performance scales on which EFA and CFA analyses were run will be discussed and be verified by SEM using the statistical package program LISREL 8.82. The scales were tested with CFA for the application of SEM. In order to measure whether the data are displayed normal distribution or not in the approved models, it is necessary to perform multivariate normality tests.

As shown in Table 6, it was determined that the variables did not provide multivariate normality due to $p < 0.05$ Therefore, the Satorra-Bentler-scaled χ^2 was used instead of the Chi-square test (χ^2) to assess the overall fit of the model. Because of the inability to provide multivariate normality, Asymptotic covariance matrix will be created to be used for the asymptotically distributed independent estimators and the data will be tested according to the Robust Maximum Likelihood (RML) (Alpar, 2013; Byrne, 2010; Jöreskog, 1999; Rex B Kline, 2011; Mardia, 1970; Yürük et al., 2017).

Based on the EFA results applied for the model, factor scores were determined by using the principal axis factoring and varimax rotation and SEM analyses were applied to the model with the help of these scores.

Table 6. Mardia's Multivariate Normality Test (Skewness and Kurtosis) Results for Research Questions and Factor Scores

Mardia Multivariate Skewness			Mardia Multivariate Kurtosis			Mardia Multivariate Skewness and Kurtosis	
Coefficient	**Z**	**p-Value**	**Coefficient**	**Z**	**p-Value**	**Chi-Square**	**p-Value**
183.765	103.990	0.000	805.565	36.073	0.000	12115.075	0.000

Hypotheses were evaluated by the SEM model. The results showed that the value of χ^2 is 89.75, the value of df is 42, the value of p is 0.00014, and the value of RMSEA is 0.042. In addition, when the other values of the compliance index were examined, Satorra-Bentler-Scaled $\chi^2 = 83.75$, χ^2 / df = 1.99, CFI = 0.98, NFI = 0.97, NNFI = 0.98 and GFI = 0.94 showed "good fit" and AGFI = 0.89, RMR = 0.057 and SRMR = 0.064 showed "acceptable fit" (Hooper et al., 2008; Hu & Bentler, 1999; Rex B Kline, 2011; Schermelleh-Engel et al., 2003).

In order to obtain meaningful t-values in SEM, values should not be within $\pm$ 1.96 at a significance level of 0.05 (Schumacker & Lomax, 2010). When the t-values in Table 7 are examined, it is seen that all values fall outside of $\pm$ 1.96 at the significance level of 0.05. In addition, as shown in Table 7, sobel tests were performed to measure the significance of the differences in mediation effects (Sobel, 1982). According to the Sobel test results, it was observed that regression loads decreased with mediation effects

Table 7. The Result of Structural Equations

Direct Effects	Hypothesis	Standardized Loadings	t-Value
LSQ→LP	H_1 (Accepted)	0.25	6.10
LSQ→FP	H_2 (Accepted)	0.15	22.14
TEC→LP	H_4 (Accepted)	0.35	7.92
TEC→FP	H_5 (Accepted)	0.27	7.80
Mediating Effects of LP		**Standardized Loadings**	**t-Value**
(s)LSQ→LP→FP	H_3 (Accepted)	0.08	5.53
(s)TEC→LP→FP	H_6 (Accepted)	0.12	5.30
Moderating Effects of TEC		**Standardized Loadings**	**t-Value**
* TEC_LSQ →LP	H_7 (Accepted)	-0.07	10.22
* TEC_LSQ→FP	H_8 (Accepted)	-0.09	8.73
Moderated Mediation Effects of TEC		**Standardized Loadings**	**t-Value**
(s) *TEC_LSQ→LP →FP	H_8 (Accepted)	-0.02	-2.08
Structural Relations			**R^2**
LP = 0.25LSQ - 0.069TEC_LSQ + 0.35TEC			0.31
FP = 0.34LP + 0.15LSQ - 0.092TEC_LSQ + 0.27TEC			0.45
FP = 0.23LSQ - 0.11TEC_LSQ + 0.39TEC			0.37

(s)Sobel test results: $Z_{(LSQ®LP®FP)}$: 4.098, p: 0.00
(s)Sobel test results: $Z_{(TEC®LP®FP)}$: 4.384, p: 0.00
(s)Sobel test results: $Z_{(TEC\_LSQ®LP®FP)}$: 2.023 p: 0.04
* TEK_LSQ = TEC x LSQ (Moderator Effect)

and this decrease was significant. Therefore, all hypotheses are accepted. In the first structural equation, it was found that the logistics service quality (LSQ) and technology (TEC) had direct effects in the same direction on logistics performance (LP), and at the same time, the technology had a direct, moderating (TEC_LSQ) and negative effect on the relationship between logistics performance and logistics service quality. The regression coefficients of equality were 0.25 for LSQ, 0.35 for TEC and -0.069 for the moderator effect of technology (TEC_LSQ). In the first structural equation, 0.31 was explained at 5% significance level of LP whereas 0.69 was not explained.

In the second structural equation, it was seen that LP, LSQ, and TEC had a direct effect in the same direction on firm performance (FP), and regression coefficients were 0.34, 0.15, and 0.27, respectively. In addition, TEC was found to have a direct, moderating and negative effect on the relations between LSQ and FP while regression coefficient was -0.092. In this structural equation, 0.45 of the firm's performance at 0.05 significance level was explained at 0.05 significance level and 0.55 was not explained.

In the third structural equation, it was seen that LSQ and TEC was related to FP in the same direction, whereas LSQ had a negative relation with the moderating effect of TEC (TEC_LSQ) on FP. The regression coefficients were found 0.23 for LSQ, -0.11 for the moderating effect of technology (TEC_LSQ), and 0.39 for the TEC. LSQ explained 0.37 of FP at 0.05 significance level alone and with the moderating effect of technology (TEC_LSQ) and TEC, and 0.63 was not explained.

Comparison of the Models

In the study, alternative models were created, and these were compared to the final model. Model-1 shows the direct effects of LSQ on LP and FP, and the indirect effects on FP. Model-2 shows that the moderating effect of technology (TEC_LSQ) on LSQ has direct effects on FP and LP and it has an indirect effect on FP. The combination of Model-1 and Model-2 in Model-3 shows that LSQ and the moderating effect of technology (TEC_LSQ) on LSQ have a direct and indirect effect on FP. In addition to the effects shown in Model-3, the direct effects of technology on logistics performance and firm performance, and indirect effects of technology on FP are shown in the final model.

As seen in Table 8, the models seemed to have fit indices that were close to each other. All models were observed to exhibit good and acceptable fit. It was determined that the Model-1 χ^2 / df goodness of fit index was not as good as the other models and that the best model of this index was Model-3.

In terms of the RMSEA goodness of fit index, the best model was the Model-3. Regarding the CFI fit indices, although there were no significant differences between the models, the index values of the final model seemed to have a lower value than the other three models. In NFI goodness of fit index, although Model-1 was observed to have a better fit than the other three models, it was quite the opposite for NNFI goodness of fit index, and Model-2, Model-3, and Final Model showed good fit. When the GFI and AGFI goodness of fit indices were compared, the model with the best index was Model-1. While Model-2 had the best goodness of fit index in the RMR compliance index, in the SRMR goodness of fit index, it was Model-1.

All the models were in the limits of good and acceptable fit. The model with the best fit was Model-1 as it had a small number of variables and was a relatively simple model compared to other models while the Final Model was in the second place. It was observed that all of the models were suitable models in the SEM framework and they also seemed to have moderating and mediating effects.

Table 8. Comparison of SEM Fit Indices of Models

Fit Indices	Good Fit	Acceptable Fit	Calculated Values			
			Model-1	Model-2	Model-3	Final Model
df			8	13	34	42
Satorra-Bentler Scaled χ^2	0 £ χ^2 £ 2df	2df < χ^2 £ 3df	22.15	22.41	55.34	83.75
χ^2/df	0 £ χ^2/df £ 2	2< χ^2/df £ 3	2.76	1.72	1.63	1.99
RMSEA	0 £ RMSEA £ 0.05	0.05 < RMSEA £ 0.08	0.056	0.036	0.033	0.042
CFI	0.97 £ CFI £ 1.00	0.95 £ CFI < 0.97	0.99	0.99	0.99	0.98
NFI	0.97 £ NFI £ 1.00	0.95 £ NFI < 0.97	0.98	0.97	0.97	0.97
NNFI	0.97 £ NNFI £ 1.00	0.95 £ NNFI < 0.97	0.97	0.98	0.98	0.98
GFI	0.95 £ GFI £ 1.00	0.90 £ GFI < 0.95	0.98	0.97	0.96	0.94
AGFI	0.90 £ AGFI £ 1.00	0.85 £ AGFI < 0.90	0.94	0.93	0.92	0.89
RMR	0 £ RMR £ 0.05	0.05< RMR £0.10	0.038	0.046	0.043	0.057
SRMR	0 £ SRMR £ 0.05	0.05 £ SRMR £0.10	0.050	0.044	0.045	0.064

PNFI, PGFI, AIC, CAIC and ECVI goodness of fit indices are frequently used to compare models. In Table 8, the measurements of the goodness of fit and calculated values of these indices are shown in accordance with the four models formed in the framework of the research.

When the PNFI and PGFI goodness fit indices were examined in Table 9, the Final Model was found better than the other three models. On the other hand, when the AIC, CAIC and ECVI goodness of fit indices used for the comparison of multiple models were examined, it was observed that the SEM Model-2 model was better than the other three models. Based on the comparison indices Model-2 was selected, that is, LSQ with moderating effect of technology (TEC_LSQ) had direct effects on LP and FP, and LSQ with mediating role of LP had an indirect effect on FP.

Table 9. Goodness of Comparative Fit Indices of the Models

Fit Indices	Good Fit	Acceptable Fit			
		Model-1	Model-2	Model-3	Final Model
PNFI	0 £ PNFI £ 1	0.37	0.60	0.60	0.62
PGFI	0 £ PGFI £ 1	0.28	0.45	0.49	0.51
AIC	In the comparative models, the lowest AIC	62.15	52.41	119.34	155.75
CAIC	In the comparative models, the lowest CAIC	169.13	132.65	290.51	348.32
ECVI	In the comparative models, the lowest ECVI	0.11	0.092	0.21	0.27

Source: (Çelik & Yılmaz, 2013; Schermelleh-Engel et al., 2003)

When the model was examined, all hypotheses were accepted and supported by the literature. In all of the models, it was determined that the LSQ had direct effects on FP and LSQ with the mediating role of LP had an indirect effect on FP.

Results of the analyses and compliance indices showed that there was a moderating role of technology (TEC_LSQ) on LSQ that firms purchase as outsourcing. LSQ seemed to have a negative and direct effect on FP with moderating effect of TEC. However, it was emerging that, the LSQ with the moderating role of technology was found to have a negative effect but an indirect effect with the mediating role of LP.

FUTURE RESEARCH DIRECTIONS

Limitations of the current study and suggestions for future research are discussed below.

- Direct effects of logistics service quality on firm performance and indirect effects of logistics service quality on firm performance with mediating effect of logistics performance are discussed in the current study. Future studies can examine that the effect of logistics service quality on logistics performance, its mediating effect of firm performance, and the moderating role of technology on these effects.
- While the current study focused on medium- and large-scale firms, future research may focus on micro and small-scale companies.
- The research was carried out without taking into consideration the fields of activity of the participating firms and the industrial areas. Future studies can focus on a particular industry group or field of activity and the results can be compared.
- The research has been carried out with the companies located in Thrace region. A general logistics service quality profile of Turkey can be created by comparing the data obtained from industrial centres in other regions.
- The research was conducted in Turkey, the effects of cultural differences on the logistics service quality can also be revealed by implementing the research model in different countries.
- The research can be repeated at periodic intervals to observe the changes in the perceptions of logistics service providers and customers concerning logistics service quality.
- The scale used in the research was developed by Thai (2013). There are many different scales in the literature to measure the logistics service quality. It is also possible to use other scales in future studies.

The results obtained from the survey are limited to the answers of the participants in this study. The results and the generalizations made are only limited to the current study.

CONCLUSION

LSQ, which is defined in relation to corporate social responsibility, participation in public service, performance notification, vision of the social responsibility, applications of information technology, quality of information, customer relationships, innovations in information technologies used in customer service (Thai, 2013), has been demonstrated to have direct effects on firm performance and indirect effects on firm performance with the mediating role of logistic performance. In addition, LSQ was found to have direct effects with the moderating effect of technology on FP while LSQ had an indirect effect with mediating effect of LP on FP.

Panayides and So (2005) showed that LSQ has an impact on LP. In their study, they investigated the logistics performance by focusing on the operational measures and found that LSQ has a direct and indirect effect on the performance of logistic service provider firms. In their work dealing with distribution service performance as operational performance, Alexander E. Ellinger et al. (2000) suggested that the relationship between marketing/logistics has a positive impact on distribution service performance in the same direction. Panayides (2007) revealed that logistics service effectiveness has a direct and positive influence on firm performance. Stank et al. (2001) found that there are differences in overall logistics performance of firms and about 30% of this difference can be explained by the customers and internal logistics integration. In addition, research show that LSQ has a positive effect on firm performance, especially financial performance (Alexander E. Ellinger et al. (2000), Zhao et al. (2001) Stank et al. (2003), Panayides (2007), Green Jr et al. (2008) Daugherty et al. (2009). The similar findings of the related literature suggest that H_1 and H_2 hypotheses are supported. The external and internal collaborations that were created in firms seem to have positive impacts on firm performance and logistics performance (Sanders & Premus, 2005). In their study, Green Jr et al. (2008) found a positive relationship between firm performance and logistics performance. The similar findings of the current study suggest that the H_3 hypothesis was supported.

While the effect of the technology dimension is generally supported by the literature, some studies suggest its moderating only. Logistics creates competitive advantages, such as distribution speed, quick response, delivery security in companies. Therefore, the use of information technology to improve these factors and to provide qualifications will positively affect the logistics output in companies (Zacharia & Mentzer, 2004). Online retailers focus on determining the qualities of customer service that will increase customer satisfaction and retention rate by using information technologies and electronic devices (Micu et al., 2013). Research indicates that information technologies play an important role on logistic performance and firm performance (Bardi et al. (1994); Daugherty et al. (2009); Lai et al. (2007); Rodrigues et al. (2004) Tippins and Sohi (2003). On the other hand, in their study, Sriram and Stump (2004) investigated the direct and indirect influences of the investments in information technology on the performance and pointed out that there is an indirect relationship only with one of the performance variables. In another study, Gil Saura, Ruiz Molina, et al. (2008) analyzed the impact of technology density on logistics service quality through the comparison of customers and retailers, and the effect of the technology on the logistics service quality have been observed neither among the customers nor the retailers. Curry and Penman (2004) who surveyed bank customers found that information technologies do not offer a competitive advantage but have a moderating effect on logistics service quality determinants. Based on the aforementioned literature, H_4, H_5, and H_6 hypotheses expressing the direct effects of technology and H_7, H_8, and H_9 hypothesis expressing the indirect effects of technology were accepted.

The findings of the study suggest that logistics service quality has a direct and indirect effect on the firm performance with the mediating role of logistic performance while technology variable seems to have a separately-moderating role on these effects, which supports all of the hypotheses.

MANAGERIAL IMPLICATIONS

Based on the results, it can be concluded that firms operating in Thrace region generally have high expectations of logistical service quality. The findings revealed that firms operating in Thrace region expect high quality services that they buy to improve their logistics performances and firm performances.

However, the results show that they are not effective enough to utilize information technologies. The reason may be that companies pay less attention to information technologies and are not quite open to innovations. The increase in innovation activities in recent times shows that companies will be able to use better and more efficient information technologies and adapt this technology on their companies more easily in the future.

According to Thai (2013), enhancing the logistics service quality and improving the performance in all logistics areas will contribute to positive, effective and sustainable logistics for supply chain members by creating a different competitive advantage in the long run on behalf of companies. It is possible for companies that provide logistic services or for companies that buy logistics services companies to increase both the performance and quality of the logistics services they offer or buy. Thus, the following suggestions are provided for practical purposes:

- **For consumers, a logistic perspective should be established. External and internal collaboration and integration should be increased in companies.** Consumers prefer "services" that include manufacturers or retailers who create an experience and take responsibility as components of customer satisfaction (Gil Saura, Ruiz Molina, et al., 2008). Firms have to manage external and internal cooperation and integration processes in order to increase customer satisfaction and achieve a position which is preferred by customers. By ensuring internal cooperation and integration, companies can improve both quality and performance, which will also improve the compatibility between functions. In addition, providing external cooperation and integration increases the quality and performance of the supply chain in which firms operate.
- **It is necessary to extend the use of technology, provide technological adaptations and invest in Information Technologies.** One of the most important activities of companies is sharing information and communication. The use of information is required in any field of business. The realization of information transfer between functions or in the supply chain effectively offers opportunities to increase the quality of the firms and to respond to customer expectation in the best way.
- **It is necessary to increase reliability in the supply chain and in the eyes of customers.** Supporting competition can bring many customers and firms together on the same platform. While the preferences of both industrial and final customers are generally within the framework of quality expectations, customers also want to trust in firms. Therefore, the communication processes between the companies and the customers can provide environment to build mutual trust.
- **The teamwork should be improved in the supply chain.** If the companies in the supply chain can act together as teams, it can foster competition. Teamwork is required between companies that are the upstream and downstream of the supply chain to increase the quality level and reduce the quality risk (Liu & Xie, 2013). The effectiveness of team work is a determinant of quality of the supply chain.
- **Order handling process and customer satisfaction should be emphasized.** The results also showed that firms do not prioritize physical delivery and punctuality during the ordering process due to the overall quality expectations of customers and inadequate basic skills of firms. Companies who wish to improve themselves must increase customer service quality, facilitate delivery conditions, and comply with the delivery conditions agreed with customers especially to improve the ordering process (Gil Saura, Servera Frances, et al., 2008).

- **Firms must engage in social responsibility activities.** According to the SEM results, order handling quality and image subdimensions of logistics service quality and social responsibility dimensions seem to have a direct effect on firm performance. Many purchasing firms are implementing related programs for workforce practices and/or environmental issues in the frame of a social responsibility within own supply chains in response to corporate social responsibility concerns that may arise in customers and shareholders (Boyd, Spekman, Kamauff, & Werhane, 2007). Firms can develop both internal and external images by carrying out activities within the framework of institutional and social responsibility. As a result, customers will choose companies which care for the environment and their health.
- **Firms need to increase their cooperation with universities and educational institutions.** During the analysis stage of the current study, it was observed that firms were not generally cooperating with universities. The results of this and other studies will likely help firms improve their performance by showing deficiencies in their activities. By contributing scientific research, companies can provide evidence for sectors, economic conditions, future prospects of the sectors, and in turn improve their activities by making use of the evidence.

ACKNOWLEDGMENT

This research was produced from the Ph.D. dissertation and it was supported by Scientific Research Project Unit of Trakya University with the project number 2015/219.

REFERENCES

Alpar, R. (2013). *Uygulamalı Çok Değişkenli İstatistiksel Yöntemler* [Applied Multivariate Statistical Methods]. Ankara: Detay Yayıncılık.

Alpar, R. (2014). *Spor, Sağlık ve Eğitim Bilimlerinden Örneklerle Uygulamalı İstatistik ve Geçerlilik-Güvenirlik-SPSS'de Çözümleme Adımları ile Birlikte* [Applied Statistics with Examples from Sports, Health and Education Sciences and Validity-Reliability-Analysis Steps in SPSS]. Ankara: Detay Yayıncılık.

Alrubaiee, L., & Al-Nazer, N. (2010). Investigate the impact of relationship marketing orientation on customer loyalty: The customer's perspective. *International Journal of Marketing Studies*, *2*(1), 155. doi:10.5539/ijms.v2n1p155

Altunışık, R., Coşkun, R., Bayraktaroğlu, S., & Yıldırım, E. (2005). *Sosyal Bilimlerde Araştırma Yöntemleri SPSS Uygulamalı* [SPSS Applied Research Methods in Social Sciences]. Sakarya: Sakarya Kitabevi.

Bardi, E. J., Raghunathan, T., & Bagchi, P. K. (1994). Logistics information systems: The strategic role of top management. *Journal of Business Logistics*, *15*(1), 71.

Berkowitz, E. N., Kerin, R. A., Hartley, S. W., & Rudelius, W. (1997). *Marketing*. Irwin/McGraw-Hill.

Bienstock, C. C., Mentzer, J. T., & Bird, M. M. (1996). Measuring physical distribution service quality. *Journal of the Academy of Marketing Science*, *25*(1), 31–44. doi:10.1177/0092070397251004

Bienstock, C. C., & Royne, M. B. (2010). Technology acceptance and satisfaction with logistics services. *International Journal of Logistics Management, 21*(2), 271–292. doi:10.1108/09574091011071951

Bienstock, C. C., Royne, M. B., Sherrell, D., & Stafford, T. F. (2008). An expanded model of logistics service quality: Incorporating logistics information technology. *International Journal of Production Economics, 113*(1), 205–222. doi:10.1016/j.ijpe.2007.03.023

Bowersox, D. J. (1969). Physical distribution development, current status, and potential. *Journal of Marketing, 33*(1), 63–70. doi:10.1177/002224296903300111

Bowersox, D. J., Mentzer, J. T., & Speh, T. W. (2008). Logistics leverage. *The Journal of Business Strategy, 25*(2), 85.

Boyd, D. E., Spekman, R. E., Kamauff, J. W., & Werhane, P. (2007). Corporate social responsibility in global supply chains: A procedural justice perspective. *Long Range Planning, 40*(3), 341–356. doi:10.1016/j.lrp.2006.12.007

Byrne, B. M. (2010). *Structural Equation Modelling with Amos, Basic Consepts, Applications, and Programing*. New York: Routledge Taylor and Francis Group.

Carroll, A. B. (1979). A three-dimensional conceptual model of corporate performance. *Academy of Management Review, 4*(4), 497–505. doi:10.5465/amr.1979.4498296

Carroll, A. B. (1991). The pyramid of corporate social responsibility: Toward the moral management of organizational stakeholders. *Business Horizons, 34*(4), 39–48. doi:10.1016/0007-6813(91)90005-G

Carter, C. R., & Jennings, M. M. (2004). The role of purchasing in corporate social responsibility: A structural equation analysis. *Journal of Business Logistics, 25*(1), 145–186. doi:10.1002/j.2158-1592.2004.tb00173.x

Carter, C. R., & Kaufmann, L. (2007). The impact of electronic reverse auctions on supplier performance: The mediating role of relationship variables. *The Journal of Supply Chain Management, 43*(1), 16–26. doi:10.1111/j.1745-493X.2007.00024.x

Çelik, H. E., & Yılmaz, V. (2013). *Lisrel 9.1 ile Yapısal Eşitlik Modellemesi Temel Kavramlar-Uygulamalar-Programlama* [Structural Equation Modeling with Lisrel 9.1 Basic Concepts-Applications-Programming]. Ankara: Anı Yayıncılık.

Chiang, C.-F., & Hsieh, T.-S. (2012). The impacts of perceived organizational support and psychological empowerment on job performance: The mediating effects of organizational citizenship behavior. *International Journal of Hospitality Management, 31*(1), 180–190. doi:10.1016/j.ijhm.2011.04.011

Ciliberti, F., Pontrandolfo, P., & Scozzi, B. (2008). Logistics social responsibility: Standard adoption and practices in Italian companies. *International Journal of Production Economics, 113*(1), 88–106. doi:10.1016/j.ijpe.2007.02.049

Cronbach, L. J. (1951). Coefficient alpha and the internal structure of tests. *Psychometrika, 16*(3), 297-334.

Curry, A., & Penman, S. (2004). The relative importance of technology in enhancing customer relationships in banking-a Scottish perspective. *Managing Service Quality: An International Journal, 14*(4), 331–341. doi:10.1108/09604520410546860

Daugherty, P. J., Chen, H., Mattioda, D. D., & Grawe, S. J. (2009). Marketing/logistics relationships: Influence on capabilities and performance. *Journal of Business Logistics, 30*(1), 1–18. doi:10.1002/j.2158-1592.2009.tb00096.x

Daugherty, P. J., Stank, T. P., & Ellinger, A. E. (1998). Leveraging logistics/distribution capabilities: The effect of logistics service on market share. *Journal of Business Logistics, 19*(2), 35.

Ellinger, A. E. (2000). Improving marketing/logistics cross-functional collaboration in the supply chain. *Industrial Marketing Management, 29*(1), 85–96. doi:10.1016/S0019-8501(99)00114-5

Ellinger, A. E., Daugherty, P. J., & Keller, S. B. (2000). The relationship between marketing/logistics interdepartmental integration and performance in U.S. manufacturing firms: An empirical study. *Journal of Business Logistics, 21*(1), 1.

Fornell, C., & Larcker, D. F. (1981). Evaluating structural equation models with unobservable variables and measurement error. *JMR, Journal of Marketing Research, 18*(1), 39–50. doi:10.1177/002224378101800104

Gil Saura, I., & Ruiz Molina, M. E. (2011). Logistics service quality and buyer–customer relationships: The moderating role of technology in B2B and B2C contexts. *Service Industries Journal, 31*(7), 1109–1123. doi:10.1080/02642060903100380

Gil Saura, I., Ruiz Molina, M. E., & Frances, D. S. (2008). Logistic service quality and technology: A comparison between supplier–retailer and retailer–consumer relationships. *International Review of Retail, Distribution and Consumer Research, 18*(5), 495–510. doi:10.1080/09593960802573385

Gil Saura, I., Servera Frances, D., Berenguer Contri, G., & Fuentes Blasco, M. (2008). Logistics service quality: A new way to loyalty. *Industrial Management & Data Systems, 108*(5), 650–668. doi:10.1108/02635570810876778

Giovanis, A. N., Tomaras, P., & Zondiros, D. (2013). Suppliers logistics service quality performance and its effect on retailers' behavioral intentions. *Procedia: Social and Behavioral Sciences, 73*, 302–309. doi:10.1016/j.sbspro.2013.02.056

Green, K. W. Jr, Whitten, D., & Inman, R. A. (2008). The impact of logistics performance on organizational performance in a supply chain context. *Supply Chain Management, 13*(4), 317–327. doi:10.1108/13598540810882206

Hair, J. F., Jr., Hult, G. T. M., Ringle, C., & Sarstedt, M. (2017). A primer on partial least squares structural equation modeling (PLS-SEM) (2nd ed.). Sage Publications.

Henseler, J., Ringle, C. M., & Sarstedt, M. (2015). A new criterion for assessing discriminant validity in variance-based structural equation modeling. *Journal of the Academy of Marketing Science, 43*(1), 115–135. doi:10.100711747-014-0403-8

Hoang, V. H., & Nguyen, T. S. (2019). *The effect of logistics service on firm financial performance in textile industry: evidence from Da Nang city, Vietnam.* Paper presented at the MATEC Web of Conferences. 10.1051/matecconf/201925904002

Hooper, D., Coughlan, J., & Mullen, M. (2008). Structural equation modelling: Guidelines for determining model fit. *Articles*, 2.

Hu, L., & Bentler, P. M. (1999). Cutoff criteria for fit indexes in covariance structure analysis: Conventional criteria versus new alternatives. *Structural Equation Modeling*, *6*(1), 1–55. doi:10.1080/10705519909540118

Innis, D. E., & La Londe, B. J. (1994). Modelling the effects of customer service performance on purchase intentions in the channel. *Journal of Marketing Theory and Practice*, *2*(2), 45–60. doi:10.1080/10696679.1994.11501650

Jöreskog, K. G. (1999). *Formulas for skewness and kurtosis*. Retrieved from http://www.ssicentral.com/lisrel

Jöreskog, K. G., & Sörbom, D. (1993). *Structural Equation Modelling With the Simplis Command Language*. Scientific Software International.

Kaiser, H. F., & Rice, J. (1974). Little jiffy, mark IV. *Educational and Psychological Measurement*, *34*(1), 111–117. doi:10.1177/001316447403400115

Kalkınma Bakanlığı, D. (2014a). *Onuncu Kalkınma Planı 2014-2018 Lojistik Hizmetlerinin Geliştirilmesi Özel İhtisas Komisyonu Raporu* [Tenth Development Plan 2014-2018 Development of Logistics Services Special Expert Commission Report]. Ankara: Kalkınma Bakanlığı Retrieved from http://www.kalkinma.gov.tr/Lists/zel%20htisas%20Komisyonu%20Raporlar/Attachments/254/Lojistik%20Hizmetlerinin%20Geli%C5%9Ftirilmesi.pdf

Kalkınma Bakanlığı, D. (2014b). *Onuncu Kalkınma Planı (2014-2018)* [Tenth Development Plan]. Ankara: T.C. Kalkınma Bakanlığı. Retrieved from http://www.kalkinma.gov.tr/Lists/Kalknma%20Planlar/Attachments/12/Onuncu%20Kalk%C4%B1nma%20Plan%C4%B1.pdf

Karatepe, O. M. (2006). Customer complaints and organizational responses: The effects of complainants' perceptions of justice on satisfaction and loyalty. *International Journal of Hospitality Management*, *25*(1), 69–90. doi:10.1016/j.ijhm.2004.12.008

Kaya, O. (2015). *Türkiye'nin Lojistik Sektörünün Büyüklüğü (resmi verilerle)* [Size of Turkey's Logistics Sector (official data)]. Retrieved from http://www.lojiport.com/turkiyenin-lojistik-sektorunun-buyuklugu-resmi-verilerle-91460yy.htm

Kim, H. J. (2017). Information technology and firm performance: the role of supply chain integration. *Operations Management Research, 10*(1-2), 1-9.

Kline, R. B. (2005). *Principles and Practice of Structural Equation Modeling*. Guilford Press.

Kline, R. B. (2011). *Principles and practice of structural equation modeling*. Guilford publications.

Lai, F., Zhao, X., & Wang, Q. (2007). Taxonomy of information technology strategy and its impact on the performance of third-party logistics (3PL) in China. *International Journal of Production Research, 45*(10), 2195–2218. doi:10.1080/00207540600693531

Liu, W., & Xie, D. (2013). Quality decision of the logistics service supply chain with service quality guarantee. *International Journal of Production Research, 51*(5), 1618–1634. doi:10.1080/00207543.2012.720390

Lohr, S. L. (2010). *Sampling: Design and Analysis*. Brooks/Cole.

Lorcu, F. (2015). *Örneklerle Veri Analizi SPSS Uygulamalı*. Ankara: Detay Yayıncılık.

Mardia, K. V. (1970). Measures of multivariate skewness and kurtosis with applications. *Biometrika, 57*(3), 519–530. doi:10.1093/biomet/57.3.519

Martenson, R. (2007). Corporate brand image, satisfaction and store loyalty: A study of the store as a brand, store brands and manufacturer brands. *International Journal of Retail & Distribution Management, 35*(7), 544–555. doi:10.1108/09590550710755921

Mentzer, J. T., Flint, D. J., & Hult, G. T. M. (2001). Logistics service quality as a segment-customized process. *Journal of Marketing, 65*(4), 82–104. doi:10.1509/jmkg.65.4.82.18390

Mentzer, J. T., Gomes, R., & Krapfel, R. E. (1989). Physical distribution service: A fundamental marketing concept? *Journal of the Academy of Marketing Science, 17*(1), 53–62. doi:10.1007/BF02726354

Micu, A., Aivaz, K., & Capatina, A. (2013). *Implications of logistic service quality on the satisfaction level and retention rate of an e-commerce retailer's customers*. Academic Press.

Nguyen, N., & LeBlanc, G. (1998). The mediating role of corporate image on customers' retention decisions: An investigation in financial services. *International Journal of Bank Marketing, 16*(2), 52–65. doi:10.1108/02652329810206707

Novack, R. A., Rinehart, L. M., & Langley, C. J. Jr. (1994). An internal assessment of logistics value. *Journal of Business Logistics, 15*(1), 113.

O'Leary-Kelly, S. W., & Flores, B. E. (2002). The integration of manufacturing and marketing/sales decisions: Impact on organizational performance. *Journal of Operations Management, 20*(3), 221–240. doi:10.1016/S0272-6963(02)00005-0

Oláh, J., Karmazin, G., Pető, K., & Popp, J. (2018). Information technology developments of logistics service providers in Hungary. *International Journal of Logistics Research and Applications, 21*(3), 332–344. doi:10.1080/13675567.2017.1393506

Panayides, P. M. (2007). The impact of organizational learning on relationship orientation, logistics service effectiveness and performance. *Industrial Marketing Management, 36*(1), 68–80. doi:10.1016/j.indmarman.2005.07.001

Panayides, P. M., & So, M. (2005). The Impact of Integrated Logistics Relationships on Third-Party Logistics Service Quality and Performance. *Maritime Economics & Logistics, 7*(1), 36–55. doi:10.1057/palgrave.mel.9100123

Paulraj, A., & Chen, I. J. (2007). Strategic buyer–supplier relationships, information technology and external logistics integration. *The Journal of Supply Chain Management*, *43*(2), 2–14. doi:10.1111/j.1745-493X.2007.00027.x

Perreault, W. D. Jr, & Leigh, L. E. (1989). Reliability of nominal data based on qualitative judgments. *JMR, Journal of Marketing Research*, *26*(2), 135–148. doi:10.1177/002224378902600201

Perreault, W. D., & Russ, F. A. (1976). Physical distribution service in industrial purchase decisions. *Journal of Marketing*, *40*(2), 3–10.

Peter, J. P. (1981). Construct validity: A review of basic issues and marketing practices. *JMR, Journal of Marketing Research*, *18*(2), 133–145. doi:10.1177/002224378101800201

Peterson, R. A. (1994). A meta-analysis of Cronbach's coefficient alpha. *The Journal of Consumer Research*, *21*(2), 381–391. doi:10.1086/209405

Rabinovich, E., & Bailey, J. P. (2004). Physical distribution service quality in Internet retailing: Service pricing, transaction attributes, and firm attributes. *Journal of Operations Management*, *21*(6), 651–672. doi:10.1016/j.jom.2003.11.004

Rahman, M. S. (2012). Service quality, corporate image and customer's satisfaction towards customers perception: An exploratory study on telecom customers in Bangladesh. *Business Intelligence Journal*, *5*(1), 56–63.

Rodrigues, A. M., Stank, T. P., & Lynch, D. F. (2004). Linking strategy, structure, process, and performance in integrated logistics. *Journal of Business Logistics*, *25*(2), 65–94. doi:10.1002/j.2158-1592.2004.tb00182.x

Sanders, N. R., & Premus, R. (2005). Modeling the relationship between firm IT capability, collaboration, and performance. *Journal of Business Logistics*, *26*(1), 1–23. doi:10.1002/j.2158-1592.2005.tb00192.x

Schermelleh-Engel, K., Moosbrugger, H., & Müller, H. (2003). Evaluating the fit of structural equation models: Tests of significance and descriptive goodness-of-fit measures. *Methods of Psychological Research Online*, *8*(2), 23–74.

Schumacker, R. E., & Lomax, R. G. (2010). *A Beginner's Guide to Structural Equation Modelling*. New York: Routledge Taylor and Francis Group.

Sin, L. Y., Tse, A. C., Yau, O. H., Lee, J. S., & Chow, R. (2002). The effect of relationship marketing orientation on business performance in a service-oriented economy. *Journal of Services Marketing*, *16*(7), 656–676. doi:10.1108/08876040210447360

Sobel, M. E. (1982). Asymptotic confidence intervals for indirect effects in structural equation models. *Sociological Methodology*, *13*, 290–312. doi:10.2307/270723

Sozuer, A., Altuntas, G., & Semercioz, F. (2017). International entrepreneurship of small firms and their export market performance. *European Journal of International Management*, *11*(3), 365–382. doi:10.1504/EJIM.2017.083874

Sriram, V., & Stump, R. (2004). Information technology investments in purchasing: An empirical investigation of communications, relationship and performance outcomes. *Omega, 32*(1), 41–55. doi:10.1016/j.omega.2003.09.008

Stank, T. P., Goldsby, T. J., Vickery, S. K., & Savitskie, K. (2003). Logistics service performance: Estimating its influence on market share. *Journal of Business Logistics, 24*(1), 27–55. doi:10.1002/j.2158-1592.2003.tb00031.x

Stank, T. P., Keller, S. B., & Daugherty, P. J. (2001). Supply chain collaboration and logistical service performance. *Journal of Business Logistics, 22*(1), 29–48. doi:10.1002/j.2158-1592.2001.tb00158.x

Tabachnick, B. G., & Fidell, L. S. (2013). *Using Multivariate Statistics*. Pearson.

Thai, V. V. (2013). Logistics service quality: Conceptual model and empirical evidence. *International Journal of Logistics Research and Applications, 16*(2), 114–131. doi:10.1080/13675567.2013.804907

Tippins, M. J., & Sohi, R. S. (2003). It Competency and Firm Performance: Is Organizational Learning a Missing Link? *Strategic Management Journal, 24*(8), 745–761. doi:10.1002mj.337

Wong, W. P., Soh, K. L., Sinnandavar, C. M., & Mushtaq, N. (2018). Could the service consumption-production interface lift national logistics performance? *Resources, Conservation and Recycling, 128*, 222–239. doi:10.1016/j.resconrec.2016.10.002

Yürük, P., Akyol, A., & Şimşek, G. G. (2017). Analyzing the effects of social impacts of events on satisfaction and loyalty. *Tourism Management, 60*, 367–378. doi:10.1016/j.tourman.2016.12.016

Zacharia, Z. G., & Mentzer, J. T. (2004). Logistics salience in a changing environment. *Journal of Business Logistics, 25*(1), 187–210. doi:10.1002/j.2158-1592.2004.tb00174.x

Zhao, M., Dröge, C., & Stank, T. P. (2001). The effects of logistics capabilities on firm performance: Customer-focused versus information-focused capabilities. *Journal of Business Logistics, 22*(2), 91–107. doi:10.1002/j.2158-1592.2001.tb00005.x

ADDITIONAL READING

Bienstock, C. C., Mentzer, J. T., & Bird, M. M. (1996). Measuring physical distribution service quality. *Journal of the Academy of Marketing Science, 25*(1), 31–44. doi:10.1177/0092070397251004

Bienstock, C. C., & Royne, M. B. (2010). Technology acceptance and satisfaction with logistics services. *International Journal of Logistics Management, 21*(2), 271–292. doi:10.1108/09574091011071951

Bienstock, C. C., Royne, M. B., Sherrell, D., & Stafford, T. F. (2008). An expanded model of logistics service quality: Incorporating logistics information technology. *International Journal of Production Economics, 113*(1), 205–222. doi:10.1016/j.ijpe.2007.03.023

Bowersox, D. J. (1969). Physical distribution development, current status, and potential. *Journal of Marketing, 33*(1), 63–70. doi:10.1177/002224296903300111

Bowersox, D. J., Mentzer, J. T., & Speh, T. W. (2008). Logistics leverage. *The Journal of Business Strategy*, *25*(2), 85.

Mentzer, J. T., Flint, D. J., & Hult, G. T. M. (2001). Logistics service quality as a segment-customized process. *Journal of Marketing*, *65*(4), 82–104. doi:10.1509/jmkg.65.4.82.18390

Panayides, P. M. (2007). The impact of organizational learning on relationship orientation, logistics service effectiveness and performance. *Industrial Marketing Management*, *36*(1), 68–80. doi:10.1016/j.indmarman.2005.07.001

Stank, T. P., Goldsby, T. J., Vickery, S. K., & Savitskie, K. (2003). Logistics service performance: Estimating its influence on market share. *Journal of Business Logistics*, *24*(1), 27–55. doi:10.1002/j.2158-1592.2003.tb00031.x

Thai, V. V. (2013). Logistics service quality: Conceptual model and empirical evidence. *International Journal of Logistics Research and Applications*, *16*(2), 114–131. doi:10.1080/13675567.2013.804907

Zhao, M., Dröge, C., & Stank, T. P. (2001). The effects of logistics capabilities on firm performance: Customer-focused versus information-focused capabilities. *Journal of Business Logistics*, *22*(2), 91–107. doi:10.1002/j.2158-1592.2001.tb00005.x

KEY TERMS AND DEFINITIONS

Firm Performance: Performance of businesses as a result of their activities.

Information Quality: The quality of the information obtained from the market by using logistics services.

Logistics Performance: Performance of logistics activities used by enterprises to carry out activities.

Logistics Service Quality: It can be expressed as the quality of the logistics services that industrial consumers generally use by purchasing from outside.

Order Handling Quality and Image: Processing orders coming from the customers of the enterprise and the business image they obtain in this direction.

Perceived Information Technologies: The perception of the technology used by the enterprises in their activities by the customers.

Personal Contact Quality: The quality and skill of communication is the first meeting of the customers when they contact the business.

Social Responsibility: The social responsibility undertaken by enterprises in carrying out their activities and the respect they have towards customers in this direction.

Chapter 7
The Role of Technological Development on Renewable Energy Usage:
An Econometric Analysis for G7 Countries

Serhat Yüksel
Istanbul Medipol University, Turkey

Hasan Dinçer
Istanbul Medipol University, Turkey

Gülsüm Sena Uluer
Istanbul Medipol University, Turkey

ABSTRACT

The aim of this study is to determine the relationship between technological development and renewable energy use. Within this framework, G7 countries were included in the scope of the review. Data for the countries in question between 1990 and 2015 were used. In order to determine the relationship between these two variables, Pedroni panel cointegration analysis was utilized. As a result, it has been determined that technological development is very effective in the use of renewable energy. Therefore, countries need to improve themselves technologically in order to increase the use of renewable energy. It is very important to have technological infrastructure in renewable energy investments. Hence, technological investments should have the priority in order to increase the use of renewable energy. With the help of this issue, it can be more possible to be successful in this kind of investment.

DOI: 10.4018/978-1-7998-4601-7.ch007

INTRODUCTION

The use of renewable energy has become very popular, especially in recent years. There are many different reasons for this. Firstly, countries that do not have energy resources attach importance to the use of renewable energy. In this way, they aim to reduce their dependence on foreign countries on energy. In addition, renewable energy is considered an environmentally friendly energy type. With the use of this energy, it becomes possible to attract the attention of environmentally sensitive investors. When these issues are considered, it is important to identify the factors that increase the use of renewable energy (Yu et al., 2019).

It is possible to talk about many different factors affecting the use of renewable energy. For example, economic factors can play a crucial role in the use of renewable energy. As can be seen here, a country can give importance to the use of renewable energy when it develops economically. In other words, a country with unemployment problems and high inflation problems will not be able to put it on its primary agenda on renewable energy use. The reason for this is that this country needs to solve these first mentioned problems (Dinçer et al., 2019d,e). Therefore, if a country attaches importance to the use of renewable energy, it should first increase its economic performance.

Political factors are another factor that can affect the use of renewable energy. In the absence of political stability in a country, investors will not want to invest in that country. This is similar for renewable energy investments. In making investment decisions, investors not only look at the economic situation in that country, but also take into account the political stability in that country (Adefarati and Bansal, 2019; Mirzaei et al., 2019). On the other hand, state support is very important in renewable energy investments. If the government provides incentives such as tax cuts to renewable energy investors, it will be easier to increase the renewable energy investments in the country (Pukšec et al., 2019; Hodges et al., 2019).

On the other hand, technological developments play an important role in increasing the use of renewable energy. Renewable energy investments are investments that require technological infrastructure. In addition, technological developments are an important factor in reducing costs in renewable energy production. Since renewable energy investments are also very costly investments, technological developments are very important. In addition, the cost-benefit analysis of renewable energy projects needs to be carried out in detail (Chen et al., 2019).

In this study, it will be tried to determine whether technological development has an effect on renewable energy use. In this context, G7 countries were included in the scope of the review. On the other hand, the relationship between these two variables are defined by Pedroni panel cointegration analysis. Thanks to the data to be obtained, it will be possible to make policy proposals for G7 countries. Therefore, it can be said that the main motivation of this study is to identify the way of improving renewable energy usage. In addition, Pedroni panel cointegration analysis is firstly considered in this study to see the relationship between these two variables.

This study consists of 5 different parts. In the first part of the study, the concept of renewable energy, its importance and the factors affecting this energy usage will be discussed. In the second part of the study, the types of renewable energy sources will be given. The literature review on the subject will be shared in the third part of the study. In the fourth part of the study, analysis results for G7 countries are given. In the last part of the study, the strategies developed for the results and suggestions for the future studies are mentioned.

BACKGROUND INFORMATION ABOUT RENEWABLE ENERGY

Energy is a phenomenon that directly affects the welfare of societies. Since energy is used in industrial production very seriously, it is an important indicator of the economic development of a country. Energy types are divided into two groups as non-renewable and renewable. Non-renewable energy sources include coal, oil, natural gas and nuclear energy (Huang, 2019; Yüksel et al., 2019; Keck et al., 2019). Renewable energy sources are wind, solar and hydrogen energy (Dinçer and Yüksel, 2019). However, the adequacy of energy resources in the world is decreasing day by day. Therefore, the continuity of energy sources has become a subject that has been discussed frequently in recent years. This situation has increased the interest in unlimited and renewable energy resources in nature instead of non-renewable energy resources which have limited resources. Many different countries are looking for ways to increase their renewable energy resources (Giddey et al., 2019; Dinçer et al., 2017; Khare, 2019).

One of the most well-known renewable energy types is wind energy. In this type of energy, the main aim is to obtain energy by using the power of the wind. Wind energy is a clean and environmentally friendly type of energy. In other words, wind energy does not harm people and natural order. Another advantage of wind energy is that it is a non-external energy type (Zhouv et al.., 2019; Dorotić et al., 2019; Yousif et al., 2019). On the other hand, wind energy also has some disadvantages. Because of their physical structure, wind power plants can create visual and aesthetic pollution. At the same time, wind energy investments are highly costly investments that require significant technological infrastructure (Draycott et al., 2019; Wang et al., 2019; Ozcan and Ozturk, 2019).

Solar energy is another important type of renewable energy. Like wind power, solar energy is environmentally friendly and easily accessible. In addition, it is a simple technology with inexhaustible energy. On the other hand, the sun is a clean source of energy and does not release harmful gases (Domínguez-Navarro et al., 2019; Pourbehzadi et al., 2019). However, the most important disadvantage of solar energy is the risk of not being present at the desired time and intensity. At the same time, solar energy is less available in winter, when energy demand and heating need increase. The high initial investment costs are another negative aspect of solar energy (Campos-Guzman et al., 2019; Baldwin et al., 2019).

Hydrogen energy means the production of energy as a result of the use of hydrogen gas in nature. Hydrogen is not a natural fuel. It is derived from primary energy sources such as fossil fuels. In this process, many different hydrogen production technologies can be utilized. Hydrogen is a fuel type suitable for electricity conversion (Lijó et al., 2019; Bekun et al., 2019). Therefore, it can be used as fuel in combustion engines, gas turbines and furnaces. In addition, hydrogen is a very promising source of energy for the automotive industry. The most important advantage of hydrogen is the low-cost energy type that does not harm the environment. Storage difficulty is the most important negative side of this energy source (Huang et al., 2019; Hassan et al., 2019; Koivisto et al., 2019).

Geothermal energy is the energy obtained from underground hot water and steam deposits. Geothermal energy is generally composed of geothermal sources which are concentrated around volcanic units (Lehmann et al., 2019; Coelho et al., 2019; Chuang et al., 2019). Geothermal energy can be used in the production of electrical energy. Geothermal energy has many advantages and disadvantages. The most important advantage is the utilization of low-level geothermal resources. However, geothermal energy is an energy source that can be used in situ. In other words, it is not possible to move over long distances (Carroquino et al., 2019; Mascaretti et al., 2019; Ali et al., 2019).

LITERATURE REVIEW

There are many studies dealing with the factors affecting the use of renewable energy. According to some studies, political factors play an important role in the use of renewable energy. Luthra et al. (2015) focused on the use of renewable energy in India. AHP method was used in the analysis stage of the study. They concluded that if renewable energy technologies can be used efficiently and governmental policy makers regulate this market effectively, India may become world leader in development renewable energy. Polzin et al. (2015) also focused on this problem for OECD countries. With the help of regression analysis, it is learnt that policy makers directly influence risk and return of renewable energy projects. Therefore, they underlined that this market should be regulated effectively. Bhattacharya et al. (2016) also made an analysis for 38 top renewable energy consuming countries. By using panel cointegration analysis, it is defined that there should be tax incentives for the renewable energy investors to improve this market. Inglesi-Lotz (2016) made a similar analysis with the help of the same methodology and found that there is a strong relationship between government policies and renewable energy consumptions.

In many studies, it is concluded that there is a significant relationship between renewable energy use and economic factors. Nematollahi et al. (2016) conducted an analysis on the use of renewable energy in Middle Eastern countries. According to the results of the analysis, it is determined that countries with economic power can give more importance to renewable energy projects. Do´ci et al. (2015) conducted a similar study for the Netherlands and emphasized the importance of the same issue. Moriarty and Honnery (2016) stated that the economic analysis of the renewable energy project should be performed. Olatomiwa et al. (2016), Olabi (2017) and Mazzucato and Semieniuk (2018) also argued that the cost-benefit analysis of the project should be carried out effectively in order to have a successful renewable energy project.

Another factor that increases the use of renewable energy is environmental sensitivity in the country. As a result of the use of fossil fuels, carbon dioxide gas is released into the atmosphere. This causes many negative factors such as global warming (Hosseini and Wahid, 2016). Since this issue causes many problems both socially and economically, the emission of carbon dioxide gas is tried to be reduced (Gils et al., 2017; Dogan and Seker, 2016). The use of renewable energy is a prominent practice in this process. Connolly et al. (2016) discussed European Union countries and stated that there is a relationship between environmental sensitivity and the use of renewable energy. Danish et al. (2017) and Jebli et al. (2016) reached the same conclusion for Pakistan and OECD countries. Zhang et al. (2017) conducted an analysis for China and stated that environmental factors have the greatest impact on the use of renewable energy.

Some researchers have stated that effective planning is very important in renewable energy investments. Kumar et al. (2017) conducted an analysis on developing countries. In this study, multi-criteria decision-making methods are taken into consideration. As a result, it was determined that effective planning plays an important role in the continuity of success in renewable energy projects. Suganthi et al. (2015) have made a similar study considering the fuzzy logic approach and reached the same result. Strantzali and Aravossis (2016) identified that energy planning is crucial because there are technical, economical environmental and social impacts. Hence, they claimed that they should be weighted with an appropriate methodology. Similarly, Khare et al. (2016) and Balın and Baraçlı (2017) tried to evaluate this situation for different countries and defined the importance of effective planning in renewable energy investment.

The relationship between technological development and the use of renewable energy has also been addressed in many studies. Parra et al. (2017) conducted an analysis of the use of renewable energy in the United Kingdom. In this study, which uses optimization method, it is concluded that technological innovations should be followed in order to be successful in renewable energy projects. Accordingly, Owusu and Asumadu-Sarkodie (2016), Kuang et al. (2016), Nizami et al. (2017) and Hemmati and Saboori (2016) also stated that technological advances are quite effective on renewable energy use. Hussain et al. (2017), Rahim et al. (2016), Dreidy et al. (2017) and Mathiesen et al. (2015) stated that it is possible to reduce the cost of renewable energy projects through technological development. This has been highlighted by many studies in the literature (Amrouche et al., 2016; Gençer and Agrawal, 2015; Bahramara et al., 2016; Hossain et al., 2016).

The literature review reveals that renewable energy is very popular. Therefore, studies are needed to determine the factors that will increase renewable energy consumption. In this context, a new method to be used will increase the authenticity of the study. In this study, the relationship between technological development and renewable energy is discussed for G7 countries. Therefore, it is thought that this need will be met in the literature.

AN ECONOMETRIC ANALYSIS ON G7 ECONOMIES

In this part of the study, details of the analysis for G7 countries will be given. In this context, firstly, the data used in the analysis and the source of this data will be explained. After that, theoretical knowledge of Pedroni panel cointegration analysis will be given. In this context, some studies considering this method will also be shared. In the last part of this section, the results of the analysis will be indicated. In this context, firstly the unit root test results and then the cointegration analysis results will be shown.

Data Set and Variables

This study aims to analyze the relationship between technological development and renewable energy usage. Annual data for these variables between 1990 and 2015 is considered and this data is provided from World Bank and OECD. On the other side, the analysis is made for G7 economies. The main reason of selecting G7 economies is that renewable energy usage in these countries significantly increased especially in the last years. Additionally, energy production increase was also higher in these countries in comparison with others. The details of this data are demonstrated in the Appendix part.

Pedroni Panel Cointegration Analysis

Cointegration analysis tries to find out if there is a long-term relationship between different factors. In Pedroni cointegration analysis, panel data can be taken into consideration to evaluate the relationship. Within this scope, 7 different tests are made that are;

- Panel v-Statistic,
- Panel rho-Statistic,
- Panel PP-Statistic,
- Panel ADF-Statistic,

- Group rho-Statistic,
- Group PP-Statistic,
- Group ADF-Statistic.

If at least 4 of these 7 tests are statistically significant, it means that there is a long-term relationship between the variables. For this purpose, probability values should be lower than 0.05 in order for the test to be accepted as significant. Pedroni panel cointegration test was used in the literature for various purposes. For instance, Dinçer and Yüksel (2019) used this approach to make an analysis in health industry. On the other side, Ersin (2020), Arabiyat et al. (2020), Dinçer et al. (2019a,b), Jäger and Schmidt (2016), Ersin and Baş (2019) and Huňady et al. (2020) considered this methodology for finance and macroeconomic purposes. There are also some studies in the literature in which Pedroni panel cointegration analysis was used for energy industry (Dinçer et al., 2019c; Zeren and Akkuş, 2020; Rahman and Velayutham, 2020; Zoundi, 2017; Streimikiene and Kasperowicz, 2016).

Analysis Results

The first step in the analysis process is to make stationary analysis. For this purpose, Im, Peseran and Shin (IPS) panel unit root test is considered. Table 1 gives information about the unit root test results.

Table 1. IPS Panel Unit Root Test Results

Variables	Level Value (prob)	First Difference Value (prob)
Technological Development	0.3573	0.0070
Renewable Energy Usage	0.9999	0.0000

Table 1 indicates that both variables are not stationary in their normal forms. On the other side, the first differences of these variables do not have unit roots. Therefore, these forms are used in the analysis. In the second stage of the analysis, Pedroni panel cointegration test is performed with these variables. Table 2 gives information about the analysis results.

Table 2. Pedroni Panel Cointegration Test Results

Relationship Type	Test Name	Probability Values
Technological Development - Renewable Energy Usage	Panel v-Statistic	0.9749
	Panel rho-Statistic	0.0000
	Panel PP-Statistic	0.0000
	Panel ADF-Statistic	0.0000
	Group rho-Statistic	0.7605
	Group PP-Statistic	0.0000
	Group ADF-Statistic	0.0000

7 different test results of Pedroni panel cointegration analysis are given on Table 2. While looking at the probability values, it can be seen that two different tests (Panel v-Statistic and Group rho-Statistic) are not statistically significant. The main reason is that probability values are greater than 0.05. In addition to this issue, other five tests (Panel rho-Statistic, Panel PP-Statistic, Panel ADF-Statistic, Group PP-Statistic and Group ADF-Statistic) are statistically significant. Since most of the tests are statistically significant, it is concluded that there is a long-term relationship between these two variables. In other saying, for G7 countries, technological development has an important influence on the renewable energy usage.

SOLUTIONS AND RECOMMENDATIONS

In this study, it has been determined that technological development has a positive effect on renewable energy use in G7 countries. Therefore, countries need to improve themselves technologically in order to increase the use of renewable energy. It is very important to have technological infrastructure in renewable energy investments. For example, renewable energy investments such as solar panels and wind power plants are investments that can be made with significant technological development. Hence, countries aiming to increase the use of renewable energy should give priority to technological investments.

FUTURE RESEARCH DIRECTIONS

In this study, the relationship between technological development and renewable energy in G7 countries is examined. In a future study, a comparative analysis can be made between the G7 and E7 countries. In addition, a different method can be considered in a new study. For example, with the help of Dumitrescu Hurlin panel causality analysis, it is possible to determine whether there is a causality relationship between said variables. On the other hand, other variables that may affect renewable energy can be included in the analysis.

CONCLUSION

In this study, we investigated whether there is a long-term relationship between technological development and renewable energy use. In order to reach this conclusion, an examination was made on G7 countries. The data of both variables between 1990 and 2015 were taken into consideration. Pedroni panel cointegration analysis was used in the analysis process of the study. First, the variables were subjected to panel unit root test. According to the results of the analysis, both variables were not stable at the level. Therefore, the first differences of both variables were used in the analysis. As a result, it has been determined that technological development is very effective in the use of renewable energy.

REFERENCES

Adefarati, T., & Bansal, R. C. (2019). Reliability, economic and environmental analysis of a microgrid system in the presence of renewable energy resources. *Applied Energy*, *236*, 1089–1114. doi:10.1016/j.apenergy.2018.12.050

Ali, G., Yan, N., Hussain, J., Xu, L., Huang, Y., Xu, S., & Cui, S. (2019). Quantitative assessment of energy conservation and renewable energy awareness among variant urban communities of Xiamen, China. *Renewable & Sustainable Energy Reviews*, *109*, 230–238. doi:10.1016/j.rser.2019.04.028

Amrouche, S. O., Rekioua, D., Rekioua, T., & Bacha, S. (2016). Overview of energy storage in renewable energy systems. *International Journal of Hydrogen Energy*, *41*(45), 20914–20927. doi:10.1016/j.ijhydene.2016.06.243

Arabiyat, T. S., Mdanat, M., & Samawi, G. (2020). Trade Openness, Inclusive Growth, And Inequality: Evidence From Jordan. *Journal of Developing Areas*, *54*(1). doi:10.1353/jda.2020.0008

Bahramara, S., Moghaddam, M. P., & Haghifam, M. R. (2016). Optimal planning of hybrid renewable energy systems using HOMER: A review. *Renewable & Sustainable Energy Reviews*, *62*, 609–620. doi:10.1016/j.rser.2016.05.039

Baldwin, E., Carley, S., & Nicholson-Crotty, S. (2019). Why do countries emulate each others' policies? A global study of renewable energy policy diffusion. *World Development*, *120*, 29–45. doi:10.1016/j.worlddev.2019.03.012

Balin, A., & Baraçli, H. (2017). A fuzzy multi-criteria decision making methodology based upon the interval type-2 fuzzy sets for evaluating renewable energy alternatives in Turkey. *Technological and Economic Development of Economy*, *23*(5), 742–763. doi:10.3846/20294913.2015.1056276

Bekun, F. V., Alola, A. A., & Sarkodie, S. A. (2019). Toward a sustainable environment: Nexus between CO2 emissions, resource rent, renewable and nonrenewable energy in 16-EU countries. *The Science of the Total Environment*, *657*, 1023–1029. doi:10.1016/j.scitotenv.2018.12.104 PMID:30677870

Bhattacharya, M., Paramati, S. R., Ozturk, I., & Bhattacharya, S. (2016). The effect of renewable energy consumption on economic growth: Evidence from top 38 countries. *Applied Energy*, *162*, 733–741. doi:10.1016/j.apenergy.2015.10.104

Campos-Guzman, V., García-Cáscales, M. S., Espinosa, N., & Urbina, A. (2019). Life cycle analysis with multi-criteria decision making: A review of approaches for the sustainability evaluation of renewable energy technologies. *Renewable & Sustainable Energy Reviews*, *104*, 343–366. doi:10.1016/j.rser.2019.01.031

Carroquino, J., Bernal-Agustín, J. L., & Dufo-López, R. (2019). Standalone Renewable Energy and Hydrogen in an Agricultural Context: A Demonstrative Case. *Sustainability*, *11*(4), 951. doi:10.3390u11040951

Chen, S., Kumar, A., Wong, W. C., Chiu, M. S., & Wang, X. (2019). Hydrogen value chain and fuel cells within hybrid renewable energy systems: Advanced operation and control strategies. *Applied Energy*, *233*, 321–337. doi:10.1016/j.apenergy.2018.10.003

Chuang, M. T., Chang, S. Y., Hsiao, T. C., Lu, Y. R., & Yang, T. Y. (2019). Analyzing major renewable energy sources and power stability in Taiwan by 2030. *Energy Policy*, *125*, 293–306. doi:10.1016/j.enpol.2018.10.036

Coelho, R. D., Lizcano, J. V., da Silva Barros, T. H., da Silva Barbosa, F., Leal, D. P. V., da Costa Santos, L., ... Martin, D. L. (2019). Effect of water stress on renewable energy from sugarcane biomass. *Renewable & Sustainable Energy Reviews*, *103*, 399–407. doi:10.1016/j.rser.2018.12.025

Connolly, D., Lund, H., & Mathiesen, B. V. (2016). Smart Energy Europe: The technical and economic impact of one potential 100% renewable energy scenario for the European Union. *Renewable & Sustainable Energy Reviews*, *60*, 1634–1653. doi:10.1016/j.rser.2016.02.025

Dinçer, H., & Yüksel, S. (2019). Identifying the causality relationship between health expenditure and economic growth: An application on E7 countries. *Journal of Health Systems and Policies*, *1*(1), 5–23.

Dinçer, H., & Yüksel, S. (2019). Multidimensional evaluation of global investments on the renewable energy with the integrated fuzzy decision-making model under the hesitancy. *International Journal of Energy Research*, *43*(5), 1775–1784. doi:10.1002/er.4400

Dinçer, H., Yüksel, S., & Adalı, Z. (2017). Identifying Causality Relationship between Energy Consumption and Economic Growth in Developed Countries. *International Business and Accounting Research Journal*, *1*(2), 71–81. doi:10.15294/ibarj.v1i2.9

Dinçer, H., Yüksel, S., & Adalı, Z. (2019b). Determining the Effects of Monetary Policies on Capital Markets of the Emerging Economies: An Evidence from E7 Countries. The Impacts of Monetary Policy in the 21st Century: Perspectives from Emerging Economies, 3-16.

Dinçer, H., Yüksel, S., & Canbolat, Z. N. (2019c). A Strategic Approach to Reduce Energy Imports of E7 Countries: Use of Renewable Energy. In Handbook of Research on Economic and Political Implications of Green Trading and Energy Use (pp. 18-38). IGI Global.

Dincer, H., Yüksel, S., & Martinez, L. (2019d). Balanced scorecard-based Analysis about European Energy Investment Policies: A hybrid hesitant fuzzy decision-making approach with Quality Function Deployment. *Expert Systems with Applications*, *115*, 152–171. doi:10.1016/j.eswa.2018.07.072

Dinçer, H., Yüksel, S., & Pınarbaşı, F. (2019e). SERVQUAL-Based Evaluation of Service Quality of Energy Companies in Turkey: Strategic Policies for Sustainable Economic Development. In The Circular Economy and Its Implications on Sustainability and the Green Supply Chain (pp. 142-167). IGI Global.

Dinçer, H., Yüksel, S., Pınarbaşı, F., & Çetiner, İ. T. (2019a). Measurement of Economic and Banking Stability in Emerging Markets by Considering Income Inequality and Nonperforming Loans. In *Maintaining Financial Stability in Times of Risk and Uncertainty* (pp. 49–68). IGI Global. doi:10.4018/978-1-5225-7208-4.ch003

Dóci, G., Vasileiadou, E., & Petersen, A. C. (2015). Exploring the transition potential of renewable energy communities. *Futures*, *66*, 85–95. doi:10.1016/j.futures.2015.01.002

Dogan, E., & Seker, F. (2016). The influence of real output, renewable and non-renewable energy, trade and financial development on carbon emissions in the top renewable energy countries. *Renewable & Sustainable Energy Reviews*, *60*, 1074–1085. doi:10.1016/j.rser.2016.02.006

Domínguez-Navarro, J. A., Dufo-López, R., Yusta-Loyo, J. M., Artal-Sevil, J. S., & Bernal-Agustín, J. L. (2019). Design of an electric vehicle fast-charging station with integration of renewable energy and storage systems. *International Journal of Electrical Power & Energy Systems*, *105*, 46–58. doi:10.1016/j.ijepes.2018.08.001

Dorotić, H., Doračić, B., Dobravec, V., Pukšec, T., Krajačić, G., & Duić, N. (2019). Integration of transport and energy sectors in island communities with 100% intermittent renewable energy sources. *Renewable & Sustainable Energy Reviews*, *99*, 109–124. doi:10.1016/j.rser.2018.09.033

Draycott, S., Sellar, B., Davey, T., Noble, D. R., Venugopal, V., & Ingram, D. M. (2019). Capture and simulation of the ocean environment for offshore renewable energy. *Renewable & Sustainable Energy Reviews*, *104*, 15–29. doi:10.1016/j.rser.2019.01.011

Dreidy, M., Mokhlis, H., & Mekhilef, S. (2017). Inertia response and frequency control techniques for renewable energy sources: A review. *Renewable & Sustainable Energy Reviews*, *69*, 144–155. doi:10.1016/j.rser.2016.11.170

Ersin, İ. (2020). Determining the Importance of Domestic Firms on Stock Market Performance in Terms of Financial Marketing: An Application on OECD Countries. In Handbook of Research on Decision-Making Techniques in Financial Marketing (pp. 269-286). IGI Global.

Ersin, İ., & Baş, H. (2019). Güney Avrupa refah ülkelerinde sosyal harcamalar ve ekonomik büyüme arasındaki ilişkinin incelenmesi. *SGD-Sosyal Güvenlik Dergisi*, *9*(1), 193–213. doi:10.32331gd.582752

Gençer, E., & Agrawal, R. (2016). A commentary on the US policies for efficient large scale renewable energy storage systems: Focus on carbon storage cycles. *Energy Policy*, *88*, 477–484. doi:10.1016/j.enpol.2015.11.003

Giddey, S., Badwal, S. P., & Ju, H. (2019). Polymer electrolyte membrane technologies integrated with renewable energy for hydrogen production. In Current Trends and Future Developments on (Bio-) Membranes (pp. 235-259). Elsevier. doi:10.1016/B978-0-12-813545-7.00010-6

Gils, H. C., Scholz, Y., Pregger, T., de Tena, D. L., & Heide, D. (2017). Integrated modelling of variable renewable energy-based power supply in Europe. *Energy*, *123*, 173–188. doi:10.1016/j.energy.2017.01.115

Hassan, M. U., Rehmani, M. H., Kotagiri, R., Zhang, J., & Chen, J. (2019). Differential privacy for renewable energy resources based smart metering. *Journal of Parallel and Distributed Computing*, *131*, 69–80. doi:10.1016/j.jpdc.2019.04.012

Hemmati, R., & Saboori, H. (2016). Emergence of hybrid energy storage systems in renewable energy and transport applications–A review. *Renewable & Sustainable Energy Reviews*, *65*, 11–23. doi:10.1016/j.rser.2016.06.029

Hodges, D. G., Chapagain, B., Watcharaanantapong, P., Poudyal, N. C., Kline, K. L., & Dale, V. H. (2019). Opportunities and attitudes of private forest landowners in supplying woody biomass for renewable energy. *Renewable & Sustainable Energy Reviews, 113*, 109205. doi:10.1016/j.rser.2019.06.012

Hossain, M. S., Madlool, N. A., Rahim, N. A., Selvaraj, J., Pandey, A. K., & Khan, A. F. (2016). Role of smart grid in renewable energy: An overview. *Renewable & Sustainable Energy Reviews, 60*, 1168–1184. doi:10.1016/j.rser.2015.09.098

Hosseini, S. E., & Wahid, M. A. (2016). Hydrogen production from renewable and sustainable energy resources: Promising green energy carrier for clean development. *Renewable & Sustainable Energy Reviews, 57*, 850–866. doi:10.1016/j.rser.2015.12.112

Huang, A. Q. (2019). Power semiconductor devices for smart grid and renewable energy systems. *Power Electronics in Renewable Energy Systems and Smart Grid: Technology and Applications*, 85-152.

Huang, Y. W., Kittner, N., & Kammen, D. M. (2019). ASEAN grid flexibility: Preparedness for grid integration of renewable energy. *Energy Policy, 128*, 711–726. doi:10.1016/j.enpol.2019.01.025

Huňady, J., Pisár, P., & Balco, P. (2020). Determinants of Employment in Information and Communication Technologies and Its Structure. In *Data-Centric Business and Applications* (pp. 277–298). Cham: Springer. doi:10.1007/978-3-030-19069-9_11

Hussain, A., Arif, S. M., & Aslam, M. (2017). Emerging renewable and sustainable energy technologies: State of the art. *Renewable & Sustainable Energy Reviews, 71*, 12–28. doi:10.1016/j.rser.2016.12.033

Inglesi-Lotz, R. (2016). The impact of renewable energy consumption to economic growth: A panel data application. *Energy Economics, 53*, 58–63. doi:10.1016/j.eneco.2015.01.003

Jäger, P., & Schmidt, T. (2016). The political economy of public investment when population is aging: A panel cointegration analysis. *European Journal of Political Economy, 43*, 145–158. doi:10.1016/j.ejpoleco.2016.04.004

Jebli, M. B., Youssef, S. B., & Ozturk, I. (2016). Testing environmental Kuznets curve hypothesis: The role of renewable and non-renewable energy consumption and trade in OECD countries. *Ecological Indicators, 60*, 824–831. doi:10.1016/j.ecolind.2015.08.031

Keck, F., Lenzen, M., Vassallo, A., & Li, M. (2019). The impact of battery energy storage for renewable energy power grids in Australia. *Energy, 173*, 647–657. doi:10.1016/j.energy.2019.02.053

Khare, V. (2019). Prediction, investigation, and assessment of novel tidal–solar hybrid renewable energy system in India by different techniques. *International Journal of Sustainable Energy, 38*(5), 447–468. doi:10.1080/14786451.2018.1529034

Khare, V., Nema, S., & Baredar, P. (2016). Solar–wind hybrid renewable energy system: A review. *Renewable & Sustainable Energy Reviews, 58*, 23–33. doi:10.1016/j.rser.2015.12.223

Koivisto, M., Das, K., Guo, F., Sørensen, P., Nuño, E., Cutululis, N., & Maule, P. (2019). Using time series simulation tools for assessing the effects of variable renewable energy generation on power and energy systems. *Wiley Interdisciplinary Reviews. Energy and Environment, 8*(3), e329. doi:10.1002/wene.329

Kuang, Y., Zhang, Y., Zhou, B., Li, C., Cao, Y., Li, L., & Zeng, L. (2016). A review of renewable energy utilization in islands. *Renewable & Sustainable Energy Reviews*, *59*, 504–513. doi:10.1016/j.rser.2016.01.014

Kumar, A., Sah, B., Singh, A. R., Deng, Y., He, X., Kumar, P., & Bansal, R. C. (2017). A review of multi criteria decision making (MCDM) towards sustainable renewable energy development. *Renewable & Sustainable Energy Reviews*, *69*, 596–609. doi:10.1016/j.rser.2016.11.191

Lehmann, P., Sijm, J., Gawel, E., Strunz, S., Chewpreecha, U., Mercure, J. F., & Pollitt, H. (2019). Addressing multiple externalities from electricity generation: A case for EU renewable energy policy beyond 2020? *Environmental Economics and Policy Studies*, *21*(2), 255–283. doi:10.100710018-018-0229-6

Lijó, L., González-García, S., Lovarelli, D., Moreira, M. T., Feijoo, G., & Bacenetti, J. (2019). Life Cycle Assessment of Renewable Energy Production from Biomass. In *Life Cycle Assessment of Energy Systems and Sustainable Energy Technologies* (pp. 81–98). Cham: Springer. doi:10.1007/978-3-319-93740-3_6

Luthra, S., Kumar, S., Garg, D., & Haleem, A. (2015). Barriers to renewable/sustainable energy technologies adoption: Indian perspective. *Renewable & Sustainable Energy Reviews*, *41*, 762–776. doi:10.1016/j.rser.2014.08.077

Mascaretti, L., Dutta, A., Kment, Š., Shalaev, V. M., Boltasseva, A., Zbořil, R., & Naldoni, A. (2019). Plasmon-Enhanced Photoelectrochemical Water Splitting for Efficient Renewable Energy Storage. *Advanced Materials*, *31*(31), 1805513. doi:10.1002/adma.201805513 PMID:30773753

Mathiesen, B. V., Lund, H., Connolly, D., Wenzel, H., Østergaard, P. A., Möller, B., ... Hvelplund, F. K. (2015). Smart Energy Systems for coherent 100% renewable energy and transport solutions. *Applied Energy*, *145*, 139–154. doi:10.1016/j.apenergy.2015.01.075

Mazzucato, M., & Semieniuk, G. (2018). Financing renewable energy: Who is financing what and why it matters. *Technological Forecasting and Social Change*, *127*, 8–22. doi:10.1016/j.techfore.2017.05.021

Mirzaei, M. A., Yazdankhah, A. S., Mohammadi-Ivatloo, B., Marzband, M., Shafie-khah, M., & Catalão, J. P. (2019). Stochastic network-constrained co-optimization of energy and reserve products in renewable energy integrated power and gas networks with energy storage system. *Journal of Cleaner Production*, *223*, 747–758. doi:10.1016/j.jclepro.2019.03.021

Moriarty, P., & Honnery, D. (2016). Can renewable energy power the future? *Energy Policy*, *93*, 3–7. doi:10.1016/j.enpol.2016.02.051

Nematollahi, O., Hoghooghi, H., Rasti, M., & Sedaghat, A. (2016). Energy demands and renewable energy resources in the Middle East. *Renewable & Sustainable Energy Reviews*, *54*, 1172–1181. doi:10.1016/j.rser.2015.10.058

Nizami, A. S., Shahzad, K., Rehan, M., Ouda, O. K. M., Khan, M. Z., Ismail, I. M. I., ... Demirbas, A. (2017). Developing waste biorefinery in Makkah: A way forward to convert urban waste into renewable energy. *Applied Energy*, *186*, 189–196. doi:10.1016/j.apenergy.2016.04.116

Olabi, A. G. (2017). *Renewable energy and energy storage systems*. Academic Press.

Olatomiwa, L., Mekhilef, S., Ismail, M. S., & Moghavvemi, M. (2016). Energy management strategies in hybrid renewable energy systems: A review. *Renewable & Sustainable Energy Reviews*, *62*, 821–835. doi:10.1016/j.rser.2016.05.040

Owusu, P. A., & Asumadu-Sarkodie, S. (2016). A review of renewable energy sources, sustainability issues and climate change mitigation. *Cogent Engineering*, *3*(1), 1167990. doi:10.1080/23311916.2016.1167990

Ozcan, B., & Ozturk, I. (2019). Renewable energy consumption-economic growth nexus in emerging countries: A bootstrap panel causality test. *Renewable & Sustainable Energy Reviews*, *104*, 30–37. doi:10.1016/j.rser.2019.01.020

Parra, D., Norman, S. A., Walker, G. S., & Gillott, M. (2017). Optimum community energy storage for renewable energy and demand load management. *Applied Energy*, *200*, 358–369. doi:10.1016/j.apenergy.2017.05.048

Polzin, F., Migendt, M., Täube, F. A., & von Flotow, P. (2015). Public policy influence on renewable energy investments—A panel data study across OECD countries. *Energy Policy*, *80*, 98–111. doi:10.1016/j.enpol.2015.01.026

Pourbehzadi, M., Niknam, T., Aghaei, J., Mokryani, G., Shafie-khah, M., & Catalao, J. P. (2019). Optimal operation of hybrid AC/DC microgrids under uncertainty of renewable energy resources: A comprehensive review. *International Journal of Electrical Power & Energy Systems*, *109*, 139–159. doi:10.1016/j.ijepes.2019.01.025

Pukšec, T., Foley, A., Markovska, N., & Duić, N. (2019). Life cycle to Pinch Analysis and 100% renewable energy systems in a circular economy at sustainable development of energy. *Water and Environment Systems 2017.*

Rahim, S., Javaid, N., Ahmad, A., Khan, S. A., Khan, Z. A., Alrajeh, N., & Qasim, U. (2016). Exploiting heuristic algorithms to efficiently utilize energy management controllers with renewable energy sources. *Energy and Building*, *129*, 452–470. doi:10.1016/j.enbuild.2016.08.008

Rahman, M. M., & Velayutham, E. (2020). Renewable and non-renewable energy consumption-economic growth nexus: New evidence from South Asia. *Renewable Energy*, *147*, 399–408. doi:10.1016/j.renene.2019.09.007

Strantzali, E., & Aravossis, K. (2016). Decision making in renewable energy investments: A review. *Renewable & Sustainable Energy Reviews*, *55*, 885–898. doi:10.1016/j.rser.2015.11.021

Streimikiene, D., & Kasperowicz, R. (2016). Review of economic growth and energy consumption: A panel cointegration analysis for EU countries. *Renewable & Sustainable Energy Reviews*, *59*, 1545–1549. doi:10.1016/j.rser.2016.01.041

Suganthi, L., Iniyan, S., & Samuel, A. A. (2015). Applications of fuzzy logic in renewable energy systems–a review. *Renewable & Sustainable Energy Reviews*, *48*, 585–607. doi:10.1016/j.rser.2015.04.037

Wang, S., Liu, Q., Yuksel, S., & Dincer, H. (2019). Hesitant Linguistic Term Sets-Based Hybrid Analysis for Renewable Energy Investments. *IEEE Access: Practical Innovations, Open Solutions*, *7*, 114223–114235. doi:10.1109/ACCESS.2019.2935427

Yousif, J. H., Al-Balushi, H. A., Kazem, H. A., & Chaichan, M. T. (2019). Analysis and forecasting of weather conditions in Oman for renewable energy applications. *Case Studies in Thermal Engineering*, *13*, 100355. doi:10.1016/j.csite.2018.11.006

Yu, Z., Liu, W., Chen, L., Eti, S., Dinçer, H., & Yüksel, S. (2019). The Effects of Electricity Production on Industrial Development and Sustainable Economic Growth: A VAR Analysis for BRICS Countries. *Sustainability*, *11*(21), 5895. doi:10.3390u11215895

Yüksel, S., Dinçer, H., & Meral, Y. (2019). Financial analysis of international energy trade: A strategic outlook for EU-15. *Energies*, *12*(3), 431. doi:10.3390/en12030431

Zeren, F., & Akkuş, H. T. (2020). The relationship between renewable energy consumption and trade openness: New evidence from emerging economies. *Renewable Energy*, *147*, 322–329. doi:10.1016/j.renene.2019.09.006

Zhang, B., Wang, B., & Wang, Z. (2017). Role of renewable energy and non-renewable energy consumption on EKC: Evidence from Pakistan. *Journal of Cleaner Production*, *156*, 855–864. doi:10.1016/j.jclepro.2017.03.203

Zhang, D., Wang, J., Lin, Y., Si, Y., Huang, C., Yang, J., ... Li, W. (2017). Present situation and future prospect of renewable energy in China. *Renewable & Sustainable Energy Reviews*, *76*, 865–871. doi:10.1016/j.rser.2017.03.023

Zhou, S., Matisoff, D. C., Kingsley, G. A., & Brown, M. A. (2019). Understanding renewable energy policy adoption and evolution in Europe: The impact of coercion, normative emulation, competition, and learning. *Energy Research & Social Science*, *51*, 1–11. doi:10.1016/j.erss.2018.12.011

Zoundi, Z. (2017). CO2 emissions, renewable energy and the Environmental Kuznets Curve, a panel cointegration approach. *Renewable & Sustainable Energy Reviews*, *72*, 1067–1075. doi:10.1016/j.rser.2016.10.018

KEY TERMS AND DEFINITIONS

E7: It explains the biggest 7 economies of emerging countries. They are Brazil, China, India, Indonesia, Mexico, Russia, and Turkey.

G7: It gives information about the biggest 7 economies in the world. They are Canada, Japan, Italy, France, United States, United Kingdom, and Germany.

OECD: The Organization for Economic Co-Operation and Development.

Stationary Analysis: It aims to identify whether there is a unit root in the series or not.

APPENDIX

Table 3. Renewable Energy Usage of G7 Economies (% of Total Energy Usage)

Years	Countries	Renewable Energy Usage	Countries	Renewable Energy Usage	Countries	Renewable Energy Usage	Countries	Renewable Energy Usage
1990	Canada	22,02	Germany	2,10	France	10,41	United Kingdom	0,65
1991	Canada	22,20	Germany	1,99	France	11,01	United Kingdom	0,61
1992	Canada	21,93	Germany	2,06	France	11,26	United Kingdom	0,84
1993	Canada	21,80	Germany	2,11	France	10,86	United Kingdom	0,78
1994	Canada	21,69	Germany	2,27	France	10,93	United Kingdom	1,02
1995	Canada	21,92	Germany	2,32	France	10,70	United Kingdom	1,06
1996	Canada	21,58	Germany	2,25	France	10,49	United Kingdom	0,94
1997	Canada	21,31	Germany	2,82	France	9,99	United Kingdom	1,03
1998	Canada	21,52	Germany	3,05	France	9,71	United Kingdom	1,03
1999	Canada	21,71	Germany	3,26	France	9,78	United Kingdom	0,95
2000	Canada	21,51	Germany	3,70	France	9,26	United Kingdom	0,96
2001	Canada	21,01	Germany	3,90	France	9,40	United Kingdom	0,85
2002	Canada	21,77	Germany	4,41	France	8,67	United Kingdom	0,97
2003	Canada	21,18	Germany	5,06	France	8,85	United Kingdom	0,93
2004	Canada	21,58	Germany	5,83	France	8,89	United Kingdom	1,14
2005	Canada	22,25	Germany	6,76	France	8,60	United Kingdom	1,35
2006	Canada	22,09	Germany	7,75	France	8,46	United Kingdom	1,55
2007	Canada	22,13	Germany	9,41	France	9,32	United Kingdom	1,84
2008	Canada	22,53	Germany	8,59	France	10,47	United Kingdom	2,78
2009	Canada	22,70	Germany	9,63	France	11,22	United Kingdom	3,38
2010	Canada	22,08	Germany	10,29	France	11,85	United Kingdom	3,64

continues on following page

Table 3. Continued

Years	Countries	Renewable Energy Usage	Countries	Renewable Energy Usage	Countries	Renewable Energy Usage	Countries	Renewable Energy Usage
2011	Canada	21,97	Germany	11,39	France	10,91	United Kingdom	4,40
2012	Canada	22,61	Germany	12,02	France	12,37	United Kingdom	4,75
2013	Canada	22,38	Germany	12,09	France	13,48	United Kingdom	6,02
2014	Canada	22,02	Germany	13,38	France	13,35	United Kingdom	7,40
2015	Canada	22,03	Germany	14,21	France	13,50	United Kingdom	8,71
1990	Italy	3,78	Japan	4,55	United States	4,18		
1991	Italy	4,67	Japan	4,73	United States	4,51		
1992	Italy	4,84	Japan	4,20	United States	4,76		
1993	Italy	4,77	Japan	4,44	United States	4,28		
1994	Italy	5,25	Japan	3,57	United States	4,09		
1995	Italy	4,46	Japan	3,92	United States	4,73		
1996	Italy	4,75	Japan	3,84	United States	4,76		
1997	Italy	4,83	Japan	4,07	United States	4,51		
1998	Italy	4,76	Japan	4,05	United States	4,53		
1999	Italy	5,02	Japan	3,83	United States	5,71		
2000	Italy	5,12	Japan	3,92	United States	5,43		
2001	Italy	5,38	Japan	3,74	United States	4,68		
2002	Italy	5,60	Japan	3,70	United States	4,84		
2003	Italy	6,24	Japan	4,08	United States	5,33		
2004	Italy	5,94	Japan	4,01	United States	5,48		
2005	Italy	6,70	Japan	3,65	United States	5,84		
2006	Italy	7,51	Japan	4,03	United States	6,40		
2007	Italy	8,73	Japan	3,75	United States	6,30		
2008	Italy	10,82	Japan	3,98	United States	6,85		
2009	Italy	12,54	Japan	4,04	United States	7,35		
2010	Italy	12,79	Japan	4,59	United States	7,51		
2011	Italy	11,90	Japan	4,69	United States	8,16		
2012	Italy	14,39	Japan	4,53	United States	8,48		
2013	Italy	16,32	Japan	4,91	United States	8,71		
2014	Italy	17,09	Japan	5,63	United States	8,75		
2015	Italy	16,52	Japan	6,30	United States	8,72		

Table 4. Total energy production (Mtoe)

Countries	1996	1997	1998	1999	2000	2001	2002	2003	2004	2005	2006	2007	2008	2009	2010	2011	2012	2013	2014	2015	2016	2017	2018	2017 - 2018 (%)	2000 - 2018 (%/year)
World	9479	9602	9718	9727	10017	10178	10258	10672	11186	11542	11870	12071	12314	12216	12791	13119	13298	13486	13716	13802	13754	14068	14468	2,8	2,1
OECD	3778	3809	3823	3799	3842	3885	3871	3843	3874	3855	3880	3870	3881	3819	3897	3876	3906	3997	4159	4180	4080	4207	4408	4,8	0,8
G7	2711	2717	2736	2716	2714	2727	2699	2658	2673	2647	2670	2663	2674	2623	2674	2676	2686	2757	2915	2945	2833	2953	3159	7,0	0,8
BRICS	2642	2626	2639	2666	2745	2838	2952	3206	3438	3626	3788	3954	4054	4115	4428	4616	4655	4735	4790	4828	4742	4901	5071	3,5	3,5
Europe	1263	1259	1227	1228	1239	1236	1245	1237	1226	1192	1169	1146	1154	1112	1118	1079	1073	1062	1044	1047	1044	1047	1043	-0,4	-1,0
European Union	1000	988	960	961	953	952	953	944	939	911	892	867	865	827	844	812	803	798	780	773	761	758	753	-0,6	-1,3
France	132	129	125	127	131	132	134	136	137	137	136	135	137	129	136	136	135	137	138	139	131	130	135	4,2	0,2
Germany	143	145	137	138	136	135	134	135	137	137	139	136	133	126	129	123	123	121	120	120	116	115	115	0,2	-0,9
Italy	31	31	31	29	28	27	29	30	29	31	30	31	33	32	33	32	35	37	37	36	34	34	36	5,4	1,4
United Kingdom	269	268	272	282	272	262	259	247	226	205	187	176	167	158	148	130	117	110	108	118	120	120	124	3,1	-4,3
Canada	361	367	371	369	377	381	386	388	400	401	418	420	409	394	401	414	425	445	468	470	474	504	526	4,2	1,9
United States	1673	1671	1691	1665	1663	1684	1656	1635	1646	1632	1655	1670	1702	1686	1725	1787	1820	1878	2015	2028	1921	2007	2175	8,4	1,5
Japan	102	107	109	105	106	105	100	87	99	104	105	94	92	98	102	54	31	30	29	34	37	42	48	12,8	-4,4

Table 5. Total energy consumption (Mtoe)

Countries	1996	1997	1998	1999	2000	2001	2002	2003	2004	2005	2006	2007	2008	2009	2010	2011	2012	2013	2014	2015	2016	2017	2018	2017 - 2018 (%)	2000 - 2018 (%/year)
World	9448	9541	9597	9790	10020	10112	10330	10692	11174	11487	11831	12152	12300	12200	12871	13071	13278	13458	13632	13675	13768	14070	14391	2,3	2,0
OECD	5027	5074	5099	5184	5303	5285	5328	5399	5499	5537	5551	5575	5499	5260	5432	5331	5293	5332	5283	5284	5293	5352	5419	1,2	0,1
G7	3835	3852	3879	3939	4027	3990	4013	4044	4118	4134	4116	4121	4036	3833	3948	3842	3794	3842	3813	3797	3765	3788	3857	1,8	-0,2
BRICS	2367	2364	2371	2434	2488	2540	2630	2854	3097	3285	3502	3709	3837	3997	4328	4588	4742	4836	4956	4972	4984	5147	5323	3,4	4,3
Europe	1847	1835	1849	1831	1853	1888	1889	1934	1955	1965	1984	1961	1959	1856	1927	1867	1856	1840	1779	1807	1824	1857	1847	-0,5	0,0
European Union	1709	1690	1700	1686	1699	1736	1734	1772	1789	1796	1802	1772	1764	1663	1729	1663	1650	1631	1570	1589	1598	1619	1602	-1,0	-0,3
France	250	244	251	252	255	260	261	267	271	272	268	265	267	255	263	254	254	255	244	248	244	244	243	-0,5	-0,3
Germany	348	346	343	335	337	346	339	337	339	337	346	328	331	310	326	310	311	318	306	308	310	312	301	-3,5	-0,6
Italy	159	162	166	169	172	172	173	182	183	186	184	184	182	170	174	168	161	156	147	153	151	154	155	0,7	-0,6
United Kingdom	226	219	221	222	223	224	220	224	222	223	219	211	208	196	203	189	194	191	180	181	179	177	176	-0,9	-1,3
Canada	238	241	240	246	254	250	251	264	270	273	278	277	273	261	263	267	268	272	280	281	281	291	301	3,4	1,0
United States	2108	2130	2156	2206	2269	2226	2256	2261	2308	2319	2297	2338	2278	2165	2218	2192	2152	2196	2217	2194	2172	2180	2258	3,5	0,0
Japan	506	511	501	509	519	511	512	509	524	523	523	518	498	475	501	463	453	455	439	432	428	430	424	-1,2	-1,1

Chapter 8
How Supply Chain Management Will Change in the Industry 4.0 Era?

Emre Aslan
https://orcid.org/0000-0002-1744-8077
Tokat Gaziosmanpasa University, Turkey

ABSTRACT

Enabled by some maturated technologies in the last decades, a new industrial revolution is predicted to arise that not only affects manufacturing or industry, but many fields of life. It is named the Fourth Industrial Revolution or Industry 4.0. The triggering technologies, concepts, or driving forces mentioned with Industry 4.0 are cyber-physical systems, vertical and horizontal integration, augmented reality, internet of things, internet of services, additive manufacturing and 3D Printers, big data analytics, cloud computing, cybersecurity. Through Industry 4.0, production activities will be made by automatic machines and robot communicating each other. Supply chains will be more integrated due to information and communication technologies based on real-time data sharing. The purpose of this study is to examine the effects of Industry 4.0 on supply chain management. For this purpose, literature is reviewed according to effects of Industry 4.0 on procurement, production, warehousing, transportation, and fulfillment functions of supply chain management.

INTRODUCTION

With the influence of globalization, developing technology and internet, manufacturing shifted to underdeveloped and developing countries where labor cost is lower when compared with developed countries. Although facilities of international corporations moved to these underdeveloped and developing countries, headquarters and critical functions like research and development or marketing were still located at home or developed countries. In this way products used to be transported and delivered to target market of developed countries cost-effectively through supply chain management.

DOI: 10.4018/978-1-7998-4601-7.ch008

Thanks to combination of some technologies that maturated, low labor cost is becoming an insignificant part of manufacturing. So, manufacturing facilities, once left their home because of labor costs, now are coming back. This wave which mainly but not only omits labor from manufacturing systems but also affects many fields of life is named Fourth Industrial Revolution or Industry 4.0.

Industry 4.0 refers to the combination of several major innovations in digital technology, all coming to maturity. Although technological infrastructure is living its infancy period, manufacturing industries started to use for traceability and upgrade of products. As technology continues to evolve, the prevalence of use and the rate at which new products and services emerge will increase (Geissbauer, Vedso & Schrauf, 2016a).

This revolution is predicted to be different than the revolutions before in some ways. First of all it is known in advance. All the previous revolutions were understood, defined and named years or decades after they happened. Secondly the effect of the revolution is predicted to be wider and deeper, not just limited with production. The whole economy of the World, daily life of people and organizations, companies, customers, nations, governments, cities, society, healthcare, education, finance, money, logistics etc. is being and going to be affected by this revolution. And lastly by the exponential development and speed of technology the spreading of new revolution is predicted to be faster.

Given that the fourth industrial revolution will radically change all production systems, it is an expected result that logistic systems or supply chains, which have a direct relationship with production, will be affected by this change. In other words, technological developments, experienced in industrial terms, affect production processes, techniques, understanding etc.; this leads to the transformation of supply chain processes like dominoes (Şekelli & Bakan, 2018: 18).

The rest of the study is as follows: Industrial revolutions, Industry 4.0 and driving forces of the revolution are presented. Afterwards Supply Chain Management and effects of Industry 4.0 on supply chains and its processes are examined. Lastly conclusions and future directions are presented.

INDUSTRY 4.0

Industrial Revolutions

Mechanical manufacturing equipment triggered industrialization (Kagermann, Wahlster & Helbig, 2013: 13). Technological leaps have led to paradigm shifts which afterwards named "industrial revolutions" (Lasi, Fettke, Kemper, Feld & Hoffman, 2014: 239). Productivity increase lies beneath every industrial revolution. The first three industrial revolutions spanned almost 200 years and had changed processes in industries, lead to increase in productivity and efficiency through disruptive innovations (Drath & Horch, 2014: 56; Pereira & Romero, 2017: 1207).

The first industrial revolution was triggered in the 18th century in England by the steam engine and mechanization of textile manufacturing (Garten, 2016: 3; Geissbauer et al., 2016a). This changed the focus of human from agriculture to the industry (Yin, Stecke & Li, 2018: 848). Extreme increase in productivity was provided by the shift of fabric production from private homes to central factories (Drath & Horch, 2014: 56). The main aim was to increase production volume, variety of products was low, mostly agricultural (Yin et al., 2018: 848).

The second industrial revolution took off in early 20th century in America with the intense use of electrical energy and innovations such as division of labor, assembly line and mass production (Garten,

2016: 3; Kagermann et al., 2013: 13; Lasi et al., 2014: 239). The production style shifted from craft production with multi-skilled qualified labor producing low volume to production lines with unqualified labor producing high volume of products, this led to productivity increase (Drath & Horch, 2014: 56). In parallel with the increasing demand, various technologies have been developed in the industry and mechanization (Pereira & Romero, 2017: 1207). Electricity, electronic and mechanical devices and cars were the featured innovations. Products of second industrial revolution are still find use in daily life and industry. Frederick Taylor, Henry Ford and Taichi Ohno are the remarkable innovators of second industrial revolution. Taylor published The Principles of Scientific Management, Ford bring assembly line and mass production to life and Ohno contributed in terms of product variety and waste elimination by developing Toyota Production System which lately called lean production (Yin et al., 2018: 848).

After World War II the invention of integrated circuit (microchip) and programmable logic controller (PLC) has triggered the third industrial revolution (Drath & Horch, 2014: 56; Geissbauer et al., 2016a; Pereira & Romero, 2017: 1207). Programmable controllers lead to automation systems to become highly flexible and efficient (Drath & Horch, 2014: 56). Electronics and information technology carried automation to an advanced stage and lead industrialization to become prevalent (Pereira & Romero, 2017: 1207). The main technological shift from analogue to digital in the third industrial revolution had big impact on the electronics industry in particular (Yin et al., 2018: 849).

A new paradigm shift in industry is beginning as a consequence of digitalization of factories, smart equipment and environment of future oriented internet technologies. Mass customization will be realized through modular and efficient manufacturing systems where the products can control their own manufacturing processes. Individualized products will be produced one by one with low cost. By this future expectation, the term fourth industrial revolution or Industry 4.0 was established (Lasi et al., 2014: 239). Industry 3.0 focused on the automation of single machines and processes, Industry 4.0 focuses on the end-to-end digitization of all physical assets and integration into digital ecosystems with the entire supply chain (Geissbauer, Vedso & Schrauf, 2016b). Technological innovations such as internet of things (IoT), big data, electric vehicles (EV), 3D printing, cloud computing, artificial intelligence and cyber-physical systems enables Industry 4.0. There is uncertainty about the effects of the revolution resulting from these technological developments, so researchers, institutes and governments concentrate on Industry 4.0 (Yin et al., 2018: 849). It is remarkable that fourth industrial revolution is announced before it happens (Drath & Horch, 2014: 56).

Industry 4.0 Concept

An agreed definition of Industry 4.0 is not found in the literature. One segment argues that this revolution will radically change existing industries, while another argues that it has been a combination of known and applied technologies and concepts. On the other hand, there is a risk that industry 4.0 would be a management fashion mentioned in the speeches of public managers (Hofmann & Rüsch, 2017: 32). The term "Industry 4.0" stands for the fourth industrial revolution. Other related terms used for similar meaning are Industrial Internet, Digital Factory, Smart Factory, Smart Industry, Advanced Manufacturing or Industrial Internet of Things (IIoT) (Geissbauer et al., 2016b; Tjahjono, Esplugues, Ares & Pelaez, 2017: 1176).

The fourth industrial revolution is possible through decentralized production processes and communication between people, machines and resources. In Industry 4.0 smart products can follow their production history, status, instruct machines about necessary tasks and transport themselves via conveyors or automated guided vehicles (Hermann, Pentek & Otto, 2016: 3929). Industry 4.0 uses a real-time network of products, processes, and infrastructure, where procurement, production, maintenance, delivery and customer service are all connected over the Internet. That is a new era in management of entire supply chain along the lifecycle of product which is directed to customization and involves all stages (Kagermann, Anderl, Gausemeier, Schuh & Wahlster, 2016: 5).

Industry 4.0 defined as;

a global transformation of the manufacturing industry by the introduction of digitalization and the Internet, these transformations consider revolutionary improvements in the design and manufacturing processes, operations and services of manufacturing products and systems (Tjahjono et al., 2017: 1176); products and services are flexibly connected via the internet or other network applications; the digital connectivity enables an automated and self-optimized production of goods and services including the delivering without human interventions; the value networks are controlled decentralized while system elements are making autonomous decisions (Hofmann & Rüsch, 2017: 25); a shift in the manufacturing logic towards an increasingly decentralized, self-regulating approach of value creation, enabled by concepts and technologies such as Cyber-Physical Systems, Internet of Things, Internet of Services, cloud computing, additive manufacturing and smart factories, so as to help companies meet future production requirements. (Hofmann & Rüsch, 2017: 33)

Hermann et al. (2016) identifies four design principles about Industry 4.0; i) interconnection (connection of machines, sensors, people over IoT), ii) information transparency (a virtual copy of physical world), iii) decentralized decisions (utilizing local and global information for better decision making) and iv) technical assistance (shifting role of humans).

Effects of Industry 4.0

The positive effects of Industry 4.0 can be summarized as follows (Barreto, Amaral & Pereira, 2017: 1247; Geissbauer et al., 2016b; Hermann et al., 2016: 3928; Hofmann & Rüsch, 2017: 23; Kagermann et al., 2013: 15-6; Thames & Schaefer, 2016: 13; Tjahjono et al., 2017: 1176; Witkowski, 2017: 769):

- Achieving operational efficiency and productivity
- Rise in the level of digitization
- New business models, services and products
- Smart systems that have autonomous properties like self-planning, self-monitoring, predictive and autonomous maintenance
- Connection between machines, human-machine collaboration and symbiotic production
- Personalized products, mass customization, highly flexible mass production
- Real time visibility, coordination and optimization of production systems and supply chains
- Cost reduction
- Big data analytics; gathering, analysis and utilization of data for decision making
- Shortened production cycles

On the other hand, some challenges with implementing Industry 4.0 are mentioned as lack of standardization between different constituents, lack of digital culture for building digital operations, operational disruption and damage to company reputation due to cybersecurity breaches (Geissbauer et al., 2016b; Kagermann et al., 2013: 25).

Driving Forces Behind Industry 4.0

Industry 4.0 is driven by digitization of vertical and horizontal value chains, products and service offerings, business models and customer access. Maturing technologies behind Industry 4.0 thought separately, however when they are used together, physical and virtual worlds are integrated (Geissbauer et al., 2016b).

The technologies, concepts and driving forces that make Industry 4.0 possible are Cyber-Physical Systems, Vertical and Horizontal Integration, Augmented Reality, Sensors, Internet of Things, Robotics, Cloud Computing, Artificial Intelligence, Additive manufacturing and 3D Printers, Autonomous vehicles (cars, trucks, ships, drones), Big Data and Analytics, Mobile devices and Wearables (smart watches, glasses, gloves), Cybersecurity and Distributed ledger systems (blockchain). Some of these are explained briefly below.

Cyber-Physical Systems (CPS)

Cyber-Physical Systems (CPS) are network of interconnected systems with physical assets and computational capabilities. CPS consists of two components: (1) the advanced connectivity that ensures real-time data collection from the physical world and information feedback from the cyber space; and (2) intelligent data management, analytics and computational capability that constructs the cyber space (Lee, Bagheri & Kao, 2015: 18). Industry 4.0 with CPS bring the physical and the virtual world together. Physical shop floor and the virtual computational space related information in manufacturing are highly synchronized allowing control, supervision, transparency and efficiency (Hofmann & Rüsch, 2017: 24-5).

Embedded software-intensive systems and global networks merge into CPS. Micro computers are embedded in a great number of devices and objects, in this way they can gather information from physical world using sensors and communicate with other devices. While millions of people use mobile devices, such as smartphones, RFID (Radio Frequency Identification) technology monitors billions of processes (Geisberger et al., 2011: 11).

Vertical and Horizontal Integration

The horizontal integration between companies and the vertical integration of a production inside a factory are two basic elements for integration across processes because supply chains involves several stages performed by different companies (Barreto et al., 2017: 1247). While vertical integration is integration of different hierarchical levels inside a factory, horizontal integration is the integration of companies across the supply chain. While vertical integration involves information and physical systems for flexibility of manufacturing, horizontal integration involves materials, energy and information exchange between different companies. The goal of the horizontal and vertical integration is to deliver an end-to-end solution which refers to the digital integration of engineering from the raw material acquisition to manufacturing product, and product in use and in the end of life (Duarte & Cruz-Machado, 2017: 1244).

Smart Factory

Smart factories in the future will find place in decentralized and digitalized production networks that autonomously control their operations (Erol, Jager, Hold, Ott & Sihn, 2016: 14). In smart factory connection and information exchange among all manufacturing resources such as machines, robots, conveyors, sensors will be realized as naturally as in a social network (Kagermann et al., 2013: 19); planning and control of production, product design are closely connected, controlled interdependently and commanded by a decentralized system (Qin, Liu & Yin, 2016: 174). Highly flexible smart factory will be able to produce customized products in small lots and profitable at the same time (Wang, Wan, Li & Zhang, 2016: 1). Smart grids supply energy to smart factories, smart logistics accomplish material flow between parties (Stock & Seliger, 2016: 538). Manufacturing structure will not be fixed in smart factories, but a specific structure automatically built for each condition (Kagermann et al., 2013: 32).

Simulation

Simulation is a key technology for smart factory concept. Different simulation types may be applied to enhance product and process on various levels. 3D-simulation for CNC machines and robotic workcells enables to detect collisions, analyze material removal, optimize cycle times, perform reachability checks (Kühn, 2006: 1899, 1902). Simulation is widely used as operational and strategic planning instrument and helps reducing costs, shorten development cycles and increase the quality of products Models that are only available to experts are replaced by models that can be easily connected to various data sources and locations and easily controlled and modified. The trend is shifting from analytical and optimization-oriented models to simulation models integrated into decision support systems that can be used repetitively. In Industry 4.0 era complex systems will be modeled and simulated automatically as virtual factory or digital twin for self-organization or autonomous adjustment (Rodic, 2017: 193-6).

Augmented Reality (AR)

The basic Augmented Reality (AR) technology is simple. The view of the person is recorded with a mini camera, the images are transferred and processed by a wearable pc running the AR system. The AR identifies the marker position and draws the additional information with correct perspective onto the image (Mueck, Höwer, Franke & Dangelmaier, 2005: 1054). The use of AR becomes more prevalent in daily life by its potential to combine real world environment with visuals. AR may be applied to all activities to augment real world environment with virtual information for enriching human senses and abilities. A simple example for AR is to display relevant statistics on the TV screen while a TV channel broadcasting sports program (Cirulis & Ginters, 2013: 17).

Internet of Things (IoT)

Internet of Things (IoT) phrase is claimed to be used first time in 1999. Most of the data on Internet used to be created by humans. The problem is the limited time, attention and accuracy of people. But things (devices, machines, robots, vehicles, elevators, refrigerators, air conditioners …, anything) can capture data more accurately and 7/24 (Ashton, 2009). The number of devices connected to the network exceeded the number of inhabitants of the globe in 2009 which was the true birth of IoT (Witkowski,

2017: 766). The IoT is expected to open up numerous economic opportunities and can be considered one of the most promising technologies with a huge disruptive potential (Hofmann & Rüsch, 2017: 25). RFID, sensors and NFC (Near Field Communication) are the main technologies used for collecting data in IoT (Borgia, 2014: 6). Main application areas of IoT are; environmental, infrastructure, industrial, energy systems, healthcare systems and logistics systems (Şekelli & Bakan, 2018: 22). The integration of business processes and IoT data also has many challenges such as distributed data source, lack of architecture design methods, diverse software modules. Without a proper modeling and design, IoT applications may encounter potential problems (Tu, Lim & Yang, 2018a: 68).

Internet of Services (IoS)

Starting from the idea of making services easily available through web and mobile technologies, Internet of Services (IoS) is emerging that allows companies and private users to combine, create and deliver new types of services. Concepts such as service-oriented architecture (SOA), software as a service (SaaS) or business process outsourcing (BPO) are closely related to the IoS (Hofmann & Rüsch, 2017: 25). IoS will bring new opportunities to the service industry as it provides the business and technical foundation for building business networks between service providers and customers. This concept follows a similar approach to IoT but applies to services rather than physical assets (Pereira & Romero, 2017: 1212).

Additive Manufacturing (AM) / 3D Printers (3DP)

Due to the necessity for mass customization in Industry 4.0, there is a need to develop non-traditional manufacturing methods. Additive Manufacturing (AM) or 3-Dimensional Printing (3DP) may become a key technology for manufacturing customized products due to its ability to create complex objects with advanced attributes. AM is currently used in a variety of industries including aerospace, biomedical and manufacturing. Although there is still some doubt about the applicability in mass production, industrial use of AM is increasing due to new technological advances. A large number of plastic/polymer materials, many metallic components aluminum, titanium, stainless steel, etc. can be used as material for AM. 3D printing may offer a simple way of instant robotic fabrication and ready-to-use functional systems. AM enables electronic circuitry to be built into the printed object. These advancements eliminate the need for an assembly operation. Moreover, AM finds application areas in construction, textile and food industries (Dilberoglu, Gharehpapagh, Yaman & Dolen, 2017: 546-9).

Big Data Analytics (BDA)

With the prevalent usage of internet by people and devices, large amount of data is produced. The data amount is over the capacity of conventional analysis methods. Big Data involves data which has been collected in various different formats, from databases, websites. Big Data consists of four dimensions: volume, variety, velocity and value (Witkowski, 2017: 767-8). Large amounts of data overwhelm managers and hinder the extraction of valuable insights. The main challenge is increasingly shifting from collection, storage and analysis of data toward the extraction of valuable insights for decision-making (Roßmann, Canzaniello, von der Gracht & Hartmann, 2018: 135-6).

Cloud Computing (CC)

Cloud Computing (CC) provides an optional, scalable network access to a pool of configurable computing resources. CC has almost unlimited capabilities in terms of storage and processing power. CC and IoT can be isolated from the limitations, heterogeneity, connectivity, identification and security of the respective devices. There are different types of categories in CC: IaaS (Infrastructure as a Service) which is the lowest layer and offers a pool of virtual machines for computing and storage, PaaS (Platform as a Service) is the middle layer which allows deploying applications and SaaS (Software as a Service) the top layer that offers accessible user applications (Diaz, Martin & Rubio, 2016: 99).

Cybersecurity

Traditional security methods against external attacks used to be physical such as access restrictions. In CPS-based manufacturing systems positioning the security at a later point is not sufficient. Real-time and high-volume data and information is transferred between the system components. Cybersecurity refers to the protection of data and services in digital systems against misuse, e.g. unauthorized access, modification or destruction. The goals of security measures are to increase confidentiality, integrity and availability (Kagermann et al., 2013: 46-7). Generally sensitive information is collected by IoT devices that must be secured from unauthorized access. If the data is stored in the cloud, the privacy and security concerns become more important. When the data is outsourced to the cloud the primary concern is loss of control over data (Henze et al., 2016: 703).

SUPPLY CHAIN MANAGEMENT IN INDUSTRY 4.0 ERA

A Supply Chain (SC) consists of suppliers, manufacturers, transporters, warehouses, retailers and customers to fulfill requests of customer. Supply Chain Management (SCM) involves the management of supply chain assets and flow of product, information and fund to maximize total supply chain profitability (Chopra & Meindl, 2007: 3, 6). It is crucial for suppliers, manufacturers and retailers to have the right good with the right quantity and right quality at the right time at the right place and in the right condition and at right price (7R), otherwise they cannot be competitive (Wang, 2016: 68). Traditional supply chains are becoming more costly and complex. For efficient supply chain management information and communication technologies (ICT) play an important role. Information and communication technologies integrate different processes, suppliers and customers internally and externally for improving supply chain performance (Abdel-Basset, Manogaran & Mohamed, 2018: 615). There is a shift from traditional supply chains to open supply network. Aspects such as flexibility, adaptability, proactivity and self-organization gain importance and can only be achieved by integration of new smart technologies to the supply chains (Wang, 2016: 68).

Industry 4.0 is strongly associated with smart products, internet platforms and the new business models (Kagermann et al., 2016: 5). Not only smart factory and smart product were defined in this new industrialized era. Other concepts defined as smart are; smart manufacturing, smart logistics, smart engineering, smart data, smart machine, smart planner, smart operator, smart customer, smart supplier, smart grid, smart energy (Duarte & Cruz-Machado, 2017: 1245).

Industry 4.0 principles and technologies are primarily considered for manufacturing; however, they can be applied to the entire supply chain (Ghadimi, Wang, Lim & Heavey, 2019: 589). Industry 4.0 describes a vision for future of the supply chains. Those applying Industry 4.0 principles and technologies to supply chain will gain competitive advantage (Duarte & Cruz-Machado, 2017: 1250-1). Industry 4.0 and supply chain 4.0 are the results of better performance desire (Dossou, 2018: 452). Traditional supply chain and digital supply chain in Industry 4.0 era differs in terms of transparency, communication, collaboration, flexibility and responsiveness (Schrauf & Berttram, 2016: 10).

To define and distinguish the new logistics and supply chain in Industry 4.0 era, Logistics 4.0 or Supply Chain 4.0 concepts are used. The aim of Logistics 4.0 is to keep away from inaccuracies and to speed up processes where the information can be shared in real time (Baretto et al., 2017: 1246).

Logistics has undergone revolutionary changes similar with industrial revolutions. The first innovation (Logistics 1.0) is caused by "mechanization of transport" from the late 19th century and early 20th century. The second innovation (Logistics 2.0) is driven by "automation of handling system" from the 1960s. The third innovation (Logistics 3.0) is represented by "the system of logistics management" from the 1980s. Now the fourth innovation of logistics, called Logistics 4.0 is beginning (Wang, 2016: 69). Logistics 4.0 refers to the combination of using logistics with the innovations and applications added by CPS (Barreto et al., 2017: 1248). What is industry 4.0 to manufacturing, that is Logistics 4.0 to supply chains (Yılmaz & Duman, 2019: 190). Logistics 4.0 definition combines two aspects: processual (supply chain processes are a subject of the Logistics 4.0 actions) and technical (tools and technologies that support internal processes in the supply chains) (Szymanska, Adamczak & Cyplik, 2017: 303).

How Supply Chain Processes Will Be Affected

In this section the effects of Industry 4.0 and driving forces on logistics and supply chains in general and particularly processes of logistics and supply chain is examined in the light of related literature.

Wang (2016) examines Logistics 4.0 in a theoretical manner. Barreto et al. (2017) examined the required significant dimensions for implementing Logistics 4.0 with an Industry 4.0 point of view. Duarte & Cruz-Machado (2017) examined Industry 4.0 paradigm in terms of lean and green supply chain. Szymanska et al. (2017) claim that Logistics 4.0 is not a new method, set of tool or paradigm but a connection of known technical, technological and organizing solutions. Abdel-Basset et al. (2018) suggested an IoT based supply chain management model for automation, identification, tracing and tracking products, transparency, cost reduction and customer satisfaction. Dossou (2018) examined the Industry 4.0 and supply chain implementation in SME's especially in metallurgy sector considering sustainability. It is told that big companies have no problem for implementing Industry 4.0 and supply chain 4.0 concepts and tools, however it is more difficult for SMEs. Large companies may invest in new technologies towards Industry 4.0 and Supply Chain 4.0. Göçmen & Erol (2018) examined the transition of a logistics company to Industry 4.0 in terms of transportation, warehousing, loading/unloading and information service units. Kaur & Singh (2018) proposed a sustainable procurement and logistics model for a supply chain using big data. Öztemel & Gürsev (2018) examined the impact of opportunities and innovations that Industry 4.0 caused on logistics management. By conducting a survey on logistic firms, it has been found that while technologies like IoT, robotics, data mining, warehouse automation systems are used by logistics firms, CPS, 3DP and other technologies are not effectively used. Roßmann et al. (2018) examined the effect of big data analytics on supply chain management with Delphi method. They suggest that big data analytics will improve demand forecasts, reduce safety stocks and improve the management of supplier performance. Tu et al (2018a, 2018b) proposed IoT system modeling approach and IoT-based cyber-physical system for production logistics and supply chain in their two-part study. Büyüközkan & Güler (2019) tried to determine which technologies have most effect on expectations of firms. For this purpose, they grouped and weighted firms' expectations from technologies within Logistics 4.0 as strategic, tactical and operational. Big data was found to be the most important technology to affect expectations. Internet of things is second and bionic reinforcement is third. Ghadimi et al. (2019) proposed a multi-agent system approach for sustainable supplier evaluation and selection process within Industry 4.0 supply chains. They implemented the system on a medical device manufacturer. Karunarathna, Wickramarachchi & Vidanagamachchi et al. (2019) analyzed the effects of logistics 4.0 on future warehousing in Sri Lanka. Yılmaz & Duman (2019) examined the effects of Industry 4.0 on logistics in a theoretical manner.

Industry 4.0 has started to shape the future of the logistics sector with the applications of Logistics 4.0 (Büyüközkan & Güler, 2019: 22). Understanding and analyzing the effects of Industry 4.0 on the entire supply chain is crucial, therefore collaboration and integration among suppliers, producers and customers is necessary from the beginning to the end (Tjahjono et al., 2017: 1176). Vertical and Horizontal Integration is the concept of Industry 4.0 which totally intersects with SCM. Vertical and Horizontal Integration is the integration of the hierarchical levels within the companies and companies in the supply chain, that means integration of the supply chain. Products, logistic operations, machines and devices used in manufacturing generate data and information used for the integration of physical and digital world (de Man & Strandhagen, 2017: 725). For reducing cost and increasing quality of product companies have to use new technologies and integrate with the supply chain (Dossou, 2018: 452). Companies in the supply chain and logistics sector need to train their current and future workforce and increase their capabilities in order to remain competitive due to the tendency of transferring repetitive and tough jobs to robots and automation, robots and people working together (DHL, 2018: 16)

Digitization makes services more valuable, accessible and affordable and has the potential to transform supply chain. A new paradigm is necessary for digital technologies to give rise to new possibilities in the supply chain. Companies must be aware that supply chain is not just about physical flow, but also ability, information and funds (Accenture, 2014: 2).

Industry 4.0 will change and improve traditional logistics. The key point is besides low-cost small batch production and high diversity of products; transparency between supplier and customer, process network and decentralized decisions. The market is offering sort of single technical solutions as a component of digital supply chain. Complete connection of the technical solutions along the entire supply chain is necessary (Wang, 2016: 68). Whole supply chain will be smart, transparent and efficient through digital transformation and intelligent systems (Barreto et al., 2017:1251).

Cyber-Physical Systems provide more flexible production, distinguished management and control possibilities of processes (Kagermann et al., 2013: 14). RFID is the digital identity and IoT is the Internet access of objects. Thanks to these technologies real-time visibility of products throughout the supply chain is realized. RFID and IoT greatly shape the evolution of production logistics in manufacturing and supply chain (Tu et al., 2018a: 65-6). Applying IoT in SCM will make it smarter and the impacts will be; 1) enhanced management of inventory, 2) real time supply chain management and 3) maximize transparency of logistics (Abdel-Basset et al., 2018: 616). Every process of supply chain such as purchasing, production, transportation, storage, sales, returns and after-sales service can be monitored real-time with RFID and NFC (Atzori, Iera & Morabito, 2010: 2793-4).

Big data analytics (BDA) finds application areas in operations optimization of supply chains (Kaur & Singh, 2018: 302). BDA applications makes supply chain operations more certain. Analysis of big data lead to more accurate demand forecasting, lower level of inventory, improved supplier management, automated operational tasks and decisions (Roßmann et al., 2018: 145).

Cloud computing is a key enabler for BDA. Cloud based digital supply networks have the advantages of being connected, intelligent, scalable and rapid. However, two categories of supply chain processes may be unsuitable for cloud computing: 1) Complex and unique processes requiring heavy degree of customized processing, 2) Processes requiring ultrafast response time (Accenture, 2014: 2, 4, 7).

With the expansion of supply chain management applications, four main component of supply chain appears: Software as a Service (SaaS) for Supply Chain Planning, Procurement, Manufacturing and Logistics (Accenture, 2014: 7). Each of the supply chain processes is being restructured with technological innovations triggering Industry 4.0 (Büyüközkan & Güler, 2019: 22). Supply chain processes may be divided into five categories. Buy process (procurement), make process (production), store process (warehousing), move process (transportation) and sell process (fulfillment) (Tjahjono et al., 2017: 1178). The effects of Industry 4.0 and its driving forces on the processes of supply chain are examined below.

Effects on Procurement

The "buy" process or procurement function involves all the processes and tasks required to purchase goods or services from suppliers. Augmented Reality, Additive Manufacturing and 3D Printing, Cloud Computing are predicted to be opportunities on procurement process of supply chain, while Big Data Analytics, Internet of Things and RFID are predicted to be both opportunities and threats on procurement process of supply chain (Tjahjono et al., 2017: 1178, 1181).

Procurement deals with the relationships at the upstream supply chain. Purchasing from a huge number of suppliers spreaded globally means thousands of transactions which arise complex data. A part of the complex data is semi-structured such as purchase orders, shipping notices, invoices. Procurement function needs a strong data gathering and analysis infrastructure (Rozados & Tjahjono, 2014: 9). Supplier selection, which is a strategic level decision rather than operational level, requires active human decision making. However, BDA may help decision making easier while managing too many suppliers. Flows of material and information are integrated across the supply chain in Industry 4.0. Due to real-time information shared with relevant members in the supply chain, suppliers obtain information and plan their production and inventory levels when a product is purchased in the supply chain. In this way bullwhip-effect may be avoided and low levels of inventory may be provided (Hofmann & Rüsch, 2017: 28, 32).

Procurement function will transform in the era of Industry 4.0 supply chains. As Industry 4.0 becomes prevalent companies will need to buy sensors, electronic components and software while purchasing raw materials and parts for production. This will change the structure of purchasing (Schrauf & Berttram, 2016: 19-21).

Effects on Production

The "make" process or production function involves production of goods or services. Production is the operations necessary to transform inputs into outputs. Inputs are raw materials, parts, resources, energy, labor, technology and information while outputs are goods or services that customers get from the company (Tjahjono et al., 2017: 1178).

Movement of goods inside the factory has been automated with autonomous forklifts, automated guided vehicles and robots (Wang, 2016: 69). Products are easily identifiable and traceable in smart factory. Since material flows can be tracked in real time and in a continuous fashion, production planning may be more accurate and even become unnecessary in deterministic environment in Industry 4.0. Customers' demand is increasing for customized products and services, but they are unwilling to pay more and wait long. This trend resulted in "batch size one" production. Producers locate production nearby customers for lower lead times (DHL, 2018: 16). Industry 4.0, paradigm gains additional flexibility. In Industry 4.0 processes are highly integrated, processes related with just-in-time system are planned and executed in an integrated manner across the supply chain. Flow of materials inbound and outbound can be traced accurately and real time with the use of CPS and automatic identification systems. Due to high integration level and shared information between suppliers and buyers, demand-oriented cross-company kanban systems will result in shortened cycle times (Hofmann & Rüsch, 2017: 25-31).

Production logistics involves manufacturing activities and logistics activities of companies in the supply chain. The activities in production logistics are sustained by various resources, involving CNC machines, robots, conveyors, operators, and all kinds of sensors. For supporting production logistics IoT, cloud and other information and communication technologies are integrated with CPS. Physical and cyber worlds are integrated, machines and information systems are collaborated for a common goal, all information between physical shop floor and virtual systems in the factory is monitored and coordinated by CPS (Tu et al., 2018b: 97-8).

Effects on Warehousing

The store process or warehousing operations, especially inventory management, have improved in the last few decades due to the short life cycles of products and demand uncertainties. Augmented Reality, Additive Manufacturing and 3D Printing, Cloud Computing, Internet of Things, RFID are predicted to be opportunities on warehousing process of supply chain, while Big Data Analytics is predicted to be both opportunity and threat on warehousing process of supply chain (Tjahjono et al., 2017: 1178, 1181).

Warehousing has been an important part of supply chains. The role of warehouse is changing since customer satisfaction and supply chain visibility are gaining significance. Market competition and changing customer demands makes meeting the requirements difficult with the traditional warehouse management. For eliminating the handicaps of traditional warehouse system, Industry 4.0 has been changing in the whole world in terms of warehousing, smart logistics and smart warehouse concepts (Karunarathna et al., 2019: 1024).

Modern identification systems like RFID changed inventory and warehouse management. Technological development in the field of material handling and packaging in terms of connectivity and intelligence through Internet of Things and sensors have been observed in recent years. Sensors are used for determining the stock presence on-shelf together with traditionally stock keeping unit levels and bill of materials (Rozados & Tjahjono, 2014: 10). RFID can be used for managing warehouses efficiently and reducing inventory inaccuracies. The entire lifecycle of objects can be tracked too. While the production process can be monitored by RFID readers located along a production line in a plant, the label can be traced all along the supply chain. Retailers and manufacturers may reduce material waste, lower cost and increase profit by advanced IoT systems which consists of items with RFID and smart shelves tracking. Products which must be stored in particular conditions like food and liquids, sensors continuously monitor temperature and humidity inside storage area and real time analysis identify deterioration (Borgia, 2014: 8).

Warehouse activities will be transformed into the future requirements of the inbound logistics according to the Industry 4.0 paradigm. Intelligent warehouse management system will assign an available docking slot for the transports on the way upon their notifications. At the same time, RFID sensors identify delivered items and send data to entire supply chain about traceability. Storage space is prepared and assigned for the specifications of delivered items automatically and appropriate equipment moves the items autonomously. As the items are moved to the location assigned, RFID tags send real time data to warehouse management system, in this way out-of-stock situations are prevented and desired service level is provided (Barreto et al., 2017:1249). Another technology that can be used for locating pallets of merchandise in a warehouse in real time is Real-time locating systems (RTLS) (Wang, 2016: 70).

One of the important tasks in warehousing and logistics is order picking. Augmented Reality (AR) can be used to avoid worker errors and decrease object pickup time in human operated warehouses (Cirulis & Ginters, 2013: 19). Improvement in workflow and efficiency of order picking in consequence of AR-based order picking is reported with test results. AR can be extremely useful as a support system for order picking to minimize the human errors and can be used at stock receipt, picking, shipping and handling, inventory processes in a warehouse (Mueck et al., 2005: 1053-6).

Industry 4.0 will provide mass customization, customized products with mass production prices. The warehouses expense can be minimized or might abolish as a result of simultaneously processing orders of customers and orders to the suppliers (Wang, 2016: 69).

Effects on Transportation

The "move" process or transportation function is liable for on-time delivery and transportation of inventories from one place to another. Augmented Reality, Additive Manufacturing and 3D Printing, Big Data Analytics, Internet of Things, RFID are predicted to be opportunities on transportation process of supply chain, while Cloud Computing is predicted to be both opportunity and threat on transportation process of supply chain (Tjahjono et al., 2017: 1178, 1181).

Industry 4.0 will change information flow fundamentally and this will have impact on the entire delivery process of supply chain (Schuh, Anderl, Gausemeier, ten Hompel & Wahlster, 2017: 39). Transportation vehicles, which have Global Positioning System (GPS) or Real Time Location System (RTLS) in order to location its position in real-time are able to be traced by the customers and suppliers (Wang, 2016: 69).

Autonomous vehicles interact with other transport units for autonomously performing vehicle and order management. Logistics platforms are used to select the best located alternative among many others to perform a given operation, instead of allocating to a person or vehicle. The selection criteria such as current location, earliest delivery time and cost are used. Last mile logistics would probably be carried out by the lowest bidder on request (Schuh et al., 2017: 40). IoT offers transformation solutions for transportation systems and automobile services. IoT can be used to enhance the capabilities of sensing, networking, communication and data processing of modern vehicles, especially electrified ones. Vehicle sharing, shared logistics, route optimization, tracing existing location, monitoring movement and predicting future location is possible with IoT (Barreto et al., 2017:1250).

Materials handling and packaging are equipped with information technologies. Technical resources used in transportation such as forklifts have the capability of self-identification, location determination and collect information about self-status and status of product carried. A digital copy of the real world is established by integrated information system in which autonomous vehicles and warehousing facilities are connected. Data, monitoring and documentation that are performed real-time and automatically, used for simulation-based control and realized through the virtual model of the process elements. Current condition is checked against purposed data. In case of difference between current and purposed condition, the plan is reviewed and current process is autonomously modified. The modifications are transmitted to the relevant vehicles or to their drivers, thus they can adapt to new conditions (Schuh et al., 2017: 39-40).

As a part of supply chain management (SCM), transportation management system realizes interactions between order management system and distribution center or a warehouse. Companies can control and manage shipment expenses, accomplish communications with stakeholders and integrate further supply chain technologies such as warehouse management through transportation management system. The number of companies using transportation management system is increasing while functionalities of transportation management systems are expanding and within Logistics 4.0 real-time data is used with IoT to achieve efficient logistic process. Thanks to GPS technology a company is able to trace vehicles and monitor movement of freight. Software provider firms are moving their solutions to cloud, in this way cloud computing based transportation management is becoming the standard. As the usage of mobile devices and services are increasing, return on investment of increases and small to mid-sized companies are adopting transportation management increases. With the increasing number of physical objects with bar codes, RFID tags or sensors, IoT will play an important role for real-time traceability of objects across the entire supply chain involving manufacturing, shipping and distribution in transportation and logistics. Transportation management systems become smart with the use of IoT devices, so supply chain management will be more flexible and efficient thanks to better decision making based on real-time and accurate data (Barreto et al., 2017:1249-50).

A smart transportation system maintains solutions for transportation partnership and platform. It in not only limited for vehicular traffic, but also implemented in navigation systems, air and water transport systems and rail systems. Electronic Toll Collection, Highway Data Collection, Traffic Management Systems, Vehicle Data Collection, Transit Signal Priority, Emergency Vehicle Preemption are some applications of smart transportation system. A fully operational smart transportation system can be used for smart truck parking and delivery areas management; multimodal cargo; estimation and monitoring of carbon dioxide footprint; priority and speed recommendation; economic driving assistance etc. (Barreto et al., 2017:1250). Last mile logistics within cities will turn into electric vehicles charged with renewable energy for green logistics (DHL, 2018: 16). Operations Research models on transportation analysis uses static data and too many assumptions that the output may not be suitable for real life. New alternative methods using real-time operational data rely on real time location of inventory on the way, traffic condition-based delivery time forecasts, weather conditions, crowd-based delivery networks among sources of Big Data (Rozados & Tjahjono, 2014: 10).

Traditional transportation model is transforming by innovative advances like RFID (Cirulis & Ginters, 2013: 16). RFID is used for identification and tracking; however, it is a passive technology and updating about location is rare. With the use of IoT and CPS in logistics integrated location and status tracking in real time become possible. Same technology can also be used for connection with electromobility, route management for electrified vehicles (Geisberger et al., 2011: 15-7). Through IoT, road transport trucks can be automatically controlled to provide fuel economy by limiting the speed. It is also possible to track the travel of shipped items with IoT. Tracking and tracing become fast, precise, predictable and safe (Witkowski, 2017: 767). IoT is also used in logistics systems for vehicle tracking, infrastructure supervision, communication and information management for traffic condition control, smart parking, fleet management and road safety (Şekelli & Bakan, 2018: 22).

Besides transported items, roads are also equipped with tags and sensors. Transportation vehicles can plan and optimize their routes according to the information sent with IoT from tags and sensors. Thanks to the combination of sensor technology, IoT and CPS, accurate information of road traffic can be used for better route planning and navigation, while policy makers may use for city and road planning purposes, transportation companies may save money and energy due to better route planning. During the transportation of the perishable goods such as fruits, meat etc. very long distances and durations are taken and the conditions like temperature, humidity need to be monitored and adjusted with IoT and sensor technology to avoid unintended consequences (Atzori et al., 2010: 2793-4). Online shopping of perishable goods will lead to fresh chain for shipping one piece of item. Logistics companies will need to innovate new kind of packaging for cold chain with fast network and guaranteed delivery time (DHL, 2018: 16).

With the prevalence of 3D printing while some companies may give up production in traditional ways, others may integrate 3D printing with mass production (DHL, 2018: 18). The use of 3D printers has prevented people and institutions from being attached to a location and thus, companies will be able to produce their products in a location close to their customers with mobile production equipment. This will have a positive impact on last mile logistics. Another effect of 3D printing will be on spare parts production. Spare parts production with 3D printers will be realized in case of need and unnecessary inventory of spare parts will be prevented (Yılmaz & Duman, 2019: 197).

During transportation truck driver may be informed about traffic and weather for optimizing the route. In fully integrated supply chains, transport and delivery processes may not be planned individually but optimized across the entire supply chain. In the future, the collection and delivery could be performed by fully autonomous and self-driving trucks (Hofmann & Rüsch, 2017: 28).

Effects on Fulfillment

The "sell" process or fulfilment function provides orders are shipped and delivered within the predetermined time. Companies have competitive advantage through fulfillment function with on-time deliveries. Increased market share and customer loyalty may be achieved by accurate management of order fulfillment. Augmented Reality, Additive Manufacturing and 3D Printing, Big Data Analytics are predicted to be opportunities on fulfillment process of supply chain, while Cloud Computing, Cybersecurity, Internet of Things, RFID are predicted to be both opportunities and threats on fulfillment process of supply chain (Tjahjono et al., 2017: 1178, 1181).

Large amount of customer information is streaming up in the supply chain through marketing. If customer data is deeply analyzed by gathering from the origins involving social media, mobile applications and loyalty programs, closer relations with customer can be established. In the same way, electronic and cloud point of sale data and transactions data generated by machine can be used for documenting multichannel sales information. Supply chain managers have propensity to regard suppliers than customers, however with the developing technology and gathered big data from different channels like social media understanding customer is unchallenging. So, customer data is able to be positioned and used in supply chain management systems (Rozados & Tjahjono, 2014: 9).

CONCLUSION

Enabled by some maturated technologies in the last decades, a new industrial revolution is predicted to arise which not only affects manufacturing or industry, but many fields of life. It is named as Fourth Industrial Revolution or Industry 4.0. The triggering technologies, concepts or driving forces mentioned together with Industry 4.0 are; Cyber-Physical Systems, Vertical and Horizontal Integration, Augmented Reality, Internet of Things, Internet of Services, Additive Manufacturing and 3D Printers, Big Data Analytics, Cloud Computing, Cybersecurity. Through Industry 4.0, production activities will be made by automatic machines and robots communicating each other. Supply chains will be more integrated due to information and communication technologies based on real time data sharing.

Although the concept is named as revolution, there is still doubt whether it is a revolution or not. While some state that the combination of those technologies changes the situations dramatically, disrupting traditional business models, therefore this must be a revolution. Others oppose that all the driving forces are known and applied technologies for some time and what's going on is usual improvement in the flow of life, therefore this must be an evolution. There may be two reasons about the transformation that human being experience at the present time is not considered as a revolution. One is the difficulty about being aware of a phenomenon that spreads decades. If people sleep one night and wake up to a completely different world next day nobody can deny the experienced revolution, however if the transformation is happening within time it is ignored by majority. The transformation will be evaluated better maybe after fifty years or a century from now. And the other is that, threshold of human being increased about what is technologically possible, so the perception of revolution. Exponential development of technology is increasing the expectations of majority.

In this study the effects of Industry 4.0 on supply chain management are examined. For this purpose, literature is reviewed according to effects of Industry 4.0 on procurement, production, warehousing, transportation and fulfillment functions of supply chain management. It will be better to examine the effects of Industry 4.0 on the supply chain related functions of firms with an empirical research it the future.

To summarize, technologies such as IoT, RFID, sensors enables information to flow accurate and real-time. This helps supply chain to be more integrated and transparent. The huge data generated by sensors and RFID is processed through big data analytics and well-directed decision can be made in this way. Augmented reality is used for order picking, autonomous vehicles inside warehouses such as forklift is used for moving objects. RFID and IoT is used for tracing products, sensors and IoT is used for information flow about weather and traffic condition; autonomous vehicles, shared logistics and logistic platforms will be used in transportation process. Additive manufacturing and 3D printing provide location-independent production and eliminates need for inventory of spare parts. It is clear that Industry 4.0 technologies will have a great impact on integrating supply chain. However, with the increasing integration and automation of supply chain processes, most decisions will be made autonomously, and this will gradually decrease the importance of management in the supply chain.

Lastly, even recent studies and their forecasts may become outdated while this paper is being written because of the exponential improvement of new technologies. Maybe this is the best proof that an industrial revolution is being lived.

REFERENCES

Abdel-Basset, M., Manogaran, G., & Mohamed, M. (2018). Internet of Things (IoT) and its impact on supply chain: A framework for building smart, secure and efficient systems. *Future Generation Computer Systems*, *86*, 614–628. doi:10.1016/j.future.2018.04.051

Accenture. (2014). *Supply Chain Management in the Cloud.* Author.

Ashton, K. (2009). That 'internet of things' thing. *RFID Journal, 22*(7), 97-114.

Atzori, L., Iera, A., & Morabito, G. (2010). The internet of things: A survey. *Computer Networks*, *54*(15), 2787–2805. doi:10.1016/j.comnet.2010.05.010

Barreto, L., Amaral, A., & Pereira, T. (2017). Industry 4.0 implications in logistics: An overview. *Procedia Manufacturing*, *13*, 1245–1252. doi:10.1016/j.promfg.2017.09.045

Borgia, E. (2014). The Internet of Things vision: Key features, applications and open issues. *Computer Communications*, *54*, 1–31. doi:10.1016/j.comcom.2014.09.008

Büyüközkan, G., & Güler, M. (2019). Lojistik 4.0 Teknolojilerinin Analizi İçin Metodolojik Yaklaşım. *Girişimcilik ve İnovasyon Yönetimi Dergisi*, *8*(1), 21–47.

Chopra, S., & Meindl, P. (2007). *Supply chain management. Strategy, planning & operation* (3rd ed.). Pearson. doi:10.1007/978-3-8349-9320-5_22

Cirulis, A., & Ginters, E. (2013). Augmented reality in logistics. *Procedia Computer Science*, *26*, 14–20. doi:10.1016/j.procs.2013.12.003

de Man, J. C., & Strandhagen, J. O. (2017). An Industry 4.0 research agenda for sustainable business models. *Procedia Cirp*, *63*, 721–726. doi:10.1016/j.procir.2017.03.315

DHL. (2018). *Logistics trend radar–delivering insight today. Creating value tomorrow*. DHL Trend Research Report.

Díaz, M., Martín, C., & Rubio, B. (2016). State-of-the-art, challenges, and open issues in the integration of Internet of things and cloud computing. *Journal of Network and Computer Applications*, *67*, 99–117. doi:10.1016/j.jnca.2016.01.010

Dilberoglu, U. M., Gharehpapagh, B., Yaman, U., & Dolen, M. (2017). The role of additive manufacturing in the era of industry 4.0. *Procedia Manufacturing*, *11*, 545–554. doi:10.1016/j.promfg.2017.07.148

Dossou, P. E. (2018). Impact of Sustainability on the supply chain 4.0 performance. *Procedia Manufacturing*, *17*, 452–459. doi:10.1016/j.promfg.2018.10.069

Drath, R., & Horch, A. (2014). Industrie 4.0: Hit or hype? *IEEE Industrial Electronics Magazine*, *8*(2), 56–58. doi:10.1109/MIE.2014.2312079

Duarte, S., & Cruz-Machado, V. (2017, July). Exploring linkages between lean and green supply chain and the industry 4.0. In *International conference on management science and engineering management* (pp. 1242-1252). Springer.

Erol, S., Jäger, A., Hold, P., Ott, K., & Sihn, W. (2016). Tangible Industry 4.0: A scenario-based approach to learning for the future of production. *Procedia CiRp*, *54*, 13–18. doi:10.1016/j.procir.2016.03.162

Garten, J. E. (2016). The man who made the computer age possible. *Strategy and Business*. Retrieved from https://www.strategy-business.com/article/The-Man-Who-Made-the-Computer-Age-Possible

Geisberger, E., Cengarle, M., Keil, P., Niehaus, J., Thiel, C., & Thönnißen-Fries, H. J. (2011). *Cyber-Physical Systems-Driving force for innovation in mobility, health, energy and production*. Acatech-Deutsche Akademie der Technikwissenschaften.

Geissbauer, R., Vedsø, J., & Schrauf, S. (2016a). *A strategist's guide to industry 4.0*. Strategy and Business.

Geissbauer, R., Vedso, J., & Schrauf, S. (2016b). *Industry 4.0–Building the digital enterprise (2016)*. PWC 2016 Global Industry 4.0 Survey. Retrieved from https://www.pwc.com/gx/en/industries/industries-4.0/landing-page/industry-4.0-building-your-digital-enterprise-april-2016.pdf

Ghadimi, P., Wang, C., Lim, M. K., & Heavey, C. (2019). Intelligent sustainable supplier selection using multi-agent technology: Theory and application for Industry 4.0 supply chains. *Computers & Industrial Engineering*, *127*, 588–600. doi:10.1016/j.cie.2018.10.050

Göçmen, E., & Erol, R. (2018). The Transition To Industry 4.0 In One Of The Turkish Logistics Company. *International Journal Of 3d Printing Technologies And Digital Industry, 2*(1), 76-85.

Henze, M., Hermerschmidt, L., Kerpen, D., Häußling, R., Rumpe, B., & Wehrle, K. (2016). A comprehensive approach to privacy in the cloud-based Internet of Things. *Future Generation Computer Systems*, *56*, 701–718. doi:10.1016/j.future.2015.09.016

Hermann, M., Pentek, T., & Otto, B. (2016, January). Design principles for industrie 4.0 scenarios. In *2016 49th Hawaii international conference on system sciences (HICSS)* (pp. 3928-3937). IEEE.

Hofmann, E., & Rüsch, M. (2017). Industry 4.0 and the current status as well as future prospects on logistics. *Computers in Industry*, *89*, 23–34. doi:10.1016/j.compind.2017.04.002

Kagermann, H., Anderl, R., Gausemeier, J., Schuh, G., & Wahlster, W. (Eds.). (2016). *Industrie 4.0 in a Global Context: strategies for cooperating with international partners*. Herbert Utz Verlag.

Kagermann, H., Wahlster, W., & Helbig, J. (2013). *Recommendations for implementing the strategic initiative Industrie 4.0: Final report of the Industrie 4.0 Working Group*. Berlin, Germany: Forschungsunion.

Karunarathna, N., Wickramarachchi, R., & Vidanagamachchi, K. (2019). A Study of the Implications of Logistics 4.0 in Future Warehousing: A Sri Lankan Perspective. *Proceedings of the International Conference on Industrial Engineering and Operations Management*, 1024-1035.

Kaur, H., & Singh, S. P. (2018). Heuristic modeling for sustainable procurement and logistics in a supply chain using big data. *Computers & Operations Research*, *98*, 301–321. doi:10.1016/j.cor.2017.05.008

Kühn, W. (2006, December). Digital factory-simulation enhancing the product and production engineering process. In *Proceedings of the 2006 winter simulation conference* (pp. 1899-1906). IEEE. 10.1109/WSC.2006.322972

Lasi, H., Fettke, P., Kemper, H. G., Feld, T., & Hoffmann, M. (2014). Industry 4.0. *Business & Information Systems Engineering, 6*(4), 239–242. doi:10.100712599-014-0334-4

Lee, J., Bagheri, B., & Kao, H. A. (2015). A cyber-physical systems architecture for industry 4.0-based manufacturing systems. *Manufacturing Letters, 3*, 18-23.

Mueck, B., Höwer, M., Franke, W., & Dangelmaier, W. (2005). Augmented reality applications for warehouse logistics. In *Soft Computing as Transdisciplinary Science and Technology* (pp. 1053–1062). Berlin: Springer. doi:10.1007/3-540-32391-0_108

Öztemel, E., & Gürsev, S. (2018). Türkiye'de Lojistik Yönetiminde Endüstri 4.0 Etkileri ve Yatırım İmkanlarına Bakış Üzerine Anket Uygulaması. *Marmara Fen Bilimleri Dergisi, 30*(2), 145–154.

Pereira, A. C., & Romero, F. (2017). A review of the meanings and the implications of the Industry 4.0 concept. *Procedia Manufacturing, 13*, 1206–1214. doi:10.1016/j.promfg.2017.09.032

Qin, J., Liu, Y., & Grosvenor, R. (2016). A categorical framework of manufacturing for industry 4.0 and beyond. *Procedia Cirp, 52*, 173–178. doi:10.1016/j.procir.2016.08.005

Rodič, B. (2017). Industry 4.0 and the new simulation modelling paradigm. *Organizacija, 50*(3), 193–207. doi:10.1515/orga-2017-0017

Roßmann, B., Canzaniello, A., von der Gracht, H., & Hartmann, E. (2018). The future and social impact of Big Data Analytics in Supply Chain Management: Results from a Delphi study. *Technological Forecasting and Social Change, 130*, 135–149. doi:10.1016/j.techfore.2017.10.005

Rozados, I. V., & Tjahjono, B. (2014, December). Big data analytics in supply chain management: Trends and related research. *6th International Conference on Operations and Supply Chain Management.*

Schrauf, S., & Berttram, P. (2016). *How digitization makes the supply chain more efficient, agile, and customer-focused.* Price Waterhouse Coopers Report.

Schuh, G., Anderl, R., Gausemeier, J., ten Hompel, M., & Wahlster, W. (2017). *Industrie 4.0 Maturity Index. Managing the Digital Transformation of Companies.* Munich: Herbert Utz.

Şekkeli, Z. H., & Bakan, İ. (2018). Endüstri 4.0'ın Etkisiyle Lojistik 4.0. *Journal of Life Economics, 5*(2), 17–36. doi:10.15637/jlecon.247

Stock, T., & Seliger, G. (2016). Opportunities of sustainable manufacturing in industry 4.0. *Procedia Cirp, 40*, 536–541. doi:10.1016/j.procir.2016.01.129

Szymańska, O., Adamczak, M., & Cyplik, P. (2017). Logistics 4.0-a new paradigm or set of known solutions? *Research in Logistics & Production, 7.*

Thames, L., & Schaefer, D. (2016). Software-defined cloud manufacturing for industry 4.0. *Procedia CIRP, 52*, 12-17.

Tjahjono, B., Esplugues, C., Ares, E., & Pelaez, G. (2017). What does industry 4.0 mean to supply chain? *Procedia Manufacturing, 13*, 1175–1182. doi:10.1016/j.promfg.2017.09.191

Tu, M., Lim, M. K., & Yang, M. F. (2018a). IoT-based production logistics and supply chain system–Part 1: Modeling IoT-based manufacturing supply chain. *Industrial Management & Data Systems, 118*(1), 65–95. doi:10.1108/IMDS-11-2016-0503

Tu, M. K., Lim, M., & Yang, M. F. (2018b). IoT-based production logistics and supply chain system–Part 2: IoT-based cyber-physical system: a framework and evaluation. *Industrial Management & Data Systems, 118*(1), 96–125. doi:10.1108/IMDS-11-2016-0504

Wang, K. (2016, November). Logistics 4.0 Solution-New Challenges and Opportunities. In *6th International Workshop of Advanced Manufacturing and Automation*. Atlantis Press. 10.2991/iwama-16.2016.13

Wang, S., Wan, J., Li, D., & Zhang, C. (2016). Implementing smart factory of industrie 4.0: An outlook. *International Journal of Distributed Sensor Networks, 12*(1), 3159805. doi:10.1155/2016/3159805

Witkowski, K. (2017). Internet of things, big data, industry 4.0–innovative solutions in logistics and supply chains management. *Procedia Engineering, 182*, 763–769. doi:10.1016/j.proeng.2017.03.197

Yılmaz, Ü., & Duman, B. (2019). Lojistik 4.0 Kavramına Genel Bir Bakış: Geçmişten Bugüne Gelişim ve Değişimi [An Overview of the Concept of Logistics 4.0: Development and Change from Past to Present]. *Bilecik Şeyh Edebali Üniversitesi Sosyal Bilimler Enstitüsü Dergisi, 4*(1), 186–200. doi:10.33905/bseusbed.465962

Yin, Y., Stecke, K. E., & Li, D. (2018). The evolution of production systems from Industry 2.0 through Industry 4.0. *International Journal of Production Research, 56*(1-2), 848–861. doi:10.1080/00207543.2017.1403664

ADDITIONAL READING

Bartodziej, C. J. (2017). The concept industry 4.0. In *The Concept Industry 4.0* (pp. 27–50). Wiesbaden: Springer Gabler. doi:10.1007/978-3-658-16502-4_3

Brynjolfsson, E., & McAfee, A. (2014). *The second machine age: Work, progress, and prosperity in a time of brilliant technologies*. WW Norton & Company.

Devezas, T., & Sarygulov, A. (2017). *Industry 4.0: Enterpreneurship and Structural Change in the New Dİgital Landscape*. Springer. doi:10.1007/978-3-319-49604-7

Ford, M. (2015). *Rise of the Robots: Technology and the Threat of a Jobless Future*. Basic Books.

Gilchrist, A. (2016). *Industry 4.0: the industrial internet of things*. Apress. doi:10.1007/978-1-4842-2047-4

Schwab, K. (2017). *The fourth industrial revolution*. Currency.

Toffler, A. (1980). *The third wave* (Vol. 484). New York: Bantam books.

Ustundag, A., & Cevikcan, E. (2017). *Industry 4.0: managing the digital transformation*. Springer.

KEY TERMS AND DEFINITIONS

Big Data Analytics: Extracting meaningful information from huge amount of data that is collected from various sources and types.

Cloud Computing: Usability of computing for storage or processing over internet.

Cyber-Physical Systems: The combination of digital and physical thing or software and hardware that becomes a system together for a common purpose.

Industry 4.0: The new industrial revolution that arise in the beginning of the 21st century with the maturation of some technologies.

Internet of Things (IoT): Connection of devices to internet

Supply Chain: The network like structure of companies in which all of them are customer of the preceding and supplier of the succeeding that begins with extraction of raw materials from nature and supplies products and services to end customer.

Supply Chain Integration: Acting of supply chain as a single company by sharing timely and accurate information.

Supply Chain Management: Management of material, information and money flow across the supply chain.

Chapter 9
Recycling Technologies for Sustainability

Sami Gören
Umm Al-Qura University, Saudi Arabia

ABSTRACT

Technology is improving every day in each aspect of daily life. This will help us to increase the sustainability rates and efficiency of recycling. In fact, waste generation is an indicator of economic activities by maintaining production output and also supplying many jobs. However, the treatment methods should also improve as the types and quantities of the wastes increase. There are many recycling technologies that are already serving mankind; however, the types of wastes are changing with composite materials. These types of "not only one origin" composite wastes make it difficult to recycle by the conventional methods. There are huge differences in the types of wastes discarded by different types of industries that make the situation more complicated. Conventional methods are no longer enough to treat and recycle all types of wastes. This chapter will discuss recent improvements and technologies about increasing the recycling rate without causing environmental impact.

INTRODUCTION

There has been a rapid increase in both the global population and its consumption rates. Manufacturing processes and materials have also increased. High production rates test our natural resources and destabilize sustainable development.

Waste is generated in all areas with living activity. A considerable amount of waste is being generated at a tremendous speed. Therefore, waste management and treatment are very important. It is important to establish an effective, integrated waste management process from its generation to its final disposal. This includes energy recovery.

Waste has no value to those who want to get rid of it. However, it may have significant value to another person or process. Waste classification is inevitable to preserve its value. Generation locations and materials help classify waste to increase its value and usability for other processes (Kinnaman, 2014).

DOI: 10.4018/978-1-7998-4601-7.ch009

In fact, the reduction of generated waste, or integrated waste management, is better than solid waste management. This process elaborates on the cost of waste management and treatment processes, boosting the economy by preserving natural resources and preventing environmental pollution.

Recycling, in general, is the collection and separation of waste materials, as well as its subsequent processing to produce marketable products. Recycling effectively supports the use of sustainable materials. Moreover, it has the advantage of minimizing the quantity of waste by using it as a resource, reducing the need for landfill sites (Goren, 2015).

Working to minimize the quantity of waste is supported by technologies that promote decreased energy use and consumption of raw materials. Termed "green technology," these tools aim to preserve nature. Otherwise, serious problems will appear, especially in rapidly developing nations.

Economic development, industrialization, and increasing populations are causing problems related to expanded consumption and depletion of resources (no more renewables). It also increases the output of dangerous (composite) wastes. For example, waste from manufacturing processes can become hazardous. Medical and radioactive wastes are also categorized as hazardous materials. Therefore, they should have strict controls related to generation, transportation, treatment, storage, and disposal.

There are increasing problems related to the growing volume of municipal and industrial waste. Human health and the natural environment should be protected from potential hazards of waste disposal. In fact, we should adopt the motto, "the practice of treasuring and using all things as long as possible," as our economies continue to grow. This enduring spirit has motivated the development of technology for reuse, recycling, and effective use through thermal processes for energy recovery.

Technology for efficient waste transport is also needed in dense cities. This can be achieved by settling transfer stations in specific regions. With this method, it will be more efficient to collect and transport waste.

The expansion of urban areas widens the waste collection zone. Waste transfer stations can be used to transfer waste from small- or medium-sized trucks to larger trucks. The cost of collecting and transporting garbage accounts for a high percentage of waste disposal operations. Improving the efficiency of collection and transportation leads to cost reductions while maintaining or improving services to residents.

The transfer of waste to larger trucks at transport stations improves transportation and reduces fuel consumption based on per garbage volume. This reduced both cost and carbon dioxide (CO2) emissions, contributing to the prevention of global climate change. This also reduces traffic loads, oil consumption, and risk of accidents.

Generally, loading and unloading the garbage is powered by an engine. Newer trucks use electricity to perform this task while the truck continues to run. This reduces the consumption of fuel and CO2 emissions. Compressor-type trucks press the garbage to the floor with a pressing plate. After breaking and reducing the volume of the waste, the garbage slides into a storage area. Due to global warming, low-pollution garbage trucks, including electric and hybrid trucks, are being developed and put into practical use.

Many materials can be recovered and used for recycling or energy recovery. High-resolution sensors sort at a rate of 320,000 scan points per second. Coupled with exclusive and application-specific electronics, sensors lead to congruent data collection across multiple material characteristics. This ensures precise identification of a range of materials. Both large and small objects can be scanned with accuracy. As resources become scarce, these alternatives are preferable to landfills or burning.

TYPES OF WASTE

There are several types of wastes. The classification differs according to generation location or generated material.

- Domestic waste (municipal solid waste [MSW]) = city waste
- Factory or industrial waste
- Construction waste
- Agricultural waste
- Food processing waste
- Biomedical waste
- Hazardous waste
- Nuclear waste
- Sewage solids (sludge, biosolids, etc.)

Domestic Waste

Domestic waste, or MSW, is generated by human activities. It is also referred to as city waste because of the type of collected waste. These organic wastes stem from cooking and feeding activities. Organic materials have the potential for quick decomposition by producing leachate and gas. Therefore, they should be quickly collected and removed from daily life. Decomposition continues at the transfer station or landfill area. In fact, this undesirable property of organic waste can be converted to an advantage through compost production.

Factory or Industrial Wastes

Factory (industrial) waste comes from manufacturing processes. These include excess raw materials, defective fabrics, or by-products. There is little similarity in the types of waste discarded by different industries. However, it can be assumed that industrial waste from within the same sector will produce similar wastes.

Predicting industrial waste production is more difficult than predicting residential waste. Less information is available due to independent handling or private disposal contractors.

Waste generation is a function of economic activity. It is related to production output and/or number of employees. Some industrial waste can become hazardous due to chemical operations and use. Therefore, these types of waste require special treatment and/or disposal methods. Disposal routes also differ from MSW based on the chemical composition of the waste.

Construction Waste

Construction waste is produced by the construction industry, particularly demolition waste and debris from old structures. They are inert wastes if construction steel bars are removed.

Agricultural Waste

Agricultural waste is generated by activities like irrigation, cultivation, and seed and pest control. Irrigation influence soil and water pollution by leaching chemical fertilizers and pesticides from the agricultural land. This also impacts underground water sources.

Food Processing Waste

This waste is generated through the cleaning, preparing, processing, and packing activities of food and drinks. They can also be accepted as industrial waste. However, due to their organic content, it is better to accept it as a separate category.

Biomedical Waste

Biomedical waste is generated at hospitals, clinics, medical laboratories, research institutes, etc. Also termed "clinical waste," it often refers to medical waste that cannot be considered general waste. This includes:

- Infectious (body parts, medical devices)
- Pathological (diagnostic samples, blood, chemicals, drugs)
- Cutter-driller (medical equipment, needles and syringes)
- Miscellaneous (radioactive materials)

This cannot be deposited in landfills because it contains infectious waste and body parts. Special treatment methods are required. Pretreatment methods for medical waste includes sterilization. Parameters for sterilization include temperature, pressure, and time. The main treatment method is incineration. Landfilling to special sites is the least preferable disposal option for this waste. In addition, it is essential that all medical waste be separated at its place of generation (i.e., hospital, clinic), appropriately treated, and safely disposed.

According to the World Health Organization (WHO), 85% of medical waste fits into the recyclable waste category. Fifteen percent are infectious and pathological (3% chemical and pharmaceutical waste; 1% needles, cutters, and drillers; 1% radioactive waste, batteries, etc.).

Hazardous Waste

Hazardous waste is dangerous to public health and the environment. Waste is hazardous if it is listed in the Title 40 Code of Federal Regulations (CFR). This is enforced by the United States Environmental Protection Agency (EPA). Organizations should have a material safety data sheet (MSDS) with necessary information. Container labels must list hazardous components as soon as waste is added to the container.

The Basel Convention's List of Hazardous Waste Categories (Y1-Y18) identifies waste from specific processes. It exhibits one or more of the following characteristics:

- Corrosive (pH less than 2.0 or greater than 12.5)
  - Hydrochloric acid, sulfuric acid, sodium hydroxide

- Ignitable (flammable, oxidizers)
    - Acetone, toluene, xylene
    - Any waste material with flashpoint < 60° C
    - Includes oxidizers (sodium nitrate, potassium permanganate)
- Reactive (shock sensitive, water reactive)
    - Shock sensitive (lithium and sodium)
    - Water reactive (calcium carbide)
    - Spontaneously combustible
    - Peroxide-forming (ethyl ether)
    - Potentially explosive (dry picric acid)
- Toxic (very broad category), includes metals [Mercury], organics [Methylene Chloride])
    - Metals like mercury, lead, methylene chloride, and chloroform
    - Acutely toxic and dangerous chemicals (sodium azide, arsenic and cyanide compounds)
    - See Environment, Health, and Safety (EHS) Website

Hazardous waste must not be discarded next to sanitary sewers, storm sewers, or regular trash. It should not be mixed with nonhazardous waste. It is also important not to leave medical wastes unattended or in open containers. A container without a lid implies evaporation for volatile substances.

Nuclear Waste

Nuclear power plants produce electricity to generate nuclear waste. The nuclear fuel turns to nuclear waste after use in reactors.

High-level and low-level waste are the two main types of nuclear waste. High-level waste makes up 3% of the total volume of waste from nuclear generation. However, they contain 95% of the radioactivity from nuclear power. Low-level waste represents 90% of the total volume of radioactive waste. However, they contain only 1% of the radioactivity.

Nuclear fuel is very hot and radioactive. Safe handling and storing can be done when cooled. Water provides both cooling and shielding. Therefore, a typical reactor will have its fuel removed underwater and transferred to a storage pool. After about five years, the fuel can be transferred to a dry, ventilated concrete container. Otherwise, it can remain in the pool indefinitely (usually up to 50 years).

Sewage Solids

Sewage solids are the by-product as solids separate from the wastewater treatment process. Most wastewater treatment processes produce a disposable substance called sludge or biosolids.

Sewage sludge contains pathogenic bacteria or viruses. These can give be hazardous to the health of humans, animals, and plants. This sludge should be treated rather than used for other purposes like agriculture. Health hazards have resulted from its agricultural use prior to treatment (EPA, 1993a).

WASTE TREATMENT METHODS

According to the World Bank, the world currently generates 4 billion tons of waste per year. The world's cities generate 1.5 billion tons of solid waste per year. This volume is expected to increase to 2.4 billion tons by 2025. In lower income countries, waste generation will more than double over the next 25 years (Hoornweg & Bhada-Tata, 2012). Currently, three-fourths of this waste is in landfills. Only one-fourth is recycled.

The fundamental principle of waste management is to reduce the amount of waste through recycling and to dispose of waste in a manner that will not impact environmental conservation (having no impact on the environment). Discharged wastes are subject to final disposal directly or after intermediate treatment. Intermediate treatment is a very effective and important process to reduce the volume of waste, stabilize waste, and make waste harmless (EPA, 1993b). In most developed countries, intermediate treatment is mainly incineration. Final disposal is the process of returning waste to nature. As for garbage (organic wastes), landfill disposal is used if there is no compost or gasification facilities.

The discharge of waste reflects lifestyles and social activities. In developed countries, discharge was on an upward trend through 1970. It declined after the 1973 oil crisis before levelling off. After 1986, the amount showed a sharp upward swing. Owing to the economic depression and progress in waste reduction policies, waste discharge has maintained its level since 1990. Technological developments and busier cities eventually caused another increase. In general, the amount of waste is larger in cities than rural areas. In high economic communities, people produce fewer organic materials, ash, ceramics, etc. Instead, they produce package waste. Existing technologies can be classified according to its process (see Table 1).

Table 1. Waste treatment technologies

Waste Treatment Technologies		
1- Biological Treatment	**2- Mechanical Treatment**	**3- Thermal Treatment**
Biomethanization Compost Bio-dry	Landfilling	Incineration Pyrolysis Gasification Plasma Others: Mechanical heat treatment (Autoclaving) Thermal depolymerisation Waste autoclaves

Biological Treatment

There are several treatment methods according to material (types of waste) and purpose. The following section will explain methods using biological reactions.

Biomethanization

Anaerobic digestion, a biological process that converts organic matter into biogas, reduces the number of microorganisms. Also termed "biomethanation," it consists of degradation in the absence of oxygen or miscellaneous organic matter. This leads to other factors like the production of methane (CH4), which is recovered in the form of heat and/or electricity.

Biochemical degradation is carried out by bacterial combinations throughout the process. The first stage, hydrolysis, is carried out by extracellular enzymes produced by bacteria. This stage, which is characterized by breaking macromolecules into smaller compounds, allows it to be easily digested by other bacteria populations (Siles, Serrano, Martín, & Martín, 2013).

Organic solid wastes, particularly those derived from households (organic fraction of MSW), are suitable for anaerobic digestion (Mata-Alvarez, 2002). Everyday food waste is mistakenly thrown in usual trash bins, ending up in landfills. The decomposition of organic wastes in landfills produces a gas mixture of approximately 50% CH4 and 50% CO2 and other trace gases. The CH4 is a greenhouse gas, which contributes to climate change. It is 21 times more potent than CO2 in terms of global warming potential. CH4 in landfill gas is poisonous, flammable, and lighter than air. Once it migrates to the surface, it poses the risk of explosion if contained in an area with an ignition source. If not contained or extracted in a controlled program, CH4 can move through the ground, entering basements of nearby buildings and creating health and explosion risks. Through landfill gas recovery, CH4 gas can be extracted from landfills and used as a natural energy source. This is extracted by wells with drills reaching up to 30 meters into a landfill. These wells are usually connected to a pipeline network that conveys the gas to a landfill gas recovery plant (Prevention CDN-NDG, 2017).

Biomethanization describes a natural process of the decomposition of organic material through microorganisms. These are activated without oxygen. The digestion of the material creates biogas, a renewable energy rich with CH4.

Biomethanization plants can treat green waste and household organic garbage. The process, which takes place in closed tunnels, extracts CH4 to reduces and recycles greenhouse gases into energy. The resulting "pre-compost" can be treated in compost plants, benefitting both gardens and agriculture.

The captured biogas can be put directly into a city's energy cycle, supporting heating systems and reducing the use of fossil fuels. One ton of organic waste produces 125 m3 (cubic meters), the energy equivalent of one barrel of oil (Prevention CDN-NDG, 2017).

Compost

Composting is the controlled decomposition process of organic material into a humus-rich residue (compost). This becomes a valuable soil conditioner and fertilizer for both gardens and agriculture. Compost is produced from biodegradable waste (organic waste) like garden waste (i.e., grass clippings, bushes, leaves) or food and kitchen waste. Organic materials inside these wastes react with microorganisms and oxygen to form heat and gas. This results in composting. This rich-in-organism compound is used for soil improvement by adding nitrogen and phosphate. Solid wastes are decomposed by manpowered stations. Fresh vegetables, kitchen wastes, and other kinds of organic wastes are used for composting.

Compost technology is a valuable tool being used to increase yields of farmers interested in sustainable agriculture. Professional growers are also discovering that compost-enriched soils can suppress disease and ward off pests. These beneficial uses of compost can help growers save money, reduce pesticides, and conserve natural resources. In the poultry industry, composting has become a cost-effective method of mortality management. It destroys disease organisms and creates a nutrient-rich product that can be used or sold. Compost technology, termed "compost bioremediation," is being used to restore contaminated soils, manage stormwater, control odors, and degrade volatile organic compounds (VOCs).

According to Goren (2005), benefits of compost use include:

1. Soil enrichment
    a. Adds organic bulk and humus to regenerate poor soils
    b. Suppresses plant disease and pests
    c. Increases soil nutrient content and water retention in both clay and sandy soils
    d. Restores soil structure after the reduction of natural soil microbes by chemical fertilizer
    e. Reduces or eliminates the need for fertilizer
    f. Combats specific soil, water, and air problems
2. Pollution remediation
    a. Absorbs odors and degrades VOCs
    b. Binds heavy metals, preventing them from migrating to water resources or being absorbed by plants
    c. Degrades, and in some cases, eliminates wood preservatives, petroleum products, pesticides, and both chlorinated and nonchlorinated hydrocarbons in contaminated soils
3. Pollution prevention
    a. Avoids CH4 production and leachate formation in landfills by diverting organics for composting
    b. Prevents pollutants in storm water runoff from reaching water resources
    c. Prevents erosion and silting on embankments parallel to creeks, lakes, and rivers
    d. Prevents erosion and turf loss on sides of roads and hills, playing fields, and golf courses
4. Economic benefits
    a. Results in significant cost savings by reducing the need for water, fertilizers, and pesticides
    b. Produces a marketable commodity and low-cost alternative to standard landfill cover and artificial soil amendments
    c. Extends municipal landfill life by diverting organic materials from the waste stream
    d. Provides an affordable alternative to conventional bioremediation techniques

The development of new composting facilities should be supported as an excellent method of managing biodegradable waste. These include garden waste, park waste, kitchen waste, and scrap paper and cardboard. In addition, it creates job opportunities.

Bio-Dry

The bio-drying process is carried out by forced aeration of waste. This enables the activation of biochemical reactions, leading to the decomposition of the easily biodegradable fraction. The result of these reactions is the production of large amounts of heat. This enhances the evaporation of moisture within the waste, as well as the destruction of pathogenic microorganisms (Mang, 2013).

The dried material produced from biological drying is:

- Stabilized

- Free of pathogenic microorganisms
- Odorless
- Manageable in bales (able to be safely stored)
- High energy content

Mechanical Treatment

Final solid waste treatment is often dumped in the ground (landfilling). Dumped wastes easily degrade. Although microbial activities are mainly biologic and chemical, landfilling is accepted as a physical or mechanical treatment because the waste is spread in thin layers, forming a "cell" within one work. Explanations regarding open dumping and modern sanitary landfills will be discussed in the following section.

Landfilling

Source reduction, reuse, recycling, composting, and thermal treatment methods can divert large portions of MSW from disposal. However, some waste must be placed in landfills using a controlled manner. In some cases, wastes are dumped irregularly (open dumping). Although this is not a method for landfilling, it is a reality. This uncontrolled manner of dumping causes soil, water, and air pollution, leading to many public health threats.

Open dumping takes place due to lack of the inspections and control, as well as the mistaken belief that it is the cheapest technique. Deposits on roads, riverbanks, or in abandoned quarries are classic types of open dumping. It seems that the owners easily dispose of waste using this method. However, it is inevitable that their chemical and biological contaminants will find their way back to humans, affecting health, quality of life, and work.

Microbiological processes in decomposing waste will cause leachate and gas problems. Leachate and gas can be controlled at modern sanitary landfills. However, open dumping poses problems related to soluble and suspended contaminants entering surface water and groundwater. Contamination may directly affect drinking water supplies and/or the aquatic food chain. Animals grazing on dumps, rodents living nearby, or flying birds and pests can spread diseases via the terrestrial food chain or infestations. People living close to such sites are at risk from hand-to-mouth transfer of contamination, as well as inhalation of volatile compounds and aerosols. CH4 explosions are another problem of such sites (Goren, 2005).

The main problem with waste stems from increased urban population and waste generation. There are insufficient resources available for solid waste management. In addition, there is a low professional status related to waste management staff. Waste management is an important municipal service. Therefore, it requires first-rate managers to make complex, authoritative decisions to achieve high-quality, sustainable operations.

Modern landfills are well-engineered facilities located, designed, operated, monitored, closed, cared, and controlled according to regulations and national laws. Regulations were established to protect human health and the environment (Goren, 2005). Sanitary landfills are an engineering solution to prevent pollution. Leachate should not penetrate the soil or cause soil and water pollution. Careful planning and preparation are required to address leachate and gas.

Leachate is a polluted liquid with high biological oxygen demand (BOD) and chemical oxygen demand (COD). This is due to the oxidation of ferrous and other metals, as well as organic and inorganic wastes' aerobic and anaerobic synthesis. Liquid waste products of microbial degradation, such as organic acids, increase the chemical activity within the fill. Biological activity in a landfill generally follows a set pattern. Solid waste initially decomposes aerobically. However, as the oxygen supply is exhausted, facultative and anaerobic microorganisms predominate and produce CH4. This odorless, colorless gas may cause explosions. Temperatures rise to the high mesophilic-low thermophilic range (15° to 65°C) due to microbial activity.

Landfill gas is produced when solid wastes decompose (regardless if located in a sanitary landfill or open dumping site). Characteristic products of aerobic decomposition of waste are CO2, water, and nitrate. Alternately, typical products of anaerobic decomposition of waste are CH4 (40% to 60%), CO2, carbon monoxide (CO), water, organic acids, nitrogen oxide (NOx), ammonia, iron sulphate, manganese, hydrogen sulphate (H_2S), and other trace gases. CH4 can be explosive when trapped in the landfill. To prevent an explosion or toxicity, landfill gas should be controlled by scientific methods. Landfill gas is removed from the fill using perforated pipes as a gas ventilation system. These are constructed with a protective steel mesh (like a cage). Stone and/or gravel fill provides "permeability." The removed landfill gas is the source of energy generation. If production of gas proves commercially feasible, recovery facilities may be installed at landfill sites. These facilities can produce electricity or upgrade pipeline quality by removing contaminants and selling the natural gas (Cord-Ruwisch, Seitz, & Conrad, 1988).

CH4 gas produced during organic decaying processes at a landfill can operate internal combustion engines, drive electric generators, and supply power. CH4 production rates may change according to the type of waste and age of the landfill. It is feasible even if the rate is less than 40%. This type of generation has become economically competitive with other fossil fuel powers.

Disadvantages of sanitary landfill technology relate to the method's applicability in urban areas. Neither the method nor its results have disadvantages.

1. In highly populated areas, suitable land may not be available within economical hauling distance.
2. Proper sanitary landfill standards must be adhered to daily or the operation may result in an open dump.
3. Sanitary landfills in residential areas can result in extreme public opposition.
4. A completed landfill will settle and require periodic maintenance.
5. Special designs and construction must be utilized for buildings on completed landfills due to settlement factors.
6. CH4, an explosive gas, and other gases produced from the decomposition of waste may become a hazard or nuisance, interfering with use of the completed landfill.

Thermal Treatment

Incineration

Incineration and other high-temperature waste treatment systems are described as thermal treatment.

Incineration is a waste treatment process that involves the combustion of organic substances in waste materials (at a temperature of 1000 – 1200°C). This process reduces volume and removes hazardous waste. It is very good for medical wastes. However, investment and operation costs are high.

Figure 1. Classical incineration process

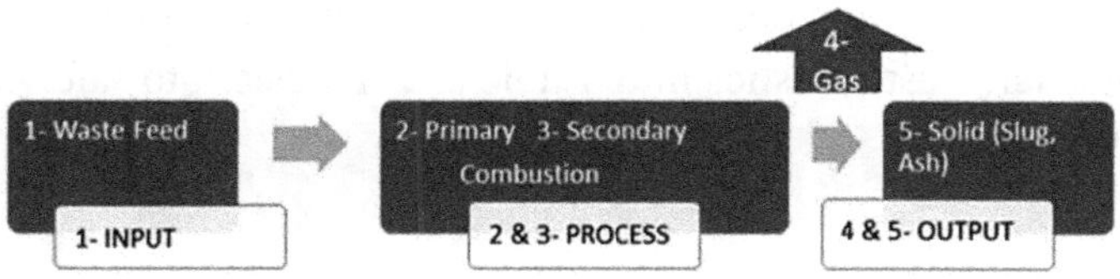

Incineration converts waste into ash, flue gas, and heat. The ash is mostly formed by the inorganic constituents of the waste. This may take the form of solid lumps or particulates carried by the flue gas. Flue gases must be cleaned of gaseous and particulate pollutants before they are dispersed into the atmosphere. In most cases, heat generated by incineration can create electric power.

Incineration with energy recovery is one of several waste-to-energy technologies, including gasification, pyrolysis, and anaerobic digestion. Incineration and gasification technologies are similar in principle. However, energy from incineration is high-temperature heat. Combustible gas is often the main energy product from gasification.

Incineration plants can treat medical/hazardous waste and MSW. It also impacts manufacturing processes (like cement kilns or steel factories) due to combustible materials. To prevent air pollution, these plants should have gas treatment and air pollution prevention facilities.

Cement kilns are used for the pyro-processing stage of the manufacturing of hydraulic cement in which calcium carbonate reacts with silica-bearing minerals to form a mixture of calcium silicates. Over a billion tons of cement is made each year, with cement kilns acting as the heart of this production process. Their capacity usually defines the capacity of the cement plant (Eunomia Research and Consulting, 2008).

Kilns serve as the main energy-consuming and greenhouse gas-emitting stage of cement manufacturing. Therefore, improvement of kiln efficiency has been a central concern of cement manufacturing technology.

Dioxin and furan emissions are the most dangerous pollutants released in the atmosphere. It is possible to prevent pollution. However, it is costly. Air pollution prevention systems are set up for incineration plants so toxic and/or hazardous gases are not released. Yet contributions to global climate change remain with hot gas emissions. On the other hand, bottom ash and fly ash from the burning chambers should also be treated.

A system should be organized to collect and transport waste before processing it through an intermediary treatment (incineration and/or other method). Finally, it is placed in landfills in a sanitary manner to prevent environmental pollution in surrounding areas and populated cities.

Pyrolysis

Pyrolysis is the thermal decomposition of materials at elevated temperatures in an inert atmosphere. Its change in chemical composition is irreversible. The word originates from the Greek-derived elements pyro "fire" and lysis "separating." Pyrolysis, which is most commonly used in the treatment of organic material, is a process used in charring wood (Tanga, Xua, Zhanga, & Lub, 2013). In general, pyrolysis of organic substances produces volatile products, leaving a solid residue enriched in carbon (char). Extreme pyrolysis leaves a carbon residue called "carbonization."

This process is used in the chemical industry (i.e., producing ethylene, forms of carbon, chemicals from petroleum, coal, wood, coke from coal). Aspirational applications of pyrolysis would convert biomass into syngas and biochar, waste plastics into usable oil, or waste into safely disposable substances.

Gasification

This process converts organic- or fossil fuel-based carbonaceous (materials containing large amount of carbon) materials into CO, hydrogen, and CO2. This is achieved by reacting the material at high temperatures (> 700°C), without combustion, with a controlled amount of oxygen and/or steam (Mata-Alvarez, 2002). The resulting gas mixture is called “syngas” (from synthesis gas) or “producer gas” (a fuel). The power from gasification and combustion of the resultant gas is a source of renewable energy if the gasified compounds are obtained from biomass.

Plasma

Plasma or plasma gasification is an extreme thermal process using plasma to convert organic matter into a syngas (synthesis gas). This is primarily made up of hydrogen and CO. A plasma torch powered by an electric arc is used to ionize gas and catalyze organic matter into a syngas. The remaining slag, or by-product, is used commercially as a form of waste treatment. It is tested for the gasification of MSW, biomass, industrial waste, hazardous waste, and solid hydrocarbons (i.e., coal, oil sands, petcoke, oil shale).

Other Treatments

- **Mechanical Heat Treatment (MHT):** MHT, also known as autoclaving, is an alternative waste treatment technology. It involves a mechanical sorting or preprocessing stage with technology found in a material recovery facility. The mechanical sorting stage is followed by a thermal treatment (in the form of a waste autoclave or processing stage) to produce a refuse-derived fuel pellet. MHT is sometimes grouped with mechanical biological treatments. However, it does not include a stage of biological degradation (anaerobic digestion or composting).
- **Thermal Depolymerization (TDP):** TDP, a depolymerization process, uses hydrous pyrolysis to reduce complex organic materials (usually waste products like a biomass or plastic) into light crude oil. Under pressure and heat, long-chain polymers of hydrogen, oxygen, and carbon decompose into short-chain petroleum hydrocarbons with a maximum length of 18 carbons.
- **Waste Autoclaves:** This form of solid waste treatment uses heat, steam, and pressure of an industrial autoclave in the processing of waste in batches or continuous-flow processes. In batch processes, saturated steam is pumped into the autoclave at temperatures around 160°C. The vessel’s steam pressure is maintained up to 6 bar (gauge) for up to 45 minutes. This allows the process to fully “cook” the waste. The autoclave process gives a very high pathogen and virus kill rate. However, the fibrous products from the process are susceptible to bacteria and fungus as they are high in starch, cellulose, and amino acids (Fichtner Consulting Engineers, 2004).

This mimics the natural geological processes thought to be involved in the production of fossil fuels. Some autoclaves (waste converters) can operate in the atmospheric pressure range to achieve full sterilization of pathogenic waste. Super heating conditions and steam generation are achieved when variable pressure controls cycle between ambient and negative pressure within the sterilization vessel. The advantage of this approach is the elimination of complexities associated with operating pressure vessels. However, steam that is not 97% saturated may not contain enough energy to kill spores on the surface of the items it encounters.

COMPARISON OF ADVANCED TREATMENT TECHNOLOGIES

Incineration, a classical method of hazardous waste treatment, falls into the thermal process category. Pyrolysis, gasification, and plasma technologies are also thermal processes because they use high temperatures to treat hazardous waste. However, they are accepted as advanced thermal treatment methods because they have an advanced control system of oxygen use while burning. Classified as incineration in the European Union (EU)'s Waste Incineration (WI) Directive, they face strict emission limits. Combustion, with or without oxygen, generates gas, solid (bottom and fly ash), and liquid residues. These gases are treated at a secondary combustion chamber.

The pyrolysis process thermally degrades waste in the absence of air (and oxygen). Gasification is a process in which materials are exposed to oxygen. However, it is not enough exposure to allow for combustion. Temperatures are usually above 750°C. In some systems, the pyrolysis phase is followed by a second gasification stage during which more of the energy-carrying gases are liberated from the waste. The main product of gasification and pyrolysis, syngas, is composed of CO and hydrogen (85%). Smaller quantities of CO2, nitrogen, CH4, and other hydrocarbon gases are also present. Syngas has a calorific value. Therefore, it can be used as a fuel to generate electricity or steam. In addition, it can serve as a basic chemical feedstock in the petrochemical and refining industries. The calorific value of a syngas will depend on the composition of the input waste to the gasifier. In plasma technologies, the waste is heated with a plasma arc (6,000° to 10,000°C) to create gas and vitrified slag. In some cases, the plasma stage may follow the gasification stage (Siles et al., 2013).

Regarding pyrolysis and gasification, less oxygen is used as compared with incineration. This gives an advantage of less air emissions. However, if there are gases and oils emitted from the first combustion chamber, they are then burnt in the second combustion chamber. This second combustion chamber process may also generate emissions that should be removed by advanced techniques.

Pyrolysis and gasification plants are modular and quick to build. As a technology, gasification takes pyrolysis to the next step by having more gas for fuel. Their small units can be added to or taken away based on changes to waste streams and/or volumes (e.g., with increased recycling). This gives the advantage of a flexible operation on a smaller scale as compared with classical incineration plants.

These processes generate more useful products as compared with incineration, including gas, oil, and char. These can be used as fuel or additives for other petrochemical processes. The produced gas, termed "synthetic gas" or "syngas," can be used to generate energy. Different brands of gas engines use the syngas as a fuel. This is an advantage as compared with steam turbines. However, the efficiency of these processes will decrease if using mixed municipal waste. On the other hand, efficiency can increase with risks during the operation of these plants. Syngas cleaning is an important issue related to gas engines. They have a low tolerance for impure gas. Therefore, operations become risky if the gas is heterogenous. To safeguard the operation, some companies choose less effective (but proven) methods for energy recovery.

Produced energy is eligible for renewables obligation certificates (ROCs). However, a dilemma exists based on recycling activities and compost manufacturing. These plants deal with all kinds of waste, regardless if it is a recyclable material. There is a tendency of less necessity for recycling and composting. For an efficient process, these plants require plastic, paper, or organic wastes (food). These are also the source of composting and recycling activities needed by certain industries. The waste stream is undermined by this application. There is still an important discussion between the proponents to identify the most beneficial. Fuel produced by pyrolysis and gasification processes will not balance the cost of fuel used to run these processes. Reduce, reuse, and recycle may be a more energy-saving process. Figure 2 shows the thermal processes at a glance to compare the technologies with products and processes.

Figure 2. Thermal Technologies at a Glance

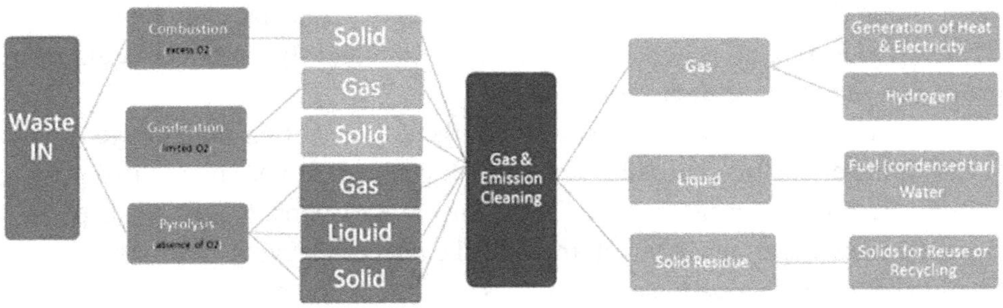

Moreover, thermal processes release fossil fuel-derived CO2 from plastics. They release biologically derived CO2 from biological materials. This can be accepted as a disadvantage, giving an advantage to conventional recycling processes in the sense of climatic impacts. However, it is clear that hazardous waste should receive thermal treatment. Yet recycling opportunities are unavailable.

Some processes use both pyrolysis and gasification (and potentially combustion) in sequential stages. In addition, there may be plasma and/or other high-temperature phases in the initial thermal stage or as a "polishing" of the syngas generated by the first process stage. The actual plant design and configuration of advanced thermal treatment facilities will differ between technology providers. Some plasma gasification technologies use high temperature methods with an electric arc. These are applied at various stages of the gasification process and in different configurations. Plasma, or another high-temperature thermal process, can be applied to fuse the ash from the process into an inert (glassy) residue. It cracks the tar to generate a relatively clean syngas.

Another advanced technology, called "hydrogen fuel cells," generates electricity. Hydrogen fuel cells are highly effective as compared with other energy-generation alternatives. In addition, they have less impact on global warming. Still, many issues should be considered to improve efficiency and safety.

One thermal process issue that should be discussed relates to the effects of technologies on human health. There is a risk for human toxicity caused by these plants. Gases from the smokestack contain furans and dioxins, acid gases, NOx, sulphur dioxide, cadmium, mercury, lead, particle materials, hydrogen sulphide, etc.

The relationship between these health issues and technologies should be resolved. Smaller scale facilities are being marketed for the treatment of MSW. This will enlarge the use of advanced treatment technologies by addressing market needs.

Raw municipal waste is usually not appropriate for gasification. In fact, it typically requires mechanical preparation and separation of glass, metals, and inert materials prior to waste processing. There are economies of scale for all thermal treatment plants. Smaller scale solutions provide for more local/integrated waste management needs. This makes it easier to locate local markets for heat generated from the facility. However, the gate fees may be higher than equivalent larger facilities.

A common issue in developed countries is the production of excessive amounts of waste per capita. As societies develop, the quantity of generated waste has increased to an unsustainable level. The general public has an increasing awareness of the damage caused to the environment. There is also an urgent need for local authorities to plan and implement sustainable, integrated strategies for managing and treating waste materials.

REFERENCES

Cord-Ruwisch, R., Seitz, H.-J., & Conrad, R. (1988). The capacity of hydrogenotrophic anaerobic bacteria to compete for traces of hydrogen depends on the redox potential of the terminal electron acceptor. *Arch Microbiol, 149*, 350-357.

EPA. (1993a). Standards for the use or disposal of sewage sludge. Final Rules, 40 CFR Parts 257, 403, and 503. *Federal Register, 58*(32), 9248–9415.

EPA. (1993b). *Pretreatment and municipal pollution prevention.* Washington, DC: U.S. Environmental Protection Agency Office of Wastewater Enforcement and Compliance.

Eunomia Research and Consulting. (2008). *Greenhouse gas balances of waste management scenarios. Report for the Greater London Authority.* Retrieved from www.london.gov.uk/mayor/environment/waste/climate-change/greenhousegas.jsp

Fichtner Consulting Engineers. (2004). *The viability of advanced thermal treatment of MSW in the UK.* Retrieved from www.esauk.org/publications/reports/thermal%20treatment%20report.pdf

Goren, S. (2005). *Sanitary landfill.* Istanbul: FU Publications.

Goren, S. (2015). Sustainable waste management. In U. Akkucuk (Ed.), *Handbook of research on developing sustainable value in economics, finance, and marketing.* Hershey, PA: IGI Global. doi:10.4018/978-1-4666-6635-1.ch009

Hoornweg, D., & Bhada-Tata, P. (2012). *What a waste.* World Bank 2012, Urban Development & Local Government Unit, No. 15.

Kinnaman, T. C., & Takeuchi, K. (2014). *Handbook on waste management.* Northampton, MA: Edward Elgar Publishing. doi:10.4337/9780857936868

Mang, H. P. (2013). Biogas Production, Developing Countries. In M. Kaltschmitt, N. J. Themelis, L. Y. Bronicki, L. Söder, & L. A. Vega (Eds.), *Renewable Energy Systems* (pp. 218–246). New York, NY: Springer. doi:10.1007/978-1-4614-5820-3_250

Mata-Alvarez, J. (2002). *Biomethanization of the organic fraction of municipal solid wastes.* London, UK: IWA Publishing.

Prevention CDN-NDG. (2017). *City of Montreal's Environmental Action Program.* Retrieved from https://preventioncdnndg.org/eco-quartier/biomethanization-2/

Siles, J. A., Serrano, A., Martín, A., & Martín, A. M. (2013, March). Biomethanization of waste derived from strawberry processing: Advantages of pretreatment. *Journal of Cleaner Production*, *42*, 190–197. doi:10.1016/j.jclepro.2012.11.012

Tanga, Y., Xua, J., Zhanga, J., & Lub, Y. (2013). Biodiesel production from vegetable oil by using modified CaO as solid basic catalysts. *Journal of Cleaner Production*, *42*, 198–203. doi:10.1016/j.jclepro.2012.11.001

Chapter 10
Sustainable Supply Chain Management and Total Quality Management in the Health Sector

İlknur Sayan
https://orcid.org/0000-0002-7133-5858
Istanbul Kent University, Turkey

Yasemin Sarıcı Aytan
https://orcid.org/0000-0002-3026-5398
Istanbul Esenyurt University, Turkey

ABSTRACT

The supply system in health sector determines effective stock management, regular material supply, speed, and quality of maintenance and service process. Elimination of all non-value-adding activities, movements, and processes in the procurement process; minimizing errors; and increasing the efficiency of the process between the inputs and outputs of the hospital is possible by applying total quality in supply management. Effective supply chain management in health institutions improves the quality of healthcare.

INTRODUCTION

Today, being good enough is not sufficient for competitive edge. Total quality management (TQM) and supply chain management (SCM) have played an incremental role in the strengthening of organizational competitiveness. In the ever-changing global market, international business competition is no longer limited to organizations, but also includes supply chains (Vanichchinchai & Igel, 2009). Despite the popularity of the term Supply Chain Management both in the academia and in practice, serious confusion remains in its meaning. Some authors see SCM as a management philosophy, while others consider it as a management process. The SCM philosophy encompasses all other functions within SCM to create

DOI: 10.4018/978-1-7998-4601-7.ch010

all customer functions and satisfaction within a company and within a supply chain. In this context, it is fundamental to understand the values and needs of customers. In other words, SCM philosophy prompts the supply chain members to be customer-oriented (Mentzer, DeWitt, Keebler, Min, Nix, Smith, & Zacharia, 2001). Besides, it is pointed out by academics and practitioners that supply chain management reduces operation costs and increases service level (Demirdöğen & Polater, 2018).

With their achievements in the global market, companies implementing Total Quality Management (TQM), and continuous improvement programs provide a significant competitive edge. While customer expectations are increasing, businesses adopting a culture of continuous learning and development create the real difference by providing for the customers' wishes and expectations (Çetin, 2010).Successful implementation of TQM requires an effective change in the culture of an organization and it is nearly impossible to change an organization without intensive effort shown by the management aiming for continuous development, open communication and cooperation throughout value development (Kaynak, 2003).

Health care involves a complex organizational structure and the balance between quality and cost has a more exquisite nature than in other industries (Abdulsalam, Gopalakrishnan, Maltz, & Schneller, 2015). Health services are different from other businesses because of their high dependence on professionals from the fields of expertise based on over-specialization and the need for further cooperation and their non-error structure. Moreover, health services are non-delay able services (Acar & Bozaykut Bük, 2017). Since health care is abstract, quality is realized or not realized when health care is provided (Ekici, 2013). Reducing the increasing medical costs and expenses, increasing quality, maximizing patient and employee satisfaction are among the main objectives of health services (Swinehart & Smith, 2005).

In health sector, implementation of Total Quality Management enables faster growth for the institutions who have the ability of providing faster and better designed service than their competitors, and adaptation, rapidly-changing requirements of customers, market and legal conditions (Swinehart & Smith, 2005). In this context, more importance has been given to supply chain management in the health sector in recent years due to the increasing pressure to reduce health care costs, reduce waste, prevent medical errors, improve service quality and increase operational efficiency.

Zairi and Liburd (2001) describe sustainability as "the ability of the organization to adapt to change in the business environment in order to capture contemporary best practices and achieve superior competitive performance". Sustainability within a business creates value for customers, investors and the environment. Without sustainable development, the benefit from Total Quality Management is minimal; because, Total Quality Management is a culture that supports business development over time, now and in the future. Also, it is a source that ensures edge in competition in the global market (Zairi & Liburd, 2001). However, quality does not emerge itself; it must be conducted (Çetin, 2010). In Supply Chain management, executive management support has a critical role in shaping an organization's values, orientation, and direction. It also has a significant impact on organizational performance (Mentzer et al. 2001).

SUSTAINABLE SUPPLY CHAIN IN HEALTH SERVICES

The Concept of Supply Chain Management

Supply Chain Management (SCM) first emerged in 1982 from the manner Toyota managed its relationships with suppliers and customers (Vanichchinchai, & Igel, 2009). The emphasis on SCM in recent years depends on trends in global resource use, onset of time and quality-based competition, and on SCM's contribution to environmental uncertainty. Supply chain management is the coordination and management of a complex network of activities involved in the delivery of a finished product or service to the end user or customer. Lambert, Stock and Ellram define the supply chain as the harmony of firms bringing products or services to the market (Mentzer et al. 2001). The American Manufacturing Management Association defines 'supply chain management' as strengthening global logistics, balancing supply and demand and measuring the target on a global basis, planning, conducting, controlling and monitoring supply chain activities (Acar & Bozaykut Bük, 2017). According to Verma and Seth (2011), the supply chain is a network that extends from suppliers to end-customers for organizations directly involved in the flow of products, services, finance, information and value (Özkan, Bayın & Yeşilaydın, 2015). In other words, the supply chain includes services starting from the raw material and delivering the product or service to the end consumer and post-sales. These services are processes such as procurement, storage, transportation, production, demand forecasting, material management and customer service (Aslantaş & Toraman, 2017).

SCM's content includes customers, suppliers, marketing, purchasing, production and logistics, product development, product return and recycling (Vanichchinchai & Igel, 2009). Structure of a company's supply chain consists of external suppliers, internal functions of the company, and external distributors and customers (commercial or end-user). Companies may be members of more than one supply chain at the same time. This includes the supply of functions, processes, raw materials and parts, manufacturing and assembly of products, storage, order entry and follow-up, distribution through various channels and ultimately delivery to the customer (Hervani, Helms, & Sarkis, 2005).

In order for all channels that comprise supply chain management to gain more profit and benefit, the relationships in the chain must be conducted properly. Successful management of a supply chain is also influenced by factors such as customer expectations, globalization, information technology, government regulation, competition and the environment (Hervani, Helms, & Sarkis, 2005). In supply chain management, the expectations of end users and the needs and expectations of all supply chain members are taken into consideration (Chang, 2009). Nowadays; customers prefer the right products or services that ensure satisfaction and reassurance in a timely manner. Supply chain management focuses on the tight integration of different rings of the chain, taking into account the changing demands of customers (Koçoğlu, 2014; Aslantaş & Toraman, 2017).

Supply Chain Management in Health Institutions

Supply chain management in health services is the material and information flow that comprises a process from production to the end user, namely, the patient (Demir & Uğuroğlu, 2015). The health sector strives to provide the services and materials needed by hospitals and suppliers in order to provide services at low costs without sacrificing patient care standards at the desired place, time, quality and price (Biçer & Ömürgönülşen, 2019).

Health care supply chains often include a function and a great number of factors linked to a high level of complexity (Abdulsalam, Gopalakrishnan, Maltz, & Schneller, 2015). In the health sector, such factors as patient density, non-error structure of the sector, sectoral and legal obligations, patient and employee health and safety, increasing costs, price competition, complexity of insurance procedures and fast changing technology make it complicated and difficult for supply management to be applied in health institutions. Furthermore, the expenses related to the supply chain have the highest share after the expenses of the employees (Demir & Uğuroğlu, 2015). In this sense, with the idea that resources are limited and needs are unlimited, effective supply chain management is a system that enables scarce resources to be used more efficiently in health institutions (Biçer & Ömürgönülşen, 2019). Supply chain members specific to the health sector are manufacturers, public and private health institutions (hospitals, oral and dental health centers, primary care clinics, etc.), pharmacies, private clinics and health care providers and financing institutions, insurance companies and regulatory institutions for economic structures, and patients (Abdulsalam, Gopalakrishnan, Maltz, & Schneller, 2015). Manufacturers, pharmacy and pharmaceuticals manufacturers, manufacturers of medical devices such as medical and surgical instruments and apparatus, prostheses, x-ray equipment, electrotherapy equipment, information systems manufacturers and medical and manufacturers of surgical equipment such as syringes, surgical knives, blood and sampling kits, hospital laboratory products, wound care units and intravenous stents could be mentioned as the important members of the supply chain for the health sector (Özkan, Bayın & Yeşilaydın G. 2015).

Despite increasing interest in supply chain management in the health sector, supply chain practices in the sector have not been adequately studied in academic research (Demirdöğen & Polater, 2018). In a number of studies, it was concluded that a less costly and more sensitive health care supply chain should be developed to meet the needs of patients and clinicians (Sweet, 2005). Bourlakis et al. (2011) state that it is necessary to establish a process to define hospital supply chains more efficiently. He also suggested that further research into demographic factors affecting patient selection and urgent transition to comprehensive information systems should be undertaken. In their study, Lee et al. (2011) concluded that impeccable suppliers of innovative supply chain design have a significant impact on selection and cooperation in promoting supply chain performance and quality management practices (Biçer & Ömürgönülşen, 2019).

The fact that, health sector supply chain management is utilized for; 1. Provision of medical supplies and equipment in the right place, time and distance with for the lowest cost; 2. Reduction of the lead time and cost of medical supplies and equipment without sacrificing quality; 3. Minimizing the storage space; 4. Enhancement of patient care service design (Acar & Bozaykut Bük, 2017).

In addition, supply chain management in the health sector will bring benefits such as reducing costs, increasing profitability and productivity, customer satisfaction, coordination and information sharing, reducing uncertainty in demand and preventing over-investment in stocks. In this way, meeting customer needs and increasing satisfaction levels of customers can be achieved and, thus, service quality increases (Özdemir, 2004). Since the services produced and offered in health institutions are related to human life; any failure in the processes can have irreversible results. Increasing productivity by putting added value to processes and preventing waste is possible with simple applications and in addition to health conceptions such as "safety," "cost effectiveness," "quality," "efficiency," "profitability," "innovation," and "quality of work life," significant changes can be created on important concepts for each business (Özkan, Bayın & Yeşilaydın G. 2015).

Difficulties Encountered in Supply Chain Management in Health Institutions

Another factor that prevents the efficient management of the supply chain in the health sector is that it has a very comprehensive and complex structure. One of the most important factors that cause complexity in the health sector supply chain is the high number of suppliers and product diversity in the chain. Therefore, it is speculated that reducing the number of suppliers will provide significant benefits due to price drops resulting from the increase in the purchase amount. Other issues that impede the supply chain management of the health sector are as follows (Biçer &Ömürgönülşen, 2019):

- Shortening of product life spans due to the constantly evolving technology,
- Expensive products that doctors prefer,
- Difficulties in forecasting disease types, frequencies and prognoses,
- Difficulties in procurement of supplies needed for treatment,
- Products not having standardized codes,
- Lack of capital to provide the infrastructure to support supply chain management implementations,
- Hospital staff's lack of adequate training and knowledge of supply chain management,
- Inadequate level of executive management support,
- Health institutions having comprehensive and complex structures.

In addition, the fact that participation of physicians in the supply selection process is absent affects medical device manufacturers and suppliers. This factor further increases the barriers to standardization and cost reduction. The products themselves and the devices purchased are very expensive, highly complex, require special use (sterilization, safety precautions, etc.) and are also frequently changing due to medical and technological innovations. These facts, especially the relative lack of data on various physician choices and objective product performance, make it even more difficult (Abdulsalam, Gopalakrishnan, Maltz, & Schneller, 2015). It is believed that supply chain operations can reduce costs and improve health care if these barriers are overcome. In this context, more attention has been paid to supply chain management in the health sector in recent years due to the increasing pressure to reduce health care costs, reduce waste, prevent medical errors, improve service quality and increase operational efficiency. Although the supply chain function in hospitals has traditionally been limited to the scope of material management, innovative hospitals have adopted a more powerful and comprehensive supply chain approach (Biçer &Ömürgönülşen, 2019).

All institutions hold responsibilities by taking prudent measures in fair use of natural resources such as not harming the environment, being socially responsible, equal human development, ensuring health and employee safety, contributing to humanity and the environment. This concept reveals the 'need for sustainability'. Ensuring sustainability requires a holistic assessment of business processes throughout the entire supply chain and management systems (Asif, Bruijn, Fisscher, O. A. M., & Steenhuis, 2008).

TOTAL QUALITY MANAGEMENT IN HEALTH SERVICES

The Concept of Total Quality Management

Quality assurance and total quality arrived late in the West, but ideas were developed by W. Edwards Deming in the US in the 1930s and 1940s. TQM attracted attention in Japan in the 1950s with the work of Deming and Juran, and changed the classical, hierarchical understanding of business and management that had prevailed in the West for a long time with quality improvement, quality control, quality circles and just-in-time production practices (Teoman 2015; Taşkın & Ekinci, 2006). Competitive companies have started to adopt productivity improvement programs, which have proven themselves particularly successful in Japan. One of these "improvement programs" is the total quality management (TQM) system (Kaynak, 2003).

Total quality management is an operating model that focuses on quality and is based on the participation of all employees, aiming to provide benefits for the employees and society providing customer satisfaction and reassurance in a continuous learning environment (Çetin, 2010). TQM can be defined as a holistic management philosophy that strives for continuous improvement in all functions of an organization (Kaynak, 2003). Total Quality Management (TQM), as a management model, enhances corporate performance by providing high quality products or services, and provides continuous improvement and development through teamwork and customer-oriented quality and inputs. According to the most accepted definition made by the American Quality Institute, 'It is a holistic organizational approach that involves continuous improvement of the processes, services and products of the organization with the participation of all managers and employees in order to meet customer needs and expectations' (Teoman, 2015). However, without sustainable development, the benefit from Total Quality Management is minimal, since Total Quality Management is an approach that supports business development over time, now and in the future. It is a significant source of competitive edge in the global market (Zairi & Liburd, 2001).

In the development stages of quality management (QM), it focused solely on the inspection stage, then included quality control, quality assurance (QA) and finally TQM. While the traditional Quality Management approach is reactive and result-oriented, the modern approach in Quality Management is broader and emphasizes the quality of process control to avoid any errors. It is a proactive process-oriented approach (Vanichchinchai, & Igel, 2009). Deming saw quality as a 'reduction of variability' in technical terms and emphasized that quality can be achieved by resetting errors in the process. Quality is a proactive process-oriented approach that establishes systems to produce quality products and ensures continuous improvement of products, services and processes (Teoman, 2015), (Vanichchinchai, & Igel, 2009). According to Deming, in order to improve production, it is necessary to first improve the process (Teoman, 2015).

Ford (1991) believes that quality is defined by the customer (Zairi & Liburd, 2001). The customer is the most important part of the production line (Teoman, 2015; Aslantaş & Toraman, 2017). Customers want products and services that meet their needs and expectations at a cost that represents their needs throughout their lives. Therefore, Total Quality Management (TQM) refers to the quality emphasis that covers the entire organization from supplier to customer (Zairi & Liburd, 2001). According to Pfau (1989) and Stevenson (2012), TQM is a culture to continuously improve the quality of goods and services offered by individuals at all levels (from executive management to the lowest level) and with the participation of all functions of the organization (Kannan 2005). Demirbağ et al. (2006) defines TQM as a holistic management philosophy that aims to continuously improve all functions of an organization in order to provide service under the leadership of senior management in line with the needs or requirements of the customer (Zairi & Liburd, 2001). Anderson et al. defines visionary leadership, internal and external cooperation, process management and employee satisfaction as the basic structures of quality management. They also demonstrated that these structures are the driving forces of customer satisfaction. It has been shown that similar structures have been identified in other studies and wider measurements of product quality and production performance have a positive effect. Nakamura et al. states that TQM has a stronger and more consistent impact on performance; Tan et al. states that TQM should be implemented in conjunction with initiatives to rationalize the supplier base in order to gain benefits in operational performance (Kannan 2005). Lee (2004) states that the benefits gained by firms, productivity increase, reduction of rejection, minimization of cost and waste and management-employee relationship turned out to be increasing with the successful implementation of TQM (Asif, Bruijn, Fisscher, OAM, & Steenhuis, 2008).

In Total Quality Management, customer needs should be continuously monitored, evaluated and products or services should be provided for these needs (Çetin, 2010). The main objective in TQM is quality coming first. A quality control mechanism designed to ensure quality standards can win the customer reliance. TQM involves quality prevention rather than eliminating errors through 'control of the result', but with the basic principle of 'do it right the first time' instead, before it occurs. TQM provides long-term institutions with internal and external customer satisfaction, productivity and profit (Ayaz & Soykan, 2002).

Total Quality Management in Health Institutions

The main purpose of health institutions is the whole of the studies conducted for the protection of health and treatment of diseases (Acar & Bozaykut Bük, 2017). In addition, diagnosis, treatment and rehabilitation of diseases, as well as prevention of diseases and improvement of the health level of the society are within the scope of health services (Ateş, 2013). Quality in health services is a service process aimed at customer focus, continuous improvement, employee empowerment (Patel, 2009), data-driven decision making, and customer loyalty. Therefore, customer satisfaction is the most important indicator of quality service (Ekici, 2013; Kannan 2005). Total Quality Management (TQM) plays a very important role in increasing the competitiveness of health institutions by enhancing the quality of the products and the quality of the services it provides. TQM is a people-oriented, customer-oriented, and measurement-oriented management philosophy that uses the well-organized working methodology and excellence in all areas of products and services that are important to the customer (Patel, 2009; Zairi & Liburd). The most important element that differentiates TQM from other approaches is the role of managers (Çetin, 2010). With the TQM approach, the decision-making and supervisory functions of the managers have become advisory functions. With this approach, although the distinction between the person making the decision and the person doing the work has not completely disappeared, yet, has decreased relatively (Koçel 2013).

Hospitals and other healthcare organizations around the world are gradually implementing TQM to reduce costs, increase productivity, and provide high quality patient care (Patel, 2009). Health institutions have a complex structure that can limit TQM due to structure, functional designs, central decision-making, strict bureaucracies, strict rules, narrowly defined job descriptions, chain of command and top-down communication (Mosadeghrad, 2014). Bureaucratic and hierarchical structure, occupational autonomy, weak leadership, resistance to employees, inappropriate organizational culture, inadequate training and insufficient resources appear to be the biggest drawbacks to TQM in the health sector (Mosadeghrad, 2014). Health care providers who want to achieve a sustainable competitive advantage must develop operational capabilities to improve quality (Swinehart & Smith, 2005; Lewisohn, & Reynoso, 1995).

Relationship of Supply Chain and Total Quality Management

Supply chain and supply chain management concepts see increasing interest as a means of competitiveness in a globally challenging environment (Cooper & Ellram, 1993).Addressing quality targets together with supply chain objectives helps to prepare the organization for global competition by strengthening its holistic capabilities (Teoman, 2015). The implementation of total quality management (TQM) in the supply chain has become an important factor of competitive superiority through innovation, flexibility, service and faster access to the market in the implementation of total quality management in businesses and health institutions (Çetin 2010). Being customer-oriented is based on the philosophy that a business determines the developments in the customer and the market as the center to guide its activities. The primary principle of TQM is determined according to the needs of the customer (Çetin, 2010). All individuals and institutions involved in the production and service process in health services are considered as customers (Ekici, 2013). In total quality management, it is essential that customer needs are constantly monitored, evaluated and the products and services that will meet these needs are provided. In this sense, the product or service should be ready, reliable and compatible with customer expectations when needed (Çetin, 2010).

In Total Quality Management, the approval and support of executive management is very important at the beginning (Khan, 2003). The impact of quality management depends on the effectiveness of the leadership, because the quality effort can have a real impact with the support of the leader. In the supply chain conditions, the leader's development of the management strategy and the goals of the supply chain's work affect the actual efficiency for leadership (Chang, 2009).

According to the results of a comprehensive survey conducted by Talip et al., in 2010, TQM focuses more on "quality" on the basis of "increasing institutional competitiveness" and "customer satisfaction", while SCM's priority is "timely delivery" and "cost" . In Table 1, TQM emphasizes the cooperation and association of internal stakeholders for continuous improvement, while SCM seeks integration and cooperation with external stakeholders. As long as the integration of these two disciplines is achieved, it is explained that the benefits such as the ability of organizations to meet customer demands, supply chain communication, the morale of the organization, continuous improvement, innovation and the adoption and support of employees' change and continuous development concept will be gained (Teoman, 2015). TQM and SCM are still being developed in terms of scope and applications. Since TQM was introduced and developed as a concept before SCM, there are now TQM frameworks that are more universally accepted than SCM. While there are commonly accepted quality standards for TQM, such as ISO 9000, SCM still does not have a comparable standard framework. TQM and SCM emerged in response to the need to develop tactical strategies for operational functions (audit and logistics). As a result, both TQM and SCM can be seen as management philosophies. Therefore, a new and well integrated framework should be developed to facilitate implementation, especially since there is no universally accepted SCM framework. TQM and SCM tend to focus on time-based performance (Vanichchinchai, & Igel, 2009).

CONCLUSION

Services produced and provided in health institutions concern human life. In each stage of health service, any fault that would possibly occur within the processes may result in irreversible consequences. Health sector is very important for maintaining human life, and its share in service industry is constantly increasing. Health institutions are making efforts to increase their market share in terms of service quality due to increasing competition. One of the common aspects of Total Quality Management and Supply Chain Management is that it is a customer-oriented management approach. TQM approach in health care institutions is important in terms of institutionalization, increasing service quality and internal and external customer satisfaction. Quality Supply Chain Management, full and timely supply of the necessary materials and products at a lower cost without compromising quality is a requirement to prevent

Table 1. Comparison of SCM and TQM Disciplines

	Total Quality Management	Supply Chain Management
Description	Customer satisfaction, quality products and services, integration-oriented management philosophy in all stages of continuous improvement and organization	Customer satisfaction, management philosophy that focuses on integration of all the stakeholders of the chain (suppliers, distributors, customers) for timely delivery of products and services
Origin	Quality	Logistics and Strategy
Development Stages	· Quality Control · Quality Circles · Quality Assurance Standards · Quality Management · Total Quality Management	· Logistics · Supply Chain Management · Integrated Supply Chain · Global Supply Chain Management
Main Goals	Increasing Corporate Competition Power and Customer Satisfaction	Increasing Corporate Competition Power and Customer Satisfaction
Focus	Product Features and Quality Performance	Delivery Time and Delivery Performance
Application Tools	Six Sigma, Taguchi Method, Quality Circle, Quality Prize Models	Agility, Just-in-time, Rapid Response
Application Principles	· Belief of Executive Management · Customer Focus · Continuous Learning and Training · Continuous Improvement · Innovation · Employee Participation · Supplier Management	· Customer Relations · Materials Management · Strategical Supplier Partnership · Information and Communication Technology · Corporate Culture · Close Cooperation with Suppliers
Field of Activity	Product safety, flexibility, improving and securing product and service quality, quality management applications, measuring quality, cost of quality, quality management systems, quality excellence models, process management, strategic, tactical, and operational issues for TQM application and its sustainability	Providing speed, flexibility, and agility to meet customer demands fast and at minimum cost, marketing, product development, product returns and recycling, purchasing, production, distribution, selling, returns (SCOR) loop, product design, logistic and inventory management, purchasing and customer relations management
Integration	Internal integration and wholeness	External integration and cooperation (suppliers, customers)

disruption of service in the health sector. In order to respond quickly to customer requests, it must be in accordance with the customer-oriented arrangements and constantly changing environmental structure. TQM and Supply Chain Management should also be considered as criteria that provide patient satisfaction in health sector and show the quality of service provided. TQM and Supply Chain Management are the models that try to prevent errors in customer satisfaction, efficiency, efficiency and processes before they occur and play a decisive role in customer reassurance. There is a need for quantitative research that examines the relationship between Total Quality and Supply Chain. In particular, an integrated management model can be set forth with the researches to be carried out to integrate Supply Chain Management into Total Quality Management.

REFERENCES

Abdulsalam, Y., Gopalakrishnan, M., Maltz, A., & Schneller, E. (2015). Health Care Matters: Supply Chains In and Of the Health Sector. *Journal of Business Logistics*, *36*(4), 335–339. doi:10.1111/jbl.12111

Acar & Bozaykut Bük. (2017). Article. *International Journal of Business and Social Sciences Research, 6*(5), 13-27.

Asif, M., de Bruijn, E. J., Fisscher, O. A. M., & Steenhuis, H.-J. (2008). Achieving sustainability three dimensionally. *2008 4th IEEE International Conference on Management of Innovation and Technology.* doi:10.1109/icmit.2008.4654402

Aslantaş Ateş, B., & Toraman, A. (2017). Basamak Bir Hastanenin Eczanesinde Yalın Tedarik Zinciri Uygulaması. *Journal Of Suleyman Demirel University Institute of Social Sciences, 29*(4), 456-469.

Ates, O. K. (2013). *Global supply chain and competitive business strategies: A case study of blood sugar monitoring industry* (Doctoral dissertation). Ohio University.

Ayaz, H., & Soykan, A. (2002). Toplam Kalite Yönetimi ve Sağlık Sektörü. *Türkiye Klinikleri Psikiyatri Dergisi, 3*, 19–26.

Biçer, İ., & Ömürgönülşen, M. (2019). Sağlık Kurumları Yöneticilerinin Tedarik Zinciri Yönetimi Algılarının Belirlenmesi. *Hacettepe Journal of Health Administration, 22*(3), 599–618.

Çetin, C. (2010). *Toplam Kalite Yönetimi.* Beta Basım Yayım Dağıtım.

Chang, G. (2009). - Total quality management in supply chain. *International Business Research, 2*(2), 82–85. doi:10.5539/ibr.v2n2p82

Cooper, M. C., & Ellram, L. M. (1993). Characteristics of Supply Chain Management and the Implications for Purchasing and Logistics Strategy. *International Journal of Logistics Management, 4*(2), 13–24. doi:10.1108/09574099310804957

Demir, İ. B., & Uğurluoğlu, Ö. (2015). Sağlık Kurumlarında Stratejik Yönetim Araçları. *Hacettepe Sağlık İdaresi Dergisi, 18*(2), 219–251.

Ekici, D. (2013). *Sağlık Hizmetinde Toplam Kalite Yönetimi.* Ankara: Sim Matbaacılık.

Hervani, A. A., Helms, M. M., & Sarkis, J. (2005). Performance measurement for green supply chain management. Benchmarking. *International Journal (Toronto, Ont.), 12*(4), 330–353. doi:10.1108/14635770510609015

Kannan, V. (2005). Just İn Time, Total Quality Management, And Supply Chain Management: Understanding Their Linkages And Impact On Business Performance. *Omega, 33*(2), 153–162. doi:10.1016/j.omega.2004.03.012

Kaynak, H. (2003). The relationship between total quality management practices and their effects on firm performance. *Journal of Operations Management, 21*(4), 405–435. doi:10.1016/S0272-6963(03)00004-4

Khan, J. H. (2003). Impact Of Total Quality Management On Productivity. *The TQM Magazine, 15*(6), 374–380.

Koçoğlu, M., & Avcı, M. (2014). *Satınalma Yönetimi: Teorik Bir Çalışma. Yüksek Lisans Tezi.* Kastamonu University Faculty of Economics and Administrative Sciences.

Lewisohn, C., & Reynoso, J. (1995). Improving health service quality from within: The case of United Leeds Teaching Hospitals NHS Trust. *International Journal of Health Care Quality Assurance*, *8*(2), 18–20. doi:10.1108/09526869510081848 PMID:10142012

McKone-Sweet, K. E., Hamilton, P., & Willis, S. B. (2005). The ailing healthcare supply chain: A prescription for change. *The Journal of Supply Chain Management*, *41*(1), 4–17. doi:10.1111/j.1745-493X.2005.tb00180.x

Mentzer, J. T., DeWitt, W., Keebler, J. S., Min, S., Nix, N. W., Smith, C. D., & Zacharia, Z. G. (2001). Defining supply chain management. *Journal of Business Logistics*, *22*(2), 1–25. doi:10.1002/j.2158-1592.2001.tb00001.x

Mosadeghrad, A. M. (2015). Developing and validating a total quality management model for healthcare organisations. *The TQM Journal*, *27*(5), 544–564. doi:10.1108/TQM-04-2013-0051

Özdemir, A. İ. (2004). Tedarik zinciri yönetiminin gelişimi, süreçleri ve yararları. *Journal of Erciyes University Faculty of Economics and Administrative Sciences*, *23*, 87–96.

Özkan, O., Bayin, G., & Yesilaydin, G. (2015). Lean Supply Chain Management In Health Sector. *AJIT-e*, *6*(18), 71–94. doi:10.5824/1309-1581.2015.1.005.x

Patel, G. (2009). *Total quality management in healthcare*. Available at: http://hdl.handle.net/10380/3062

Polater, A. (2015). *Sağlık Sektöründe Tedarik Zinciri Yönetimi ve Müşteri Memnuniyetinin İncelenmesi: Bazı İllerde İkinci ve Üçüncü Basamak Hastaneler ve Tedarikçileri Üzerine Bir Uygulama* (PhD thesis). Atatürk University Institute of Social Sciences.

Polater, A., & Demirdogen, O. (2018). An investigation of healthcare supply chain management and patient responsiveness. *International Journal of Pharmaceutical and Healthcare Marketing*, *12*(3), 325–347. doi:10.1108/IJPHM-07-2017-0040

Swinehart, K. D., & Smith, A. E. (2005). Internal supply chain performance measurement: A health care continuous improvement implementation. *International Journal of Health Care Quality Assurance*, *18*(7), 533–542. doi:10.1108/09526860510627210 PMID:16335618

Taşkın, E., & Ekinci, K. M. (2006). *Toplam Kalite Yönetimi ve Kamu Sektörü. 1*. Ankara: Basım, Turan Kitabevi.

Teoman, S. (2015). *Tedarik zinciri kalite yönetiminde liderlik etkisi-Türkiye'de faaliyet gösteren işletmeler evreninde deneysel bir araştırma*. Academic Press.

Vanichchinchai, A., & Igel, B. (2009). Total quality management and supply chain management: Similarities and differences. *The TQM Journal*, *21*(3), 249–260. doi:10.1108/17542730910953022

Zairi & Liburd. (2001). TQM sustainability-a roadmap for creating competitive advantage. *Integrated Management: 6th International conference on ISO 9000 and TQM*, 452-461.

Chapter 11
Analysis of the Barriers to Green Supply Chain Management Implementation:
An Application on the BIST Sustainability Index

Merve Eser
Arel University, Turkey

Gülay İrak
https://orcid.org/0000-0002-0756-7937
Bulent Ecevit University, Turkey

ABSTRACT

The statistical analysis of the data obtained by the survey method was performed with SPSS 22.0 program. According to the findings of the research, the most important barriers in the implementation of green supply chain management are green projects with high investment costs in construction, changing facilities and equipment, as well as the international crisis and economic downturn. These barriers are raw material costs are higher in green applications, green projects having high operating costs, and high prices in green applications unable to compete with lower prices of competitors, respectively. Another finding of the study is that there is no significant difference between the implementation status of the green projects and the duration of the export activity on the barriers encountered in the implementation of GSCM.

INTRODUCTION

Conventional supply chain management focuses on the final product, without considering environmental degradation. In contrast, green supply chain management reorganizes environmental concerns and supply chain activities within the framework of environmental management principles. Companies that adopt the green supply chain may face some restrictive factors in the transition from the traditional supply

DOI: 10.4018/978-1-7998-4601-7.ch011

chain to the green supply chain. These constraints, defined as barriers, adversely affect the success of "green" initiatives. Barriers face to green supply chain management vary according to the size of the business and the area in which it operates. Therefore, companies that have adopted the "green" initiative should first try to eliminate barriers by identifying them according to their field of activity and size. In this study, operating in different sectors in Turkey "green" initiative adopted in the company of green supply chain management practices most frequently encountered barriers has been revealed as a result of an extensive review of the literature. The contribution of this study is provided with to be handled companies operating in different sectors related to barriers encountered in the management of green supply chain in Turkey. In the first part of the study, the green supply chain management and the barriers faced by the companies in the green supply chain management are discussed at the conceptual level. Then, the literature on the barriers encountered in green supply chain management was tabulated and explanations about the methodology followed in the study were made. Finally, the analyzes conducted according to the method of the research are presented with the results and the results obtained are summarized and recommendations are made for future studies.

CONCEPTUAL FRAMEWORK

In this part of the study, the barriers encountered in green supply chain management and implementation are expressed in a conceptual framework.

Green Supply Chain Management (GSCM)

In 1990s, as a result of the increase in the trade volume of products and services at national and international level, enterprises became inadequate to manage their own companies. In this way, the companies have started to strengthen the practices in which back and forward processes are integrated, which include all processes suppliers ensure raw material as well as the delivery of the final product to the consumer and after-sales processes. Thus, the companies started to control the processes before and after production efficiently by combining all functions under one roof. In this context, the concept of supply chain was born with the need to create a structure in which all components are connected to a single network and to control this structure transparently in order to meet the increasing consumer demand and provide competitive advantage (Baki, 2018). However, due to the decrease in raw material resources due to industrialization, increasing social pressures on effective environmental management due to increased environmental pollution, legal measures on packaging and green consumption, the supply chain activities have directed the attention to the impact on the natural environment and to create environmental performance changes (Muduli et al, 2013). Thus, the concept of green supply chain, which evaluates business processes in traditional supply chain management in the most efficient way with an environmental perspective, has emerged (Thun & Müller, 2010). The concept of GSCM dates back to the 1960s in the context of environmental management. However, the concept was put forward as a new discipline after the 1990s. The popularization of the green supply chain approach has been due to the increase in academic studies carried out in this field after 2000 (Tseng et al 2019; Zhu, & Sarkis, 2006). In the period of rapid industrialization that coincided with the 1960s after World War II, the use of resources by neglecting the environmental factor caused the ecological balance to deteriorate. Therefore, at the end of the 1960s, the concept of environmental management was started to be discussed. In the

1970s, the importance of the concept of environmental management has been increasingly considered by enterprises as reducing environmental pollution and managing waste. With the rapid destruction of natural resources in the 1980s, production processes were redesigned by the enterprises to generate the lowest amount of waste. In the 1990s, with the increasing consumer awareness in environmental management, businesses started to focus on the environmental impacts of product processes and product life cycle. The awareness of the GSCM concept has increased as a result of the increase in the green supply chain studies in 2000s. Thus, GSCM has become a necessity decrease in raw material resources, increase of environmental pollution, insufficient waste sites etc. in terms of sustainability of enterprises since 2000 (Ergülen & Büyükkeklik 2008; Beamon, 1999; Ay, & Ecevit, 2005; Baki, 2018). GSCM; it is a concept that integrates the traditional supply chain management approach with environmental sensitivity by adding the management of end-of-life products to traditional supply chain activities such as product design, raw material selection, production process, delivery of the final product to consumers (Srivastava 2007; Zhu, & Sarkis, 2004). GSCM is a strategy for companies to gain market superiority and increase profits by minimizing environmental risks and increasing productivity throughout the supply chain (Wang et al, 2013). Today, GSCM is widely applied by many companies operating in different sectors in order to reduce the environmental impact of their activities, increase brand image and provide competitive advantage (Muduli et al, 2013). Hervani et al. defined green supply chain management as follows (Hervani et al, 2005):

$$GSCM = \frac{Green\ Purchasing + Green\ Production}{Materials\ Management + Green\ Distribution + Green\ Marketing + Reverse\ Logistics}.$$

GSCM's activities include raw material selection, production, handling, transportation, waste management and recycling of products using the materials and technology that less harmful the environment with the addition of the "green ine component to the supply chain (Srivastava, 2007; Muduli, 2013; Diabat, 2011; Wang et al, 2013). Descriptions of these activities are as follows:

Green purchasing; is to pay attention to environment-friendly feature in the selection of materials to be used in product inputs. The support of suppliers and the selection of the appropriate supplier is crucial to the success of the green purchasing component. Green production; to ensure that the environmental impacts are kept to a minimum in all processes from product design to acquire of the final product, together with selection and supply of inputs required for production (Dubey et al, 2017). Green distribution; determination of forward and reverse logistics distribution locations, the choice of transport mode, production policies include full-time decisions (Sarkis, 2003). Green marketing; the marketing mix of enterprises in accordance with the concept of "green" (Özesen, 2009). Green packaging; is the selection of recyclable and environmentally friendly materials in accordance with the characteristics and size of the product in order to increase efficiency in distribution, handling and transportation activities. Reverse logistic is collecting, separating, recycling, reusing, disposing of products that have expired, warranty expired, returned or defective or spoiled (Zhang & Zhao, 2012).

For a successful GSCM, "green" activity components in the supply chain, such as green purchasing, green production, green distribution, green marketing and reverse logistics, should be well understood.

Barriers to the Implementation of GSCM

Nowadays, many enterprises have adopted green supply chain management and started to implement it. However, enterprises face a number of restrictive factors during implementation. These limiting factors that prevent the success of GSCM are defined as "barriers" in the literature. For a successful GSCM implementation, these barriers need to be identified and detected (Dhull, 2016). The barriers encountered during GSCM implementation may vary depending on the size and scope of the business. However, many barriers are standard features for businesses of all sizes and sectors (Baki, 2018). In this context, the most common barriers were identified by academicians and experts as a result of a wide literature review. The identified barriers are described in the literature by the researchers in various classifications. Govindan et al. explained the barriers encountered in GSCM practices in five main categories as outsourcing, participation and support, technology, information and financial (Govindan et al, 2014). Walker et al, (2008) explained the barriers under two main headings as internal and external barriers (Walker et al, 2008). In his study, Rahman explained the lack of information and support in four classes as the inadequacy of the enterprise, in terms of GSCM support and operational policies, lack of infrastructure-technology and financial constraints (Rahman, 2018). In his study Zailani on the other hand, explained four categories as institutional, organizational, financial and information-based (Zailani, 2009). In this study, the barriers encountered in the implementation of GSCM that are based upon internal and external barriers will explained with the classifications of Balasubramanian and Mehrabi et al, (Balasubramanian, 2012; Mehrabi et al, 2012).

External Barriers to the Implementation of GSCM

Regardless of the size of the enterprise, the constraints that affect outside the jurisdiction of the enterprise are defined as external barriers.

Lack of resources: Technical experts that have inadequate qualification and equipment to carry out "green" projects in the region are barriers to a successful GSCM (Baki, 2018).

Lack of understanding of GSCM among supply chain members: The lack of cooperation, strong communication and information sharing among supply chain members is one of the constraints to the success of green supply chain management practices (Balasubramanian, 2012).

Inadequate state support: Failure to provide appropriate support with government policies and regulations on sustainability may prevent companies from adopting and implementing green supply chain management (Govindan et al, 2014).

Competition and uncertainty: A company's activities are influenced by its external environment. The external environment of the company may influence the company's decisions in adopting innovations. In this context, competition and uncertainty in the market can be an barrier to the implementation of "green" initiatives (Baki, 2018).

Lack of demand and public awareness: Consumers' awareness of green products increases their demand for environmentally friendly products. This means that companies change production processes and technologies for green products. In this respect, inadequate consumer awareness and demand for "green" products may prevent the adoption and implementation of green supply chain management (Luthra et al, 2011).

Internal Barriers to the Implementation of GSCM

In the implementation of GSCM, the limiting factors that affect within the scope of the authority of the enterprise are defined as internal barriers.

Lack of GSCM practices in the company's mission and vision: The absence of "green" projects in the vision and mission of the enterprise in the long term may prevent GSCM implementation (Balasubramanian, 2012).

Lack of corporate leadership and support: The failure of senior management to show the necessary commitment to the adoption and implementation of GSCM policies is an barrier to a successful GSCM (Lamba & Thareja, 2016).

Lack of knowledge and experience: Proper training, support and information on GSCM should be provided to supply chain members and employees. Lack of knowledge and inexperience among the supply chain members may prevent GSCM practices (Rahman, 2018).

Poor organizational culture: A long-term vision of GSCM policies and practices by senior management is an barrier to GSCM (Lamba & Thareja, 2016).

Lack of technological infrastructure: Green production activity, which is one of the most important components of GSCM applications, requires having innovative technology and infrastructure in production processes. Lack of green technology in production processes may prevent GSCM implementation (Govindan et al, 2014).

Lack of green initiatives: The lack of training in GSCM, the company's lack of ISO environmental standards certificates, and the lack of intraco and inter-supplier control constitute a barrier to the adoption and implementation of "green" initiatives (Balasubramanian, 2012).

Financial constraints: The high investment costs required for "green" activities, the disposal of waste and the innovative technology required for environmentally friendly production processes create a huge cost for companies. Despite the costs to be incurred for "green" activities, the company's low economic benefit or uncertainty in this regard emerges as a limiting factor in the adoption and implementation of green supply chain management (Majumdar & Sinha, 2018).

LITERATURE REVIEW

In the literature, GSCM has become a remarkable concept in the context of corporate environmental management by researchers after the 2000s. The studies in this field vary at conceptual, empirical and analytical level. In the context of the barriers encountered in GSCM applications, there are many scientific studies in the literature. Data analysis with SPSS, DEMATEL, AHP, ISM methods were applied frequently by using survey technique. According to the method of the research, the barriers encountered in green supply chain applications were analyzed and the prominent factors were revealed. The studies in the literature regarding the factors that come forward from the barriers encountered in the implementation of GSCM can be seen in the table below.

Table 1. Literature Review of Barriers of GSCM

Author	Industry (Country)	Method	Major Barriers of GSCM
Majumdar and Sinha (2019)	•Textile (Southeast Asian Countries)	•ISM	•The complexity of the "green" process •System design •Inadequate consumer support for green •Inadequate support and guidance from regulatory agencies
Rahman (2018)	•Plastic (Bangladesh)	•FUZZY VIKOR	•Lack of knowledge, training and support
Da Silva, Shiboa, Barbieri, Librantz and Santos (2018)	•Automotive (Brazil)	•AHP	•High costs in GSCMimplementation
Sarker, Ahmed, Deb and Chowdhury (2018)	•Footwear (Bangladesh)	•DELPHI	•Inadequate participation of senior management in the field of GSCM •Inadequacy of the top management's policy on the GSCM
Kaur, Sidhu, Awasthi, Chauhan and Goyal (2018)	•Electronics (Canada)	•DEMATEL	•Lack of information and training on GSCM •Lack of senior management participation and policy
Majumdar and Sinha (2018)	•Clothing (India)	•ISM	•The complexity of the "green" process •System design •Inadequate regulatory support •The economic benefit does not meet the high investment cost
Wang, Mathiyazhagan, Xu and Diabat (2016)	•Packaging (North India)	•DEMATEL	•Lack of training in environmental management concepts •Inadequate process tracking •Lack of customer awareness of GSCM
Malviya and Kant (2016)	•Automotive (India)	•AHP	•Inadequate involvement of the senior management in terms of GSCM •The inadequacy of the top management's policy on the issue
Nieman, Kotze and Adamo (2016)	•Manufacturing (Mozambique)	•Interview	•High costs •Lack of legislation on GSCM •Organizational culture policies
Koska, Göksu and Sünbül (2016)	•Paper (Turkey)	•AHP	•Inadequate government support in adopting environmentally friendly policies
Faisal (2015)	•Pharmaceutical (Pakistan)	•ISM •SPSS	•High investment costs •The cost of training required for training in GSCM •Cost of procurement of equipment required for "green" production
Govindan, Kaliyan, Kannan and Haq (2014)	•Various Industrial Sectors (South India)	•AHP	•Lack of "green" technology
Jayant and Ashar (2014)	•Manufacturing (India)	•ISM	•Lack of government support for GSCM. •Lack of bank loans to promote "green" products •Economic impacts of GSCMimplementation •Lack of environmental awareness of consumers about "green" products •Lack of training on GSCM practices •Lack of environmental awareness of suppliers about GSCM. •Poor organizational culture in the adoption of GSCM. •Lack of determination and support of senior management.
Nigam (2014)	•Various Industrial Sectors (India)	•ISM	•High costs in GSCM application •Lack of consumer demand for "green" products

continues on following page

Table 1. Contineud

Author	Industry (Country)	Method	Major Barriers of GSCM
Ojo, Mbowa and Akinlabi (2014)	•Construction (Nigeria)	•SPSS	•High costs for investment •Resistance of suppliers to change •Lack of awareness about GSCM
Muduli and Barve (2013)	•Mining (India)	•SPSS	•Technological and financial deficiencies •Disruptions in the functioning of legislation on GSCM •Lack of social concerns about environmental management •Lack of knowledge of managers about GSCM
Khiewnavawongsa and Schmidt (2013)	•Electronics (USA)	•SPSS	•High costs in GSCMimplementation
Mehrabi, Jalalifar, Gharakhani and Rahmati (2012)	•Petrochemical (Iran)	•ANP	•Lack of understanding of supply chain members about GSCM •Lack of "green" initiatives •Inadequate corporate leadership and support
Balasubramanian (2012)	•Construction (United Arab Emirates)	•ISM •DDPA	•Lack of government support •Lack of environmental awareness of consumers •Lack of demand from consumers
Luthra, Kumar, Kumar and Haleem (2011)	•Automotive (India)	•ISM	•Market competition and uncertainty •Failure to implement green practices •Financial impacts of GSCM implementation •Lack of environmental awareness of consumers
Walker, Di Sisto and McBain (2008)	•Manufacturing (China)	•Interview	•High costs in GSCM implementation •Reluctance of suppliers to change •Gaps in legislation

METHODOLOGY

The aim of this study is to identify the barriers encountered in the application of GSCM. The field of application of the study is the companies registered in the BIST Sustainability Index and the statistical analysis of the data obtained from the participants through the survey was conducted with SPSS 22.0 program. The methodology followed in the study is stated below.

Research Gap

There are many studies in the Turkish literature towards the adoption and implementation of green supply chain management. However, the literature on the barriers faced by enterprises in the application of GSCM is limited. Koska et al, (2016) application on the Kipaş paper factory with the AHP method in the paper sector is the only study to analyze the barriers encountered in the application of GSCM in the Turkish literature take parts in Table 1. Therefore, there is a research gap regarding the inclusion of different sectors in the analysis. This gap in the literature has led to the choice of the research topic. In this context, the application area of the study; designate as companies registered to BIST Sustainability Index, which operates in different sectors and is valued according to international sustainability criteria. BIST Sustainability Index; is an index of the aim to increase understanding, information and applications on sustainability created with Turkey, especially involving companies performing higher performance between in Borsa Istanbul companies in terms of corporate sustainability level. BIST Sustainability Index has been started to be calculated and published as price and return with the code of XUSRD since date of 4 November 2014 (Borsa İstanbul, 2019).

Survey Questions

In the study, questionnaire consists of two parts. In the first part of the study, there are 7 questions. In the second part, 37 questions were asked to the participants. In this section, the extent to which the participants participated in the questions in the scale was determined by the five-point Likert scale.(1-Very Weak; 2-Weak; 3-Ineffective; 4-Strong; 5-Very Strong)

The questions in the first section aim to reveal business history and demographic characteristics. In addition, in this section to the participants were asked questions searches the preparation degree and willingness about implementing the "green" projects of the enterprise that they are working. The questions in the second part are aimed at identifying the barriers encountered in the application of GSCM. As a result of a wide literature review, Balasubramanian (2012), Govindan et al. (2014), Kaur et al. (2018), 37 barriers obtained by Dhull and Narwall (2016) are divided into 12 categories identified by Balasubramanian (2012).

These are: lack of resources (3 barriers), lack of understanding about GSCM between supply chain members (2 barriers), inadequate state support (3 barriers), competition and uncertainty (3 barriers), lack of demand and public awareness (2 barriers), the lack of GSCM practices in mission and vision of enterprise (2 barriers), lack of corporate leadership and support (2 barriers), lack of knowledge and experience (3 barriers), poor organizational culture (3 barriers), lack of technological infrastructure (3 barriers), inadequate green initiatives (4 barriers), financial constraints (7 barriers).

Data Collection

The universe of the research consists of 50 companies in the index between November 2018 - October 2019. Survey questions; sent to white collar employees who are expected to have knowledge about GSCM via e-mail and linkedin like senior managers, branch managers, procurement, sales, logistics, etc. in 50 companies that make up the universe of the research. The data collection process in the research was between 05.04.2019 - 16.05.2019 and 24 of the questionnaires sent at the end of the process were answered. All 24 questionnaires answered by the participants were found to be valid and included in the study. Thus, the valid response rate is 48% and the sample size is considered to represent the universe.

Data Analysis

The data about the valid questionnaires answered by the participants were analyzed in SPSS 22.0 program. The stages of statistical analysis are as follows: First, reliability test was applied to measure the consistency of the responses to the questionnaire. In the second stage, the scales were averaged and the results were interpreted by applying descriptive statistical analysis. The normality and homogeneity test were applied to the data according to the hypotheses formed in the fourth stage. In the fifth stage, T Test and One Way Analysis of Variance were applied to test whether the characteristics of company differed averages over the barriers meaningfully. At this stage, the variance between the groups was found to be homogeneous and the sub-criteria were compared with the Scheffe test.

RESEARCH FINDINGS

In this section, the results of statistical analysis of the data are expressed.

Reliability Analysis

Cronbach Alpha test is the most commonly used reliability calculation method. Cronbach Alpha coefficient is between 0 and 1. If this coefficient is equal to or higher than 0.70, it is statistically acceptable (the consistency level increases as the coefficient approaches to 1) (Gliem & Gliem, 2003). In this study, the consistency calculations of the criteria were performed by using Cronbach Alpha test. Cronbach Alpha coefficient for each criterion is presented in Table 2.

Table 2. Cronbach Alpha Analysis Results

Barrier Criteria	Number of Items	Cronbach Alpha Coefficient
Lack of GSCM practices in business mission and vision	2	0,904
Lack of corporate leadership and support	2	0,935
Financial constraints	7	0,907
Poor organizational culture	3	0,861
Lack of technological infrastructure	3	0,906
Lack of green initiatives	4	0,819
Lack of knowledge and experience	3	0,873
Lack of resources	3	0,669
Lack of demand and public awareness	2	0,890
Lack of government support	3	0,853
Competition and uncertainty	3	0,711
Lack of understanding of the GSCM among supply chain members	2	0,830
Total	37	0,925

As shown in Table 2, it was concluded that the Cronbach Alpha coefficient of 0.925 was statistically highly rate consistent for all criteria.

Demographic Characteristics and Company Characteristics According to Participants' Responses

According to the results of the frequency analysis, 16.7% of the participants were active in energy, 12.5% in electrical-electronics, 20.8% in finance, 8.3% in food and 16.7% in automotive shows.

16.7% of the companies in which the participants operate are engaged in export activities between 1-5 years, 8.3% between 11-20 years, and 75% of them are 21 years or more.

On the question on the rate of aproximate use of green project in all the sales for the last 5 years, 50% of participants have replied as "I don't know". On the question on the aproximate investment rate for the next five years, 62.5% of the participants answered "I don't know".

66.7% of the participants confirmed that their company has recently implemented a "green" project.

Descriptive Statistics Analysis

Table 3 presents the responses of the participants regarding the grading of the barriers encountered in GSCM implementation.

Tablo 3. Most Affected Barriers in GSCM Implementation

Barrier Criteria	Mean
Competition and uncertainty	3,31
Lack of demand and public awareness	3,19
Financial constraints	3,17
Lack of understanding of the GSCM among supply chain members	3,08
Lack of corporate leadership and support	3,04
Lack of government support	3,01
Poor organizational culture	3,00
Lack of knowledge and experience	3,00
Lack of green initiatives	2,96
Lack of resources	2,93
Lack of technological infrastructure	2,90
Lack of GSCM practices in business mission and vision	2,83

According to Table 3, competition and uncertainty criterion has the highest level among the barriers encountered in the implementation of "green" projects. This criterion is followed by lack of demand, public awareness and financial constraints, respectively. The first three criteria with the lowest ratings are the lack of GSCM practices, lack of technological infrastructure and insufficient resources in the mission and vision of the enterprise.

Table 4. Most Affected Sub-Criteria Barriers in GSCM Implementation

Sub-Criteria Barrier	Barrier Criteria	Mean
"Green" projects have a high investment cost in construction, transfering facilities and equipment.	Financial constraints	3,500
The international crisis and economic decline are barriers.	Competition and uncertainty	3,500
Costs of raw materials for "green" initiatives are higher.	Financial constraints	3,375
"Green" projects have high operating costs.	Financial constraints	3,333
High prices in "green" practices prevent competitors from competing with lower prices.	Competition and uncertainty	3,292

3 of the 5 most important barriers encountered in the implementation of GSCM presented in Table 4 are financial constraints from the internal barriers encountered in GSCM implementation; the others belong to the criteria of competition and uncertainty from external barriers.

Testing the Hypotheses

In this study, the relationship between the demographic characteristics of the companies registered in BIST Sustainability Index of 2018-2019 and the criteria and sub-criteria related to the barriers encountered in the application of GSCM was investigated by independent sample T test and One Way Analysis of Variance (ANOVA). With these analyzes, it can be investigated whether there is a significant difference between the demographic characteristics of the companies and the barriers encountered during the application of GSCM. For this purpose; with the independent sample T test, it is possible to investigate whether the application status of the "green" projects constitutes a significant difference on the barriers encountered in the implementation of GSCM, and the One-Way Analysis of Variance (ANOVA) can be used to investigate whether the type of activity of the company and the duration of export activity make a significant difference on the barriers encountered in the implementation of GSCM. Before the tests, normal distribution test was applied to the data. The normality test is a test designed to test whether a random variable distribution is normal (D'Agostino et al, 1990). If the p value calculated as a result of normality test is greater than 0.05, it is considered that the data are distributed normally (Demir et al, 2016).

As a result of the analysis conducted in this study, it was found that the data were distributed normally. Then, it was investigated whether the groups had equal variance. For this purpose, Levene covariance test was performed. In Levene co-variance test p value greater than 0.05 is obtained shows that the variance of the groups equal.

According to Levene Co-variance test results; p value 0,339 for "lack of resources" factor, p value 0,072 for "lack of understanding of the GSCM among supply chain members" factor, p value 0,633 for "lack of government support" factor, p value 0,160 for "competition and uncertainty" factor, p value 0,347 for "lack of demand and public awareness" factor, p value 0,654 for "lack of GSCM practices in business mission and vision" factor, p value 0,680 for "lack of corporate leadership and support" factor, p value 0,826 for "lack of knowledge and experience" factor, p value 0,173 for "poor organizational culture" factor, p value 0,235 for "lack of technological infrastructure" factor, p value 0,209 for "lack of green initiatives" factor, p value 0,510 for "financial constraints" factor. The p value for all factors is greater than 0.05, which means that the variance of these factors does not change according to the application situation of the company's "green" projects. Therefore, the statistic t, which gives reliable results in the case of homogenitiy of variance, was calculated for the barrier factors encountered in GSCM.

According to independent sample T test results; p value 0,354 for "lack of resources" factor, p value 0,386 for "lack of understanding of the GSCM among supply chain members" factor, p value 0,392 for "lack of government support" factor, p value 0,960 for "competition and uncertainty" factor, p value 0,656for "lack of demand and public awareness" factor, p value 0,632 for "lack of GSCM practices in business mission and vision" factor, p value 0,384 for "lack of corporate leadership and support" factor, p value for 0,868 "lack of knowledge and experience" factor, p value 0,287 for "poor organizational culture" factor, p value 0,305 for "lack of technological infrastructure" factor, p value 0,558 for "lack of green initiatives" factor, p value 0,903 for "financial constraints" factor. The p value of t statistic for all factors was greater than 0.05. The results show that the implementation status of the "green" projects of the company does not make a significant difference on the barriers faced in the implementation of GSCM.

According to Levene Co-variance test results; p value 0,734 for "lack of resources" factor, p value 0,110 for "lack of understanding of the GSCM among supply chain members" factor, p value 0,434 for "lack of government support" factor, p value 0,283 for "competition and uncertainty" factor, p value 0,261 for "lack of demand and public awareness" factor, p value 0,519 for "lack of GSCM practices in business mission and vision" factor, p value 0,191 for "lack of corporate leadership and support" factor, p value for 0,192 "lack of knowledge and experience" factor, p value 0,973for "poor organizational culture" factor, p value 0,443 for "lack of technological infrastructure" factor, p value 0,628 for "lack of green initiatives" factor, p value 0,141 for "financial constraints" factor. According to ANOVA test, p values of these factors were found to be greater than 0.05. ANOVA test results, p value greater than 0.05 shows that the type of activity of the company does not make a significant difference on the barriers faced in the implementation of GSCM.

According to Levene Co-variance test results; p value 0,477 for "lack of resources" factor, p value 4,271 for "lack of understanding of the GSCM among supply chain members" factor, p value 0,149 for "lack of government support" factor, p value 0,334 for "competition and uncertainty" factor, p value 0,184 for "lack of demand and public awareness" factor, p value 1,208 for "lack of GSCM practices in business mission and vision" factor, p value 2,019 for "lack of corporate leadership and support" factor, p value 0,277 for "lack of knowledge and experience" factor, p value 0,141 for "poor organizational culture" factor, p value 0,521 for "lack of technological infrastructure" factor, p value 0,574 for "lack of green initiatives" factor, p value 0,882 for "financial constraints" factor. According to ANOVA test results; p values of all factors were found to be greater than 0.05. As a result of the findings, it was evaluated that the export period of the company did not create a significant difference on the barriers faced in the implementation of GSCM.

CONCLUSION

The aim of this study; in implementation of GSCM is to identify the barriers faced by enterprises and the prominent factors. The implementation area of the study is the companies registered in BIST Sustainability Index treated on Borsa Istanbul.

In the Turkish literature about barriers to GSCM implementation, there is only an application on paper sector. For this reason, it is aimed to include different sectors in this study. The companies included in the BIST Sustainability Index are suitable for the purpose of the study as they operate in many different sectors. In addition, the companies included in this index have ISO 14001 Environmental Management Certificate and are members of organizations that audit environmental management policies such as Coalition for Environmentally Responsible Economies (CERES) and Eco Management and Audit Scheme (EMAS) (Borsa İstanbul, 2019). The fact that the companies in the index operate in different sectors and implement environmental management policies has shaped the selection decision of the study field.

The barriers encountered in the application of GSCM in the study; is split in half as internal and external. In this study, the barrier criteria were arranged according to the study conducted by Balasubramanian (2012). Accordingly, internal barriers; lack of GSCM practices in the mission and vision of the enterprise, lack of corporate leadership and support, lack of knowledge and experience, poor organizational culture, financial constraints, inadequate green initiatives, inadequate technological infrastructure. External barriers; inadequate resources, lack of understanding about GSCM among members of the supply chain, lack of demand and public awareness, competition and uncertainty, and inadequate state support. The sub-criteria were extended by a wide literature review. According to the results of the reliability analysis, it was concluded that all criteria were highly consistent.

The online questionnaire was sent to the related people in electronic environment and 24 responses were obtained. The data obtained were analyzed in SPSS 22.0 program. According to the survey responses, most of the respondents are active in the energy, electrical-electronics, finance and automotive sectors. According to the findings of the research, the top 5 barriers are as follows: "Green" projects have high investment costs in construction, changing facilities and equipment, international crisis and economic decreases, raw material costs are higher in "green" applications, "green" projects have high operating costs and high prices in "green" applications unable to compete with lower prices of competitors.

On the other hand, the major barriers in the study of Majumdar and Sinha (2019) are the complexity of the "green" process, the system design, the insufficient support and incentives of consumers on the issue of "green" and the lack of adequate support and guidance from the regulatory institutions. Sarker et al. (2018), the prominent barriers in his study are the inadequate participation of senior management in GSCM and the inadequacy of the policy of senior management in GSCM. Koska et al. (2016) the prominent barriers in his study are the inadequate state support in adopting environmentally-friendly policies.

In this case, the barrier criterion that prominent in the "green" initiatives of the enterprises is the financial constraints of the internal barriers within the jurisdiction of the enterprise. Another criterion is the competition and uncertainty factor from external barriers encountered outside the competence areas of the enterprise. Another finding obtained by evaluating the normal distribution of the data in the study is as follows: The activity area of the company, the implementation status of the "green" projects and the duration of export activity do not make a significant difference on the barriers encountered in the implementation of GSCM.

According to the results of the research, if the companies concentrate on the prominent barriers and eliminate these barriers, they will be able to develop more green projects, increase customer satisfaction by increasing their green activities, and gain a competitive advantage by placing green policies on company visions and missions. Accordingly, the company; with the organizational factors like the management, employees and partners; must cooperate with out of organization factors such as customers, government, creditors and suppliers.

The most important limitation of the research is that the employees do not want to respond to the surveys. Another limitation is; The number of companies registered in the index of 2018-2019 which constitutes the universe of the study is low (there are 50 companies in the list). Therefore, in order to generalize the results obtained in the study, it is recommended that researchers work with larger sample groups in future studies. However, depending on the field of activity of businesses in "green" applications may vary due to barriers encountered in so it is recommended to repeat the studies in other sectors such as textiles, plastics, packaging, etc.

REFERENCES

Ay, C., & Ecevit, Z. (2005). Çevre bilinçli tüketiciler. *Journal of Akdeniz University Faculty of Economics and Administrative Sciences*, *5*(10), 238–263.

Ayant, A., & Azhar, M. (2014). Analysis of the barriers for implementing green supply chain management (GSCM) practices: An interpretive structural modeling (ISM) approach. *Procedia Engineering*, *97*, 2157–2166. doi:10.1016/j.proeng.2014.12.459

Baki, R. (2018). Literature review on green supply chain management concept and problems during it's implementation. *The Journal of International Scientific Researches*, *3*(2), 114–122.

Balasubramanian, S. (2012). A hierarchical framework of barriers to green supply chain management in the construction sector. *Journal of Sustainable Development*, *5*(10), 15–27. doi:10.5539/jsd.v5n10p15

Beamon, M. B. (1999). Designing the gren supply chain. *Logistics Information Management*, *10*(4), 132–142.

Borsa İstanbul. (2019). *Bist sürdürülebilirlik endeksi*. Retrieved from https://www.borsaistanbul.com/endeksler/bist-pay-endeksleri/surdurulebilirlik-endeksi

D'Agostino, R. B., Belanger, A., & D'agostino, R. B. Jr. (1990). A suggestion for using powerful and informative tests of normality. *The American Statistician*, *44*(4), 316–321.

Da Silva, F. C., Shibao, F. Y., Barbieri, J. C., Librantz, A. F. H., & Dos Santos, M. R. (2018). Barriers to green supply chain management in the automotive industry. *Revista De Administração De Empresas*, *58*(2), 149–162.

Demir, E., Saatçioğlu, Ö., & İmrol, F. (2016). Uluslararası dergilerde yayımlanan eğitim araştırmalarının normallik varsayımları açısından incelenmesi. *Current Research in Education*, *3*(3), 130–148.

Dhull, S., & Narwal, M. S. (2016). Drivers and barriers in green supply chain management adaptation: A state-of-art review. *Uncertain Supply Chain Management*, *4*, 61–76. doi:10.5267/j.uscm.2015.7.003

Diabat, A., & Govindan, K. (2011). An analysis of the drivers affecting the implementation of green supply chain management. *Resources, Conservation and Recycling*, *55*(6), 659–667. doi:10.1016/j.resconrec.2010.12.002

Dubey, R., Gunasekaran, A., & Papadopoulos, T. (2017). Green supply chain management: Theoretical framework and further research directions. *Benchmarking: An International Journal*, *24*(1), 184–218. doi:10.1108/BIJ-01-2016-0011

Ergülen, A., & Büyükkeklik, A. (2008). Çevre yönetiminde yeni bir yaklaşım yeşil tedarik zinciri yönetimi [A new approach in environmental management green supply chain management]. *Selçuk University Journal of Vocational School of Social Sciences*, *10*(1-2), 33–50.

Faisal, M. (2015). Research analysis on barriers to green supply chain management in pharmaceutical industries. *Review of Public Administration and Management*, *3*(1). doi:10.4172/2315-7844.1000176

Gliem, J. A., & Gliem, R. R. (2003). Calculating, interpreting, and reporting cronbach's alpha reliability coefficient for likert-type scales. In *2003 Midwest Research to Practice Conference in Adult, Continuing, and Community Education* (pp.82-88). Academic Press.

Govindan, K., Mathiyazhagan, K., Kannan, D., & Haq, A. N. (2014). Barriers analysis for green supply chain management implementation in Indian industries using analytic hierarchy process. *International Journal of Production Economics, 147*, 555–568. doi:10.1016/j.ijpe.2013.08.018

Hervani, A. A., Helms, M. M., & Sarkis, J. (2005). Performance measurement for green supply chain management. *Benchmarking: An International Journal, 12*(4), 330–353. doi:10.1108/14635770510609015

Kaur, J., Sidhu, R., Awasthi, A., Chauhan, S., & Goyal, S. (2018). A DEMATEL based approach for investigating barriers in green supply chain management in Canadian manufacturing firms. *International Journal of Production Research, 56*(1-2), 312–332. doi:10.1080/00207543.2017.1395522

Khiewnavawongsa, S., & Schmidt, E. K. (2013). Barriers to green supply chain implementation in the electronics industry. *International Conference on Industrial Engineering and Engineering Management*, 226-230. 10.1109/IEEM.2013.6962408

Koska, A., Göksu, N., & Sünbül, M. B. (2016). Barriers of green supply chain management implementation: An application in Kipaş paper factory. *Journal of Social and Humanities Sciences Research, 6*(2), 117–140.

Lamba, N., & Thareja, P. (2016). Barriers of green supply chain management: A review. Journal of Advanced Research In Manufacturing. *Material Science & Metallurgical Engineering, 3*(3-4), 4–15.

Luthra, S., Kumar, V., Kumar, S., & Haleem, A. (2011). Barriers to implement green supply chain management in automobile industry using interpretive structural modeling technique an Indian perspective. *Journal of Industrial Engineering and Management, 4*(2), 231–257. doi:10.3926/jiem.2011.v4n2.p231-257

Majumdar, A., & Sinha, S. K. (2018). Modeling the barriers of green supply chain management in small and medium enterprises: A case of Indian clothing industry. *Management of Environmental Quality, 29*(6), 1110–1122. doi:10.1108/MEQ-12-2017-0176

Majumdar, A., & Sinha, S. K. (2019). Analyzing the barriers of green textile supply chain management in South-East Asia using interpretive structural modelling. *Sustainable Production and Consumption, 17*, 176–187. doi:10.1016/j.spc.2018.10.005

Malviya, R. K., & Kant, R. (2016). A comprehensive analysis of the barriers to green supply chain management implementation. *International Journal of Decision Sciences, Risk Management, 6*(4), 331–362.

Mehrabi, J., Gharakhani, D., Jalalifar, S., & Rahmati, H. (2012). Barriers to green supply chain management in the petrochemical sector. *Life Science Journal, 9*(4), 3438–3442.

Muduli, K., & Barve, A. (2013). Empirical Investigation of the Barriers of Green Supply Chain Management Implementation in Indian Mining Industries. In *3rd International Conference on Business, Economics, Management and Behavioral Sciences* (pp. 290-294). Singapore: Academic Press.

Niemann, W., Kotze, T., & Adamo, F. (2016). Drivers and barriers of green supply chain management implementation in the Mozambican manufacturing industry. *Journal of Contemporary Management, 13*(1), 977–1013.

Nigam, P. (2014). Interpretive structural modelling (ISM) of the barriers to green supply chain management in Indian companies. *International Journal of Business Performance and Supply Chain Modelling, 6*(2), 183. doi:10.1504/IJBPSCM.2014.062466

Ojo, E., Mbowa, C., & Akinlabi, E. T. (2014). Barriers in implementing green supply chain management in construction industry. In *4th International Conference on Industrial Engineering and Operations Management* (pp. 1974-1981). Bali, Indonesia: Academic Press.

Özesen, E. (2009). *Yeşil tedarik zinciri yönetimi ve ambalaj sanayinde bir uygulama* [An application in green supply chain management and packaging industry] (Unpublished master's thesis). Marmara University Institute of Social Sciences. Turkey, Istanbul.

Rahman, T. (2018). *Analysis of barriers in implementing green supply chain management in plastic industry* (Unpublished master's thesis). Bangladesh University of Engineering and Technology. Department of Industrial and Production Engineering.

Sarker, M., Ahmed, F., Deb, A. K., & Chowdhury, M. (2018). Identifying barriers for implementing green supply chain management (GSCM) in footwear industry of Bangladesh: A Delphi Study Approach. *Leather and Footwear Journal, 18*(3), 175–186. doi:10.24264/lfj.18.3.1

Sarkis, J. (2003). A strategic decision framework for gren supply chain management. *Journal of Cleaner Production, 11*(4), 397–409. doi:10.1016/S0959-6526(02)00062-8

Srivastava, S. K. (2007). Green supply chain management: A state of the art literature review. *International Journal of Management Reviews, 9*(1), 53–80. doi:10.1111/j.1468-2370.2007.00202.x

Thun, J. H., & Müller, A. (2010). An empirical analysis of green supply chain management in the German automotive industry. *Business Strategy and the Environment, 19*(2), 119–132.

Tseng, M.-L., Islam, M., Karia, N., Fauzi, F. A., & Afrin, S. (2019). A literature review on green supply chain management: Trends and future challenges. *Resources, Conservation and Recycling, 141*, 145–162. doi:10.1016/j.resconrec.2018.10.009

Walker, H., Di Sisto, L., & McBain, D. (2008). Drivers and barriers to environmental supply chain management practices: Lessons from the public and private sectors. *Journal of Purchasing and Supply Management, 14*(1), 69–85. doi:10.1016/j.pursup.2008.01.007

Wang, Y.-F., Chen, S.-P., Lee, Y.-C., & Tsai, C.-T. (2013). Developing green management standards for restaurants: An application of green supply chain management. *International Journal of Hospitality Management, 34*, 263–273. doi:10.1016/j.ijhm.2013.04.001

Wang, Z., Mathiyazhagan, K., Xu, L., & Diabat, A. (2016). A decision making trial and evaluation laboratory approach to analyze the barriers to green supply chain management adoption in a food packaging company. *Journal of Cleaner Production, 117*, 19–28. doi:10.1016/j.jclepro.2015.09.142

Zhang, G., & Zhao, Z. (2012). Green packaging management of logistics enterprises. *Physics Procedia, 24*, 900–905. doi:10.1016/j.phpro.2012.02.135

Zhu, Q., & Sarkis, J. (2004). Relationships between operational practices and performance among early adopters of green supply chain management practices in Chinese manufacturing enterprises. *Journal of Operations Management*, *22*(3), 265–289. doi:10.1016/j.jom.2004.01.005

Zhu, Q., & Sarkis, J. (2006). An inter-sectoral comparison of green supply chain management in China: Drivers and practices. *Journal of Cleaner Production*, *14*(5), 472–486. doi:10.1016/j.jclepro.2005.01.003

Chapter 12
Ensuring the Relevance of Independent Smallholder Farmers (ISHFs) Through Sustainable Sourcing Practices:
A Model to Track and Trace Within the Malaysian Palm Oil Industry

Muhilan Ratnam
https://orcid.org/0000-0003-4217-2524
Malaysia Institute for Supply Chain Innovation, MIT Global SCALE Network, Malaysia

ABSTRACT

Malaysia and Indonesia have been the main sources of supply for palm oil (PO), palm kernel oil (PKO), and other palm-related derivatives for most multi-national companies (MNCs). However, deforestation, new legislation in Europe, and stakeholder expectations have posed significant challenges to this industry. In response to these challenges, companies are looking at driving key sustainability initiatives in palm oil supply chains while remaining beneficial to the farmers. This chapter discusses the findings of a collaborative research project conducted through active academic-industry collaboration in South East Asia and shares an approach to identify and incorporate traceability within the supply chain. Critically, it also aims to provide a framework for both academicians and practitioners towards developing a collaborative approach of driving sustainability goals in difficult to measure parts of the supply chain. Importantly, this work also highlights the key aspects of implementing sustainability practices in the upstream palm oil supply chains, which are often ignored.

DOI: 10.4018/978-1-7998-4601-7.ch012

INTRODUCTION

MNCs face constant challenges in trying to balance concerns related to the socio-economic and environmental aspects of palm oil production and at the same time, keeping organizational goals of maintaining procurement excellence to meet strategic business goals. Increasing pressure through global regulations on sustainable sourcing of palm oil has also forced organizations to relook at traceability in their supply chains. For instance, regulations enacted by European economies propose new requirements to adopt sustainable practices of palm oil production in Malaysia and Indonesia (MPOC,2019).

For organizations to establish high traceability of their supply chains, it is imperative that all stakeholders and actors must be tracked and transparent in terms of physical movement of crops, information sharing, and financial flows. This research study, conducted in collaboration with a large Consumer Packaged Goods (CPG) company (which is one of the largest buyers of palm oil in the world) revealed that there were a significant number of Independent Smallholder Farmers (ISHFs) in its supply base who were difficult to trace. Smallholders are divided into two groups: organized and unorganized or independent. A significant share of planted area in Malaysia is under the ownership of ISHFs. In general, ISHFs have contributed a substantial amount towards the Malaysian Palm Oil Industry, in spite of the land size holdings of less than 50 Hectares (Ha). ISHFs in Malaysia represents 17% of total palm oil plantations, or an equivalent of approximately 980,000 hectares of land, and consist of more than 250,000 ISHFs. (MPOB 2018). ISHFs are independent farmers, in the sense of self-managing and financing their plantations. Since they are not contractually bound and part of any corporate scheme, they receive limited technical, institutional and financial support, which makes it challenging for them to adopt sustainability initiatives. These posed a challenge in tracking their locations and mapping their agricultural practices.

Given this context, the author is addressing the following research questions in the study:

1. How can suitable trace and track methodologies be designed and adopted to help identify small and marginal farmers in upstream palm oil supply chains?
2. How can sustainable supply chain practices be adopted by small and marginal farmers in upstream palm oil supply chains?

Broadly, the objective of this research is to design a methodology to trace the farmers across multiple collection centers, spanning through various networks of Super Dealers, tracking the existing practices and design interventions to ascertain sustainability gaps while improving their livelihood.

BACKGROUND

The palm oil industry in Malaysia is organized into four segments. The *plantation* segment includes seed nursery, planting, harvesting, collecting, and milling. The second segment includes refining, bulking and trading activities. The remaining two downstream segments are non-food downstream as well as food and health-based downstream (PEMANDU, 2010).

The Oil palm tree starts to bear fruits after 30 months of field planting and continues to be productive for the next 20 to 30 years; thus ensuring a consistent supply of ripe palm fruit, commonly known as Fresh Fruit Bunch (FFB). In Malaysia, the oil palm trees planted are mainly the *tenera* variety, a hybrid between the *dura* and *pisifera*. The *tenera* variety yields about 4 to 5 tons of crude palm oil (CPO) per hectare per year and about 1 ton of palm kernels. The oil palm is the most efficient oil-bearing crop in the world, requiring only 0.26 hectares of land to produce one ton of crude palm oil while sunflower, soybean, and rapeseed require 2, 2.22 and 1.52 hectares, respectively, to produce the same (MPOC, 2016).

Malaysia is one the largest producers and exporters of palm oil in the world, amounting to 11% of the world's oils & fats production and 27% of export trade of oils & fats. It is about 4.49 million hectares of land in Malaysia that is cultivated with oil palm; producing 17.73 million tons of palm oil and 2.13 tons of palm kernel oil. The industry provides employment to more than half a million people and livelihoods to an estimated one million people (MPOC, 2016).

The oil palm plantations in Malaysia are largely dependent on smallholder schemes and estate management systems, better known as organized farmers. These scheme smallholders are structurally bound to a particular mill and do not have much degree of freedom in their crop management. They are supervised, managed and organized in their crop management system by the scheme or the mill they are associated with. They receive support in the forms of seedlings, fertilizers, pesticides, technical assistance, and credit support. This helps them attain sustainability certifications such as RSPO and MSPO and fulfills the requirements for certified sustainable palm oil. On the other hand, ISHFs are self-managed, self-organized and self-financed, and thus more autonomous and independent in comparison to scheme and associated smallholders. Since they are not contractually bound and part of an extension scheme, they receive limited technical, institutional and financial support, which makes it more difficult to persuade them to adopt Good Agricultural Practices (GAP) and Best Management Practices (BMP) within the upstream supply chain. These ISHFs play an important role in the Malaysian landscape and are considered as key actors in the palm oil supply chain, due to their contribution in terms of the planted area towards FFB production.

In 2014, smallholders represented about 40% (MPOB 2014) of the total planted area and played an important role in the upstream supply chain in producing quality fresh fruit bunches (FFB) supplied to mills. Out of this, 17% is contributed by ISHFs. Challenge has always been procuring sustainably and holding social responsibility towards the various stakeholders, especially the Independent Smallholder Farmers (ISHF) and Small Growers within the supply chain.

Interestingly, while the efforts on sustainability and certification have gained momentum in the region, the main challenge for the processors and buyers of palm related products is to adopt sustainable sources, processes, and practices at the upstream stage. In Malaysia, most scheme farmers are associated with big plantation companies who adopt a three-element approach in their corporate social responsibility (CSR) plan, which is, People, Planet, and Profit commonly referred to as 3Ps. These 3Ps eventually aim to strike a balance between social, environmental and economic needs.

However, the adoption of sustainable practices poses a big challenge to ISHFs, who own small land sizes and manage their farms with limited funding vis-à-vis other scheme farmers who are largely corporate supported with more backing for sustainability programs and funding.

Therefore, to keep the ISHFs relevant in the supply network, it was important to assess their current condition, practices, and in finding ways to improve their practices, productivity, and livelihood.

Preliminary findings revealed that the MNC procured one-third of its supply from ISHFs and small growers within Malaysia. This implied a land-use of approximately 200,000 Ha to procure. The average landholding size in Malaysia for ISHFs for palm oil varies between 2.5 Ha to 50 Ha, with more farmers working on smaller land sizes. Computations showed that this implied dealing with approximately 20,000 to 30,000 ISHFs.

LITERATURE REVIEW

Challenges of World Palm Oil

The world production of palm oil has doubled over the last decade. In the year 2000, palm oil was and still the most produced and traded vegetable oil amounting to 40% of overall traded vegetable oil. Global demand is expected to increase again in 2050 to 240 million mt, which will result in the expansion of many new palm oil plantations in Malaysia, Indonesia, Thailand, Africa, and Latin America. (FAO, 2015).

The highest production globally among all oils and fats produced is contributed by the palm oil industry. (Green Palm, 2016). This is proven by the unique characteristic of oil palm crops that has the highest productivity in terms of yield per hectare cultivated.

Furthermore, the global consumption of palm oil products is predominantly distributed in the Asia region where India, Indonesia, China, and Malaysia together account for almost half of the world's consumption of palm oil. (USDA, 2014).

Malaysia is one of the major players in the palm oil industry globally. Malaysia and Indonesia alone contributed 86% of the overall world palm oil production in 2014. Palm oil is the largest agricultural contributor to Malaysia's gross domestic product (GDP) with a total of RM44. 8 billion or 3.8 percent of the GDP contribution in 2017. (Rasiah and Shahrin, 2004)

However, both of these economies have faced restrictions on exports of palm oil, specifically from European nations with the new requirements to adopt sustainable practices of palm oil production *(MPOC, 2019*). Such policy changes have the potential to affect exports and create significant financial hardship for Independent Smallholder Farmers (ISHF).

Challenges in Upstream Palm Oil Supply Chain

Being one of the biggest producers and exporters of palm oil and palm oil products, Malaysia has an important role to play in fulfilling the growing global need for oils and fats sustainably. (MPOC, 2016). Handfield and Nichols (1999) emphasized the importance of managing the entire supply chain encompassing all activities associated with the flow and transformation of goods from raw materials to the end product.

As far as the scope of this project is concerned, over these years the oil palm industry has been a major contributor towards poverty eradication by closing the gap between rural and urban lifestyle. (Abazue et.al, 2015)

Arif Simeh and Tengku (2001) has stressed on the impacts of smallholders' scheme on rural livelihood; found that poverty amongst the rural livelihoods was significantly reduced from 68.3% in 1970 to a mere 11.8% in 1997. On the economic sustainability of the smallholders, the result shows a strong indication that the sector has positively impacted on the lives of the smallholders.

Although traceability schemes have slightly different definitions for traceability, they all reference a process by which a product moves from its original raw material extraction and production phase to the final customer. The original ISO definition of traceability is "the ability to identify and trace the history, distribution, location, and application of products, parts, and materials". (UN Global Compact & BSR, 2014) This report stressed that it is difficult for companies to trace each and every step in the journey of a given product. A combination of stakeholders with different systems and requirements may contribute to production across international borders, and some areas in a supply chain may be especially opaque.

This is a complex issue as traceability requires the engagement and collaboration of actors along the entire supply chain to trace a product's history. However, developments in technology and demands for greater transparency from both business and government sectors are making this increasingly more manageable. This pressure will eventually move from downstream towards the upstream of the supply chains.

CHALLENGES OF TRACING AND TRACKING

Often the expansion of palm oil industry has environmental and social costs where the expansion takes place at the expense of forest area, peatlands and local communities land that lead to environmental degradation, loss of ecosystem services, loss of biodiversity, increasing land conflict and anthropogenic climate change (WWF, 2008). Therefore, large-scale palm oil production and growth have increased public concerns regarding the environmental and social impact and an increased need for sustainability and accountability. These have created a domino effect for sustainable supply from all stakeholders within the supply chain. However, the impact of sustainability requirements is more obvious in the downstream rather than the upstream supply chain. The awareness, acceptance, and adaptability level is much lower at the upstream source of supply.

MNCs face constant challenges in trying to balance concerns related to the socio-economic and environmental aspects of palm oil production and at the same time up-keeping company goals by maintaining procurement excellence to meet strategic business goals.

For companies to establish 100% traceability in its supply chain, all stakeholders and actors must be traceable. Transparency must be established within the supply chain to track physical, information, and financial flows.

As per our research, one of the largest buyers of palm oil in the world realized that there was a significant amount of Independent Smallholder Farmers upstream in its supply base which was difficult to trace. This posed the obvious challenge of tracking their locations and mapping the AS-IS condition and agricultural practices. To keep these ISHFs relevant in the supply network, it's important to assess their current condition, practices, and move ahead by finding ways to improve their practices, productivity, and livelihood.

The different ways in which the Palm Kernel Oil is sourced and produced in the current value chain is shown in Figure 1. The red dotted line represents the scope of our project.

Traceability for MNC's PKO supply chain was carried out in various stages. Tracing is done backward from fork to farm, which is from the Oleo chemical plant to the plantation and Independent Smallholder Farmers (ISHF). During this initial stage, many actors were identified which eventually turned out to be key stakeholders within the Supply Chain. Naming a few are ISHFs, Estates, Contractors, Collection Centers (CC), Dealers, Transporters, Harvesters, Palm Oil Mills (POM), Kernel Crusher Plants (KCP), Refinery and Oleo Chemical Plant.

MISI's role mainly focused on tracing ISHFs that supply to the MNC's network. With the help of supporting bodies, MISI researchers managed to leverage on their databank to come up with a mill analysis that comprise of Palm Oil Mills and Kernel Crusher Plants which brings us to the Dealer prioritization, based on critical and chosen criteria, such as mill dependency on any dealer's supply, dealer's contribution to a mill, and dealer's dependency on ISHFs supply.

Although ISHFs contribute a small volume to the network, it is still deemed significant for large MNCs to track and trace their source of supply to be justified as sustainable producers. This initiative will also

Figure 1. The Palm Kernel Oil Value Stream
(CSVN,2016)

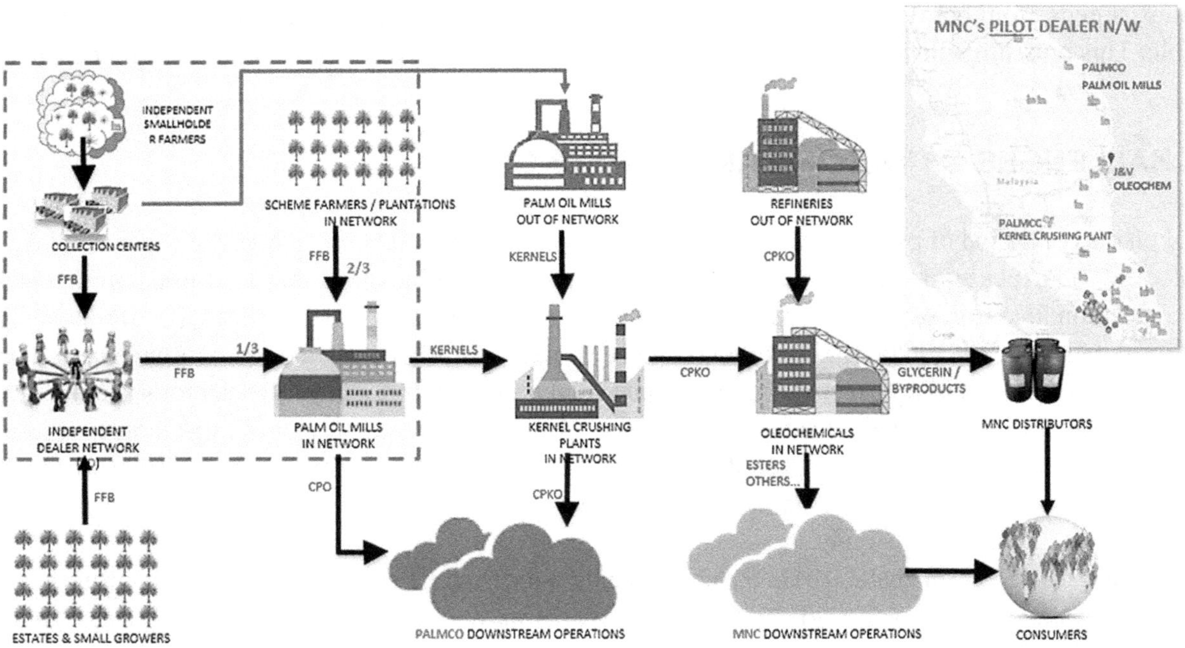

be part of any company's corporate social responsibility by taking into account the livelihood and survival of ISHFs who are not affiliated to any company or mills, nor bound by any contractual obligations.

While ISHFs contribute significantly because of their sheer volume, with farm sizes as low as two and a half hectares, an average yearly production of eight to twelve metric tons per hectare per year and a population size of approximately thirty-four thousand, it poses an enormous challenge to provide transparency into these supply chains.

SCOPE

The supply chain in the palm oil industry consists of many businesses from the upstream FFB growers to the downstream Oleo chemical manufacturer. These businesses are interlinked together across the value chain.

This study is primarily based upon three of the thirty-three collection centers as depicted in Figure 2, which also shows the geographic scope and relevance of the overall study. Pilot 1 study was focused at Parit Raja, which is in Batu Pahat district within the state of Johor, south of Malaysia.

CCs under network means aggregation centers which supplied to a relevant mill in scope under the account of a Dealer, who is officially registered with the particular MNC's source of supply.

Out of the total CCs under the dealer's network, three was selected and clustered based on various selection criteria and chosen to be the pilot area. Selection criteria does include data availability, records up-keeping, homogeneity, proximity, quantum of ISHF, constant supply back to POMs under network, and cooperation by both CC and ISHFs.

Figure 2. Survey Scope

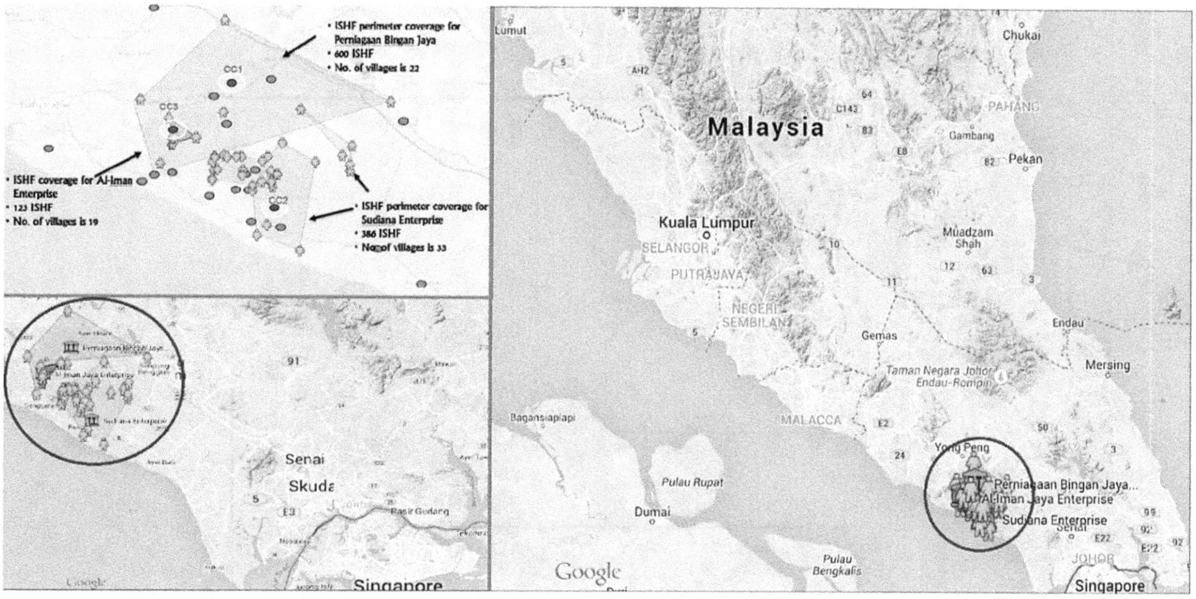

This scope of work henceforth called as the AM Network is based upon 'One' primary dealer acting as the core supplier to Downstream of the supply chain via POMs under network. This is shown in Figure 3. The figure shows that while the dealer is central to the information and money flow, the physical flow of FFB happens directly from the collection centers to the mills. Dealers do act as an intermediary between the seller and buyer. Their value-add within the upstream supply chain is critical and his/her influence is vital for the research team to leverage on for building inroads to gain transparency towards ISHFs, CCs, and POMs.

The upstream supply system is autonomous and indicates that they are not bound to sell their FFB to the dealer and may sell directly to the mills. Thus, the dealer can get the FFB supply from the upstream: ISHF, contractor, scheme or collection center. The collection center in return may have his suppliers from many different sources. The system shows a complex upstream supply network and it has been a challenging task to identify the specific source of FFB supply. What may be identified here is that there are two aggregating points for the product. Crops can be aggregated either at the collection centers or directly at the Palm Oil Mills. Only selected mills deal directly with Individual farmers, for the sake of either fulfilling mill capacity due to limited supply from organized plantations and smallholders, or genuinely safeguarding the livelihood of the ISHFs as part of their CSR.

ROLES OF KEY STAKEHOLDERS (UPSTREAM SUPPLY CHAIN)

Stakeholder: Smallholders

Smallholders are generally defined in Malaysia as having less than 40 Ha of land and legally holding the land title. They are divided into two categories, depending on the extent of external support they receive:

Figure 3. AM Dealer Network – Upstream Supply Chain
(CSVN,2016)

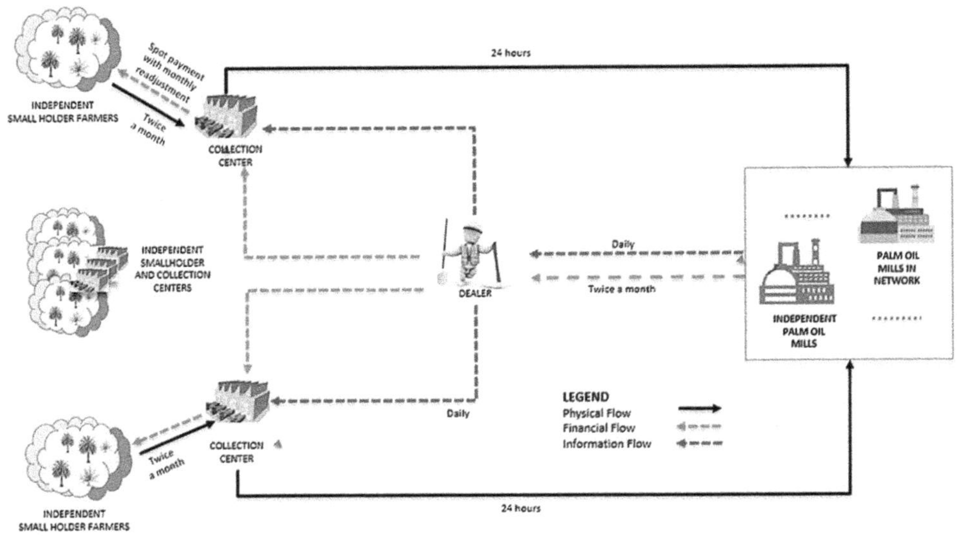

organized or scheme smallholders, which refers to smallholders that are managed by governmental agencies such as FELDA or FELCRA, and unorganized or independent smallholders that are self-managed and self-financed without or with limited support from the government.

Scheme smallholders are farmers who are structurally bound to a particular mill and do not have much degree of freedom in their crop management. They are supervised, managed and organized in their crop management techniques by the scheme or the mill they are linked with, such as FELDA or the Federal Land Consolidation and Rehabilitation Authority (FELCRA), Sime Darby, KLK and many other big players. They may receive support in the form of seedlings, fertilizers, pesticides, technical assistance, and credit support. On the other hand, ISHFs are more independent, in the sense of self-managing and financing their plantations. Since they are not contractually bound and part of an extension scheme, they receive limited technical, institutional and financial support.

Stakeholder: Dealer / Mill Account Holder

Dealers can be considered as intermediaries between the ISHFs and the mills where they buy FFB from the upstream supply chain and sells it to the palm oil mills. They act essentially as a license holder that a collection center or an ISHF uses to sell its FFB to the mills. Dealers play an essential role in the upstream supply chain of the palm oil industry in Malaysia as they represent the main link between growers and millers. Their relationship with ISHFs and mills allow them to collect the FFB supply from various sources and supply the mills in response to the orders the mills placed. The dealers usually manage one or more collection centers. They may also own one or several collection centers in different regions and supply FFB to different mills. The dealers are autonomous in their management of supply of FFB from ISHF sources and in their order treatment placed from the mills. Results from a survey carried out by (Rahman, et al. 2008), identified 1860 dealers operating in the palm oil industry with more than 120'000 ISHFs. This number is estimated to be higher in 2015 as the number of ISHF, as well as the planted area and palm oil production, increased considerably since then. Depending on the size of its business, a dealer may have few hundreds up to thousands of ISHF sources through multiple Collection Centers.

Due to the nature of the FFB and its perishability, the dealer delivers usually all its supply from ISHFs on the same day to the mills. Delay in transporting the FFB to the mill can cause infections to overripe FFB and it allows the bunches to be affected by microorganisms thereby resulting in rotting fruits (Mat Sharif, et al., 2017). Moreover, the late delivery will contribute to the lower quality of oil. The quality of crude palm oil (CPO) is determined based on the free fatty acid (FFA) content in FFB and high oil extraction rate (OER) (Amponsah, et al., 2012).

Dealers may have different business models and pricing systems. This study only considers a simple dealer model where the dealer charges a small amount for each FFB traded under his license from CC or smallholder to the mills. The mills generally prefer to deal with licensed dealers as they receive a large daily supply volume. The dealers also have their supply network ranging from CCs, smallholder farmers, and even small growers.

In this study, the dealers are also known as traders and official account holders under a particular supply network that supplies consistent volume to Palm Oil Mills. This consistent supply is enabled through a network of CCs under his/her control.

Stakeholder: Collection Center (CC)

Collection centers are generally managed or owned by the dealers'/traders network. A collection center can supply FFB to multiple mills. To sell their supply of FFB, the CC must use a dealers' account as a point of sale at the palm oil mills. The dealers may possess more than one account at various mills. In this way, they will be able to mitigate supply risks during high crop seasons. Thus, the CCs and dealers work hand in hand to match daily supply and demand at the upstream of the supply chain.

The main function of a CC is an aggregation point of FFB supplied by smallholders and small growers within a certain radius of their center. A typical collection center works with a few hundred of ISHFs. Each ISHF usually supplies the FFB twice a month to the collection center. In the Malaysian landscape, the collection center may have other functions than aggregating the FFB from ISHFs and smallholders. Indeed, the CC may also work as an input material supplier by providing ISHFs with young palms, fertilizers, pesticides or other tools. Besides that, the CC also offers additional services such as transportation of FFB, construction work, MPOB license renewal and replanting for ISHFs or also in some cases they may provide small personal loans.

The collection center receives its supply from various sources such as ISHFs, governmental schemes or other collection centers. These sources need governmental authorization to trade the FFB they grow. The authorization includes all details about the ISHF such as the land area and the address. The relationship between the CC and ISHFs is essentially based on verbal agreements and the farmers are not bound to any contract. The ISHFs ae free to sell their crops to any CCs. Collection centers usually receive the supply from any particular ISHF twice a month. Payment to ISHFs are done either on the day of the supply or paid out once every beginning of the month through various payment methods. The most common payment method is cash payment. However, some ISHFs prefer to have direct bank transfer, and a handful of them requests payment by cheque.

Apart from the mentioned stakeholders, contractors play an important role within the upstream supply chain. They act as an intermediary between an ISHF and CC. They are engaged by ISHFs to manage their farms in terms of farm management and the sale of crops. They are given autonomy by the farmers to manage harvesting, pruning, weeding, etc. In this case, the ISHF only owns the land and takes a percentage of the profit obtained from the contractor.

The heads of collection centers act as key resources connecting the ISHFs with the dealers. They maintain the MPOB licenses for the farmers and are aware of the day to day needs and demands of the ISHFs. They also maintain the records of the yearly supply from their ISHF base to provide transportation to collect the FFB from the farms and to deliver it to the mills.

Stakeholder: Palm Oil Mill (POM)

The mill is the key buyer and last actor in the upstream value chain of the palm oil industry. The mills are responsible for converting the Fresh Fruit Bunches (FFB) into 3 main products, which are Crude Palm Oil (CPO), Palm Kernel (PK) and Palm Oil Biomass. Each of these products takes a different direction as it moves downstream the value chain. The purified CPO is transferred to a Bulk Storage Tank (BST) for storage at the mill level before dispatch from the mill. CPO may be transported to refiners for further use and processing or exported. The Palm Kernel is transported to a Kernel Crushing Plant (KCP) where it is turned into Palm Kernel Oil (PKO). The palm oil biomass is composed of 3 different forms, namely Empty Fruit Bunch (EFB), Dried Long Fiber (DLF) and Mesocarp Fiber (MF).

Apart from the core products produce in a POM, there are also byproducts generated through the milling process. Some value-adding byproducts are as follows:

- Sludge cake from sludge oil – to be used for life stocks feeding
- Sludge palm oil (SPO) – the lower quality of palm oil. It is darker in color and averages 20% of CPO price. It can be used for animal feed, soap, etc.
- Bio decomposing fertilizer – from EFB
- Jute like product from EFB via Long Fibre Technology – to make ropes

The main role(s) of the Palm Oil Mill is to purchase FFB from Smallholders, Small growers, Collection Centers, and Plantations. In principle, all scheme smallholders are associated to a particular mill, and priority is always given to these associated smallholders. However, for a mill to fulfill its capacity, they consistently buy from external suppliers such as Independent Smallholders and growers through an aggregator (Collection Center), via a registered account holder (Dealer). All financial and information transactions happen only between the mill and the registered account holder, as shown in Figure 3. However, the physical flow of products will go directly to the mills. External dealers not only play an important role in assisting the mills in carrying out their activities more efficiently but also helping the mills to run in full capacity through their network of suppliers.

RESEARCH APPROACH

Researchers from Malaysia Institute for Supply Chain Innovation (MISI) adopted a multi-stakeholder pronged approach encompassing subject matter experts, policymakers, NGOs, plantation companies, crop dealers, and farming contractors to identify the critical supply chain issues about ISHFs. Multiple brainstorming sessions within the working group led to the design and development of a sustainability gap assessment (SGA) tool which resulted in a scorecard. This was further used to develop a multi-phase sustainability model that could be implemented at the upstream supply chain involving ISHFs.

The approach to reach out to the ISHFs is based on questions developed and mapped to the principles, criteria, and indicators as set out by the RSPO P&Cs. There are 8 principles, 43 criteria and 138 indicators in the RSPO P&Cs.

To understand the context, background research and study was done to map the overall PKO supply chain for the MNC. Questions addressing the RSPO P&Cs for the relevant stakeholders were designed and framed into four groups, as shown in Figure 4 below. These are enabled through survey tools such as individual questionnaires, focus group discussions (FGDs), key informant interviews (KIIs) and a general census survey for the entire collection center population in the network under study.

Figure 4. Survey Approach and Enablers

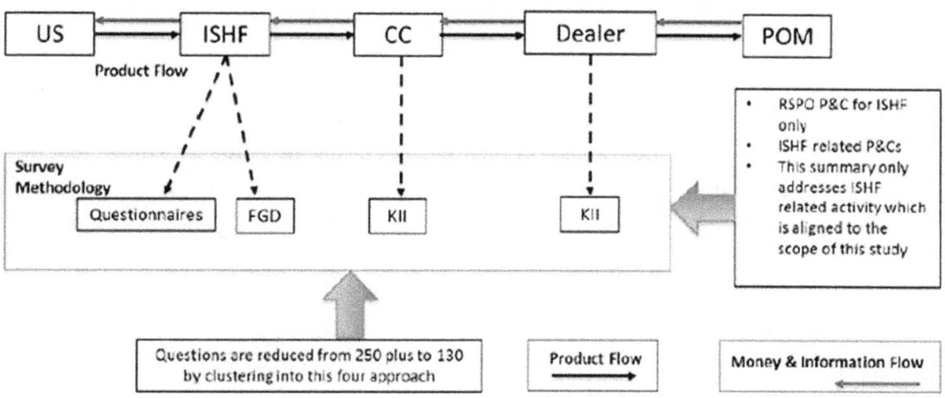

Initially, questions developed in MISI's Question Bank were 250 plus and it was narrowed down to 130 by clustering into the 4 approaches, as shown in Figure 4. This consists of 45 individual questionnaires which are carried out face-to-face for 303 ISHFs, 32 questions for 11 groups of FGD consisting 6 ISHFs in each group, 14 questions of KII for 7 collection centers, 7 short census questions on 33 collection centers, and 32 question KII for 1 main dealer, as shown in Table 1.0.

Every question developed in the question bank can be mapped back to RSPOs P&Cs. These questions were purely developed for ISHFs only and it doesn't cover miller and growers. The survey tools were separated into 4 different categories:

Category 1: Questionnaires were developed mainly for ISHFs who required to be interviewed face to face under semi-structured interviews. Individual interviews were more focused on demographics and field information. The farmers were requested to identify their farm management and practices, working conditions and labor rights and experience of disruptions or losses in their firm. The individual ISHF has 6 main sections. The 6 main sections include owner's profile, traceability information, planting and replanting information, intercropping and livestock information, high conversation value and high carbon stock areas, and training.

Category 2: MISI's research team also facilitated 11 sessions of Focus Group Discussion (FGD) to get a more consistent response towards the scope of the study. FGD was carried out to break the ice further with the farmers in the presence of their peers. This approach certainly did break the barrier and made the farmers more open towards information related to weed, pest, diseases, nutrient, and harvesting management. In addition to this, the respondents were further requested to provide information on harvesting practices, transportation, costs for smallholders' activities in terms of direct cost, operational cost, opportunity cost, replanting cost, and other related information.

Category 3: KIIs are catered for two groups: Collections Center Heads (CC) and Super Dealer. These interviews were conducted one on one with mostly open-ended questions to understand the operations, financing, practices, and value add within the supply chain.

Category 4: Short questions or census were developed for the remaining 29 CCs which were not directly under the pilot study. This data was collected either face to face or via telephone conversations.

DATA COLLECTION

The baseline survey was conducted over a span of approximately 9 months with a sample size of 303 ISHFs from a population of approximately 1100 farmers as shown in Table 1. The survey revealed critical gaps in the area of sustainable practices of the farmers. The outcome of the gap analysis was further used to design and develop a structured approach to help the farmers adopt sustainable practices and scale up while maintaining their livelihoods.

SURVEY RESULTS

Demographics

Based on the survey approach designed in Table 1, results have shown that more than half of the 303 ISHFs interviewed were aged more than 50 years old and possess basic primary and secondary education. This is an expected phenomenon in most farms and rural areas as the youngsters tend to move to urban areas for better jobs and quality of life. The majority of these respondents were male, and the handful of female respondents were the farm owners' wives and they were not directly involved in farming. They have been long enough in the oil palm field that over 65% of ISHFs have a minimum of 12 years of experience. In spite of the age and lack of long work experiences in the industry, nearly 35% of the respondents claimed they do not have license to cultivate and sell FFB. The most common issue here is due to missing documents and physical license through farm inheritance.

Farm Profile

From the perspective of farm profiles, on average the farmers at this pilot owned a land size of between 2 to 2.5Ha. This is in parallel with the findings obtained from the interview sessions with the CC owners. The average FFB yield recorded is approximately 12 metric tons (MT) per Hectare (Ha) per year (Yr). The lowest production recorded is 6MT/Ha/Yr, and the highest is 17MT/Ha/Yr. Various factors may contribute to this high yield gap, such as the age of palm trees, farm management, quality of input materials, and the financial strength of these farmers.

Farm Management

For farm operations, close to 80% of the respondents chose to manage their farms themselves. Only a small number decided to sub-contract it to a 3rd party to manage. The main reason for this decision is to save costs despite their old age and limited physical capabilities. Most of the ISHFs did not receive any assistance from their family members in terms of farming activities. This is due to the lack of interest and motivation among youngsters towards farming activities. More than half of the respondents employ external labour to carryout farm-related activities.

Naturally, an oil palm tree is ready to be harvested on a fortnightly basis. Although survey results showed close to 80% of the ISHFs harvest 24 times a year, it is noticed that there were farmers who harvested more than 24 times in a year. Based on the interview, some farmers only harvest 12 times a year. They claimed to be choosy by only selecting matured fruits and prefers to sell in smaller quantity with high quality. However, this method may pose a different set of problems to the aggregator or CC, which means the turnaround from CC to the mill has to be faster to avoid quality deterioration during mill processing.

In terms of awareness and training, most farmers are the least exposed in terms of capacity building. They are fortunate that their practices through intuition and gut feelings have been keeping them abreast of the most minimal requirements. Some of them do not follow the basic sustainability field requirements. Our survey results have revealed most of the ISHFs were not trained to use herbicide and pesticides on the farm. Most of them learned either from their peers based on their trial and error experience. More than half of the respondents store their chemicals at designated areas and only mix the chemicals at their farms. This is the easiest and safest method rather than doing it at home, which will expose their family members to potential hazards. The empty chemical containers are collected and sold, thrown, or recycled into vase, bailer, or shovel.

Most of the ISHFs (63.7%) claimed that they did not have Riparian Buffer Zone nearby to their farm. This is because most of these farmers are old villagers and they live in remote areas, hence their awareness level on Riparian Buffer Zones is extremely low and out of their concern. This could also be due to the proximity of one farm from another. Thus these farms were isolated from any Riparian Buffer Zone.

Only a small number of ISHFs practiced burning for land preparation and replanting during the early days of planting. As of now, they don't practice burning unless there is a need for controlled burnings, to prevent the spread of Ganoderma disease. The most common method for ISHFs to replant is through the injection of decay agents into the tree trunk. The trees will fall and decompose by itself while the replanting is being done in parallel.

Income

Most of these ISHFs relied solely on income through oil palm plantation. However, some of them cultivated oil palm as a side income. These farmers have other permanent jobs such as working as government servants and other stable jobs in the private sector.

The lowest monthly income recorded was RM200, from an old farmer who relied solely on oil palm plantation. The highest total income recorded was RM24,600, which was from a businessman cum farmer owning approximately 80 acres of oil palm plantation. Most of these respondents did not have any other source of income, besides oil palm plantation. However, some of them worked as casual labourers, factory workers, government servants, and other private sectors.\

Table 1. Data Collection Framework

Survey Approach	Target Respondents	Question	Sample Size	Methodology
Questionnaires	Independent Smallholder Farmers (Licensed & Unlicensed)	45	303	Face to face (F2F)
Focus Group Discussions (FGD)	Independent Smallholder Farmers (Licensed & Unlicensed)	32	11 groups of 6	Facilitation
Key Informant Interview (KII)	Collection Center (CC)	14	7	Face to face (F2F)
Key Informant Interview (KII)	Dealer	32	1	Face to face (F2F)
Census (7 questions)	Remaining CCs	7	33	F2F / Telephone

KEY FINDINGS

The MNC had made progress in the Independent Smallholder program for the trader/dealer supply network under the project with Malaysia Institute for Supply Chain Innovation (MISI). The clarification of a subset to the trader/dealer supply chain and value chain provided the perspective for designing the plans and actions to improve the practices and productivity of the large complex network. This led to smallholder management pilots with NGOs to develop models that can be reapplied to improve the larger national footprint for Independent Smallholders to meet their sustainability milestones.

MISI's traceability exercise had unearthed a substantial amount of traceable supply within the MNC from the Independent Smallholder Farmers. Crops from these pilots under AM Network contributes close to 1% of Crude Palm Kernel Oil (CPKO) back to the MNC's plant. A total of 1100 farmers under 3 Collection Centers with an aggregate land size of 2750 Hectares was traced and able to produce 22,000 to 25,000 MT of FFB/year collectively regardless of individual yield performances.

At a higher level, secondary data and surveys conducted within CCs under AM Network have traced CPKO contribution of approximately 7% back to the MNC's Network through a single Dealer within the Southern Region Corridor of Peninsular Malaysia. On average, a total of approximately 6000 farmers under 33 Collection Centers, with a land bank of ~15,000Ha was able to contribute to approximately 260,000mt of FFB/year.

The sustainability gap assessment analysis allows us to appreciate the overall gaps that exist today which needs to be addressed in order of priority to help the ISHFs attain sustainability standards. These need to be built upon to design interventions for smallholder certification. Extension of this work is based upon the sustainability gap assessment to understand and have a transparent view of the AS-IS condition and the GAP towards sustainability certification.

The following *Table 2* assesses the gap as High, Medium and Low for ISHF on farm status and practices. A High Gap indicates the existence of greater risk and a higher intervention and larger investment required to move closer to the RSPO certification standard. A Low Gap indicates an existing Gap which can be easily filled or one which requires a simpler corrective action involving zero or low cost.

As per project scope, majority of MISI's question bank developed, revolves around RSPO Principles and Criteria No.2 and No.4 that focusses on transparency and farm practices. The remainder relevant questions were developed based on P&C No. 1, 3, 6 and 7. Principles 5 and 8 were deemed not relevant to our scope of project and denoted as Not Applicable (NA) as shown in *Table 2*.

Our findings reveal majority of the farmers interviewed are transparent in terms of sharing and reporting data, but their practices have not shown evidence of compliance to sustainability regulation and standards. In general, the yield has been relatively low at 4-8 mt/ha/yr versus the national average of 18-20mt/ha/yr. This is mainly due to the aged palm trees that required replanting. These aging trees require more care in terms of fertilizer and pesticides as they are prone to disease attacks such as Ganoderma and pests. Some plantations are located on peat soil, but there has been no evidence of peat soil management or riparian zone management. They have not been formally trained in fertilizer application and practices are based on peer to peer guidance and own judgments.

As far as principle 4 is concerned, there is no compliance with the requirement use of pesticides, chemical handling, and scheduled waste management

Table 2. SGA Summary

RSPO P&C	Relevance to Project Scope	SGA Risk Level		
		High	Medium	Low
1. Commitment to Transparency	✓			
2. Compliance with Applicable Laws and Regulations	✓			
3. Commitment to long term Economic and Financial Viability	✓			
4. Use of Appropriate Best Practices	✓			
5. Environmental Responsibilities and Conservation of Natural Resources & Biodiversity	NA	NA	NA	NA
6. Responsible Consideration of Employees, and Individuals and Communities affected by Growers and Millers	✓			
7. Responsible Development of New Plantings	✓			
8. Commitment to Continuous Improvement in key areas of Activity	NA	NA	NA	NA

PRACTICAL OUTCOME AND CONCLUSION

Palm oil producers in the Asian region are in a challenging period driven by continuous changes to European regulations which potentially cause a dent to their production and overall survival.

Malaysia and Indonesia combined production amounts to 85% of the total production of world palm oil. The largest buying nations are India, China, and Europe. Therefore, Asia and the EU are and will always be the key region for the palm oil market. Hence, adopting sustainable practices and producing Certified Sustainable Palm Oil (CSPO) should continue to be of utmost importance across the value chain.

The sustainability gap assessment analysis allows us to appreciate the overall gaps that exist today which need to be addressed in order of priority to help the ISHFs attain sustainability standards and being relevant in this era of sustainability. These need to be built upon to design interventions for smallholder certification. Extension of this work is based upon the sustainability gap assessment to understand and have a transparent view of the AS-IS condition and the GAP towards sustainability certification.

The survey findings provide some key takeaways associated with responsible sourcing for supply chain managers addressing sustainability issues within PO supply chains.

1. Large multinationals must be responsible for their entire supply chain. It is recommended to include subject matter experts with existing supply chain needs into their sustainability program. These subject matter experts can be from local authorities, governmental bodies, or NGOs, who will be a catalyst towards the creation of a viable economic model for sustainability certification.
2. Clustering ISHFs for group certification rather than individual certification. This step will ensure cost savings by achieving economies of scale. These groups will be managed by a 'Group Manager' who will manage the demand, sale, quality, and payments for ISHF.
3. Outreach to the next generation of farmers is critical to creating a pool of potential young ISHFs. These will sustain the continuous contribution of ISHF towards the Palm Oil industry. One approach is by incorporating technology and innovation into existing farming practices. Such an approach may untangle farmers from existing practices and motivate them to adopt this trade through sustainable practices.

Going forward, the research team proposes to conduct similar assessments and pilots for ABC's network at different geographical locations to comprehensively understand, validate and propose mechanisms to enable smallholder certifications and help them scale up.

FUTURE RESEARCH DIRECTIONS

The research team would like to reiterate the quotes by Inke van der Sluijs, Head of European Operations of the Roundtable on Sustainable Palm Oil (RSPO), said in an exclusive ICIS interview:

The main challenge is to transform this sector. What we need is change. Palm oil is the most consumed vegetable oil in the world, but we don't want to see deforestation, planting on peat soil or violations of workers' rights continue, therefore the production of the product must change.

These quotes are very much in line with the researcher's scaling-up business model which involves a multi-pillar approach, mainly Traceability and Expansion; Certification; Livelihood Improvement; and Digitalization. This model is being developed to safeguard the interest of the small farmers and improve their livelihood while ensuring ethical and responsible sourcing for oil palm with commitments to no deforestation, no new plantation on peatlands and no exploitation (NDPE) in the supply chain.

Detailed future research work aims to engage directly with more 6,000 of these farmers across 77 collection centers, spanning through eight super-dealer networks in the next four years, empowering them to achieve endorsement towards sustainability while improving their livelihood. As of early 2019, five thousand farmers have been approached, of which 1,200 are engaged directly.

A large volume of potentially certifiable ISHF base today, supplies to mills out of network i.e. outside the MNC's footprint. One of the goals is to reduce this supply leak and regain the in-network supply. These FFB leakages can be reduced by developing an upstream stakeholder loyalty program. Modeling around the diffusion of innovations principle, the research team aims to address the issue of scalability and implement a solution capable of disseminating good agricultural practices and yield improvement across the footprint. These initiatives aim to reach approximately 23,000 independent smallholder farmers in the next four years. This should allow tracing and verifying as much of the external dealer supply base through independent smallholder farmers and small growers.

ACKNOWLEDGMENT

This book chapter became a reality with the kind support and help of many individuals in so many ways. The author would like to take this opportunity to express his sincere gratitude and appreciation to all of them

First and foremost, the author would like to express his sincere gratitude and thanks to the Director of Center for Sustainable Value Networks (CSVN) and Associate Professor, Dr. Asad Ata for leading this project and sharing his knowledge and expertise throughout this study. In addition to this, he would like to thank Dr. Debabrata Ghosh, Associate Professor at Malaysia Institute for Supply Chain Innovation (MISI) for his support towards the success of this chapter.

Finally, the author would like to thank the entire research team he worked with, Siti Salmah Abu Bakar and Rosdiyani Massaguni, for their continuous assistance and input.

REFERENCES

Abazue, C. M., Er, A. C., Ferdous Alam, A. S. A.., & Begum, H. (2015). Oil palm smallholders and its sustainability practices in Malaysia. *Mediterranean Journal of Social Sciences, 6*(S4), 482-488.

Amponsah, C., Visser, L., Adjei-Nsiah, S., Struik, P., Sakyi-Dawson, O., & Stomph, T. (2012). Processing practices of small-scale palm oil producers in the Kwaebibirem. *NJAS Wageningen Journal of Life Sciences, 60-63*, 49–56. doi:10.1016/j.njas.2012.06.006

CSVN. (2016). Sustainability Gap Assessment Survey and Insights I. Selangor: Center for Sustainable Value Network (CVSN). Malaysia Institute for Supply Chain Innovation.

FAO. (2015). Retrieved from http://faostat3.fao.org/download/Q/QC/E

Global Palm Oil Production. (2016). Retrieved from https://www.slideshare.net/GreenPalmOil/2015-global-palm-oil-production-by-country

Handfield, R.B., & Nicoles, E.L. (1999). *Introduction to Supply Chain Management*. Prentice-Hall International.

Malaysia's Performance Management and Delivery Unit (PEMANDU). (2010). Retrieved from https://www.centreforpublicimpact.org/case-study/performance-management-delivery-unit-kuala-lampur/

Malaysian Palm Oil Council (MPOC). (2016). *Annual Report*. Retrieved from http://www.mpoc.org.my/pubs_view.aspx?id=94b4276f-4b4e-438a-b503-7726e933a07a

Malaysian Palm Oil Council (MPOC). (2016). *Annual Report*. Retrieved from http://www.mpoc.org.my/pubsView.aspx?catid=e1755218-c298-4d85-ba649e9beb584463&id=5ab6aafb-7ce5-406a-b48e-64d1022b736b&ddlID=e1755218-c298-4d85-ba64-9e9beb584463&print=1

Mat Sharif, Z., Mohd Taib, N., Yusof, M., Rahim, M., Mohd Tobi, A., & Othman, M. (2017). Study on handing process and quality degradation of oil palm fresh fruit bunches (FFB). *Mechanical Engineering, Science and Technology International Conference* (pp. 1-9). IOP Publishing.

MPOB. (2018). *Overview of the Malaysian Oil Palm Industry 2017*. Retrieved from http://palmoilis.mpob.gov.my/index.php/overview-of-industry/593-overview-of-industry-2017

MPOC. (2019). *The Implications of EU Resolution to the Malaysian palm oil Industry*. Retrieved from http://www.mpoc.org.my/The_implications_of_EU_Resolution_to_the_Malaysian_Palm_Oil_Industry.aspx

Rahman, Abdullah, Shariff, & Simeh. (2008). The Malaysian Palm Oil supply Chain: The Role of the Independent Smallholders. *Oil Palm Industry Economic Journal, 8*(2).

Rasiah, R., & Shahrin, A. (2004). *Development of Palm Oil and Related Products in Malaysia and Indonesia*. Academic Press.

Simeh & Ahmad. (2001). *The Case Study on the Malaysia Oil Palm*. http://www.rehdainstitute.com/research-a-resources/etp.html

Vision and Missions of RSPO. (n.d.). Retrieved from https://www.rspo.org/about

WWF. (2008). *Palm oil, soy and tropical forests: a strategy for life*. WWF.

KEY TERMS AND DEFINITIONS

CC: Collection centre where the ISHF send their produce.
CC Head: Dealers who manage a collection centre.
CPKO: Crude palm kernel oil.
CPO: Crude palm oil.

FELDA: Federal Land Development Authority.

FFB: Fresh fruit bunch or palm fruit.

ISHF: Independent smallholder farmers. Oil palm farmers with less than 40 Ha of farmland. These are not under any contractual obligation to any party in the supply chain.

KCP: Kernel crushing plant.

POM: Palm oil mill, which receives FFB and converts to palm oil.

SG: Small grower who are farmers or cooperatives with more than 40 Ha of farmland.

Super Dealer: Dealers with accounts at the palm oil mill through which the collection centres sell their produce.

Chapter 13
Unified Approach to Integrated Food Quality and Safety Management

Antoaneta Petrova Stoyanova
https://orcid.org/0000-0002-5186-1498
University of Economics, Varna, Bulgaria

ABSTRACT

The market development and globalization requires for every organization to seek assurance in its supply chain in order to ensure that the products manufactured meet the requirements. Production quality is considered as a socio-economic category and is perceived as an aggregation of properties and features that are to satisfy the ever-growing customer needs and requirements in terms of consumption. Health insurance of all food consumers target groups is the basis of the global food safety policies. The goal of the present study is to analyze the requirements of ISO 9001:2015 and ISO 22000:2018 standards for food quality and safety management systems and thus identify the opportunities for a unified approach towards an integrated management to be implemented through risk-based thinking at all management levels. It is necessary for the assurance of food safety; it being the most important element of quality, to be perceived as an essential part of all management activities.

INTRODUCTION

Sustainable development is objectively necessary for the future of any society. Its goals are directed toward satisfying the current needs without jeopardizing the possibilities for satisfying the needs of future generations. This task is a responsibility for each and every society and all of its economic actors should be directly engaged for achieving this goals.

The Sustainable Development Goals of EU until 2030 are directed toward reduction of food waste per person worldwide on the retail trade and consumers level, as well as minimalization of food losses in the production and distribution processes, including losses of primary production, transportation and storage (Griggs, 2013).

DOI: 10.4018/978-1-7998-4601-7.ch013

Food management systems are becoming more complex. Primely consumers expect that food is not only safe, but also produced without significant environmental impact and simultaneously on affordable prices (Wognum, N., & Bremmers, H., 2009).

Global food quality and safety solutions would be essential to meet the requirements and fully satisfy the customer needs within the entire food chain.

The adopted sustainability measures apply to the food supply chain in the European Union as well as at every stage of the food chain, from production, through processing, transportation, storage, retailing, placing on the market to consumption. In the definitions of the food chain and the supply chain, the unifying is that they cover the product's path from raw materials to its consumption (ISO, 2018). The sustainability measures are imposed by the fact that in highly industrialized countries most food is wasted in the sale and consumption phase, and in the developing countries food is lost even in the production and processing phase. The customer increasingly dominates customer-seller relationships, and, therefore, manufacturers are striving to reduce cases of expressed end-user dissatisfaction. In many cases, the consumers perception for the quality of the food overlaps with the perception of its safety. With supply chains becoming increasingly globalized and complex, the need for standardized, internationally accepted food safety audits has grown. The debate around these topics focuses on several aspects of the product: from organoleptic characteristics to health and hygiene safety, from health and nutrition properties to the place of production and related ethical and social aspects (Frewer, 2008).

This focus is closely related to the achievement of better financial results by the manufacturers. From this perspective, the food quality and safety are simply paramount to a company engaged in the manufacture and supply of food products, in both national and global markets. Food safety audits provide transparency and traceability in the supply chain, enhance quality and efficiency, while also reduce cost and risk.

The production quality is seen as a socio-economic category and is perceived as a set of properties and characteristics that must meet the ever-increasing demands in terms of consumer needs and consumption. The economic importance is determined by the ratio quality-pace of economic development and efficient utilization of raw and processed materials, and thereby more consumer value is being created (Vukasović, T., 2015).

The social importance of the problem with product quality increase is expressed by the ability to meet as many and as more growing customer needs as possible. The quality of the products produced is the result of the manufacturer's activity, however, the specific assessment is to be given by the market and so by the consumer.

Consumption processes are constantly evolving and becoming more complex, as food products are being evaluated for both their material values and their perceived value. For each consumer, the intention to buy and subsequently to consume the food is determined not only by the characteristics of the product itself but also by the impact of various factors such as consumer's social, environmental and health culture. In defining their identity and attitude towards the society, consumers are paying more attention to other aspects of the food production and food origin. Food is becoming a mean of communication and socialization (Wognum, 2009).

It could be said that quality is also perceived as an added value based on customer benefit (ISO, 2015 a).

There is a growing critical attitude and strictness from the side of the consumers with regards to the consumption of safe food of good quality. In recent years, their concerns have been related to the widely discussed problems among the food industry. The emergence of new human and animal diseases and the occurrence of epidemic cases of illness resulting in the death of a significant number of people/animals outline the framework of a crisis situation (EFSA, 2012). This problem draws attention to the adoption of measures aimed at making landmark decisions for proper response. Some known infectious agents, which were assumed to have been contained and placed under control, are presently considered to be one of the causes of severe epidemics. This requires a thorough examination of the reasons for such rapid evolution of some infectious agents and drives the search for impact mechanisms (EFSA, 2014).

Based on data published in its report, the World Health Organization (WHO, 2015) has estimated the global burden of foodborne diseases caused by microbiological and chemical contaminants. Food-related scandals make an increasing number of consumers look for guarantees from the producers on the quality and safety of their food products, or cause them to switch to organic food (Vasileva, E. & Ivanova, D.& Tipova, N.& Stefanov, S., 2019). According to the Directorate General for Agriculture and Rural Development of the European Commission organic food is "food that is grown without most artificial fertilizers or pesticides in a way that emphasizes crop rotation, makes the most of natural fertilizers and ensures that the life of soil is maintained" (Berge, H.F.M. ten, Schroder, J.J., Olesen, J.E. and Giraldez Cervera, J.V., 2017).

Various authors have emphasized the importance of the steadily growing consumer's interest in the origin and place of production of the food product, especially for those products that have been certified (Dimara, E. & Skuras, D., 2003).

Over the last few years, product quality and safety management has been perceived by many national and international organizations as a precise and clearly defined approach to identifying and meeting requirements in all aspects. In this sense, food quality and safety management consists in the application of certain methods of operation and interaction with consumers. The globalization of food trade makes the manufacturers' use of established international tools mandatory, in order to prove that the quality and safety throughout the production cycle and market placement of foodstuffs is ensured and achieved. Such tools are the various widely used international standards such as ISO 9001, ISO 22000, etc.

The implementation of standardised quality and safety management systems in the production of foods protects manufacturers from unwanted costs, poor reputation, loss of market share, loss of competitiveness, loss of customers and business partners, etc. There are many examples from the global practice that demonstrate the great importance of these systems, which encompass the entire production cycle and facilitate the adoption of adequate corrective actions when the production process control shows deviation from the input parameters for quality and safety (Khorsandi, J., Aven, T., 2013).

According to the terminology of ISO 9001:2015, the quality system is a component of the management system of an organization aimed at proper satisfaction of the needs, expectations and requirements of interested parties. Using a quality management system, the senior management plans the use of resources necessary to achieve results defined in the strategic and operational objectives. The quality objectives complement other objectives of the organization, such as those related to growth, funding, profitability, environmental protection and safety.

The competitive advantage in the food business involves not only controlling safety and efficiency, but also the ability of each company to add value. The concept of value-adding is strictly customer-oriented. The management emphasizes the production processes and the place of production of the goods.

Therefore, it is essential for the functioning of the multi-stage food production chain that it is effectively planned, coordinated, maintained and enhanced in order for the associated characteristics of the product to be assured. Meeting a variety of specific requirements makes it difficult for firms to implement them simultaneously.

The relationship between quality and safety has always been in the prioritisation of these categories, which are treated as separate elements of a single issue. In fact, the reasoning behind separating food safety from food quality was the need to place the concept of safety first and above all the other quality aspects (Rotaru, 2005).

The implementation of a unified approach towards integrated quality and safety management is associated with adding value by potentially reducing costs by deploying and certifying a single system that meets multiple requirements, as different resources are optimized, most notably through the reducement of personnel costs, materials, certification costs, etc. The involvement of specialists from different areas and the creation of an opportunity for enhanced cooperation are a prerequisite for designing adequate documentation. Combining different, but at the same time, compatible requirements reduces the time and amount of documentation required by the individual standards.

One of the most important reasons to seek the possibility for a unified approach to food quality and safety is, above all, compliance with a multitude of legal and regulatory requirements.

The integrated management of various aspects of the business minimizes errors and inconsistencies in the organization's operations. This is practically ensured by a detailed presentation of the process and identification of responsibilities and authorities. Eliminating unnecessary bureaucracy offers additional opportunities to focus on other crucial aspects of the business.

Last but not least, the use of internationally recognized standards and their unification enables a better representation of the organization in front of partners, customers and society. In this way, trust and stability in the diverse stages of the supply chain are built, which further enhance the trade relations.

In this study, the objective is to analyse the possibilities of applying a unified approach to integrated management of quality and safety in accordance with the requirements laid down in the latest editions of the international standards ISO 9001:2015 and ISO 22000:2018 for the food sector.

The benchmarking method is used to determine similarities and differences between the requirements of the international standards ISO 9001:2015 and ISO 22000:2018, taking into account also the current regulatory requirements for food safety. This is executed through comparing requirements, defining differences and identifying common elements in order to derive opportunities to integrate particular standards into a single consolidated approach based on the adopted management principles.

It has been shown that the management of interrelated processes as a system in the activity of food sector operators contributes to achieving effective results for the organization, taking into consideration the impact of external and internal environment circumstances according to risk-based thinking.

BACKGROUND

The food quality and safety terms which one would seek the most often are categories that are interchangeable and interconnected, as in fact their interpretation is the subject of various discussions and interpretations. (Röhr, A., Lüddecke, K., Drusch, S., Müller, M. J., & Alvensleben, R. V., 2005).

In the literature, there are different approaches to defining the concept of food quality, especially for the analysis of the perception of food quality (Brunsø K., Ahle Fjord T, Grunert KG, 2002) focus on the distinction between objective and subjective quality. They present several categories for different understandings of food quality. According to their work, food quality can be seen as product-oriented quality, process-oriented quality, user-oriented quality, and quality control.

Product-oriented quality is measured by the different physical or physicochemical properties of a product (fat percentage, moisture content, etc.). Finished product quality is ensured by applying visual and instrumental control by means of measuring the values of various quality indicators of the finished product, included in standardization documents Food safety is not identified as an independent term or characteristic.

The use and application of different classifications of food properties relevant to the quality formation is determined by the specific composition and construction of each food, as well as by the degree of specific needs satisfaction, ones that determine their usefulness. Depending on the nature of the needs they meet, the main nutritional properties of food are energy, nutritional and physiological value, harmlessness, digestibility etc. (Wilcock, A., Pun, M., Khanona, J., & Aung, M., 2004).

Whereas, process-oriented quality is associated with the production stages in which the product is created in a way so that these processes meet the pre-planned parameters. Quality control refers to adherence to specific product standards. Meanwhile, User-oriented quality is considered and interpreted as subjective quality because its rating is given by the degree of consumer perception in the food chain.

In the current conditions the consumers are however not only guided by the given quality of the food. Essential is also the so-called desired quality, the quality the consumer wishes to receive. In many cases this quality differs, firstly, from the actual quality, achieved in the production process through the available facilities, the qualification of the actors involved; and secondly, from the so-called normative quality defined by the requirements of the relevant standards.

Quality assessment is a complex process and thus, the consumer often feels insecure in her choice because the evaluation of some product characteristics could be challenging. This lays most often in the lack of information at the time of purchase. Moreover, consumer perception of safety is directly related to the conceptual model for quality assessment, known as the Total Food Quality Model (TFQ Model) (Grunert, K.G., Larsen, H.H., Madsen, T.K. & Baadsgaard, A., 1996). This model shows what functional or psychological consequences the product characteristics have and how these are related to the personal values of the user. Expected quality for consumers is directly dependent on her food models, food preparation habits, and current intentions and purchasing decisions (Grunert, K.G., 2011). Quality assessment plays a key role in the model, as the goal is reaching the extent to which the purchase motives and associated values are met.

Thus, defining quality as terminology is significantly broader concept than the food safety related terminology (Sikora, T., & Strada, A., 2005). The consumers' attitude towards food choice has changed immensely over the last couple of decades (Rosak-Szyrocka, J., & Blažević, L. B., 2019).

Typically, deficiencies in food quality can result in consumers' refusal to buy the product and respectively to decline of sales, to the detriment of the manufacturer or the retailer, while the hazards for the product may remain hidden and not be identified before the product has been consumed. The occurrence of various food safety incidents has increased the consumer concerns and at the same time, decreased the public confidence in food safety and food-related hazards management (Verbeke, W., Frewer, L. J., Scholderer, J., & de Brabander, H. F., 2007).

Conducted studies have shown that consumers are much more able to judge and perceive the quality of the foods when they are produced in certified quality and safety systems. These circumstances turn into indicators that guarantee some of the product's characteristics (Grunert, 2002). According to some authors (Powell, 2013), the combination of food safety audits and the consumer's culture towards food safety is the basis for achieving an overall effect in food safety management.

This underscores once again the need to implement customer-focused approaches and requirements (Verbeke, Vermeir, & Brunso, 2007).

In order to effectively manage the food quality, it is necessary to make an objective assessment of the quality of production at all stages of its production according to precisely defined indicators (Greit,

1992) . According to the author, the consumer's value estimate of the product results as a combination of the objective product-oriented quality and the user-oriented quality, which stems from the subjective consumer's perception of the good.

Food Safety Legislative Framework

The occurrence of increased risk incidents with hazard foods covering a large number of consumers is difficult to manage in a company or sector level and it requires the use of market-based and institutionally imposed mechanisms.

Safety has begun to be viewed as an independent priority food feature with the advent of policies worldwide, which not only focuses on the quality of the finished foods but also emphasizes on food safety (Food safety in the EU, 2003). The uniform policy of the EU regarding food safety aims to achieve the highest possible level of human health protection and consumer's interests regarding foods (European, 2014). Food safety is becoming a leading strategy for manufacturers and retailers, it is now a characteristic of product quality more significant than any other feature, and, it is perceived as an identification and implementation mechanism for strategic planning and resource provision measures. At an international level these policies are turning into a development and appliance initiator for numerous legislative acts that set considerable science-based demands to all participants in food manufacturing and food realization.

European legislation on food safety first appeared in 1964 when the generally valid directives (Directive 64/433/EEC and Directive 64/432/EEC) were adopted. Legislation was further developed in Council (Directive 85/374/EE Council Directive 92/59/EEC) regulating the manufacture and supply of safe and high-quality foods (Parliament European, 01.1964, 29.06.1992). Protecting high safety standards, European legislation was harmonized (by means of Directive 93/43/EEC of 14.07.1993) with established international standards, in particular with the rules formulated in the Agreement on the Application of Sanitary and Phytosanitary Measures of the Food and Agriculture Organization (FAO) and by the Codex Alimentarius of the World Trade organization. With the European Council Decision 2003/822/EC of 17.11.2003, the European Community joins the Commission on Codex Alimentarius (Council of Europe, 26.11.2003). Thus unified and internationally valid rules and procedures are introduced in order to increase consumer's trust in the food products on the market. Food safety turns into a vital feature that is legally regulated in public health care.

Fulfilling the requirements laid down by legislation calls for the creation of a control system which should prescribe, monitor and control compliance with these established regulatory measures. This circumstance determines *the adoption of effective regulatory measures along the entire food chain* which should identify specific hazards for each particular product by planning appropriate measures aimed at controlling the risk entailed (WHO, 1998 jun 2-6).

As a term Food Safety Management System is deemed to comprise a set of programs and procedures, based on the good manufacturing practices and the principles of HACCP (Hazard Analysis Critical Control Point), the implementation of which generates conditions for independent control and ensuring food safety, or it is a system that conforms to the requirements of Codex Alimentarius or the standard ISO 22000 (Parliament, European, 1.2.2002).

The overall legislative approach to food safety is based on HACCP (Article 5 of Regulation (EC) No 852/2004) and requires food business operators to introduce, implement and maintain FSMS (Parliament, 30.4.2004). Subject of validation are the general principles in the field of foods, related to risk analysis and risk assessment, the precautionary principle, protection of consumers' interests (Commission, 2003).

With the implementation of HACCP specification (7 principles and 12 steps) conditions for independent control are created, the necessary conditions and resources are planned, so that manufacturing processes are carried out and thus the level of various product-specific hazards is surveyed, identified, eliminated or reduced (Lunin, Marcelis, & Rovira, 2009). Steps of the technological process are subjected to evaluation by means of the familiar Decision Tree tool, which results in the identification of the steps, designed to eliminate a certain hazard or reduce it to an acceptable level. These steps are known as critical control points (CCP) in regard to food safety. A HACCP plan is developed for said steps and monitoring and control measures are identified (including their range, periodicity and associated corrective activities), should there be found a trend of the identified CCP deviating from the established critical limits. What is specific in safety management by applying HACCP, is to make decisions based on scientifically supported and proven approaches.

The adopted legislative changes result in a shift of the status of responsibility by transferring responsibility regarding food quality and food safety from the particular government institutions to food manufacturers and food retailers themselves. Every participant in the food chain is given the privilege of building and implementing in their own practice the appropriate management systems. Food industry operators face the need to plan measures and prove they have achieved compliance with standards and regulatory requirements (Orriss & Whitehead, 2000; Boutrif, 2003). Consequently, global harmonization of requirements is a key step to world population sharing the same degree of protection against foodborne hazards. Owing to the adopted regulatory framework, consumers today are able to make a more informed choice (Boisrobert, Stjepanovic, Oh, & Lelieveld, 2009). Dynamic changes in regulatory requirements on food safety are a logical result of the industrialization and automation of food manufacturing according to each company's peculiarities and structure, the trans-border supply of foods across the world due to liberalization of trade, changes in the eating habits and lifestyle of the population, legislative and market –generated requirements and the ever increasing influence of certain countries on the business environment (Garengo & Biazzo, 2012).Good knowledge of food properties and comparison to other foods of the same or similar function provides the opportunity to identify the factors that contribute to higher quality and the instruments for its management. The food safety challenges that the industry is facing at present are the limited resources in terms of necessary materials, a growing competition in the sector, and continuous improvement of staff qualifications and competence in order to satisfy the increasingly higher requirements and expectations of customers and other stakeholders (Dora, M., Kumar, M., Van Goubergen, D., Molnar, A., & Gellynck, X., 2013). These factors are beginning to influence the strategically important decisions in the food manufacturing sector, as in many cases the finished products manufactured by a particular food operator are themselves a material for another manufacturer and are necessary for the manufacturing of other end products across the entire food chain. Therefore, every notification of a food-related incident, the registration of cases of foods on the market well beyond their expiry date, inconsistency of finished food quality stemming from mistakes made by staff during the management and execution of technological and control processes, can be perceived as real prerequisites for compromising ready foods safety (Fielding LM, 2005).

The growing number of food-related incidents in an international and regional perspective is one of the reasons for the increase in food safety and food quality regulations (Lelieveld, 2009). The enormous number of acts, regulations, standards, good practices and codes call for in-depth knowledge regarding their implementation (Fulponi, 2007). Over time, attention has been turned to a new, broader strategic direction, where there are already many other interrelated objective factors, committed to global scale policies.

In order to successfully manage these risky situations, it is necessary to create legislative changes that would be a legal framework and would integrate the whole agri-food chain business by identifying each and every single one of its elements as a whole and continuous process. This is being made through a comprehensive risk assessment along the whole agri-food chain, by introducing a policy and linking the activities to the control type and frequency according to Regulation (EU) 2017/625 (Parliament European, 2017). The Union legislation is currently providing a set of harmonized rules in order to ensure that the food and feed are safe and healthy, and that activities that could affect the agri-food chain safety or the protection of consumers' interests related to the food and the information regarding food shall be carried out in accordance with specific requirements. The correct application of these rules, hereinafter collectively named "Union agri-food chain legislation", contributes to the successful functioning of the internal (local) market.

These rules may be considered measures of considerable public interest, because, each Member State through its competent authorities, achieves the objectives of eliminating, limiting or reducing any type of hazard that may affect human or animal/plant health, as well as the environment.

The international regulations state the criteria and requirements for the quality and safety of foodstuffs but do not specify the mechanisms, approaches, and methods for their implementation.

INTEGRATION OF MANAGEMENT PRINCIPLES IN QUALITY AND SAFETY MANAGEMENT SYSTEMS

Development of the Standards ISO 9001 and ISO 22000

Entering a market, expanding and maintaining established market positions on the part of food manufacturers makes quality and safety standards a widely preferred and prioritized marketing tools of methodological character (ISO 9001and ISO 22000 international standards). These recognizable and globally unified requirements reveal numerous opportunities for food manufacturers to position themselves on international standards under conditions of severe competition (Gereffi & Lee, 2002; Henson, 2008). In the last years, international standards of quality and food safety management have been updated and they have expanded their scope and structure, with a lasting tendency of close ties between them and in the chronology of their amendments. (Reardon, Codron, & Busch, 2000; Jaffee, 2004; Thomas, 2000; Havinga, 2008).

Many countries develop voluntary standards also known as Safe Quality Foods (SQF) (1994) i.e. the British Retail Consortium for retail trade (BRC) in England (1998) (British Retail Consortium, 2018) or the voluntary standards of traders in Europe – International Food Standard (IFS). The specific requirements of these de/facto standards focus mainly on specific food production. Their requirements are aiming to prove the authenticity of the product and to point out the risks of counterfeiting, as well as manipulation of products during storage.

The majority of specific standards adopted are similar but not identical in structure and requirements. This creates inconvenience for food operators in documentation development in cases when several standards need to be met at once. The strict provisions of the BRS, SCV or IFS standards require the design of a safety system with numerous requirements that are difficult to reconcile and integrate simultaneously. It is practically impossible to combine the requirements of different private standards with a single audit by a third party. This is the reason for the access restriction and gives an opportunity for positioning of the above-mentioned standards in different regional markets. It results in the need for the application of cross-standardization approaches between such requirements and criteria in order for a recognizable market-based instrument to be unified.

Standards of the ISO 9001 and ISO 22000 series represent common requirements towards the development and implementation of management systems, with ISO 9001 respectively towards quality management system and ISO 22000 towards food safety management system.

The dynamic growth of the total number of certified companies worldwide in accordance to ISO 9001 (from 980 322 in 2008 to 1 055 028 companies in 2018) shows the continuous strive of producers and traders to proof the conformity of their activities to the requirements of the international standards. The number of certified food companies according to the standard ISO 22000 has increased from 26 652 in 2008 to 27 091 in 2018. (Charlet, 2018)

This data shows that an increasing number of companies choose to be certified as an adequate market strategy which gives them access to stable market positions. The number of companies worldwide certified according to "de-facto" standards for Food Management System such as the BRC Global Standards is 27 628 for over 20 years (Betts, 2019). It is clear that for merely a half of this period the number of companies certified according to ISO 22000 is almost equal to the number of certified companies in accordance to BRC. This information leads to the conclusion that the market is more accessible for companies certified according to ISO 22000 and ISO 9001.

As early as the year 2000, the ISO 9000 standard (ISO, 2000) stipulates that quality management is directly related to the firm's activity and is viewed as an aggregate of numerous processes and follows eight basic principles: client orientation, leadership, staff involvement, process approach, systemic approach to management, constant improvement, fact-based decision-making, and mutually beneficial relationships with suppliers. With the application of the principles of management, quality management begins to be perceived as a function of all participants in the manufacturing process directly related to product quality. ISO 9001:2000 standard lays the foundations for quality management to be perceived as coordinated activities for directing the firm towards quality and how to control it. Therefore, ensuring food safety, as the most important property of quality, needs to be thought of and managed as an element of all activities associated with management.

Principles of quality management begin to be successfully introduced in safety management and in 2005 the ISO 22000 standard, defining the requirements to safety management systems, was published (ISO, 2005).

Expanding the food supply chain from regional to international level requires engagement and communication between different government bodies, manufacturers and customers regarding requirements (Korada, S. K., Yarla, N. S., Putta, S., Hanumakonda, A. S., Lakkappa, D. B., Bishayee, A., ... & Lu, D. Y., 2018). Liberalization and cross-border food production and trade establish unified approaches in supply chain management to coordinate activities between independent and interconnected actors in the chain (Молов, 2017). The aim is to ensure continuity and integration, coherence of business processes in the chain to add value to customers. From the definitions presented, there are many significant similarities in quality, safety and supply chain management. It can be perceived that by integrating the various aspects of the business, integrated management is achieved in the direction of efficiency and effectiveness of the results achieved. The focus of such management in the supply chain is to achieve customer satisfaction in the most efficient way possible. The implementation of standardized and internationally recognized management approaches is a prerequisite for the planning and the fulfillment of processes in the food trade sector (Henson, S., 2008).

The requirements of the ISO 22000:2005 define the scope and structure of the food safety management system and are perceived as an instrument that can guarantee all potential food-related hazards (of biological, chemical or physical origin) are correctly identified, analyzed and controlled so that they do not present a potential or real risk for consumer health (Domenech, E., Escriche, I. and Martorell, S., 2008). Standard requirements do not exclude the application of all generally valid specific regulatory requirements for the food sector, which automatically involves the application of HACCP principles, as well. Requirements refer to food operators' need to also plan, design, implement and support an updated food safety management system with the intention of supplying end products which, in accordance with their envisaged usage, will be safe for the customer (Varzakas & Tzia, 2016).

Quality and food safety management as a system is viewed as a means, whereby each manufacturer in the food sector will maintain their role, position and mission in the food chain and will be able to exchange information across all levels of the chain on matters of food safety (Panghal, 2018).

Achieving customer satisfaction and prevention of negative health effects from the consumption of food is the basis for strategy development on the part of manufacturers, with which many social opportunities can be realized (Klassen, 2012). This requires the managers' focus on the market already in the initial stage of the planning of the production process.

Research shows that standardized management systems are necessary for supply chain risk management, regardless of the role the organization plays in the supply chain (Zimon, 2019).

Since their adoption the ISO 9001 and ISO 22000 international standards have undergone continuous improvement to the extent of their overlapping and towards a unified management of various aspects of activity through unified approaches. The latest update of ISO 9001 standard took place in 2015, where a specific difference is the new structure, compared to that of the 2000 edition or the 2008 edition. The said change is a result of strategic choice and is the foundation for gradual restructuring of all management standards with the objective to help adopting organizations to easily integrate all or parts of their own systems into a uniform system for integrated management of various aspects of company activity. In the previous versions of the ISO 9001 standards a clear difference could be observed in the definition and interpretation of the process approach in management systems.

Quality requirements pertained to the identification of the interconnection of processes involved in product creation, as well as processes of control of product parameters. It is worth pointing out that in previous revisions of the 22000 standard, safety requirements mostly emphasized on defining the technological sequence of steps (developing a diagram of the process) during the product manufacturing stage, as well as on specific programs as a basis for ensuring the necessary safety conditions, while various hazards were analyzed (Wallace C, 2012).

Standards ISO 9001 and ISO 22000: Unified Approach to Management

By applying the basic principles of management, the relevant organisation can bind together various standards with specific requirements using a unified management system. As early as 10 years ago some authors realised that in order to function effectively, an organization needs to coordinate multiple related activities through methodological tools enshrined in the relevant international standards (Riehard, 2001). In this sense, the international standard ISO 9001:2015 allows an organization to integrate into its quality management system any other food safety system (ISO, 2015).

The application of a unified approach to bringing together the divergent requirements a food producing company has to meet, was made difficult by the different structure and scope of requirements featuring in the adopted ISO 9001 and ISO 22000 standards. According to Bennet, despite the unambiguous understanding of the requirements of standards, there are different interpretations of integration (Bennet, W., L. Steed, 1999). It is characteristic and essential that the ISO 9001 standard defines the general requirements for system development, regardless of whether the object of management is a product or service, which determines the universality of the scope of the standardAnother significant point is that the ISO 9001 standard imposes requirements on the organization with respect to the quality management system, but does not regulate the mechanisms by which these requirements are applied in the organization. The development and implementation of a quality management system is based on the interpretation and applicability of these requirements to the specific organization. Unlike ISO 9001, the Food Safety Management System, ISO 22000, together with HACCP, guarantees food safety by analyzing the hazards of a specific product as well as the specific risk that will arise with the consumption of that product.

This is a foundation which facilitates the creation of necessary and sufficient conditions for executing contemporary requirements in order to ensure compliance with the current regulatory and standard requirements (Khalili, Ismail, & Karim, 2017). Consequently, under conditions of market globalization, a unified approach can be enforced in certification of various management systems, including specific customer requirements, and thus opportunities for new business partnerships and clients can expand (Fulponi, 2007).

Changes in the food safety requirements set out in ISO 22000 from 2018 are driven by a change in attitudes and strategic guidelines to address global food risks. In 2005, food safety was defined as "the concept that food will not cause harm to the consumer when cooked and / or consumed according to the intended use" (ISO, 2018 a; ISO, 2005). The change made in 2018 is essential, with the main focus in the standard being the change in the food safety definition, with food safety being perceived as "ensuring that the food does not cause an adverse health effect to the consumer when cooked and/or consumed according to the intended use". The emphasis is on moving from "concept" to "making sure", and from "harm" to "adverse health effect" (Raybould, 2018).

Until 10 years ago food quality and food safety were perceived as planning a set of measures and actions designed to provide conditions for the manufacturing of a quality and safe product through the preventive approach. At present food operators are required to implement contemporary systems for safety management and provide objective evidence that the planned measures are effectively and efficiently applied in company practice, and the achieved results match the planned objectives. For over 20 years the application of the process approach combined with the PDCA cycle (Plan-Do-Check-Act) has established itself as an effective approach to problem-solving and change management, and is further developing and applicable as an underlying principle in the latest editions of the standards, which regulate the requirements for quality and safety management systems(Samani, Ismail, & Leman, 2017). The major difference between the management process of the past and the present is that previous versions of the quality and safety requirements accentuated on processes of monitoring the existing state of the process and product, not considering the impact of various external and internal factors on the company performance. According to various authors, the integration of the requirements of both standards even before the release of their latest versions can facilitate planning, allocation of resources, setting goals and assessing the overall efficiency of the organization (Stefanova, M &Gotcheva, V, 2016).

Trends in the development of food quality and food safety standards point to an approach related to risk management of the identified processes of company operations (Baines, 2010; Mena & Graham, 2010; Soon, 2013).

By defining the processes through which the organization functions, the following can also be defined and planned:

- *elements, factors and criteria* which make up product quality and product safety and which fulfill the requirements of stakeholders and ensure stakeholder trust and confidence;
- the impact of *external and internal circumstances* of the business environment, which determine the identification *of risks or the opening of new opportunities;*
- *statutory requirements* regulating the quality and safety of materials and the finished product;
- optimum *financial and human resources*, the necessary *infrastructure* and the appropriate *working environment, technological processes* for manufacturing high quality and safe products;
- focus on the key operation processes and possibilities for improving *product and process parameters,* including periodicity of control to be exercised in order to confirm compliance with the requirements regarding quality and safety of materials, intermediate and end products;
- identification, elimination and reduction of any *potential hazard*за for the end product in the technological process;
- *supervision and control* на of the activities involved in testing and studying the changes which may entail losses and a decline in quality levels.

SOLUTIONS AND RECOMMENDATIONS

Contemporary quality and safety management systems, according to the requirements of ISO 9001 and ISO 22000 standards, which encompass the basic management principles, lay the foundations for successful implementation of activities, control and analysis of process results and demonstrate that the above-mentioned sequence can be followed across all levels of the management system–from strategic to operating processes, with clearly defined responsibilities.

This is determined by the fact that these two quality and safety management systems are customer-oriented by applying the principles of leadership, processes, continuous improvement and risk-based thinking.

- **Customer Orientation:** Both systems pursue the main goal of meeting the ever higher and more clearly defined needs of the customers by providing them with high-quality safe food products. Among the most important expectations of today's consumer (most often in latent form) is his or her desire to consume healthy and safe food products. Food safety is defined as the assurance that the food product will not have an adverse health effect on the consumer, when it is prepared and/or consumed according to its intended use (Parliament, European, 1.2.2002). It is essential to note that the definition of food safety does not include certain health-related aspects, such as malnutrition.
- **Orientation Towards the Process:** Identification, co-ordination and management of all basic and ancillary activities throughout the technological cycle of production. This is a fundamental principle of the ISO 9001:2015 and ISO 22000:2018 standards. Any activity that uses "inputs" and turns them into "results" may be seen as a process, i.e. the application of a "process approach". The process approach is a systematic identification and management of both the processes and the relationships between them (ISO, 2015). The advantage of the process model enshrined in both

standards is in the continuous control exercised over the processes and the relationships between them. The ISO 22000:2018 standard integrates the principles of HACCP specification, which also monitor the process, but from the viewpoint of product safety in the production process only (analysis of the various biological, physical and chemical hazards specific for the particular product). In many cases the possibilities of one process may be the hazards of another, and the process approach in the safety systems is applied on two levels (organizational and operational – implementation and control of activities). In management systems complying with the requirements of ISO 9001:2015 and ISO 22000:2018 the process approach combines the PDCA (Plan-Do-Check-Act) cycle and relies on one of its key management principles, namely the risk-based thinking.
- **Determining the Context of the Organization:** Both standards focus on defining the effects of the factors of the external and internal ussues on the quality and safety of manufactured food products, as well as on the overall management of processes and activities. Through examination and evaluation of the degree of influence of these external and internal issues, each manufacturer can quantitatively determine how much it is dependent on the external environment and how it affects its business. The context is a new requirement in ISO 9001:2015 and ISO 22000:2018 and now it puts the management of quality and safety on a whole new level: not as isolated and separate management activity, but as a socio-economic factor in the macro scale (ISO, 2018). The identification of all interested parties helps to better identify their requirements, and thus the issues of concern for the company and which of those constitute real or potential risks or opportunities.

The application of approaches to managing relationships with the specific stakeholders that each company identifies is, on the one hand, the basis for fulfilling stakeholders' requirements, and on the other – a guarantee for the company's success in creating added value.

- **Risk-based Thinking:** The production and marketing of food products to the customer is inevitably associated with the occurrence of a variety of hazards, some of which have a high potential to generate risks with very serious consequences for each manufacturer. Risk management is seen as a systematic application of policies, procedures and practices for managing exchange of information, as well as the identification, analysis, evaluation, influence, monitoring and review of the risk (Kaplan, S., Garrick, B. J., 2017). The agrarian sector produces commodities that are the main raw materials for foods. Kirechev discusses key strategic actions and solutions for agricultural risk management including informal and formal mechanisms (Kirechev, 2018). The agrarian sector is exposed to various types of risks that occur at high frequency and result in many variable outputs for the foods.

So far the food safety management practice has conducted only the Hazard Analysis by applying the 7 principles and 12 steps of the HACCP specification. Characteristic of the HACCP system is that it only covers the hazards in the technological process stages. The focus is on defining control measures in the analysis of each hazard aimed at its mitigation or elimination

It should be pointed out that the requirements of ISO 22000:2018 and ISO 9001:2015 as regards management of food safety and quality provide for assessment of all processes and the associated risks that arise from the impact of external and internal factors. Using the risk-based thinking principle, one can examine in detail the likelihood, cause and source of the risk, as well as the factors that may influence the effects of a risk situation. The results of the risk assessment can be a basis for planning and implementing a set of measures and actions aimed at achieving the potential impact on risk, thus achieving an effective reduction of the residual risk to safety and subsequently reduction of morbidity caused by food infections and intoxications (Zwietering, 2015). This step is the basis for increased efficiency and continuous improvement of quality and safety management systems.

Both systems are based on the principle of continuous improvement and refinement through objective evaluations. ISO 9001 lays down continuous improvement as a requirement for the quality management system. The implementation of the two systems (ISO 9001:2015 and ISO 22000:2018) is a choice of the management of the organization. In both cases, it needs to put in place and maintain policies that allow the participation of all employees. The management as a leader has the overall responsibility for the organization's quality and safety policies and performs the task of documenting, guaranteeing and communicating these policies, as well as of conducting regular checks on their application as required. Improvements in the company's business processes are carried out by the senior management in accordance with the organization's context, strategy, policy and objectives and thus conditions are generated for making use of new opportunities. In each company the degree of improvements feasibility and compatibility with the remaining activities of the firm are related to a feasibility study and assessment of the system's general efficiency. Continuous improvement is the basis for the sustainable development of a company.

- **Possibility of External Recognition:** The above-mentioned series of standards, namely ISO 9000:2015 for quality systems and ISO 22000:2018 for food safety systems are implemented through a system of voluntary certification. Based on the principle of compliance/non-compliance with the international standard, a certificate is awarded by an independent certification organization.

A certified quality and safety management system is one of the most important factors for market stability. Having a certificate is a means of positioning the market because it guarantees confidence in all stakeholders about the degree to which their expectations are fulfilled. It is a major contractual requirement in international trade channels and a proof of stability in the commitments made.

Certified organizations which support food quality and safety management system need to ensure that the envisaged hazards associated with the products within the system's scope, have been identified, assessed and controlled in such a way that the organization's products do not inflict direct or indirect harm for the consumer, and that there is regular exchange of information about product safety across all levels of the food chain (Soares, Martins, & Vicente, 2016). The aim of food quality and food safety management is to supply end products, which, according to their intended usage, will be safe for the customer (Tzia, Tzia, & Tzia, 2015) .

Nevertheless, the analysis of the two systems shows certain differences. The HACCP system as part of the food safety management system under the requirements of ISO 22000:2018 is a legislatively regulated procedure, subject to government control and inspection by a competent authority. In the European Union, the legal basis for implementation of the HACCP system is Regulation 178/2002 (Parliament, European, 1.2.2002). The use of the HACCP approach only is insufficient for food safety management, because some of the risks for the food products remain outside the scope of this regulatory management concept. It is essential to note that the developed HACCP plan only sets out measures in the Critical Control Points, in order to reduce the hazards in the relevant process stage (Lelieveld H, Holah, J., Napper, D. (2013).

Both systems are internationally recognized approaches to food safety and quality management. The respective contents of the two standards reveal an almost complete match between the elements of the two systems. There is a general focus on the dynamics of risk assessment. The application of a unified approach to integrated management can achieve better results in terms of food quality and safety, as opposed to the separate introduction of only ISO 9001:2015 or ISO 22000:2018. As in other industries, food companies strive to implement in their work approaches that can improve their own processes to avoid a situation of instability. The integrity of the system allows continuous assurance of food safety by maintaining and monitoring all changes within the scope of its management. This approach can also be successfully implemented in integrating the requirements of other management standards for other business aspects such as ISO 14000: 2015; ISO 45000 and more.

FUTURE RESEARCH DIRECTIONS

Due to the overlapping structure in terms of scope and content of the two standards (ISO 9001:2015 and ISO 22000:2018), an integrated management system can be put into practice by adopting a unified approach in the creation of documentation and in the continuous control on the satisfaction of the relevant requirements. The integration of the requirements of ISO 9001: 2015 and ISO 22000: 2018 is the basis for the development of an integrated system that helps to integrate all the elements in the supply chain quality management. The development and implementation of an integrated management system can identify and assess the various risks to food quality and safety, including the risks associated with the supply chain resulting from the impact of the business environment. Using standardized and validated assessment methods (such as PESTLE and FMEA) in the development of an integrated system for a given sector or manufacturer/trader, specific risks can be identified and analyzed according to the internal and external environment. From external issues: Political factors intersect Legislative factors directly depending on the action of the Environmental and Technological. However, the main difference is that political factors are governed by government policy, while legislative factors must be respected and subject to legislation approved by many governments. This creates the conditions for practically proposing concrete measures to manage the risks involved.

CONCLUSION

From the analysis and presentation of the similarities in the application of the management principles in the selected standards, it can be summarized that the introduction of a unified management approach covers the processes from the supply of raw materials to the sale of the products on the market. Combining compatible requirements is the basis for creating strategy, interpreted as a policy and translated into specific management activities. In conclusion, it can be said that the common thing between management systems (whether quality or safety management) is their applicability to organizations of different size, subject of activity, cultural and social conditions of realization. The common management system creates unified strategic goals and their resulting goals. The implementation of a common system for maintaining and controlling the required documentation helps to carry out adequate product control and subsequent analysis of the activity.

Bringing together the requirements of standards into a unified approach is more cost-effective and efficient than independently applying each of them individually. A single standardized approach can achieve sustainable quality and safety of manufactured foods. Food quality and safety management mechanisms also create the conditions for their implementation in the quality management of their supply chain.

The implementation of quality and safety management systems in various aspects of economic activity achieves sustainability and development in both the specific business activity and the overall economic development. In the context of the above, we can summarize the same for the single European market as a whole. It is possible to minimize the impact of prepared foods of unknown origin on the health of the general public.

REFERENCES

Baines, N. (2010). *Delivering Performance in Food Supply Chains. Quality and safety standards in food supply chains* (1st ed.). Cambridge: Woodhead Publishing.

Bennet, W., & Steed, L. (1999). An Integrated Approach to Food Safety. *Quality Progress, 32*(2), 37–42.

Betts, K. (2019). https://www.brcgs.com/media/1621646/brgcs-compliance-report-2019-digital.pdf

Boisrobert, C., Stjepanovic, A., Oh, S., & Lelieveld, H. (2009). *Ensuring global food safety: Exploring global harmonization* (1st ed.). New York: Academic Press.

Boutrif, E. (2003). The new role of Codex Alimentarius in the context of WTO/SPS agreement. *Food Control, 14*(2), 81–88. doi:10.1016/S0956-7135(02)00113-5

Brunsø, K., Ahle Fjord, T., & Grunert, K. G. (2002). *Consumers' Food Choice and Quality Perception.* Working paper no 77. The Aarhus School of Business.

Carlson, C. (2012). *Effective FMEAs: Achieving safe, reliable, and economical products and processes using failure mode and effects analysis.* Hoboken, NJ: John Wiley & Sons. doi:10.1002/9781118312575

CharletL. (2018). https://www.iso.org/the-iso-survey.html

Commission, C. (2003). *General principles of food hygiene CAC/RCP 1–1969.* Available online: http://www.fao.org/input/download/standards/23/CXP_001e.pdf

Council of Europe. (2003). Decision 2003/822/EO of 17.11.2003. *OB. L 309.*

Dimara, E., & Skuras, D. (2003). Consumer evaluations of product certification, geographic association and traceability in Greece. *European Journal of Marketing, 37*(5/6), 690–705. doi:10.1108/03090560310465099

Domenech, E., Escriche, I., & Martorell, S. (2008). Assessing the effectiveness of critical control points to guarantee food safety. *Food Control, 19*(6), 557–565. doi:10.1016/j.foodcont.2007.06.015

Dora, M., Kumar, M., Van Goubergen, D., Molnar, A., & Gellynck, X. (2013). Food quality management system: Reviewing assessment strategies and a feasibility study for European food small and medium-sized enterprises. *Food Control, 31*(2), 607–616. doi:10.1016/j.foodcont.2012.12.006

EFSA. (2012). BIOHAZ Panel (EFSA Panel on Biological Hazards), Scientific Opinion on public health risks represented by certain composite products containing food of animal origin. *EFSA Journal, 10*(5). doi:10.2903/j.efsa.2012.2662

EFSA. (2014). *Drivers of emerging risks and their interactions in the domain of biological risks to animal, plant and public health: a pilot study, EFSA supporting publication, EN-588*. European Food Safety Authority.

Environmental transparency of food supply chains-Current status and challenges. (n.d.). *Global Perspective for Competitive Enterprise, Economy and Ecology*, 275-285.

European, C. (2014). *Food safety. Ensuring a high level of protection of human health and consumers' interests*. Brussels: Publications Office.

Fielding, L. M., Ellis, L., Beveridge, C., & Peters, A. C. (2005). An evaluation of HACCP implementation status in UK small and medium enterprises in food manufacturing. *International Journal of Environmental Health Research, 15*(2), 117–126. doi:10.1080/09603120500061583 PMID:16026023

Food safety in the EU. (2003). Retrieved from Official website of the European Union: https://europa.eu/european-union/topics/food-safety_en

Frewer, V. R. (2008). Consumer perceptions of food quality and safety and their relation to traceability. *British Food Journal, 110*(10), 1034–1046. doi:10.1108/00070700810906642

Fulponi, L. (2007). *The globalization of private standards and the agri-food system. Global Supply Chains, Standards and the Poor* (1st ed.). Cambridge: CAB International.

Garengo, P., & Biazzo, S. (2012). From ISO quality standards to an integrated management system: An implementation process in SME. *Total Quality Management & Business Excellence, 24*(3-4), 310–335. doi:10.1080/14783363.2012.704282

Gereffi, G., & Lee, J. (2002). *A global value chain approach to food safety and quality standards*. Global Health Diplomacy for Chronic Disease Prevention Working Paper Series. Duke University.

Greit, M. (1992). *The Visual Factory*. Portland, OR: Productivity Press.

Griggs, D. M.-S., Stafford-Smith, M., Gaffney, O., Rockström, J., Öhman, M. C., Shyamsundar, P., ... Noble, I. (2013). Policy: Sustainable development goals for people and planet. *Nature, 495*(7441), 305–307. doi:10.1038/495305a PMID:23518546

Grunert, K. (2002). Current issues in the understanding of consumer food choice. *Trends in Food Science & Technology, 13*(8), 275–285. doi:10.1016/S0924-2244(02)00137-1

Grunert, K. G. (2011). Sustainability in the food sector: A consumer behaviour perspective. *International Journal on Food System Dynamics, 2*(3), 207–218.

Grunert, K. G., Larsen, H. H., Madsen, T. K., & Baadsgaard, A. (1996). *Market orientation in food and agriculture*. Norwell, MA: Kluwer Academic. doi:10.1007/978-1-4613-1301-4

Havinga, T. (2008). Retail driven food safety regulation. In *Food safety, market organization, trade and development* (1st ed., Vol. 1). Geneva: Springer International Publishing.

Henson, S. (2008). The role of public and private standards in regulating international food markets. *Journal of International Agricultural Trade and Developments*, *4*(1), 63–81.

ISO. (2005). ISO 22000:2005 Food safety management systems. Requirements for any organization in the food chain. Geneva: ISO.

ISO. (2015a). ISO 9000:2015 – Quality management systems — Fundamentals and vocabulary. Geneva: ISO.

ISO. (2015b). ISO 9001:2015 – Quality management systems — Requirements. Geneva: ISO.

ISO. (2018a). *22000:2018 Food safety management systems — Requirements for any organization in the food chain*. ISO.

ISO. (2018b). ISO 31000:2018 – Risk management. Principles and instructions. Geneva: ISO.

Jaffee, S. H. (2004). Standards and agro-food exports from developing countries: Rebalancing the debate. *World Bank Policy Research Working*, *3348*(1), 44–50.

Jodkowski, L. (2015). Possibilities and Methods of Risk Assessment under ISO 9001:2015. *International Journal of Managerial Studies and Research*, *3*(10), 14–23.

Kaplan, S., & Garrick, B. J. (2017). On the quantitative definition of risk. *Risk Analysis*, *1*(1), 11–27. doi:10.1111/j.1539-6924.1981.tb01350.x PMID:11798118

Khalili, A., Ismail, M. Y., & Karim, A. (2017). Integration of lean manufacturing and quality management system through structural equation modelling. *(2017). International Journal of Productivity and Quality Management*, *20*(4), 534–556. doi:10.1504/IJPQM.2017.082835

Khorsandi, J., & Aven, T. (2013). A risk perspective supporting organizational efforts for achieving high reliability. *Journal of Risk Research*.

Kirechev, D. (2018). Risk Management Mechanisms in Agricultural Holdings in Bulgaria. *Fourth International Scientific Business Conference LIMEN 2018*, 597-602. 10.31410/limen.2018.597

Klassen, R. D., & Vereecke, A. (2012). Social issues in supply chains: Capabilities link responsibility, risk (opportunity), and performance. *International Journal of Production Economics*, *140*(1), 103–115. doi:10.1016/j.ijpe.2012.01.021

Korada, S. K., Yarla, N. S., Putta, S., Hanumakonda, A. S., Lakkappa, D. B., Bishayee, A., . . . Lu, D. Y. (2018). A critical appraisal of different food safety and quality management tools to accomplish food safety. Food Safety and Preservation, 1-12.

Lelieveld, H. (2009). Progress with the global harmonization initiative. *Trends in Food Science & Technology*, *20*(1), 82–84. doi:10.1016/j.tifs.2009.01.025

Lelieveld, H., Holah, J., & Napper, D. (2013). *Hygiene in Food Processing. Principles and Practice*. Woodhead Publishing.

Lunin, P., Marcelis, W., & Rovira, J. (2009). Systematic assessment of core assurance activities in a company specific food safety management system. *Trends in Food Science & Technology*, *20*(6), 300–312. doi:10.1016/j.tifs.2009.03.003

Mena, C., & Graham, S. (2010). *Delivering performance in food supply chains* (3rd ed.). Cambridge: Elsevier. doi:10.1533/9781845697778

Ministry of Agriculture and Food. (1999). Food Act, promulgated in State Gazette No. 90 of 15 October 1999, amended in State Gazette No. 106 of 21 December 2018. *Promulgated in State Gazette No. 90 of 15 October 1999, amended in State Gazette No. 106 of 21 December 2018.*

Molov, D. (2017). Globalni Verigi za Dostovka - Kontseptsii. Sofia: Izdatelski Kompleks - UNSS.

Orriss, G., & Whitehead, A. (2000). Hazard analysis and critical control point (HACCP) as a part of an overall quality assurance system in international food trade. *Food Control*, *11*(5), 345–351. doi:10.1016/S0956-7135(99)00094-8

Panghal, A. C., Chhikara, N., Sindhu, N., & Jaglan, S. (2018). Role of Food Safety Management Systems in safe food production. *Journal of Food Safety*, *38*(4), e12464. doi:10.1111/jfs.12464

Parliament, E. (2002). Regulation (EC) no 178/2002 of the European Parliament and of the council laying down the general principles and requirements of food law, establishing the European Food Safety Authority and laying down procedures in matters of food safety. *OJ L 031.*

Parliament, E. (2004). Regulation (EC) No 882/2004 and of the Council of 29 April 2004 on official controls performed to ensure the verification of compliance with feed and food law, animal health and animal welfare rules. *OJ L 165*1–141.

Parliament European. (2017). Regulation (EU) 2017/625 of the European Parliament and of the Council of 15 March 2017 on official controls and other official activities performed to ensure the application of food and feed law, rules on animal health and welfare, plant health and plant. *OJ L 95,* 1–142.

Parliament European. (1992). *Council Directive 85/374/EEC and Council Directive 92/59/EEC on General Product Safety.*

Powell, D. A., Erdozain, S., Dodd, C., Costa, R., Morley, K., & Chapman, B. J. (2013). Audits and inspections are never enough: A critique to enhance food safety. *Food Control*, *30*(2), 686–691. doi:10.1016/j.foodcont.2012.07.044

Raybould, A. a. (2018). Policy- led comparative environmental risk assessment of genetically modified crops: Testing for increased risk rather than profiling phenotypes leads to predictable and transparent decision-making. *Frontiers in Bioengineering and Biotechnology*, *§§§*, 6. PMID:29755975

Reardon, T., Codron, J., & Busch, L. (2000). Global change in agrifood grades and standards: Agribusiness strategic responses in developing countries. *The International Food and Agribusiness Management Review*, *2*(4), 421–435.

Riehard, T. P. (2001). *The Art of Japanese Management*. New York: Simon & Sehuster.

Röhr, A., Lüddecke, K., Drusch, S., Müller, M. J., & Alvensleben, R. V. (2005). Food quality and safety—consumer perception and public health concern. *Food Control*, *16*(8), 649–655. doi:10.1016/j.foodcont.2004.06.001

Rosak-Szyrocka, J., & Blažević, L. B. (2019). Food Safety in Quality Mark Aspect. *System Safety: Human-Technical Facility-Environment*, *1*(1), 558–565.

Rotaru, G. B. (2005). Food Quality and Safety Management Systems: A Brief Analysis of the Individual and Integrated Approaches. *Technologies*, *11*(1), 229–236.

Samani, M. A., Ismail, N., & Leman, Z. (2017). Development of a conceptual model for risk-based quality management system. *Total Quality Management & Business Excellence*, *14*(4), 1–16.

Sikora, T., & Strada, A. (2005). *Safety and quality assurance and management systems in food industry: An overview.* The Food Industry in Europe, Agricultural University of Athens.

Soares, N. F., Martins, C., & Vicente, A. A. (2016). *Food safety management system EN ISO 22000: 2005. Food Safety in the Seafood Industry: A practical guide for ISO 22000 and FSSC 22000 implementation* (1st ed.). Oxford: John Wiley & Sons. doi:10.1002/9781118965108

Soon, J. M., & Baines, R. (2013). Public and Private Food Safety Standards: Facilitating or Frustrating Fresh Produce Growers? *Laws*, *2*(1), 1–19. doi:10.3390/laws2010001

Stefanova, M., & Gotcheva, V. (2016). Possibilities for Integrating the Requirements of Food Quality and Safety Management Standards. In Scientific works of University of Food technologies 2016, (pp. 111 - 118). Plovdiv: University of Food Technologies.

ten Berge, H. F. M., Schroder, J. J., Olesen, J. E., & Giraldez Cervera, J. V. (2017). *Research for AGRI Committee – Preserving agricultural soils in the EU, European Parliament.* Brussels: Policy Department for Structural and Cohesion Policies.

Thomas, R. (2000). Agrifood grades and standards in the extended Mercosur: Their role in the changing agrifood system. *American Journal of Agricultural Economics*, *82*(5), 1170–1176. doi:10.1111/0002-9092.00116

Tzia, V., Tzia, T., & Tzia, C. (2015). Handbook of Food Processing: Food Safety, Quality, and Manufacturing Processes (35th ed.). CRC Press.

Varzakas, T., & Tzia, C. (2016). Handbook of food processing: food safety, quality, and manufacturing processes (1st ed.). Boca Raton: CRC Press.

Vasileva, E. & Ivanova, D.& Tipova, N.& Stefanov, S. (2019.). Quality of organic foods—a model for comparative analysis. *Organic Agriculture Official Journal of the International Society of Organic Agriculture Research*, *9*(1).

Verbeke, W., Frewer, L. J., Scholderer, J., & de Brabander, H. F. (2007). Why consumers behave as they do with respect to food safety and risk information. *Analytica Chimica Acta*, *586*(1-2), 2–7. doi:10.1016/j.aca.2006.07.065 PMID:17386689

Verbeke, W., Vermeir, I., & Brunsø, K. (2007). Consumer evaluation of fish quality as a basis for fish market segmentation. *Food Quality and Preference*, *18*(4), 651–661. doi:10.1016/j.foodqual.2006.09.005

Vukasović, T. (2015). Food quality and safety: Added value in a customer-oriented concept. *International Journal of Value Chain Management*, *7*(3), 241–254. doi:10.1504/IJVCM.2015.079208

Wallace, C. H. L., Holyoak, L., Powell, S. C., & Dykes, F. C. (2012). Re-thinking the HACCP team: An investigation into HACCP team knowledge and decision-making for successful HACCP development. *Food Research International*, *47*(2), 236–245. doi:10.1016/j.foodres.2011.06.033

WHO. (1998). *Guidance on regulatory assessment of HACCP. Report of a join FAO/WHO consultation on the role of government agencies in assessing HACCP.* WHO.

WHO. (2015). *WHO estimates of the global burden of foodborne diseases" has been launched on 3 December.* WHO.

Wilcock, A., Pun, M., Khanona, J., & Aung, M. (2004). Consumer attitudes, knowledge and behaviour: A review of food safety issues. *Trends in Food Science & Technology*, *15*(2), 56–66. doi:10.1016/j.tifs.2003.08.004

Wognum, N. (2009). Environmental transparency of food supply chains-Current status and challenges. In *Global Perspective for Competitive Enterprise, Economy and Ecology* (pp. 645–652). London: Springer. doi:10.1007/978-1-84882-762-2_61

Wognum, N., & Bremmers, H. (2009). Environmental transparency of food supply chains-Current status and challenges. In *Global Perspective for Competitive Enterprise, Economy and Ecology* (pp. 645–652). London: Springer. doi:10.1007/978-1-84882-762-2_61

Zimon, D., & Madzík, P. (2019). Standardized management systems and risk management in the supply chain. *International Journal of Quality & Reliability Management*, *37*(2), 305–327. doi:10.1108/IJQRM-04-2019-0121

Zwietering, M. (2015). Risk assessment and risk management for safe foods: Assessment needs inclusion of variability and uncertainty, management needs discrete decisions. *International Journal of Food Microbiology*, *213*, 118–123. doi:10.1016/j.ijfoodmicro.2015.03.032 PMID:25890788

ADDITIONAL READING

Cvetkova, T., Stoyanova, K., & Paunov, T. (2018). Contamination with Toxocara spp. eggs of environmental samples of public places of Varna city, Bulgaria. *Journal of IMAB–Annual Proceeding Scientific Papers*, *24*(3), 2177–2180. doi:10.5272/jimab.2018243.2177

Ivanova, D., Naradinova, A., & Vasileva, E. (2019). Eco-Innovations in Bulgarian Companies with Pro-Environmental Policy. *Quality-Access to Success*, *20*, 168.

Nováková, R., Cekanova, K., & Pauliková, A. (2016). Integration management system–new of requirements of ISO 9001: 2015 and ISO 14001: 2015 standards. *Production Engineering Archives, 13*(4), 35–40. doi:10.30657/pea.2016.13.08

Pashova, S. (2015) Food safety in the dynamic developing economy - ensuring the protection of consumers` health and interests. *Proceedings of the International Conference "Business Education and Market Dynamics", Varna: STENO Publishing House,* pp. 84-99.

Stefanova, M., & Pashova, S. (2018) Analysis of the risks of circular contamination in fruit processing products. *Commodity science - traditions and relevance: Proceedings of the 13th Scientific Conference with International Participation: Dedicated to the 70th Anniversary of the Establishment of the Department of Commodity Science and Specialty of Commodity Science, Varna, October 18th - 19th, 2018, Varna: "Science and Economy", University of Economics-Varna, Bulgaria, 2018,* pp. 180 – 187.

Vasileva, E. (2019). *Education About Standardization in the Context of Sustainable Development* (pp. 79–94). Sustainable Development Knowledge and Education About Standardization.

Vasileva, E., Ivanova, D., Tipova, N., & Stefanov, St. (2018). Quality of organic foods—a model for comparative analysis. *Springer Netherlands Organic Agriculture, 9*(1), 1–12.

Zhechev, V. (2018). Measuring Brand Competitive Performance – a Focus on Ethical Brand Positioning, *Conference: The 12th International Days of Statistics and Economics, Prague, September 6-8, 2018, At Prague, Czech Republic, Volume:1*

KEY TERMS AND DEFINITIONS

Food: Substance (ingredient), whether processed, semi-processed or raw, which is intended for consumption, and includes drink, chewing gum and any substance which has been used in the manufacture, preparation or treatment of "food" but does not include cosmetics or tobacco or substances (ingredients) used only as drugs.

Food Safety: Assurance that food will not cause an adverse health effect for the consumer when it is prepared and/or consumed in accordance with its intended use.

Food Safety Hazard: Biological, chemical, or physical agent in food with the potential to cause an adverse health effect.

HACCP-Based Procedures or "HACCP": Procedures based on the hazard analysis and critical control point (HACCP) principles, that is, an auto-control system which identifies, evaluates and controls hazards which are significant for food safety consistent with the HACCP principles.

Operational Prerequisite Programme (OPRP): Control measure or combination of control measures applied to prevent or reduce a significant food safety hazard to an acceptable level, and where action criterion and measurement or observation enable effective control of the process and/or product.

Risk: Effect of uncertainty.

Validation: Food safety obtaining evidence that a control measure (or combination of control measures) will be capable of effectively controlling the significant food safety hazard.

Verification: Confirmation, through the provision of objective evidence, that specified requirements have been fulfilled.

Chapter 14
A Comparison of Population Growth Rate and the Rate of Increase in Food Crop Production in Africa

Emmanuel Kofi Ankomah
https://orcid.org/0000-0002-2346-8736
Mendel University in Brno, Czech Republic

ABSTRACT

Millions of people in Africa require sufficient food for healthy living. However, inefficient farming practices are making a lot more people hungry and poor. Simultaneously, the population keeps on increasing. The legitimate question that this study seeks to address is how the production capacity can meet the needs of the increasing population in the future. The chapter examines the increase in population growth and its consequences on food production with the consideration of the theory of population growth by Thomas Malthus. The result of time series data analyzed shows that population growth is increasing at a high rate whereas food production growth is increasing at a decreasing rate. The trend seems to confirm that the Malthus population theory is still relevant in Africa. The study recommends that stewards and policymakers invest immensely in agriculture to improve technology, skills, methods, and know-how to boost food production and invest in women in adopting family planning to decrease population growth for the solution of food deficiency.

INTRODUCTION

The inception of the agricultural revolution has brought about a significant change to the world food supply and this, in turn, made the population theory of Malthus irrelevant in the developed nations where agriculture has seen a tremendous improvement. The drastic improvement in the methods of crop cultivation has brought about a significant improvement in agricultural yields. The growth of total world food production has been increasing over the years.

DOI: 10.4018/978-1-7998-4601-7.ch014

In general, the growth in food production exceeds the growth of population (Yanjiu, 1982). Despite the increases in world food production, the supply of food within countries are not the same. There is an inequality in food supply among countries around the world, Bellis (2017). Food production is continually increasing in abundance in the developed countries. Some of the food produced is sometimes deliberately disposed of as waste. But the situation is different in developing countries. The food crops produced in developing countries is deficient. The reason is that developing countries are still using the old traditional hand tools and depending on physical weather conditions (Mendelsohn, 2008). The farmers are mostly illiterate peasant farmers who use their human power on the farms. (Temesgen, 2017) Lack of knowledge and technology aggravate the extreme weather prevalence in many developing countries to decrease food production (Ochieng, Kirimi, & Mathenge, 2016).

The quality and quantity of food supply and consumption by the world population are different between social classes within countries and between countries. World Bank statistics show that one billion or more of the world population are suffering from malnutrition and that many of these people are living in developing countries, including Africa.

Foodgrains are very important in the world. It is produced and consumed in many countries. Man consumes about half of the grains produced in the world. Wheat flour bread is one of the staple foods eaten by people around the world. Rice, corn and wheat are the most common staple foods that are mostly consumed by man and animals on earth.

In developed countries, about half of the increase in the food supply is from food grains. They follow the policy of reducing farmland to maintain stable grain prices, especially in Europe. In 1981 the world population growth rate decreased from 2% to about 1.7%. Birth control and an increase in the food supply has brought new hope to the world's problems of overpopulation and food supply.

To this date, cereal food prices remain unstable and keep increasing. The rising costs of cereals have become a huge economic problem for many developing nations. Policymakers have realised the importance of boosting agriculture productivity as a solution to the problem. In this respect, many of the countries in the developing world are adopting strategies to motivate the numerous small-scale farmers to increase grain production. Farmers are provided with agriculture inputs to increase yields. Subsidised equipment is being made available, and the peasant farmers are being encouraged to adopt modern farming techniques to increases the arable land area yield and to enhance their methods of cultivation to decrease postharvest loses. However, the farmers are facing problems of funding and harsh weather conditions. Water supply and agricultural inputs like fertilizer and pesticides are woefully inadequate. The high population growth in the developing countries turns to neutralised and diminished the endeavours of the farmers in their struggle for high productivity. In recent years, developing counties have realized the importance of population growth measures and applying it to augment the progress towards the achievement of food sufficiency.

The recent population estimates show that rapid population growth rate in Africa will eventually impact negatively on the development efforts, (Boadu, 1994; Ofosu-Amaah, 2006). This consensus usually stems from economic development, Benneh (1987). Often, writers associate a nation's development mainly with economic growth. Nevertheless, population growth has some amount of effects on economic growth and development.

The paper focuses on the relationship between population growth and economic growth in Africa with food crop production. The paper examines the trend in population growth in Africa and its consequences on food grain productivity, taking into consideration of the fact that corn, rice and wheat are the most important and most common food grains consumed in the world.

The increasing trend of population growth in Africa is a significant setback to food sustainability policies that are being undertaken by many of the countries. The theory of population growth (Malthus, 1798) stated that food production grows at the arithmetical rate, whereas the population grows at a geometric rate. His argument revolved around population pressure on food crop production.

There are many food crops produced and consumed locally in the countries in Africa. Examples of such food crops include the varieties of yams (Dioscoreaceae), cocoyams with the family name Araceae, plantains with the family name Musaceae and many other food crops, fruits and also vegetables which are not found or eaten in many parts of the world. Many food crops are known and consumed in the localities within which they are grown. Such food crops contribute immensely to the reduction of famine and hunger in Africa, yet the production of such food crops are in smaller quantities. The principal food crops that are produced and consumed in larger quantities in Africa are maize, rice, millet, wheat, sorghum, teff, yam, cocoyam and plantains. Cereals are easy to store by the peasant farmer using sun drying and also keeping them in reserve room or by storing it on top of traditional improvised open-air cribs.

The production of cereals which are the most import staple crops has been growing very slow or has become stagnant in the last five years whereas the output of starchy food which are cassava and other tubers are increasing in recent years. Unfortunately, the tubers are highly perishable, and lack of storage facilities has made these crops highly seasonal. They are produced in abundance during the harvesting season but becomes scarce shortly after the harvesting period due to lack of storage facilities couple with other causes of post-harvest losses.

Agriculture contributes immensely to the economy of most of the countries in Africa. In Ghana, for instance, agriculture contributed 36 per cent to the GDP in 1997, and in 2003 it increased to 40.4 per cent. Cocoa is an important tree crop in West Africa. The young fresh green fruit of the cocoa is a nutritious ingredient for preparing the sauce. When the cocoa fruit matures, the seeds are taken out of the pods and dried. The countries produce cocoa beans mainly produced for export, but they use a small amount for the preparation of cocoa drinks and chocolate for the local market. It is the most important cash crop in La Cote d'Ivoire and Ghana. The cocoa plant contributed $1 billion, which is about 39.2% to the national income of Ghana in 2004 and has increased to about $2 billion annually in recent years. It employs more 800,000 farm families in Ghana. Agricultural growth is vital for Africa. About 80 per cent of poor people living in rural areas in Africa depends on agriculture but are not able to meet their basic food needs. The population pressure on land is increasingly growing, land and water resources are becoming scarce, making agricultural productivity growth increasing at a decreasing rate.

The total land area of Africa is about 11,724,000 square miles which are 30,365,000 square km. The uncultivated arable land is about 60% of the world's entire arable land. The small scale farmers whose poor farming practices produce meagre crop yields of about one-third of the global average dominate.

If Africans can combine land and water appropriately suitable to the labour and farming technology, food production in many countries in Africa will exceed available demand. The advanced countries have proven from the start of the industrial and agricultural revolution that proper combination of suitable technologies, labour, investment, land and water can enable global agrarian production to outpace the growing demand. In Africa, there is a lack of process to build up soil fertility and the moisture-holding capacity of the soils, equipped land with irrigation and small-scale water control systems. The percentage of irrigated arable land in Africa is 7 per cent and just about half of it (3.7 per cent) is found in Sub-Saharan Africa whereas, in South Asia alone the figure for the same facility stands at 41 per cent. It has become an essential issue as technological advancement has made the world becomes one big global village, to revisit the Malthusian theory and its relevance to present-day Africa. And to analyse the assumption that population growth rate in Africa will not exceed the growth rate of the production of the leading staple food, which includes maize, rice, millet, sorghum and other cereals.

In the case of Ghana, for instance, the aggregate land is about 23.8 million hectares. Still, just about 57.1 per cent, which is about 13.6 million hectares are arable, which is suitable for agricultural. Yet, only 7.2 million hectares (30.2 per cent) is under development according to data released in 2004 by FAO. The agriculture sector is the most significant labour employer and so as the population grows the land area accessible for cultivation by individual farmers diminishes. This situation does not exist only peculiar to Ghana but the whole of Africa. At a Total Fertility Rate of 3.6 as estimated for 2019, there will be less arable land accessible per individual for food production and cash crops in support of individual households' food consumption needs as well as the sale of any surpluses generated.

BACKGROUND

Africa is a vast continent with a diverse climate ranging from high rainfall in the equatorial rain forest region and the tropical wetlands to the arid climatic zones of the semi-desert and the hyper-arid territories. There are sporadic cases of temperate climate which appear on the high elevations and fringes of the continent. The climate varies more in terms of the amount of rainfall than temperature.

Agriculture is the mainstay of the people of Africa. It is the oldest civilization and the means of livelihood. The culture and the traditions of the people of Africa promote the practices of subsistence farming (Darkwah & Ankomah, 2010). This system of agriculture in Africa has been there for centuries. It is a means to meet the nutritional needs of the people and their families. Accordingly, the peasant farmers produced a variety of crops for their households.

In recent years, the high population growth has generated constant land division and fragmentation, making it difficult for the peasants' farmers to meet the required varieties of sustainable food for their families. The African continent is full of natural resources and fertile pastoral land. Food crops can be grown continuously to produce food throughout the year. The African continent is the place suitable for the cultivation of the world's essential plants and vegetables which are facing extinction. The continent is a land of plants and crops, which exist in an incredible variety. It is surprising to see that, Africa cannot feed its people with the diverse food crops under the relatively conducive climatic and ecological condition.

The system of agriculture in a country is supposed to provide food security and nutrition for the population. Food crop cultivation system in Africa follows the path of hand to mouth with a small fraction going from producer to consumer. The role of agriculture in human development in Africa is an essential linkage between agriculture and nutrition of its people and the development of the continent which emphasize the need for Africa to develop its vast arable land and the productive capacity of its young population, (Grega & Ankomah, 2016).

The African agricultural system provides a livelihood for about 70 per cent of the economically active labour force, of which many are small scale farmer (Grega, Ankomah & Darkwah, 2015). The availability of quality and quantity of resources, and investment capacity of the continent and on the traditions and culture of the people will increase land and labour productivity. The higher number of the African population dwells in rural communities in a social setting where the producer and the consumer are living in the same household and as neighbours, and they are often relatives from the same family. Their decision and actions have a significant impact on the future of the whole economy of Africa and therefore, must contribute to the source of information for policy-makers. The implication of the patterns of consumption and the effects of agricultural decisions of the households has a high impact on food availability and nutritional status of the producers and consumers in both rural and urban communities.

Such implications can affect the food supply chain, and their decisions can bring about changes in the consumption of food quality, quantity, safety and varieties (Horák, Darkwah, & Verter, 2014). The repercussions can also bring changes in food supply for a particular community due to fluctuations in food supply and changes in prices. All of these changes can result in a decreasing household income and increase poverty, especially among the peasant farmers. A breakdown of food production and supply management in households and a lack of adequate food for consumption will result in health deterioration and early death. Life expectancy at birth will eventually become very low.

Population growth is a challenge to food production and its availability in terms of both access to land and consumption pattern. The rapid population growth and the increasing number of fertility rate imply that there is a need to produce more food for the people. Africa is becoming more urbanized with a growing trend of rural-urban migration which is a crucial contributing factor to poor food crop productivity.

MAIN FOCUS OF THE CHAPTER

As stated by the United Nations Food and Agriculture Organization (FAO), there are only twelve crops which provide about 75 per cent of the food consumed in the world today. There are three of these crops, which are rice, maize, and wheat that contribute nearly 60 per cent protein and calories needed by human beings from food crops. From the beginning of the 20th century, studies have shown that more than 70 per cent of crop genetic diversity is missing particularly in Africa.

Building the interest and investment capabilities of the indigenous people in the production of the indigenous crops may bring relief to Africa and offer a means of solution to the food scarcity and food insecurity and improve the problem of losing biodiversity. Many traditional varieties of crops can withstand the harsh climatic conditions and survive poor agricultural practices until today but facing extinction and only got lost due to lack of interest in their cultivation. Cultivating such crops can help improve nutrition and health and improve the standard of living of the indigenous farmers and the local economies, and enhance climatic condition by rejuvenating biodiversity, whiles upholding the tradition and culture of the communities.

The work of the Slow Food International's Ark of Taste which is going around the world, taking inventory of indigenous species of fruits and vegetables provides a lot of experience. Besides, the Biodiversity International, an Italian research organization, has been providing scientific evidence, on management practices with policies that can safeguard biodiversity in agriculture to advance the work in agriculture sustainability and global food security.

Africans must take an interest in cultivating the many indigenous foods in addition to the thirty-one crops listed by the Food Tank. It will help preserve species and varieties that are facing extinction and improve not only biodiversity but make diverse food available to the people and the world over.

Materials and Methods

The chapter reviews a comprehensive list of articles published in journals, books, reports and working papers in the examination of the notion that Africa has the capacity and potentials to feed itself. The result of the study is the outcome of time series data extracted from the FAO statistics' recent data array on cereal crops production in Africa. A compilation of a 25-year population data from the World Bank databank prepared for a comparison of the annual growth rate of cereals and yearly population growth rate in Africa. The linear trend analysis of the 25 years of data extracted from FAO statistics recent data array and the World Bank databank. The data allowed for the assessment of the population growth rate in Africa detailing the trend over time and the production of cereal crops. Based on data compiled for the observed variables, the study used the linear trend analysis. Linear trend analysis is suitable for analyzing figures to predict future patterns in data movements. The study determined the growth rate from the data. It explained the trends and patterns in the historical data obtained from the Food and Agriculture Organization (FAO) Statistics and the World Bank population data. The aim is to predict the future pattern of growth in the production of the staple food produced and consumed in Africa, which are mainly cereals. The cereals are also known as cereal grains are the grains of the cereal food crops, and they serve as the staple food for the majority of the people living in Africa.

The term cereal refers to the grass family grown purposely for its edible grains or fruits. The types, such as rice, wheat, maize and many more are for feeding people, animal husbandry, and the making of alcoholic drinks and beverages.

In recent years the typical breakfast meals are made from different kinds of cereal. The cereals eaten for breakfast are also called breakfast cereal or cereals in short. Though the study covers the use of cereal grains as in breakfast cereals, the consumption analysis focuses on seeds in the form grains produced by all the edible grasses and the comestibles created out of them.

The trend of the growth rate of the cereal production compared to that of the growth rate of the population by the historical data for the same period establishes the difference between the amount of cereal food crop produced and the amount needed for consumption in Africa. By calculating the rate of change in the population growth variable and the rate of change in the food crop variable over the 25 years, the study predicts their relationship. The period for the calculation of the percentage rate of change from the time series is from 1992 to 2016, which is the most recent data reported by the two internationally recognized bodies. The calculation is done by subtracting the immediate past year value from the year under observation and dividing the result by the immediate previous year value and then multiply by 100. The results are given in percentages to make comparisons meaningful. When the effect is negative, it implies the rate has decreased, and vice versa. Therefore, negative numbers represent a negative trend rate and the positive rate represent a positive trend.

The foundation for the analysis is the population and the cereals produced in Africa. Grains are the crops mainly consumed as a staple food, the chief of which are maize, millet, rice and sorghum.

In the calculation of the annual growth rate from one year to the other, the paper used the following formula.

$$\text{Growth Percentage Over One Year} = \{(\text{Final Value} - \text{Start Value}) / \text{Start Value}\} * 100$$

The formula for calculating the annual growth rate for the time in years is as follows:

$$\text{Growth Percentage Over One Year} = \{((f/s)^{1/y}-1)\} * 100$$

where f is the final closing value, s is the initial starting value, and y is the number of years between the time frame

An average increase refers to the average rate of growth of a variable within a given period. The mathematical theory for average increase or decrease is calculated just as in accounting, financing or the population growth. The underlying algebraic method and principles in the calculation of average growth rate are applied. It is appropriate in cases where there are finite start time and an end time value.

The initial value and the end value for the given period under consideration are determined and label V_1 for the initial and V_2 for the end value. The calculation of the percentage change is by the equation $(V_2 - V_1)/ V_1$ and then divided by the time T, thus $[(V_2 - V_1)/ V_1]/T$ to arrive at the percentage change as a function of time. The result of the percentage change is multiplied by 100 to arrive at the annual percentage change. The calculation is presented as $\{[(V_2 - V_1)/ V_1]/T\} *100$ in line with the presentation by Beck (2018)

SOLUTIONS AND RECOMMENDATIONS

Due to the range of different climatic conditions prevailing in Africa, the continent can pride itself on many food crops (Freda, 2019). There are varieties of tree crops, cereals, pulses, roots and tubers, and vegetables and greens that grow very well in Africa (Food and Agriculture Organization of the United Nations, 1997).

Food Crops

The African continent is the origin of the major cereal crops like sorghum, pearl millet, finger millet, teff, fonio, and African rice (Taylor & Naushad, 2008). The dependence on the development of new crop varieties is not always the best way to find a solution to hunger and famine, but increasing the interest in indigenous food crops can improve nutrition, increase incomes, restore agricultural biodiversity and preserve the ecosystem. (Amanda, et al., 2011) Table 1 shows some of the indigenous food crops that are grown in Africa. Cereals, roots and tubers and, the main starchy fruits are the staple foods. However, many other plants alongside the staples crops especially cocoa, coffee, cashew, avocado, mango, orange, lemon, lime and others are grown as cash crops, and the farmers consume part of the yields.

Population Growth in Africa

The Table 2 below shows 64 years of historical data of the population growth in Africa from 1955 to the year 2019 with yearly changes in percentage as well as in absolute values with the annual fertility rate and the annual share of the world population in proportion. On the table, the 2019 total population of Africa stands at 1,320,038,716, which makes it the second-most populous continent after Asia. With the total land area of 29,648,481 square kilometres and a population density of 44 persons per square kilometre, an equivalent of 114 persons per square miles and about 43.4% which is approximately 567,387,619 people urbanised, there is still more room for agricultural activities. With the median age of 19.4 years, the continent has more active labour force to undertake the production of food crops. Still, with the rise in population growth and the yearly percentage changes, the study of the population growth concerning the growth of other economic development variables has become significant. According to the World

Table 1. Prevalent indigenous food crops in Africa

Staple Crops		Cash Crops		Minor Crops	
Starchy/Cereals	**Others**	**Tree Crops**	**Others**	**Tree Crops**	**Others**
Maize	Lettuce	Cacao	Tobacco	Marula tree	African Eggplant
Rice	Pineapple	Coconut	Sugar cane	Monkey Orange	Ceylon spinach
Sorghum	Groundnuts	Oil-palm	Orange	Moringa Tree	Lablab
Millet	Cowpea	Coffee	Cotton	Locust Bean	Marama
Wheat/Barley	Groundnuts	Avocado	Ginger	Baobab	Fonio cereal
Finger Millet	Baobab	Shear butter	Tobacco	Dika	Teff
Potatoes	Beans	Orange	Soybean	Guava	Safou
Yam	Kukumba	Lemon	Sesame	Custard apple	Pigeonpea
Cassava	Carrot	Lime	Sugar cane		Coleus
Cocoyam	Pepper	Cashew,	Bambara nut		Egusi
sweet potato	Melons	Mango	Onion		Enset
Banana	Cabbage	Passion fruit	Spring onion		Gourd
Plantain	mustard				squash
	Tomato				pumpkin
	Papaya				Okra

Source: Sanginga 2015 Root and tuber crops

Economic Forum (2016) reported that all the first ten youngest populated countries in the world are in Africa. Niger has the world's, most youthful population with a median age of 14.8, which is half of the global average figure of 29.6. Uganda is the second youngest country with a median age of 15.9, Chad comes third to complete the list of the top three with a median age of 16 and is followed by Angola, 16.1; Mali, 16.2; Somali, 16.5; Gambia, 16.8; Zambia,16.9; Democratic Republic of Congo, 16.9 and Burkina Faso, 17.0. The report stated in also that the average birth rate for a woman in Niger is 7.6 children, whereas the global average is 2.5. The high birth rate, combined with the low life expectancy, which is about 58 years, is part of the conditions responsible for the life expectancy of the population in the Niger and Africa in general.

Young Population and Productivity

The young population of Africa is an advantage due to the notion that young people are the economically active labour force. The economically active people are all the people who make up the labour force in producing economic goods and services by definition provided by the United Nations System of National Accounts. The young population is an opportunity for economic growth in Africa. The United Nations has estimated that the increases in population growth of Africa have the potential to generate between 11 and 15 per cent of gross domestic product from 2011 to 2030. By taken advantage of providing adequate education and jobs to the young population, Africa will gain billions of dollars a year to its economy. Nevertheless, lack of employment and other economic opportunities couple with the social stress of unemployment leads the young population into poverty. A report of the United Nations in 2014 asserted that the risk of lack of jobs among young people in Africa has brought about frustration which has contributed to high risk of unmanaged migration and that African nations are yet to face the most significant challenges from youthful populations growth.

The part of the population living in extreme poverty has been declining globally. Nevertheless, the story is different in Africa. The World Bank estimates support the notion that the number of people living under extreme poverty in Africa is increasing. The estimate by the World Bank in 2015 shows that more than half of the people who earn less than $1.90 in a day are living in Africa though the global number of impoverished people who are living on less than $1.90 a day reduced by more than half between 1990 and 2015 from 1.9 billion to about 736 million.

The prevailing condition is an indication that the poverty numbers will keep growing in Africa. The World Bank forecast has indicated that about nine out of every ten extremely poor will be in Africa by the year 2030. According to Hans-Peter (2013), the majority of the population in Africa are living in regions where there are high fertility rate and poor reproductive health, and low per capita income regions. The assertion is right in the case of Niger, Angola, Mali, Burundi, and Somalia, among others. Scholars have given many reasons for the rapid population growth in developing countries which are not different from each other. However, in the case of Ghana and other countries with high Gross Domestic Product growth rate, there is the double condition of being a highly populated as compared to the average population density in Africa and being a highly specialized exporter of resource and commodities such as cocoa, minerals, and, oil (Nin-Pratt & McBride, 2014).

With the presence of different agroecological regions in terms of rainfall, climate, vegetation, soil, and growing seasons, Africa provides a varied environment for agricultural production from the south to the north, (Nin-Pratt & McBride, 2014). The agroecological zones are the Tropics, Sub-tropics, Coastal, Forest, South Savannah, and North Savannah, Arid, Semi-arid, Sub-humid, and humid regions. Data from the Food and Agriculture Organization([FAO], 2013) indicate that the Forest region receives more rainfall, the Coastal and the South Savannah regions receive between 800 and 1300 mm yearly. The same data also suggests that precipitation levels are both lower and more erratic in the Arid and semi-arid areas. The climatic variations across the continent make the length of the growing period varies from the south to the north and makes it possible to grow varieties of food within the continent. The climatic variations establish the fact that aside from the relationship between population and food production in Africa, other factors also contribute to the cultivation of food crops.

Population Growth in Africa

The data array available at the FAO Statistics shows the population growth trend in Africa in Figure 1. The trend lines are drawn based on available population data from the year 1992 to 2016, which covers 25-year span.

The graphs show decreases in population growth rate. However, there is a steady increase in the total yearly population. The reductions and increases between 1995 and 2000 must have happened as a result of civil wars and the deliberate attempt by some government and policymakers to increase their population. The growth is steady throughout the 25 years under study. Scholars have been alarmed at the constant rate of population growth in Africa. Engelman (2016) described Africa as a crowded confrontational and urban continent with prospects which has begun to worry its leaders, most of whom traditionally favour population growth.

Table 2. Population growth in Africa (2019 and historical data)

Year	Population	Yearly % Change	Yearly Change	Fertility Rate	Density (P/ Km^2)	Africa's Share of World Pop
1955	253,995,025	2.12	5,065,001	6.62	9	10.00%
1960	285,142,006	2.34	6,229,396	6.66	10	10.30%
1965	322,470,634	2.49	7,465,726	6.62	11	10.60%
1970	366,458,929	2.59	8,797,659	6.72	12	11.00%
1975	417,898,074	2.66	10,287,829	6.71	14	11.30%
1980	480,012,209	2.81	12,422,827	6.64	16	11.80%
1985	552,796,228	2.86	14,556,804	6.48	19	12.40%
1990	634,567,044	2.80	16,354,163	6.18	21	13.00%
1995	722,921,961	2.64	17,670,983	5.72	24	13.60%
2000	817,566,004	2.49	18,928,809	5.34	28	14.20%
2005	924,757,708	2.49	21,438,341	5.08	31	15.00%
2010	1,049,446,344	2.56	24,937,727	4.89	35	16.00%
2015	1,194,369,908	2.62	28,984,713	4.72	40	17.20%
2016	1,225,080,510	2.57	30,710,602	4.66	41	16.40%
2017	1,256,268,025	2.55	31,187,515	4.66	42	16.60%
2018	1,287,920,518	2.52	31,652,493	4.66	43	16.90%
2019	1,320,038,716	2.49	32,118,198	4.66	45	17.10%

Source: World Bank databank

Evidently, in the case of some of the low-income countries, there has been an absolute population increment in millions just within ten years. The estimate shows that the population of some of the countries in Africa increase by about half a million per year and over two million absolutes in every five years. All things being equal, this slow and steady growth should not be alarming if the increase in food production corresponds to the rise in population.

Figure 1. The trend of population growth in Africa
Source: FAO Statistics (2017)

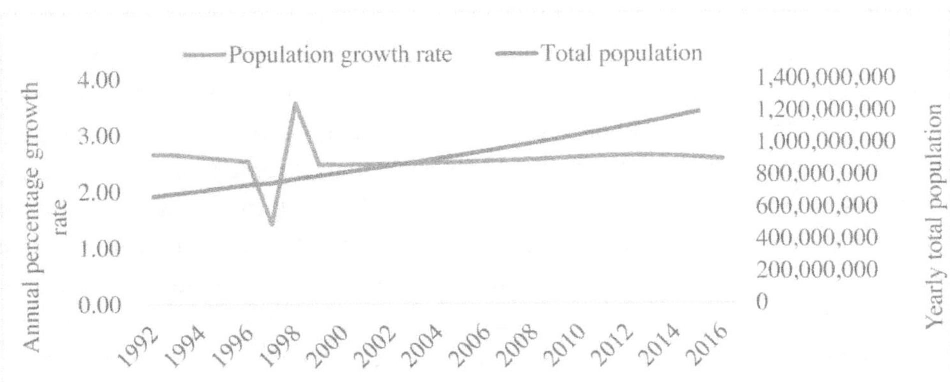

Cereal Food Crop Production Between 1992 and 2016

In consideration of Africa's food production, the total output of cereals which are the leading staple food, are analysed. The main four, which are grown in many of the countries are Maize, millet, sorghum, and rice. These food crops and many other kinds of cereal are having fluctuating yield over the years. Table 3 below depicts the production quantity of cereals crops, the annual growth rate, the yearly population increase figure and the population growth rate in percentage.

It is evident from Figure 2 that the graph of crop production growth rate has a series of peaks and troughs. The situation is unstable for most farmers and households in Africa (Doss & Morris, 2001) as the food crops produced are not enough to meet the growing urban and rural consumer demand in food deficit areas (Smith et al., 1997). The Food Research Institute of Ghana (1986) and Boateng et al. (1990) observed that maize-based foods in many countries in Africa are more than twenty-four food items and that maize-based food accounts for more than 10% of total food expenditures of all households in Africa. Cereals are, therefore, prominent in the agricultural sector and have the potential to address food insecurity problems. It could play a role in the future strategy to reverse Africa's seemingly declining trend in per capita food productivity (Tachie-Obeng et al., 2013).

A Comparison of Population Growth and Food Production

By observing the trend of population growth rate in Figure 1, it is clear that the population in Africa has been increasing at a constant rate. Though the rate of increase has been decreasing in recent times, the percentage growth in food production falls below the population percentage growth, as shown in Figure 2. On the order hand, the cultivation of food crops either grow with a slow increase, or it does not grow at all. Among the cereals, maize is the main crop cultivated in a higher quantity in Africa. Like all cereals, the rate of production increases to some extent and then drops. Rice is another cereal crop which is being produced much more steadily but has not yet reached the level of maize and many other kinds of cereal. The bulk of rice eaten in Africa is mostly imported.

The Figure 2 below shows that the theory of Malthus is still relevant in agrarian developing countries in Africa more especially the Sub-Saharan African countries where the peasant farmers dominate with outmoded agricultural practices (Ankomah & Adjei, 2019). It contributes to the reasons for the high importation of rice and other food crops in Africa.

With the conducive climatic conditions in 2002, crop production surpassed population growth, pushing down costs of a portion of the real staple foods including yam and cassava and other traditional crops. The growth endured a setback in 2004 due to the 2002 and 2003 terrible climatic conditions. It brought about a decrease in food crop production. Notwithstanding, the population increase and food production deficits, low interest in farming and low per capita nourishment contribute to food insecurity (National Population Council, 2006). In the economics of agrarian change under population pressure, it is asserted that increasing population pressure mostly leads to an increase in land-use intensity in agriculture (Boserup, 1965; Blitz, 1965/1967; Abernethy, 1965/2005). And that mainly after the agricultural and industrial revolutions, conditions suggested that increasing population pressure can lead to an increase in market price incentives, (Schultz, 1964). The situation can also bring about a diminishing return on labour and capital that has been invested (Chayanov, 1966). In the same vein, it will increase the total agricultural output and (Turner et al., 1993). The high market price of food crops will cause farmers to intensify the cultivation of those crops (John W. Mellor, 1969). It will also increase the farm holdings to

Table 3. Production of cereal and population growth in Africa

Year	Production In Tonnes	Annual Growth Rate	Total Population	Population Growth Rate (%)
1992	5618987	2.16	669,221,342	2.66
1993	5500370	2.20	686,916,862	2.64
1994	5381738	7.24	704,820,799	2.61
1995	5018225	14.22	722,921,961	2.57
1996	4393501	14.19	741,220,519	2.53
1997	3847427	-18.08	751,752,789	1.42
1998	4696666	28.86	778,592,236	3.57
1999	3644724	17.74	797,836,027	2.47
2000	3095451	-0.46	817,566,004	2.47
2001	3109846	12.78	837,820,928	2.48
2002	2757410	-22.38	858,622,597	2.48
2003	3552574	42.08	880,016,866	2.49
2004	2500468	6.56	902,048,601	2.50
2005	2346432	23.66	924,757,708	2.52
2006	1897545	-8.43	948,156,166	2.53
2007	2072203	5.86	972,265,961	2.54
2008	1957433	0.65	997,144,670	2.56
2009	1944785	22.77	1,022,858,654	2.58
2010	1584039	-29.03	1,049,446,344	2.60
2011	2231843	12.49	1,076,933,813	2.62
2012	1983950	29.42	1,105,285,268	2.63
2013	1532917	3.47	1,134,398,192	2.63
2014	1481445	-0.65	1,164,129,782	2.62
2015	1491085	11.62	1,194,369,908	2.60

Source: FAO Statistics (2017)

the advancement of food crop cultivation (Wharton, 1969). The population problem in Africa is about the numbers and the welfare of the people, which is always questionable. The agricultural sector is the largest sector of the African economy. According to the National population council, over 60 per cent of the labour force in Africa engages directly or indirectly in agricultural activities. The sector has a vital role to play in the poverty reduction and economic growth of Africa.

Analysis of Per Capita Consumption and Cereal Food Crop Production

Africans highly consumes cereal crops. The reason is that the use of cereals and wholegrain foods are essential for human health, and they form part of the oldest domesticated staple foods if not the oldest staple crops in Africa. Health workers have emphasized that at least two-thirds of grain foods that are consumed by man should be wholegrain. The Food and Agriculture Organization has confirmed that

Figure 2. Percentage growth of cereals production and population comparison
Source: FAO Statistics (2017)

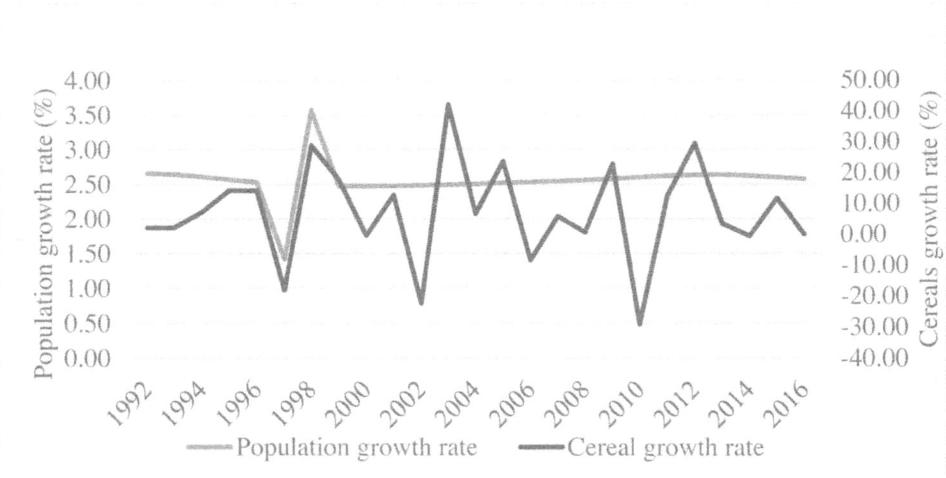

cereals comprising, maize, rice and wheat are the three vital grain crops that constitute 51 per cent of the global calorie's intake out of the main staple foods that are consumed mostly around the world. The consumption of maize alone amount to 16.9 per cent of total global food consumption, followed by rice, and then wheat. The three cereal crops provide more than half of the world caloric intake. The type of food crops consumed in various countries differs most because of climatic conditions, culture, and how the system of government facilitate trade and the popularity of the type of food crop. There are more than 50,000 edible plants around the world. Still, a few of these plants make any significant way of contributing to the supply of food for human consumption. Table 4 below provides a look at the few most essential staples crops. The table shows that root and tuber crops are the second most important staple foods. They produce about 5.3 per cent of the global caloric intake of human energy, but this number does not come anywhere near the amount of the world caloric intake from cereal grains.

The root crops which are also known as tubers grow well in a climatic condition that does not often favour the growth of some types of cereals like rice. Manihot esculenta also called cassava, tapioca, yuca or manioc, is the most common of all the tubers eaten in Africa. It provides 2.6 per cent of global calorie intake, but the 5.3 per cent total human energy intake from root and tuber crops does not come anywhere near the consumption of cereal grains. However, the tubers provide many of the diets in Africa to supplement the cereal crops. Potatoes provide up to 1.7 per cent of the world's calorie consumption. Other conventional root crops that are also sources of energy include sweet potato and yams, which provide 0.6 per cent and 0.4 per cent global calories respectively.

To justify population growth impact on cereal production, the assumption of consumption per capita at 5kg, 10kg and 20kg, as shown in Table 5 is paramount. The weight of the minimum amount of food needed by a person in a day is determined based on data provided by Australian Dietary Guidelines (2015). According to the guidelines, one whole-wheat English-muffin, a small round size bread weighs 35 grams. One slice of bread weighs 40g. A half of medium roll weighs 40g. Half-cup cooked rice, pasta, noodles, barley, buckwheat, semolina, polenta, bulgur or quinoa weigh from 75 grams and more and in the Kids for Health (2014) guidelines, toddlers from 1 year to 3 years old must eat food that contains at least 19 grams of fibre each day. Children from 4 years to 8 years old should be given food with at

Table 4. Global caloric intake of the most important staple crops

Staple Food by Order of Importance	Share of Total Global Caloric Intake
Maize Corn	19.5%
Rice	16.5%
Wheat	15.0%
Cassava	2.6%
Soybeans	2.1%
Potatoes	1.7%
Sorghum	1.2%
Sweet Potato	0.6%
Yams	0.4%
Plantain	0.3%

Source: FAO according to World Atlas

least 25 grams of fibre a day. Older female children from 9 years to 18 years must consume food that contains 26 grams of fibre each day and older male children from 9 years to 13 years should take in food that contains at least 31 grams of fibre and teenagers from 14 to 18 years should take in a minimum of 38 grams of fibre per day.

By taking into consideration the amount of weight of minimum fibre in food recommended for toddlers from one year to three years, the least amount of total weight of food fibre per a person in one year is:

19g X 365 = 6,935g

6,935g ÷ 1000 = 6.935kg

Much the same way, using the least amount of weight of food fibre which must be consumed by teenagers, the consumption per capita for one year can be calculated as:

38g X 365 = 13,870g

13,870g ÷ 100 = 13.870kg

Realistically, the average consumption of cereal/grains in Africa for a whole year can be more than 20 kilograms. Table 5 shows the actual amount of cereals produced yearly in tonnes and the population growth from 1992 to 2015. With the yearly per capita consumption pegged as low as 5 kilograms. At a maximum of 10 kilograms, the total quantity of grains needed for consumption in tonnes is by multiplying the yearly population growth by the per capita quantity and dividing by 1000 kilograms.

Though the actual quantity of cereals produced in the 1990s was enough to sustain the population consumption needs at a level of 5 kilograms per capita consumption rate, the whole situation changed from the year 2000. The analysis of the 2012 figures for the cereals needed for consumption and the actual quantity of grains produced from 2012 to 2015, shows clearly that, as shown in Table 5 that population increases in a more dramatic rate in Africa but cereal food production falls short far below the needed amount for consumption. Not even the high number of deaths of about 8 million to 10 million people yearly as reported in some population study reports could reduce the needed amount of cereals for consumption since 10,000,000 multiply by the assumed maximum consumption per capita of 20 kilograms divided by 1000 gives only 200,000 tonnes. The 200,000 tonnes is far below the over 3,000,000 tonnes needed in 2012 at 5kg consumption per capita which is above the actual cereals produced even in 2015. It is an accepted fact that a child born in 2012 will be old enough to eat food prepared from grains either directly or indirectly in the year 2015. It is possible beyond a reasonable doubt that such a child can consume more than 5 kilograms of cereal foods in a year. Therefore, the assumption that the minimum per capita consumption of cereal grain is 5 kilograms is acceptable as justified in the calculation above. It is also reasonable to assume that each person can consume an average of 20 kilograms of cereal or grain food products per year base on the fact that many people in Africa depend more on cereal crops or grain foods than any other plant. Based on these assumptions the Table 5 compares the deductions of the total population in Africa and the consumption of cereal foods and shows that the difference between the actual product and the amount needed is far more than the effect of deaths as postulated in the population theory.

When 5kg, 10 kg or 20kg is multiplied by the total yearly populations and divided by 1000, it converts the results into tonnes. When compared the consumption per capita at 5 kilograms column to the actual production in tonnes column, it is clear that there is a vast difference between the cereals produced and the amount consumed yearly. The difference becomes more evident when the consumption per capita quantity increased to 10 kg or 20 kg.

The Food and Agriculture statistics reported that cereals produced in 2012 were 1,983,950 tonnes, and that of 2015 was 1,491,085 tonnes. When consumption per capita is presumed to be at 10 kilograms, the total quantity of cereals needed to feed the population comes to 11,052,852.68 tones, and 11,943,699.08 in the respective years (see Table 5). Comparing the figures for 2012 and 2015 shows that there is a vast difference between the quantity produced and the quantity needed for consumption.

The yearly population is made-up of babies which do not eat solid food and therefore depends on breastmilk only, and then children and adults. The study avoids the effect of breastfeeding babies on the needed quantity for consumption by taking the cereals consumed by people in 2012 and production quantity in 2015 and comparing them. It is acceptable to say that all babies born in 2012 will be old enough to eat cereal food in different forms.

CONCLUSION

Food crops in Africa are many different varieties of crops which are dominated by the production of cereals. It employs more than half of the active labour force in both the formal and informal sectors. Crops in Africa, include varieties of tubers, starchy fruits, vegetables, cereal grains, tree crops, among others. The food crops are grown in different climatic zones which ranges from dry savanna, arid, tropical rainforest to grassland, employing traditionally outmoded farming practices. The main staple food consumed in Africa are mostly cereals of which Maize, Rice, Millet and Sorghum are the most common among the increasing population.

The total population of Africa continues to increase year after year. The rate of growth, even though decreasing, it has not reduced enough to have an impact on total population growth. The growth rate has to reduced to its bare minimum, to minimise the overall population growth. More than half of the

Table 5. Estimated yearly consumption of cereals

Year	Actual Production in Tonnes	Total Population	Tons of Consumption Per Capita at 5kg	Tons of Consumption Per Capita at 10kg	Tons of Consumption Per Capita at 20kg
1992	5618987	669,221,342	3346106.71	6692213.42	13384426.84
1993	5500370	686,916,862	3434584.31	6869168.62	13738337.24
1994	5381738	704,820,799	3524104	7048207.99	14096415.98
1995	5018225	722,921,961	3614609.81	7229219.61	14458439.22
1996	4393501	741,220,519	3706102.6	7412205.19	14824410.38
1997	3847427	751,752,789	3758763.95	7517527.89	15035055.78
1998	4696666	778,592,236	3892961.18	7785922.36	15571844.72
1999	3644724	797,836,027	3989180.14	7978360.27	15956720.54
2000	3095451	817,566,004	4087830.02	8175660.04	16351320.08
2001	3109846	837,820,928	4189104.64	8378209.28	16756418.56
2002	2757410	858,622,597	4293112.99	8586225.97	17172451.94
2003	3552574	880,016,866	4400084.33	8800168.66	17600337.32
2004	2500468	902,048,601	4510243.01	9020486.01	18040972.02
2005	2346432	924,757,708	4623788.54	9247577.08	18495154.16
2006	1897545	948,156,166	4740780.83	9481561.66	18963123.32
2007	2072203	972,265,961	4861329.81	9722659.61	19445319.22
2008	1957433	997,144,670	4985723.35	9971446.7	19942893.4
2009	1944785	1,022,858,654	5114293.27	10228586.54	20457173.08
2010	1584039	1,049,446,344	5247231.72	10494463.44	20988926.88
2011	2231843	1,076,933,813	5384669.07	10769338.13	21538676.26
2012	1983950	1,105,285,268	5526426.34	11052852.68	22105705.36
2013	1532917	1,134,398,192	5671990.96	11343981.92	22687963.84
2014	1481445	1,164,129,782	5820648.91	11641297.82	23282595.64
2015	1491085	1,194,369,908	5971849.54	11943699.08	23887398.16

Source: Estimates were calculated based on FAO Statistics (2017)

labour force is engaged in the agriculture sector, yet there is still a deficit of food availability to the total population. The main reason for this as shown in the trend line comparison is because the population growth in Africa keeps on increasing at a steady rate whereas the total production of the cereal crops which the people depend on keeps on decreasing. The comparison of the percentage growth rate of the population in Africa and the percentage growth rate of the cereal crop production proves that the population theory of Thomas Malthus is still relevant in Africa. And that policymakers must do well to invest in population control measures whiles expanding measures and policies for food crop production.

FUTURE RESEARCH DIRECTIONS

Recent reports show that some individual countries in Africa are making commendable progress in food crop production. A country like Ghana in the Sub-Sahara African region has progressed in the agricultural sector, maintaining an annual average agrarian GDP growth rate of about 5 per in cent years. The increases in staple crop production in some specific countries like Ghana is bringing self-sufficiency and reducing child malnutrition, undernourishment, and poverty. The growth in productivity and progress in social standards brings a nation to the position of achieving the Sustainable Development Goals. It is, therefore, necessary to do further research into the growth of the maintenance of agricultural reforms in the individual countries and the regions that have ushered in a favourable environment for increasing private investment to determine the relevance of the population theory on food crop production. The specific countries to study are the countries within the Northern, the Southern and West African regions of Africa. There have been favourable reports of increases in food crop production. They have restructured the food market and reform the agriculture system to increase expenditure for a primary drive in progress.

ACKNOWLEDGMENT

This research received no specific grant from any funding agency in the public, commercial, or not-for-profit sectors.

REFERENCES

Abernethy, V. D. (2005). *Ester Boserup a new introduction by Virginia Deane Abernethy and a forward by Nicholas Kaldor* [Review of the book *The Conditions of Agricultural Growth: The Economics of Agrarian Change under Population Pressure*, by E. Boserup]. New York: Routledge. (Original work published 1814)

Amanda, S., Massey, A., Theobald, M., Styslinger, M., Kane, D., Kandy, D., … Davert, E. (2011). Africa's indigenous crops. State of the world innovations that nourish the planet. Worldwatch Institute.

Ankomah, E. K., & Adjei, R. K. (2019). *Population growth and food production in Ghana. A region in the development of society*. Brno: Mendel University in Brno.

Australian Dietary Guidelines. (2015). *Advice about the amount and kinds of foods that we need to eat for health and wellbeing*. Retrieved from Eatforhealth.gov.au.

Beck, K. (2018). How to Calculate an Average Percent Change. *Sciencing*. Retrieved from https://sciencing.com/calculate-average-increase-7479420.html

Bellis, M. (2017). *History of the agricultural revolution*. Retrieved from https://www.Thoughtco.Com/Agricultural-Revolution-1991931

Benneh, G. (1987). *Population growth and development in Ghana, Legon*. University of Ghana, Dept. of Geography.

Blitz, R. C. (1967). Environment, population, and technology in primitive societies [Review of the book *The conditions of agricultural growth: The Economics of Agrarian Change under Population Pressure,* by E. Boserup]. *Journal of Political Economics.* (Original work published 1965)

Boadu, E. A. (1994). Rapid Population Growth and Development in Ghana. Department of Geography & Resource Development, University Of Ghana Legon-Accra.

Boateng, E. O., Ewusi, K., Kanbur, R., & Mckay, A. (1990). *A poverty profile for Ghana, 1987–88.* Social Dimensions of Adjustment in Sub-Saharan Africa Working Paper No. 5. The World Bank.

Boserup, E. (1965). *Food and Agriculture Organization of the United Nations.* Retrieved from http://Agris.Fao.Org/Agris-Search/Search.Do?Recordid=Us201300593530

Chayanov, A. V. (1966). The theory of peasant economy. In D. Thorner, B. Kerblay, & R. E. F. Smith (Eds.), *The American economic association translation series* (pp. 1–301). Birmingham, UK: Richard D. Irwin, Inc.

Darkwah, S. A., & Ankomah, E. K. (2010). Developing the Least Developed Countries in the Larger spectrum of Globalized Economy. In *Proceedings of International Conference on Applied Business Research 2010* (CD-ROM). Ras Al Khaimah, UAE: Mendel University in Brno.

Djameh, C., Saalia, F. K., Sinayobye, E., Budu, A., Essilfie, G., Mensah-Brown, H., & Sefah-Dedeh, S. (2015). Optimization of the sorghum malting process for "Pito" production in Ghana. *Journal of the Institute of Brewing, 121*(1), 106–112. doi:10.1002/jib.191

Doss, C. (2001). How does gender affect the adoption of agricultural innovations? The case of improved maize technology in Ghana. *Agricultural Economics, 25*(1), 27–39. doi:10.1016/S0169-5150(00)00096-7

Engelman, R. (2016). Six billion in Africa. *Scientific American,* 31, 56-63.

Food and Agricultural Organization of the United Nations. (2013). FAO Country Profiles: Ghana. *Food and Agricultural Organization of the United Nations.* Retrieved from http://www.fao.org/countryprofiles/index/en/?iso3=GHA

Food and Agricultural Organization of the United Nations. (2017). *Crop.* Retrieved from http://www.fao.org/faostat/en/#data/QC

Food and Agriculture Organization of the United Nations. (1997). *Agriculture food and nutrition for Africa - A resource book for teachers of agriculture (FAO Information Division).* Rome: Author.

Freda, M. (2019). *Cereal Grains of Africa.* Retrieved from https://www.thespruceeats.com/cereal-grains-of-Africa-39517

GavinM. L. (2014). *Figuring out fibre.* Retrieved from https://kidshealth.org/en/parents/ fiber.html

Grega, L. & Ankomah, E. K. (2016). The environmental effect of land use in the tenure systems in Ghana. *Acta of Mendel University of agriculture and forestry Brno, 64*(6), 1211-8516. doi:10.11118/actaun201664061889

Grega, L., Ankomah, E. K., & Darkwah, S. A. (2015). Analysis of land tenure systems and its relationship with productivity in the agricultural sector in Ghana. *Acta of Mendel University of agriculture and forestry Brno, 63*(3), 893-902.

Hans-Peter, K. (2013). Population growth. In B. Lomborg (Ed.), *Global Problems, Smart Solutions: Costs and Benefits* (pp. 510–596). Cambridge: Cambridge University Press. doi:10.1017/CBO9781139600484.011

Horák, M., Darkwah, S. A., & Verter, N. (2014). Tourism as a Poverty Reduction Tool: The Case of Mukuni Village in the Southern Province of Zambia. *Acta Universitatis Agriculturae et Silviculturae Mendelianae Brunensis, 62*(6), 1287-1292.

Malthus, T. (1798). *An essay on the principle of population*. St. Paul's Church-Yard.

Mellor, J. W., & James D. (1969). Production Economics and The Modernization of Traditional Agricultures. *The Agrarian Journal of Agriculture and Resource Economics,* 25-34.

Mendelsohn, R. (2008). The impact of climate change on agriculture. *Journal of Natural Resources Policy Research*, 5-19.

Muyambo, F. (2019). Cereal Grains of Africa. *The Spruce Eats, 3*(23). Retrieved from https://www.thespruceeats.com/cereal-grains-of-africa-39517

National Population Council. (2006). *Ghana's Development Agenda and Population Growth: The Unmet Need for Family Planning*. Accra, Ghana: Government Printing Office.

Nin-Pratt, A., & Mcbride, L. (2014). Agricultural Intensification in Ghana: Evaluating the optimist's case for a green revolution. In *Boserup and Beyond: Mounting Land Pressures and Development Strategies in Africa*. (Original work published 1965)

Ochieng, J., Kirimi, L., & Mathenge, M. (2016). Effects of Climate Variability and Change on Agricultural Production. *NJAS Wageningen Journal of Life Sciences, 77*, 71–78. doi:10.1016/j.njas.2016.03.005

Ofosu-Amaah, V. (2006). *Chairperson National Population Council Accra*. Ghana's Development Agenda and Population HP EliteBook.

Sanginga, N. (2015). Root and tuber crops (cassava, yam, potato and sweet potato). *African Development Bank Group*. Retrieved from https://www.afdb.org/fileadmin/uploads/afdb/documents/events/dakagri2015/root_and_tuber_crops__cassava__yam__potato_and_sweet_ potato_.pdf

Smith, J., Cadavid, A., Rincón, R. V., & Vera, R. (1997). Land speculation and intensification at the frontier: A seeming paradox in the Colombian savanna. *Agricultural Systems, 54*(4), 501–520. doi:10.1016/S0308-521X(96)00088-1

Tachie-Obeng, E., Akponikpè, P., & Adiku, S. (2013). *Considering effective adaptation options to impacts of climate change for maize production in Ghana*. Environmental. doi:10.1016/j.envdev.2012.11.008

Taylor, R. N. J., & Naushad, E. M. (2008). Traditional African Cereal Grains - Overview. Pretoria: Academic Press.

Temesgen, G. B. (2017). Poverty, peasantry and agriculture in Ethiopia. *Annals of Agrarian Science*, 420-430.

Turner, M. G., Romme, W. H., Gardner, R. H., O'neill, R. V., & Kratz, T. K. (1993). A revised concept of landscape equilibrium: Disturbance and stability on scaled landscapes. *Landscape Ecology*, *8*(3), 213–227. doi:10.1007/BF00125352

Wharton, C. J. (1969). The challenge of population and food. In *Proceedings of Conference on Subsistence and Peasant Economics*. Chicago: Aldine Pub. Co.

World Economic Forum. (2016). *The world's ten youngest populations are all in Africa*. Genève, Switzerland: Author.

Yanjiu, R. (1982). *World population growth and the food supply*. Retrieved from https://www.ncbi.nlm.nih.gov/ PubMed/12265442

ADDITIONAL READING

De Graaff, J., & Kessler, A. & Nibbering. (2011). Agriculture and food security in selected countries in Sub-Saharan Africa: Diversity in trends and opportunities. *Sec.*, *3*, 195. doi:10.100712571-011-0125-4

Dorélien, A. (2008). *Population's Role in the Current Food Crisis: Focus on East Africa*. Washington, DC: Population Reference Bureau.

Hall, C., Dawson, T. P., Macdiarmid, J. I., Matthews, R. B., & Smith, P. (2017). The impact of population growth and climate change on food security in Africa: Looking ahead to 2050. *Journal International Journal of Agricultural Sustainability*, *15*(2), 124–135.

Msangi, J. P. (2014). *Food Security Among Small-Scale Agricultural Producers in Southern Africa*. New York, NY: Springer. doi:10.1007/978-3-319-09495-3

Muimba-Kankolongo, A. (2018). *Food Crop Production in Southern Africa: Challenges and Opportunities for Improvement*. London, UK: Academic Press.

Obasanjo, O., & d'Orville, H. (2012). The Challenges of Agricultural Production and Food Security. In *Africa*. New York, NY: Routledge.

Paulino, L. A. (1986). *Food in the Third World: Past Trends and Projection To 2000*. Washington, DC: International Food Policy Research Institute.

Pendleton, J. W., & Lawson, T. L. (1989). *Climate and Food Security. Climate Variability and Food Security in Developing Countries*. New Delhi, India: International Rice Research Institute.

Shaw, T. M. (Ed.). (1982). *Alternative futures for Africa*. New York, NY: Taylor & Francis.

Szabo, S. (2015). Urbanisation and Food Insecurity Risks: Assessing the Role of Human Development. *Journal of Oxford Development Studies*, *44*(1), 28–48. doi:10.1080/13600818.2015.1067292

Thornton, P. K. (2010). Livestock production: recent trends, future prospects. Journal of the Philosophical Transaction B. Retrieved from DOI: 10.1098/rstb.2010.0134

Zepeda, L. (Ed.). (2001). *Agricultural Investment and Productivity in Developing Countries*. Rome, Italy: Food and Agriculture Organization of the United Nations.

KEY TERMS AND DEFINITIONS

Araceae: Is a family of monocotyledonous flowering plants. The flowers borne are on a type of inflorescence called a spadix.

Cash Crops: Are the crops produced for their commercial value.

Consumption per Capita: An average consumption per person in a country or a region.

Dioscoreaceae: A family of monocotyledonous flowering plants.

Food Security: Is the access by all people at all times to food for a healthy life.

Formal Sector: The jobs registered and contributes to the gross national product (GNP) and gross domestic product (GDP) of a country.

Indigenous Crops: Crops that originated from Africa and vegetables that were introduced into countries in Africa and are now recognised as naturalised or traditional plants.

Informal Sector: The jobs which are not recognized and registered as standard income sources.

Manihot esculenta: A deciduous shrub food crop of the cassava family that can grow up three metres.

Minor Crops: The crops that are grown in a smaller amount.

Monocotyledonous: A class of angiosperm plants having a single cotyledon in the seed.

Musaceae: A banana family of plants.

Pastoral Land: The land use and managed as land resources which allow grazing in animal husbandry.

Staple Crops: The food items that can be stored easily and eaten throughout the year.

Chapter 15

Behavioral Economics:
New Dimension in Understanding the Real Economic Behavior

Miloš Krstić
Faculty of Science and Mathematics, University of Niš, Serbia

Nebojša Pavlović
Faculty of Hotel and Tourism, University Kragujevac, Serbia

ABSTRACT

The idea of the significance of the psychological dimension of human behavior is not new and has existed in the social sciences since ancient times. Accordingly, there is an endeavor to place economic analysis on the foundations of psychological research, which takes its form of expression in economic theory through the affirmation of behavioral economics. The aim of this chapter is to critically analyze various normative research programs in behavioral economics and to consider the importance of alternative concepts, models, and theories from the point of view of improving understanding of real economic and social behavior. The particular value of this chapter lies in affirming the importance of a program of behavioral economics known as new paternalism, which is based on challenging the concept of maximizing rationality and opens a new dimension of understanding the justification of state interference in the sphere of economy and society.

INTRODUCTION

Economic theory has traditionally analyzed the world inhabited by calculated, insensitive maximizers called *homo economicus*. In a sense, economic theory defines itself as explicitly "anti-behavioral" Virtually, all behaviors studied by cognitive and social psychologists are either ignored or excluded in a rational model. *Homo economicus* or non-behavioral actor is defended on many grounds (Askari, & Eshaghi Gordji, 2018). Some have argued that the rational model is "correct"; most others have simply argued that this model is easier to formalize and is practically relevant (Thaler, 1980). Behavioral eco-

DOI: 10.4018/978-1-7998-4601-7.ch015

nomic theory considers that the claims mentioned above are not true. Behavioral economics explores the constraints of human rationality. The findings of this area of economic theory are not related only to market decisions, but to, almost, all areas of human decision-making: politics, medicine, the tax system, and daily life. It is a combination of economics and psychology that explains in very understandable and attractive way why humans are not rational beings and why they often do own harm? Further work about behavioral economics has clearly demonstrated that psychological ideas could be formalized into an alternative model and used to form predictions that could be applied in real economic environment (Krstić & Đekić, 2018).

The aim of this chapter is to critically analyze different normative research programs in behavioral economics and to consider the importance of alternative concepts, models and theories from the point of view of improving understanding of real economic and social behavior. The chapter itself consists of five interconnected parts. In the introduction, the authors present basic information about behavioral decision theory (or behavioral economics) as an alternative to classical or orthodox economic theory. Then the authors give a detailed overview of some significant theorists whose work has left an indelible mark in this field. In the third, fourth and fifth parts of the paper, the authors describe the normative research programs that emerged within behavioral decision theory. The particular value of the chapter lies in affirming the importance of the normative program of behavioral economics known as "new paternalism", that, on the basis of refuting the concept of "maximizing rationality", "opens" a "new dimension" to understanding the justification of state intervention in the sphere of economy and society. In this regard, in this chapter, the authors will discuss on the need to apply new paternalism measures in order to moderate (reduce) the degree of the irrationality of citizens and economic entities in the Republic of Serbia and stimulate their action towards making better decisions on the use of restricted resources.

BACKGROUND

In the theoretical literature, the emergence of new analytical direction, by which the name behavioral economics has become "domesticated" and "consolidated", has the status of one of the most interesting and significant events in economic science in recent decades. The ideas and approaches developed within behavioral economics quickly gained "academic recognition". This allowed behavioral theory to partly penetrate into the economic mainstream, which, among other things, led to certain changes and transformations of some of its segments and parts. In the continuation of this chapter, the authors present behavioral ideas of Adam Smith, Robert Maltus, John Stuart Mill, and other "giants" of economic science who, through their theoretical considerations, determined the "path" of developing the behavioral economics as we know it today.

In *The Theory of Moral Sentiments*, Adam Smith, before writing *The Wealth of Nations*, dealt in detail, with what would today be considered psychological problems (feelings, pleasure, human nature). Although skilled in that kind of analysis, he did not see reason for explicit exposure of his view of human nature in *The Wealth of Nations*. Indeed, the impression is that Adam Smith considers people as they are. He had, mainly, acquired knowledge of human nature in Scotland and assumed that there was one "Scot" in each individual. It is quite natural that he believes that the constant and consistent driving of a man to make his position better is understandable in itself. This premise about human nature is a key feature Smith's "system of natural freedom" (Smith, 1998).

The ideas of Robert Maltus also played a significant role in the formation of theoretical understandings of behavioral economics. Robert Maltus is known for understanding that passion (or love) between the sexes is an indestructible human instinct. In the first edition of the *Essay on the Principles of Population*, he assumed that this passion would remain unchanged and saw no other factors that could limit population growth. But in the second edition (of the same book), Maltus modified his understanding, recognizing that sex drive can control. Morality, according to him, is a key psychological factor influencing population decline (Malthus, 1998).

According to William Senior, the next representative of the classical political economy who had a significant influence on the economic politics of his time, two of the four general assumptions on which political economy rests relate to the characteristics of human nature. When it comes to the first assumption, which states that every person strives to further increase personal wealth with the fewest possible casualties, Senior emphasized that this hypothesis has the same meaning as the law of gravity in physics – the "final fact" beyond whose bounds reasoning never reaches. The second premise that Senior pointed out is, in fact, a summary of Malthus's theory of population (Senior, 1965).

The tradition of thinking about the psychological assumptions on which economic science is postulated is continued in the work of John Stuart Mill, called *Identifying objects and methods of political economy*. More clearly than Senior, John Stuart Mill recognized that political economy is an abstract science in the sense that it does not consider human nature as a whole, but deals with humans only as a beings who wish to possess wealth and is able to evaluate the comparative effectiveness of the various means of achieving that goal (Wesley, 1910, Krstić, 2012).

Although the leading English economists were recognized hedonists, the hedonistic interpretation of the desire for wealth was not fully adopted in economics by the time of Stanley Jevons. William Stanley Jevons is an English economist and logician who based his discussion of value and distribution on the theory of pleasure and pain, which is derived from Bentham's hedonistic doctrine. In that way, he acknowledged hedonism as the official psychology of economic science. With "astonishing" consistency, he excludes the inappropriate instinct of "sex" from the principles of human nature and focuses his attention on the "static" area in which hedonistic principles can logically be applied (Jevons, 1965).

In the preface to the first edition of the book *Principles of Political Economy*, Alfred Marshall wrote that attempts to create an abstract science of the actions of *homo economics* were unsuccessful. He suggested eliminating the influence of habits (actions without motives or actions that are common and permanent) in economic models, and emphasized that the *homo economicus*, which is able to "translate" any initial allocation of resources into Pareto's optimum, should be replaced by analysis of an "outsider" who has neither the strength nor the will to act in accordance with the assumptions of classical economic theory (rational choice theory) (Krstić, 2012).

Sigmund Freud also had great importance in terms of popularizing psychological ideas in economic models. Freud is known as the first author to formulate the concept of "psychological man". According to Freud, a real man is an impulsive and emotional being, and his activities are determined by internal unconscious and uncontrollable "forces" that make him contradictory and unpredictable (Krstić, 2014).

Some researchers refer to the concept of "psychological man" as to the model of motivation proposed by Abraham Maslow. According to Maslow, every individual has motives that he strives to satisfy. These motives are organized hierarchically into 5 levels: 1) biological motives (thirst, hunger, sexual motive, etc.); 2) safety motives (avoidance of pain, illness, and loss of job); 3) love and belonging needs (friendship, love, relationships, sympathy); 4) esteem needs (a motive for social recognitions that bring to life rewards and praise for professional work); 5) self-actualization needs (Maslow, 1970).

In the following, the authors examine normative research programs emerging in behavioral economics. To narrow their considerations, the authors focus on the Kahneman/Tversky program (heuristics-and-biases research program), Gerd Gigerenzer et al's *FFH* program and "new paternalism". In addition to the emphasis on the importance of behavioral decision theory for understanding economic behavior, the authors also point to its importance for understanding social behavior in general.

THE HEURISTICS-AND-BIASES PROGRAM

In a great series of experiments on what psychologists call "judgments" and what economists might call "expectations" or "beliefs", Amos Tversky and Daniel Kahneman have shown that people make estimates which are mostly biased (or wrong) (Tversky & Kahneman, 1974). These errors were predictable based on the theory of human cognition. The hypothesis of Kahneman and Tversky was that people often make judgments, applying "rule of thumb" or heuristics (Kahneman, 2015). A good example is "availability heuristic". The availability heuristic is the idea that people evaluate the frequency of events on the basis of the "ease" with which they can recall instances of that event (Camerer et al., 2004; Kahneman, 2003). The application of this heuristic is rational given that the frequency and "ease" of remembering an event are usually in a positive relationship. However, the use of this heuristic leads to errors in those cases in which the likelihood of event realization and the "ease" of remembering the event deviate greatly. For example, when respondents were asked to estimate the relationship between the number of homicides and the number of suicides committed by guns, most thought that gun homicide was more frequent, while in fact almost twice as many suicides. These expectations are nowhere near as rational. They represent behavioral biases (Thaler, 1989).

Another influential line in Kahneman's and Tversky's research concerns decision making. In 1979, Kahneman and Tversky published a paper on the. Prospect theory, which was proposed as a descriptive (or what Milton Friedman would call "positive") model of decision making under uncertainty (Kahneman & Tversky, 1979). Their theory is based on empirical observation and describes how individuals experience their gains and losses. Kahneman and Tversky found that most people have aversion to loss (Mathis & Steffen, 2015). Thus, the increase in assets from $ 1000 to $ 2000 is quantitatively equal to the increase from 10,000 to 11,000, but the first difference is perceived by the individual as greater than the second. In addition, the conclusion that gains are slower to grow and losses sharply decrease means that the reaction to realized gains is far weaker than the negative reaction to the loss of the same amount (Pavličić, 2010). Prospect theory seemed to be a descriptive alternative to the theory of the expected utility of John Von Neumann and Oscar Morgenstern which was considered by most economists to be normative decision theory (Von Neumann & Morgenstern, 1947). Kahneman's and Tversky's research has documented numerous choices that violate any reasonable definition of rational (Krstić, 2014). The following problems, posed to the respondents, are a good illustration (Table 1).

First, examine both decisions (decision I and decision II), and then show the options that you prefer. It is not explicitly clear is there something contradictory about these choices, until problem no. 2 is considered (Table 2).

Check reveals that, although problem no. 2 differently formulated, choices in problem no. 2 have been formally (quantitative) identical to those (with the choices) in the problem no.1. Difficulties related to the choices in task no. 2, is that the option E, that no one chooses (in problem no. 2), represents combination of options A and D, that chosen by the majority of respondents in the problem no. 1, while

Table 1. The problem no. 1.

Imagine that you are facing the following options.
Decision (I). Choose between:
Option A. Safe win of $ 240 [84%] and
Option B. 25% chance to get $ 1,000 and 75% chance you do not get anything or lose nothing [16%]
Decision (II). Choose between:
Option C. Reliable loss of $ 750 [13%] and
Option D. 75% chance of losing $ 1,000 and 25% chance of not losing anything [87%]
Note: Numbers in square brackets show the percentage of respondents who chose.

Source: (Thaler, 2016, p.1583).

Table 2. The problem no. 2.

Choose between
Option E. 25% chance to get $ 240 and 75% chance to lose $ 760 [0%] and
Option F. 25% chance to get $ 250 and 75% chance to lose $ 750 [100%]

Source: (Thaler, 2016, p. 1583)

Table 3. Expected value of options

The problem no. 1
Decision (i)
Option A *EV* (*A*) = 240*1= 240
Option B *EV* (*B*) = (1000*0.25)+(+0-0*0.75)= 250
Decision (ii)
Option C *EV* (*C*) = -750*1 = -750
Option D *EV* (*D*) = (-1000*0.75)+(-0*0.25) = -750
The problem no. 2
Option *E EV*(*E*) = (240*0.25) – (760*0.75) = 60 – 570 = - 510
Option *EV* (*A+D*) = *EV*(*A*) + *EV* (*D*) = 240 – 750 = - 510 = *EV* (*E*)
EV (B+C) = *EV* (*B*)+ *EV* (*C*) = 250 – 750 = - 500 = *EV* (*F*)

Source: The authors' calculation

option F, that everyone chooses in problem no. 2, represents combination of options B and C that were very unpopular in task no. 1 (Table 3).

Problems no. 1 and no. 2 shows two results that are surprising to supporters of classical, orthodox economic theory. First, respondents' answers depend on how the problem is "framed". Second, the "smart" framed problem may encourage respondents to choose a pair of options (suboptimal option *E*) dominated by the other pair. This behavior is not in line with the idea (supporters of classic or orthodox economic theory) that people choose *as if* they are rational.

The cognitive anomalies associated with heuristics, irrational behavior and biases of economic actors have become a serious problem for economic theories. Even economists who believe that such problems can be solved within traditional, classical or orthodox economic theory (such as rational choice theory), generally agree that cognitive anomalies should be "solved". But there is also a differently reaction (to anomalies). Perhaps a change in traditional theory (rational choice theory) is not needed. There may be an honorable way out. The rational choice theory "lives a double life":1) as a descriptive/scientific theory of (individual) decision making and 2) as a normative theory of rationality (Heukelom, 2011). Although anomalies in the decision process are a serious challenge to rational choice theory as a descriptive theory of (individual) decision making, they do not necessarily represent a "threat" to normative interpretation. Namely, the fact that (real) people violate the RCT-based norms of rationality does not diminish, in any way, the credibility of this theory. Behavior that is contrary to rational norms based on RCT shows that people are incapable of behaving rationally, not that rational choice theory or classical economic theory is wrong (Krstić & Krstić, 2015).

The foregoing suggests that we can identify the elements of the dual relationship of behavioral economics representatives to rational choice theory. When they keep in mind its descriptive character, they vigorously reject it. However, opposing the "illusory" model of complete rationality does not mean that the existence of rational aspirations of economic actors should be negated, i.e. Individuals' intentions to be rational were not called into question. Instead, is it desirable to reconstruct the actions of individuals in particular situations, owing to what can be assumed in specific circumstances, in the case of purely rational activities? Because of all this, behavioral economics representatives have retained the basic "architecture" of rational choice when they hypothetically treat rational choice, attributing it to the trait of a normative ideal (Lee, 2011; Hands, 2015; Neto et al., 2019; Krol & Sokolov, 2018; Gaweł, 2012).

The following is a summary of basic information about Gerd Gigerenzer's et al.'s "fast and frugal heuristics" program. This will allow a better understanding of the rational behavior of real economic actors and the entire economic system.

RESEARCH PROGRAM OF "FAST AND FRUGAL HEURISTICS"

The *heuristics-and-biases program* is not the only program in behavioral economics that deals with the analysis of heuristics, bias, uncertainty decision making, etc. Another approach has been developed over the last few decades. It is a program of "fast and economical heuristics" by Gerd Gigerenzer and his associates (hereinafter referred to as the *FFH* program) (Gigerenzer, 2008; Gigerenzer et al., 2011). The basic idea of this program is that the rationality of decisions depends on the environment in which people make decisions. In this sense, heuristics are not a reflection of human irrationality. More specifically, human behavior is rational if studied in the environment in which it developed (Polšek & Bolukić, 2013).

According to Giderenzer and his associates, the *FFH* program is essentially empirical and descriptive research, i.e. consideration of how and in what environments heuristics work well (otherwise Gierenzer heuristics are called "adaptive tools")? If a particular heuristics is found to be good in an environment, that is what decision-makers should do instead of maximizing the utility suggested by rational choice theory (classical or orthodox economic theory) (Hands, 2015). The *FFH* program is based on a particular understanding of rationality which is also known as "bounded rationality". Although Herbet Simon introduced some ideas of bounded rationality in his book *Administrative Behavior*, published in 1945, there is an explicit application of this term in Simon's (scientific) work entitled *Models of Man* published in 1957 (Klaes & Sent, 2005).

This psychologist believed that the idea of rationality in the rational choice theory must be abandoned, because people lack complete and reliable (quality) information and the perfect intellectual "gift" that requires rational choice theory. He, therefore, proposes to replace the idea of rationality in terms of rational choice theory with the concept of "bounded rationality". Because they conscious their imperfections and face different objective constraints, economic actors are guided by the satisficing principle instead of the principle of maximizing personal utility (Simon, 1961). Real people tend to behave rationally, but in fact they can only do so to a certain extent (Simon, 1961; Krstić & Krstić, 2016). In other words, there are practical limits to rationality. The potential rational actor makes a simplified model of the real situation. He is rational only within this model. In order to predict his behavior, one should consider not only the rationality of the choice, but also the rationality of the procedures used in choosing the solution ("procedural rationality") (Krol & Sokolov, 2019). For economic theory, this means that seeking the maximum of the utility function will be replaced by the procedure of finding a satisfactory solution (Simon, 1967; Pavlović, 2016).

Representatives of the *FFH* program rejected the idea of man as rational, autonomous *homo economicus*. *FFH* is based on *homo heuristicus* that has a biased mind and ignores some of the information available. However, *homo heuristicus* manages risk more effectively than *homo economicus*, because it relies on more resources and strategies for "general purposes". Gigerenzer and others who support the *FFH* program often insist that it is a normative program that provides advice on what an individual should do (or which heuristics should apply) in certain circumstances. Gigerenzer and associates suggest that the advice of this program is often better than the advice offered by rational choice theory (classical and orthodox economic theory). We say "often" because representatives of the *FFH* program do not think that rational choice theory cannot provide adequate guidance regarding rational decision making. Representatives of the *FFH* program say that rational choice theory does not always do this, and that what this theory proposes can be classified as a broader concept of ecological rationality. Ecological rationality "begins" with instrumental rationality. „Our psychological program has chosen one specific sense of the notion of rationality ... a kind of rationality of means and ends, but continues to supplement the instrumental notion of rationality with an ecological "(Gigerenzer & Sturm, 2012, p. 245).

In the following, the authors examine the prominent understandings of a normative program of behavioral economics known as the "new paternalism". Also, guided by the experience where citizens of the Republic of Serbia have shown a particular preference for cognitive errors and psychological anomalies, special attention in this part of the chapter will be given to the behavioral economist's recommendations, which should be taken into account when the Government of the Republic of Serbia designing program of operation.

NEW PATERNALISM

Behavioral economics questions the interpretation of economic behavior according to the standard rational choice model. Its representatives insist that real people are *homo sapiens* (Mankiw, 2005). Although they largely resemble rational, calculated people who are assumption of economic theory, they are far more complex beings. They can be forgetful, sudden, emotional, confused and myopic (Diamond & Hannu, 2007). Empirical reality abounds in examples of irrational behavior. This is primarily related to psychological limitations and anomalies. In this regard, behavioral imperfections related to discounting inconsistencies, psychological and emotional state variability, context dependency, lack of self-control, over-optimism, *status quo* orientation, etc. are most mentioned (Neto et al., 2019).

Emphasizing the fact that people can make decisions that are not in line with their best interests, representatives of the behavioral economics come up with the idea that paternalistic-oriented state can help individuals make better decisions. In this way, a new normative program of behavioral economics, known as "new paternalism", was affirmed. In principle, paternalism means the restriction on freedom of individual action, that is exclusively justified by reasons relating to the realization of personal well-being, well-being, happiness, needs, interests, or values. Although it does not have the mark of state engagement, it is common for paternalism to mean, above all, activity in the field of law-making and measures that relax the decision-making process. Depending on how deeply it goes into the individual decision-making process, we can distinguish between "hard" and "soft" paternalism (Alm & Bourdeaux, 2014; Madhadam, & Gutmann, 2013). While "soft" paternalism and its inherent minimum restriction on freedom of choice are preferred, the justification for introducing some direct bans, direct organizations, as well as high taxes and other state levies should not be underestimated. When measures of "soft" paternalism do not produce the desired results, the state justifiably seeks interventions with "hard" restrictions on free choice.

Economic theory, in principle, has a negative view of the politics of paternalism and the restriction of freedom of individuals' choice. The traditionally stated argument about when to make an exception and limit the freedom of choice of individuals refers to a situation where the activity of one economic actor "threatens" the interests of others. However, the idea behind behavioral economics is to add a behavioral reason to the above reason for justified state interventionism. Namely, if people are not "immune" to the emergence of systemic decision-making errors, the state's task, from the point of view of behavioral economics, is to help them, directing their behavior towards the rational use of scarce resources.

Among the various forms of state intervention in the field of individual decision-making that are recommended by behavioral economists, the "strongest" are those that impose explicit prohibitions and restrictions on the choice of the individual ("severe" paternalism). Measures of hard paternalism, in the view of representatives of behavioral economics, are justified when the irrationality of economic actors is so pronounced that it is almost impossible to correct "soft" paternalistic measures (providing necessary information, "architecture of choice manipulating", etc.). This is why representatives of the behavioral economics propose the adoption of appropriate legislation in all areas where there is a high risk of irrational action by economic actors (Conly, 2014; Sunstein, 2012; Thaler & Sunstein, 2003).

The relatively simple way recommended to correct mistakes, which people make in emotionally and psychologically "hot" states, is to legally determine the so-called a *cooling-off* period. Such periods can be predicted, both before and after important decisions are made (Camerer et al., 2003). When it comes to buying a car, for example, there are the following options. The first is that when a buyer signs a car purchase agreement, he can wait, for example, three days, before picking up the car. During this time, he may change his mind. Alternatively, the car can be picked up immediately, with the option of returning it within three days. One of the instruments actively supported by "new paternalists" and behavioral economists relates to the mandatory publication of certain information. The mandatory disclosure policy for certain information is particularly effective when it comes to consumer lending. Since irrational behavior is widespread in the financial sphere and their "price" is quite high, behavioral recommendations are that consumers be adequately informed about all banking products (Wright & Ginsburg, 2012).

In the next part, the authors will try to explain the measures of a "new paternalism" that could lead to the reduction of numerous cognitive errors and psychological anomalies and to reduce the degree of irrationality of economic actors in the Republic of Serbia. Due to the accumulating social and economic problems, slow acceptance of market norms of behavior, irrational behavior of a large number of economic actors, skepticism towards entrepreneurship, etc., it seems that the Republic of Serbia and its political authorities are facing "enormous" tasks and "determined struggle" to create preconditions necessary for the development of a "healthy" market economy.

Examining the Possibility of Implementing Measures and Recommendations of New Paternalism in the Republic of Serbia

The citizens of Serbia are still characterized by a great aversion to individualistic arrangements, entrepreneurship and development impulses based on the realization of individualistic motives and actions (Pavlović, 2018). Instead, it is possible to recognize the collectivist mentality of our community (Katić, 2018; Katić, 2019). Citizens of Serbia expect the assistance of every kind from the state (jobs, solving the problem of unpaid wages and cash benefits to workers who lose their jobs in the transition process, to the widespread belief that the state should protect domestic producers from "relentless" foreign competition). In view of all the challenges facing the state of Serbia, it seems quite justified that the Government of the Republic of Serbia, in the implementation of its program of activities, largely respects some of the recommendations of the representatives of the behavioral economy and the "new paternalism". Significant experience with the problems that accompany the process of economic and social behavior in conditions of transition from a planned to a market economy leads us to the conclusion that the authors can draw the following areas and domains of economic and social life that specifically require a "protective arm" of the state:

1) The choice between legal and illegal activities is a subject of interest in various social sciences (Uggen & Thompson, 1999). A common sociological view is that lawbreakers (law abusers) are completely irrational. In contrast, according to classical economic interpretation (or a rational choice-based approach), violators act rationally because they decide whether to break the law or not, comparing the expected net utility they can gain from committing a crime and the expected net utility they might accomplish if they do not break the law (Hafner & Krstić, 2011). Representatives of behavioral economics indicate that human beings (due to their egoistic nature) can "put" economic interest above the behaviors followed by the law, without considering all the potential costs. Research by eminent sociologist Oleinik has shown that by moving into the illegal sphere of business, economic agents save on one type of cost, but on the other hand, pay a high "cost of illegality" (Oleinik, 2002). The impression is that, unlike citizens of the developed market economy, the Serbian population is still not aware of the high costs of committing crimes (figure 1). Numerous tax evasion scandals (figure 2), high levels of "undeclared work", high levels of corruption (figure 3), etc., confirm this. Overall government engagement in these areas should contribute to raising awareness of acceptable ways of gaining economic benefits, as well as enhancing the belief that, in the long run, it is most profitable to comply with the law.

2) Choice of work area - public or private sector. According to research by the Statistical Office of the Republic (Statistical Office of the Republic of Serbia, 2019; Jakopin & Čokorilo, 2019; Gavrilović, 2019), after graduating from schools and colleges, many citizens first try to find work in the public sector (Pavlović et al., 2012). Almost half of the citizens with formal employment work in the public sector. Giving preference to the public sector in employment, from the perspective of behavioral economics, results from a cognitive failure (or behavioral anomaly) that is labeled "context dependent". Namely, under the influence of the traditional cultural pattern (the general context in which Serbian citizens live), which does not approve of complete dominance of private property over state property and individualism over collectivism, Serbian citizens are subject to thinking in certain frames. Therefore, it should come as no surprise that after graduating from schools and colleges, Serbian citizens first seek employment in the public sector. If they fail to do the following, they will face a relatively longer period of job searching or starting their own business. When it comes to the second variant, the choice is likely to fall to the service sector (due to the lack of new ideas and information from Serbian citizens).

Figure 1. The Republic of Serbia – The Size of the Serbian shadow economy, from 2001 to 2010
Note: Shadow economy is defined as the set of all market-based legal productive activities that are intentionally hidden from government by one or more reasons: to avoid paying income, value added or other taxes, avoid paying social security contributions, avoid certain legal labor market standards (such as minimum wages, maximum working hours, safety standards, etc.), and avoiding certain administrative procedures (such as completing statistical questionnaires or administrative forms).*
*Note**: The size of the Serbian shadow economy has been reduced from 33.2% to 30.1% of GDP in the selected period, but still every third firm operates in the shadow zone. We also note that the analysis conducted by NALED showed that entrepreneurs and small firms are more prone to the shadow economy in relation to firms with large numbers of employees. From the standpoint of behavioral economics, this result shows extreme impatience of many business owners and tom managers in Serbia. This can lead to decisions that are supposed to immediately bring present benefits, and that the high costs, incurred as a result of the process of irrational decision-making (the choice of the illegal sphere of business) will gradually accrue over time. In addition, the state of extreme impatience may result in underestimation of the long-term benefits arising from the choice of the legal sphere of business. The tendency of leaders and prominent individuals in an organizations to prefer the present in relation to the future benefits is known as hyperbolic discounting in behavioral economics.*
Source: The authors 'calculation in Matlab based on following researches: 1) (Schneider,2011); 2) (National Agency for Local Development (NALED), 2017); 3)(Petrović et al., 2017); 4) (Kyvelou & Chiotinis, 2013).

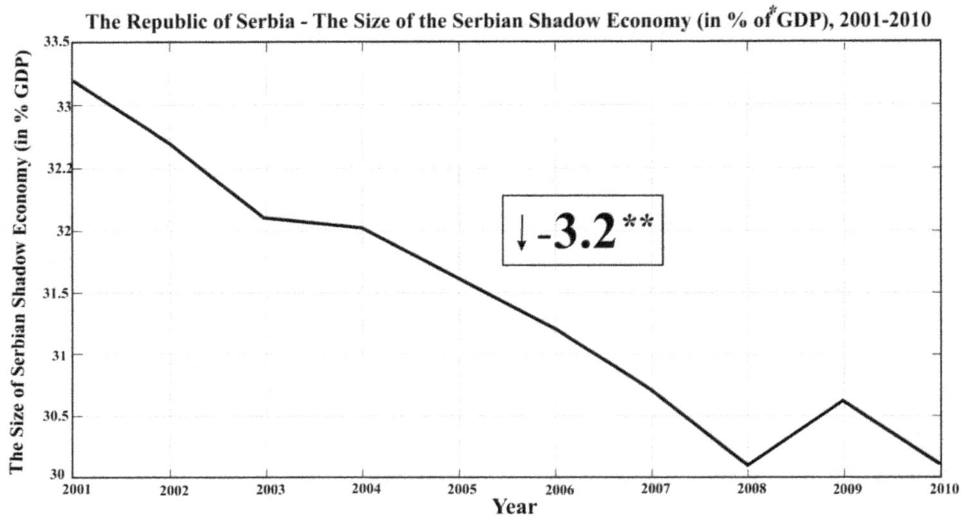

However, the state can be involved in the decision-making process on which fields it is profitable for Serbs to invest their human capital (knowledge and skills). Giving the necessary information and advice ("soft" paternalism), as well as an adequate combination of legal, fiscal and other administrative measures ("hard" paternalism), the state can significantly influence Serbian citizens to test their knowledge and skills in the productive sector of the economy.

3) Crediting of the population is a typical area of economic life that belongs to priority areas of interest to the representatives of behavioral economics and to "new paternalism". The primary reason for this is that the behavior of a significant proportion of people deviates from the rationality hypothesis (or assumption of maximizing behavior) in the sphere of taking out credit and using credit cards. Thus, citizens of the Republic of Serbia often take out loans without adequate information on: 1) the "cost" of consumer loans; 2) processing and administration costs; 3) real (or total) interest rate on credit cards. Behaviorist's recommendations in this sphere of life need not be confined to meeting justifiable requirements for disclosure of all relevant information related to the credit process. More importantly, the government supports the conclusion of credit agreements, in which the mandatory elements of standard banking products will take precedence over the default credit clauses. When it comes to credit cards, it

Figure 2. The Republic of Serbia – The Rate of Evasion of Tax on labor Income, from 2007 to 2012
Note: The labor income tax evasion rate is defined as the share of undeclared labor income in real, total labor income.*
*Note**: According to the Living Standards Survey, the share of undeclared work income in real, total labor income is close to 21% . Later studies show that labor income tax evasion has increased to over 27% in 2010-2012. The data also show that undeclared work and tax evasion is significantly (five times) higher in the case of the self-employed (freelancers, entrepreneurs who have their own businesses, start-ups or agencies, etc.) than employed individuals (persons working for a particular employer). These results show that the self-employed are characterized by excessive optimism (high self-esteem) that causes the self-employed to have low risk aversion. Emphasized risk appetite can cause irreparable harm to an individual.*
Source: The authors' calculation in Matlab based on following researches: 1)(Ranđelović, 2015); 2) (Krstić et al., 2017); 3) (World Bank, 2007).

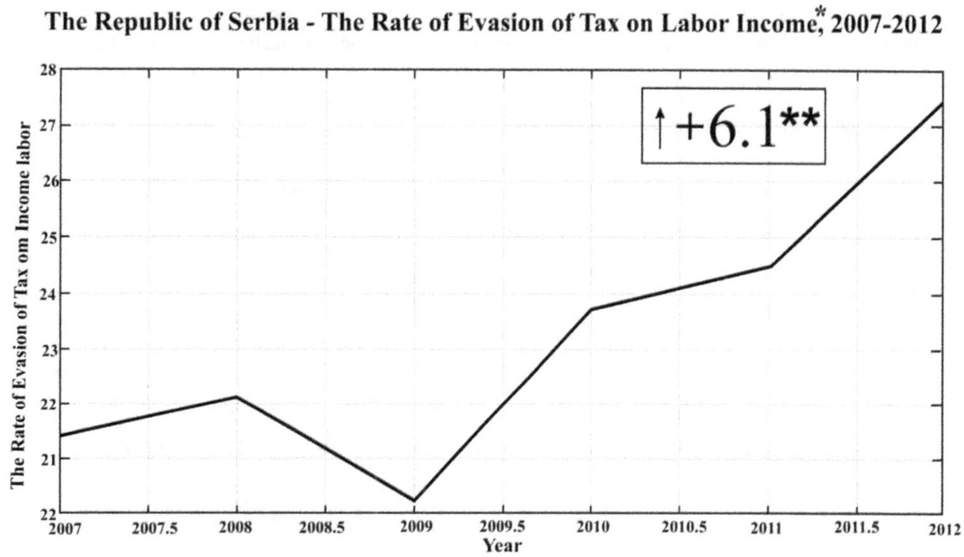

would be worth considering the rationality of separating their savings and transaction function, where, for example, one type of credit card would only serve to raise money while the other would buy goods and services. Finally, given the many negative experiences associated with the misuse of credit cards by Serbian citizens, and the warnings of some behaviorists about these limited rational individuals, they are definitely unable to use such complex financial instruments without adversely affecting their own well-being, ideas should probably be considered regarding the introduction of more restrictive credit card rules (Wright & Ginsburg, 2012).

From all the following, it is advisable that the Government of the Republic of Serbia take into account numerous paternalistic recommendations. The practical implementation of paternalistic recommendations involves "adopting" measures different in "character" and intensity of action. In some cases, paternalistic recommendations regarding persuasion, advice, education, and the like should be preferred. However, the justification for introducing some direct prohibitions and restrictions, as well as high taxes and other taxes, should not be underestimated. When measures of "soft" paternalism do not produce the desired results, the state may apply strict restrictions on free choice.

Figure 3. The Republic of Serbia – Scores and Ranks of Corruption Perception Index, from 2014 to 2018
Note: The objectives of the Global (180 countries/territories) Aggregate Index (up to 13 different data sources), which measure perceptions (experts/businesspeople) of corruption ("misuse of public powers of private utterance") in the public sector are: 1) improving comparative understanding of the level of corruption, 2) stimulating scientific research into the causes and consequences of corruption at the international and domestic levels, 3) contributing to raising public awareness of corruption, 4) creating a climate for change and the like.*
*Note**: According to Transparency Serbia website, Serbia ranked 89th in terms of the Corruption Perceptions Index in 2018. Compared to 2014, the value of the Corruption Perceptions Index decreased by 2, which led to a negative shift of Serbia by 9 positions. Figure 6 shows the results and ranks of the Corruption Perceptions Index for Serbia from 2014 to 2018. The thick line in Figure 6 shows the shift in Corruption Perceptions Index results, while the dashed line shows the movements of the ranks of this Index between 2014 and 2018. Representatives of the behavioral economics link high levels of corruption to behavioral research findings that indicate that people, in the desire to find the best solution in the short term, suppress unfavorable moral judgments about a particular action, rationalize warnings (ignore environmental signals), create the illusion of invulnerability that leads to over optimism and emphasized risk appetite, choose alternatives without serious evaluation, set unrealistically high goals, etc.*
Source: The authors' calculation in Matlab based on: 1) (Transparency Serbia, 2019); 2) (Pavličić, 2010)

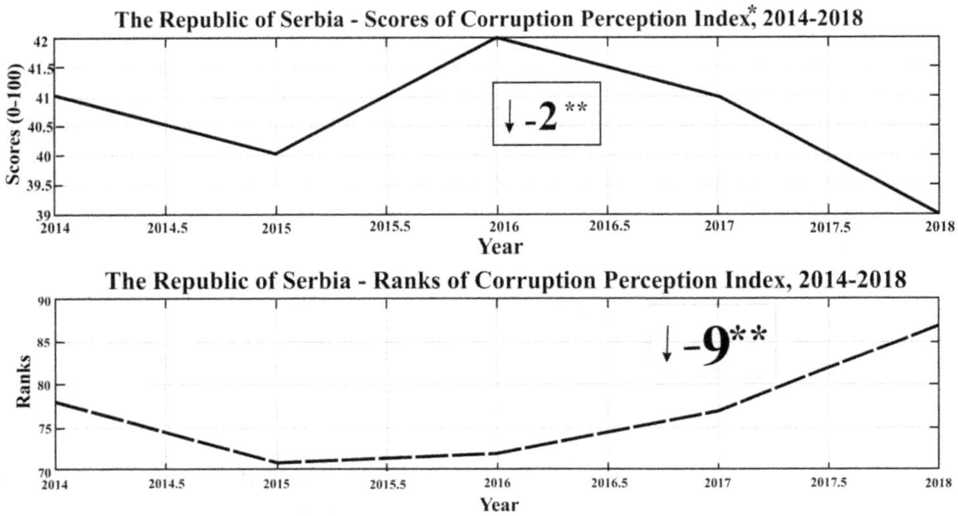

CONCLUSION

In recent years there has been an increasing interest in the combination of psychology and economics known as behavioral economics. This discipline enhances the explanatory power of economic science, combining it with more realistic psychological settings and using social, emotional and cognitive factors in an attempt to explain the economic decisions of individuals and institutions. At the heart of this sub-discipline within economic science is the idea that the increased realism of the psychological underpinnings of economic analysis will improve the standard economic model in terms of generating theoretical knowledge, making good predictions about different phenomena, and creating better economic policies. This idea does not imply a rejection of the standard economic model. A rational model is useful because it provides a theoretical framework that can be practically applied to any form of economic or even non-economic behavior and allows rebuttable predictions.

Recognizing the fact that individuals may exhibit numerous cognitive and behavioral "failures" when making decisions about the use of scarce resources and thus making decisions that are not in their best interests, representatives of behavioral economics propose a "strong turn" against the traditional antipaternalistic view of classical or orthodox economic theories. In their deep conviction, only a paternalist-oriented state can help individuals make better decisions, which is accompanied by the affirmation of a new normative programmatic behavioral economy known as "new paternalism".

When it comes to the Republic of Serbia, numerous economic and social problems have led to the creation of excessive, even unreasonable expectations regarding the implementation of various state activities and measures. In light of the negative experiences of the state's involvement so far, the argument of supporters of the behavioral economy and of "new paternalism" is quite encouraging. It seems justifiable for the government when designing economic measures and programs, to take into account some recommendations of the representatives of the behavioral economy and the "new paternalism" with the aim of reducing the degree of irrationality and direct actions of economic actors towards better decision-making on the use of scarce resources. Such measures may be especially useful in reducing the illegal economic activities, increase incentives for private entrepreneurship or soft regulation of banking services costs.

ACKNOWLEDGMENT

Funding for the publicationof this chapter provided by the Ministry of Education, Science and Technological Development of the Republic of Serbia (the number of contractof the realization and financing of scientific research work:451-03-68/2020-14/200124).

REFERENCES

Alm, J., & Bourdeaux, C. J. (2014). *Applying behavioral economics to the public sector*. New Orleans, LA: Tulane University.

Askari, G., & Eshaghi Gordji, M. (2018). Hyper-rational choice and economic behaviour. *Advances in Mathematical Finance and Applications*, *3*(3), 69–76.

Camerer, C., Issachoroff, S., Loewenstein, G., O'Donoghue, T., & Rabin, M. (2003). Regulation for conservatives: Behavioral economics and the case for asymmetric paternalism. *University of Pennsylvania Law Review*, *151*(1), 1211–1254. doi:10.2307/3312889

Camerer, C., Loewenstein, G., & Rabin, M. (2004). *Advances in behavioral economics*. Princeton, NJ: Princeton University Press. doi:10.1515/9781400829118

Conly, S. (2014). Against autonomy: Justifying coercive paternalism. *Journal of Medical Ethics*, *40*(5), 349–349. doi:10.1136/medethics-2013-101444 PMID:24335658

Diamond, P., & Vartiainen, H. (2007). *Introduction to behavioral economics and its applications*. Princeton, NJ: Princeton University Press. doi:10.1515/9781400829149

Gavrilović, D. (2019). Regions in Serbia. Belgrade: Statistical office of the Republic of Serbia. (in Serbian)

Gaweł, A. (2012). Entrepreneurship and sustainability: do they have anything in common? Poznan University of Economics Review, 12(1), 5-16.

Gigerenzer, G. (2008). Why heuristics work. *Perspectives on Psychological Science, 3*(1), 20–29. doi:10.1111/j.1745-6916.2008.00058.x PMID:26158666

Gigerenzer, G., Hertwig, R., & Thorsten, P. (2011). *Heuristics: the foundations of adaptive behavior*. New York: Oxford University Press. doi:10.1093/acprof:oso/9780199744282.001.0001

Gigerenzer, G., & Sturm, T. (2012). How (far) can rationality be naturalized? *Synthese, 187*(1), 243–268. doi:10.100711229-011-0030-6

Hafner, P., & Krstić, M. (2011). Application of rational choice theory in the analysis of criminal behavior. [in Serbian]. *Ekonomika (Nis), 57*(1), 37–47.

Hands, D. W. (2014). Normative ecological rationality: Normative rationality in the fast-and-frugal-heuristics research program. *Journal of Economic Methodology, 21*(4), 396–410. doi:10.1080/1350178X.2014.965907

Hands, D. W. (2015). *Normative rational choice theory: past, present, and future*. Retrieved from https://www.researchgate.net/publication/228319027_Normative_Rational_Choice_Theory_Past_Present_and_Future

Heukelom, F. (2011). Behavioral economics. In J. B. Davis & D. W. Hands (Eds.), *The elgar companion to recent economic methodology* (pp. 19–38). Cheltenham: Edward Elgar Publishing. doi:10.4337/9780857938077.00007

Jakopin, E., & Čokorilo, N. (2019). Trends - analysis of work of public and state-owned firms in the Republic of Serbia 2015-2017. Belgrade: Statistical office of the Republic of Serbia. (in Serbian)

Jevons, W. S. (1965). The theory of political economy. New York: Kelley. (Original publication 1871)

Kahneman, D. (2003). Maps of bounded rationality: Psychology for behavioral economics. *The American Economic Review, 93*(5), 1449–1475. doi:10.1257/000282803322655392

Kahneman, D. (2015). *Thinking, fast and slow*. Smederevo: Heliks. (in Serbian)

Kahneman, D., & Tversky, A. (1979). Prospect theory: An analysis of decision under risk. *Econometrica, 47*(2), 363–391. doi:10.2307/1914185

Katić, N. (2018). *Is Orthodoxy Guilty to All?* Retrieved from http:// nkatic.wordpress.com (in Serbian)

Katić, N. (2019). *When Abnormal Becomes Normal*. Retrieved from http:// nkatic.wordpress.com (in Serbian)

Klaes, M., & Sent, E. M. (2005). A conceptual history of the emergence of bounded rationality. *History of Political Economy, 37*(1), 27–59. doi:10.1215/00182702-37-1-27

Krol, O., & Sokolov, V. (2018). Rational choice of machining tools using prediction procedures. *EUREKA: Physics and Engineering*, (4), 14-20.

Krol, O. S., & Sokolov, V. I. (2019). Rational choice of machine tools for designers. Sofia: Academy publishing house of Bulgarian Academy of Sciences. doi:10.7546/RCMTD.2019

Krstić, B., & Krstić, M. (2015). Normative theory of rational choice: Past, present, and future. [in Serbian]. *Theoria, 58*(2), 49–64. doi:10.2298/THEO1502049K

Krstić, B., & Krstić, M. (2016). Rational choice theories and social research. [in Serbian]. *Sociologija, 58*(4), 598–611. doi:10.2298/SOC1604598K

Krstić, G., Schneider, F., Arandarenko, M., Arsić, M., Radulović, B., Ranđelović, S., & Janković, I. (2013). The shadow economy in serbia–new findings and recommendations for reform. Belgrade: Foundation for the advancement of economics.

Krstić, M. (2012). The role of rules in the evolution of the market system: Hayek's concept of evolutionary epistemology. *Economic Annals, 57*(194), 123–140. doi:10.2298/EKA1294123K

Krstić, M. (2014). Rational choice theory and addiction behaviour. *Market-Tržište, 26*(2), 163–177.

Krstić, M., & Đekić, I. (2018). Behavioral economics and standard economic theory. *Kultura polisa,* (37), 397-410. (in Serbian)

Kyvelou, S., & Chiotinis, N. (2013). La politique regionale et la democratisation de l'Europe: La lutte a la corde Europeenne. *Géographies. Géopolitiques et Géostratégies Régionales, 1*(1), 89–96.

Lee, K. S. (2011). Three ways of linking laboratory endeavours to the realm of policies. *European Journal of the History of Economic Thought, 18*(5), 755–776. doi:10.1080/09672567.2011.616593

Madhadam, B. F., & Gutmann, T. (2013). Governing (through) autonomy: the moral and legal limits of "soft paternalism". Münster, 60, 1-20.

Malthus, T. (1998). *An essay on the principle of population*. London, UK: J. Johnson.

Mankiw, G. N. (2005). *Principles of economics*. Belgrade: Publishing Center of Faculty of Economics in Belgrade. (in Serbian)

Maslow, A. (1970). *Motivation and personality*. New York: Harper and Row.

National agency for local development (NALED). (2017). *Shadow book*. Belgrade: NALED. (in Serbian)

Neto, J. C., Filipe, J. A., & Caleiro, A. B. (2019). Creativity and innovation: a contribution of behavioral economics. *International Journal of Innovation Studies, 3*(1), 12-21.

Oleinik, A. (2002). The costs and prospects of reforms in Russia: An institutional approach. *Teme, 4*, 491–517.

Pavličić, D. (2010). *The theory of decision making*. Belgrade: Publishing Center of Faculty of Economics. (in Serbian)

Pavlović, N. (2016). Are authentic leaders satisfied with their job? *International Journal of Qualitative Research, 10*(2), 325–340.

Pavlović, N. (2018). Developing an innovation culture. In D. Karabašević & S. Vukotić (Eds.), *Innovation as an Initiator of the Development "Innovations – Basis for Development"* (pp. 193–212). Belgrade: Faculty of Applied Management, Economy, and Finance.

Pavlović, N., Oljaca, M., & Kostović, S. (2012). Integration of leadership styles of school director. *Educational Research Review, 7*(2), 31–35.

Petrović, D., Stefanović, Z., & Marković, I. (2017). Behavioral models in economics as a framework for individual adaptation to the institutional environment. *Ekonomski horizonti, 19*(1), 17-30. (in Serbian)

Polšek, D., & Bokulić, M. (2013). Two paradigms in bihevioral economics. In *An introduction to the behavioral economics of heuristics and bias* (pp. 5–24). Zagreb: Institute of Social Sciences Ivo Pilar. (in Croatian)

Ranđelović, S. (2015). Tax design-tax evasion relationship in Serbia: New empirical approach to standard theoretical model. *Industrija, 43*(1), 73–89. doi:10.5937/industrija43-6963

Schneider, F. (2011). *Handbook on the shadow economy.* Cheltenham, UK: Edward Elgar Publishing Company. doi:10.4337/9780857930880

Senior, N. (1965). *An outline of the science of political economy.* London, UK: Unwin Library of Economics.

Simon, H. (1961). *Administrative behaviour.* New York: Macmillan.

Simon, H. (1967). *Models of man: social and rational.* New York: John Wiley and Sons.

Smith, A. (1998). *An Inquiry into the Nature and Causes of the Wealth of Nations.* Belgrade: Global Book. (in Serbian)

Statistical Office of the Republic of Serbia. (2019). *Labor Force Survey, II quarter 2019.* Belgrade: Statistical Office of the Republic of Serbia. (in Serbian)

Sunstein, C. R. (2012). The storrs lectures: Behavioral economics and paternalism. *The Yale Law Journal, 122*(7), 1826–1899.

Thaler, R. (1980). Toward a positive theory of consumer choice. *Journal of Economic Behavior & Organization, 1*(1), 39–60. doi:10.1016/0167-2681(80)90051-7

Thaler, R. (1989). Anomalies: Interindustry wage differentials. *The Journal of Economic Perspectives, 3*(2), 181–193. doi:10.1257/jep.3.2.181

Thaler, R. (2016). Behavioral economics: Past, present, and future. *The American Economic Review, 106*(7), 1577–1600. doi:10.1257/aer.106.7.1577

Thaler, R. H., & Sunstein, C. R. (2003). Libertarian paternalism. *The American Economic Review, 93*(2), 175–179. doi:10.1257/000282803321947001

Transparency Serbia. (2019). *The EC report highlighted significant problems in the fight against corruption.* Belgrade: Transparency Serbia. (in Serbian)

Tversky, A., & Kahneman, D. (1974). Judgment under uncertainty: Heuristics and biases. *Science, 185*(4157), 1124–1131. doi:10.1126cience.185.4157.1124 PMID:17835457

Uggen, C., & Thompson, M. (2003). The socioeconomic determinants of ill-gotten gains: Within-person changes in drug use and illegal earnings. *American Journal of Sociology*, *109*(1), 146–185. doi:10.1086/378036

Von Neumann, J., & Morgenstern, O. (1947). *Theory of games and economic behavior*. Princeton, NJ: Princeton University Press.

Wesley, M. (1910). The rationality of economic activity. *Journal of Political Economy*, *18*(2), 97–113. doi:10.1086/251657

World Bank. (2007). *The Living Standards Survey*. Washington, DC: World Bank.

Wright, D. J., & Ginsburg, D. H. (2012). Behavioral law and economics: Its origins, fatal flaws and implications for liberty. *Northwestern University Law Review*, *106*(3), 1033–1089.

ADDITIONAL READING

Barberis, N. (2018). Richard Thaler and the rise of behavioral economics. *The Scandinavian Journal of Economics*, *120*(3), 661–684. doi:10.1111joe.12313

DellaVigna, S. (2009). Psychology and economics: Evidence from the field. *Journal of Economic Literature*, *47*(2), 315–372. doi:10.1257/jel.47.2.315

MacGregor, S. (1999). Welfare, neo-liberalism and new paternalism: Three ways for social policy in late capitalist societies. *Capital and Class*, *23*(1), 91–118. doi:10.1177/030981689906700104

Mathis, K., & Steffen, A. D. (2015). From rational choice to behavioural economics. In *European perspectives on behavioural law and economics* (pp. 31–48). Cham: Springer.

Osmani, S. R. (2019). Rationality, Behavioural Economics and Amartya Sen. *Journal of Human Development and Capabilities*, *20*(2), 162–180. doi:10.1080/19452829.2019.1565631

Pavlović, D. (2019). Prospect theory and presidential elections: Two cases from Yugoslavia and Serbia. *Communist and Post-Communist Studies*, *52*(1), 11–24. doi:10.1016/j.postcomstud.2019.01.002

Rizzo, M. J., & Whitma, D. G. (2009). The knowledge problem of new paternalism. *BYU Law Review*, (4), 904-968.

Smith, V. L. (2003). Constructivist and ecological rationality in economics. *The American Economic Review*, *93*(3), 465–508. doi:10.1257/000282803322156954

Urbina, D. A., & Ruiz-Villaverde, A. (2019). A critical review of homo economicus from five approaches. *American Journal of Economics and Sociology*, *78*(1), 63–93. doi:10.1111/ajes.12258

Whitman, G. (2006). Against the new paternalism. *Policy Analysis*, *563*, 1–16.

KEY TERMS AND DEFINITIONS

Behavioral Economics: Behavioral economics is an area of economic science where economists use basic understandings of psychology to explain the behavior of real economic actors.

Cognitive Biases: Cognitive biases are manifested as systematic deviations from the results of thinking, judgment, reasoning, memory, and decision-making processes from normative standards.

Hard Paternalism: Hard paternalism implies the introduction of some direct bans, direct organizations, as well as high taxes and other government benefits to help real economic players make better and better decisions.

Heuristics: Heuristics are simple mental strategies that we use to make our decisions.

Homo Economicus: Standard economic theory is based on a special kind of orgasm which we sometimes call homo economic. Members of that sort are always rational. As managers in factories, they maximize profits. As consumers, they maximize utility or, equivalently, choose the point on the highest indifference curve. With the limitations they face, they rationally measure all the costs and benefits and always choose the best course of action.

Normative Statements: Normative statements are statements that prescribe what the world should be like.

Prospect Theory: The descriptive theory of Amos Tversky and Daniel Kahneman describes and explains the choices of ordinary people.

Positive Testimonials: Positive testimonials are statements that describe the world as it is.

Soft Paternalism: Soft paternalism means providing the necessary information or manipulating the architecture of choice in order to reduce or eliminate the irrationality of real business entities.

Chapter 16
Ethics in Management:
Ethical Leadership and Culture

Yasemin Sarıcı Aytan
https://orcid.org/0000-0002-3026-5398
Istanbul Esenyurt University, Turkey

İlknur Sayan
https://orcid.org/0000-0002-7133-5858
Istanbul Kent University, Turkey

ABSTRACT

Recently, ethics is one of the fundamental issues that companies had to pay attention to because of global economic crises, corporate scandals, and rising importance of environmental concerns. Furthermore, scarcity of resources forced companies to think about sustainability within ethical issues. Devastating effects of the problems that companies dealing with have some consequences at the last instance. Ethics in management is becoming an ascending subject with all stakeholders, from a single customer to governmental practices. In this chapter, ethics in management will be discussed with its theoretical development, relation with organizational culture, and leadership.

ETHICS AND ETHICAL MANAGEMENT

Ethics

Ethics is the search for the general character that makes right acts right (Ross, 1930). It is the study of what is good or right for human beings (Hoffman and Moore, 1984). Ethics, has been defined by De-George as 'a systematic attempt through the use of reason to make sense of our individual and social moral experience in such a way as to determine the rules which ought to govern human conduct and the values worth pursuing in life' (1982). Singer (1994) writes on 'what is ethics?' that it stands for systematic studying of reasoning about how we ought to act. Ethics can be seen as a guide to action

DOI: 10.4018/978-1-7998-4601-7.ch016

while asking the question 'what shall we do?' Ethics is the evaluative study of what actors ought to do, rather than the descriptive study of what they have done, or are doing (Baylis, Smith,& Owens, 2008).

Since the beginning of the human race, doing the right thing for the sake of community is the matter of ethics. It is a timeless phenomenon. On the other side, there are no written rules, obligations or enforcements for ethical applications. Ethics could not be measured as concrete scientific experiments done under stable conditions.

Furthermore, every ethical belief contains a subject and a predicate. A subject is defined as what the belief is concerning while a predicate is what is said about the subject. Actions or practices such as capital punishment, adultery, lying could be count as regular subjects. "Wrong, unfair, bad, good" are examples of ethical predicates. Hence, for the person who believes that assisted suicide is wrong, "assisted suicide" is the subject of the belief and "wrong" is the ethical predicate. The subject of an ethical belief is usually an action or practice, but sometimes is a system or institution. Intentional actions we designate as "ethical" or "unethical" are usually actions that benefit or harm other people or ourselves in some serious ways (Duska, R., Duska, B., Ragatz, 2011).

To comprehend ethics more obviously Hosmer (1994) summarized general ethical principles under 10 groups:

1. **Self- interest (ethical egoism):** The first principle can be expressed as never take any action that is not in the long-term self-interests of yourself and/or of the organization to which you belong.
2. **Personal virtues (Aristotle):** Second principle defined as never take any action which is not honest, open and truthful, and which you would not be proud to see reported widely in national newspapers and on network news programs.
3. **Religious injunctions (St. Augustine and St. Thomas Aquinas):** Third one never take any action that is not kind and compassionate, and that does not build a sense of community, a sense of all of us working together for a commonly accepted goal.
4. **Government requirements (Hobbes and Locke):** The principle, then, can be expressed as never take any action that violates the law, for the law represents the minimal moral standards of our society.
5. **Utilitarian benefits (Bentham and Mill):** explained as never take any action that does not result in greater good than harm for the society of which you are a part.
6. **Universal Rules (Kant):** never take any action that you would not be willing to see others, faced with the same or a closely similar situation, also be free or even encouraged to take.
7. **Individual rights (Jefferson and King):** summarized as never take any action that abridges the agreed-upon and accepted rights of others.
8. **Economic efficiency (Smith, Friedman and Blinder):** always act to maximize profits subject to legal and market constraints, for maximum profits are evidence of the most efficient production.
9. **Distributive justice (Rawls):** defined as never take any action in which the least among us are harmed in some way.
10. **Contributive liberty (Nozick):** last grouping expressed as never take any action that will interfere with the right of all of us for our self-development and self-fulfillment to the limit of our abilities.

Also Klikauer (2010) classified ethics under three aspects. Table 1 shows us this grouping:

Table 1.

Traditional Ethics	Sittlichkeit(Morality)	Communicative Ethics
Core Ethical Question: What shall I do and How shall I live?	**Core Ethical Question:** How shall we live ethically in society	**Core Ethical Question:** How can we communicate ethically?
Meta-Ethical Perspective: Philosophy about ethics and moral behaviour	**Meta-Ethical Perspective:** Philosophy about socially constructed ethics and moral behavior (Hegel)	**Meta-Ethical Perspective:** Ethics of communicatively established dialogue (Habermas)
Normative Viewpoint: Norms, values, rules, standards and principles that guide actions	**Normative Viewpoint:** Ethical institutions organized and run by morally conscious actors (Mündigkeit-resposibility)	**Normative Viewpoint:** Ethical communication organized by participants in discourse ethics
Form of Ethics: Universalism, Moral Relativism, Irrationalism, Act and Rule Utilitarianism, Greek and Modern Virtue Ethics, Social Contract Theory, Kant's Universalism and Morality, Nihilism and Egoism	**Form of Ethics:** End of master-slave relationship, serving a purpose- having a purpose end of alienation and deception, Mündigkeit, autonomy, self-reflection, self-determination, self-actualization, social development of ethical standarts and moral institutions	**Form of Ethics:** Overcoming distorted communication, end of colonization and manipulation of speech, symmetrical relations, domination-free dialogue, establishing ideal speech and communicative action, moral dialogue-moral action

In Table 1. we can see the developmental stages of ethics under four aspects as core ethical question, meta-ethical perspective, normative viewpoint and form of ethics according to Klikauer. The core difference between a) and b) is that the latter is no longer based on formulas, categorical imperatives, rules, principles, etc. that are developed by a philosopher. Instead, those to whom ethics is applied become the very foundation of ethics which moves ethics from being constructed by an individual philosopher or a small group of philosophers towards socially constructed ethics developed by society. To achieve this, human beings are no longer seen as atomized individuals but as moral actors inside an ethical society engaged in ethical life. This is what Hegel calls Sittlichkeit. At the next stage (b®c) the need for communication becomes highly relevant. Moral actors need to communicate when creating their own ethical rules, principles, and codes of conduct. This needs to happen under ethical principles that are developed inside a particular framework called communicative ethics. Transition from (a) to (b), and eventually to (c) is established with this logic (Klikauer, 2010).

Lawrence Kohlberg, mostly known for his cognitive moral theory, defined Virtue as a unique, regardless of climate or culture, and always the same ideal form. The name of this ideal form is justice. According to him, virtue is not only the "good", it is also the knowledge of the "good". Therefore, "good" could be taught (Kohlberg, 1970). So ethics became the issue of education as well as other disciplines. Kolhberg's contributions to managerial ethics later will be discussed.

Ethics in Management

'Management of ethics or ethics of management' is the basic question behind the studies conducted in that area. Management and ethics follow two different sets of epistemological – knowledge creating – philosophical questions. Ethical knowledge is predominantly concerned with human subjects, while managerial knowledge is dealing with objects, facts and figures, and numbers directed towards profit-making. Management ethics is not viewed as a philosophical study of morals but a study of management morality. Consequently, it has been degraded from being a philosophy to being merely knowledge in the service of power. Only when something – marketing, sales, operations, HRM, and even ethics – adds to shareholder value, it is of value to management. As a result, management allocates and transforms human and material resources into profit-making operations (Magretta 2002).

The core of management's own existence is represented as follows:

- what is profitable?
- what is relevant to improve shareholder values?
- how can my company be profitable?
- do I have the right cost-benefit strategy?
- do I allocate labour and capital in the best way?
- am I efficient in what I do?; and later maybe
- why should I act ethically?

Moral issues such as every human being think about how to live a good life are simply no issues for management. However, rapid changes in the technology, information channels forced companies to re-think about what is right to do or what is best for all? Scandals, harmful products, environmental pollution give the deserved position to ethics. Nowadays, organizations respect ethics for the best practices of strategic management.

Kohlberg, after WW2, try to answer the question "how could a developed nation be so evil?" Nazi Holocaust was the worst example of systematic managerial applications. As a result, he established a seven step general and managerial orientations (Klikauer, 2010).

In Table 2 Kohlberg numbered seven stage for general ethical orientation form the infant period to the more complex one as respecting the cosmos as an integral whole. Furthermore, Table 3 explains stages of moral motives of management.

Table 2. Kohlberg's Seven Stages of Morality: General Moral Orientations

Stage	General Orientation
0	Impulsive and amoral
1	Obedience and avoidance of punishment
2	Personal benefits and rewards and getting a good deal for oneself
3	Conforming to social expectations and gaining approval
4	Protecting law and order; maintaining existing systems of official arrangements; and supporting existing structures unquestioned as a given
5	Promoting justice and welfare within a wider community, as defined in open and reasonable debate
6	Defending everyone's right to justice; supporting and promoting universal welfare; and the universal application of ethical actions
7	Respecting the cosmos as an integral whole; an openness that extends well beyond humanity

In Table 3, Kohlberg examine moral motives of management in seven stages excluding infant stage. Rationally, stage 0, unconscious stage do not need to self orientation of morality. At stage 1, fear and obedience appears and developed itself through stage 7, respecting, preserving and supporting all universal values of the cosmos with its environmental harmonies. Social responsibility projects of today's organizations may probably are the result of stage 7 (Klikauer, 2010).

Table 3. Kohlberg's Seven Stages of Morality: Management's Moral Orientations

Stage	Moral Motives of Management
0	None (unconscious stage or babies and newborns), pre-ethics
1	People act irrational to the threat of punishment through management Guiding principle are fear of those in managerial authority
2	Management gets selfish pleasure and gains are for managers Calculating managerial risks and payoffs of management actions
3	Avoiding disapproval by other managers and top-management Waiting to be praised, liked admired, rather than shamed
4	Performing managerial and formal duties and responsibilities Meeting company standards as set by management Working for the best interest of the company
5	Following principles that serve the best interest of the great majority Striving for reasonable, just and purposeful managerial action
6	Applying well- thought principles to management and the company Share information in an open debate beyond corporate boundaries Act non-defensive with other managers and employees
7	Respecting, preserving, and supporting all intrinsic values of the cosmos with its wider environmental harmonies (animals and plants)

According to Hosmer (1994), ethics should be considered at the beginning of the strategic planning beside analytical aspects. Freeman and Gilbert (1988), took a major step in that direction that "if corporate strategy did not recognize the individual values and goals (or 'projects') of the members, both internal and external to the firm, then those members could not be expected to cooperate to achieve organizational goals". Ethical analysis, in the view of the authors, is the only means available to resolve conflicts in values, goals, and 'projects,' and consequently essential in the processes of corporate strategy.

Today, ethical principles reflect the expectations of an organization's customers and the public. The changing and developing socio-cultural structure increased social sensitivity. Due to the awareness of societies and changing social needs, the importance given to ethical values has increased. The fact that the leaders act in accordance with ethical values and principles is considered as an important success criterion and the discussions have been raised in this issue (Sayan, 2018, & Akkucuk, 2015).

Ethical Leadership and Culture

Leaders are expected to have some qualifications according to organization needs. Unavoidable of these qualifications are the provision of justice in organizational environment and commitment to moral values. Disagreements in human relations, developments in social and economic life change the perspective of leadership and bring new tasks and responsibilities to leaders. As a result of these new responsibilities, some ethical principles are expected to be implemented by the leaders in the organizational environment. Above all, it is expected that moral values will be taken into account at the level of individuals, groups and organizations. In this respect, the leader should adopt different approaches to both internal and external organizations dealing with ethics and justice (Aytan, 2018).

Five principles form the basis for the development of ethical leadership: These basic principles are respect, service, justice, honesty and social structure (Northouse, 2016).

- Serving Others: Serving leaders care about the well-being of their followers. In organizations, activities such as service principle, guidance and empowerment behaviors, team building and citizenship behaviors have gained importance. Servant leaders have a social responsibility and strive to eliminate inequalities and social injustices. Leaders who implement the service principle act in a way that benefits others (Northouse, 2016).
- Respect for others: Leaders who respect others feel that they are valuable and establish close relationships with individuals. Respect for the existence and personality of individuals means that a leader is close and empathetic to his followers. When a leader respects his followers, his followers can feel competent in their work. In short, leaders who respect other people have a positive impact on their followers (Northouse, 2016).
- Acting Fairly: The fair decisions taken by ethical leaders are assessed by their followers. Ethical leaders treat their followers equally. Justice is the lack of special treatment of leaders in their decision-making except in special circumstances. When people are treated differently, their justification should be clear and reasonable and should be based on moral values (Sayan, 2018).
- Honesty: Being honest is not just about telling the truth. It has nothing to do with being open to others and telling the truth as completely and completely as possible. Sometimes there are times when saying the full truth can be destructive or inefficient. The challenge for the leaders is to create a balance between being open and sincere, while in a particular situation they need to be outspoken. Most of the time, there are organizational restrictions that prevent leaders from disclosing information to their followers. It is important for the leaders to be authentic, but it is also important that they are sensitive to the attitudes and feelings of others. To be honest to the leaders in the organization means "don't promise anything you can't do, don't make false statements, don't avoid accountability"(Sayan, 2018).
- Community Creation: An ethical leader deals with the common interest in the broadest sense. Leaders should take into account the goals of both themselves and their followers when working towards the objectives that are appropriate for both. According to Burns, leadership as a result of leader-follower relationship, based on personal relations. Leaders must participate in the aims and objectives of the community (Sayan, 2018).

Ethical leaders determine clear ethical standards and follow the implementation of these standards. They use reward and punishment methods when necessary. Ethical leaders are honest and reliable. In addition, they take fair and principled decisions and act ethically in personal and professional lives n people. Researchers describe this aspect of the leader as a moral and ethical aspect. Ethical leaders apply what they say and are proactive role models in ethical behavior (Brown & Treviño, 2016).

Ethical leader's behavior and attitudes can be attributed to ethical principles and ethical values are placed in organizational culture and rewarded by employees who exhibit ethical behaviors. This creates a positive outlook on ethical principles and trust among the employees.

According to Association of Professionals in Business Managements Best Practices (2008), Vallabhaneni mentions that, The Chief Ethics Officer is a key person for creating an ethical culture and has the following roles and responsibilities:

- Promote a positive ethical climate in the organization through his leadership skills.
- Develop an ethics manual describing company policy, codes of conduct, and expected behavior; reporting of ethical violations; and referencing to all the applicable laws and regulations.

- Annually require each and every employee in the organization to sign a corporate ethics document that lays out the organization's requirements concerning employee ethics and stipulates that the signer has received, read, and understood the document and agrees to abide by its requirements.
- Conduct training classes for managers and nonmanagers in ethical principles, with attention to actions and consequences.
- Work with the internal audit department in developing audit plans and identifying areas of audit that address ethical violations
- Work with the legal department in pursuing cases that violated ethical principles either inside the company (e.g., employees and management) or outside (e.g., customers, suppliers, vendors, and contractors).
- Conduct ethics audits, special management reviews, and self-assessment reviews periodically and proactively to ensure continuous improvement in ethical matters.
- Analyze outside-in views (i.e., views of stakeholders about company management) and inside-out views (i.e., views of company management about stakeholders) to identify disconnections between these views and to integrate them in a coherent manner.

Ethics and Organizational Culture

Nelson and Trevino (2011), define ethical behavior in business as "consistent with the principles, norms, and standards of business practice that have been agreed upon by society". Ethics become significantly important for the management issues in every aspect of social life. Public organizations, non- governmental organizations, business& industrial organizations, religious organizations, basically every unit in social life concern about ethics to compete with rivals. Without ethics, trust and commitment may not be assured among the shareholders and stakeholders of the organization.

Culture defines the identity of individuals in a society; composed of norms, customs, artistic compositions of music, literature, art and have similarities in form, style or subject matters (Baylis, Smith, Owens, 2008). Organizational culture is a certain value system that distinguishes the business from other enterprises by the norms and standards created on this subject consisting of common assumptions, thoughts, opinions and value judgments of all individuals in the enterprise. It creates a high identity for the members of the organization and creates a responsibility for the employees to achieve the objectives of the business (Greenberg, 2002).

Organizational culture is a mosaic in which basic approaches and opinions such as behaviors, beliefs and values shared by members of the organization are discussed (Vries. M., Miller.D., 1988).

There some basic factors that define organizational culture, the importance and weight given to these factors determine the organizational culture of the enterprise and differentiate it from other enterprises (Ülgen,H., Mirze, K., 2013):

- **Hypercritical:** while some businesses carry out their activities, they organize everything in the finest detail and perform it in accordance with the rules and procedures.
- **Aggressive:** some businesses are characterized by their fighter and aggressive behavior in business life.
- **Balanced:** oppose to the aggressive ones, some enterprises tend to keep its position.
- **Result Oriented:** one of the most valuable elements is how and in what way to achieve target results.

- **People Oriented**: is the culture of human-oriented enterprises that takes care of the welfare and comfort of employees, believes in values.
- **Team Oriented:** Businesses that focus on team-based work, give a premium to cooperation and togetherness, are companies with a team culture.
- **Risk Management:** In some businesses, the dominant idea is innovation and risk overload, while in others there is a traditional culture and risk aversion seen as organizational culture.

An organization's beliefs and values affect the behavior of its members. It is important to create an organizational culture on ethical codes which accepted within the organization to reach success in any environment of management.

The Hofstede's Cultural Dimensions Theory, developed by Geert Hofstede, is a framework used to understand the differences in culture across countries and to discern the ways that business is done across different cultures. In other words, the framework is used to distinguish between different national cultures, the dimensions of culture, and their impact on a business setting.

1. **Individualism–collectivism:** Describes the relationships individuals have in each culture. In individualistic societies, individuals look after themselves and their immediate family only whereas in collectivistic cultures, individuals belong to groups that look after them in exchange for loyalty. Personal goals are important for individualistic cultures while 'we' is important in collectivist ones.
2. **Uncertainty Avoidance**: Refers to "The extent to which people feel threatened by uncertainty and ambiguity and try to avoid these situations" (Hofstede, 1991: 113). This dimension deals with the need for well-defined rules for prescribed behavior. Strict rules are needed for high fears of uncertainty; on the other hand lax rules are important for highly risk taker societies.
3. **Power Distance:** Dimension reflects the consequences of power inequality and authority relations in society. It influences hierarchy and dependence relationships in the family and organizational contexts. High power distance societies need bureaucratic organizations while less power distance societies have flat, decentralized structures.
4. **Masculinity–femininity**: Dominant values in masculine countries are achievement and success and in feminine countries are caring for others and quality of life. Distinct gender roles, are important for masculine cultures while fluid gender roles.
5. **Long-term Orientation**: "stands for the fostering of virtues oriented towards future rewards, in particular perseverance and thrift" (Hofstede, 2001: 359). A late addition to the initial four (Bond, 1987), this dimension represents a range of Confucian like values and was termed Confucian Dynamism. Hofstede (1991) later proposed the long-versus short-term designation as more appropriate for this dimension (Soares, A.M., Farhangmehr, M., Shoham, A. 2007)

Organizations have taken many different approaches to implementing an ethics strategy. According to objectives of the organizations most common ethics strategy could be summarized as follows (Vallabhaneni, 2008):

- To avoid any behavior, legal, or otherwise, that violates company policy and negatively affects its interests
- To satisfy the concerns of company stakeholders and thereby capture the benefits that derives from a reputation for ethical behavior

- To create a culture in which each employee and manager pursues a set of ethical and social values to which the company is firmly committed.

Successful corporate ethics could be developed in three stages (2008):

Stage 1: Managing for Compliance. Organizations see the tremendous damage that can be done to corporate reputation and momentum by incidents of illegal or blatantly unethical behavior. To prevent such occurrences, the organization establishes a program to ensure compliance with both the law and ethical standards demanded by the public and stakeholders. Such programs include prohibitions against conflicts of interest, theft of company property, and disclosure of trade secrets. The primary objective is to prevent lawbreaking and scandals. Standards for judging behavior include laws, regulations, and the rights of the corporation. Strengths of the approach include clear standards and clear penalties for violations. Weaknesses of the approach include addressing too few issues, hampering empowerment, and possibly implying that the company expects only the minimum. Action steps include:

- Adopt a code of ethics, practice, or conduct to address specific behaviors.
- Ensure board-level and senior management support.
- Assign responsibility for the ethics and compliance strategy to an appropriate function in the organization.
- Identify and communicate compliance standards.
- Train employees to use compliance standards.
- Establish clear channels of communications.
- Ensure supervision to compliance standards.
- Make periodic reports to senior management and the board of directors.

Stage 2: Managing Stakeholder Relations. Organizations become increasingly sophisticated and see the long-term value to be gained from maintaining good relations with key stakeholders. Self-interest drives the organization to monitor its reputation among these stakeholders and to initiate programs to address their ethical concerns. The primary objective is to create value by meeting stakeholder expectations. Standards for judging behavior include stakeholder demands and expectations. Strengths of the approach include clear payoffs for the organization; stakeholders can be surveyed for expectation and attitudes. Weaknesses of the approach include the changeability of stakeholder views' with time and location, the probability that some expectations cannot be met, an absence of guidance on many issues, and a lack of clear values behind behaviors. Action steps include:

- Define corporate stakeholders.
- Evaluate the attitudes and opinions of stakeholder groups.
- Design programs to address stakeholder concerns.
- Audit the effectiveness of stakeholder programs.

Stage 3: Creating a Value-Based Organization. Many organizations have found it difficult to manage compliance or stakeholder relations without creating a genuine change in corporate culture. As a result, instinct rather than strategy dominates responses to the breadth of ethical issues held important by stakeholders. Such organizations define their values and invest considerable effort and expense in making those values permeate all aspects of their work. They find it productive to make decisions consistent with these values even when short-term payoffs are not apparent. In reality, very few organizations reach this stage. The primary objective is to create an organization that has enduring value. Standards for judging behavior include the company's own values and beliefs. Strengths of the approach include bolstering corporate culture, with desired behavior becoming instinctive. Weaknesses of the approach include the need to wait for a long-term payoff, the high costs needed for implementation, and the possibility that empowered employees may interpret and misinterpret values in their own ways. Action steps include:

- Define the organization's values.
- Communicate the organization's values.
- Create systems that support corporate values.
- Ensure supervision of corporate values.
- Establish an ethics or corporate values function.
- Assign responsibility for interpreting values.
- Recruit and promote employees of strong moral character.
- Train employees in ethical decision making and application of the values.
- Encourage employees to report behavior inconsistent with the values.
- Reward managers and employee behavior consistent with the values.
- Renew the values.
- Conduct policy and practice review

As a result, establishment of an ethical culture within an organization is essential, not only for the achievement of desired business goals, but also necessary for the proper management of key risks in its business environment. To avoid questionable practices, reaching the spirit of doing the right, fair and just on behalf of others would be the fringe benefits of ethical culture among the organizations. Beside the economic, legal and philanthropic responsibilities, ethical responsibility becomes also important for the business management.

CONCLUSION

Defending everyone's right to justice; supporting and promoting universal welfare; and the universal application of ethical actions are the basic motives behind the orientation of ethics in society also in business management.

Nowadays, corporate scandals, economic crises, environmental issues and sensitivity of the public obligate organizations to think about ethics. Even strategic management tools also used hand in hand with ethical codes. Organizations, especially in business management, understand the importance of ethics to be successful among the rivals. Even consumers could give buying decisions according to ethical principles of the firm that produce the product or giving the service.

Organizational culture is defined as the underlying assumptions, beliefs, values, attitudes, and expectations shared by an organization's members (i.e., managers and nonmanagers). An organization's beliefs and values affect the behavior of its members. It is important to create an organizational culture on ethical codes which accepted within the organization to reach success in any environment of management. Organizational culture based on ethical codes provides superiority over the competitors in business life.

REFERENCES

Akkucuk, U. (2015). *Handbook of Research on Developing Sustainable Value in Economics, Finance, and Marketing*. IGI Global. doi:10.4018/978-1-4666-6635-1

Aytan, Y. (2018). *A case study on the affect of organizational justice, trust, commitment and citizenship on worker's performance* (Unpublished doctoral dissertation). Istanbul Aydın University, Istanbul, Turkey.

Baylis, J., Simith, S., & Owens, P. (2008). *The Globalization of World Politics*. New York: Oxford University Press.

DeGeorge, R. (1982). *Business Ethics* (1st ed.). New York: Macmillan.

Duska, Shay, & Ragatz. (2011). Accounting Ethics. John Wiley & Sons, Ltd.

Greenberg, J. (2002). *Managing Behavior in Organizations*. Prentice Hall.

Hoffman, W. M., & Moore, J. M. (1984). *Business Ethics* (1st ed.). New York: McGraw Hill.

Hosmer, L. T. (1994). Strategic Planning as if Ethics Mattered. *Strategic Management Journal*, 15.

Klikauer, T. (2010). *Critical Management Ethics*. Palgrave Macmillan. doi:10.1057/9780230281776

Kohlberg, L. (1970). *Education for Justice: A modern Statement of the Platonic View in moral Education*. Harvard University Press.

Magretta, J. (2002). *What Management is – How It Works and Why It's Everyone's Business*. New York: Free Press.

Nelson & Trevino. (2011). Managing Business Ethics: Straight Talk About How To Do It Right (5th ed.). John Wiley & Sons, Inc.

Northouse, P. G. (2016). Leadership: Theory and Practice (7th ed.). Thousand Oaks, CA: Sage.

Ross, W. D. (1930). *The Right and the Good*. Oxford: Clarendon Press.

Sayan, İ. (2018). *Kurumsal liderlik tarzlarını algılamanın örgütsel bağlılık ve vatandaşlığa etkisinde çalışanların motivasyon seviyelerinin rolü ve bir araştırma*. İstanbul, Turkey: Yayınlanmamış Doktora Tezi, İstanbul Aydın Üniversitesi Sosyal Bilimleri Enstitüsü.

Singer, P. (1994). *The Oxford Reader on Ethics*. Oxford: Oxford University Press.

Soares, A. M., Farhanmeghr, M., & Shoham, A. (2007). Hofstede's dimension of culture in international marketing studies. *Journal of Business Research*, *60*(3), 277–284. doi:10.1016/j.jbusres.2006.10.018

Ulgen, H., & Mirze, K. (2013). *İşletmelerde Stratejik Yönetim*. Istanbul: Beta Yayınları.

Vallabhaneni, S. R. (2008). *Corporate Management, Governance, and Ethics: Best Practices. Association of professionals in Business Management*. Wiley.

Chapter 17
Supervising System and Business Control of Local Self-Government Units in Performance Audit Function

Jelica Eremić-Đođić
University EDUCONS, Serbia

Ivan Bosnjak
Ministry of Public Administration and Local Self-Goverment, Serbia

ABSTRACT

As everywhere in the world, resources in the Republic of Serbia are limited. Almost half of the resources are covered by public spending. A well-established oversight of the budget process provides real assistance in performance audit, and it is also an instrument of a permanent guidance and correction. The State Audit Office is often assigning itself tasks to carry out the activities related to the performance audit process. In this way, the state audit approaches systematically to the examination of business activities of all budget users. The basic task of the performance audit lies in examining the economy, efficiency, and effectiveness of the use of public funds by using various analyses, making comparisons, and analyzing indicators. This chapter will describe the proposal for a procedure that ensures a continuous process of supervision and control of business operations in local self-government units in the function of performance audits.

INTRODUCTION

The purpose of the performance audit should be to assess the of disposing performance of an income: both from own and earmarked funds received by the state as well as the process of spending. In order to carry out such an assessment, it is necessary to consider the way in which one's own income is generated; criteria for acquiring them, as well as to determine to what extent the way of spending own revenues

DOI: 10.4018/978-1-7998-4601-7.ch017

of budget users is useful. In this case, the research will be applied to local government units as one of the significant budget users.At the same time, it is also a way of assessing whether local governments adhere to the principles of economy, efficiency and effectiveness in their work.

BACKGROUND

However, there are few studies on the use of resources and costs for local government, which can be used for this purpose. Considering that financial management and control are an area of implementation in local governments, practice shows that there have been no comprehensive studies on the use of resources and associated costs so far that we can accept or disrupt their results. That is why this research is a novelty because it speaks about the steps that need to be taken in order to establish continuous supervision over financial management and control in local governments, which, in addition to numerous advantages, would definitely ensure the tracking of documents which we can say with certainty that signifies both innovations in Serbia and relevant developing countries. (D. Coderre, 2011)

Internal auditors / controllers who provide consulting services to their organizations are in a position where they can contribute to the improvement of the overall control system. The data they collect through any type of consulting assignment can almost always be used to develop control throughout the organization. In addition, an increasing number of audit teams are giving management advice on designing new processes and systems. (M. Stanišić, 2015)

The management of a legal entity has the primary responsibility for designing, implementing and overseeing the operation of internal control systems, with a view to pursuing the specific objectives of the organization, including the prevention and detection of criminal acts. (A. Petković, 2010)

The Performance Audit of Budget Users

In order to make a more realistic assessment of the use of public funds and to determine whether the principles of economy (Table 1) are respected, it is necessary to use certain analyses and observe indicators in order to draw conclusions that describe their comparability and affect realization of business tasks.

Table 1. Principles of economy

Cost-effectiveness	Minimizing the cost of resources used with the right quality of products or services.
Efficiency	In its relation to cost-effectiveness, it provides an answer if the funds have been used optimally and appropriately. So, it can be evaluated whether similar results can be achieved with fewer resources.
Effectiveness	It refers to the goals achievement and the relationship between them, the outcomes, ie. purpose. The way in which it can be measured is the effects on the assets used to realize them.
Impartiality	A defined concept on equal opportunities

Source: authors (2019)

Developing the modern economy, the professional profile of auditing is changing as well. The purpose of the audit is not to have one structure controling other, but to assist the company to which it is intended. (J.Eremić-Đođić, B.Laban & A. Tomić, 2017).

The performance audit is made up of connected elements that have repercussions on each other. These elements are usually the findings, tasks, inputs, activities, results and outcomes, ie effects on the whole process. Most auditors use the input-output model for this purpose to successfully create the elements for their audit analysis based on which the audit report is prepared.

Because of the fact that performance audit is more flexible than other audits (such as business audits), it does not use predefined templates and forms in its work. Its work is based on research and valuation method and is not uniform.However it is based on its own assessments and interpretations.

Supervising System (Control) of Business in Local Self-Government Units

In order that performance audit achieve its full success, the assistance of the government, the National Assembly and the interested public is needed. The best means by which the executive, the Ministry of Finance, the tax administration, the public can accurately grasp the spending of funds is performance audit. In fact, it provides the ability to control public or budgetary resources. It can clearly see the effects of the business of all government sectors, and especially local governments.

In its interconnections with other business activities, performance audit provides clear answers to the most important questions:

- Is the legislation in local self-government units properly implemented and to what extent?
- Are the prescribed internal acts applied to the local self-government units and to what extent?
- Does the local government operate in accordance with the decisions made?
- Does the spending of funds in local self-government units proceed in accordance with the adopted plans?
- Does the local government operate in accordance with the principles of economy?

These are just some of the most basic requirements that need to be fulfilled in order to set up a sound financial management and control system and make sure that local government managers make more secure decisions.

An efficient management and control system helps to track the budgeting program in the most correct and successful way possible by ensuring economic and financial responsibility at all levels of business. The achieved results are monitored so the one of the essential tasks of performance audit is being realized.

Of course, the mentioned conditions can not be sufficient for the performance audit. In order to have full benefit, it needs answers to the essential questions:

- Are there any written and adopted procedures, guidelines and policies in local government in all its areas of business?
- Is their implementation adequately implemented?
- Is the verification of their implementation continuous?
    - In order to get answers to the defined questions, it is necessary that the audited entity, ie local self-government, prepares a business program which, in addition to legal regulations, will fully enable the implementation of all business policies and decisions adopted as well as full implementation of adopted procedures, instructions and other of internal acts.

Local government work is of public interest. In its main activity, local self-government works for the general interest and serves the society as a whole. Local government development also affects the development of the state. Therefore, it is very important to establish quality control and continuous monitoring of its activities.

Only on time controls bring multiple benefits. It is a signpost to the responsible person to prevent any deviation from the planned activities. Just as current controls can help to correct bad business activities on the spot and prevent them from occurring in the future, so it enables responsible persons to prevent the recurrence of mistakes from the previous period. (Eremić-Đođić, J., Laban, B., Bošnjak, I., Ćirić, I., Škatarić, G. & Sedlak, O., 2018)

A well-designed internal control framework in each budget institution, and especially in local government, greatly helps the proper and safe functioning of local government. And as such, it is subject to change. There is no universal control framework that covers every control and whose application eliminates errors by one hundred percent. The reason for this lies in the legal and economic changes that affect the business of all institutions. Therefore, it is necessary to update the control box and put its leakage power under continuous monitoring.

Each institution has its own management style. Local governments are also distinguished by their way of organizing and managing, which is reflected in the internal controls applicable in such an environment.

It has been searching for the long time, for the best control framework and how to manage it. All analyzes and conclusions led to only one prerequisite: co-operation between employees and management is necessary. Since the control framework cannot exist in isolation, this is another reason why it is necessary for management to allow the internal control process to be revised on a regular basis. That is why local self-government should strive to improve skills and provide professional development of its executors, ensure a smooth flow of information in it and provide selfless support to all this.

What is the management of internal control?

COSO defines internal control as follows:

Internal control is a process, affected by an entity' board of directors, management, and other personnel, designed to provide reasonable assurance regarding the achievement of objectives in the following categories:

- **Operations Objective**: Affecting the effectiveness and efficiency of operations
- **Reporting Objective**: Enhancing the reliability of reporting
- **Compliance Objective:** Encouraging adherence with applicable laws and regulation. (Dutta K.S, 2013)

Since internal control is embraced into all local government business activities, its monitoring, involves the function of a precise description of each role and a clear division of responsibilities throughout its business process. That is why when it comes to performance audit, it is useful to:

- Look at the performance audit file from last year (if any)?
- The audit manager must familiarize the audit team with the subject matter and subject of the audit
- The audit manager is tasked with carrying out the audit in the planned manner, or in accordance with the approved audit plan of the performance audit;

- There is a need for several interviews with senior management. There is no need to go into the details of auditing the financial statements on this occasion; more experienced auditors are required to evaluate the feasibility audit;
- Perform all preparatory actions to detect irregularities. This also implies the usage of internal controls;
- Before going to a place where a performance audit is performed, it is extremely important that the auditor reads all domestic and foreign material related to it;
- Since communication is crucial in this type of audit, it is necessary to ensure a high level of trust between participants in both parties in the audit review process;
- If appropriate records are available from the audite, the auditor's findings on what he or she has observed and expected should be thoroughly recorded;
- If there is no proper record by the auditee, there is no information available and the auditor is forced to make proposals. The proposals contain the types of information and reviews required for the audite to make certain conclusions in future;
- In a situation where there is time and cash available and when it covers the cost of the audit, the auditor may collect the necessary information himself;
- Performance audit is an independent research and is very flexible which means that it chooses the subject, method and opinion;
- Regarding that it does not consist of an audit with a pre-defined form of opinion, it is exposed to its own judgments and interpretations;
- Research and evaluation methods are used in conducting the audit;
- In an optional audit, one sometimes considers only a particular activity, sometimes a specific subject that makes an audit, and sometimes an entire study of a particular system with an emphasis on management activities, organization and business policy;
- It is essential to follow the strategic and annual plan adopted throughout the audit process;
- It is necessary for the auditor to make a comparison of the effects and objectives achieved, as well as to determine their connection with the resources as to what the audit objective is;
- These may be questions of organization, program, activity or service to which the auditor finds answers through research and analysis processes;
- The following is considered when determining the scope of the audit:
    - The relevance of the competent State Audit Institution (SAI) that does not threat the goals of the National Assembly, the government, etc.),
    - The importance of the SAI in its strategic plan,
    - Auditability (the ability to perform audits in accordance with professional standards and guidelines);
- One of the most difficult tasks of an auditor is to evaluate cost effectiveness since neither quality nor quantity should be neglected in its assessment. In order to provide recommendations in the audit findings as instruments that can act to reduce costs without affecting service quality and quantity, the financial plan should include all the necessary details;
- It is also necessary to evaluate the most rational method of work - thus avoiding duplicating the jobs which could increase the costs;
- It is necessary to consider and evaluate if the audited entity operates in accordance with the applicable business regulations;

- If the application of the provisions of a law contravenes the principle of efficiency, the auditor cannot take a position on it, but it would be useful to draw attention to such a case so that the legislative authorities can make a possible change in the legislation.

With the performance audit, the state apparatus acquires control over the spending of all budget users: health care, school, public enterprises, local governments

The research in this paper will be applied to local government units. Its main point is to define a model that, in the form of controls, will help to spend money in the mildest possible way, as smart as possible.

There is no universal control framework that covers every control and whose application eliminates errors by one hundred percent. The reason for this lies in the legal and economic changes that affect the business of all institutions. Therefore, it is necessary to update the control box and put its leakage power under continuous monitoring.

THE PROCEDURE FOR CONTINUOUS MONITORING AND OPERATIONS CONTROLING IN LOCAL SELF-GOVERNMENT UNITS IN THE FUNCTION OF THE PERFORMANCE AUDIT

Research done in this paper is presented in the questionnaire shown in Table 2.

Practically applied specifics that form a part of the performance audit can best be seen by answering the questions **in Table 2**.

Responses received by an anonymous survey lead to the following conclusions:

- The assessment of the coverage of business activities in local self-governments by procedures and instructions was assessed as towards the medium, which means that additional engagement in this field should be undertaken;
- The legal obligation to regulate internal controls in accordance with the COSO model has been respected the same way and it should be completed;
- The legal obligation of introducing a system of a management control somewhere has been fully respected, in some cases they are working on it, while in in certain local governments this process is at its beginning.

Considering that these activities represent the basic preparatory actions necessary to create a favorable basis for the most positive evaluations of any audit, and therefore the performance audit. The conclusion that can be drawn from this research leads us to think that additional engagement is needed in this field, which is primarily reflected in providing training to all levels of management and employees. In this way, employees become aware of the importance of the project of implementing financial management control in local governments. In order for the project to be as successfully implemented as possible, the main task is to encourage employees to participate in it. Their daily contribution would significantly shorten its implementation time.

Table 2. Questionnaire - anonymous survey

Importance of General Characteristics: (Score from 1 to 5, with 1 -insufficient, 2 -poor, 3- medium, 4- sufficient, 5- more than sufficient)		1	2	3	4	5
1.	Evaluate the coverage of the business with the procedures and guidelines available at your organization.					
2.	Evaluate how well employees apply procedures and instructions in their work?					
3.	Evaluate people's training in procedures and instructions.					
4.	Assess how well the training has prepared you to work in financial management and control.					
5.	Evaluate the implementation of internal control according to the COSO model in your organization.					
7.	Evaluate how much control has saved your institution's assets and other resources from a negative business result.					
8.	Evaluate how much the application of internal controls has helped to realize business activities in a proper, effective and efficient manner?					
9.	Assess how much the control system has reduced the risk in your organization.					
10.	Assess how well the internal control system has been monitored.					
11.	Evaluate how much the financial management and control system has helped reduce budget expenditures.					
12.	Evaluate the business activities undertaken as a result of responding to the recommendations received from the audit findings to date.					
13.	Evaluate the continuity of internal controls in your organization.					
14. Do you have a perormance audit file from last year? Answer: **No.** 15. Have you implemented internal control -COSO in your organization? Answer: **Yes.** 16. Do you continuously monitor the identified risk and how much is it under control? Answer: **Partially.** 17. Have you implemented financial management and control in your organization? Answer: **Preparatory activities have just begun**..						

Source: authors (2019)

Steps of the Procedure of Continuous Supervision and Operations Control in Local Self-Government Units

The results of the conducted research in local self-governments indicate that it is necessary to design and implement a certain audit procedure for continuous supervision of business operations, which could find application in local self-government units. There are various control methods and techniques that executives rely on.They are the necessary instrument which is used for measuring and evaluating. Control is also necessary to establish standards of behavior for the individual and business standards as well. (Eremić-Đođić, J., Tomić, A.,2018)

However, by applying such a control procedure, the local government would be well prepared for any type of audit, and therefore a performance audit.

Analyzing the documentation submitted in this research, some of its institutions have found incomplete records that indicate the loss of documents visibility, which may lead to errors in the record of spending the funds. That is why it is necessary to prescribe internal control also in this part. Wherever there is a possible availability or disagreement in the records, it must be covered by internal control. Control mechanisms influence more accurate record keeping, primarily analytical records in the ledgers, reduce the risk of misuse of budget funds.

The following processes are steps of such a procedure that ensures continuous monitoring and implementation of internal business controls in local governments:

1. **Planning**: The supervising area should be selected and the criterion for selecting internal controls should be determined in order to evaluate them and make recommendations for improvements which will gain new benefits, and thus help the competent state institutions to identify risk areas so could be analysed; Consider whether there is an **application of an electronic document** flow that:
   a. unload the work processes in local self-government,
   b. accelerates the flow of documents to clients,
   c. speeds up information about the case as well as the way of submitting the necessary documentation,
   d. **provides accurate tracking of the entire business records.**
2. **Review the Risk**: accurately reviewing and analyzing risk, following the provisions of the COSO model, as follows:
   a. Risk Identification: for each risk, analysis and description should be thoroughly done by filling in the information shown in Table 3.

Table 3. Risk description

The Organizational Part to which the Risk Belongs	Risk Description	Cause of Risk	Consequences of Risk	Objectives of the Organizational Unit

Source: authors (2019)

Using a risk assessment methodology, it is necessary to determine its impact and probability. They are determined for each risk individually, by filling in certain fields in the risk management form as shown in Table 4.

Table 4. Risk Management Form

Risk Assessment – Inherent Risk	Influence			Probability		
	High	Medium	Low	High	Medium	Low
Reasons						

Source: authors (2019)

b. Total risk of an audit is rarely quantitatively determined. The results of the impact and probability risk studies on this way, are presented in the matrix form shown in Table 5.

Table 5. Risk matrix

<table>
<tr><td colspan="2"></td><td colspan="4">Total Risk Assessment</td></tr>
<tr><td rowspan="4">RISK ASSESMENT – INHERENT RISK</td><td>High</td><td rowspan="4">ESTIMATION OF RISKS DETECTION</td><td>High</td><td>Medium</td><td>Low</td></tr>
<tr><td>Medium</td><td>Very low</td><td>Low</td><td>Medium</td></tr>
<tr><td rowspan="2">Low</td><td>Low</td><td>Medium</td><td>Higher</td></tr>
<tr><td>Medium</td><td>Higher</td><td>The highest</td></tr>
</table>

Source: Andrić, M., Krsmanović.,B. & Jakšić, D, 2012.

This will rank the risk and determine whether it is high, medium or low. This creates the condition that the risk is really resolved.

4. **Risk Management** is closely linked to the tolerance that local government has. Namely, after assessing the inherent risks for each risk, it will be considered individually whether it will be tolerated, treated, transfered or abolished.

Risk management is the documentation which is kept and done by filling in the fields in Table 6.

Table 6. Risk solving form

<table>
<tr><td colspan="10">Risk Solve</td></tr>
<tr><td colspan="3">Risk</td><td colspan="2">Procedure With Risk</td><td colspan="2">Risk Solve</td><td>Responsible Person and Organization Unit in Which Responsible Person Works</td><td>Time Period for Resolving the Risk</td><td>Detailed Report About Resolving Risk</td></tr>
<tr><td>Higher</td><td>Medi-um</td><td>Low</td><td>Acceptable</td><td>Unacceptable</td><td>Internal control</td><td>Organization Unit</td><td rowspan="3"></td><td></td><td></td></tr>
<tr><td></td><td></td><td></td><td></td><td></td><td></td><td></td><td></td><td></td></tr>
<tr><td></td><td></td><td></td><td></td><td></td><td></td><td></td><td></td><td></td></tr>
</table>

Source: authors (2019)

When all risks are solved, there is always a certain level of risk that remains after controlling activities that eliminate the risk itself. That remaining part, cannot be completely eliminated and can occur. It is called residual risk. Therefore, it is necessary to find activities that would be undertaken if it happen. In this case, it is necessary to make a plan for situations that cannot be foreseen but can still occur.

5. **Risk monitoring or Reporting**: Involves the part of the procedure in which the holder is determined for each risk and defines a hierarchy of its responsibility. In this step it is necessary to define one or two indicators that would be put under control, on the basis of which the risk would be easier to monitor. Risk assessment should be carried out regularly, every 12 to 24 months. According to the requirements of Section 404 of the Sarbanes-Oxley Act, it is necessary to carry out an internal control evaluation every year to achieve compliance with Section 404. Suitable performance of this

assessment is not easy so it is not often performend. (Singleton, T.W., Singleton,A.J., Bologna, J. & Lindquist, R, 2006).

6. **Monitoring:** The auditor makes the internal control plan, the method of its implementation and the work program. Conducting a preliminary examination, the internal controller finds the volume of the control, identify potential problems and consider whether or not a detailed control plan is required. Control plan consists the testing subject and control objectives, defines the scope and organization of control and defines the quality controls, deadlines and means by which they will perform the audit and the criteria by which they will evaluate its quality.
7. Check whether in their work they have and act on the following acts:
    a. Statute;
    b. Decision on Local Communities;
    c. Local action plan for young people for a specific period ________;
    d. Rulebook on Budget Accounting;
    e. Rulebook on the use of official vehicles;
    f. Local Sustainable Development Strategy of the Municipality _____ for the period _______;
    g. Government (Municipal) Bodies Fact Sheet;
    h. Decision on fees for use of public lands;
    i. Decision on local utility taxes;
    j. Decision on environmental compensation;
    k. Decision on the amount of municipal property tax rate ___________;
    l. Rulebook on the use of mobile phones;
    m. Internal acts governing the manner, conditions, procedures and criteria for the use and use of representation funds;
    n. A general act governing the conditions, criteria, manner and procedure of allocation of funds;
    o. A legal act establishing the right to assistance for the elimination of damage due to natural disasters (Article 56, Paragraph 2 of the Law on the Budget System);
    p. General acts and regulations governing other rights in relation to the rights prescribed by the Law on Financial Support to Families with Children, in accordance with the competences of local self-government bodies prescribed by the Law on Local Self-Government, adopted by the Municipal Assembly at the proposal of the Municipal Council;
    q. Acts on disposal of property and property owned by the municipality on the basis of which the contracts will be concluded;
    r. Risk management strategy, and other internal acts.
8. Establish record controlling and make their comparability such as:
    a. Determine the alignment of the 2018 Census List and the 2018 Budget Accounts Decisions of specific Municipalities published in the Official Gazette:
    b. Compare the gross balance sheet (closing sheet) and the Decision on the final statement of the municipal budget for 2018 adopted and published in the Official Gazette of the Municipality: as of January 1, 2019. ;
    c. Compare the records of the “List of short-term and long-term claims and financial placements with the balance as of 31.12.2018”, closing sheet for the period 01.01.2019-30.09.2019. and “List of earmarked assets as of December 31, 2018” in the municipality;
    d. Determine what records have a substantive check of the data monitored on a daily basis with monthly reporting, so we could monitor more accurately the realization of funds spent on public

procurement and compare them with the approved procurement plan, contracts, invoices; and other records.

These are just some of the many controls that need to be designed and applied to local government work.

9. **The internal control report** should be reliable and should contain: objectives, scope, methodology, sources used, findings, conclusions and recommendations, and at the same time it should be understandable and clear. At the same time, the principles of suitability, completeness, reliability and credibility, accuracy, impartiality, comparability, accessibility, persuasiveness, relevance, clarity, scope of reporting and intelligibility must be respected.
10. **Continuous surveillance** is the last step in controlling a business and is a preventive model for early detection and prevention of business errors. Monitoring - is an activity that is carried out concealed and continuously in order to gather information about people, places and things to determine the activity and the identity of persons suspected of behavior who may break (or not), civil and criminal law. (Hoopwood, S.,W. Leiner, J.Jay & Young, R.G. 2008)

In this part, it would be good to design a local government team to take care of and assist in the successful implementation of all recommendations by any type of control, especially the audit, thus eliminating any possible risk of mistakes being repeated in the future. However, many auditors are hesitant even today, and being confused by the concept of continuous oversight, this approach has not become widely accepted in the audit profession. One of the main reasons for misunderstanding is the term supervision itself, which is seen as a function of management. The second barrier is early attempts to apply continuous monitoring to both the current audit (real-time transaction review) and the concept of recurring audits, but not in real time. Most audit organizations do not yet have the capacity for real-time analysis.(D. Coderre, 2011)

The steps of this audit procedure are a safe way to apply an adequate control framework in the operations of local governments and, with the help of its continuous oversight, complete the performance audit process. All that remains is to solve dilemma about the necessary costs for this type of control. Although we believe that a cost analysis could provide useful information in terms of different budgetary implications (Perin, J., Eremić-Đođić, J., Potić, Z., Zarić, B., Sekeruš, V., Perin, B., 2018) in this case it is sufficient to consider the benefits it provides and put them in relation to the legislation.

Operating in accordance with the law, preserving the assets of state institutions, local governments and other organizations is a key task of any successful business. However, there are few studies on the use of resources and costs (Perin, J., Eremić-Đođić, J., Potić, Z., Zarić, B., Sekeruš, V., Perin, B., 2018) for local government, which can be used for this purpose. Considering that financial management and control are an area of implementation in local governments, practice shows thatthere have been no comprehensive studies on the use of resources and associated costs (Perin, J., Eremić-Đođić, J., Potić, Z., Zarić, B., Sekeruš, V., Perin, B., 2018)so far that we can accept or disrupt their results. That is why this research is a novelty because it speaks about the steps that need to be taken in order to establish continuous supervision over financial management and control in local governments, which, in addition to numerous advantages, would definitely ensure the tracking of documents which we can say with certainty that signifies both innovations in Serbia and relevant developing countries. (Perin, J., Eremić-Đođić, J., Potić, Z., Zarić, B., Sekeruš, V., Perin, B., 2018)

Internal auditors / controllers who provide consulting services to their organizations are in a position where they can contribute to the improvement of the overall control system. The data they collect through any type of consulting assignment can almost always be used to develop control throughout the organization. In addition, an increasing number of audit teams are giving management advice on designing new processes and systems. (M. Stanišić, 2015)

This dual role: advisory and control will be crowned with good recommendations that are necessary to be:

Fully supported by findings and conclusions as the only relevant basis;

- Clear and precise recommendations;
- Understandable and detailed;
- Suggestive procedures need to be clarified;
- Their practical feasibility is necessary;
- The benefit must be evident;
- Design an activity that will continuously monitor the implementation of the recommendations and benefits of them, etc.

The management of a legal entity has the primary responsibility for designing, implementing and overseeing the operation of internal control systems, with a view to pursuing the specific objectives of the organization, including the prevention and detection of criminal acts. (A. Petković, 2010)

That is why this procedure of continuous monitoring and control in the function of performance audit provides the answers to the following questions:

- whether the adopted procedures, business policies, decisions have been followed;
- whether they are implemented in accordance with the regulations, taking into account the economy and efficiency of business;
- whether the adopted documents have been implemented in an appropriate manner, which will be proven by the preparation of various analyzes and reports;
- review the performance of local government employees or the government program implemented through an appropriate package of measures to evaluate its success.

SOLUTIONS AND RECOMMENDATIONS

The performance audit in the function of the principles of economy is importance for the state apparatus because it is the instrument by which the state acquires control over the spending of all budgetary resources.

It also clarifies the role of control local government units, the role of the financial management and control system, the responses it provides, what internal control is, and how to manage it.

The results we get, we use to make the procedure of continuous supervision and control of business operations in local self-government units. This procedure should be periodically used in order to be revised in accordance to the regulations.

FUTURE RESEARCH DIRECTIONS

This paper is a base for future research regarding the introduction of new procedural rules for the application of continuous business monitoring and control in the function of the performance auditing in local governments.

Developing the procedural steps as a type of supervision and control of business in local governments provides answers to unsolved problems encountered in literature and practice, and outlines the perspective and possible directions for the further development of the audit profession. Therefore, this research provides useful information on specific solutions that can reduce the risk in local government operations, thus preventing the consequences of negative business on each state's budget.

CONCLUSION

The work and development of local governments directly affects the development of the state. Since these are institutions whose work is of public interest, the whole public is interested in it. This is why the state strives to put the entire activity of local self-government under control.

In addition to the regular control that local governments have by the state, it is necessary to design an additional activity that will help them to be managed with as much security as possible. This type of management is provided by a system of financial management and control that is also their legal obligation.

Besides the analyzed facts obtained through the research in this paper, it is necessary to point out the insufficient training of employees in local self-governments when it comes to financial management and control. It has been evaluated in the direction of moving from weak towards medium and it is necessary to intensify activities to fulfill this legal obligation.

Since the performance audit provides an explanation of whether the local government based its business on economic principles and in accordance with the adopted planning indicators, continuous controls can serve as the best instrument for this purpose. This in fact points to the justification of this research, which has shown that more effort is needed to ensure positive results when the responses to the recommendations are based on the audit findings in question. Continuity of control has also been assessed as weak, which is why this research has designed and created a continuous monitoring and control procedure that, assists activities which ultimately move towards the function of perfprmance audit.

Since it is still a novelty, after this research we will look at the effects of its implementation in the future.

ACKNOWLEDGMENT

This research received no specific grant from any funding agency in the public, commercial, or not-for-profit sectors.

REFERENCES

Andrić, M., Krsmanović, B., & Jakšić, D. (2012). Revizija teorija I praksa, V izmenjenoi dopunjeno izdanje [Revision theory and practice, edited edition]. "Proleter", A.D. Bečej, Subotica.

Coderre, D. (2011). Internal Audit, Efficiency Through Automation. John Wiley & Sons, Inc.

Dutta, K. S. (2013). *Statistical Techniques For Forensic Accounting. In Understanding The Theory and Application of Data Analysis*. Upper Saddle River, NJ: FT Press.

Eremić-Đođić, J., & Tomić, A. (2018). Development of the finance model for tourism of local goverments in the function of the performance audit. In *3th International Scientific Conference* (pp. 692-707). University of Крагујевац, Republic of Serbia.

Eremić-Đođić, J., Laban, B., Bošnjak, I., Ćirić, I., Škatarić, G., & Sedlak, O. (2018). An Audit of the Financing Models for Agricultural Housejolds in Local Goverments in Serbia. *Green Room Sessions 2018. Internationa GEA (Geo Eco – Eco Agro) Conference Book of Proceedings, 2,* 301-317.

Eremić-Đođić, J., Laban. B.& Tomić, A. (2017). Forenzička revizija-sprečavanje, otkrivanje i odgovornosti za finansijske kriminalne radnje u kompanijama, časopis „Poslovna ekonomija", Univerzitet Edukons, Sr.Kamenica, godina XI, broj 2 [Forensic Audit - Prevention, Detection and Responsibility for Financial Crimes in Companies]. *Journal of Business Economics, Educational University, 11*(2).

Perin, J., Eremić-Đođić, J., Potić, Z., Zarić, B., Sekeruš, V., & Perin, B. (2018). The cost of hospital treatment of advanced stage lung cancer patients in a developing South East European country. *International Journal of Cancer, 9*(17), 3038-3045.

Petković, A. (2010), *Forenzička revizija, Kriminalne radnje u finansijskim izveštajima* [Forensic Audit, Criminal Investigation in Financial Statements]. Novi Sad, Republic of Serbia: Orfelin Publishing.

Singleton, T. W., Singleton, A. J., Bologna, J., & Lindquist, R. (2006). *Fraud Auditing and Forensic Accounting*. John Wiley & Sons, Inc.

Stanišić, M. (2015). *Interna kontrola i revizija* [Internal Control and Audit]. Belgrade, Republic of Serbia: Singidunum University.

ADDITIONAL READING

Bellino, C., Wells, J., & Hunt, S. (2007). *GTAG Auditing Aplication Controls*. Alamonte Springs, FL: The Institute of Internal Auditors.

Coderre, D. (2011.), Internal Audit, Efficiency Through Automation, The Institute of Internal Auditors, John Wiley & Sons, Inc. translated bySerbian Association of Accountants and Auditors, Belgrade, Republika Srbija: Serbian Association of Accountants and Auditors.

Dutta, K. S. (2013). *Statistical Techniques For Forensic Accounting, Understanding The Theory and Application of Data Analysis* (p. 07458). Upper Saddle River, New Jersey: FT Press.

Eremić-Đođić, I. Bošnjak, S.Rakočević, S.Popović, O.Sedlak, Z.Cirić & A.Tomić, (2019). *Application of financial management and control in Institutions of education in The Republic of Serbia*, (1st-3RD of July, 2019., 11th International Conference on Education and nwew Learning Technologies page 4382-4388.), Edulearn 19, Palma (Spain), IATED Academy.

Eremić-Đođić, J., Laban, B., Bošnjak, I., Ćirić, I., Škatarić, G., & Sedlak, O. (2018)., An Audit of the Financing Models for Agricultural Housejolds in Local Goverments in Serbia, *Green Room Sessions 2018. Internationa GEA(Geo Eco – Eco Agro) Conference Book of Proceedings 2,* 2018., (pp 301-317.) 1-3. Novembar, Podgoroica, Montenegro, publisher: University of Montengro, Faculty of Philosophy, Geography.

Eremić-Đođić, J., & Tomić, A. (2018). *Development of the finance model for tourism of local goverments in the function of the performance audit*, (3th International Scientific Conference, 31 May-2 June, 2018. god., pp 692-707). Publisher:University of Kragujevac, Republic of Serbia.

Hoopwood, S.,W. Leiner, J.Jay, & Young, R.G. (2008), The McGraw-Hill Companies, Inc.

Singleton, T. W., Singleton, A. J., Bologna, J., & Lindquist, R. (2006). *Fraud Auditing and Forensic Accounting*. John Wiley&Sons, Inc.

Stanišić, M. (2015.), *Interna kontrola i revizija,*Beograd, Republika Srbija: Univerzitet Singidunum

Wallace, A., W. (2004). Internal Control Guide. New Jerk: John Wiley & Son.

KEY TERMS AND DEFINITIONS

Business Plan: A plan for spending the organization funds that has been accepted by the state and should be complied with.

Continuous Control: Control that continuously checks the application of procedures and regulations in an entity's business discovering the weaknesses of individuals, parts, and functions at the same time.

Control Procedure: A procedure for controlling specific business activities designed for a specific purpose.

COSO: Committee of Sponsoring Organizations of the Treadway Commission.

Earmarked Funds: Funds whose spending and purpose are determined by the contract and the decision of the local self-government unit.

Local Government: Local self-government is an autonomous system of local community management, which is based on inner parts of the state territory.

Performance Audit: It means examining the use of budgetary and other public funds to obtain sufficient, adequate and reliable evidence to report. It explains whether the assets of the audited have been used in accordance with the principles of economy, efficiency and effectiveness and in accordance with the intended goals.

Procedure: Issued process activities (in this case the control process) that takes place in the local government.

Risk: Implies that a particular activity will not be successfully performed because there is a lack of control over that activity, which can cause consequences and has to be removed from that activity.

Chapter 18
Digitalization of the Development of the Fuel and Energy Balance of Russia's Northern Territories:
Example of the Republic of Sakha (Yakutia)

Izabella Elyakova
North-Eastern Federal University, Russia

Aleksandr Elyakov
North-Eastern Federal University, Russia

ABSTRACT

The urgency of the energy budget research practice in the Republic of Sakha (Yakutia) on settlements with software for effective formation, implementation, management, monitoring, analysis, evaluation, rapid response, and strategic management of the entire complex of the energy budget is substantiated. The chapter reveals the lack of problems of unified methodology for the development of the energy budget and the use of different fundamentals of its preparation. The necessity of using digital technologies to develop a control system for a complex network of production and consumption of fuel and energy resources is rationalized.

INTRODUCTION

This chapter of the book demonstrates the importance of energy security for all, without exception, the world's northern regions with severe climatic conditions. Hence, it means a need to develop optimal and long-term fuel and energy balances (FEB) of the region in the context of each population item and consumer groups. In the long term, it is possible to effectively develop the fuel and energy balance for

DOI: 10.4018/978-1-7998-4601-7.ch018

each region, which takes into account the fuel and energy potential of neighboring territories only using digital technology programs.

This work aims at compiling a large number of digital and analytical materials on the production and consumption of energy resources; analysis and assessment of the effectiveness of their use; compiling and selecting from many forecast scenarios for the development and use of different types of fuel and energy the one that is the most effective in a specific period of time, in the context of each settlement and consumer groups, including households, organizations and large industrial companies.

The main goal of such a digital FEB is to provide data analysis and digital modeling to efficiently generate, implement and modify a prospective FEB for the long-term period, for example, 100 years ahead. It is important even in using such types of energy as the friendliest for the environment for 100-150 years ahead. Digital technological software enables future generations to quickly respond and adapt the digital FEB. It will be modified to meet the conditions of the global energy and power markets, global and regional energy sectors, including potential generation, on a large scale, of renewable energy.

The chapter identifies the lack of a unified methodology for the development of FEB, the use of different fundamental principles of its compilation. It presents examples of compiling an information and analytical database for fuel and energy indicators in the Western economic zone of the Republic of Sakha (Yakutia) in the context of its villages and various consumer groups, using the example of the region. The balance development stages for settlements in the region are presented.

The chapter substantiates the use of digital technologies to develop a control system for a complex network of production and consumption of fuel and energy resources. Using a digital fuel and energy balance facilitates to expansive and efficient monitoring, analyzing, and evaluation the effectiveness of each type of local, regional or imported energy resources. It also enables operational and strategic management of the entire fuel and energy complex of the regions, taking into account the long-term energy needs of consumers. The ultimate goal of the fuel and energy balance is the continuous and reliable supply of high-quality and efficient fuel and energy resources to all consumers for the long-term period.

BACKGROUND

The strategy for sustainable development of regions provides for the prevention and protection from existing and new dangers and threats. All kinds of challenges and threats imply the creation of appropriate security systems, including an energy security system in a particular region, taking into account the development of an integrated system of social, economic and energy security across the country and each territory. One of the priority factors of sustainable social and economic development of the region that determine the life of economic facilities and the standard of living of the population is to ensure its energy security.

Security is the state of an object in the system of its connections in terms of its ability to self-preserve and develop in the face of internal and external threats, as well as the actions of unpredictable and difficult to predict factors (Ilyin et al., 2015). Ensuring the energy security of the region is a primary state task, since it is so important for any state to reliably provide its citizens with heat and light, and to freeze life-supporting facilities without any special threats or dangers, especially in the extreme climatic conditions of the North and the Arctic. Therefore, the State energy policy and Energy strategies for sustainable energy development of the regions and countries are based on a competent compilation of fuel and energy balances of these territories, taking into account the mutual flows of energy and fuel for effective interaction to ensure the reliability of energy supply to consumers.

The energy budget contains representative and systematic information on the flows of all types of energy resources and energy between the stages of production, transformation, transport, distribution, storage and final use (Zyryanov, 2011). Despite the fact that the role of the Energy budget is realized by the administrations of the subjects of the Federation, its development at the regional level is currently a big problem, despite the solid experience gained by our country in this area (Zyryanov, 2011).

Currently, according to the Protocol of the meeting of Prime Minister of the Republic of Sakha (Yakutia) Solodov V.V. "On the effectiveness of the organization of cargoes delivery to the territory of the Republic of Sakha (Yakutia)" of 29.03.19. Federal Research Center "Siberian Branch of the Russian Academy of Sciences prepared draft technical specifications for R&D "Fuel and energy balance of the Republic of Sakha (Yakutia) for the period until 2050" and in accordance with the Protocol of the meeting of the 1st Deputy Prime Minister of the RS (Y) Kolodeznikov A.Z. on the project for the implementation of research "Energy strategy of the Republic of Sakha (Yakutia) for the period up to 2032 with a target vision up to 2050" of 13.09.10.

Both projects propose to create the Energy budget of the Republic until 2050 and only differ, in my opinion, in different key approaches to the fundamental research – in the first project in the application, and in the second project - the refusal to create the Energy budget of the Republic with software and in the Energy budget development in the context of settlements of the Republic (1 project) and in general by regions of the Republic (2 project). This leads to the question: which of the projects will be more effective for producers and consumers of energy resources, for local governments and Executive authorities of the Republic for the interaction of fuel and energy enterprises and utilities with interrelated industries and the social sphere?

JUSTIFICATION FOR DIGITALIZATION OF FEB

The development of the energy strategy of the state and its regions is based on the preparation of a prospective energy budget, which in our opinion should include the following interrelated stages of effective formation, implementation, management, monitoring, analysis, evaluation, rapid response and strategic management of the entire complex of the energy budget. Only transition to digital technologies, devices of management and rendering of services of the power enterprises and municipal services will allow managing flexibly the flows of energy and deliveries and consumption of fuel. We need control systems for a complex network of production and consumption of fuel and energy resources, which will require the consideration of a huge number of factors, and according to the experts - that is not yet under the force of existing information algorithms (a precisely defined sequence of actions for the performer that were performed according to the strictly defined rules that leading to the solution of the problem). But the age of technology does not stand still. The main thing is to start developing our own software corresponding to high-tech automation tools and our young scientists-programmers of NEFU together with specialists in the housing sector are ready to work on the development of appropriate software of the Energy balance in the Republic of Sakha (Yakutia).

The methodological basis for the development of a perspective energy budget of the Republic of Sakha (Yakutia) is as follows:

- in the need to solve new problems of transformation of industries of the regions. It is the implementation of the digital economy or the digitalization of all branches of the fuel and energy complex of the Republic of Sakha (Yakutia), which is aimed at using digital technologies to raise the efficiency of the energy sector and related industries for the smooth and reliable provision of fuel and energy resources (FER) consumers in the Republic and adjacent territories;
- In justifying the novelty and efficiency of achieving the goal and task of creating the Energy budget of the Republic of Sakha (Yakutia) in a section of settlements with its software on formation, implementation, monitoring, the analysis, forecasting and response for timely strategic, tactical and operational management of all complex of providing production and consumption with fuel and energy resources (FER);
- in the need to create a basic Energy budget in the software, to assess the effectiveness of the use of fuel and energy resources in each locality and in general in municipalities and in the Republic, taking into account the existing and prospective resource and production potential of the fuel and energy complex and transport enterprises.

The need to use digital technologies is caused, first of all, by the fact that software, computerization, and digitization in general are needed to develop a management system for a complex network of production and consumption of fuel and energy resources (FER). With the help of a digital FEB, it is possible to monitor, analyze, and evaluate the efficiency of using each type of local and imported energy resources, as well as rapid response and strategic management of the entire fuel and energy complex of the regions, taking into account the long-term needs for energy resources of consumers. The ultimate goal of developing a digital FEB is the uninterrupted and reliable supply of high-quality and efficient fuel and energy resources to all consumers in the long term.

STUDY OF BASIC FEB CREATION IN WESTERN ECONOMIC ZONE OF THE REPUBLIC OF SAKHA (YAKUTIA) IN TERMS OF SETTLEMENTS AND GROUPS OF CONSUMERS

Results of the analysis of energy production and consumption in the Western economic zone of the Republic of Sakha (Yakutia) for 2016 and estimation of electric energy consumption in settlements of seven districts in WEZ of RS(Y) for 2012-2019 years will become the basis for the long-term perspective fuel and energy balance of the Republic of Sakha (Yakutia) with consideration to its cost indicators in the selection of effective energy resources and energy sources with the aim of the energy supply of each municipal district in terms of its settlements, taking into account the integrated efficiency of their production and consumption in general in the Republic.

The volume assessment of production and consumption of energy resources in the Western economic zone of the Republic of Sakha (Yakutia) for 2016, may be the basis for the future drafting of a long-term fuel and energy balance of the Republic taking into account the value of the indicators for choice of efficient energy and power sources to supply power to each municipal district in the context of its settlements based on the integrated efficiency of their production and consumption in the Republic.

In 2017, we have implemented the section 3.8. "Analysis of consumption and production of fuel and energy resources in order to develop fuel and energy balance in the Republic of Sakha (Yakutia) considering the development of alternative energy", research work under the state contract N° 5327

"Evaluation, the main trends in natural and socio-economic status, human potential of the Western economic zone of the Republic of Sakha (Yakutia)". As a result, the basic fuel and energy balance for settlements of municipal districts of the Western economic zone of the Republic of Sakha (Yakutia) was created in 2016 (table 1).

In 2017, according to the results of the study on the implementation of research work under the state contract No. 5327 "Assessment, the main trends in the natural and socio-economic condition and human potential of the Western Economic Zone of the Republic of Sakha (Yakutia)" section 3.8. Analysis of consumption and production of fuel and energy resources in order to develop the Energy budget of the Republic considering the development of alternative energy was created a database of prospective Energy budget in the context of settlements in the two conditional economic zones in the Eastern Economic Zone and the Western Economic Zone of the Republic of Sakha (Yakutia). Based on the analysis of the volume of production and consumption of energy resources in the settlements of seven districts of the Western Economic Zone, its assessment in quantitative and cost indicators for municipal districts is presented (table 1).

On the basis of the treated analysis of the energy resources production and consumption of settlements in 7 districts in the Western economic zone is the basic energy balance in the municipal areas in the West economic zone of the Republic of Sakha (Yakutia) in quantitative and cost indicators for municipal areas.

Table 1 shows the actual established fuel and energy balance for the 2016 year: production and consumption of fuel and energy resources for all seven areas of the Western economic zone of the RS(Y) in natural and cost terms.

In this work we introduce an example of analysis of the volume of electricity consumption by the main groups of consumers in the settlements of the West for 2012 and 2019 years, given in natural and cost indicators for estimation of its use efficiency by consumers.

The volume of electricity consumption by the main consumer groups in the Western energy district is shown in table 2.

In 2019, the largest consumers of electricity in the WEZ are enterprises that produce and distribute electricity (33.8%). In 2000, the largest share of consumption was occupied by companies engaged in mining and manufacturing (57%). The second place in terms of consumption is occupied by the population (27.5%), and in 2000 this figure was equal to 7.1%. There is a big change in the structure of consumers.

The sharpest decrease in consumption is observed in the agricultural sector, which, unfortunately, implies a reduction in agricultural complexes in the Republic, and not the effective use of electricity associated with the intensification (through the use of more advanced means and methods of production) of local products.

The largest consumers in the WEZ are AK ALROSA (PJSC), Transneftenergo LLC and Teploenergoservice JSC (Vilyui branch), which are shown in table 4.

In 2012-2019, there was a sharp decrease in the volume of electricity consumption by PJSC "ALROSA" from 961 to 237 million kW. This is mainly due to the structural changes in the diamond mining company, the release of non-core subsidiaries and structural divisions from their main activities by transferring them or converting them into independent joint-stock companies with the sale of the share of the parent company's shares or retaining the corresponding share in newly created enterprises. As well as it was due to the diversification of crude diamond production and modernization and improvement of mining equipment and mechanisms. In 2019, the decrease in electricity consumption of LLC "Transneftenergo" was due to the energy consumption from the wholesale energy and capacity market.

Table 1. Basic fuel and energy balance for settlements of municipal districts of the Western economic zone in the Republic of Sakha (Yakutia) for the 2016 year.

Indicator	Units	Mirninsky District	Lensky District	Olekminsky District	Suntarsky District	Nyurbinsky District	Verkhnevilyuysky District	Vilyuysky District	Total in WEZ
Production of Fuel and Energy Resources									
Electricity	Million kWh	1762	326	144	130	87	26	35	2548
Thermal energy	Thousand Gcal	1749	552	219	127	195	123	247	3211
Natural gas	Million cub. m	220	50					1735	2005
Oil	Thousand tons	1207	8894						10101
Coal	Thousand tons				26	25			51
Gas liquid	Thousand tons	3	2					107	112
Fuel and Energy Consumption									
Electricity	Million kWh	1762	326	144	130	87	26	35	2548
	Million RUB	8822	1649	1039	277	280	122	179	10673
Thermal energy	Thousand Gcal	1406	448	177	101	150	95	173	2550
	Million RUB	4868	1992	867	686	979	509	871	10772
Including Boiler and Furnace Fuel, in Total									
Natural gas	Million cub. m	171	59				12	32	274
	Million RUB	876	432				45	123	1476
Oil	Thousand tons	4	12	17	5	13	0		52
	Million RUB	68	227	290	82	187	2		856
Coal	Thousand tons	2	2	20	29	28	8		89
	Million RUB	4	10	84	66	88	29		282
Gas liquid	Thousand tons				0,1	0,8	1,1	4,2	6
	Million RUB				2	13	16	63	95
Electricity for electric heating	Million kWh	501		1		3			505
	Million RUB	1575		3		13			1591
Firewood	Thousand cub.m		6	20			0,3		26
	Million RUB		6	16			0		22
Diesel fuel	Thousand tons	0	1	0,0		0,0	0	0	1
	Million RUB	5	40	0		1	0	9	56

The analysis of energy consumption in the regions of the Western economic zone of the Republic of Sakha (Yakutia), including by consumer groups for the period 2000-2019 is given in table 5.

On the basis of the analysis of the dynamics of electricity consumption in the WEZ areas in terms of natural and cost indicators over the last 7 years, it can be stated that electricity consumption has increased significantly by 402%, mainly due to the growth index in housing and communal infrastructure and due to the growth of population consumption by 35%. At the same time, there is a sharp decrease in electricity consumption by other industrial enterprises (the reasons for the sharp decrease will be considered and justified in each particular area below). Respectively growth in incomes (the revenues of PJSC Yakutskenergo - the main producer of electric energy in areas) is connected with the growth of electricity tariffs, higher growth rates of which occurred for the population for this studied period (88%).

The analysis of energy consumption in the settlements of the Mirninsky district of the Western economic zone of the Republic of Sakha (Yakutia), for the period 2000-2019 is shown in table 6.

Table 2. Volumes of electricity consumption by the main consumer groups in the settlements of the Western energy district for 2000–2019, million kWh.

Western Energy District	2000	2015	2016	2017	2018	2019	2017/2000, in%	2018/ 2000, in%	2019/ 2000, in %
Electricity consumption by indusry, total	2519	2467	2548	1771	2163	1514	70	86	60
including:									
- agriculture, hunting and forestry	164	10	9	9	10	7	6	6	4
- mining	1945	1407	1453	228	294	203	12	15	10
- manufacturing		93	95	93	72	78			
- production and distribution of electricity	-	136	197	520	494	511			
- building		6	11	15	16	20			
- transport and communication	62	311	238	324	674	47	523	1086	77
- other utilities and social services	17	33	34	42	41	44	249	241	258
- others	151	151	152	142	144	186	94	96	123
- population	180	320	357	397	418	417	221	232	232

Table 3. Share of electricity consumption by major consumer groups in the WEZ for 2000–2019, mln kWh

Western Energy District	2000	2010	2015	2016	2017	2018	2019	2017 / 2000, %	2018 / 2000, %	2019 / 2000, %
Electricity consumption by type of economic activity, including					100	100	100	100	100	100
including:										
- agriculture, hunting and forestry	6,5	1,1	0,4	0,35	0,5	0,5	0,5	8	7	7
- mining	77,2	61,6	57,0	57,0	12,9	13,6	13,4	17	18	17
- manufacturing		4,1	3,8	3,7	5,2	3,3	5,1			
- production and distribution of electricity		8,9	5,5	7,7	29,4	22,9	33,8			
- building		0,5	0,2	0,4	0,8	0,8	1,3			
- transport and communication	2,4	1,3	12,6	9,3	18,3	31,1	3,1	744	1265	127
- the provision of other utilities and social services	0,7	3,0	1,3	1,3	2,4	1,9	2,9	354	281	430
- other types of economic activity	6,0	7,5	6,1	6,0	8,0	6,7	12,3	134	111	205
- population	7,1	12,1	13,0	14,0	22,4	19,3	27,6	314	270	386

Table 4. The list of major consumers of electricity of PJSC "Yakutskenergo" at WEZ for 2017-2019

ZER	2012		2018		2019	
	m. kWh	m. rub	m. kWh	m. rub	m. kWh	m. rub.
Population, total	308	308	418	972	417	1009
including Electric heating *	57	57	221	171	230	202
Budget, total	65	65	58	243	56	305
Federal budget	9	9	8	31	7	37
Republican budget	18	18	16	68	15	85
Local budget	38	38	34	145	34	183
Housing and communal services enterprises, including:	160	160	524	2027	519	2732
TES JSC (Vilyui branch)	126	126	100	399	95	516
Others, including:	1 161	1 161	1163	4681	522	2703
PJSC AK ALROSA, total	961	961	235	929	237	1245
Transneftenergo LLC total, including:	85	85	638	2442	10	27
Oil pumping station -14	85	85	143	511		
Oil pumping station -13			134	479		
Oil pumping station -12			266	1054		
Oil pumping station -11			93	392		
Oil pumping station -8.9					9	20
Distribution network			2	6	2	7
TOTAL			2163	7922	1513	6749

In 2019, the Mirninsky district of the Western economic zone of the Republic of Sakha (Yakutia), more electricity was consumed than all other settlements in Udachny (40.6%), as well as in Mirny (28.4%) and in Aikhal (11.7%). This is due to the fact that the main industrial enterprises of PJSC "ALROSA" (the flagship of the Republic's economy) are located in the center of this district in Udachny and Aikhal. For the same period in 2012, more than all other settlements electric energy was consumed in the Mirny (64.3%), as well as in Aikhal village (21%) and in Udachny village (37.6%). There was also a large increase in average electricity tariffs in the district only for the population (62%).

The analysis of energy consumption in localities in the Lensky district of the Western economic zone of the Republic of Sakha (Yakutia), for the period 2000-2019 is shown in table 7.

For the period 2012-2019, in the Lensky district of the Western economic zone of the Republic of Sakha (Yakutia), electric energy was consumed the most of all other settlements in Lenks (73,5%), as well as in Vitim (11.2%) and Peleduy (10.3%). This is due to the fact that the main industrial enterprises PJSC "Surgutneftegaz", LLC "Transneftenergo" are located in the center of Lenskiy district.

The analysis of energy consumption in the settlements of the Olekminsky district of the Western economic zone of the Republic of Sakha (Yakutia) for the period 2000-2019 is given in table 8.

For the period 2012-2019 in the Olyokminsky district of the Western economic zone of the Republis of Sakha (Yakutia), electric energy was consumed in the district center Olekminsk (92,1%) more than any other villages. This is what the population and enterprises are located in the centre of the area and in the village of Peleduy.

Table 5. Analysis of energy consumption for all seven Western economic zones (WEZ) of the Republic of Sakha (Yakutia), for the period 2012-2019.

Consumers	2012			2019			2019/2012		
	Volume	Revenue	Tariff	Volume	Revenue	Tariff	Volume	Revenue	Tariff
	Thousand kWh	Thousand rubles	Rubles/ kWt	Thousand kWh	Thousand rubles.	Rubles/ kWt	%	%	%
Western Economic Zone									
TOTAL	1695	6508	3,84	1514	6749	4,28	89	104	111
Population	308	577	1,87	417	1 010	3,41	135	175	182
Budget	65	275	4,26	56	304	4,48	87	111	105
Enterprises of housing and utilities infrastructure	37	160	4,28	519	2 732	4,37	1402	1708	102
OTHER	1285	5497	4,28	522	2 702	4,32	41	49	101
Mirny District									
TOTAL	1233	4875	3,96	933	4786	4,28	76	98	108
Population, total	115	243	2,10	74	303	3,41	64	124	162
Budget, total	20	82	4,07	17	90	4,48	84	110	110
Enterprises of housing and utilities infrastructure	1	6	4,03	467	2448	4,37	46680	40795	108
Other	1096	4544	4,15	375	1946	4,32	34	43	104
Lensky District									
TOTAL	132	549	4,15	177	792	4,46	134	144	108
Population, total	53	132	2,49	60	190	3,20	112	144	128
Budget, total	11	53	4,85	9	51	5,42	85	96	112
Enterprises of housing and utilities infrastructure enterprises	7	33	4,75	22	118	5,41	310	356	114
Other	61	331	5,39	87	433	4,99	142	131	93
Olekminsky District									
TOTAL	129	582	4,5	76	247	3,25	59	42	72
Population, total	21	51	2,41	47	92	1,95	225	181	81
Budget, total	5	26	4,75	4	21	5,41	78	81	114
Enterprises of housing and utilities infrastructure	5	23	4,78	7	37	5,50	136	163	115
Other	98	482	4,92	18	96	5,36	18	20	109

continues on following page

Table 5. Continued

Consumers	2012			2019			2019/2012		
	Volume	Revenue	Tariff	Volume	Revenue	Tariff	Volume	Revenue	Tariff
	Thousand kWh	Thousand rubles	Rubles/ kWt	Thousand kWh	Thousand rubles.	Rubles/ kWt	%	%	%
Nyurba District									
TOTAL	62	170	2,76	112	317	2,37	181	186	86
Population, total	33	45	1,38	78	132	1,42	236	294	103
Budget, total	8	33	4,08	8	46	4,58	106	141	112
Enterprises of housing and utilities infrastructure	9	38	4,05	9	50	4,58	102	133	113
Other	12	55	4,66	17	88	4,41	139	160	95
Suntar District									
TOTAL	86	158	1,85	144	298	1,72	167	189	93
Population, total	61	52	0,86	120	163	1,13	196	313	131
Budget total	11	44	4,04	10	53	4,62	87	121	114
Enterprises of housing and utilities infrastructure	5	21	4,04	5	28	4,63	100	132	115
Other	9	41	4,64	10	55	4,68	108	133	101
Verkhnevilyuiskiy District									
TOTAL	23	71	3,08	35	132	3,125	153	186	101
Population, total	12	23	1,96	22	61	2,28	186	266	116
Budget, total	4	16	4,07	4	21	4,55	98	133	112
Enterprises of housing and utilities infrastructure	4	16	4,06	4	21	4,59	93	128	113
Other	4	17	4,65	5	29	4,55	133	170	98
Vilyuiskiy District									
TOTAL	30	102	3,38	36	177	4,05	121	173	120
Population, total	13	30	2,27	17	69	3,46	128	230	152
Budget, total	5	20	4,06	4	21	4,55	78	107	112
Enterprises of housing and utilities infrastructure	6	23	4,07	6	31	4,57	94	134	112
Other	6	27	4,66	10	56	4,53	171	206	97

Table 6. Analysis of energy consumption by the settlements in the Mirninsky district for the period 2012-2019.

Consumers	2012			2019			2019/2012		
	Volume	Revenue	Tariff	Volume	Revenue	Tariff	Volume	Revenue	Tariff
	Thousand kWh	Thousand rubles.	Rubles/ kWt	Thousand kWh	Thousand rubles.	Rubles/ kWt	%	%.	%
TOTAL	1232585	4874949	3,96	932785	4786146	4,28	76	98	108
Population, total	115407	242730	2,10	73 864	302463	3,41	64	125	162
Budget, total	20210	82356	4,07	16 827	90 327	4,48	83	110	110
Enterprises of housing and utilities infrastructure	1428	5748	4,03	466 849	244724	4,37	327	425	108
Other	1095540	4544114	4,15	375 244	1 945 632	4,32	34	43	104
City of Mirny									
TOTAL	792423	1995725	2,52	265832	1369061	4,29	34	69	170
Population, total	61750	129345	2,09	39706	158220	3,32	64	122	159
Budget, total	9711	39477	4,07	7351	39063	4,43	76	99	109
Enterprises of housing and utilities infrastructure	1379	5548	4,02	52610	268697	4,26	3815	4843	106
Other	719583	1821355	2,53	205872	1061301	4,3	29	58	170
Settlements of Mirny District									
Chernyshevsky	127373	510928	4,01	93923	503864	4,47	74	99	111
Svetly	12610	45539	3,61	10085	51355	4,24	80	113	117
Udachnyi	463413	1857910	4,01	378697	1966090	4,33	82	106	108
Aikhal	258833	1028226	3,97	108567	554549	4,26	42	54	107
Almazny	16300	69621	4,27	22017	112781	4,27	135	162	100
Zarya	1323	4936	3,73	937	4770	4,24	71	97	114
Arylakh	56432	228147	4,04	8504	42996	4,21	15	19	104
Suldyukar	1534	5390	3,51	1027	5288	4,29	67	98	122
Taas Yuryakh	3637	14190	3,90	3256	16328	4,18	90	115	107
Berezovyi	43	168	3,90	76	320	3,49	177	190	89
Novyi	59	115	1,96	159	524	2,75	269	456	140

The analysis of energy consumption in the settlements of the Nyurbinsky district of the Western economic zone of the Republic of Sakha (Yakutia) for the period 2000-2019 is given in table 9.

During the period 2012-2019 in the Nurbinskiy district of the Western economic zone of the RS(Y) most of all other villages consume electric energy in the district center of Nurba (28.0%) and Antonovka village (18.2), this is due to the fact that the population and enterprises are located in the center of this district.

The analysis of energy consumption in settlements of Suntar district of the Western economic zone of the RS(Y) for 2000-2019 is given in Table 10.

The largest consumer of electricity in the Suntarsky district is Suntar (45.6%).

The analysis of energy consumption in settlements of Verhneviluiskiy district of the Western economic zone of the RS(Y) for 2000-2019 is given in Table 11.

Table 7. Analysis of energy consumption in the settlements in the Lenskiy district for 2012-2019 years.

Consumers	2012			2019			2019/2012		
	Volume	Revenue	Tariff	Volume	Revenue	Tariff	Volume	Revenue	Tariff
	Thousand kWh	Thousand rubles.	Rubles/ kWt	Thousand kWh	Thousand rubles.	Rubles/ kWt	%	%.	%
TOTAL	131465	545250	4,15	177393	791685	4,46	135	145	108
Population, total	10461	50018	4,78	9367	50750	5,42	90	101	113
Budget, total	22259	115510	5,19	21721	117506	5,41	98	102	104
Enterprises of housing and utilities infrastructure	49964	258156	5,17	86764	433160	4,99	174	168	97
Other	48781	121566	2,49	59541	190269	3,20	122	157	128
Lensk									
TOTAL	91517	383159	4,19	130494	596055	4,57	143	156	109
Population, total	33200	83383	2,51	37877	127943	3,38	114	153	134
Budget, total	6021	28594	4,75	5661	30636	5,41	94	107	114
Enterprises of housing and utilities infrastructure	17611	92361	5,24	16679	90740	5,44	95	98	104
Other	34684	178831	5,16	70276	346734	4,93	203	194	96
Settlements of the Lensky District									
Vitim	18681	82065	4,39	19802	90428	4,57	106	110	104
Peledui	13370	53340	3,99	18286	74910	4,10	137	140	103
South Nuya	2833	7928	2,80	1988	7528	3,79	70	95	135
North Nuya	300	959	3,20	443	1576	3,56	148	164	111
Road	347	1413	4,07	625	3204	5,13	180	227	126
Murya	284	934	3,29	345	1337	3,88	121	143	118
Yaroslavsky	1330	5692	4,28	504	2494	4,95	38	44	116
Bechencha	858	2775	3,23	2183	5170	2,37	254	186	73
Chamcha	348	1146	3,29	1226	3167	2,58	352	276	78
Batamai	517	2319	4,49	19802	90428	5,20	3830	3899	116

The largest consumer of electricity in the Verchneviluysky district is Verkhneviluisk (83.0 per cent).

Analysis of energy consumption in settlements of Vilyuiskiy district of the Western economic zone of the RS(Y) for 2000-2019 is given in Table 12

The largest consumer of electricity in the Vilyuysky district is Vilyuysk (30.3%).

Table 8. Analysis of energy consumption by the settlements in the Olekminsky district for the period 2012-2019.

Consumers	2012			2019			2019/2012		
	Volume	Revenue	Tariff	Volume	Revenue	Tariff	Volume	Revenue	Tariff
	Thousand kWh	Thousand rubles.	Rubles/ kWt	Thousand kWh	Thousand rubles.	Rubles/ kWt	%	%.	%
TOTAL	129371	582181	4,50	82304	272501	3,26	70	50	70
Population, total	21109	50946	2,41	47151	92081	1,95	438	402	92
Budget, total	5448	25903	4,75	3850	21054	5,47	92	101	110
Housing and communal services enterprises	4872	23274	4,78	6764	37385	5,53	153	174	114
Other	97942	482058	4,92	18102	96460	5,33	19	20	108
Olekminsk and Nearby Villages									
TOTAL	116976	545633	4,66	75868	246980	3,26	65	45	70
Population, total	10764	22892	2,13	47151	92081	1,95	438	402	92
Budget, total	4183	20754	4,96	3850	21054	5,47	92	101	110
Housing and communal services enterprises	4422	21467	4,86	6764	37385	5,53	153	174	114
Other	97608	480520	4,92	18102	96460	5,33	19	20	108
Settlements of Olekminsky District									
Sakhaenergo, including	4273	10752	2,52	6436	25521		151	237	0
Beating Kuel	118	255	2,16	139	538	3,87	118	211	179
Daban	317	719	2,27	437	1756	4,02	138	244	177
Dapparay	580	1756	3,02	982	4089	4,16	169	233	138
Delgay	62	259	4,16	485	1907	3,93	782	736	95
Innyakh	93	203	2,19	93	345	3,71	100	170	169
Kudu Kuel	182	394	2,16	225	836	3,72	124	212	172
Malykan	100	209	2,10	125	494	3,95	125	236	188
Marha	165	351	2,12	157	581	3,70	95	166	175
Macha	297	698	2,35	339	1304	3,85	114	187	164
Snyahtakh	76	328	4,31	864	3429	3,97	1137	1045	92
Muddy	49	117	2,41	47	179	3,81	96	153	158
Tocco	958	2444	2,55	1093	4402	4,03	114	180	158
Pull	289	663	2,29	336	1316	3,92	116	198	171
Uritsky	232	492	2,12	294	1147	3,90	127	233	184
Chapaevo	754	1862	2,47	820	3198	3,90	109	172	158
Yakutskenergo, including	125098	571429	4,57	82304	272501	3,26	66	48	71
Olekminsk and nearby villages	116976	545633	4,66	75868	246980	3,26	65	45	70

Table 9. Analysis of energy consumption in the settlements in the Nyurbinsky district for the period 2012-2019 years.

Consumers	2012			2019			2019/2012		
	Volume	Revenue	Tariff	Volume	Revenue	Tariff	Volume	Revenue	Tariff
	Thousandk Whe	Thousand rubles.	Rubles/ kWhe	Thousandk Whe	Thousand rubles.	Rubles/ kWhe	%	%	%
Totalamount	61730	170419	2,76	111632	317360	2,37	181	186	86
Population, total	32621	45077	1,38	77749	132144	1,42	238	293	103
Budget, total	8078	32955	4,08	8444	46376	4,58	105	141	112
Enterprises of housing and utilities infrastructure	9296	37644	4,05	9181	50468	4,58	99	134	113
Others	11736	54743	4,66	16258	88372	4,53	139	161	97
Nyurba									
Population, total	18741	27327	1,46	31274	59554	1,59	167	218	109
Budget, total	4770	19493	4,09	3310	18122	4,56	69	93	111
Enterprises of housing and utilities infrastructure	5666	22842	4,03	6405	34895	4,54	113	153	113
Others	9852	44822	4,55	9774	53265	4,54	99	119	100
Total	39028	114484	2,93	19489	106282	4,54	50	93	155
Settlements in the Nyurbinsky District									
Akana	1121	2164	1,93	1743	4165	1,99	155	192	103
Antonovka	7390	16387	2,22	20330	39606	1,62	275	242	73
Bysyttakh	494	1436	2,91	760	2721	2,99	154	189	103
Dikimde	376	1037	2,76	713	2240	2,62	190	216	95
Gharkhan	751	1602	2,13	3231	12813	3,3	430	800	155
Kirov	374	1255	3,36	1106	2855	2,15	296	227	64
Mar	2168	5728	2,64	3838	9345	2,03	177	163	77
Neftebaza	378	1347	3,56	333	1693	4,24	88	126	119
Nyurbachan	1175	3399	2,89	1916	5297	2,3	163	156	80
Engoldja	631	1839	2,92	1479	3767	2,12	234	205	73
Ynakhsyt	881	2061	2,34	2464	5360	1,81	280	260	77
Chukar	923	2661	2,88	1897	5298	2,33	206	199	81
Chappanda	1399	4126	2,95	3222	7312	1,89	230	177	64
Khatyn-Sysy	1289	2472	1,92	2794	5821	1,74	217	235	91
Khaty	659	1950	2,96	1064	2715	2,13	161	139	72
Syule	556	1619	2,91	1511	3617	1,99	272	223	68
Saiylyk	1250	4203	3,36	1550	5100	2,74	124	121	82
Malykai	2223	6064	2,73	3214	11415	2,96	145	188	108
Kyundede	5710	9880	1,73	6589	16027	2,03	115	162	117
Edei	342	1092	3,20	6589	1653	2,2	183	151	69

Table 10. Analysis of energy consumption by settlements in Suntarskiy district for 2012-2019

Consumers	2012			2019			2019/2012		
	Volume	Revenue	Tariff	Volume	Revenue	Tariff	Volume	Revenue	Tariff
	Thousandk Whe	Thousand rubles.	Rubles/ kWhe	Thousandk Whe	Thousand rubles.	Rubles/ kWhe	%	%	%
Totalamount	85716	158267	1,85	144228	297677	1,72	168	188	93
Population, total	60844	52496	0,86	119731	162489	1,13	197	310	131
Budget, total	10947	44202	4,04	9574	53249	4,63	87	120	115
Enterprises of housing and utilities infrastructure	5071	20510	4,04	5021	27816	4,62	99	136	114
Others	8853	41059	4,64	9901	54124	4,56	112	132	98
Suntar									
Population, total	30800	25053	0,81	57971	77769	1,12	188	310	138
Budget, total	3286	13358	4,07	2432	13401	4,59	74	100	113
Enterprises of housing and utilities infrastructure	2158	8711	4,04	2249	12470	4,62	104	143	114
Population, total	4782	22182	4,64	5827	31756	4,54	122	143	98
Total	41026	69304	1,69	68478	135395	1,65	167	195	98
Settlements in the Suntarskiy District									
Allaga	1569	2219	1,41	2124	4847	1,9	135	218	135
Arylakh	2476	4438	1,79	2099	4980	1,98	85	112	111
Arylakh(Gharkhan)	1569	2219	1,41	2743	5466	1,66	175	246	118
Ilimniir	632	912	1,44	1881	3481	1,54	298	382	107
Kempendyai	2290	4110	1,79	2537	5813	1,91	111	141	107
Krestyakh	3838	7210	1,88	5116	11035	1,8	133	153	96
Kuokunu	1530	3078	2,01	2953	6788	1,92	193	221	96
Kutana	1662	3277	1,97	3984	7326	1,53	240	224	78
Kyukei	760	1841	2,42	1369	3811	2,32	180	207	96
Kyundeya	1257	2445	1,94	3580	6825	1,59	285	279	82
Mar-keol	690	1391	2,02	2004	3578	1,49	290	257	74
Nakhara	353	878	2,49	724	1838	2,11	205	209	85
Sardanga	2650	6175	2,33	4531	9350	1,72	171	151	74
Agdary	1381	1720	1,24	1890	3237	1,43	137	188	115
Toibikhoi	9162	15878	1,73	11461	22933	1,67	125	144	97
Tolon	172	518	3,01	428	1242	2,42	249	240	80
Tuoidakh	458	1208	2,64	1109	2738	2,06	242	227	78
Tenke	705	1546	2,19	838	2579	2,57	119	167	117
Tyubei	643	1239	1,93	1062	2325	1,82	165	188	94
Ustie	757	1810	2,39	1769	3793	1,79	234	210	75
Uhun-Keol	404	1379	3,42	3770	6340	1,4	933	460	41
Khordogoi	1152	2807	2,44	3573	7817	1,82	310	278	75
Khoro	467	1246	2,67	1234	2406	1,62	264	193	61
Sheya	3036	9004	2,97	3977	13377	2,8	131	149	94
Yguatta	103	230	2,22	112	188	1,4	109	82	63
Elgyai	4969	10179	2,05	8882	18167	1,7	179	178	83

Table 11. Electricity Consumption by consumer groups in Verhnevilyuiskiy district for 2012-2019.

Consumers	2012 год			2019 год			2019/2012		
	Volume	Revenue	Tariff	Volume	Revenue	Tariff	Volume	Revenue	Tariff
	Thousandk Whe	Thousand rubles.	Rubles/ kWhe	Thousandk Whe	Thousand rubles.	Rubles/ kWhe	%	%	%
Totalamount	23155	71314	3,08	35201	132022	3,13	152	185	102
Population, total	11833	23226	1,96	22262	61138	2,29	188	263	117
Budget, total	3878	15766	4,07	3910	21339	4,55	101	135	112
Enterprises of housing and utilities infrastructure	3892	15799	4,06	3730	20550	4,59	96	130	113
Others	3553	16524	4,65	5299	28995	4,56	149	175	98
Verhneviljujsk									
Population, total	2897	5769	1,99	17663	72889	3,44	610	1263	173
Budget, total	2092	8526	4,07	1852	10086	4,54	89	118	112
Enterprises of housing and utilities infrastructure	1905	7711	4,05	1873	10322	4,59	98	134	113
Others	2270	10583	4,66	12958	25836	1,66	571	244	36
Total	9164	32589	3,56	29205	99171	2,83	319	304	79
Settlements in the Verhneviljujsky District									
Tuobuynskynasleg	348	774	2,23	444	1857	4,18	128	240	188
Khorinskynasleg	932	3096	3,32	2836	7459	2,19	304	241	66
Onkhoiskynasleg	382	1124	2,94	1427	3413	1,99	374	304	68
Dyullyukinskynasleg	1478	3555	2,40	2587	5968	1,92	175	168	80
Dalyrskynasleg	578	1906	3,30	1755	4548	2,16	304	239	65
Meyikskynasleg	964	1995	2,07	1318	3798	2,4	137	190	116
Botulinskynasleg	1373	3665	2,67	1682	4241	2,1	123	116	79
Surgulukskynasleg	391	1073	2,74	758	2277	2,5	194	212	91
Kyrykyiskynasleg	389	1179	3,03	618	1950	2,63	159	165	87
Magaskiynasleg	1104	2440	2,21	857	2607	2,53	78	107	114
Khomustakhskynasleg	309	808	2,61	473	1546	2,73	153	191	105
Balagannakh VVU	241	737	3,06	406	1362	2,8	168	185	92
Khomustakh of Namskiynasleg	1642	5362	3,27	1439	6667	3,86	88	124	118
Orosu	638	1865	2,92	714	3292	3,84	112	177	132
Tamalakan	489	1354	2,77	542	2448	3,76	111	181	136
Khatbalakh	454	1402	3,09	473	2229	3,93	104	159	127
Orget	548	1670	3,05	1156	3113	2,24	211	186	73
Byrakan	602	1117	1,86	594	1563	2,19	99	140	118
Kharuyalakh	755	2021	2,68	768	3670	3,98	102	182	149
Andreevsky	374	1583	4,23	2667	11646	3,64	713	736	86

Table 12. Electricity Consumption by consumer groups in the Vilyuiyskiy district for 2012-2019

Consumers	2012			2019			2019/2012		
	Volume	Revenue	Tariff	Volume	Revenue	Tariff	Volume	Revenue	Tariff
	Thousandk Whe	Thousand rubles.	Rubles/ kWhe	Thousandk Whe	Thousand rubles.	Rubles/ kWhe	%	%	%
Population, total	13416	30484	2,27	33255	131547	3,3	248	432	145
Budget, total	5033	20433	4,06	3920	21400	4,55	78	105	112
Enterprises of housing and utilities infrastructure	5710	23229	4,07	5610	30790	4,57	98	133	112
Others	5897	27454	4,66	10240	55610	4,53	174	203	97
Total	30056	101600	3,38	36400	176900	4,05	121	174	120
Vilyuysk									
Population, total	6988	17755	2,54	8072	33261	3,43	116	187	135
Budget, total	2914	11829	4,06	2407	13081	4,53	83	111	112
Enterprises of housing and utilities infrastructure	3085	12588	4,08	3096	16952	4,56	100	135	112
Others	4203	19525	4,65	6317	23628	3,12	150	121	67
Total	16178	58788	3,63	11821	53660	3,78	73	91	104
Settlements in the Vilyuysky District									
Balagatchy	735	2416	3,29	1354	5102	3,14	184	211	95
Betung	337	938	2,78	430	2055	3,98	128	219	143
Ekundu	276	831	3,01	332	1623	4,08	120	195	136
Ilbenge	794	2323	2,93	520	2764	3,98	65	119	136
Kyunde	186	573	3,09	122	537	3,68	66	94	119
Kyrova	393	1255	3,19	537	2623	4,07	137	209	128
Kyubeinde	386	1109	2,87	361	1701	3,92	94	153	137
Kyulekyan	410	1168	2,85	511	2424	3,95	125	208	139
Lekechen	384	1108	2,89	692	2720	3,93	180	245	136
Satagai	642	1855	2,89	665	3135	3,93	104	169	136
Sosnovka	408	1441	3,53	373	1911	4,27	91	133	121
Starovatova	124	512	4,13	97	494	4,24	78	96	103
Syudybyl	777	2551	3,28	802	3956	4,11	103	155	125
Tasagar	374	1038	2,78	431	2040	3,95	115	197	142
Terbyas	488	1411	2,89	920	4736	4,29	189	336	148
Tosu	944	2751	2,92	1518	4626	2,54	161	168	87
Tympy	575	1848	3,22	602	2944	4,08	105	159	127
Usun	475	1355	2,85	479	2202	3,83	101	163	134
Khampa	912	3437	3,77	1575	7964	4,21	173	232	112
Chai	430	1350	3,14	393	1914	4,06	91	142	129
Chineke	510	1763	3,46	735	3445	3,91	144	195	113
Ebya	638	1919	3,01	1633	4015	2,05	256	209	68
Arylakh	94	350	3,73	51	217	3,56	54	62	95
Bagadya	125	439	3,52	167	817	4,08	134	186	116
Mastakh	405	1382	3,41	492	2398	4,06	121	174	119
Saiylyk	1045	2776	2,66	1191	5838	4,09	114	210	154

In the studied areas of WEZ of the RS(Y) according to the table 12 above, traditional energy sources mainly function:

- In the production of electric energy it is the Cascade of Vilyuiskiy HPP - energy source of renewable energy on the hydraulic resources of the Vilyu river;
- In the production of thermal energy - boiler rooms, operating on natural gas, crude oil, gas condensate and coal.

In the Western energy district there are significant costs for imported fuel (coal, gas condensate, oil, diesel fuel) problems of its transportation and storage, difficulties of operation of boilers on organic fuel put forward the need to find alternative options for obtaining heat. One of the effective uses of renewable energy sources for heating the private residential sector in these areas is electricity for electric heating of houses and apartments using wood for heating (Elyakova I.D. & Koryagina J.N. (2015). In seven districts of WEZ RS(Y) in 2013-2019, the residential sector was transferred to electric heating (Table 13).

Table 13. Net supply of electricity for electric heating in the WEZ for 2013-2019., thousand kWh

District	2013	2014	2015	2016	2017	2018	2019
Suntarskiy district	52776	69701	78995	87182	93 458	99 724	101 887
Nuyrbinsky district	19869	28283	31213	40139	48 011	54 233	58 280
Mirninsky district	1971	2242	2015	2320	3 194	3 356	4 001
Verkhnevilyuisky district		158	574	1775	4 325	7 784	9 741
Vilyuisky district		53	1184	1774	1 983	2 382	2 645
Olekminsky district		237	2408	10600	19725	26940	31800
Lensky district		60	1684	6588	2641	16483	20821

The efficiency of electric heating of private houses consists in the non-heating of furnaces with the help of firewood, which leads to the exhaustion of forest resources, environmental cleanliness, reduction of labor intensity of thermal energy production and reduction of its cost, and subsequently to reduction of electricity tariffs for the population. High electricity consumption is observed in Suntarskiy and Nurbinskiy districts, where the majority of the population lives in the private sector. In Suntarskiy district the transfer to electric heating is connected with the completion of construction of high-voltage power transmission lines to Suntarskiy village, reduction of losses on low-voltage electric networks, In Nurbinskiy district due to the high cost of thermal energy produced on traditional sources of fuel (coal and firewood) the majority of the population switched to electric heating, instead of using firewood for furnace heating.

Low dynamics of growth of electric heating volumes in Mirninsky district is explained by the fact that heating is mainly in centralized boiler rooms on natural gas. The increase in the volume of electric heating is observed in the Verhnevilyiskiy and Vilyuiskiy districts, despite the gasification of settlements, so it is more convenient and economically feasible to use electricity as electric heating. The potential for electric heating in all seven areas is huge, taking into account the construction of large electric boilers, due to its efficiency, environmental friendliness, operational feasibility, cheap electricity tariffs for electric heating for many consumers of thermal energy. Due to this circumstances, it is necessary to build high-voltage electric transmission lines for efficient operation of electric power and thermal engineering enterprises in WEZ of the RS(Y).

As a result of the analysis of the natural and cost parameters of the change in the volume of electric energy consumption in seven regions of the Western economic zone according to the above tables, it can be concluded:

- large areas with settlements in terms of electric energy consumption in WEZ of the RS(Y) are Mirninsky, Lensky and Nurbinskiy districts;
- over the past 7 years, the highest growth of consumption has occurred in the population (35%) and in housing and utilities enterprises (402%), this is due to the growth of the introduced housing stock in the WEZ and the transfer of communal infrastructure to housing and utilities enterprises. This factor is also related to the growth of revenues at PJSC "Yakutskenergo";
- high rates of growth of tariffs for electric energy are also observed in the population (82%), in the budget (5%) and in housing and utilities enterprises (402%),
- At the same time, there is the lowest rate of growth of tariffs for electric energy for industrial enterprises (by 1%), due to the reduction of tariffs for industrial enterprises of the Far East region taking into account the adoption by the Government of the Russian Federation of the mechanism of levelling tariffs for electric energy.
- one of the ways to solve the problem, primarily in relation to dispersed, small consumers is the elimination of uneconomical small boilers, as well as for heating the private residential sector, which uses firewood is the use of electric energy for heating purposes.
- it is possible to compile a database in software with the help of digital technologies for creation and realization of digital perspective fuel and energy balance (FEB) of electricity consumption volumes in settlements of seven districts of Western economy zone of the Republic of Sakha (Yakutia).

SOLUTIONS AND RECOMMENDATIONS

In order to draw up a promising digital FEB of the RS(Y) for the long term, it is necessary to solve scientific and practical problems consistently:

1. To create an algorithm for creating and implementing digital perspective FEB on software using digital and information technologies, using methods and models of economic and mathematical forecasting of demand, use (application, consumption) and production of energy resources for a very long period.
2. To carry out an analysis of the demand for fuel and energy resources: the necessary volume of demand for fuel for electric-heat plants and boiler facilities, the necessary demand for the production of electric and thermal energy in the extremely harsh conditions of the North and the Arctic. This means forecasting socio-economic development in these areas, in terms of energy demand.
3. To carry out the comparative assessment of efficiency of application (use) of traditional and renewable all types of fuel and energy on concrete settlements (first of all to calculate and prove

environmental, technological, technical, social and cost efficiency of use and production of energy resources).

4. To justify and calculate the necessity of production and delivery of energy resources of each type for the necessary demand of consumers:
    a. taking into account natural resource potential (their reserves of proved and potential),
    b. industrial (functioning, ready to transformation and potential enterprises of fuel and energy complex (TEC) and public utilities (HUE)
    c. labour potential taking into account demographic indicators and labour migration.
5. To justify the ecological, technological, technical, social and economic efficiency of the use and production of fuel and energy resources for the preparation of a promising long-term FEB of each district, economic zone and republic of the territory at the level of each settlement.

FUTURE RESEARCH DIRECTIONS

In order to create and implement the Energy budget in the Republic until 2050, that meet the modern requirements of economic and social development with the prospect of accelerated introduction of digital technologies in the energy sector, it is necessary:

1. The working group establishment of comprehensive team of researchers, specialists of energy companies and utilities and local Executive authorities and local self-government that work not only in the Republic but also in other regions.
2. Determine which body will be constantly engaged in the process of managing the Energy budget in the Republic of Sakha (Yakutia).
3. To develop the agreed TK research project "Energy strategy of the Republic of Sakha (Yakutia) for the period up to 2032 with a target vision up to 2050", which includes a separate unit for the creation of the Energy budget settlements with software.

Table 14. Development phases of digital fuel and energy balance by settlements in the Republic of Sakha (Yakutia)

Development Phases of Digital Fuel and Energy Balance by Settlements	Expected Result
Phase I	
1. Creation the fuel and energy balance database on the Republic of Sakha (Yakutia) for 2017-2018; 2. Software architecture development	Demonstration of the main indicators of fuel and energy balance in the Republic of Sakha (Yakutia)

continues on following page

Table 14. Continued

Development Phases of Digital Fuel and Energy Balance by Settlements	Expected Result
Phase II	
1. The application software development of perspective fuel and energy balance of the Republic of Sakha (Yakutia) on the municipalities and settlements (in natural and cost indicators) 1.1. Creation a user interface for software 1.2. Creation a client-server interaction to synchronize with remote companies 1.3. Study of data formats for the implementation of the software 1.4. Creation of analytical software core	
2. Comprehensive analysis of the current state of the economy and energy of the Republic of Sakha (Yakutia) on the basis of the created Database (in the context of municipalities and settlements of the Republic of Sakha (Yakutia)) for 2017-2018. 2.1. Assessment of the socio-economic status of the Republic of Sakha (Yakutia) 2.2. Analysis of the current state of the energy infrastructure of the Republic of Sakha (Yakutia) 2.3. Analysis and evaluation of efficiency of production and consumption of electric energy 2.4. Analysis and evaluation of efficiency of production and consumption of heat energy 2.5. Analysis and evaluation of production and consumption efficiency of fuel resources (boiler and furnace fuel; motor fuel) 2.6. Analysis and evaluation of the effectiveness of fuel and energy resources' supply from outside of the Republic of Sakha (Yakutia)	
3. Comprehensive assessment of the potential of the fuel and energy resources of the Republic of Sakha (Yakutia) on the basis of the created Database 3.1 Electricity 3.2. Thermal energy 3.3. Natural gas 3.4. Oil 3.5. Coal 3.6. Other solid fuels (including wood for heating, solid domestic and industrial waste) 3.7. Peat (including peat fuel briquettes and semi-briquettes) 3.8. Renewable energy sources (RES): - solar energy; - wind energy; - hydro energy; - energy from waste 3.9. Petroleum products (including liquefied gas, automobile and aviation gasoline, kerosene, diesel fuel, heating oil, domestic furnace fuel, fleet fuel oil, gas turbine and motor fuel) 3.10. Atomic energy 4. Development scenarios of FEC (Fuel and Energy Complex) and performance evaluation of major investment projects of the Republic of Sakha (Yakutia) in conjunction with neighboring territories until 2023 and in the future up to 2050 on the basis of the developed software	Creation the most important tool used for formation, planning and implementation of strategy of development of fuel and energy complex of the Republic of Sakha (Yakutia) - Assessment of production and consumption efficiency of fuel and energy resources (in the context of municipalities and settlements)
4.1. Forecast of energy demand and prices in the world energy markets NEA and APR 4.2. Evaluation of the forecast of energy intensity of GRP of adjacent territories of the Eastern Siberia and the Far East. 4.3. Prospects for the development of small energy: - optimization of diesel power plants; - application of low-power CHP on coal of local producers; - use of renewable energy sources (Solar power plants); 4.4. Prospects for the development of enterprises in coal deposits: - "Nadezhdinskoye" (JSC "Zyryansky ugolnuy razrez"); - "Dzhebariki-Khayinskoe" (branch of JSC HC "Yakutugol"); - "Kharbalakhskoye" (JSC "Telen"); - "Belogorskoye" (LLC "Sangar coal mine"); - "Kularskoe" and "Uyandinskoe"; - "Krasnorechenskoe"; - "Buolkalakhskoe"; - "Soginskoe". 4.5. Scenarios of efficient production and consumption of gas resources (natural gas and associated petroleum gas) with comparative calculation of LNG production:	

continues on following page

Table 14. Continued

Development Phases of Digital Fuel and Energy Balance by Settlements	Expected Result
Phase III	
1. Development of a model of the consolidated fuel and energy balance of the Republic of Sakha (Yakutia) for the period up to 2023 and for the future up to 2050 (in the context of municipalities and settlements) on the basis of the developed software 1.1. The balance of secondary energy resources: - electric energy balance; - balance of thermal energy 1.2. Balance of primary fuel and energy resources (boiler-furnace and motor fuel) 1.3. Integrated fuel and energy balance of the Republic of Sakha (Yakutia) for the period up to 2023 and for the future up to 2050 2. Software approbation of fuel and energy balance on the Central power district of the Republic of Sakha (Yakutia) with start-up and adjustment of the program complex.	The development of the fuel and energy sector will ensure a deficit-free balance of primary energy resources of the Republic; it will improve the structure of consumption of boiler and furnace fuel. Demonstration of performance on fuel and energy balance of the Republic of Sakha (Yakutia).

CONCLUSION

The results of the study can be summarized as follows:

- estimation of energy production and consumption in Western economic zone of the Republic of Sakha (Yakutia) for 2016, which can be the basis for the future development of the long-term perspective fuel and energy balance of the Republic taking into account its cost indicators for the selection of effective energy resources and energy sources for the energy supply of each municipal district in terms of its settlements, taking into account the integrated efficiency of their production and consumption in the Republic as a whole;
- database creation for the development of perspective Energy budget on settlements, municipal organizations;
- consumption and production analysis of fuel and energy resources in the context of settlements, the main consumer groups of fuel and energy resources: population, budget, utilities and other enterprises in the Western Economic Zone, in quantitative and cost indicators for the period 2012-2016;
- assessment of energy supply problems to the consumers of fuel and energy resources by municipalities;
- development and evaluation of energy-efficient organizational, economic and technological mechanisms of production, distribution and transmission of electricity and heat for producers and consumers of fuel and energy resources of the Western Economic Zone;
- assessment of the use of local energy resources and renewable energy sources (RES) for the production of electricity and heat (Elyakova, I.D. & et al, 2016);
- identification of the main trends and production and consumption potentials of fuel and energy resources in WEZ Republic of Sakha (Yakutia);
- construction of electric boiler houses and conversion to electric consumption of consumers is in our opinion the most effective solution - provision of reliable and high-quality electric and heat supply to all groups of consumers of WEZ of the RS(Y);

- transfer to electric heating in WEZ districts and connection to the centralized electricity supply of large oil and gas enterprises of Lensky, Mirninsky districts of enterprises of diamond mining company Nakynsky GOK of JSC "ALROSA-Nurba" AK "ALROSA (PJSC), as well as the construction of high-voltage power transmission lines VL-220 kV Suntar-Nurba for the Vilyu group of districts, would reduce the tariff for electricity for electric boilers (it is necessary to construct), to save exhaustible organic fuel as coal, crude oil, natural gas, gas condensate, to refusal of heating of houses firewood due to transfer to electric heating. The increase in electricity consumption leads to lower tariffs, which ultimately has a positive impact on increasing the income of enterprises and improving the standard of living of the population.

The main goal of digital FEB is to efficiently generate, implement and manage promising FEB for the long term, and even, for example, 100 years ahead, to use those types of energy that are most environmentally friendly.

REFERENCES

Annual reports of PJSC "Sakhaenergo" for 2011-2019. (n.d.)

Annual reports of PJSC "Yakutskenergo" for 2011-2019. (n.d.)

Digest of UK Energy Statistics 2017 (DUKES). (2017). Retrieved from www.gov.uk/government/statistics/electricity-chapter-5-digest-of-united-kingdom-energy-statisticsdukes

Electricity generation and supply figures for Scotland, Wales, Northern Ireland and England, 2012 to 2015. (2016). Retrieved from www.gov.uk/government/publications/energy-trends-december-2016-special-feature-articles

Elyakova, I. D., & Koryagina, J. N. (2015). *Efficiency of electric heating in the Western districts of Yakutia. Min. of education and science of the Russian Federation; NEFU; The Yakut Scientific Centre of the Siberian Branch of the Russian Academy of Sciences.* Yakutsk: NEFU Publisher.

Elyakova, I. D., Pakhomov, A. A., Poiseyev, I. I., Yefremov, E. I., Darbasov, V. R., Noyeva, E. Y., ... Elyakov, A. L. (2016). Prospects for development of renewable energy sources to preserve the ecosystem of arctic zone of Russia. *Indian Journal of Science and Technology*, *9*(46), 1–9.

Official materials of the Ministry for Price Policy of the Republic of Sakha (Yakutia).

Official materials of the Ministry of Housing and Utilities of the Republic of Sakha (Yakutia).

Petrov, N. A. (2005). *The fuel and energy balance of the Republic of Sakha (Yakutia). Part. 1. V.P. Larionov's Institute of Physical-Technical Problems of the North SB RAS.* Yakutsk: Sakhapoligrafizdat.

Petrov, O. N., Saneyev, B. G., Alekseyev, G. F., & Safronov, A. F. (2010). The Energy Strategy of the Republic of Sakha (Yakutia) for the Period Up to 2030. Government of the Republic of. Sakha (Yakutia). Yakutsk: Media Holding "Yakutia".

The General Layout of Power Facilities Up to 2035. (2017) (Approved by the Order of the Government of the Russian Federation) No. 1209.

The Russian Statistical Yearbook Rosstat. (2016). Retrieved from http://www.gks.ru/bgd/regl/b16_13

The Scheme and Program for the Development of the Energy Industry of the Republic of Sakha (Yakutia) for 2017-2021. (Established by the Decree of the Head of the Republic of Sakha (Yakutia) No. 1908 of May 9, 2017).

The Scheme for Integrated Development of Productive Forces, Transport and Energy of the Republic of Sakha (Yakutia) up to 2020. (2016).

Zyryanov, V.V. (2011). Fuel and energy balance in the management system of the regional fuel and energy complex. *Bulletin of the Academician M.F. Reshetnev Siberian state aerospace, 3*(34), 111-114.

Compilation of References

Abazue, C. M., Er, A. C., Ferdous Alam, A. S. A.., & Begum, H. (2015). Oil palm smallholders and its sustainability practices in Malaysia. *Mediterranean Journal of Social Sciences, 6*(S4), 482-488.

Abbasi, F., & Riaz, K. (2016). CO2 emissions and financial development in an emerging economy: An augmented VAR approach. *Energy Policy*, *90*, 102–114. doi:10.1016/j.enpol.2015.12.017

Abbasi, M., & Nilsson, F. (2016). Developing environmentally sustainable logistics: Exploring themes and challenges from a logistics service providers' perspective. *Transportation Research Part D, Transport and Environment*, *46*, 273–283. doi:10.1016/j.trd.2016.04.004

Abdel-Basset, M., Manogaran, G., & Mohamed, M. (2018). Internet of Things (IoT) and its impact on supply chain: A framework for building smart, secure and efficient systems. *Future Generation Computer Systems*, *86*, 614–628. doi:10.1016/j.future.2018.04.051

Abdulsalam, Y., Gopalakrishnan, M., Maltz, A., & Schneller, E. (2015). Health Care Matters: Supply Chains In and Of the Health Sector. *Journal of Business Logistics*, *36*(4), 335–339. doi:10.1111/jbl.12111

Abernethy, V. D. (2005). *Ester Boserup a new introduction by Virginia Deane Abernethy and a forward by Nicholas Kaldor* [Review of the book *The Conditions of Agricultural Growth: The Economics of Agrarian Change under Population Pressure*, by E. Boserup]. New York: Routledge. (Original work published 1814)

Abokyi, E., Appiah-Konadu, P., Abokyi, F., & Oteng-Abayie, E. F. (2019). Industrial growth and emissions of CO2 in Ghana: The role of financial development and fossil fuel consumption. *Energy Reports*, *5*, 1339–1353. doi:10.1016/j.egyr.2019.09.002

Acar & Bozaykut Bük. (2017). Article. *International Journal of Business and Social Sciences Research*, *6*(5), 13-27.

Accenture. (2014). *Supply Chain Management in the Cloud.* Author.

Acciaro, M., & Wilmsmeier, G. (2015). Energy efficiency in maritime logistics chains. *Research in Transportation Business & Management*, *17*, 1–7. doi:10.1016/j.rtbm.2015.11.002

Adefarati, T., & Bansal, R. C. (2019). Reliability, economic and environmental analysis of a microgrid system in the presence of renewable energy resources. *Applied Energy*, *236*, 1089–1114. doi:10.1016/j.apenergy.2018.12.050

Adenso-Díaz, B., Lozano, S., & Moreno, P. (2016). How the environmental impact affects the design of logistics networks based on cost minimization. *Transportation Research Part D, Transport and Environment*, *48*, 214–224. doi:10.1016/j.trd.2016.08.022

Aditjandra, P. T., Zunder, T. H., Islam, D. M. Z., & Palacin, R. (2016). Green rail transportation: Improving rail freight to support green corridors. In H. N. Psaraftis (Ed.), *Green Transportation Logistics, the Quest for Win-Win Solutions* (pp. 413–454). Springer International Publishing. doi:10.1007/978-3-319-17175-3_12

Ahi, P., & Searcy, C. (2015). An analysis of metrics used to measure performance in green and sustainable supply chains. *Journal of Cleaner Production, 86*, 360–377. doi:10.1016/j.jclepro.2014.08.005

Ahmad, A., Zhao, Y., Shahbaz, M., Bano, S., Zhang, Z., Wang, S., & Liu, Y. (2016). Carbon emissions, energy consumption and economic growth: An aggregate and disaggregate analysis of the Indian economy. *Energy Policy, 96*, 131–143. doi:10.1016/j.enpol.2016.05.032

Ahmad, M., Khan, Z., Ur Rahman, Z., & Khan, S. (2018). Does financial development asymmetrically affect CO2 emissions in China? An application of the nonlinear autoregressive distributed lag (NARDL) model. *Carbon Management, 9*(6), 631–644. doi:10.1080/17583004.2018.1529998

Akkucuk, U. (2011a). *Veri Madenciliği: Kümeleme ve Sınıflama Algoritmaları*. İstanbul: Yalın Yayıncılık.

Akkucuk, U. (2011b). A Study on the Competitive Positions of Countries Using Cluster Analysis and Multidimensional Scaling. *European Journal of Economics Finance and Administrative Sciences, 37*, 17–26.

Akkucuk, U. (2011c). *Görselleştirme Teknikleri: Pazarlama ve Patent Analizi Örnek Uygulamaları İle*. İstanbul: Yalın Yayıncılık.

Akkucuk, U. (2015). *Handbook of Research on Developing Sustainable Value in Economics, Finance, and Marketing*. IGI Global. doi:10.4018/978-1-4666-6635-1

Akkucuk, U. (2016). SCOR Model and the Green Supply Chain. In U. Akkucuk (Ed.), *Handbook of Research on Waste Management Techniques for Sustainability* (pp. 108–124). Hershey, PA: IGI Global. doi:10.4018/978-1-4666-9723-2.ch006

Akkucuk, U., & Artemel, M. N. (2016). Patent Data Visualization: A Regional Study. *International Journal of Research in Business and Social Science, 5*(3), 66–79.

Akkucuk, U., Carroll, J. D., & France, S. L. (2013). *Visualizing Data in Social and Behavioral Sciences: An Application of PARAMAP on Judicial Statistics. In Algorithms from and for Nature and Life* (pp. 147–154). Springer International Publishing.

Akkucuk, U., & Kucukkancabas, S. (2007). Analyzing the Perceptions of Turkish Universities Using Multidimensional Scaling (MDS) Analysis. *Bogazici Journal, 21*(1-2), 125–141. doi:10.21773/boun.21.1.8

Akkucuk, U., & Sekercioglu, C. H. (2016). NGOs for Environmental Sustainability: The Case of Kuzeydoga Foundation. *Fresenius Environmental Bulletin, 25*(12), 6038–6044.

Akkucuk, U., & Turan, C. (2016). Mobile use and online preferences of the millenials: A study in Yalova. *Journal of Internet Banking and Commerce, 21*(1), 142.

Alam, M. M., Murad, M. W., Noman, A. H. M., & Ozturk, I. (2016). Relationships among carbon emissions, economic growth, energy consumption and population growth: Testing Environmental Kuznets Curve hypothesis for Brazil, China, India and Indonesia. *Ecological Indicators, 70*, 466–479. doi:10.1016/j.ecolind.2016.06.043

Alberro, H. (2019). *Utopia isn't just idealistic fantasy – it inspires people to change the world*. Retrieved November 20, 2019, from https://theconversation.com/utopia-isnt-just-idealistic-fantasy-it-inspires-people-to-change-the-world-118962

Ali, G., Yan, N., Hussain, J., Xu, L., Huang, Y., Xu, S., & Cui, S. (2019). Quantitative assessment of energy conservation and renewable energy awareness among variant urban communities of Xiamen, China. *Renewable & Sustainable Energy Reviews, 109*, 230–238. doi:10.1016/j.rser.2019.04.028

Allen, J. G., MacNaughton, P., Satish, U., Santanam, S., Vallarino, J., & Spengler, J. D. (2015). Associations of cognitive function scores with carbon dioxide, ventilation, and volatile organic compound exposures in office workers: A controlled exposure study of green and conventional office environments. *Environmental Health Perspectives, 124*(6), 805–812. doi:10.1289/ehp.1510037 PMID:26502459

Alm, J., & Bourdeaux, C. J. (2014). *Applying behavioral economics to the public sector*. New Orleans, LA: Tulane University.

Alpar, R. (2013). *Uygulamalı Çok Değişkenli İstatistiksel Yöntemler* [Applied Multivariate Statistical Methods]. Ankara: Detay Yayıncılık.

Alpar, R. (2014). *Spor, Sağlık ve Eğitim Bilimlerinden Örneklerle Uygulamalı İstatistik ve Geçerlilik-Güvenirlik-SPSS'de Çözümleme Adımları ile Birlikte* [Applied Statistics with Examples from Sports, Health and Education Sciences and Validity-Reliability-Analysis Steps in SPSS]. Ankara: Detay Yayıncılık.

Alrubaiee, L., & Al-Nazer, N. (2010). Investigate the impact of relationship marketing orientation on customer loyalty: The customer's perspective. *International Journal of Marketing Studies, 2*(1), 155. doi:10.5539/ijms.v2n1p155

Altunışık, R., Coşkun, R., Bayraktaroğlu, S., & Yıldırım, E. (2005). *Sosyal Bilimlerde Araştırma Yöntemleri SPSS Uygulamalı* [SPSS Applied Research Methods in Social Sciences]. Sakarya: Sakarya Kitabevi.

Álvarez, J. F. G., & de Grado, J. G. (2016). Study of a modern industrial low pressure turbine for electricity production employed in oxy-combustion cycles with CO2 capture purposes. *Energy, 107*, 734–747. doi:10.1016/j.energy.2016.04.038

Amanda, S., Massey, A., Theobald, M., Styslinger, M., Kane, D., Kandy, D., … Davert, E. (2011). Africa's indigenous crops. State of the world innovations that nourish the planet. Worldwatch Institute.

Amponsah, C., Visser, L., Adjei-Nsiah, S., Struik, P., Sakyi-Dawson, O., & Stomph, T. (2012). Processing practices of small-scale palm oil producers in the Kwaebibirem. *NJAS Wageningen Journal of Life Sciences, 60-63*, 49–56. doi:10.1016/j.njas.2012.06.006

Amrouche, S. O., Rekioua, D., Rekioua, T., & Bacha, S. (2016). Overview of energy storage in renewable energy systems. *International Journal of Hydrogen Energy, 41*(45), 20914–20927. doi:10.1016/j.ijhydene.2016.06.243

Andrić, M., Krsmanović, B., & Jakšić, D. (2012). Revizija teorija I praksa, V izmenjenoi dopunjeno izdanje [Revision theory and practice, edited edition]. "Proleter", A.D. Bečej, Subotica.

Angeleanu, A. (2015). New technology trends and their transformative impact on logistics and supply chain processes. *International Journal of Economic Practices and Theories, 5*(5), 413–419.

Angelovska, N. (2019). *Top 5 online retailers*. Retrieved November 30, 2019, from https://www.forbes.com/sites/ninaangelovska/2019/05/20/top-5-online-retailers-electronics-and-media-is-the-star-of-e-commerce-worldwide/#6c9267bb1cd9

Ankomah, E. K., & Adjei, R. K. (2019). *Population growth and food production in Ghana. A region in the development of society*. Brno: Mendel University in Brno.

Annual Energy Outlook. (2019). Retrieved from https://www.eia.gov/outlooks/aeo/pdf/aeo2019.pdf

Annual reports of PJSC "Sakhaenergo" for 2011-2019. (n.d.)

Annual reports of PJSC "Yakutskenergo" for 2011-2019. (n.d.)

Apergis, N., Gupta, R., Lau, C. K. M., & Mukherjee, Z. (2018). US state-level carbon dioxide emissions: Does it affect health care expenditure? *Renewable & Sustainable Energy Reviews, 91*, 521–530. doi:10.1016/j.rser.2018.03.035

Arabiyat, T. S., Mdanat, M., & Samawi, G. (2020). Trade Openness, Inclusive Growth, And Inequality: Evidence From Jordan. *Journal of Developing Areas*, *54*(1). doi:10.1353/jda.2020.0008

Aronsson, H., & Brodin, M. H. (2006). The environmental impact of changing logistics structures. *International Journal of Logistics Management*, *17*(3), 394–415. doi:10.1108/09574090610717545

Ashrafzadeh, M., Rafiei, F. M., Isfahani, N. M., & Zare, Z. (2012). Application of fuzzy TOPSIS method for the selection of Warehouse Location: A Case Study. *Interdisciplinary Journal of Contemporary Research in Business*, *3*(9), 655–671.

Ashton, K. (2009). That 'internet of things' thing. *RFID Journal*, *22*(7), 97-114.

Asif, M., de Bruijn, E. J., Fisscher, O. A. M., & Steenhuis, H.-J. (2008). Achieving sustainability three dimensionally. *2008 4th IEEE International Conference on Management of Innovation and Technology*. doi:10.1109/icmit.2008.4654402

Askari, G., & Eshaghi Gordji, M. (2018). Hyper-rational choice and economic behaviour. *Advances in Mathematical Finance and Applications*, *3*(3), 69–76.

Aslantaş Ateş, B., & Toraman, A. (2017). Basamak Bir Hastanenin Eczanesinde Yalın Tedarik Zinciri Uygulaması. *Journal Of Suleyman Demirel University Institute of Social Sciences*, *29*(4), 456-469.

Ates, O. K. (2013). *Global supply chain and competitive business strategies: A case study of blood sugar monitoring industry* (Doctoral dissertation). Ohio University.

Atzori, L., Iera, A., & Morabito, G. (2010). The internet of things: A survey. *Computer Networks*, *54*(15), 2787–2805. doi:10.1016/j.comnet.2010.05.010

Australian Dietary Guidelines. (2015). *Advice about the amount and kinds of foods that we need to eat for health and wellbeing*. Retrieved from Eatforhealth.gov.au.

Ayant, A., & Azhar, M. (2014). Analysis of the barriers for implementing green supply chain management (GSCM) practices: An interpretive structural modeling (ISM) approach. *Procedia Engineering*, *97*, 2157–2166. doi:10.1016/j.proeng.2014.12.459

Ayaz, H., & Soykan, A. (2002). Toplam Kalite Yönetimi ve Sağlık Sektörü. *Türkiye Klinikleri Psikiyatri Dergisi*, *3*, 19–26.

Ay, C., & Ecevit, Z. (2005). Çevre bilinçli tüketiciler. *Journal of Akdeniz University Faculty of Economics and Administrative Sciences*, *5*(10), 238–263.

Aytan, Y. (2018). *A case study on the affect of organizational justice, trust, commitment and citizenship on worker's performance* (Unpublished doctoral dissertation). Istanbul Aydın University, Istanbul, Turkey.

Bahmani, M., Shariati, J., & Rouzbahani, A. N. (2017). Simulation and optimization of an industrial gas condensate stabilization unit to modify LPG and NGL production with minimizing CO2 emission to the environment. *Chinese Journal of Chemical Engineering*, *25*(3), 338–346. doi:10.1016/j.cjche.2016.07.006

Bahramara, S., Moghaddam, M. P., & Haghifam, M. R. (2016). Optimal planning of hybrid renewable energy systems using HOMER: A review. *Renewable & Sustainable Energy Reviews*, *62*, 609–620. doi:10.1016/j.rser.2016.05.039

Baines, N. (2010). *Delivering Performance in Food Supply Chains. Quality and safety standards in food supply chains* (1st ed.). Cambridge: Woodhead Publishing.

Baki, R. (2018). Literature review on green supply chain management concept and problems during it's implementation. *The Journal of International Scientific Researches*, *3*(2), 114–122.

Balasubramanian, S. (2012). A hierarchical framework of barriers to green supply chain management in the construction sector. *Journal of Sustainable Development*, *5*(10), 15–27. doi:10.5539/jsd.v5n10p15

Baldwin, E., Carley, S., & Nicholson-Crotty, S. (2019). Why do countries emulate each others' policies? A global study of renewable energy policy diffusion. *World Development, 120*, 29–45. doi:10.1016/j.worlddev.2019.03.012

Balin, A., & Baraçli, H. (2017). A fuzzy multi-criteria decision making methodology based upon the interval type-2 fuzzy sets for evaluating renewable energy alternatives in Turkey. *Technological and Economic Development of Economy, 23*(5), 742–763. doi:10.3846/20294913.2015.1056276

Barbosa-Póvoa, A. P., da Silva, C., & Carvalho, A. (2017). Opportunities and challenges in sustainable supply chain: An operations research perspective. *European Journal of Operational Research, 268*(2), 399–431. doi:10.1016/j.ejor.2017.10.036

Bardi, E. J., Raghunathan, T., & Bagchi, P. K. (1994). Logistics information systems: The strategic role of top management. *Journal of Business Logistics, 15*(1), 71.

Barreto, L., Amaral, A., & Pereria, T. (2017) Industry 4.0 implications in logistics: an overview. *Proceedings of the Manufacturing Engineering Society International Conference MESIC 2017*. DOI: 10.1016/j.promfg.2017.09.045

Bartholdi, J. J., & Hackman, S. T. (2014). *Warehouse & Distribution Science: Release 0.96*. Atlanta, GA: Supply Chain and Logistics Institute, School of Industrial and Systems Engineering, Georgia Institute of Technology.

Bartolini, M., Bottani, E., & Eric, H. (2019). Green warehousing: Systematic literature review and bibliometric analysis. *Journal of Cleaner Production, 226*, 242–258. doi:10.1016/j.jclepro.2019.04.055

Bask, A., Rajahonka, M., Laari, S., Solakivi, T., Töyli, J., & Ojala, L. (2018). Environmental sustainability in shipper-LSP relationships. *Journal of Cleaner Production, 172*, 20. doi:10.1016/j.jclepro.2017.11.112

Baylis, J., Simith, S., & Owens, P. (2008). *The Globalization of World Politics*. New York: Oxford University Press.

Beamon, M. B. (1999). Designing the gren supply chain. *Logistics Information Management, 10*(4), 132–142.

Beck, K. (2018). How to Calculate an Average Percent Change. *Sciencing*. Retrieved from https://sciencing.com/calculate-average-increase-7479420.html

Bekhet, H. A., Matar, A., & Yasmin, T. (2017). CO2 emissions, energy consumption, economic growth, and financial development in GCC countries: Dynamic simultaneous equation models. *Renewable & Sustainable Energy Reviews, 70*, 117–132. doi:10.1016/j.rser.2016.11.089

Bekun, F. V., Alola, A. A., & Sarkodie, S. A. (2019). Toward a sustainable environment: Nexus between CO2 emissions, resource rent, renewable and nonrenewable energy in 16-EU countries. *The Science of the Total Environment, 657*, 1023–1029. doi:10.1016/j.scitotenv.2018.12.104 PMID:30677870

Bellis, M. (2017). *History of the agricultural revolution*. Retrieved from https://www.Thoughtco.Com/Agricultural-Revolution-1991931

Benneh, G. (1987). *Population growth and development in Ghana, Legon*. University of Ghana, Dept. of Geography.

Bennet, W., & Steed, L. (1999). An Integrated Approach to Food Safety. *Quality Progress, 32*(2), 37–42.

Berkowitz, E. N., Kerin, R. A., Hartley, S. W., & Rudelius, W. (1997). *Marketing*. Irwin/McGraw-Hill.

Beske, P., & Seuring, S. (2014). Putting sustainability into supply chain management. *Supply Chain Management, 19*(3), 322–331. doi:10.1108/SCM-12-2013-0432

Betts, K. (2019). https://www.brcgs.com/media/1621646/brcgs-compliance-report-2019-digital.pdf

Bhattacharya, M., Paramati, S. R., Ozturk, I., & Bhattacharya, S. (2016). The effect of renewable energy consumption on economic growth: Evidence from top 38 countries. *Applied Energy*, *162*, 733–741. doi:10.1016/j.apenergy.2015.10.104

Biçer, İ., & Ömürgönülşen, M. (2019). Sağlık Kurumları Yöneticilerinin Tedarik Zinciri Yönetimi Algılarının Belirlenmesi. *Hacettepe Journal of Health Administration*, *22*(3), 599–618.

Bienstock, C. C., Mentzer, J. T., & Bird, M. M. (1996). Measuring physical distribution service quality. *Journal of the Academy of Marketing Science*, *25*(1), 31–44. doi:10.1177/0092070397251004

Bienstock, C. C., & Royne, M. B. (2010). Technology acceptance and satisfaction with logistics services. *International Journal of Logistics Management*, *21*(2), 271–292. doi:10.1108/09574091011071951

Bienstock, C. C., Royne, M. B., Sherrell, D., & Stafford, T. F. (2008). An expanded model of logistics service quality: Incorporating logistics information technology. *International Journal of Production Economics*, *113*(1), 205–222. doi:10.1016/j.ijpe.2007.03.023

Black, W. R. (2010). *Sustainable transportation: problems and solutions*. New York, NY: Guilford Press.

Blitz, R. C. (1967). Environment, population, and technology in primitive societies [Review of the book *The conditions of agricultural growth: The Economics of Agrarian Change under Population Pressure,* by E. Boserup]. *Journal of Political Economics*. (Original work published 1965)

Boadu, E. A. (1994). Rapid Population Growth and Development in Ghana. Department of Geography & Resource Development, University Of Ghana Legon-Accra.

Boateng, E. O., Ewusi, K., Kanbur, R., & Mckay, A. (1990). *A poverty profile for Ghana, 1987–88.* Social Dimensions of Adjustment in Sub-Saharan Africa Working Paper No. 5. The World Bank.

Boeras, D. I., Collins, B. C., & Peeling, R. W. (2019). *The Use of Drones in the Delivery of Rural Healthcare. In Revolutionizing Tropical Medicine: Point-of-Care Tests, New Imaging Technologies and Digital Health* (p. 618). John Willey and Sons.

Boisrobert, C., Stjepanovic, A., Oh, S., & Lelieveld, H. (2009). *Ensuring global food safety: Exploring global harmonization* (1st ed.). New York: Academic Press.

Bonilla, D. (2016). Urban vans, e-commerce and road freight transport. *Production Planning and Control*, *27*(6), 433–442. doi:10.1080/09537287.2016.1147093

Borda, J. (2016). La Fábrica del Futuro: Humana, inteligente, tecnológica y digital [The Factory of the Future: Human, intelligent, technological and digital]. Sisteplant.

Borda, J. (2018). Hombre y Tecnología: 4.0 y más [Man and Technology: 4.0 and more]. Sisteplant.

Borgia, E. (2014). The Internet of Things vision: Key features, applications and open issues. *Computer Communications*, *54*, 1–31. doi:10.1016/j.comcom.2014.09.008

Borsa İstanbul. (2019). *Bist sürdürülebilirlik endeksi.* Retrieved from https://www.borsaistanbul.com/endeksler/bist-pay-endeksleri/surdurulebilirlik-endeksi

Boserup, E. (1965). *Food and Agriculture Organization of the United Nations.* Retrieved from http://Agris.Fao.Org/Agris-Search/Search.Do?Recordid=Us201300593530

Bouchard, D. (2015). *What is globalization doing to the world of logistics*. Retrieved from https://www.inboundlogistics.com/cms/article/what-is-globalization-doing-to-the-world-of-logistics/

Boudoin, D., Morel, C., & Gardat, M. (2014). Supply Chains and Urban Logistics Platforms. In J. Gonzalez-Feliu, F. Semet, & J. L. Routhier (Eds.), *Sustainable Urban Logistics: Concepts, Methods and Information Systems. Environmental Issues in Logistics and Manufacturing*. Berlin, Germany: Springer; doi:10.1007/978-3-642-31788-0_1

Boutrif, E. (2003). The new role of Codex Alimentarius in the context of WTO/SPS agreement. *Food Control*, *14*(2), 81–88. doi:10.1016/S0956-7135(02)00113-5

Bowersox, D. J. (1969). Physical distribution development, current status, and potential. *Journal of Marketing*, *33*(1), 63–70. doi:10.1177/002224296903300111

Bowersox, D. J., Mentzer, J. T., & Speh, T. W. (2008). Logistics leverage. *The Journal of Business Strategy*, *25*(2), 85.

Bowersox, D. J., Stank, T. P., & Daugherty, P. J. (1999). Lean launch: Managing product introduction risk through response-based logistics. *Journal of Product Innovation Management*, *16*(6), 557–568. doi:10.1111/1540-5885.1660030

Boyd, D. E., Spekman, R. E., Kamauff, J. W., & Werhane, P. (2007). Corporate social responsibility in global supply chains: A procedural justice perspective. *Long Range Planning*, *40*(3), 341–356. doi:10.1016/j.lrp.2006.12.007

Boyer, K. K., Frohlich, M. T., & Hult, G. T. M. (2005). *Extending the supply chain – How cutting-edge companies bridge the critical last mile into customers' homes*. New York: Amacom.

Boysen, N., de Koster, R., & Weidinger, F. (2019). Warehousing in the e-commerce era: A survey. *European Journal of Operational Research*, *277*(2), 396–411. doi:10.1016/j.ejor.2018.08.023

Boysen, N., Fedtke, S., & Weidinger, F. (2018). Optimizing automated sorting in warehouses: The minimum order spread sequencing problem. *European Journal of Operational Research*, *270*(1), 386–400. doi:10.1016/j.ejor.2018.03.026

Brandenburg, M., Govindan, K., Sarkis, J., & Seuring, S. (2014). Quantitative models for sustainable supply chain management: Developments and directions. *European Journal of Operational Research*, *233*(2), 299–312. doi:10.1016/j.ejor.2013.09.032

Brown, J. R., & Guiffrida, A. L. (2014). Carbon emissions comparison of last mile delivery versus customer pickup. *International Journal of Logistics Research and Applications*, *17*(6), 503–521. doi:10.1080/13675567.2014.907397

Brundtland, G. H. (1987). *Our Common Future. Report of the World Commission on Environment and Development*. United Nations Comm.

Brunsø, K., Ahle Fjord, T., & Grunert, K. G. (2002). *Consumers' Food Choice and Quality Perception*. Working paper no 77. The Aarhus School of Business.

Buckley, P. J., Chen, L., Clegg, L. J., & Voss, H. (2020). The role of endogenous and exogenous risk in FDI entry choices. *Journal of World Business*, *55*(1), 101040. doi:10.1016/j.jwb.2019.101040

Büyüközkan, G., & Güler, M. (2019). Lojistik 4.0 Teknolojilerinin Analizi İçin Metodolojik Yaklaşım. *Girişimcilik ve İnovasyon Yönetimi Dergisi*, *8*(1), 21–47.

Büyüksaatçi, S., & Esnaf, Ş. (2014). Carbon emission based optimization approach for the facility location problem. *TOJSAT*, *4*(1), 9–20.

Byrne, B. M. (2010). *Structural Equation Modelling with Amos, Basic Consepts, Applications, and Programing*. New York: Routledge Taylor and Francis Group.

Caiado, R. G., Filho, W. L., Quelhas, O. L. G., de Mattos, D. L., & Avila, L. V. (2018). A literature-based review on potentials and constraints in the implementation of the sustainable development goals. *Journal of Cleaner Production*, *198*, 10.

Cairns, S. (2007). Delivering supermarket shopping: More or less traffic? *Transport Reviews*, *§§§*, 51–84.

Cambra-Fierro, J., & Ruiz-Benitez, R. (2009). Advantages of intermodal logistics platforms: Insights from a Spanish platform. *Supply Chain Management*, *14*(6), 418–421. doi:10.1108/13598540910995183

Camerer, C., Issachoroff, S., Loewenstein, G., O'Donoghue, T., & Rabin, M. (2003). Regulation for conservatives: Behavioral economics and the case for asymmetric paternalism. *University of Pennsylvania Law Review*, *151*(1), 1211–1254. doi:10.2307/3312889

Camerer, C., Loewenstein, G., & Rabin, M. (2004). *Advances in behavioral economics*. Princeton, NJ: Princeton University Press. doi:10.1515/9781400829118

Campos-Guzman, V., García-Cáscales, M. S., Espinosa, N., & Urbina, A. (2019). Life cycle analysis with multi-criteria decision making: A review of approaches for the sustainability evaluation of renewable energy technologies. *Renewable & Sustainable Energy Reviews*, *104*, 343–366. doi:10.1016/j.rser.2019.01.031

Caris, A., Macharis, C., & Janssens, G. K. (2013). Decision support in intermodal transport: A new research agenda. *Computers in Industry*, *64*(2), 105–112. doi:10.1016/j.compind.2012.12.001

Carlson, C. (2012). *Effective FMEAs: Achieving safe, reliable, and economical products and processes using failure mode and effects analysis*. Hoboken, NJ: John Wiley & Sons. doi:10.1002/9781118312575

Carroll, A. B. (1979). A three-dimensional conceptual model of corporate performance. *Academy of Management Review*, *4*(4), 497–505. doi:10.5465/amr.1979.4498296

Carroll, A. B. (1991). The pyramid of corporate social responsibility: Toward the moral management of organizational stakeholders. *Business Horizons*, *34*(4), 39–48. doi:10.1016/0007-6813(91)90005-G

Carroquino, J., Bernal-Agustín, J. L., & Dufo-López, R. (2019). Standalone Renewable Energy and Hydrogen in an Agricultural Context: A Demonstrative Case. *Sustainability*, *11*(4), 951. doi:10.3390u11040951

Carter, C. R., & Jennings, M. M. (2004). The role of purchasing in corporate social responsibility: A structural equation analysis. *Journal of Business Logistics*, *25*(1), 145–186. doi:10.1002/j.2158-1592.2004.tb00173.x

Carter, C. R., & Kaufmann, L. (2007). The impact of electronic reverse auctions on supplier performance: The mediating role of relationship variables. *The Journal of Supply Chain Management*, *43*(1), 16–26. doi:10.1111/j.1745-493X.2007.00024.x

Carter, C. R., & Rogers, D. S. (2008). A framework of sustainable chain management: Moving toward new theory. *International Journal of Physical Distribution & Logistics Management*, *38*(5), 360–387. doi:10.1108/09600030810882816

Çelik, H. E., & Yılmaz, V. (2013). *Lisrel 9.1 ile Yapısal Eşitlik Modellemesi Temel Kavramlar-Uygulamalar-Programlama* [Structural Equation Modeling with Lisrel 9.1 Basic Concepts-Applications-Programming]. Ankara: Anı Yayıncılık.

Çetin, C. (2010). *Toplam Kalite Yönetimi*. Beta Basım Yayım Dağıtım.

Chaabane, A., Ramudhin, A., & Paquet, M. (2012). Design of sustainable supply chains under the emission trading scheme. *International Journal of Production Economics*, *135*(1), 37–49. doi:10.1016/j.ijpe.2010.10.025

Chaabouni, S., Zghidi, N., & Mbarek, M. B. (2016). On the causal dynamics between CO2 emissions, health expenditures and economic growth. *Sustainable Cities and Society, 22*, 184-191.

Chaabouni, S., & Saidi, K. (2017). The dynamic links between carbon dioxide (CO2) emissions, health spending and GDP growth: A case study for 51 countries. *Environmental Research*, *158*, 137–144. doi:10.1016/j.envres.2017.05.041 PMID:28624630

Chang, G. (2009). - Total quality management in supply chain. *International Business Research, 2*(2), 82–85. doi:10.5539/ibr.v2n2p82

Charfeddine, L., & Kahia, M. (2019). Impact of renewable energy consumption and financial development on CO2 emissions and economic growth in the MENA region: A panel vector autoregressive (PVAR) analysis. *Renewable Energy, 139*, 198–213. doi:10.1016/j.renene.2019.01.010

CharletL. (2018). https://www.iso.org/the-iso-survey.html

Chayanov, A. V. (1966). The theory of peasant economy. In D. Thorner, B. Kerblay, & R. E. F. Smith (Eds.), *The American economic association translation series* (pp. 1–301). Birmingham, UK: Richard D. Irwin, Inc.

Chen, C., & Pan, S. (2015). Using the Crowd of Taxis to Last Mile Delivery in E-Commerce: a methodological research. Proceedings of SOHOMA15, 640, 61-70.

Chen, L., Zhuo, Y., Xu, Z., Xu, X., & Gao, X. (2019). Is Carbon Dioxide (CO2) Emission an Important Factor Affecting Healthcare Expenditure? Evidence from China, 2005–2016. *International Journal of Environmental Research and Public Health, 16*(20), 3995. doi:10.3390/ijerph16203995 PMID:31635413

Chen, S., Kumar, A., Wong, W. C., Chiu, M. S., & Wang, X. (2019). Hydrogen value chain and fuel cells within hybrid renewable energy systems: Advanced operation and control strategies. *Applied Energy, 233*, 321–337. doi:10.1016/j.apenergy.2018.10.003

Cherrafi, A., Garza-Reyes, J. A., Kumar, V., Mishra, N., Ghobadian, A., & ElFezazi, S. (2018). Lean, green practices and process innovation: A model for green supply chain performance. *International Journal of Production Economics, 206*(December).

Chiang, C.-F., & Hsieh, T.-S. (2012). The impacts of perceived organizational support and psychological empowerment on job performance: The mediating effects of organizational citizenship behavior. *International Journal of Hospitality Management, 31*(1), 180–190. doi:10.1016/j.ijhm.2011.04.011

Chopra, S., & Meindl, P. (2007). *Supply chain management. Strategy, planning & operation* (3rd ed.). Pearson. doi:10.1007/978-3-8349-9320-5_22

Chopra, S., & Meindl, P. (2015). *Supply Chain Management Strategy Planning, and Operation.* Edinburgh, UK: Pearson.

Chuang, M. T., Chang, S. Y., Hsiao, T. C., Lu, Y. R., & Yang, T. Y. (2019). Analyzing major renewable energy sources and power stability in Taiwan by 2030. *Energy Policy, 125*, 293–306. doi:10.1016/j.enpol.2018.10.036

Chuang, Y. Y., Wang, J. J., Chao, P. Y., Tsai, C. T., Tsai, Y. C., Chen, W. C., & Tsai, T. C. (2018). Evaluation of on-stream industrial CO2 adsorbent in air pretreatment for cryogenic production of oxygen. *Journal of the Taiwan Institute of Chemical Engineers, 84*, 41–48. doi:10.1016/j.jtice.2017.12.030

Ciliberti, F., Pontrandolfo, P., & Scozzi, B. (2008). Logistics social responsibility: Standard adoption and practices in Italian companies. *International Journal of Production Economics, 113*(1), 88–106. doi:10.1016/j.ijpe.2007.02.049

Cirulis, A., & Ginters, E. (2013). Augmented reality in logistics. *Procedia Computer Science, 26*, 14–20. doi:10.1016/j.procs.2013.12.003

Clement, J. (2019). *Retail e-commerce sales worldwide from 2014 to 2023.* Retrieved 11 11, 2019 from https://www.statista.com/statistics/379046/worldwide-retail-e-commerce-sales/

Clive, M. (2015). Reducing the environmental impact of warehousing. In Green logistics: Improving the environmental sustainability of logistics (pp. 167-190). Kogan Page Publishers.

Closs, D. J., Roath, A. S., Goldsby, T. J., Eckert, J. A., & Swartz, S. M. (1998). An empirical comparison of anticipatory and response-based supply chain strategies. *International Journal of Logistics Management*, *9*(2), 21–34. doi:10.1108/09574099810805816

Coderre, D. (2011). Internal Audit, Efficiency Through Automation. John Wiley & Sons, Inc.

Coelho, R. D., Lizcano, J. V., da Silva Barros, T. H., da Silva Barbosa, F., Leal, D. P. V., da Costa Santos, L., ... Martin, D. L. (2019). Effect of water stress on renewable energy from sugarcane biomass. *Renewable & Sustainable Energy Reviews*, *103*, 399–407. doi:10.1016/j.rser.2018.12.025

Colicchia, C., Marchet, G., Melacini, M., & Perotti, S. (2013). Building environmental sustainability: Empirical evidence from Logistics Service Providers. *Journal of Cleaner Production*, *59*, 197–209. doi:10.1016/j.jclepro.2013.06.057

Collom, L. (2018). *Electric-Powered Forklift Benefits in the Warehouse*. Retrieved (December 9, 2019) from https://www.toyotaforklift.com/blog/electric-powered-forklifts-benefits-in-the-warehouse

Commission, C. (2003). *General principles of food hygiene CAC/RCP 1–1969*. Available online: http://www.fao.org/input/download/standards/23/CXP_001e.pdf

Conly, S. (2014). Against autonomy: Justifying coercive paternalism. *Journal of Medical Ethics*, *40*(5), 349–349. doi:10.1136/medethics-2013-101444 PMID:24335658

Connolly, D., Lund, H., & Mathiesen, B. V. (2016). Smart Energy Europe: The technical and economic impact of one potential 100% renewable energy scenario for the European Union. *Renewable & Sustainable Energy Reviews*, *60*, 1634–1653. doi:10.1016/j.rser.2016.02.025

Cook, P., & Sproul, A. (2011). Towards low-energy retail warehouse building. *Architectural Science Review*, *54*(3), 206–214. doi:10.1080/00038628.2011.590055

Cooper, M. C., & Ellram, L. M. (1993). Characteristics of Supply Chain Management and the Implications for Purchasing and Logistics Strategy. *International Journal of Logistics Management*, *4*(2), 13–24. doi:10.1108/09574099310804957

Cord-Ruwisch, R., Seitz, H.-J., & Conrad, R. (1988). The capacity of hydrogenotrophic anaerobic bacteria to compete for traces of hydrogen depends on the redox potential of the terminal electron acceptor. *Arch Microbio1, 149*, 350-357.

Council of Europe. (2003). Decision 2003/822/EO of 17.11.2003. *OB. L 309.*

Cronbach, L. J. (1951). Coefficient alpha and the internal structure of tests. *Psychometrika, 16*(3), 297-334.

CSVN. (2016). Sustainability Gap Assessment Survey and Insights I. Selangor: Center for Sustainable Value Network (CVSN). Malaysia Institute for Supply Chain Innovation.

Curry, A., & Penman, S. (2004). The relative importance of technology in enhancing customer relationships in banking-a Scottish perspective. *Managing Service Quality: An International Journal*, *14*(4), 331–341. doi:10.1108/09604520410546860

D'Agostino, R. B., Belanger, A., & D'agostino, R. B. Jr. (1990). A suggestion for using powerful and informative tests of normality. *The American Statistician*, *44*(4), 316–321.

Da Silva, F. C., Shibao, F. Y., Barbieri, J. C., Librantz, A. F. H., & Dos Santos, M. R. (2018). Barriers to green supply chain management in the automotive industry. *Revista De Administração De Empresas*, *58*(2), 149–162.

Dadhich, P., Genovese, A., Kumar, N., & Acquaye, A. (2015). Developing sustainable supply chains in the UK construction industry: A case study. *International Journal of Production Economics*, *164*, 271–284. doi:10.1016/j.ijpe.2014.12.012

Darkwah, S. A., & Ankomah, E. K. (2010). Developing the Least Developed Countries in the Larger spectrum of Globalized Economy. In *Proceedings of International Conference on Applied Business Research 2010* (CD-ROM). Ras Al Khaimah, UAE: Mendel University in Brno.

Datta, S. (2008). *WiFi meet FuFi: Disruptive innovation in logistics catalysed by energy.* Academic Press.

Daugherty, P. J., Chen, H., Mattioda, D. D., & Grawe, S. J. (2009). Marketing/logistics relationships: Influence on capabilities and performance. *Journal of Business Logistics, 30*(1), 1–18. doi:10.1002/j.2158-1592.2009.tb00096.x

Daugherty, P. J., Stank, T. P., & Ellinger, A. E. (1998). Leveraging logistics/distribution capabilities: The effect of logistics service on market share. *Journal of Business Logistics, 19*(2), 35.

Davarzani, H., Fahimnia, B., Bell, M. G. H., & Sarkis, J. (2015). A Review of the literature of green ports and maritime logistics. In B. Fahimnia, M. G. H. Bell, D. A. Hensher, & J. Sarkis (Eds.), *Green Logistics and Transportation a Sustainable Supply Chain Perspective* (pp. 149–158). Springer International Publishing. doi:10.1007/978-3-319-17181-4_9

Davis, D. (2019). *Guide to Warehouse Lighting.* Retrieved December 5, 2019, from https://blog.1000bulbs.com/home/guide-to-warehouse-lighting

De Koster, R., Le-Duc, T., & Roodbergen, K. J. (2007). Design and control of warehouse order picking: A literature review. *European Journal of Operational Research, 182*(2), 481–501. doi:10.1016/j.ejor.2006.07.009

de Man, J. C., & Strandhagen, J. O. (2017). An Industry 4.0 research agenda for sustainable business models. *Procedia Cirp, 63*, 721–726. doi:10.1016/j.procir.2017.03.315

DeGeorge, R. (1982). *Business Ethics* (1st ed.). New York: Macmillan.

Dekker, R., Bloemhof, J., & Mallidis, I. (2012). Operations Research for green logistics–An overview of aspects, issues, contributions and challenges. *European Journal of Operational Research, 219*(3), 671–679. doi:10.1016/j.ejor.2011.11.010

Deloitte. (2014). *The shed of the future E-commerce: its impact on warehouses.* London: Deloitte LPP.

Demir, İ. B., & Uğurluoğlu, Ö. (2015). Sağlık Kurumlarında Stratejik Yönetim Araçları. *Hacettepe Sağlık İdaresi Dergisi, 18*(2), 219–251.

Demir, E., Bektaş, T., & Laporte, G. (2014). A review of recent research on green road freight transportation. *European Journal of Operational Research, 237*(3), 775–793. doi:10.1016/j.ejor.2013.12.033

Demir, E., Saatçioğlu, Ö., & İmrol, F. (2016). Uluslararası dergilerde yayımlanan eğitim araştırmalarının normallik varsayımları açısından incelenmesi. *Current Research in Education, 3*(3), 130–148.

Demirel, T., Demirel, N. Ç., & Kahraman, C. (2010). Multi-criteria warehouse location selection using Choquet integral. *Expert Systems with Applications, 37*(5), 3943–3952. doi:10.1016/j.eswa.2009.11.022

Dhillon, G., Coss, D., & Hackney, R. (2001). Interpreting the role of disruptive technologies in e-businesses. *Logistics Information Management, 14*(1/2), 163–171. doi:10.1108/09576050110363167

DHL. (2010). *Delivering Tomorrow: Towards Sustainable Logistics. Deutsche Post DHL.* Bonn: Christof E. Ehrhart.

DHL. (2016). *Robotic in logistics: A DPDHL perspective on implications and use cases for the logistics industry. ST. Onge Company.* Tom Bonkenburg.

DHL. (2018). *Logistics trend radar–delivering insight today. Creating value tomorrow.* DHL Trend Research Report.

Dhull, S., & Narwal, M. S. (2016). Drivers and barriers in green supply chain management adaptation: A state-of-art review. *Uncertain Supply Chain Management, 4*, 61–76. doi:10.5267/j.uscm.2015.7.003

Diabat, A., & Govindan, K. (2011). An analysis of the drivers affecting the implementation of green supply chain management. *Resources, Conservation and Recycling*, *55*(6), 659–667. doi:10.1016/j.resconrec.2010.12.002

Diamond, P., & Vartiainen, H. (2007). *Introduction to behavioral economics and its applications*. Princeton, NJ: Princeton University Press. doi:10.1515/9781400829149

Díaz, M., Martín, C., & Rubio, B. (2016). State-of-the-art, challenges, and open issues in the integration of Internet of things and cloud computing. *Journal of Network and Computer Applications*, *67*, 99–117. doi:10.1016/j.jnca.2016.01.010

Digest of UK Energy Statistics 2017 (DUKES). (2017). Retrieved from www.gov.uk/government/statistics/electricity-chapter-5-digest-of-united-kingdom-energy-statisticsdukes

Dilberoglu, U. M., Gharehpapagh, B., Yaman, U., & Dolen, M. (2017). The role of additive manufacturing in the era of industry 4.0. *Procedia Manufacturing*, *11*, 545–554. doi:10.1016/j.promfg.2017.07.148

Dimara, E., & Skuras, D. (2003). Consumer evaluations of product certification, geographic association and traceability in Greece. *European Journal of Marketing*, *37*(5/6), 690–705. doi:10.1108/03090560310465099

Dinçer, H., Yüksel, S., & Adalı, Z. (2019b). Determining the Effects of Monetary Policies on Capital Markets of the Emerging Economies: An Evidence from E7 Countries. The Impacts of Monetary Policy in the 21st Century: Perspectives from Emerging Economies, 3-16.

Dinçer, H., Yüksel, S., & Canbolat, Z. N. (2019c). A Strategic Approach to Reduce Energy Imports of E7 Countries: Use of Renewable Energy. In Handbook of Research on Economic and Political Implications of Green Trading and Energy Use (pp. 18-38). IGI Global.

Dinçer, H., Yüksel, S., & Pınarbaşı, F. (2019e). SERVQUAL-Based Evaluation of Service Quality of Energy Companies in Turkey: Strategic Policies for Sustainable Economic Development. In The Circular Economy and Its Implications on Sustainability and the Green Supply Chain (pp. 142-167). IGI Global.

Dinçer, H., & Yüksel, S. (2019). Identifying the causality relationship between health expenditure and economic growth: An application on E7 countries. *Journal of Health Systems and Policies*, *1*(1), 5–23.

Dinçer, H., & Yüksel, S. (2019). Multidimensional evaluation of global investments on the renewable energy with the integrated fuzzy decision-making model under the hesitancy. *International Journal of Energy Research*, *43*(5), 1775–1784. doi:10.1002/er.4400

Dinçer, H., Yüksel, S., & Adalı, Z. (2017). Identifying Causality Relationship between Energy Consumption and Economic Growth in Developed Countries. *International Business and Accounting Research Journal*, *1*(2), 71–81. doi:10.15294/ibarj.v1i2.9

Dinçer, H., Yüksel, S., & Canbolat, Z. N. (2019a). A strategic approach to reduce energy imports of E7 countries: use of renewable energy. In *Handbook of research on economic and political implications of green trading and energy use* (pp. 18–38). IGI Global. doi:10.4018/978-1-5225-8547-3.ch002

Dincer, H., Yüksel, S., & Martinez, L. (2019d). Balanced scorecard-based Analysis about European Energy Investment Policies: A hybrid hesitant fuzzy decision-making approach with Quality Function Deployment. *Expert Systems with Applications*, *115*, 152–171. doi:10.1016/j.eswa.2018.07.072

Dinçer, H., Yüksel, S., Pınarbaşı, F., & Çetiner, İ. T. (2019c). Measurement of economic and banking stability in emerging markets by considering income inequality and nonperforming loans. In *Maintaining financial stability in times of risk and uncertainty* (pp. 49–68). IGI Global. doi:10.4018/978-1-5225-7208-4.ch003

Djameh, C., Saalia, F. K., Sinayobye, E., Budu, A., Essilfie, G., Mensah-Brown, H., & Sefah-Dedeh, S. (2015). Optimization of the sorghum malting process for "Pito" production in Ghana. *Journal of the Institute of Brewing*, *121*(1), 106–112. doi:10.1002/jib.191

Dóci, G., Vasileiadou, E., & Petersen, A. C. (2015). Exploring the transition potential of renewable energy communities. *Futures*, *66*, 85–95. doi:10.1016/j.futures.2015.01.002

Dogan, E., & Seker, F. (2016). The influence of real output, renewable and non-renewable energy, trade and financial development on carbon emissions in the top renewable energy countries. *Renewable & Sustainable Energy Reviews*, *60*, 1074–1085. doi:10.1016/j.rser.2016.02.006

Domenech, E., Escriche, I., & Martorell, S. (2008). Assessing the effectiveness of critical control points to guarantee food safety. *Food Control*, *19*(6), 557–565. doi:10.1016/j.foodcont.2007.06.015

Domínguez-Navarro, J. A., Dufo-López, R., Yusta-Loyo, J. M., Artal-Sevil, J. S., & Bernal-Agustín, J. L. (2019). Design of an electric vehicle fast-charging station with integration of renewable energy and storage systems. *International Journal of Electrical Power & Energy Systems*, *105*, 46–58. doi:10.1016/j.ijepes.2018.08.001

Dora, M., Kumar, M., Van Goubergen, D., Molnar, A., & Gellynck, X. (2013). Food quality management system: Reviewing assessment strategies and a feasibility study for European food small and medium-sized enterprises. *Food Control*, *31*(2), 607–616. doi:10.1016/j.foodcont.2012.12.006

Dorotić, H., Doračić, B., Dobravec, V., Pukšec, T., Krajačić, G., & Duić, N. (2019). Integration of transport and energy sectors in island communities with 100% intermittent renewable energy sources. *Renewable & Sustainable Energy Reviews*, *99*, 109–124. doi:10.1016/j.rser.2018.09.033

Doss, C. (2001). How does gender affect the adoption of agricultural innovations? The case of improved maize technology in Ghana. *Agricultural Economics*, *25*(1), 27–39. doi:10.1016/S0169-5150(00)00096-7

Dossou, P. E. (2018). Impact of Sustainability on the supply chain 4.0 performance. *Procedia Manufacturing*, *17*, 452–459. doi:10.1016/j.promfg.2018.10.069

Drath, R., & Horch, A. (2014). Industrie 4.0: Hit or hype? *IEEE Industrial Electronics Magazine*, *8*(2), 56–58. doi:10.1109/MIE.2014.2312079

Draycott, S., Sellar, B., Davey, T., Noble, D. R., Venugopal, V., & Ingram, D. M. (2019). Capture and simulation of the ocean environment for offshore renewable energy. *Renewable & Sustainable Energy Reviews*, *104*, 15–29. doi:10.1016/j.rser.2019.01.011

Dreidy, M., Mokhlis, H., & Mekhilef, S. (2017). Inertia response and frequency control techniques for renewable energy sources: A review. *Renewable & Sustainable Energy Reviews*, *69*, 144–155. doi:10.1016/j.rser.2016.11.170

Duarte, S., & Cruz-Machado, V. (2017, July). Exploring linkages between lean and green supply chain and the industry 4.0. In *International conference on management science and engineering management* (pp. 1242-1252). Springer.

Dubey, R., Gunasekaran, A., & Papadopoulos, T. (2017). Green supply chain management: Theoretical framework and further research directions. *Benchmarking: An International Journal*, *24*(1), 184–218. doi:10.1108/BIJ-01-2016-0011

Duffy, V. G., Wu, F. F., & Ng, P. P. (2003). Development of an internet virtual layout system for improving workplace safety. *Computers in Industry*, *50*(2), 207–230. doi:10.1016/S0166-3615(02)00121-5

Dumitrescu, E. I., & Hurlin, C. (2012). Testing for Granger non-causality in heterogeneous panels. *Economic Modelling*, *29*(4), 1450–1460. doi:10.1016/j.econmod.2012.02.014

Du, Q., Zhou, J., Pan, T., Sun, Q., & Wu, M. (2019). Relationship of carbon emissions and economic growth in China's construction industry. *Journal of Cleaner Production*, *220*, 99–109. doi:10.1016/j.jclepro.2019.02.123

Duska, Shay, & Ragatz. (2011). Accounting Ethics. John Wiley & Sons, Ltd.

Dutta, K. S. (2013). *Statistical Techniques For Forensic Accounting. In Understanding The Theory and Application of Data Analysis*. Upper Saddle River, NJ: FT Press.

Edwards, H. A., Dixon-Hardy, D., & Wadud, Z. (2016). Aircraft cost index and the future of carbon emissions from air travel. *Applied Energy*, *164*, 553–562. doi:10.1016/j.apenergy.2015.11.058

EFSA. (2012). BIOHAZ Panel (EFSA Panel on Biological Hazards), Scientific Opinion on public health risks represented by certain composite products containing food of animal origin. *EFSA Journal*, *10*(5). doi:10.2903/j.efsa.2012.2662

EFSA. (2014). *Drivers of emerging risks and their interactions in the domain of biological risks to animal, plant and public health: a pilot study, EFSA supporting publication, EN-588*. European Food Safety Authority.

Ekici, D. (2013). *Sağlık Hizmetinde Toplam Kalite Yönetimi*. Ankara: Sim Matbaacılık.

Electric Power Research Institute (EPRI). (2004). Evaluating Opportunities for Fast Charging Application at Del Monte Foods. Electric Power Research Institute Report 1002237. Palo Alto, CA: EPRI.

Electricity generation and supply figures for Scotland, Wales, Northern Ireland and England, 2012 to 2015. (2016). Retrieved from www.gov.uk/government/publications/energy-trends-december-2016-special-feature-articles

Elhedhli, S., & Merrick, R. (2012). Green supply chain network design to reduce carbon emissions. *Transportation Research Part D, Transport and Environment*, *17*(5), 370–379. doi:10.1016/j.trd.2012.02.002

Elkington, J. (1998). Partnerships from cannibals with forks: The triple bottom line of 21st-century business. *Environmental Quality Management*, *8*(1), 37–51. doi:10.1002/tqem.3310080106

Ellinger, A. E. (2000). Improving marketing/logistics cross-functional collaboration in the supply chain. *Industrial Marketing Management*, *29*(1), 85–96. doi:10.1016/S0019-8501(99)00114-5

Ellinger, A. E., Daugherty, P. J., & Keller, S. B. (2000). The relationship between marketing/logistics interdepartmental integration and performance in U.S. manufacturing firms: An empirical study. *Journal of Business Logistics*, *21*(1), 1.

Ellram, L. M., & Murfield, M. L. U. (2017). Environmental sustainability in freight transportation: A systematic literature review and agenda for future research. *Transportation Journal*, *56*(3), 263–298. doi:10.5325/transportationj.56.3.0263

Elyakova, I. D., & Koryagina, J. N. (2015). *Efficiency of electric heating in the Western districts of Yakutia. Min. of education and science of the Russian Federation; NEFU; The Yakut Scientific Centre of the Siberian Branch of the Russian Academy of Sciences*. Yakutsk: NEFU Publisher.

Elyakova, I. D., Pakhomov, A. A., Poiseyev, I. I., Yefremov, E. I., Darbasov, V. R., Noyeva, E. Y., ... Elyakov, A. L. (2016). Prospects for development of renewable energy sources to preserve the ecosystem of arctic zone of Russia. *Indian Journal of Science and Technology*, *9*(46), 1–9.

Engelman, R. (2016). Six billion in Africa. *Scientific American*, 31, 56-63.

Environmental Protection Agency. (2015). *2015 Green Communities Criteria*. Retrieved January 13, 2020, from https://www.enterprisecommunity.org/solutions-and-innovation/green-communities/criteria

Environmental Protection Agency. (2019). *Greenhouse Gas Emissions*. Retrieved November 12, 2019, from https://www.epa.gov/ghgemissions/sources-greenhouse-gas-emissions

Environmental transparency of food supply chains-Current status and challenges. (n.d.). *Global Perspective for Competitive Enterprise, Economy and Ecology*, 275-285.

EPA. (1993a). Standards for the use or disposal of sewage sludge. Final Rules, 40 CFR Parts 257, 403, and 503. *Federal Register*, *58*(32), 9248–9415.

EPA. (1993b). *Pretreatment and municipal pollution prevention*. Washington, DC: U.S. Environmental Protection Agency Office of Wastewater Enforcement and Compliance.

Eremić-Đođić, J., & Tomić, A. (2018). Development of the finance model for tourism of local goverments in the function of the performance audit. In *3th International Scientific Conference* (pp. 692-707). University of Крагујевац, Republic of Serbia.

Eremić-Đođić, J., Laban, B., Bošnjak, I., Ćirić, I., Škatarić, G., & Sedlak, O. (2018). An Audit of the Financing Models for Agricultural Housejolds in Local Goverments in Serbia. *Green Room Sessions 2018. Internationa GEA (Geo Eco – Eco Agro) Conference Book of Proceedings, 2,* 301-317.

Eremić-Đođić, J., Laban. B.& Tomić, A. (2017). Forenzička revizija-sprečavanje, otkrivanje i odgovornosti za finansijske kriminalne radnje u kompanijama, časopis „Poslovna ekonomija", Univerzitet Edukons, Sr.Kamenica, godina XI, broj 2 [Forensic Audit - Prevention, Detection and Responsibility for Financial Crimes in Companies]. *Journal of Business Economics, Educational University, 11*(2).

Ergülen, A., & Büyükkeklik, A. (2008). Çevre yönetiminde yeni bir yaklaşım yeşil tedarik zinciri yönetimi [A new approach in environmental management green supply chain management]. *Selçuk University Journal of Vocational School of Social Sciences*, *10*(1-2), 33–50.

Eroglu, C., Kurt, A. C., & Elwakil, O. S. (2016). Stock Market Reaction to Quality, Safety, and Sustainability Awards in Logistics. *Journal of Business Logistics*, *37*(4), 329–345. doi:10.1111/jbl.12145

Erol, S., Jäger, A., Hold, P., Ott, K., & Sihn, W. (2016). Tangible Industry 4.0: A scenario-based approach to learning for the future of production. *Procedia CiRp*, *54*, 13–18. doi:10.1016/j.procir.2016.03.162

Ersin, İ. (2020). Determining the Importance of Domestic Firms on Stock Market Performance in Terms of Financial Marketing: An Application on OECD Countries. In Handbook of Research on Decision-Making Techniques in Financial Marketing (pp. 269-286). IGI Global.

Ersin, İ., & Baş, H. (2019). Güney Avrupa refah ülkelerinde sosyal harcamalar ve ekonomik büyüme arasındaki ilişkinin incelenmesi. *SGD-Sosyal Güvenlik Dergisi*, *9*(1), 193–213. doi:10.32331gd.582752

Eskandarpour, M., Dejax, P., Miemczyk, J., & Péton, O. (2015). Sustainable supply chain network design: An optimization-oriented review. *Omega*, *54*, 11–32. doi:10.1016/j.omega.2015.01.006

Eunomia Research and Consulting. (2008). *Greenhouse gas balances of waste management scenarios. Report for the Greater London Authority*. Retrieved from www.london.gov.uk/mayor/environment/waste/climate-change/greenhousegas.jsp

European Commission. (2011). *Science for environment report*. Bristol: The University of the West of England.

European Union's Council of Ministers. (2001). *2340th Council meeting Transport / Telecommunications*. Retrieved November 26, 2019, from https://ec.europa.eu/commission/presscorner/detail/en/PRES_01_131

European, C. (2014). *Food safety. Ensuring a high level of protection of human health and consumers' interests*. Brussels: Publications Office.

Evangelista, P. (2012). Disruptive innovation trends in transport and logistics. INNO-GripsWorkshop on Disruptive Innovation, Brussels, Belgium.

Evtodieva, T. E., Chernova, D. V., Ivanova, N. V., & Kisteneva, N. S. (2019). Logistics 4.0. In S. Ashmarina & M. Vochozka (Eds.), *Sustainable Growth and Development of Economic Systems. Contributions to Economics*. Cham: Springer. doi:10.1007/978-3-030-11754-2_16

Evtodieva, T. E., Chernova, D. V., Voitkevich, N. I., Khramtsova, E. R., & Gorgodze, T. E. (2017). Transformation of logistics organization forms under the conditions of modern economy. In E. G. Popkova (Ed.), *Contributions to Economics*. Cham: Springer.

Facchini, F., Mummolo, G., Mossa, G., Digiesi, S., Boenzi, F., & Verriello, R. (2016). Minimizing the carbon footprint of material handling equipment: Comparison of electric and LPG forklifts. *Journal of Industrial Engineering and Management*, *9*(5), 1035–1046. doi:10.3926/jiem.2082

Fahimnia, B., Farahani, R. Z., Marian, R., & Luong, L. (2013). A review and critique on integrated production-distribution planning models and techniques. *Journal of Manufacturing Systems*, *32*(1), 1–19. doi:10.1016/j.jmsy.2012.07.005

Faisal, M. (2015). Research analysis on barriers to green supply chain management in pharmaceutical industries. *Review of Public Administration and Management*, *3*(1). doi:10.4172/2315-7844.1000176

FAO. (2015). Retrieved from http://faostat3.fao.org/download/Q/QC/E

Farahani, R. Z., Rezapour, S., Drezner, T., & Fallah, S. (2014). Competitive supply chain network design: An overview of classifications, models, solution techniques and applications. *Omega*, *45*, 92–118. doi:10.1016/j.omega.2013.08.006

Fernández-Villacañas, M. A. (2008). *Reflexiones en torno al logro de una Logística Global Sostenible* [Reflections on the achievement of a Sustainable Global Logistics]. V Congreso Internacional ACOLOG - Asociación Colombiana de Logística, Bogotá (Colombia).

Fernández-Villacañas, M. A. (2019b). Strategies for the Digital Transformation for the In-Service Support Phase of the Aerospace Weapon Systems. *Proceedings of the Third International Joint Conference of Logistics by EPFAC & UMNG*.

Fernández-Villacañas, M.A. (2018) *Las plataformas logística 4.0 y la mejora del comercio global: Creando ventaja competitiva logística y desarrollo sostenible* [Logistics 4.0 platforms and the improvement of global trade: Creating competitive logistics advantage and sustainable development]. VI Simposio Internacional Online de Logística y Competitividad, High Logistics Simposios, Medellín, Colombia.

Fernández-Villacañas, M. A. (2019a). Desarrollo e Implementación de Plataformas Logísticas de Carga 4.0 [Development and Implementation of Logistics Cargo Platforms 4.0]. *Proceedings of Primer Congreso Internacional de Tecnología e Innovación en Logística 4.0*.

Fichtner Consulting Engineers. (2004). *The viability of advanced thermal treatment of MSW in the UK*. Retrieved from www.esauk.org/publications/reports/thermal%20treatment%20report.pdf

Fielding, L. M., Ellis, L., Beveridge, C., & Peters, A. C. (2005). An evaluation of HACCP implementation status in UK small and medium enterprises in food manufacturing. *International Journal of Environmental Health Research*, *15*(2), 117–126. doi:10.1080/09603120500061583 PMID:16026023

Food and Agricultural Organization of the United Nations. (2013). FAO Country Profiles: Ghana. *Food and Agricultural Organization of the United Nations*. Retrieved from http://www.fao.org/countryprofiles/index/en/?iso3=GHA

Food and Agricultural Organization of the United Nations. (2017). *Crop*. Retrieved from http://www.fao.org/faostat/en/#data/QC

Food and Agriculture Organization of the United Nations. (1997). *Agriculture food and nutrition for Africa - A resource book for teachers of agriculture (FAO Information Division)*. Rome: Author.

Food safety in the EU. (2003). Retrieved from Official website of the European Union: https://europa.eu/european-union/topics/food-safety_en

Fornell, C., & Larcker, D. F. (1981). Evaluating structural equation models with unobservable variables and measurement error. *JMR, Journal of Marketing Research*, *18*(1), 39–50. doi:10.1177/002224378101800104

Franco-Luesma, S., Cavero, J., Plaza-Bonilla, D., Cantero-Martínez, C., Arrúe, J. L., & Álvaro-Fuentes, J. (2020). Tillage and irrigation system effects on soil carbon dioxide (CO2) and methane (CH4) emissions in a maize monoculture under Mediterranean conditions. *Soil & Tillage Research*, *196*, 104488. doi:10.1016/j.still.2019.104488

Frazzon, E., Rodriguez, C. M., Pereira, M., Pires, M., & Uhlmann, I. (2019). Towards Supply Chain Management 4.0. *Brazilian Journal of Operations & Production Management, Volume*, *16*(2).

Freda, M. (2019). *Cereal Grains of Africa*. Retrieved from https://www.thespruceeats.com/cereal-grains-of-Africa-39517

Freis, J., Vohlidka, P., & Gunthner, W. (2016). Low-carbon warehousing: Examining impacts of building and intra-logistics design options on energy demand and the CO^2 emissions of logistics centers. *Sustainability*, *8*(5), 448. doi:10.3390u8050448

Frewer, V. R. (2008). Consumer perceptions of food quality and safety and their relation to traceability. *British Food Journal*, *110*(10), 1034–1046. doi:10.1108/00070700810906642

Fuc, P., Kurczewski, P., Lewandowska, A., Nowak, E., Selech, J., & Ziolkowski, A. (2016). An environmental life cycle assessment of forklift operation: A well-to-wheel analysis. *The International Journal of Life Cycle Assessment*, *21*(10), 1438–1451. doi:10.100711367-016-1104-y

Fulponi, L. (2007). *The globalization of private standards and the agri-food system. Global Supply Chains, Standards and the Poor* (1st ed.). Cambridge: CAB International.

Gajšek, B., & Grzybowska, K. (2013). A cross-county contextual comparison of the understanding of the term logistics platforms in practice. Research in Logistics & Production, 3(2).

Gajšek, B., & Grzybowska, K. (2016) Supply Chain Logistics Platform as a Supply Chain Coordination Support. Highlights of Practical Applications of Scalable Multi-Agent Systems. Proceedings of Collection International Workshops of PAAMS 2016. Doi:10.1007/978-3-319-39387-2_6

Garengo, P., & Biazzo, S. (2012). From ISO quality standards to an integrated management system: An implementation process in SME. *Total Quality Management & Business Excellence*, *24*(3-4), 310–335. doi:10.1080/14783363.2012.704282

Garten, J. E. (2016). The man who made the computer age possible. *Strategy and Business*. Retrieved from https://www.strategy-business.com/article/The-Man-Who-Made-the-Computer-Age-Possible

GavinM. L. (2014). *Figuring out fibre*. Retrieved from https://kidshealth.org/en/parents/ fiber.html

Gavrilović, D. (2019). Regions in Serbia. Belgrade: Statistical office of the Republic of Serbia. (in Serbian)

Gaweł, A. (2012). Entrepreneurship and sustainability: do they have anything in common? Poznan University of Economics Review, 12(1), 5-16.

Geerlings, H., & Van Duin, R. (2011). A new method for assessing CO^2-emissions from container terminals: A promising approach applied in Rotterdam. *Journal of Cleaner Production*, *19*(6-7), 657–666. doi:10.1016/j.jclepro.2010.10.012

Geisberger, E., Cengarle, M., Keil, P., Niehaus, J., Thiel, C., & Thönnißen-Fries, H. J. (2011). *Cyber-Physical Systems-Driving force for innovation in mobility, health, energy and production.* Acatech-Deutsche Akademie der Technikwissenschaften.

Geissbauer, R., Vedso, J., & Schrauf, S. (2016b). *Industry 4.0–Building the digital enterprise (2016).* PWC 2016 Global Industry 4.0 Survey. Retrieved from https://www.pwc.com/gx/en/industries/industries-4.0/landing-page/industry-4.0-building-your-digital-enterprise-april-2016.pdf

Geissbauer, R., Vedsø, J., & Schrauf, S. (2016a). *A strategist's guide to industry 4.0.* Strategy and Business.

Gençer, E., & Agrawal, R. (2016). A commentary on the US policies for efficient large scale renewable energy storage systems: Focus on carbon storage cycles. *Energy Policy*, *88*, 477–484. doi:10.1016/j.enpol.2015.11.003

Gencer, Y. G. (2016). Mystery of Recycling: Glass and Aluminum Examples. In U. Akkucuk (Ed.), *Handbook of Research on Waste Management Techniques for Sustainability* (pp. 172–191). Hershey, PA: IGI Global. doi:10.4018/978-1-4666-9723-2.ch009

Gencer, Y. G., & Akkucuk, U. (2016). Reverse Logistics: Automobile Recalls and Other Conditions. In U. Akkucuk (Ed.), *Handbook of Research on Waste Management Techniques for Sustainability* (pp. 125–154). Hershey, PA: IGI Global. doi:10.4018/978-1-4666-9723-2.ch007

Gereffi, G., & Lee, J. (2002). *A global value chain approach to food safety and quality standards.* Global Health Diplomacy for Chronic Disease Prevention Working Paper Series. Duke University.

Gevaers, R., Voorde, E. V., & Vanelslander, T. (2009). Characteristics of Innovations in Last-Mile Logistics - Using Best Practices, Case Studies and Making the Link with Green and Sustainable Logistics. In Proceedings of the E. T. Conference. Association for t European Transport and Contibutors.

Gevaers, R., Voorde, E. V., & Vanelslander, T. (2014). Cost Modelling and Simulation of Last-mile Characteristics in an Innovative B2C Supply Chain Environment with Implications on Urban Areas and Cities. *8th International Conference on City Logistics*, *125*(2014), 398-411. 10.1016/j.sbspro.2014.01.1483

Gevaers, R., Van de Voorde, E., & Vanelslander, T. (2011). *Characteristics and Typology of Last-Mile Logistics from an Innovative Perspective in an Urban Context.* Presented at the *Transportation Research Board Annual Meeting*, Washington, DC.

Ghadimi, P., Wang, C., Lim, M. K., & Heavey, C. (2019). Intelligent sustainable supplier selection using multi-agent technology: Theory and application for Industry 4.0 supply chains. *Computers & Industrial Engineering*, *127*, 588–600. doi:10.1016/j.cie.2018.10.050

Ghayur, A., & Verheyen, T. V. (2018). Technical evaluation of post-combustion CO2 capture and hydrogen production industrial symbiosis. *International Journal of Hydrogen Energy*, *43*(30), 13852–13859. doi:10.1016/j.ijhydene.2018.02.069

Ghiani, G., Manni, E., Quaranta, A., & Triki, C. (2009). Anticipatory algorithms for same-day courier dispatching. *Transportation Research Part E, Logistics and Transportation Review*, *45*(1), 96–106. doi:10.1016/j.tre.2008.08.003

Giddey, S., Badwal, S. P., & Ju, H. (2019). Polymer electrolyte membrane technologies integrated with renewable energy for hydrogen production. In Current Trends and Future Developments on (Bio-) Membranes (pp. 235-259). Elsevier. doi:10.1016/B978-0-12-813545-7.00010-6

Gigerenzer, G. (2008). Why heuristics work. *Perspectives on Psychological Science*, *3*(1), 20–29. doi:10.1111/j.1745-6916.2008.00058.x PMID:26158666

Gigerenzer, G., Hertwig, R., & Thorsten, P. (2011). *Heuristics: the foundations of adaptive behavior*. New York: Oxford University Press. doi:10.1093/acprof:oso/9780199744282.001.0001

Gigerenzer, G., & Sturm, T. (2012). How (far) can rationality be naturalized? *Synthese*, *187*(1), 243–268. doi:10.100711229-011-0030-6

Gil Saura, I., & Ruiz Molina, M. E. (2011). Logistics service quality and buyer–customer relationships: The moderating role of technology in B2B and B2C contexts. *Service Industries Journal*, *31*(7), 1109–1123. doi:10.1080/02642060903100380

Gil Saura, I., Ruiz Molina, M. E., & Frances, D. S. (2008). Logistic service quality and technology: A comparison between supplier–retailer and retailer–consumer relationships. *International Review of Retail, Distribution and Consumer Research*, *18*(5), 495–510. doi:10.1080/09593960802573385

Gil Saura, I., Servera Frances, D., Berenguer Contri, G., & Fuentes Blasco, M. (2008). Logistics service quality: A new way to loyalty. *Industrial Management & Data Systems*, *108*(5), 650–668. doi:10.1108/02635570810876778

Gill, A., & Ishaq Bhatti, M. (2007). Optimal model for warehouse location and retailer allocation. *Applied Stochastic Models in Business and Industry*, *23*(3), 213–221. doi:10.1002/asmb.666

Gils, H. C., Scholz, Y., Pregger, T., de Tena, D. L., & Heide, D. (2017). Integrated modelling of variable renewable energy-based power supply in Europe. *Energy*, *123*, 173–188. doi:10.1016/j.energy.2017.01.115

Giovanis, A. N., Tomaras, P., & Zondiros, D. (2013). Suppliers logistics service quality performance and its effect on retailers' behavioral intentions. *Procedia: Social and Behavioral Sciences*, *73*, 302–309. doi:10.1016/j.sbspro.2013.02.056

Gliem, J. A., & Gliem, R. R. (2003). Calculating, interpreting, and reporting cronbach's alpha reliability coefficient for likert-type scales. In *2003 Midwest Research to Practice Conference in Adult, Continuing, and Community Education* (pp.82-88). Academic Press.

Global Palm Oil Production. (2016). Retrieved from https://www.slideshare.net/GreenPalmOil/2015-global-palm-oil-production-by-country

Göçmen, E., & Erol, R. (2018). The Transition To Industry 4.0 In One Of The Turkish Logistics Company. *International Journal Of 3d Printing Technologies And Digital Industry*, *2*(1), 76-85.

Golini, R., Caniato, F., & Kalchschmidt, M. (2016). Linking global value chains and supply chain management: Evidence from the electric motors industry. *Production Planning and Control*, *27*(11), 934–951. doi:10.1080/09537287.2016.1170225

Gong, M., Liu, H., Atif, R. M., & Jiang, X. (2019). A study on the factor market distortion and the carbon emission scale effect of two-way FDI. *Chinese Journal of Population Resources and Environment*, *17*(2), 145–153. doi:10.1080/10042857.2019.1574487

Gonzalez, E. D. R. S., Sarkis, J., Huisingh, D., Huatuco, L. H., Maculan, N., Montoya-Torres, J. R., & De Almeida, C. M. V. B. (2015). Making real progress toward more sustainable societies using decision support models and tools: Introduction to the special volume. *Journal of Cleaner Production*, *105*, 1–13. doi:10.1016/j.jclepro.2015.05.047

Goodland, R., & Bank, W. (2002). Sustainability: Human, Social, Economic and Environmental. *Social Science*, *6*, 220–225.

Gordon, D. (1995). Sustainable transportation: what do we mean and how do we get there. *Transportation and Energy: Strategies for a sustainable transportation system*, 1-11. doi:. doi:10.3141/1670-05

Goren, S. (2005). *Sanitary landfill*. Istanbul: FU Publications.

Goren, S. (2015). Sustainable waste management. In U. Akkucuk (Ed.), *Handbook of research on developing sustainable value in economics, finance, and marketing*. Hershey, PA: IGI Global. doi:10.4018/978-1-4666-6635-1.ch009

A. Gosavi, & S. E. Grasman (Eds.). (2009). Simulation-based optimization for determining AGV capacity in a manufacturing system. In *IIE Annual Conference Proceedings*. Institute of Industrial and Systems Engineers.

Gourdin, K. N. (2006). *Global logistics management: A competitive advantage for the 21st century* (2nd ed.). Wiley-Blackwell Publishing.

Govindan, K., Fattahi, M., & Keyvanshokooh, E. (2017). Supply chain network design under uncertainty: A comprehensive review and future research directions. *European Journal of Operational Research*, *263*(1), 108–141. doi:10.1016/j.ejor.2017.04.009

Govindan, K., Garg, K., Gupta, S., & Jha, P. C. (2016). Effect of product recovery and sustainability enhancing indicators on the location selection of manufacturing facility. *Ecological Indicators*, *67*, 517–532. doi:10.1016/j.ecolind.2016.01.035

Govindan, K., Mathiyazhagan, K., Kannan, D., & Haq, A. N. (2014). Barriers analysis for green supply chain management implementation in Indian industries using analytic hierarchy process. *International Journal of Production Economics*, *147*, 555–568. doi:10.1016/j.ijpe.2013.08.018

Greenberg, J. (2002). *Managing Behavior in Organizations*. Prentice Hall.

Green, K. W. Jr, Whitten, D., & Inman, R. A. (2008). The impact of logistics performance on organizational performance in a supply chain context. *Supply Chain Management*, *13*(4), 317–327. doi:10.1108/13598540810882206

Grega, L. & Ankomah, E. K. (2016). The environmental effect of land use in the tenure systems in Ghana. *Acta of Mendel University of agriculture and forestry Brno, 64*(6), 1211-8516. doi:10.11118/actaun201664061889

Grega, L., Ankomah, E. K., & Darkwah, S. A. (2015). Analysis of land tenure systems and its relationship with productivity in the agricultural sector in Ghana. *Acta of Mendel University of agriculture and forestry Brno, 63*(3), 893-902.

Greit, M. (1992). *The Visual Factory*. Portland, OR: Productivity Press.

Griggs, D. M.-S., Stafford-Smith, M., Gaffney, O., Rockström, J., Öhman, M. C., Shyamsundar, P., ... Noble, I. (2013). Policy: Sustainable development goals for people and planet. *Nature*, *495*(7441), 305–307. doi:10.1038/495305a PMID:23518546

Grunert, K. (2002). Current issues in the understanding of consumer food choice. *Trends in Food Science & Technology*, *13*(8), 275–285. doi:10.1016/S0924-2244(02)00137-1

Grunert, K. G. (2011). Sustainability in the food sector: A consumer behaviour perspective. *International Journal on Food System Dynamics*, *2*(3), 207–218.

Grunert, K. G., Larsen, H. H., Madsen, T. K., & Baadsgaard, A. (1996). *Market orientation in food and agriculture*. Norwell, MA: Kluwer Academic. doi:10.1007/978-1-4613-1301-4

Gružauskas, V., Baskutis, S., & Navickas, V. (2018). Minimizing the trade-off between sustainability and cost effective performance by using autonomous vehicles. *Journal of Cleaner Production*, *184*, 709–717. doi:10.1016/j.jclepro.2018.02.302

Gue, K. R., & Meller, R. D. (2009). Aisle configurations for unit-load warehouses. *IIE Transactions*, *41*(3), 171–182. doi:10.1080/07408170802112726

Gue, K., Ivanovi'c, G., & Meller, R. (2012). A unit-load warehouse with multiple pickup and deposit points and non-traditional aisles. *Transportation Research Part E, Logistics and Transportation Review*, *48*(4), 795–806. doi:10.1016/j.tre.2012.01.002

Gurtu, A. (2019). A pioneering approach to reducing fuel cost and carbon emissions from transportation. *Transportation Journal*, *58*(4), 309–322. doi:10.5325/transportationj.58.4.0309

Gurtu, A., Jaber, M. Y., & Searcy, C. (2015). Impact of fuel price and emissions on inventory policies. *Applied Mathematical Modelling*, *39*(3-4), 1202–1216. doi:10.1016/j.apm.2014.08.001

Hafner, P., & Krstić, M. (2011). Application of rational choice theory in the analysis of criminal behavior. [in Serbian]. *Ekonomika (Nis)*, *57*(1), 37–47.

Hair, J. F., Jr., Hult, G. T. M., Ringle, C., & Sarstedt, M. (2017). A primer on partial least squares structural equation modeling (PLS-SEM) (2nd ed.). Sage Publications.

Han, L., Chin, S.-M., Franzese, O., & Hwang, H.-L. (2005). Estimating the impact of pickup-and delivery-related illegal parking activities on traffic. *Transportation Research Record Journal of the Transportation Research Board,* (1906), 49-55 Doi:10.3141/1906-06

Handfield, R.B., & Nicoles, E.L. (1999). *Introduction to Supply Chain Management*. Prentice-Hall International.

Hands, D. W. (2015). *Normative rational choice theory: past, present, and future*. Retrieved from https://www.researchgate.net/publication/228319027_Normative_Rational_Choice_Theory_Past_Present_and_Future

Hands, D. W. (2014). Normative ecological rationality: Normative rationality in the fast-and-frugal-heuristics research program. *Journal of Economic Methodology*, *21*(4), 396–410. doi:10.1080/1350178X.2014.965907

Hans-Peter, K. (2013). Population growth. In B. Lomborg (Ed.), *Global Problems, Smart Solutions: Costs and Benefits* (pp. 510–596). Cambridge: Cambridge University Press. doi:10.1017/CBO9781139600484.011

Hassan, M. U., Rehmani, M. H., Kotagiri, R., Zhang, J., & Chen, J. (2019). Differential privacy for renewable energy resources based smart metering. *Journal of Parallel and Distributed Computing*, *131*, 69–80. doi:10.1016/j.jpdc.2019.04.012

Hassini, E., Surti, C., & Searcy, C. (2012). A literature review and a case study of sustainable supply chains with a focus on metrics. *International Journal of Production Economics*, *140*(1), 69–82. doi:10.1016/j.ijpe.2012.01.042

Havinga, T. (2008). Retail driven food safety regulation. In *Food safety, market organization, trade and development* (1st ed., Vol. 1). Geneva: Springer International Publishing.

Hemmati, R., & Saboori, H. (2016). Emergence of hybrid energy storage systems in renewable energy and transport applications–A review. *Renewable & Sustainable Energy Reviews*, *65*, 11–23. doi:10.1016/j.rser.2016.06.029

Henseler, J., Ringle, C. M., & Sarstedt, M. (2015). A new criterion for assessing discriminant validity in variance-based structural equation modeling. *Journal of the Academy of Marketing Science*, *43*(1), 115–135. doi:10.100711747-014-0403-8

Henson, S. (2008). The role of public and private standards in regulating international food markets. *Journal of International Agricultural Trade and Developments*, *4*(1), 63–81.

Henze, M., Hermerschmidt, L., Kerpen, D., Häußling, R., Rumpe, B., & Wehrle, K. (2016). A comprehensive approach to privacy in the cloud-based Internet of Things. *Future Generation Computer Systems*, *56*, 701–718. doi:10.1016/j.future.2015.09.016

Hermann, M., Pentek, T., & Otto, B. (2016, January). Design principles for industrie 4.0 scenarios. In *2016 49th Hawaii international conference on system sciences (HICSS)* (pp. 3928-3937). IEEE.

Hervani, A. A., Helms, M. M., & Sarkis, J. (2005). Performance measurement for green supply chain management. Benchmarking. *International Journal (Toronto, Ont.)*, *12*(4), 330–353. doi:10.1108/14635770510609015

Heukelom, F. (2011). Behavioral economics. In J. B. Davis & D. W. Hands (Eds.), *The elgar companion to recent economic methodology* (pp. 19–38). Cheltenham: Edward Elgar Publishing. doi:10.4337/9780857938077.00007

Hitchcock, F. L. (1941). The distribution of a product from several sources to numerous locations. *Journal of Mathematics and Physics*, *20*(1-4), 224–230. doi:10.1002apm1941201224

Hoang, V. H., & Nguyen, T. S. (2019). *The effect of logistics service on firm financial performance in textile industry: evidence from Da Nang city, Vietnam*. Paper presented at the MATEC Web of Conferences. 10.1051/matecconf/201925904002

Hodges, D. G., Chapagain, B., Watcharaanantapong, P., Poudyal, N. C., Kline, K. L., & Dale, V. H. (2019). Opportunities and attitudes of private forest landowners in supplying woody biomass for renewable energy. *Renewable & Sustainable Energy Reviews*, *113*, 109205. doi:10.1016/j.rser.2019.06.012

Hoffman, A.J. (2006, Sept. 5). The Real Thing. Coca-Cola learns a tough lesson about corporate sustainability. *Grist Magazine: Environmental News and Commentary*.

Hofmann, E., & Osterwalder, F. (2017). Third-party logistics providers in the digital age: Towards a new competitive arena? *Logistics*, *1*(2), 9. doi:10.3390/logistics1020009

Hofmann, E., & Rüsch, M. (2017). Industry 4.0 and the current status as well as future prospects on logistics. *Computers in Industry*, *89*, 23–34. doi:10.1016/j.compind.2017.04.002

Hooper, D., Coughlan, J., & Mullen, M. (2008). Structural equation modelling: Guidelines for determining model fit. *Articles*, 2.

Hoornweg, D., & Bhada-Tata, P. (2012). *What a waste*. World Bank 2012, Urban Development & Local Government Unit, No. 15.

Horák, M., Darkwah, S. A., & Verter, N. (2014). Tourism as a Poverty Reduction Tool: The Case of Mukuni Village in the Southern Province of Zambia. *Acta Universitatis Agriculturae et Silviculturae Mendelianae Brunensis*, *62*(6), 1287-1292.

Hosmer, L. T. (1994). Strategic Planning as if Ethics Mattered. *Strategic Management Journal*, 15.

Hossain, M. S., Madlool, N. A., Rahim, N. A., Selvaraj, J., Pandey, A. K., & Khan, A. F. (2016). Role of smart grid in renewable energy: An overview. *Renewable & Sustainable Energy Reviews*, *60*, 1168–1184. doi:10.1016/j.rser.2015.09.098

Hosseini, S. E., & Wahid, M. A. (2016). Hydrogen production from renewable and sustainable energy resources: Promising green energy carrier for clean development. *Renewable & Sustainable Energy Reviews*, *57*, 850–866. doi:10.1016/j.rser.2015.12.112

Hsu, J. (2019). *Out of the Way, Human! Delivery Robots Want a Share of Your Sidewalk*. Retrieved November 22, 2019, from https://www.scientificamerican.com/article/out-of-the-way-human-delivery-robots-want-a-share-of-your-sidewalk/

Huang, A. Q. (2019). Power semiconductor devices for smart grid and renewable energy systems. *Power Electronics in Renewable Energy Systems and Smart Grid: Technology and Applications*, 85-152.

Huang, Y. W., Kittner, N., & Kammen, D. M. (2019). ASEAN grid flexibility: Preparedness for grid integration of renewable energy. *Energy Policy*, *128*, 711–726. doi:10.1016/j.enpol.2019.01.025

Hübner, A., Holzapfel, A., Kuhn, H., & Obermair, E. (2019). Distribution in Omnichannel Groccery Retailing. In *Operations in an Omnichannel World /Springer Series in Supply Chain Management* (pp. 293–294). Cham: Springer Nature.

Hu, L., & Bentler, P. M. (1999). Cutoff criteria for fit indexes in covariance structure analysis: Conventional criteria versus new alternatives. *Structural Equation Modeling*, *6*(1), 1–55. doi:10.1080/10705519909540118

Huňady, J., Pisár, P., & Balco, P. (2020). Determinants of Employment in Information and Communication Technologies and Its Structure. In *Data-Centric Business and Applications* (pp. 277–298). Cham: Springer. doi:10.1007/978-3-030-19069-9_11

Huppertz, P. (1999). Market changes require new supply chain thinking. *Transportation & Distribution*, 70-4.

Hussain, A., Arif, S. M., & Aslam, M. (2017). Emerging renewable and sustainable energy technologies: State of the art. *Renewable & Sustainable Energy Reviews*, *71*, 12–28. doi:10.1016/j.rser.2016.12.033

IEA. (2019). *Tracking Transport*. Retrieved December 16, 2019, https://www.iea.org/reports/tracking-transport-2019

Inglesi-Lotz, R. (2016). The impact of renewable energy consumption to economic growth: A panel data application. *Energy Economics*, *53*, 58–63. doi:10.1016/j.eneco.2015.01.003

Inman, R. R., & Bhaskaran, S. (2019). Empirical evaluation of the delivery risk of extended supply chains. *International Journal of Production Research*, *57*(11), 3466–3477. doi:10.1080/00207543.2018.1539264

Innis, D. E., & La Londe, B. J. (1994). Modelling the effects of customer service performance on purchase intentions in the channel. *Journal of Marketing Theory and Practice*, *2*(2), 45–60. doi:10.1080/10696679.1994.11501650

Işik, C., Kasımatı, E., & Ongan, S. (2017). Analyzing the causalities between economic growth, financial development, international trade, tourism expenditure and/on the CO2 emissions in Greece. *Energy Sources. Part B, Economics, Planning, and Policy*, *12*(7), 665–673. doi:10.1080/15567249.2016.1263251

ISO. (2005). ISO 22000:2005 Food safety management systems. Requirements for any organization in the food chain. Geneva: ISO.

ISO. (2015a). ISO 9000:2015 – Quality management systems — Fundamentals and vocabulary. Geneva: ISO.

ISO. (2015b). ISO 9001:2015 – Quality management systems — Requirements. Geneva: ISO.

ISO. (2018a). *22000:2018 Food safety management systems — Requirements for any organization in the food chain*. ISO.

ISO. (2018b). ISO 31000:2018 – Risk management. Principles and instructions. Geneva: ISO.

Jaffee, S. H. (2004). Standards and agro-food exports from developing countries: Rebalancing the debate. *World Bank Policy Research Working*, *3348*(1), 44–50.

Jäger, P., & Schmidt, T. (2016). The political economy of public investment when population is aging: A panel cointegration analysis. *European Journal of Political Economy*, *43*, 145–158. doi:10.1016/j.ejpoleco.2016.04.004

Jakopin, E., & Čokorilo, N. (2019). Trends - analysis of work of public and state-owned firms in the Republic of Serbia 2015-2017. Belgrade: Statistical office of the Republic of Serbia. (in Serbian)

Jamel, L., & Maktouf, S. (2017). The nexus between economic growth, financial development, trade openness, and CO2 emissions in European countries. *Cogent Economics & Finance*, *5*(1), 1341456. doi:10.1080/23322039.2017.1341456

Janic, M. (2007). Modelling the full costs of an intermodal and road freight transport network. *Transportation Research Part D, Transport and Environment*, *12*(1), 33–44. doi:10.1016/j.trd.2006.10.004

Jebli, M. B., Youssef, S. B., & Ozturk, I. (2016). Testing environmental Kuznets curve hypothesis: The role of renewable and non-renewable energy consumption and trade in OECD countries. *Ecological Indicators*, *60*, 824–831. doi:10.1016/j.ecolind.2015.08.031

Jevons, W. S. (1965). The theory of political economy. New York: Kelley. (Original publication 1871)

Jiang, Y., Zhou, X., & Xu, Q. (2019). Scenario analysis-based decision and coordination in supply chain management with production and transportation scheduling. *Symmetry*, *11*(2), 160. doi:10.3390ym11020160

Jodkowski, L. (2015). Possibilities and Methods of Risk Assessment under ISO 9001:2015. *International Journal of Managerial Studies and Research*, *3*(10), 14–23.

Joerss, M., Neuhaus, F., & Schröder, J. (2016b). How customer demands are reshaping last-mile delivery. *The McKinsey Quarterly*, *17*, 1–5.

Joerss, M., Schröder, J., Neuhaus, F., Klink, C., & Mann, F. (2016a). *Parcel delivery: The future of last mile*. McKinsey & Company.

Johnson, E. (2008). Disagreement over carbon footprints: A comparison of electric and LPG forklifts. *Energy Policy*, *36*(4), 1569–1573. doi:10.1016/j.enpol.2008.01.014

Jones, K. (2010). *Aircraft Noise and Children's Learning. Civil Aviation Authority*. Norwich: The Stationery Office.

Jöreskog, K. G. (1999). *Formulas for skewness and kurtosis*. Retrieved from http://www.ssicentral.com/lisrel

Jöreskog, K. G., & Sörbom, D. (1993). *Structural Equation Modelling With the Simplis Command Language*. Scientific Software International.

Kabe, T., Tanaka, K., Ikeda, H., & Sugimoto, N. (2010). Consideration on safety for emerging technology–Case studies of seven service robots. *Safety Science*, *48*(3), 296–301. doi:10.1016/j.ssci.2009.11.008

Kaddoussi, A., Zoghlami, N., Zgaya, H., Hammadi, S., & Bretaudeau, F. (2011, October). A preventive anticipation model for crisis management supply chain. In *2011 IEEE International Conference on Systems, Man, and Cybernetics* (pp. 109-114). IEEE. 10.1109/ICSMC.2011.6083651

Kagermann, H., Anderl, R., Gausemeier, J., Schuh, G., & Wahlster, W. (Eds.). (2016). *Industrie 4.0 in a Global Context: strategies for cooperating with international partners*. Herbert Utz Verlag.

Kagermann, H., Wahlster, W., & Helbig, J. (2013). *Recommendations for implementing the strategic initiative Industrie 4.0: Final report of the Industrie 4.0 Working Group*. Berlin, Germany: Forschungsunion.

Kahn Ribeiro, S., Figueroa, M. J., Creutzig, F., Dubeux, C., Hupe, J., & Kobayashi, S. (2012). Energy end-use: Transport. In Global Energy Assessment-Toward a Sustainable Future. Cambridge University Press.

Kahneman, D. (2003). Maps of bounded rationality: Psychology for behavioral economics. *The American Economic Review*, *93*(5), 1449–1475. doi:10.1257/000282803322655392

Kahneman, D. (2015). *Thinking, fast and slow*. Smederevo: Heliks. (in Serbian)

Kahneman, D., & Tversky, A. (1979). Prospect theory: An analysis of decision under risk. *Econometrica*, *47*(2), 363–391. doi:10.2307/1914185

Kaiser, H. F., & Rice, J. (1974). Little jiffy, mark IV. *Educational and Psychological Measurement*, *34*(1), 111–117. doi:10.1177/001316447403400115

Kais, S., & Sami, H. (2016). An econometric study of the impact of economic growth and energy use on carbon emissions: Panel data evidence from fifty eight countries. *Renewable & Sustainable Energy Reviews*, *59*, 1101–1110. doi:10.1016/j.rser.2016.01.054

Kalkınma Bakanlığı, D. (2014a). *Onuncu Kalkınma Planı 2014-2018 Lojistik Hizmetlerinin Geliştirilmesi Özel İhtisas Komisyonu Raporu* [Tenth Development Plan 2014-2018 Development of Logistics Services Special Expert Commission Report]. Ankara: Kalkınma Bakanlığı Retrieved from http://www.kalkinma.gov.tr/Lists/zel%20htisas%20Komisyonu%20Raporlar/Attachments/254/Lojistik%20Hizmetlerinin%20Geli%C5%9Ftirilmesi.pdf

Kalkınma Bakanlığı, D. (2014b). *Onuncu Kalkınma Planı (2014-2018)* [Tenth Development Plan]. Ankara: T.C. Kalkınma Bakanlığı. Retrieved from http://www.kalkinma.gov.tr/Lists/Kalknma%20Planlar/Attachments/12/Onuncu%20Kalk%C4%B1nma%20Plan%C4%B1.pdf

Kämäräinen, V., Saranen, J., & Holmström, J. (2001). The reception box impact on home delivery efficiency in the e-grocery business. *International Journal of Physical Distribution & Logistics Management, 31*(6), 414–426. doi:10.1108/09600030110399414

Kannan, V. (2005). Just İn Time, Total Quality Management, And Supply Chain Management: Understanding Their Linkages And Impact On Business Performance. *Omega, 33*(2), 153–162. doi:10.1016/j.omega.2004.03.012

Kaplan, D. A. (2019). *7 elements of the sustainable warehouse.* Retrieved November 22, 2019 from https://www.supplychaindive.com/news/building-sustainable-warehouse-shippers-cost-benefits/549625/

Kaplan, S., & Garrick, B. J. (2017). On the quantitative definition of risk. *Risk Analysis, 1*(1), 11–27. doi:10.1111/j.1539-6924.1981.tb01350.x PMID:11798118

Karatepe, O. M. (2006). Customer complaints and organizational responses: The effects of complainants' perceptions of justice on satisfaction and loyalty. *International Journal of Hospitality Management, 25*(1), 69–90. doi:10.1016/j.ijhm.2004.12.008

Karunarathna, N., Wickramarachchi, R., & Vidanagamachchi, K. (2019). A Study of the Implications of Logistics 4.0 in Future Warehousing: A Sri Lankan Perspective. *Proceedings of the International Conference on Industrial Engineering and Operations Management*, 1024-1035.

Kasarda, J. D., & Lindsay, G. (2011). Aerotropolis: The Way We'll Live Next (A. Lane, Ed.). London, UK: Academic Press.

Kasarda, J.D. (2000). Logistics & the rise of aerotropolis. *Real Estate Issues, 25*(4).

Kasarda, J.D. (2006a). The rise of the aerotropolis. *The Next American City, 10*(10), 35-7.

Kasarda, J.D. (2006b). Asia's emerging airport cities. *International Airport Review, 10*(2).

Kasarda, J.D. (2011). Creating an Aerotropolis. How Indianapolis Is Strategically Charting Its Airport's and Region's Future. *Global Airport Cities, 5*(1).

Kasarda, J.D. (2013). Aerotropolis: Business mobility and urban competitiveness in the 21st century. *Urban Insight, 2*(7).

Kasarda, J. D. (2004). *Aerotropolis. The Wiley Blackwell Encyclopedia of Urban and Regional Studies.*

Kasarda, J. D. (2019). Aerotropolis. In A. Orum (Ed.), *The Wiley Black well Encyclopedia of Urban and Regional Studies*. John Wiley & Sons Ltd.; doi:10.1002/9781118568446.eurs0436

Kasarda, J. D., & Appold, S. J. (2014). Planning a competitive Aerotropolis. In *The economics of international airline transport*. Emerald Group Publishing Limited. doi:10.1108/S2212-160920140000004010

Katić, N. (2018). *Is Orthodoxy Guilty to All?* Retrieved from http:// nkatic.wordpress.com (in Serbian)

Katić, N. (2019). *When Abnormal Becomes Normal.* Retrieved from http:// nkatic.wordpress.com (in Serbian)

Kaur, H., & Singh, S. P. (2018). Heuristic modeling for sustainable procurement and logistics in a supply chain using big data. *Computers & Operations Research, 98*, 301–321. doi:10.1016/j.cor.2017.05.008

Kaur, J., Sidhu, R., Awasthi, A., Chauhan, S., & Goyal, S. (2018). A DEMATEL based approach for investigating barriers in green supply chain management in Canadian manufacturing firms. *International Journal of Production Research, 56*(1-2), 312–332. doi:10.1080/00207543.2017.1395522

Kawa, A. (2017). Fulfillment service in e-commerce logistics. *LogForum, 13*(4), 429–438. doi:10.17270/J.LOG.2017.4.4

Kaya, O. (2015). *Türkiye'nin Lojistik Sektörünün Büyüklüğü (resmi verilerle)* [Size of Turkey's Logistics Sector (official data)]. Retrieved from http://www.lojiport.com/turkiyenin-lojistik-sektorunun-buyuklugu-resmi-verilerle-91460yy.htm

Kaynak, H. (2003). The relationship between total quality management practices and their effects on firm performance. *Journal of Operations Management, 21*(4), 405–435. doi:10.1016/S0272-6963(03)00004-4

Keck, F., Lenzen, M., Vassallo, A., & Li, M. (2019). The impact of battery energy storage for renewable energy power grids in Australia. *Energy, 173*, 647–657. doi:10.1016/j.energy.2019.02.053

Kelle, P., Song, J., Jin, M., Schneider, H., & Claypool, C. (2019). Evaluation of operational and environmental sustainability tradeoffs in multimodal freight transportation planning. *International Journal of Production Economics, 209*, 411–420. doi:10.1016/j.ijpe.2018.08.011

Khalili, A., Ismail, M. Y., & Karim, A. (2017). Integration of lean manufacturing and quality management system through structural equation modelling. *(2017). International Journal of Productivity and Quality Management, 20*(4), 534–556. doi:10.1504/IJPQM.2017.082835

Khan, J. H. (2003). Impact Of Total Quality Management On Productivity. *The TQM Magazine, 15*(6), 374–380.

Khare, V. (2019). Prediction, investigation, and assessment of novel tidal–solar hybrid renewable energy system in India by different techniques. *International Journal of Sustainable Energy, 38*(5), 447–468. doi:10.1080/14786451.2018.1529034

Khare, V., Nema, S., & Baredar, P. (2016). Solar–wind hybrid renewable energy system: A review. *Renewable & Sustainable Energy Reviews, 58*, 23–33. doi:10.1016/j.rser.2015.12.223

Khiewnavawongsa, S., & Schmidt, E. K. (2013). Barriers to green supply chain implementation in the electronics industry. *International Conference on Industrial Engineering and Engineering Management*, 226-230. 10.1109/IEEM.2013.6962408

Khorsandi, J., & Aven, T. (2013). A risk perspective supporting organizational efforts for achieving high reliability. *Journal of Risk Research.*

Khoshnevis Yazdi, S., & Ghorchi Beygi, E. (2018). The dynamic impact of renewable energy consumption and financial development on CO2 emissions: For selected African countries. *Energy Sources. Part B, Economics, Planning, and Policy, 13*(1), 13–20. doi:10.1080/15567249.2017.1377319

Kim, H. J. (2017). Information technology and firm performance: the role of supply chain integration. *Operations Management Research, 10*(1-2), 1-9.

Kinnaman, T. C., & Takeuchi, K. (2014). *Handbook on waste management.* Northampton, MA: Edward Elgar Publishing. doi:10.4337/9780857936868

Kirechev, D. (2018). Risk Management Mechanisms in Agricultural Holdings in Bulgaria. *Fourth International Scientific Business Conference LIMEN 2018*, 597-602. 10.31410/limen.2018.597

Klaes, M., & Sent, E. M. (2005). A conceptual history of the emergence of bounded rationality. *History of Political Economy, 37*(1), 27–59. doi:10.1215/00182702-37-1-27

Klassen, R. D., & Vereecke, A. (2012). Social issues in supply chains: Capabilities link responsibility, risk (opportunity), and performance. *International Journal of Production Economics, 140*(1), 103–115. doi:10.1016/j.ijpe.2012.01.021

Klibi, W., Martel, A., & Guitouni, A. (2010). The design of robust value-creating supply chain networks: A critical review. *European Journal of Operational Research, 203*(2), 283–293. doi:10.1016/j.ejor.2009.06.011

Klikauer, T. (2010). *Critical Management Ethics*. Palgrave Macmillan. doi:10.1057/9780230281776

Kline, R. B. (2005). *Principles and Practice of Structural Equation Modeling*. Guilford Press.

Kline, R. B. (2011). *Principles and practice of structural equation modeling*. Guilford publications.

Kocaman, Y., Öztürkoğlu, Ö., & Gümüşoğlu, Ş. (2019). Aisle designs in unit-load warehouses with different flow policies of multiple pickup and deposit points. *Central European Journal of Operations Research*, *§§§*, 1–33.

Koçoğlu, M., & Avcı, M. (2014). *Satınalma Yönetimi: Teorik Bir Çalışma. Yüksek Lisans Tezi*. Kastamonu University Faculty of Economics and Administrative Sciences.

Kohlberg, L. (1970). *Education for Justice: A modern Statement of the Platonic View in moral Education*. Harvard University Press.

Koivisto, M., Das, K., Guo, F., Sørensen, P., Nuño, E., Cutululis, N., & Maule, P. (2019). Using time series simulation tools for assessing the effects of variable renewable energy generation on power and energy systems. *Wiley Interdisciplinary Reviews. Energy and Environment*, *8*(3), e329. doi:10.1002/wene.329

Kopidou, D., & Diakoulaki, D. (2017). Decomposing industrial CO2 emissions of Southern European countries into production-and consumption-based driving factors. *Journal of Cleaner Production*, *167*, 1325–1334. doi:10.1016/j.jclepro.2017.05.183

Korada, S. K., Yarla, N. S., Putta, S., Hanumakonda, A. S., Lakkappa, D. B., Bishayee, A., . . . Lu, D. Y. (2018). A critical appraisal of different food safety and quality management tools to accomplish food safety. Food Safety and Preservation, 1-12.

Koska, A., Göksu, N., & Sünbül, M. B. (2016). Barriers of green supply chain management implementation: An application in Kipaş paper factory. *Journal of Social and Humanities Sciences Research*, *6*(2), 117–140.

Krol, O. S., & Sokolov, V. I. (2019). Rational choice of machine tools for designers. Sofia: Academy publishing house of Bulgarian Academy of Sciences. doi:10.7546/RCMTD.2019

Krol, O., & Sokolov, V. (2018). Rational choice of machining tools using prediction procedures. *EUREKA: Physics and Engineering*, (4), 14-20.

Krstić, G., Schneider, F., Arandarenko, M., Arsić, M., Radulović, B., Ranđelović, S., & Janković, I. (2013). The shadow economy in serbia–new findings and recommendations for reform. Belgrade: Foundation for the advancement of economics.

Krstić, M., & Đekić, I. (2018). Behavioral economics and standard economic theory. *Kultura polisa,* (37), 397-410. (in Serbian)

Krstić, B., & Krstić, M. (2015). Normative theory of rational choice: Past, present, and future. [in Serbian]. *Theoria*, *58*(2), 49–64. doi:10.2298/THEO1502049K

Krstić, B., & Krstić, M. (2016). Rational choice theories and social research. [in Serbian]. *Sociologija*, *58*(4), 598–611. doi:10.2298/SOC1604598K

Krstić, M. (2012). The role of rules in the evolution of the market system: Hayek's concept of evolutionary epistemology. *Economic Annals*, *57*(194), 123–140. doi:10.2298/EKA1294123K

Krstić, M. (2014). Rational choice theory and addiction behaviour. *Market-Tržište*, *26*(2), 163–177.

Krüger, J., Lien, T. K., & Verl, A. (2009). Cooperation of human and machines in assembly lines. *CIRP Annals*, *58*(2), 628–646. doi:10.1016/j.cirp.2009.09.009

Kuang, Y., Zhang, Y., Zhou, B., Li, C., Cao, Y., Li, L., & Zeng, L. (2016). A review of renewable energy utilization in islands. *Renewable & Sustainable Energy Reviews*, *59*, 504–513. doi:10.1016/j.rser.2016.01.014

Kühn, W. (2006, December). Digital factory-simulation enhancing the product and production engineering process. In *Proceedings of the 2006 winter simulation conference* (pp. 1899-1906). IEEE. 10.1109/WSC.2006.322972

Kumar, A., Sah, B., Singh, A. R., Deng, Y., He, X., Kumar, P., & Bansal, R. C. (2017). A review of multi criteria decision making (MCDM) towards sustainable renewable energy development. *Renewable & Sustainable Energy Reviews*, *69*, 596–609. doi:10.1016/j.rser.2016.11.191

Kumar, P. K., Krishna, S. V., Naidu, S. S., Verma, K., Bhagawan, D., & Himabindu, V. (2019). Biomass production from microalgae Chlorella grown in sewage, kitchen wastewater using industrial CO2 emissions: Comparative study. *Carbon Resources Conversion*, *2*(2), 126–133. doi:10.1016/j.crcon.2019.06.002

Kyvelou, S., & Chiotinis, N. (2013). La politique regionale et la democratisation de l'Europe: La lutte a la corde Europeenne. *Géographies. Géopolitiques et Géostratégies Régionales*, *1*(1), 89–96.

Lagorio, A., Pinto, R., & Golini, R. (2016). Research in urban logistics: A systematic literature review. *International Journal of Physical Distribution Management*, *46*(10). doi:10.1108/IJPDLM-01-2016-0008

Lai, F., Zhao, X., & Wang, Q. (2007). Taxonomy of information technology strategy and its impact on the performance of third-party logistics (3PL) in China. *International Journal of Production Research*, *45*(10), 2195–2218. doi:10.1080/00207540600693531

Lamba, N., & Thareja, P. (2016). Barriers of green supply chain management: A review. Journal of Advanced Research In Manufacturing. *Material Science & Metallurgical Engineering*, *3*(3-4), 4–15.

Lasi, H., Fettke, P., Kemper, H. G., Feld, T., & Hoffmann, M. (2014). Industry 4.0. *Business & Information Systems Engineering*, *6*(4), 239–242. doi:10.100712599-014-0334-4

Laudon, K., & Traver, C. (2016). *E-commerce: business, technology, society*. Boston: Pearson.

Lawrence, E. C. (1998). *Internet Commerce: Digital Models for Business*. Sydney, Australia: John Wiley & Sons.

Le, F.; Olivier, B. & Mognol, J.H. (2013). Sustainable manufacturing: Evaluation and modeling of environmental impacts in additive manufacturing. *International Journal of Advance Manufacturing Technology, 69*.

Lee, J., Bagheri, B., & Kao, H. A. (2015). A cyber-physical systems architecture for industry 4.0-based manufacturing systems. *Manufacturing Letters, 3*, 18-23.

Lee, K. L., Huang, W. C., & Teng, J. Y. (2009). Locating the competitive relation of global logistics hub using quantitative SWOT analytical method. *Quality & Quantity*, *43*(1), 87–107. doi:10.100711135-007-9087-1

Lee, K. S. (2011). Three ways of linking laboratory endeavours to the realm of policies. *European Journal of the History of Economic Thought*, *18*(5), 755–776. doi:10.1080/09672567.2011.616593

Lee, Y. H., Lee, M. H., & Hur, S. (2005). Optimal design of rack structure with modular cell in AS/RS. *International Journal of Production Economics*, *98*(2), 172–178. doi:10.1016/j.ijpe.2004.05.018

Lehmann, P., Sijm, J., Gawel, E., Strunz, S., Chewpreecha, U., Mercure, J. F., & Pollitt, H. (2019). Addressing multiple externalities from electricity generation: A case for EU renewable energy policy beyond 2020? *Environmental Economics and Policy Studies*, *21*(2), 255–283. doi:10.100710018-018-0229-6

Lelieveld, H. (2009). Progress with the global harmonization initiative. *Trends in Food Science & Technology*, *20*(1), 82–84. doi:10.1016/j.tifs.2009.01.025

Lelieveld, H., Holah, J., & Napper, D. (2013). *Hygiene in Food Processing. Principles and Practice*. Woodhead Publishing.

Lenzini, J. M. (2002). Anticipatory logistics: The army's answer to supply chain management. *Army Logistician, 34*(5), 11–13.

Lewisohn, C., & Reynoso, J. (1995). Improving health service quality from within: The case of United Leeds Teaching Hospitals NHS Trust. *International Journal of Health Care Quality Assurance, 8*(2), 18–20. doi:10.1108/09526869510081848 PMID:10142012

F. Li, T. Liu, H. Zhang, R. Cao, W. Ding, & J. P. Fasano (Eds.). (2008). Distribution center location for green supply chain. In *Proceedings of 2008 IEEE International Conference on Service Operations and Logistics, and Informatics*. IEEE.

Lijó, L., González-García, S., Lovarelli, D., Moreira, M. T., Feijoo, G., & Bacenetti, J. (2019). Life Cycle Assessment of Renewable Energy Production from Biomass. In *Life Cycle Assessment of Energy Systems and Sustainable Energy Technologies* (pp. 81–98). Cham: Springer. doi:10.1007/978-3-319-93740-3_6

Lim, S. F., Jin, X., & Srai, J. S. (2018). Consumer-driven e-commerce: A literature review, design framework, and research agenda on last-mile logistics models. *International Journal of Physical Distribution & Logistics Management, 48*(3), 308–332. doi:10.1108/IJPDLM-02-2017-0081

Li, S., Wu, W., Xia, Y., Zhang, M., Wang, S., & Douglas, M. A. (2019). How do crowd logistics platforms create value? An exploratory case study from China. *International Journal of Logistics Research and Applications, 22*(5), 5. doi:10.1080/13675567.2019.1628929

Litman. (2017). Developing Indicators for Comprehensive and Sustainable Transport Planning. *Transportation Research Record: Journal of the Transportation Research Board, 2017*(1), 10–15. doi:10.3141/2017-02

Liu, W., & Xie, D. (2013). Quality decision of the logistics service supply chain with service quality guarantee. *International Journal of Production Research, 51*(5), 1618–1634. doi:10.1080/00207543.2012.720390

Lohr, S. L. (2010). *Sampling: Design and Analysis*. Brooks/Cole.

Lorcu, F. (2015). *Örneklerle Veri Analizi SPSS Uygulamalı*. Ankara: Detay Yayıncılık.

Lunin, P., Marcelis, W., & Rovira, J. (2009). Systematic assessment of core assurance activities in a company specific food safety management system. *Trends in Food Science & Technology, 20*(6), 300–312. doi:10.1016/j.tifs.2009.03.003

Luthra, S., Kumar, S., Garg, D., & Haleem, A. (2015). Barriers to renewable/sustainable energy technologies adoption: Indian perspective. *Renewable & Sustainable Energy Reviews, 41*, 762–776. doi:10.1016/j.rser.2014.08.077

Luthra, S., Kumar, V., Kumar, S., & Haleem, A. (2011). Barriers to implement green supply chain management in automobile industry using interpretive structural modeling technique an Indian perspective. *Journal of Industrial Engineering and Management, 4*(2), 231–257. doi:10.3926/jiem.2011.v4n2.p231-257

Lyu, G., Chen, L., & Huo, B. (2019). The impact of logistics platforms and location on logistics resource integration and operational performance. *International Journal of Logistics Management, 30*(2), 549–568. doi:10.1108/IJLM-02-2018-0048

MacNaughton, P., Satish, U., Laurent, J. G. C., Flanigan, S., Vallarino, J., Coull, B., ... Allen, J. G. (2017). The impact of working in a green certified building on cognitive function and health. *Building and Environment, 114*, 178–186. doi:10.1016/j.buildenv.2016.11.041 PMID:28785124

Madhadam, B. F., & Gutmann, T. (2013). Governing (through) autonomy: the moral and legal limits of "soft paternalism". Münster, 60, 1-20.

Magretta, J. (2002). *What Management is – How It Works and Why It's Everyone's Business*. New York: Free Press.

Maharloo, D. G., Darvishi, A., Davand, R., Saidi, M., & Rahimpour, M. R. (2017). Process intensification and environmental consideration of sodium bicarbonate production in an industrial soda ash bubble column reactor by CO2 recycling. *Journal of CO2 Utilization, 20*, 318-327.

Majumdar, A., & Sinha, S. K. (2018). Modeling the barriers of green supply chain management in small and medium enterprises: A case of Indian clothing industry. *Management of Environmental Quality, 29*(6), 1110–1122. doi:10.1108/MEQ-12-2017-0176

Majumdar, A., & Sinha, S. K. (2019). Analyzing the barriers of green textile supply chain management in South-East Asia using interpretive structural modelling. *Sustainable Production and Consumption, 17*, 176–187. doi:10.1016/j.spc.2018.10.005

Malaysia's Performance Management and Delivery Unit (PEMANDU). (2010). Retrieved from https://www.centreforpublicimpact.org/case-study/performance-management-delivery-unit-kuala-lampur/

Malaysian Palm Oil Council (MPOC). (2016). *Annual Report.* Retrieved from http://www.mpoc.org.my/pubs_view.aspx?id=94b4276f-4b4e-438a-b503-7726e933a07a

Malaysian Palm Oil Council (MPOC). (2016). *Annual Report.* Retrieved from http://www.mpoc.org.my/pubsView.aspx?catid=e1755218-c298-4d85-ba649e9beb584463&id=5ab6aafb-7ce5-406a-b48e-64d1022b736b&ddlID=e1755218-c298-4d85-ba64-9e9beb584463&print=1

Malthus, T. (1798). *An essay on the principle of population.* St. Paul's Church-Yard.

Malviya, R. K., & Kant, R. (2016). A comprehensive analysis of the barriers to green supply chain management implementation. *International Journal of Decision Sciences, Risk Management, 6*(4), 331–362.

Mandel, M. (2017). *How e-commerce is raising pay and creating jobs around the country.* Retrieved November 11, 2019, from https://www.forbes.com/sites/realspin/2017/04/03/how-e-commerce-is-raising-pay-and-creating-jobs-around-the-country/#aa393d76dff5

Mang, H. P. (2013). Biogas Production, Developing Countries. In M. Kaltschmitt, N. J. Themelis, L. Y. Bronicki, L. Söder, & L. A. Vega (Eds.), *Renewable Energy Systems* (pp. 218–246). New York, NY: Springer. doi:10.1007/978-1-4614-5820-3_250

Mankiw, G. N. (2005). *Principles of economics.* Belgrade: Publishing Center of Faculty of Economics in Belgrade. (in Serbian)

Manners-Bell, J., & Lyon, K. (2019). *The Logistics and Supply Chain Innovation Handbook: Disruptive Technologies and New Business Models.* Kogan Page Publishers.

Manuj, I., & Mentzer, J. T. (2008). Global supply chain risk management. *Journal of Business Logistics, 29*(1), 133–155. doi:10.1002/j.2158-1592.2008.tb00072.x

Manupati, V. K., Jedidah, S. J., Gupta, S., Bhandari, A., & Ramkumar, M. (2019). Optimization of a multi-echelon sustainable production-distribution supply chain system with lead time consideration under carbon emission policies. *Computers & Industrial Engineering, 135*, 1312–1323. doi:10.1016/j.cie.2018.10.010

Mardia, K. V. (1970). Measures of multivariate skewness and kurtosis with applications. *Biometrika, 57*(3), 519–530. doi:10.1093/biomet/57.3.519

Marks, M. (2019). *Robots in space: Sharing our world with autonomous delivery vehicles.* SSRN 3347466.

Martenson, R. (2007). Corporate brand image, satisfaction and store loyalty: A study of the store as a brand, store brands and manufacturer brands. *International Journal of Retail & Distribution Management*, *35*(7), 544–555. doi:10.1108/09590550710755921

Mascaretti, L., Dutta, A., Kment, Š., Shalaev, V. M., Boltasseva, A., Zbořil, R., & Naldoni, A. (2019). Plasmon-Enhanced Photoelectrochemical Water Splitting for Efficient Renewable Energy Storage. *Advanced Materials*, *31*(31), 1805513. doi:10.1002/adma.201805513 PMID:30773753

Maslow, A. (1970). *Motivation and personality*. New York: Harper and Row.

Mat Sharif, Z., Mohd Taib, N., Yusof, M., Rahim, M., Mohd Tobi, A., & Othman, M. (2017). Study on handing process and quality degradation of oil palm fresh fruit bunches (FFB). *Mechanical Engineering, Science and Technology International Conference* (pp. 1-9). IOP Publishing.

Mata-Alvarez, J. (2002). *Biomethanization of the organic fraction of municipal solid wastes*. London, UK: IWA Publishing.

Mathers, J., Craft, E., Norsworthy, M., & Wolfe, C. (2020). *The Green Freight Handbook: A Practical Guide for Developing a Sustainable Freight Transportation Strategy for Business*. Retrieved from http://business.edf.org/projects/green-freight-handbook

Mathiesen, B. V., Lund, H., Connolly, D., Wenzel, H., Østergaard, P. A., Möller, B., ... Hvelplund, F. K. (2015). Smart Energy Systems for coherent 100% renewable energy and transport solutions. *Applied Energy*, *145*, 139–154. doi:10.1016/j.apenergy.2015.01.075

Mazzucato, M., & Semieniuk, G. (2018). Financing renewable energy: Who is financing what and why it matters. *Technological Forecasting and Social Change*, *127*, 8–22. doi:10.1016/j.techfore.2017.05.021

McKee, J. (2018). *Global Digital Commerce Sales to Near $6 Trillion By 2022*. Retrieved from https://www.forbes.com/sites/jordanmckee/2018/09/11/global-digital-commerce-sales-to-near-6-trillion-by-2022/#11f0874f4c5a

McKenzie, S. (2004). *Social Sustainability: Towards Some Definitions*. Hawke Research Institute Working Paper Series 27.

McKone-Sweet, K. E., Hamilton, P., & Willis, S. B. (2005). The ailing healthcare supply chain: A prescription for change. *The Journal of Supply Chain Management*, *41*(1), 4–17. doi:10.1111/j.1745-493X.2005.tb00180.x

Mehrabi, J., Gharakhani, D., Jalalifar, S., & Rahmati, H. (2012). Barriers to green supply chain management in the petrochemical sector. *Life Science Journal*, *9*(4), 3438–3442.

Meixell, M. J., & Gargeya, V. B. (2005). Global supply chain design: A literature review and critique. *Transportation Research Part E, Logistics and Transportation Review*, *41*(6), 531–550. doi:10.1016/j.tre.2005.06.003

Mellor, J. W., & James D. (1969). Production Economics and The Modernization of Traditional Agricultures. *The Agrarian Journal of Agriculture and Resource Economics*, 25-34.

Memari, A., Rahim, A. R. A., Ahmad, R., & Hassan, A. (2016). A literature review on green supply chain modelling for optimising CO2 emission. *International Journal of Operational Research*, *26*(4), 509–525. doi:10.1504/IJOR.2016.077725

Mena, C., & Graham, S. (2010). *Delivering performance in food supply chains* (3rd ed.). Cambridge: Elsevier. doi:10.1533/9781845697778

Mendelsohn, R. (2008). The impact of climate change on agriculture. *Journal of Natural Resources Policy Research*, 5-19.

Mentzer, J. T., DeWitt, W., Keebler, J. S., Min, S., Nix, N. W., Smith, C. D., & Zacharia, Z. G. (2001). Defining supply chain management. *Journal of Business Logistics*, *22*(2), 1–25. doi:10.1002/j.2158-1592.2001.tb00001.x

Mentzer, J. T., Flint, D. J., & Hult, G. T. M. (2001). Logistics service quality as a segment-customized process. *Journal of Marketing*, *65*(4), 82–104. doi:10.1509/jmkg.65.4.82.18390

Mentzer, J. T., Gomes, R., & Krapfel, R. E. (1989). Physical distribution service: A fundamental marketing concept? *Journal of the Academy of Marketing Science*, *17*(1), 53–62. doi:10.1007/BF02726354

Meunier, N., Chauvy, R., Mouhoubi, S., Thomas, D., & De Weireld, G. (2020). Alternative production of methanol from industrial CO2. *Renewable Energy*, *146*, 1192–1203. doi:10.1016/j.renene.2019.07.010

Micu, A., Aivaz, K., & Capatina, A. (2013). *Implications of logistic service quality on the satisfaction level and retention rate of an e-commerce retailer's customers*. Academic Press.

Ministry of Agriculture and Food. (1999). Food Act, promulgated in State Gazette No. 90 of 15 October 1999, amended in State Gazette No. 106 of 21 December 2018. *Promulgated in State Gazette No. 90 of 15 October 1999, amended in State Gazette No. 106 of 21 December 2018.*

Mirzaei, M. A., Yazdankhah, A. S., Mohammadi-Ivatloo, B., Marzband, M., Shafie-khah, M., & Catalão, J. P. (2019). Stochastic network-constrained co-optimization of energy and reserve products in renewable energy integrated power and gas networks with energy storage system. *Journal of Cleaner Production*, *223*, 747–758. doi:10.1016/j.jclepro.2019.03.021

Mirza, F. M., & Kanwal, A. (2017). Energy consumption, carbon emissions and economic growth in Pakistan: Dynamic causality analysis. *Renewable & Sustainable Energy Reviews*, *72*, 1233–1240. doi:10.1016/j.rser.2016.10.081

Mladenow, A., Bauer, C., & Strauss, C. (2016). "Crowd logistics": The contribution of social crowds in logistics activities. *International Journal of Web Information Systems*, *12*(3), 379–396. doi:10.1108/IJWIS-04-2016-0020

Mohr, S., & Khan, O. (2015). 3D printing and its disruptive impacts on supply chains of the future. *Technology Innovation Management Review*, *5*(11), 20–25. doi:10.22215/timreview/942

Mokhtarian, P. L. (2004). A conceptual analysis of the transportation impacts of B2C e-commerce. *Transportation*, *31*(3), 257–284. doi:10.1023/B:PORT.0000025428.64128.d3

Molov, D. (2017). Globalni Verigi za Dostovka - Kontseptsii. Sofia: Izdatelski Kompleks - UNSS.

Montreuil, B. (2011). *Toward a Physical Internet: Meeting the global logistics sustainability grand challenge. Logistics Research*, 3, 2-3.

Montreuil, B., Meller, R. D., & Ballot, E. (2010). Towards a physical internet: the impact on logistics facilities and material handling systems design and innovation. In K. Gue (Ed.), *Progress in material handling research*. Material Handling Industry of America.

Morana, J. (2014). Sustainable Supply Chain Management in Urban Logistics. In J. Gonzalez-Feliu, F. Semet, & J. L. Routhier (Eds.), *Sustainable Urban Logistics: Concepts, Methods and Information Systems. Environmental Issues in Logistics and Manufacturing*. Berlin, Germany: Springer. doi:10.1007/978-3-642-31788-0_2

Morel, J. C., Mesbah, A., Oggero, M., & Walker, P. (2001). Building houses with local materials: Means to drastically reduce the environmental impact of construction. *Building and Environment*, *36*(10), 1119–1126. doi:10.1016/S0360-1323(00)00054-8

Morelli, J. (2011). Environmental Sustainability: A Definition for Environmental Professionals. *Journal of Environmental Sustainability*, *1*(1), 1–9. doi:10.14448/jes.01.0002

Morgan, T. R., Tokman, M., Richey, R. G., & Defee, C. (2016). Resource commitment and sustainability: A reverse logistics performance process model. *International Journal of Physical Distribution & Logistics Management*, *46*(3), 4.

Moriarty, P., & Honnery, D. (2016). Can renewable energy power the future? *Energy Policy*, *93*, 3–7. doi:10.1016/j.enpol.2016.02.051

Mosadeghrad, A. M. (2015). Developing and validating a total quality management model for healthcare organisations. *The TQM Journal*, *27*(5), 544–564. doi:10.1108/TQM-04-2013-0051

MPOB. (2018). *Overview of the Malaysian Oil Palm Industry 2017*. Retrieved from http://palmoilis.mpob.gov.my/index.php/overview-of-industry/593-overview-of-industry-2017

MPOC. (2019). *The Implications of EU Resolution to the Malaysian palm oil Industry*. Retrieved from http://www.mpoc.org.my/The_implications_of_EU_Resolution_to_the_Malaysian_Palm_Oil_Industry.aspx

Muduli, K., & Barve, A. (2013). Empirical Investigation of the Barriers of Green Supply Chain Management Implementation in Indian Mining Industries. In *3rd International Conference on Business, Economics, Management and Behavioral Sciences* (pp. 290-294). Singapore: Academic Press.

Mueck, B., Höwer, M., Franke, W., & Dangelmaier, W. (2005). Augmented reality applications for warehouse logistics. In *Soft Computing as Transdisciplinary Science and Technology* (pp. 1053–1062). Berlin: Springer. doi:10.1007/3-540-32391-0_108

Muhammad, B., & Khan, S. (2019). Effect of bilateral FDI, energy consumption, CO2 emission and capital on economic growth of Asia countries. *Energy Reports*, *5*, 1305–1315. doi:10.1016/j.egyr.2019.09.004

Murad, M. W., Alam, M. M., & Islam, M. M. (2019). *Dynamics of Japan's Industrial Production and CO2 Emissions: Causality*. Long-Run Trend and Implication.

Murray, C. C., & Chu, A. G. (2015). The flying sidekick traveling salesman problem: Optimization of drone-assisted parcel deliveryThe flying sidekick traveling salesman problem: Optimization of drone-assisted parcel delivery. *Transportation Research Part C, Emerging Technologies*, *54*, 86–109. doi:10.1016/j.trc.2015.03.005

Muyambo, F. (2019). Cereal Grains of Africa. *The Spruce Eats*, *3*(23). Retrieved from https://www.thespruceeats.com/cereal-grains-of-africa-39517

MWPL International Inc. (2019). *The Walmart distribution center network in the United States*. Retrieved November 11, 2019, from http://www.mwpvl.com/html/walmart.html

Napolitano, M. (2013). *7 Trends in Sustainable Warehouse Design*. Retrieved November 25, 2019, from https://www.supplychain247.com/article/7_trends_in_sustainable_warehouse_design/green

Narayan, P. K., Saboori, B., & Soleymani, A. (2016). Economic growth and carbon emissions. *Economic Modelling*, *53*, 388–397. doi:10.1016/j.econmod.2015.10.027

Nasiri, G. R., & Jolai, F. (2018). Supply chain network design in uncertain nnvironment: A review and classification of related models. In S. L. Tilahun & J. M. T. Ngnotchouye (Eds.), *Optimization Techniques for Problem Solving in Uncertainty* (pp. 262–282). IGI Global. doi:10.4018/978-1-5225-5091-4.ch010

National agency for local development (NALED). (2017). *Shadow book*. Belgrade: NALED. (in Serbian)

National Bureau of Economic Research. (2017). *Economies of Density in E-Commerce: A Study of Amazon's Fulfillment Center Network (No. w23361)*. Cambridge: Author.

National Population Council. (2006). *Ghana's Development Agenda and Population Growth: The Unmet Need for Family Planning*. Accra, Ghana: Government Printing Office.

Navarro, M., & Sabalza, X. (2016). Reflexiones sobre la Industria 4.0 desde el caso vasco [Reflections on Industry 4.0 from the Basque case]. *Ekonomiaz, 89*(1).

Nelson & Trevino. (2011). Managing Business Ethics: Straight Talk About How To Do It Right (5th ed.). John Wiley & Sons, Inc.

Nematollahi, O., Hoghooghi, H., Rasti, M., & Sedaghat, A. (2016). Energy demands and renewable energy resources in the Middle East. *Renewable & Sustainable Energy Reviews, 54*, 1172–1181. doi:10.1016/j.rser.2015.10.058

Neto, J. C., Filipe, J. A., & Caleiro, A. B. (2019). Creativity and innovation: a contribution of behavioral economics. *International Journal of Innovation Studies, 3*(1), 12-21.

Neto, J. Q. F., Walther, G., Bloemhof, J., Van Nunen, J. A. E. E., & Spengler, T. (2009). A methodology for assessing eco-efficiency in logistics networks. *European Journal of Operational Research, 193*(3), 670–682. doi:10.1016/j.ejor.2007.06.056

Nguyen, K. H., & Kakinaka, M. (2019). Renewable energy consumption, carbon emissions, and development stages: Some evidence from panel cointegration analysis. *Renewable Energy, 132*, 1049–1057. doi:10.1016/j.renene.2018.08.069

Nguyen, N., & LeBlanc, G. (1998). The mediating role of corporate image on customers' retention decisions: An investigation in financial services. *International Journal of Bank Marketing, 16*(2), 52–65. doi:10.1108/02652329810206707

Niemann, W., Kotze, T., & Adamo, F. (2016). Drivers and barriers of green supply chain management implementation in the Mozambican manufacturing industry. *Journal of Contemporary Management, 13*(1), 977–1013.

Nigam, P. (2014). Interpretive structural modelling (ISM) of the barriers to green supply chain management in Indian companies. *International Journal of Business Performance and Supply Chain Modelling, 6*(2), 183. doi:10.1504/IJBPSCM.2014.062466

Nin-Pratt, A., & Mcbride, L. (2014). Agricultural Intensification in Ghana: Evaluating the optimist's case for a green revolution. In *Boserup and Beyond: Mounting Land Pressures and Development Strategies in Africa*. (Original work published 1965)

Nizami, A. S., Shahzad, K., Rehan, M., Ouda, O. K. M., Khan, M. Z., Ismail, I. M. I., ... Demirbas, A. (2017). Developing waste biorefinery in Makkah: A way forward to convert urban waste into renewable energy. *Applied Energy, 186*, 189–196. doi:10.1016/j.apenergy.2016.04.116

Northouse, P. G. (2016). Leadership: Theory and Practice (7th ed.). Thousand Oaks, CA: Sage.

Novack, R. A., Rinehart, L. M., & Langley, C. J. Jr. (1994). An internal assessment of logistics value. *Journal of Business Logistics, 15*(1), 113.

O'Leary-Kelly, S. W., & Flores, B. E. (2002). The integration of manufacturing and marketing/sales decisions: Impact on organizational performance. *Journal of Operations Management, 20*(3), 221–240. doi:10.1016/S0272-6963(02)00005-0

Ochieng, J., Kirimi, L., & Mathenge, M. (2016). Effects of Climate Variability and Change on Agricultural Production. *NJAS Wageningen Journal of Life Sciences, 77*, 71–78. doi:10.1016/j.njas.2016.03.005

Official materials of the Ministry for Price Policy of the Republic of Sakha (Yakutia).

Official materials of the Ministry of Housing and Utilities of the Republic of Sakha (Yakutia).

Ofosu-Amaah, V. (2006). *Chairperson National Population Council Accra*. Ghana's Development Agenda and Population HP EliteBook.

Ojo, E., Mbowa, C., & Akinlabi, E. T. (2014). Barriers in implementing green supply chain management in construction industry. In *4th International Conference on Industrial Engineering and Operations Management* (pp. 1974-1981). Bali, Indonesia: Academic Press.

Olabi, A. G. (2017). *Renewable energy and energy storage systems*. Academic Press.

Oláh, J., Karmazin, G., Pető, K., & Popp, J. (2018). Information technology developments of logistics service providers in Hungary. *International Journal of Logistics Research and Applications, 21*(3), 332–344. doi:10.1080/13675567.2017.1393506

Olatomiwa, L., Mekhilef, S., Ismail, M. S., & Moghavvemi, M. (2016). Energy management strategies in hybrid renewable energy systems: A review. *Renewable & Sustainable Energy Reviews, 62*, 821–835. doi:10.1016/j.rser.2016.05.040

Oleinik, A. (2002). The costs and prospects of reforms in Russia: An institutional approach. *Teme, 4*, 491–517.

Orriss, G., & Whitehead, A. (2000). Hazard analysis and critical control point (HACCP) as a part of an overall quality assurance system in international food trade. *Food Control, 11*(5), 345–351. doi:10.1016/S0956-7135(99)00094-8

Owusu, P. A., & Asumadu-Sarkodie, S. (2016). A review of renewable energy sources, sustainability issues and climate change mitigation. *Cogent Engineering, 3*(1), 1167990. doi:10.1080/23311916.2016.1167990

Ozcan, B., & Ozturk, I. (2019). Renewable energy consumption-economic growth nexus in emerging countries: A bootstrap panel causality test. *Renewable & Sustainable Energy Reviews, 104*, 30–37. doi:10.1016/j.rser.2019.01.020

Özdemir, A. İ. (2004). Tedarik zinciri yönetiminin gelişimi, süreçleri ve yararları. *Journal of Erciyes University Faculty of Economics and Administrative Sciences, 23*, 87–96.

Özesen, E. (2009). *Yeşil tedarik zinciri yönetimi ve ambalaj sanayinde bir uygulama* [An application in green supply chain management and packaging industry] (Unpublished master's thesis). Marmara University Institute of Social Sciences. Turkey, Istanbul.

Özkan, O., Bayin, G., & Yesilaydin, G. (2015). Lean Supply Chain Management In Health Sector. *AJIT-e, 6*(18), 71–94. doi:10.5824/1309-1581.2015.1.005.x

Öztemel, E., & Gürsev, S. (2018). Türkiye'de Lojistik Yönetiminde Endüstri 4.0 Etkileri ve Yatırım İmkanlarına Bakış Üzerine Anket Uygulaması. *Marmara Fen Bilimleri Dergisi, 30*(2), 145–154.

Öztürkoğlu, Ö. (2015). *Investigating the robustness of aisles in a non-traditional unit-load warehouse design: Leverage. In 2015 IEEE congress on evolutionary computation (CEC)* (pp. 2230–2236). IEEE. doi:10.1109/CEC.2015.7257160

Öztürkoğlu, Ö. (2016). The Effects of Manual Material Handling Equipment on Loading and Unloading Time of a Case in a Pallet. *Journal of Yaşar University, 11*(44), 278–290.

Öztürkoğlu, Ö. (2018). Lean and Sustainable Warehousing. In U. Akküçük (Ed.), *Handbook of Research on Supply Chain Management for Sustainable Development* (pp. 218–241). IGI Global. doi:10.4018/978-1-5225-5757-9.ch012

Öztürkoğlu, Ö., Gue, K. R., & Meller, R. D. (2012). Optimal unit-load warehouse designs for single-command operations. *IIE Transactions, 44*(6), 459–475. doi:10.1080/0740817X.2011.636793

Öztürkoğlu, Ö., Gue, K. R., & Meller, R. D. (2014). A constructive aisle design model for unit-load warehouses with multiple pickup and deposit points. *European Journal of Operational Research, 236*(1), 382–394. doi:10.1016/j.ejor.2013.12.023

Öztürkoğlu, Ö., & Hoşer, D. (2018). A new warehouse design problem and a proposed polynomial-time optimal order picking algorithm. *Journal of the Faculty of Engineering and Architecture of Gazi University, 33*(4), 1569–1588.

Öztürkoğlu, Ö., & Hoser, D. (2019a). A discrete cross aisle design model for order-picking warehouses. *European Journal of Operational Research*, *275*(2), 411–430. doi:10.1016/j.ejor.2018.11.037

Öztürkoğlu, Ö., & Hoser, D. (2019b). An evaluation of order picking tour efficiency in two-block warehouses. *Operations and Supply Chain Management: An International Journal*, *12*(2), 74–78. doi:10.31387/oscm0370225

Öztürkoğlu, Ö., Kocaman, Y., & Gümüşoğlu, Ş. (2018). Evaluating Chevron aisle design in unit load warehouses with multiple pickup and deposit points. *Journal of the Faculty of Engineering and Architecture of Gazi University*, *33*(3), 793–807.

Pagh, J. D., & Cooper, M. C. (1998). Supply chain postponement and speculation strategies: How to choose the right strategy. *Journal of Business Logistics*, *19*(2), 13.

Panayides, P. M. (2007). The impact of organizational learning on relationship orientation, logistics service effectiveness and performance. *Industrial Marketing Management*, *36*(1), 68–80. doi:10.1016/j.indmarman.2005.07.001

Panayides, P. M., & So, M. (2005). The Impact of Integrated Logistics Relationships on Third-Party Logistics Service Quality and Performance. *Maritime Economics & Logistics*, *7*(1), 36–55. doi:10.1057/palgrave.mel.9100123

Pan, F., & Nagi, R. (2010). Robust supply chain design under uncertain demand in agile manufacturing. *Computers & Operations Research*, *37*(4), 668–683. doi:10.1016/j.cor.2009.06.017

Panghal, A. C., Chhikara, N., Sindhu, N., & Jaglan, S. (2018). Role of Food Safety Management Systems in safe food production. *Journal of Food Safety*, *38*(4), e12464. doi:10.1111/jfs.12464

Pan, Y., Qiao, F., Tang, K., Chen, S., & Ukkusuri, S. V. (2020). Understanding and estimating the carbon dioxide emissions for urban buses at different road locations: A comparison between new-energy buses and conventional diesel buses. *The Science of the Total Environment*, *703*, 135533. doi:10.1016/j.scitotenv.2019.135533 PMID:31767339

Park, C. D., Kim, S. W., & Park, J. G. (2019). An Analysis on Causalities Among GDP, Electricity Consumption, CO 2 Emission and FDI Inflow in Korea. *Journal of Energy Engineering*, *28*(2), 1–17.

Parliament European. (1992). *Council Directive 85/374/EEC and Council Directive 92/59/EEC on General Product Safety.*

Parliament European. (2017). Regulation (EU) 2017/625 of the European Parliament and of the Council of 15 March 2017 on official controls and other official activities performed to ensure the application of food and feed law, rules on animal health and welfare, plant health and plant. *OJ L 95,* 1–142.

Parliament, E. (2002). Regulation (EC) no 178/2002 of the European Parliament and of the council laying down the general principles and requirements of food law, establishing the European Food Safety Authority and laying down procedures in matters of food safety. *OJ L 031.*

Parliament, E. (2004). Regulation (EC) No 882/2004 and of the Council of 29 April 2004 on official controls performed to ensure the verification of compliance with feed and food law, animal health and animal welfare rules. *OJ L 165*1–141.

Parra, D., Norman, S. A., Walker, G. S., & Gillott, M. (2017). Optimum community energy storage for renewable energy and demand load management. *Applied Energy*, *200*, 358–369. doi:10.1016/j.apenergy.2017.05.048

Pata, U. K. (2018). Renewable energy consumption, urbanization, financial development, income and CO2 emissions in Turkey: Testing EKC hypothesis with structural breaks. *Journal of Cleaner Production*, *187*, 770–779. doi:10.1016/j.jclepro.2018.03.236

Patel, G. (2009). *Total quality management in healthcare*. Available at: http://hdl.handle.net/10380/3062

Paulraj, A., & Chen, I. J. (2007). Strategic buyer–supplier relationships, information technology and external logistics integration. *The Journal of Supply Chain Management, 43*(2), 2–14. doi:10.1111/j.1745-493X.2007.00027.x

Pavličić, D. (2010). *The theory of decision making.* Belgrade: Publishing Center of Faculty of Economics. (in Serbian)

Pavlović, N. (2016). Are authentic leaders satisfied with their job? *International Journal of Qualitative Research, 10*(2), 325–340.

Pavlović, N. (2018). Developing an innovation culture. In D. Karabašević & S. Vukotić (Eds.), *Innovation as an Initiator of the Development "Innovations – Basis for Development"* (pp. 193–212). Belgrade: Faculty of Applied Management, Economy, and Finance.

Pavlović, N., Oljaca, M., & Kostović, S. (2012). Integration of leadership styles of school director. *Educational Research Review, 7*(2), 31–35.

Payne, L. M., Peltier, J. W., & Barger, V. A. (2017). Omni-channel marketing, integrated marketing communications and consumer engagement: A research agenda. *Journal of Research in Interactive Marketing, 11*(2). doi:10.1108/JRIM-08-2016-0091

Pazienza, P. (2019). The impact of FDI in the OECD manufacturing sector on CO2 emission: Evidence and policy issues. *Environmental Impact Assessment Review, 77*, 60–68. doi:10.1016/j.eiar.2019.04.002

Pazienza, P., & De Lucia, C. (2019). How does FDI in the "agricultural and fishing" sector affect methane emission? Evidence from the OECD countries. *Economics and Politics, §§§*, 1–22.

Pedroni, P. (1999). Critical values for cointegration tests in heterogeneous panels with multiple regressors. *Oxford Bulletin of Economics and Statistics, 61*(s1S1), 653–670. doi:10.1111/1468-0084.61.s1.14

Peerless research group. (2019). *The Impacts of e-Commerce: Fulfillment Challenges and Improvement Priorities.* Retrieved November 30, 2019, from https://scg-peerless.s3.amazonaws.com/reseach_briefs/Honeywell-Intelligrated_RB5.pdf

Pereira, A. C., & Romero, F. (2017). A review of the meanings and the implications of the Industry 4.0 concept. *Procedia Manufacturing, 13*, 1206–1214. doi:10.1016/j.promfg.2017.09.032

Perin, J., Eremić-Đođić, J., Potić, Z., Zarić, B., Sekeruš, V., & Perin, B. (2018). The cost of hospital treatment of advanced stage lung cancer patients in a developing South East European country. *International Journal of Cancer, 9*(17), 3038-3045.

Perreault, W. D. Jr, & Leigh, L. E. (1989). Reliability of nominal data based on qualitative judgments. *JMR, Journal of Marketing Research, 26*(2), 135–148. doi:10.1177/002224378902600201

Perreault, W. D., & Russ, F. A. (1976). Physical distribution service in industrial purchase decisions. *Journal of Marketing, 40*(2), 3–10.

Persdotter, M., Hulthén, H., & Forslund, H. (2019). Environmentally Sustainable Logistics Performance Management Process Integration between Buyers and 3PLs. *Sustainability, 11*(11), 3061. doi:10.3390u11113061

Pervez, H., & Haq, I. U. (2019, March). Blockchain and IoT Based Disruption in Logistics. In *2019 2nd International Conference on Communication, Computing and Digital systems (C-CODE)* (pp. 276-281). IEEE. 10.1109/C-CODE.2019.8680971

Peter, J. P. (1981). Construct validity: A review of basic issues and marketing practices. *JMR, Journal of Marketing Research, 18*(2), 133–145. doi:10.1177/002224378101800201

Peterson, R. A. (1994). A meta-analysis of Cronbach's coefficient alpha. *The Journal of Consumer Research, 21*(2), 381–391. doi:10.1086/209405

Peterson, S. B., & Michalek, J. J. (2013). Cost-effectiveness of plug-in hybrid electric vehicle battery capacity and charging infrastructure investment for reducing US gasoline consumption. *Energy Policy*, *52*, 429–438. doi:10.1016/j.enpol.2012.09.059

Petković, A. (2010), *Forenzička revizija, Kriminalne radnje u finansijskim izveštajima* [Forensic Audit, Criminal Investigation in Financial Statements]. Novi Sad, Republic of Serbia: Orfelin Publishing.

Petrov, O. N., Saneyev, B. G., Alekseyev, G. F., & Safronov, A. F. (2010). The Energy Strategy of the Republic of Sakha (Yakutia) for the Period Up to 2030. Government of the Republic of. Sakha (Yakutia). Yakutsk: Media Holding "Yakutia".

Petrović, D., Stefanović, Z., & Marković, I. (2017). Behavioral models in economics as a framework for individual adaptation to the institutional environment. *Ekonomski horizonti, 19*(1), 17-30. (in Serbian)

Petrov, N. A. (2005). *The fuel and energy balance of the Republic of Sakha (Yakutia). Part. 1. V.P. Larionov's Institute of Physical-Technical Problems of the North SB RAS.* Yakutsk: Sakhapoligrafizdat.

Planners, C. (2014). A Global Survey of Urban Sustainability Rating Tools. *Global Symposium on Urban Sustainability Rating Tool.*

Polater, A. (2015). *Sağlık Sektöründe Tedarik Zinciri Yönetimi ve Müşteri Memnuniyetinin İncelenmesi: Bazı İllerde İkinci ve Üçüncü Basamak Hastaneler ve Tedarikçileri Üzerine Bir Uygulama* (PhD thesis). Atatürk University Institute of Social Sciences.

Polater, A., & Demirdogen, O. (2018). An investigation of healthcare supply chain management and patient responsiveness. *International Journal of Pharmaceutical and Healthcare Marketing*, *12*(3), 325–347. doi:10.1108/IJPHM-07-2017-0040

Polšek, D., & Bokulić, M. (2013). Two paradigms in bihevioral economics. In *An introduction to the behavioral economics of heuristics and bias* (pp. 5–24). Zagreb: Institute of Social Sciences Ivo Pilar. (in Croatian)

Polzin, F., Migendt, M., Täube, F. A., & von Flotow, P. (2015). Public policy influence on renewable energy investments—A panel data study across OECD countries. *Energy Policy*, *80*, 98–111. doi:10.1016/j.enpol.2015.01.026

Porter, J. (2019). *Google's Wing drones approved to make public deliveries in Australia.* Retrieved December 11, 2019, from https://www.theverge.com/2019/4/9/18301782/wing-drone-delivery-google-alphabet-canberra-australia-public-launch

Pourbehzadi, M., Niknam, T., Aghaei, J., Mokryani, G., Shafie-khah, M., & Catalao, J. P. (2019). Optimal operation of hybrid AC/DC microgrids under uncertainty of renewable energy resources: A comprehensive review. *International Journal of Electrical Power & Energy Systems*, *109*, 139–159. doi:10.1016/j.ijepes.2019.01.025

Powell, D. A., Erdozain, S., Dodd, C., Costa, R., Morley, K., & Chapman, B. J. (2013). Audits and inspections are never enough: A critique to enhance food safety. *Food Control*, *30*(2), 686–691. doi:10.1016/j.foodcont.2012.07.044

Prevention CDN-NDG. (2017). *City of Montreal's Environmental Action Program.* Retrieved from https://preventioncdnndg.org/eco-quartier/biomethanization-2/

Progressive Policy Institute. (2017). *How ecommerce creates jobs and reduces income inequality.* Washington, DC: Author.

Prologis. (2017). *Sustainability Report.* San Francisco: Author.

Pudleiner, D., & Colton, J. (2015). Using sensitivity analysis to improve the efficiency of a Net-Zero Energy vaccine warehouse design. *Building and Environment*, *87*, 302–314. doi:10.1016/j.buildenv.2014.12.026

Pukšec, T., Foley, A., Markovska, N., & Duić, N. (2019). Life cycle to Pinch Analysis and 100% renewable energy systems in a circular economy at sustainable development of energy. *Water and Environment Systems 2017.*

Punakivi, M., Yrjölä, H., & Holmström, J. (2001). Solving the last mile issue: Reception box or delivery box? *International Journal of Physical Distribution & Logistics Management, 31*(6), 427–439. doi:10.1108/09600030110399423

Qiao, W., Lu, H., Zhou, G., Azimi, M., Yang, Q., & Tian, W. (2020). A hybrid algorithm for carbon dioxide emissions forecasting based on improved lion swarm optimizer. *Journal of Cleaner Production, 244*, 118612. doi:10.1016/j.jclepro.2019.118612

Qin, J., Liu, Y., & Grosvenor, R. (2016). A categorical framework of manufacturing for industry 4.0 and beyond. *Procedia Cirp, 52*, 173–178. doi:10.1016/j.procir.2016.08.005

Rabinovich, E., & Bailey, J. P. (2004). Physical distribution service quality in Internet retailing: Service pricing, transaction attributes, and firm attributes. *Journal of Operations Management, 21*(6), 651–672. doi:10.1016/j.jom.2003.11.004

Radhi, H. (2010). On the optimal selection of wall cladding system to reduce direct and indirect CO^2 emissions. *Energy, 35*(3), 1412–1424. doi:10.1016/j.energy.2009.11.026

Rahim, S., Javaid, N., Ahmad, A., Khan, S. A., Khan, Z. A., Alrajeh, N., & Qasim, U. (2016). Exploiting heuristic algorithms to efficiently utilize energy management controllers with renewable energy sources. *Energy and Building, 129*, 452–470. doi:10.1016/j.enbuild.2016.08.008

Rahman, Abdullah, Shariff, & Simeh. (2008). The Malaysian Palm Oil supply Chain: The Role of the Independent Smallholders. *Oil Palm Industry Economic Journal, 8*(2).

Rahman, T. (2018). *Analysis of barriers in implementing green supply chain management in plastic industry* (Unpublished master's thesis). Bangladesh University of Engineering and Technology. Department of Industrial and Production Engineering.

Rahman, M. M., & Velayutham, E. (2020). Renewable and non-renewable energy consumption-economic growth nexus: New evidence from South Asia. *Renewable Energy, 147*, 399–408. doi:10.1016/j.renene.2019.09.007

Rahman, M. S. (2012). Service quality, corporate image and customer's satisfaction towards customers perception: An exploratory study on telecom customers in Bangladesh. *Business Intelligence Journal, 5*(1), 56–63.

Rai, H. B., Verlinde, S., Merckx, J., & Macharis, C. (2017). Crowd logistics: an opportunity for more sustainableurban freight transport? *Eur. Transp. Res. Rev.*, 9-39 . doi:10.100712544-017-0256-6

Rai, D., Sodagar, B., Fieldson, R., & Hu, X. (2011). Assessment of CO^2 emissions reduction in a distribution warehouse. *Energy, 36*(4), 2271–2277. doi:10.1016/j.energy.2010.05.006

Ranđelović, S. (2015). Tax design-tax evasion relationship in Serbia: New empirical approach to standard theoretical model. *Industrija, 43*(1), 73–89. doi:10.5937/industrija43-6963

Rao, S., Goldsby, T., & Iyengar, D. (2009). The marketing and logistics efficacy of online sales channels. *International Journal of Physical Distribution & Logistics Management, 39*(2), 106–130. doi:10.1108/09600030910942386

Rasiah, R., & Shahrin, A. (2004). *Development of Palm Oil and Related Products in Malaysia and Indonesia*. Academic Press.

Raut, R. D., Narkhede, B. E., Gardas, B. B., & Raut, V. (2017). Multi-criteria decision making approach: A sustainable warehouse location selection problem. *International Journal of Management Concepts and Philosophy, 10*(3), 260–281. doi:10.1504/IJMCP.2017.085834

Raybould, A. a. (2018). Policy- led comparative environmental risk assessment of genetically modified crops: Testing for increased risk rather than profiling phenotypes leads to predictable and transparent decision-making. *Frontiers in Bioengineering and Biotechnology*, *§§§*, 6. PMID:29755975

Reagan, C. (2018). *Walmart saves $200 million by changing its light bulbs and $20 million with a new floor wax.* Retrieved December 4, 2019, from https://www.cnbc.com/2018/10/16/walmart-saves-200-million-by-changing-its-light-bulbs.html

Reardon, T., Codron, J., & Busch, L. (2000). Global change in agrifood grades and standards: Agribusiness strategic responses in developing countries. *The International Food and Agribusiness Management Review*, *2*(4), 421–435.

Ren, R., Hu, W., Dong, J., Sun, B., Chen, Y., & Chen, Z. (2020). A systematic literature review of green and sustainable logistics: Bibliometric analysis, research trend and knowledge taxonomy. *International Journal of Environmental Research and Public Health*, *17*(1), 261. doi:10.3390/ijerph17010261 PMID:31905934

Reyes, D., Savelsbergh, M., & Toriello, A. (2017). Vehicle routing with roaming delivery locations. *Transportation Research Part C, Emerging Technologies*, *80*, 71–91. doi:10.1016/j.trc.2017.04.003

Ricker, F., & Kalakota, R. (1999). Order fulfillment: the hidden key to e-commerce success. *Supply Chain Management Review, 11*(3), 60-70.

Riehard, T. P. (2001). *The Art of Japanese Management*. New York: Simon & Sehuster.

Ries, J. M., Grosse, E. H., & Fichtinger, J. (2017). Environmental impact of warehousing: A scenario analysis for the United States. *International Journal of Production Research*, *55*(21), 6485–6499. doi:10.1080/00207543.2016.1211342

Rivera, A. E. P., & Mes, M. R. (2017). Anticipatory freight selection in intermodal long-haul round-trips. *Transportation Research Part E, Logistics and Transportation Review*, *105*, 176–194. doi:10.1016/j.tre.2016.09.002

Rodič, B. (2017). Industry 4.0 and the new simulation modelling paradigm. *Organizacija*, *50*(3), 193–207. doi:10.1515/orga-2017-0017

Rodrigue, J. P., & Dablanc, L. (2020) What is City Logistics? In *City Logistics: Concepts, Policy and Practice*. MetroFreight Consortium, Dept. of Global Studies & Geography, Hofstra University. https://globalcitylogistics.org/

Rodrigues, A. M., Stank, T. P., & Lynch, D. F. (2004). Linking strategy, structure, process, and performance in integrated logistics. *Journal of Business Logistics*, *25*(2), 65–94. doi:10.1002/j.2158-1592.2004.tb00182.x

Röhr, A., Lüddecke, K., Drusch, S., Müller, M. J., & Alvensleben, R. V. (2005). Food quality and safety—consumer perception and public health concern. *Food Control*, *16*(8), 649–655. doi:10.1016/j.foodcont.2004.06.001

Rosak-Szyrocka, J., & Blažević, L. B. (2019). Food Safety in Quality Mark Aspect. *System Safety: Human-Technical Facility-Environment*, *1*(1), 558–565.

Rosati, F., & Diniz, L. G. (2019). Addressing the Sustainable Development Goals in sustainability reports: The relationship with institutional factors. *Journal of Cleaner Production*, *215*, 1. doi:10.1016/j.jclepro.2018.12.107

Roso, V. (2013). Sustainable intermodal transport via dry ports–importance of directional development. *World Review of Intermodal Transportation Research*, *4*(2/3), 140–156. doi:10.1504/WRITR.2013.058976

Roßmann, B., Canzaniello, A., von der Gracht, H., & Hartmann, E. (2018). The future and social impact of Big Data Analytics in Supply Chain Management: Results from a Delphi study. *Technological Forecasting and Social Change*, *130*, 135–149. doi:10.1016/j.techfore.2017.10.005

Ross, W. D. (1930). *The Right and the Good*. Oxford: Clarendon Press.

Rotaru, G. B. (2005). Food Quality and Safety Management Systems: A Brief Analysis of the Individual and Integrated Approaches. *Technologies*, *11*(1), 229–236.

Rozados, I. V., & Tjahjono, B. (2014, December). Big data analytics in supply chain management: Trends and related research. *6th International Conference on Operations and Supply Chain Management.*

Sabattini, L., Digani, V., Secchi, C., Cotena, G., Ronzoni, D., Foppoli, M., & Oleari, F. (Eds.). (2013). Technological roadmap to boost the introduction of AGVs in industrial applications. In *Proceedings* of *2013 IEEE 9th International Conference on Intelligent Computer Communication and Processing (ICCP)*. IEEE. 10.1109/ICCP.2013.6646109

Saini, N., & Sighania, M. (2019). *Environmental impact of economic growth, emission and FDI: systematic review of reviews*. Qualitative Research in Financial Markets.

Salahuddin, M., Alam, K., Ozturk, I., & Sohag, K. (2018). The effects of electricity consumption, economic growth, financial development and foreign direct investment on CO2 emissions in Kuwait. *Renewable & Sustainable Energy Reviews*, *81*, 2002–2010. doi:10.1016/j.rser.2017.06.009

Samani, M. A., Ismail, N., & Leman, Z. (2017). Development of a conceptual model for risk-based quality management system. *Total Quality Management & Business Excellence*, *14*(4), 1–16.

Sanders, N. R., & Premus, R. (2005). Modeling the relationship between firm IT capability, collaboration, and performance. *Journal of Business Logistics*, *26*(1), 1–23. doi:10.1002/j.2158-1592.2005.tb00192.x

Sanginga, N. (2015). Root and tuber crops (cassava, yam, potato and sweet potato). *African Development Bank Group*. Retrieved from https://www.afdb.org/fileadmin/uploads/afdb/documents/events/dakagri2015/root_and_tuber_crops__cassava__yam__potato_and_sweet_ potato_.pdf

Sarker, M., Ahmed, F., Deb, A. K., & Chowdhury, M. (2018). Identifying barriers for implementing green supply chain management (GSCM) in footwear industry of Bangladesh: A Delphi Study Approach. *Leather and Footwear Journal*, *18*(3), 175–186. doi:10.24264/lfj.18.3.1

Sarkis, J. (2003). A strategic decision framework for gren supply chain management. *Journal of Cleaner Production*, *11*(4), 397–409. doi:10.1016/S0959-6526(02)00062-8

Sayan, İ. (2018). *Kurumsal liderlik tarzlarını algılamanın örgütsel bağlılık ve vatandaşlığa etkisinde çalışanların motivasyon seviyelerinin rolü ve bir araştırma*. İstanbul, Turkey: Yayınlanmamış Doktora Tezi, İstanbul Aydın Üniversitesi Sosyal Bilimleri Enstitüsü.

Schermelleh-Engel, K., Moosbrugger, H., & Müller, H. (2003). Evaluating the fit of structural equation models: Tests of significance and descriptive goodness-of-fit measures. *Methods of Psychological Research Online*, *8*(2), 23–74.

Schmidt, J., Meyer-Barlag, C., Eisel, M., Kolbe, L. M., & Appelrath, H. J. (2015). Using battery-electric AGVs in container terminals—Assessing the potential and optimizing the economic viability. *Research in Transportation Business & Management*, *17*, 99–111. doi:10.1016/j.rtbm.2015.09.002

Schneider, F. (2011). *Handbook on the shadow economy*. Cheltenham, UK: Edward Elgar Publishing Company. doi:10.4337/9780857930880

Schrauf, S., & Berttram, P. (2016). *How digitization makes the supply chain more efficient, agile, and customer-focused.* Price Waterhouse Coopers Report.

Schuh, G., Anderl, R., Gausemeier, J., ten Hompel, M., & Wahlster, W. (2017). *Industrie 4.0 Maturity Index. Managing the Digital Transformation of Companies*. Munich: Herbert Utz.

Schumacker, R. E., & Lomax, R. G. (2010). *A Beginner's Guide to Structural Equation Modelling*. New York: Routledge Taylor and Francis Group.

Şekkeli, Z. H., & Bakan, İ. (2018). Endüstri 4.0'ın Etkisiyle Lojistik 4.0. *Journal of Life Economics*, *5*(2), 17–36. doi:10.15637/jlecon.247

Senior, N. (1965). *An outline of the science of political economy*. London, UK: Unwin Library of Economics.

Sesso, P. P., Amâncio-Vieira, S. F., Zapparoli, I. D., & Sesso Filho, U. A. (2020). Structural decomposition of variations of carbon dioxide emissions for the United States, the European Union and BRIC. *Journal of Cleaner Production*, *252*, 119761. doi:10.1016/j.jclepro.2019.119761

Sgouridis, S., Bonnefoy, P. A., & Hansman, R. J. (2011). Air transportation in a carbon constrained world: Long-term dynamics of policies and strategies for mitigating the carbon footprint of commercial aviation. *Transportation Research Part A, Policy and Practice*, *45*(10), 1077–1091. doi:10.1016/j.tra.2010.03.019

Sikora, T., & Strada, A. (2005). *Safety and quality assurance and management systems in food industry: An overview.* The Food Industry in Europe, Agricultural University of Athens.

Siles, J. A., Serrano, A., Martín, A., & Martín, A. M. (2013, March). Biomethanization of waste derived from strawberry processing: Advantages of pretreatment. *Journal of Cleaner Production*, *42*, 190–197. doi:10.1016/j.jclepro.2012.11.012

Simeh & Ahmad. (2001). *The Case Study on the Malaysia Oil Palm*. http://www.rehdainstitute.com/ research-a-resources/etp.html

Simon, H. (1961). *Administrative behaviour*. New York: Macmillan.

Simon, H. (1967). *Models of man: social and rational*. New York: John Wiley and Sons.

Singer, P. (1994). *The Oxford Reader on Ethics*. Oxford: Oxford University Press.

Singh, S. (2015). Critical Reasons for Crashes Investigated in the National Motor Vehicle Crash Causation Survey. U.S. Department of Transportation. Washington, DC: NHTSA's National Center for Statistics and Analysis.

Singh, A. P., Avinash, A. D., & Agarwal, K. (2017). *Evolving Energy Scenario: Role and Scope for Alternative Fuels in Transport Sector. In Prospects of Alternative Transportation Fuels. Energy, Environment, and Sustainability* (pp. 7–19). Singapore: Springer.

Singleton, T. W., Singleton, A. J., Bologna, J., & Lindquist, R. (2006). *Fraud Auditing and Forensic Accounting*. John Wiley & Sons, Inc.

Sin, L. Y., Tse, A. C., Yau, O. H., Lee, J. S., & Chow, R. (2002). The effect of relationship marketing orientation on business performance in a service-oriented economy. *Journal of Services Marketing*, *16*(7), 656–676. doi:10.1108/08876040210447360

Slabinac, M. (2015). Innovative Solutions For A "Last-Mile" Delivery – A European Experience. *Proceedings of The 15th International Scientific Conference Business Logistics in Modern Management.*

Smith, A. (1998). *An Inquiry into the Nature and Causes of the Wealth of Nations*. Belgrade: Global Book. (in Serbian)

Smith, J., Cadavid, A., Rincón, R. V., & Vera, R. (1997). Land speculation and intensification at the frontier: A seeming paradox in the Colombian savanna. *Agricultural Systems*, *54*(4), 501–520. doi:10.1016/S0308-521X(96)00088-1

Soares, A. M., Farhanmeghr, M., & Shoham, A. (2007). Hofstede's dimension of culture in international marketing studies. *Journal of Business Research*, *60*(3), 277–284. doi:10.1016/j.jbusres.2006.10.018

Soares, N. F., Martins, C., & Vicente, A. A. (2016). *Food safety management system EN ISO 22000: 2005. Food Safety in the Seafood Industry: A practical guide for ISO 22000 and FSSC 22000 implementation* (1st ed.). Oxford: John Wiley & Sons. doi:10.1002/9781118965108

Sobel, M. E. (1982). Asymptotic confidence intervals for indirect effects in structural equation models. *Sociological Methodology, 13*, 290–312. doi:10.2307/270723

Soltani, M., Rahmani, O., Ghasimi, D. S., Ghaderpour, Y., Pour, A. B., Misnan, S. H., & Ngah, I. (2020). Impact of household demographic characteristics on energy conservation and carbon dioxide emission: Case from Mahabad city, Iran. *Energy, 194*, 116916. doi:10.1016/j.energy.2020.116916

Soon, J. M., & Baines, R. (2013). Public and Private Food Safety Standards: Facilitating or Frustrating Fresh Produce Growers? *Laws, 2*(1), 1–19. doi:10.3390/laws2010001

Sozuer, A., Altuntas, G., & Semercioz, F. (2017). International entrepreneurship of small firms and their export market performance. *European Journal of International Management, 11*(3), 365–382. doi:10.1504/EJIM.2017.083874

Spisak, K. (2019). *How Can Drone Delivery Change E-commerce?* Retrieved December 09, 2019, from https://www.business2community.com/ecommerce/how-can-drone-delivery-change-e-commerce-02198890

Sriram, V., & Stump, R. (2004). Information technology investments in purchasing: An empirical investigation of communications, relationship and performance outcomes. *Omega, 32*(1), 41–55. doi:10.1016/j.omega.2003.09.008

Srivastava, S. K. (2007). Green supply-chain management: A state-of-the-art literature review. *International Journal of Management Reviews, 9*(1), 53–80. doi:10.1111/j.1468-2370.2007.00202.x

Stanišić, M. (2015). *Interna kontrola i revizija* [Internal Control and Audit]. Belgrade, Republic of Serbia: Singidunum University.

Stank, T. P., Goldsby, T. J., Vickery, S. K., & Savitskie, K. (2003). Logistics service performance: Estimating its influence on market share. *Journal of Business Logistics, 24*(1), 27–55. doi:10.1002/j.2158-1592.2003.tb00031.x

Stank, T. P., Keller, S. B., & Daugherty, P. J. (2001). Supply chain collaboration and logistical service performance. *Journal of Business Logistics, 22*(1), 29–48. doi:10.1002/j.2158-1592.2001.tb00158.x

Stanley Frederick, W.T., & Lim, X. J. (2018). Consumer-driven e-commerce: A literature review, design framework, and research agenda on last-mile logistics models. *International Journal of Physical Distribution & Logistics Management, 48*(3), 308-332.

Starcke, D. (2018). *Creative Crowdsourcing for Last Mile Efficiency.* Retrieved August 12, 2019, from https://firstflight-solutions.com/creative-crowdsourcing-last-mile-efficiency/

Statistica. (2019a). *Retail e-commerce sales worldwide from 2014 to 2023.* Retrieved Nov 11, 2019 from statista.com: https://www.statista.com/statistics/379046/worldwide-retail-e-commerce-sales/

Statistica. (2019b). *B2C e-commerce as percentage of GDP in Western Europe from 2009 to 2018.* Retrieved Nov 3, 2019 from https://www.statista.com/statistics/324588/b2c-e-commerce-as-percentage-of-gdp-western-europe/

Statistica. (2019c). *B2C e-commerce as percentage of GDP in the United States from 2009 to 2018.* Retrieved Nov 3, 2019 from https://www.statista.com/statistics/324582/b2c-e-commerce-as-percentage-of-gdp-usa/

Statistical Office of the Republic of Serbia. (2019). *Labor Force Survey, II quarter 2019.* Belgrade: Statistical Office of the Republic of Serbia. (in Serbian)

Stefanova, M., & Gotcheva, V. (2016). Possibilities for Integrating the Requirements of Food Quality and Safety Management Standards. In Scientific works of University of Food technologies 2016, (pp. 111 - 118). Plovdiv: University of Food Technologies.

Stindt, D. (2017). A generic planning approach for sustainable supply chain management—How to integrate concepts and methods to address the issues of sustainability? *Journal of Cleaner Production, 153*, 1. doi:10.1016/j.jclepro.2017.03.126

Stock, T., & Seliger, G. (2016). Opportunities of sustainable manufacturing in industry 4.0. *Procedia Cirp, 40*, 536–541. doi:10.1016/j.procir.2016.01.129

Strandhagen, J.O., Vallandingham, L.R., Fragapane, G., Strandhagen, J.W., Stangeland, A.B.H., & Sharma, N. (2019). Logistics 4.0 and emerging sustainable business models. *Advance Manufacturing, 5*(4).

Strantzali, E., & Aravossis, K. (2016). Decision making in renewable energy investments: A review. *Renewable & Sustainable Energy Reviews, 55*, 885–898. doi:10.1016/j.rser.2015.11.021

Streimikiene, D., & Kasperowicz, R. (2016). Review of economic growth and energy consumption: A panel cointegration analysis for EU countries. *Renewable & Sustainable Energy Reviews, 59*, 1545–1549. doi:10.1016/j.rser.2016.01.041

Suganthi, L., Iniyan, S., & Samuel, A. A. (2015). Applications of fuzzy logic in renewable energy systems–a review. *Renewable & Sustainable Energy Reviews, 48*, 585–607. doi:10.1016/j.rser.2015.04.037

Sunstein, C. R. (2012). The storrs lectures: Behavioral economics and paternalism. *The Yale Law Journal, 122*(7), 1826–1899.

Swinehart, K. D., & Smith, A. E. (2005). Internal supply chain performance measurement: A health care continuous improvement implementation. *International Journal of Health Care Quality Assurance, 18*(7), 533–542. doi:10.1108/09526860510627210 PMID:16335618

Szymańska, O., Adamczak, M., & Cyplik, P. (2017). Logistics 4.0-a new paradigm or set of known solutions? *Research in Logistics & Production, 7.*

Tabachnick, B. G., & Fidell, L. S. (2013). *Using Multivariate Statistics*. Pearson.

Tachie-Obeng, E., Akponikpè, P., & Adiku, S. (2013). *Considering effective adaptation options to impacts of climate change for maize production in Ghana*. Environmental. doi:10.1016/j.envdev.2012.11.008

Tambovcevs, A., & Tambovceva, T. (2012). Logistic system ıntegration with environmental management system: A case study of ınternational company. ISEE 2012 Conference "Ecological Economics and Rio+20": Abstracts and Full Papers.

Tanga, Y., Xua, J., Zhanga, J., & Lub, Y. (2013). Biodiesel production from vegetable oil by using modified CaO as solid basic catalysts. *Journal of Cleaner Production, 42*, 198–203. doi:10.1016/j.jclepro.2012.11.001

Tang, C. S., & Veelenturf, L. P. (2019). The Strategic Role of Logistics in the Industry 4.0 Era. *Transportation Research Part E, Logistics and Transportation Review, 6*(June).

K. S. Tan, M. D. Ahmed, & D. Sundaram (Eds.). (2009). Sustainable warehouse management. In *Proceedings of the International Workshop on Enterprises & Organizational Modeling and Simulation*. New York: Association for Computng Machinery.

Tappia, E., Marchet, G., Melacini, M., & Perotti, S. (2015). Incorporating the environmental dimension in the assessment of automated warehouses. *Production Planning and Control, 26*(10), 824–838. doi:10.1080/09537287.2014.990945

Taşkın, E., & Ekinci, K. M. (2006). *Toplam Kalite Yönetimi ve Kamu Sektörü. 1.* Ankara: Basım, Turan Kitabevi.

Tavasszy, L. A., Behdani, B., & Konings, R. (2015). *Intermodality and Synchromodality*. Available at SSRN: https://ssrn.com/abstract=2592888

Taylor, R. N. J., & Naushad, E. M. (2008). Traditional African Cereal Grains - Overview. Pretoria: Academic Press.

Taylor, J. (2015). Crowdsourcing IT Work: A Three-Fold Perspective from the Workers, Buyers, and Platform Providers. *Proceedings of the 2015 ACM SIGMIS conference on computers and people research*. 10.1145/2751957.2755504

Temesgen, G. B. (2017). Poverty, peasantry and agriculture in Ethiopia. *Annals of Agrarian Science*, 420-430.

ten Berge, H. F. M., Schroder, J. J., Olesen, J. E., & Giraldez Cervera, J. V. (2017). *Research for AGRI Committee – Preserving agricultural soils in the EU, European Parliament*. Brussels: Policy Department for Structural and Cohesion Policies.

Teoh, L. E., & Khoo, H. L. (2016). Green air transport system: An overview of issues, strategies and challenges. *KSCE Journal of Civil Engineering*, *20*(3), 1040–1052. doi:10.100712205-016-1670-3

Teoman, S. (2015). *Tedarik zinciri kalite yönetiminde liderlik etkisi-Türkiye'de faaliyet gösteren işletmeler evreninde deneysel bir araştırma*. Academic Press.

Texas A&M Transportation Institute. (2017). *How will e-commerce growth impact our transportation network? Final report* (No. PRC 17-79 F). Author.

Thai, V. V. (2013). Logistics service quality: Conceptual model and empirical evidence. *International Journal of Logistics Research and Applications*, *16*(2), 114–131. doi:10.1080/13675567.2013.804907

Thaler, R. (1980). Toward a positive theory of consumer choice. *Journal of Economic Behavior & Organization*, *1*(1), 39–60. doi:10.1016/0167-2681(80)90051-7

Thaler, R. (1989). Anomalies: Interindustry wage differentials. *The Journal of Economic Perspectives*, *3*(2), 181–193. doi:10.1257/jep.3.2.181

Thaler, R. (2016). Behavioral economics: Past, present, and future. *The American Economic Review*, *106*(7), 1577–1600. doi:10.1257/aer.106.7.1577

Thaler, R. H., & Sunstein, C. R. (2003). Libertarian paternalism. *The American Economic Review*, *93*(2), 175–179. doi:10.1257/000282803321947001

Thames, L., & Schaefer, D. (2016). Software-defined cloud manufacturing for industry 4.0. *Procedia CIRP, 52*, 12-17.

The General Layout of Power Facilities Up to 2035 . (2017) (Approved by the Order of the Government of the Russian Federation) No. 1209.

The Russian Statistical Yearbook Rosstat. (2016). Retrieved from http://www.gks.ru/bgd/regl/b16_13

The Scheme and Program for the Development of the Energy Industry of the Republic of Sakha (Yakutia) for 2017-2021. (Established by the Decree of the Head of the Republic of Sakha (Yakutia) No. 1908 of May 9, 2017).

The Scheme for Integrated Development of Productive Forces, Transport and Energy of the Republic of Sakha (Yakutia) up to 2020 . (2016).

Thomas, R. (2000). Agrifood grades and standards in the extended Mercosur: Their role in the changing agrifood system. *American Journal of Agricultural Economics*, *82*(5), 1170–1176. doi:10.1111/0002-9092.00116

Thun, J. H., & Müller, A. (2010). An empirical analysis of green supply chain management in the German automotive industry. *Business Strategy and the Environment*, *19*(2), 119–132.

Tippins, M. J., & Sohi, R. S. (2003). It Competency and Firm Performance: Is Organizational Learning a Missing Link? *Strategic Management Journal*, *24*(8), 745–761. doi:10.1002mj.337

Tjahjono, B., Esplugues, C., Ares, E., & Pelaez, G. (2017). What does industry 4.0 mean to supply chain? *Procedia Manufacturing*, *13*, 1175–1182. doi:10.1016/j.promfg.2017.09.191

Tompkins, J. A., White, J. A., Bozer, Y. A., & Tanchoco, J. M. A. (2003). *Facilities Planning*. John Wiley & Sons.

Transparency Serbia. (2019). *The EC report highlighted significant problems in the fight against corruption*. Belgrade: Transparency Serbia. (in Serbian)

Transport & Environment. (2019). *Low-Emission Zones are a success - but they must now move to zero-emission mobility*. Retrieved 02 07, 2020, from https://www.transportenvironment.org/sites/te/files/publications/2019_09_Briefing_LEZ-ZEZ_final.pdf

Tseng, M.-L., Islam, M., Karia, N., Fauzi, F. A., & Afrin, S. (2019). A literature review on green supply chain management: Trends and future challenges. *Resources, Conservation and Recycling*, *141*, 145–162. doi:10.1016/j.resconrec.2018.10.009

Tu, M. K., Lim, M., & Yang, M. F. (2018b). IoT-based production logistics and supply chain system–Part 2: IoT-based cyber-physical system: a framework and evaluation. *Industrial Management & Data Systems*, *118*(1), 96–125. doi:10.1108/IMDS-11-2016-0504

Tu, M., Lim, M. K., & Yang, M. F. (2018a). IoT-based production logistics and supply chain system–Part 1: Modeling IoT-based manufacturing supply chain. *Industrial Management & Data Systems*, *118*(1), 65–95. doi:10.1108/IMDS-11-2016-0503

Turner, M. G., Romme, W. H., Gardner, R. H., O'neill, R. V., & Kratz, T. K. (1993). A revised concept of landscape equilibrium: Disturbance and stability on scaled landscapes. *Landscape Ecology*, *8*(3), 213–227. doi:10.1007/BF00125352

Tversky, A., & Kahneman, D. (1974). Judgment under uncertainty: Heuristics and biases. *Science*, *185*(4157), 1124–1131. doi:10.1126cience.185.4157.1124 PMID:17835457

Tzia, V., Tzia, T., & Tzia, C. (2015). Handbook of Food Processing: Food Safety, Quality, and Manufacturing Processes (35th ed.). CRC Press.

Uggen, C., & Thompson, M. (2003). The socioeconomic determinants of ill-gotten gains: Within-person changes in drug use and illegal earnings. *American Journal of Sociology*, *109*(1), 146–185. doi:10.1086/378036

Ulgen, H., & Mirze, K. (2013). *İşletmelerde Stratejik Yönetim*. Istanbul: Beta Yayınları.

Ülkü, M. A. (2012). Dare to care: Shipment consolidation reduces not only costs, but also environmental damage. *International Journal of Production Economics*, *139*(2), 438–446. doi:10.1016/j.ijpe.2011.09.015

Ulmer, M. W., Brinkmann, J., & Mattfeld, D. C. (2015). Anticipatory planning for courier, express and parcel services. In *Logistics Management* (pp. 313–324). Cham: Springer. doi:10.1007/978-3-319-13177-1_25

United Nations Department of Economic and Social Affairs. (2019). *Population Prospects 2019*. New York: Population Division. Retrieved from https://population.un.org/wpp2019/Publications/Files/WPP2019_Volume-I_Comprehensive-Tables.pdf

United Nations. (2019). *World Urbanization Prospects. The 2018 Revision*. Department of Economic and Social Affairs: Population Division. Access https://population.un.org/wup/Publications/Files/WUP2018-Report.pdf

United States Department of Labor. (2019). *Industries at a glance: Warehousing and storage (NAICS 493)*. Retrieved Nov 30, 2019 from https://www.bls.gov/iag/tgs/iag493.htm#workplace_trends

United States Energy Information Administration. (2019). *Use of energy explained: Energy use for transportation*. Retrieved November 11, 2019, from https://www.eia.gov/energyexplained/use-of-energy/transportation.php

United States Environmental Protection Agency. (2019). *Greenhouse Gas Emissions*. Retrieved December 12, 2019 from https://www.epa.gov/ghgemissions/sources-greenhouse-gas-emissions

University of Minnesota Center for Urban and Regional Affairs. (2010). *Framework for Measuring Sustainable Regional Development for the Twin Cities Region*. University of Minnesota Center for Transportation Studies.

Ürge-Vorsatz, D., Cabeza, L. F., Serrano, S., Barreneche, C., & Petrichenko, K. (2015). Heating and cooling energy trends and drivers in buildings. *Renewable & Sustainable Energy Reviews*, *41*, 85–98. doi:10.1016/j.rser.2014.08.039

US Energy Information Administration. (2016). *Energy use in commercial buildings*. Retrieved Dec 5, 2019 from https://www.eia.gov/energyexplained/use-of-energy/commercial-buildings.php

Valev, J.; Mitković, P. & Vasilevska, L. (2011). Spatial and functional transformation of the city center structure in the process of transition. *Facta universitatis - Series Architecture and Civil Engineering*, *9*(3). Doi:10.2298/FUACE1103455V

Vallabhaneni, S. R. (2008). *Corporate Management, Governance, and Ethics: Best Practices. Association of professionals in Business Management*. Wiley.

Vanichchinchai, A., & Igel, B. (2009). Total quality management and supply chain management: Similarities and differences. *The TQM Journal*, *21*(3), 249–260. doi:10.1108/17542730910953022

Varzakas, T., & Tzia, C. (2016). Handbook of food processing: food safety, quality, and manufacturing processes (1st ed.). Boca Raton: CRC Press.

Vasileva, E. & Ivanova, D.& Tipova, N.& Stefanov, S. (2019.). Quality of organic foods—a model for comparative analysis. *Organic Agriculture Official Journal of the International Society of Organic Agriculture Research*, *9*(1).

Ventura, J. A., & Rieksts, B. Q. (2009). Optimal location of dwell points in a single loop AGV system with time restrictions on vehicle availability. *European Journal of Operational Research*, *192*(1), 93–104. doi:10.1016/j.ejor.2007.09.014

Verbeke, W., Frewer, L. J., Scholderer, J., & de Brabander, H. F. (2007). Why consumers behave as they do with respect to food safety and risk information. *Analytica Chimica Acta*, *586*(1-2), 2–7. doi:10.1016/j.aca.2006.07.065 PMID:17386689

Verbeke, W., Vermeir, I., & Brunsø, K. (2007). Consumer evaluation of fish quality as a basis for fish market segmentation. *Food Quality and Preference*, *18*(4), 651–661. doi:10.1016/j.foodqual.2006.09.005

Viet, N. Q., Behdani, B., & Bloemhof, J. (2019). Data-driven process redesign: Anticipatory shipping in agro-food supply chains. *International Journal of Production Research*, 1–17.

Vision and Missions of RSPO. (n.d.). Retrieved from https://www.rspo.org/about

Von Neumann, J., & Morgenstern, O. (1947). *Theory of games and economic behavior*. Princeton, NJ: Princeton University Press.

Vukasović, T. (2015). Food quality and safety: Added value in a customer-oriented concept. *International Journal of Value Chain Management*, *7*(3), 241–254. doi:10.1504/IJVCM.2015.079208

Walker, H., Di Sisto, L., & McBain, D. (2008). Drivers and barriers to environmental supply chain management practices: Lessons from the public and private sectors. *Journal of Purchasing and Supply Management*, *14*(1), 69–85. doi:10.1016/j.pursup.2008.01.007

Wallace, C. H. L., Holyoak, L., Powell, S. C., & Dykes, F. C. (2012). Re-thinking the HACCP team: An investigation into HACCP team knowledge and decision-making for successful HACCP development. *Food Research International, 47*(2), 236–245. doi:10.1016/j.foodres.2011.06.033

Wang, G., Gunasekaran, A., & Ngai, E. W. (2018). Distribution network design with big data: Model and analysis. *Annals of Operations Research, 270*(1-2), 539–551. doi:10.100710479-016-2263-8

Wang, K. (2016, November). Logistics 4.0 Solution-New Challenges and Opportunities. In *6th International Workshop of Advanced Manufacturing and Automation.* Atlantis Press. 10.2991/iwama-16.2016.13

Wang, Q., Zhao, M., Li, R., & Su, M. (2018). Decomposition and decoupling analysis of carbon emissions from economic growth: A comparative study of China and the United States. *Journal of Cleaner Production, 197*, 178–184. doi:10.1016/j.jclepro.2018.05.285

Wang, S., Liu, Q., Yuksel, S., & Dincer, H. (2019). Hesitant Linguistic Term Sets-Based Hybrid Analysis for Renewable Energy Investments. *IEEE Access: Practical Innovations, Open Solutions, 7*, 114223–114235. doi:10.1109/ACCESS.2019.2935427

Wang, S., Wan, J., Li, D., & Zhang, C. (2016). Implementing smart factory of industrie 4.0: An outlook. *International Journal of Distributed Sensor Networks, 12*(1), 3159805. doi:10.1155/2016/3159805

Wang, X., Zhan, L., Ruan, J., & Zhang, J. (2014). How to choose "last mile" delivery modes for e-fulfillment. *Mathematical Problems in Engineering.*

Wang, Y.-F., Chen, S.-P., Lee, Y.-C., & Tsai, C.-T. (2013). Developing green management standards for restaurants: An application of green supply chain management. *International Journal of Hospitality Management, 34*, 263–273. doi:10.1016/j.ijhm.2013.04.001

Wang, Y., Zhang, D., Liu, Q., Shen, F., & Lee, L. (2016). Towards enhancing the last-mile delivery: An effective crowd-tasking model with scalable solutions. *Transportation Research Part E, Logistics and Transportation Review, 93*, 279–293. doi:10.1016/j.tre.2016.06.002

Wang, Z., Mathiyazhagan, K., Xu, L., & Diabat, A. (2016). A decision making trial and evaluation laboratory approach to analyze the barriers to green supply chain management adoption in a food packaging company. *Journal of Cleaner Production, 117*, 19–28. doi:10.1016/j.jclepro.2015.09.142

Watanabe, E. H., Da Silva, R. M., Blos, M. F., Junqueira, F., Filho, D. J., & Miyagi, P. E. (2018). Framework to evaluate the performance and sustainability of a disperse productive system. *Journal of the Brazilian Society of Mechanical Sciences and Engineering, 40*(277).

Wen, W., & Wang, Q. (2020). Re-examining the realization of provincial carbon dioxide emission intensity reduction targets in China from a consumption-based accounting. *Journal of Cleaner Production, 244*, 118488. doi:10.1016/j.jclepro.2019.118488

Wesley, M. (1910). The rationality of economic activity. *Journal of Political Economy, 18*(2), 97–113. doi:10.1086/251657

Wharton, C. J. (1969). The challenge of population and food. In *Proceedings of Conference on Subsistence and Peasant Economics.* Chicago: Aldine Pub. Co.

WHO. (1998). *Guidance on regulatory assessment of HACCP. Report of a join FAO/WHO consultation on the role of government agencies in assessing HACCP.* WHO.

WHO. (2015). *WHO estimates of the global burden of foodborne diseases" has been launched on 3 December.* WHO.

WHO. (2019). *Air pollution.* Retrieved December 15, 2019, from www.who.int: https://www.who.int/sustainable-development/transport/health-risks/air-pollution/en/

WHO. (2019). *Noise.* Retrieved November 27, 2019, from https://www.who.int/sustainable-development/transport/health- www.who.int/.risks/noise/en

Wilcock, A., Pun, M., Khanona, J., & Aung, M. (2004). Consumer attitudes, knowledge and behaviour: A review of food safety issues. *Trends in Food Science & Technology, 15*(2), 56–66. doi:10.1016/j.tifs.2003.08.004

Willsher, K. (2019). *Drones used to deliver parcels to remote Alpine villages.* Retrieved November 23, 2019, from https://www.theguardian.com/technology/2019/dec/02/drones-used-to-deliver-parcels-to-remote-alpine-villages

Winkelhaus, S., & Grosse, E. (2019). Logistics 4.0: A systematic review towards a new logistics system. *International Journal of Production Research, 11*(April).

Witkowski, K. (2017). Internet of things, big data, industry 4.0–innovative solutions in logistics and supply chains management. *Procedia Engineering, 182*, 763–769. doi:10.1016/j.proeng.2017.03.197

Wognum, N. (2009). Environmental transparency of food supply chains-Current status and challenges. In *Global Perspective for Competitive Enterprise, Economy and Ecology* (pp. 645–652). London: Springer. doi:10.1007/978-1-84882-762-2_61

Wong, W. P., Soh, K. L., Sinnandavar, C. M., & Mushtaq, N. (2018). Could the service consumption-production interface lift national logistics performance? *Resources, Conservation and Recycling, 128*, 222–239. doi:10.1016/j.resconrec.2016.10.002

World Bank. (2007). *The Living Standards Survey.* Washington, DC: World Bank.

World Commission on Environment and Development. (1987). *Our Common Future.* New York: Oxford University Press.

World Economic Forum. (2009). *Supply Chain Decarbonization.* Geneva: World Economic Forum.

World Economic Forum. (2016). *The world's ten youngest populations are all in Africa.* Genève, Switzerland: Author.

Wright, D. J., & Ginsburg, D. H. (2012). Behavioral law and economics: Its origins, fatal flaws and implications for liberty. *Northwestern University Law Review, 106*(3), 1033–1089.

Wu, C., & Barnes, D. (2018). Design of agile supply chains including the trade-off between number of partners and reliability. *International Journal of Advanced Manufacturing Technology, 97*(9-12), 3683–3700. doi:10.100700170-018-2205-5

WWF. (2008). *Palm oil, soy and tropical forests: a strategy for life.* WWF.

Xia, X. (2019, February). FDI, Economic Growth and China's Carbon Emission Intensity: An Empirical Study Based on Spatial Panel Econometric Model. In *IOP Conference Series: Earth and Environmental Science* (Vol. 237, No. 5). IOP Publishing. 10.1088/1755-1315/237/5/052078

Xu, Q., & Yang, R. (2019). The sequential collaborative relationship between economic growth and carbon emissions in the rapid urbanization of the Pearl River Delta. *Environmental Science and Pollution Research International, 26*(29), 30130–30144. doi:10.100711356-019-06107-9 PMID:31420837

Yang, L., Yang, Y., Zhang, X., & Tang, K. (2018). Whether China's industrial sectors make efforts to reduce CO2 emissions from production?-A decomposed decoupling analysis. *Energy, 160*, 796–809. doi:10.1016/j.energy.2018.06.186

Yanjiu, R. (1982). *World population growth and the food supply.* Retrieved from https://www.ncbi.nlm.nih.gov/PubMed/12265442

Yao, X., Zhang, X., & Guo, Z. (2020). The tug of war between local government and enterprises in reducing China's carbon dioxide emissions intensity. *The Science of the Total Environment*, *710*, 136140. doi:10.1016/j.scitotenv.2019.136140 PMID:31923656

Yılmaz, Ü., & Duman, B. (2019). Lojistik 4.0 Kavramına Genel Bir Bakış: Geçmişten Bugüne Gelişim ve Değişimi [An Overview of the Concept of Logistics 4.0: Development and Change from Past to Present]. *Bilecik Şeyh Edebali Üniversitesi Sosyal Bilimler Enstitüsü Dergisi*, *4*(1), 186–200. doi:10.33905/bseusbed.465962

Yin, Y., Stecke, K. E., & Li, D. (2018). The evolution of production systems from Industry 2.0 through Industry 4.0. *International Journal of Production Research*, *56*(1-2), 848–861. doi:10.1080/00207543.2017.1403664

Yousif, J. H., Al-Balushi, H. A., Kazem, H. A., & Chaichan, M. T. (2019). Analysis and forecasting of weather conditions in Oman for renewable energy applications. *Case Studies in Thermal Engineering*, *13*, 100355. doi:10.1016/j.csite.2018.11.006

Yu, Y., Wang, X., Zhong, R. Y., & Huang, G. Q. (2016). *E-commerce logistics in supply chain management*. Academic Press.

Yüksel, S., Dinçer, H., & Meral, Y. (2019). Financial analysis of international energy trade: A strategic outlook for EU-15. *Energies*, *12*(3), 431. doi:10.3390/en12030431

Yun, G., Yalcin, M. G., Hales, D. N., & Kwon, H. Y. (2019). Interactions in sustainable supply chain management: A framework review. *International Journal of Logistics Management*, *30*(1), 140–173. doi:10.1108/IJLM-05-2017-0112

Yürük, P., Akyol, A., & Şimşek, G. G. (2017). Analyzing the effects of social impacts of events on satisfaction and loyalty. *Tourism Management*, *60*, 367–378. doi:10.1016/j.tourman.2016.12.016

Yu, Z., Liu, W., Chen, L., Eti, S., Dinçer, H., & Yüksel, S. (2019). The Effects of Electricity Production on Industrial Development and Sustainable Economic Growth: A VAR Analysis for BRICS Countries. *Sustainability*, *11*(21), 5895. doi:10.3390u11215895

Zacharia, Z. G., & Mentzer, J. T. (2004). Logistics salience in a changing environment. *Journal of Business Logistics*, *25*(1), 187–210. doi:10.1002/j.2158-1592.2004.tb00174.x

Zairi & Liburd. (2001). TQM sustainability-a roadmap for creating competitive advantage. *Integrated Management: 6th International conference on ISO 9000 and TQM*, 452-461.

Zeren, F., & Akkuş, H. T. (2020). The relationship between renewable energy consumption and trade openness: New evidence from emerging economies. *Renewable Energy*, *147*, 322–329. doi:10.1016/j.renene.2019.09.006

Zhang, B., Wang, B., & Wang, Z. (2017). Role of renewable energy and non-renewable energy consumption on EKC: Evidence from Pakistan. *Journal of Cleaner Production*, *156*, 855–864. doi:10.1016/j.jclepro.2017.03.203

Zhang, D., Wang, J., Lin, Y., Si, Y., Huang, C., Yang, J., ... Li, W. (2017). Present situation and future prospect of renewable energy in China. *Renewable & Sustainable Energy Reviews*, *76*, 865–871. doi:10.1016/j.rser.2017.03.023

Zhang, G., & Zhao, Z. (2012). Green packaging management of logistics enterprises. *Physics Procedia*, *24*, 900–905. doi:10.1016/j.phpro.2012.02.135

Zhao, M., Dröge, C., & Stank, T. P. (2001). The effects of logistics capabilities on firm performance: Customer-focused versus information-focused capabilities. *Journal of Business Logistics*, *22*(2), 91–107. doi:10.1002/j.2158-1592.2001.tb00005.x

Zhao, X., Zhang, X., Li, N., Shao, S., & Geng, Y. (2017). Decoupling economic growth from carbon dioxide emissions in China: A sectoral factor decomposition analysis. *Journal of Cleaner Production*, *142*, 3500–3516. doi:10.1016/j.jclepro.2016.10.117

Zheng, J., Sun, X., Jia, L., & Zhou, Y. (2020). Electric passenger vehicles sales and carbon dioxide emission reduction potential in China's leading markets. *Journal of Cleaner Production*, *243*, 118607. doi:10.1016/j.jclepro.2019.118607

Zhou, S., Matisoff, D. C., Kingsley, G. A., & Brown, M. A. (2019). Understanding renewable energy policy adoption and evolution in Europe: The impact of coercion, normative emulation, competition, and learning. *Energy Research & Social Science*, *51*, 1–11. doi:10.1016/j.erss.2018.12.011

Zhu, Q., & Sarkis, J. (2004). Relationships between operational practices and performance among early adopters of green supply chain management practices in Chinese manufacturing enterprises. *Journal of Operations Management*, *22*(3), 265–289. doi:10.1016/j.jom.2004.01.005

Zhu, Q., & Sarkis, J. (2006). An inter-sectoral comparison of green supply chain management in China: Drivers and practices. *Journal of Cleaner Production*, *14*(5), 472–486. doi:10.1016/j.jclepro.2005.01.003

Zimon, D., & Madzík, P. (2019). Standardized management systems and risk management in the supply chain. *International Journal of Quality & Reliability Management*, *37*(2), 305–327. doi:10.1108/IJQRM-04-2019-0121

Zoundi, Z. (2017). CO2 emissions, renewable energy and the Environmental Kuznets Curve, a panel cointegration approach. *Renewable & Sustainable Energy Reviews*, *72*, 1067–1075. doi:10.1016/j.rser.2016.10.018

Zwietering, M. (2015). Risk assessment and risk management for safe foods: Assessment needs inclusion of variability and uncertainty, management needs discrete decisions. *International Journal of Food Microbiology*, *213*, 118–123. doi:10.1016/j.ijfoodmicro.2015.03.032 PMID:25890788

Zyryanov, V.V. (2011). Fuel and energy balance in the management system of the regional fuel and energy complex. *Bulletin of the Academician M.F. Reshetnev Siberian state aerospace, 3*(34), 111-114.

About the Contributors

Ulas Akkucuk is an Associate Professor of Quantitative Methods at Bogazici University Department of Management, Istanbul, Turkey. Dr. Akkucuk has a BS in Industrial Engineering from Bilkent University (1997), an MBA from Bogazici University (2000), and a PhD in Management Science and Information Systems from Rutgers University (2004). His research interests focus on the methodological development of multivariate techniques such as Clustering and Multidimensional Scaling and novel applications into fields, such as global competitiveness, CRM, technology management, and sustainable development. He has taught Statistics, CRM and Data Mining, and Global Aspects of Management courses, among others, at both graduate and undergraduate levels. He is associate editor and editorial board member of International Journal of Research in Business and Social Science (IJRBS) and has been an ad hoc reviewer for journals such as Journal of Multivariate Analysis, Bogazici Journal, and International Journal of Business Economics and Management. He is a member of the Classification Society and Society for the Study of Business and Finance. He has edited eight books with IGI Global, two indexed by WoS. He is also the editor-in-chief of International Journal of Environmental Sustainability and Green Technologies (IJESGT).

* * *

Emmanuel Kofi Ankomah is an assistant professor of management and economics at Mendel University in Brno. He received his MSc and Ph.D. from the faculty of Business and Economics of Mendel University in Brno. He has been on the faculty of Regional Development and International Studies as an academic researcher and a lecturer. He is also a member of the organizing committee of the Institute of Research and International Symposiums IRIS – ALKONA for international scientific and practical symposiums and he serves as a reviewer for management, economics, and development economics journals indexed on SCOPUS and several others. His areas of research interest are the management of resources, land tenure systems, development economic issues on productivity and capital funding.

Emre Aslan was born in 1981. Graduated Department of Business Administration in Ege University in 2004. Completed his MBA in 2007 and PhD in 2014 from Erciyes University Department of Business Administration. Worked as a research assistant between 2004-2014 and as an instructor till 2014 in Tokat Gaziosmanpaşa University.

Yasemin Sarıcı Aytan graduated from Public Administration and Political Science, Bilkent University, in 1998. Worked as a manager in various management levels in the banking sector for 5 years dealing with SME's, e-commerce solutions (B2C&B2B), credit card suppliers. Organization marketing plans of Commercial Banking products especially on e-commerce solutions for merchants. Planning and giving in-company training courses. After that she has NGO experience as a strategic consultant for 4 years about women studies. She completed her master's degree in Political Sciences and International Relations. Worked as a Vice President of a Municipality. Areas of responsibility: Cultural and Educational Affairs, Women and Family Centers, Drug Addiction Rehabilitation Center, Libraries, Kindergartens. She earned her Ph.D. in Business Administration from Istanbul Aydın University and is lecturer at Istanbul Esenyurt University.

Ivan Bošnjak was born on 4 November 1974 in Zrenjanin. He graduated in 2000 at the Faculty of Veterinary Medicine, University of Belgrade. He obtained his Masters of Science degree in 2010 and the title of Doctor of Veterinary Science in 2016 at the Faculty of Veterinary Medicine, University of Belgrade. Since 2015. he started as associate lecturer in Agricultural college in Sabac, In 2018 become a lecturer in Academia for medical and educational studies in Kruševac, section in Ćuprija. As a candidate of the Serbian Progressive Party, he was elected in 2012 as a deputy in the Assembly of the AP Vojvodina, and then for the mayor of Zrenjanin. During his tenure, Zrenjanin again became a desirable place for life and business, as confirmed by the FDI Magazine Financial Times, 2012 and 2014, as well as the election to chair the Presidency of the Standing Conference of Cities and Municipalities in 2013. After the formation of the Government in 2014, he assumed the position of State Secretary in the Ministry of State Administration and Local Self-Government, and on September 13, 2016 and july 13, 2017, he was reappointed to the same post. During this period he attended several professional development courses - at School of National Defence in Serbia, and international at GCMC Garmisch-Partenkirhen,Germany; EIPA Barcelona, Spain; l'ENA France... He is in charge of monitoring the activities in the fields of the Sector for EU Integration and International Cooperation and the Human and Minority Rights Sector, where he is the president of several working groups for amendments to the legislation. Dr Bosnjak is the president of the Council for professional development of employees in local self-government units since December 2016. Co-chairing the Intergovernmental Mixed Committee for Improving the Position of Minorities with the Republic of Croatia and Romania, as well as the Commission for Coordination of the Process of Permanent Integration of Refugees. He is a member of the Gender Equality Council, the Gender Equality Coordination Body and the Council for Monitoring the Implementation of the Recommendations of the United Nations Human Rights Mechanisms. Speaks English and Russian. Mr Bosnjak is married, and also the father of three children.

Yeliz Demirkıran graduated from the Department of Industrial Engineering at Yaşar University. She completed her Master and PhD degree at Business Administration. She started her academic career as a research assistant in the Department of Industrial Engineering at Yaşar University in 2007 and continues as a lecturer in the Department of Logistics at Yaşar University. Her research areas are warehouse layouts, optimization and multi-criteria decision making.

Hasan Dinçer is a professor of finance at Istanbul Medipol University, Faculty of Economics and Administrative Sciences, Istanbul-Turkey. Dr. Dinçer has BAs in Financial Markets and Investment Management at Marmara University. He received PhD in Finance and Banking with his thesis entitled "The

Effect of Changes on the Competitive Strategies of New Service Development in the Banking Sector". He has work experience in finance sector as portfolio specialist and his major academic studies focusing on financial instruments, performance evaluation, and economics. He is the executive editor of the International Journal of Finance and Banking Studies (IJFBS) and the founder member of the Society for the Study of Business and Finance (SSBF).

İkbal Dizbay, after completing her undergraduate studies at the Faculty of Engineering, Yasar University, completed her Master degree at the Business Administration Department. She received her Ph.D. on Business at Yasar University. She started her academic career as a research assistant at the Yasar University Industrial Engineering Department in 2007 and continued her academic career at Vocational School/ Management and Organization Department as a lecturer. She is currently working as a full-time lecturer at Yasar University Vocational School. Her research interests include transportation management and optimization.

Jelica Eremić-Đođić is Assistant Professor in the Department of Accounting and Business Finance at the University of Education, Sremska Kamenica and in full-time employment as a Chief Expert Associate at EPS Distribution LLC Belgrade. After finishing elementary and high school of economics, she graduated from the Faculty of Economics in Subotica, majoring in "Business Informatics"; science. She completed Master's thesis at the Faculty of Economics in Subotica under the title: "Information Systems in Support of Procurement of Trade Enterprises", and earned a Master's degree in Information Science. She completed my doctoral thesis entitled "AUDIT PROCEDURES FOR EVALUATION OF INTERNAL CONTROLS OF THE INFORMATION SYSTEM OF THE BASIS OF CONTROL OBJECTIVES" at the Faculty of Economics in Subotica in 2013 and obtained the title of Doctor of Economic. Sciences. Research interest: Accounting, financial management and control, internal audit, audit IT audit, forensic audit, Due diligence.

Manuel Antonio Fernández-Villacañas Marín is a Consultant in Logistics & Management at M&M Planning and Project Management, an Associate Professor at the School of Aeronautical and Space Engineering and member of the Research Group in Organization Engineering and Logistics, Technical University of Madrid (Spain), and a Colonel of the Spanish Air Force (R). After finishing his military studies for officer at the Spanish Air Force Academy and was graduated as Lieutenant, he received a Degree in Statistics and Operational Research from the University of Granada (Spain), a Bachelor degree in Economics and Business Sciences from the University of Murcia (Spain), a Masters degree in Security and Defence form the University Complutense of Madrid (Spain), a Masters degree in Business Studies from the IE University (Spain), a Masters degree in Public Management from the IE University (Spain), a Ph.D. in Economic and Business Sciences from the University of Granada (Spain), and a Ph.D. in Administration and Logistics of Security and Defence Systems from the Rey Juan Carlos University (Sapin). He has been director of the Department of Logistics, Economy and Administration of Spanish Air Force Academy, general manager at the Polytechnic University of Cartagena (Spain), academic director for postgraduate and research initiatives of the Executive Logistics Centre (CELOGIS) of Monterrey (Mexico) and of the Metropolitan University of Quito (Ecuador), professor at the Spanish Universities of Granada, Murcia, CEU San Pablo, Catholic San Antonio of Murcia, Polytechnic of Cartagena, Rey Juan Carlos, Alcalá de Henares, ENAE Business School and Air Warfare School of the Spanish Air Force, and out of Spain, among others, at the Technological and Higher Studies Institute of

Monterrey (Mexico), Metropolitan University (Ecuador), University of Monterrey (Mexico), University of Wales (UK), Autonomous University of Yucatán (Mexico), Aristotle University of Thessaloniki (Greece), etc. In the field of logistics he has been director of the Master in Logistics and International Trade (Metropolitan University, Ecuador), International Master in Logistics (University of Monterrey, México), Master in Logistics Management (University of Monterrey, México), and Masters Course in Logistics Management Techniques (Air Warfare School of the Spanish Air Force). He is the author of six technical books and co-author in four others, and of many research articles, monographs and technical-scientific presentations at international conferences in the field of logistics, management and technology.

Yasin Galip Gencer is currently an Associate Professor in Yalova University. He worked on a thesis with his advisor Dr. Ulas Akkucuk, in the Operations Management & Information Systems – PhD program in Boğaziçi University. Before joining this PhD program, he graduated from the Management Department and also has an MBA degree from Bogazici University. He is lecturing in Yalova University in the Department of International Trade and Finance as well. Furthermore, he also has a Leadership Communication certificate from Harvard Business School and has engaged in many business ventures in a family run company specializing in automotive and household appliance sales. Besides extensive business experience, he has also studied in Universiteit de Maastricht within the scope of an Erasmus exchange program.He has participated in a number of international conferences, published in proceedings volumes indexed in CPCI and journals indexed by SSCI and ESCI. His research interests are in forecasting automotive demand, determination of productivity and quality in the automotive sales and service sector.

Sami Gören was graduated from Technical University of Istanbul as a Civil Engineer. He got his MS and PhD degree from Kanazawa University in Japan. He has worked as faculty in the universities of different countries. He has worked as main investigator of a project for waste-water treatment technologies under the fund of TUBITAK (Scientific Board of Turkey) with a number of 109G095, Ankara / Turkey. He has conducted undersea tunnel crossing (MARMARAY) project, as Project Coordinator and Founder of "Project Implementation Unit" for this huge engineering project. He served as consultant to three different ministries (Ministry of Transportation, Ministry of Health and Ministry of Environment). He has taught courses like geotechnical engineering, landfill design and remediation, solid & hazardous waste management, natural disasters, project management, etc. at both graduate and undergraduate level. He is a member of Japanese Society of Civil Engineers, Japanese Society for Soil Mechanics and Foundation Engineering, Saudi Arabian Water Environment Association and Gulf Engineering Forum. He is doing editorial job in the journals such as; CLEAN (Soil, Air, Water), J. of the Air & Waste Management Ass, International Journal of Environmental Sustainability and Green Technologies (IJESGT), etc.

Alfred L. Guiffrida is an Emeritus Associate Professor of Management & Information Systems in the Graduate School of Business Administration at Kent State University, Kent, Ohio. He received his Ph.D. in Industrial Engineering from the State University of New York at Buffalo. His research interests are in supply chain performance measurement, sustainability and last mile delivery.

Gülay Irak was born on 13.04.1982 in Zonguldak. She completed her primary, middle and high school in Zonguldak. She completed her undergraduate education in Zonguldak Karaelmas University Faculty of Economics and Administrative Sciences, Department of Business Administration in 2000-

2004.She graduated from master's degree in 2006 and doctorate in 2013. She started her career as an assistant professor at Bulent Ecevit University in 2014 and still continues her duty at the same university.

Hüsne Karakuş is an undergraduate student of Banking and Insurance department in Istanbul Medipol University. Her research interests are energy economics, wind energy and renewable energy projects.

Özgür Kayapinar is an Assistant Professor in the Uzunköprü Applied Sciences Schooll at Trakya University. She received a BA degree in Business from Cumhuriyet University, MA degree in Akdeniz University and Ph. D degree in Trakya University. His research interest's logistics, logistics service quality, supply chain management, and research, marketing, marketing research, quantitive research methods, statistics, and contemporary marketing research.

Miloš Krstić is research associete who is employed at Faculty of Science and Mathematics in Niš. He earned his MSc and PhD degree at the Faculty of Economics in Niš. He is a member of the editorial board of the *Ekonomika – Journal for Economic Theory and Practice and Social Issues* and a member of publishing council of the scientific journal *Economics of Sustainable Development*. He is an assembly member of the Society of Economists "Економика" Niš and Scientific Society of Economists of Serbia. His main research interests include contemporary economic paradigms (rational choice theory, game theory, social choice theory, rational expectations theory), and macroeconomics. He is an author or coauthor of one book and more than 50 scientific papers.

Heather Lincecum graduated from The University of Edinburgh with a masters in Education and Kent State University with an MBA with a focus on Supply Chain Management. She has interned at the International Centre for Trade and Sustainable Development and is currently working as a Logistics Coordinator for a mercury detecting instrument company.

Fatma Lorcu is working as Professor of Numerical Methods in the Department of Business Administration, Faculty of Economics and Administrative Sciences, at Trakya University, Turkey. She received a BA degree in Mathematics from Yildiz Technical University, Turkey; MA, and Ph. D degree in Numerical Methods from Istanbul University, Turkey. She also worked as a postdoctoral researcher at the University of Wane State, USA. Her research interests are multivariate statistical methods, quantitative decision-making techniques, operations research, SPSS statistical program, and contemporary issues in numerical methods.

Kelly McQuade is an Enterprise Account Manager at MRI Real Estate Software in Solon, Ohio. She received her Master of Business Administration in Management from Kent State University.

Nebojsa Pavlović graduated at Faculty for political sciences. He graduated postgraduate and PhD studies at Faculty for philosophy in Novi Sad. Nebojsa is employed at Faculty for tourism in Vrnjacka Banja which belongs to University in Kragujevac. Also, Nebojsa works as teacher for subjects HR management, Entrepreneurship and management and business communications. His fields of management, entrepreneurship, and education.

Iknur Sayan worked as a manager in various management levels in the health sector for 23 years. Contributed in carrying out TS-EN-ISO 9000 Quality Assurance System activities, and establishing and improving ISO 10002: 2004, OHSAS 18001: 2007, ISO 9001: 2008, 14001: 2004 Environmental Management Systems. Improvement and development of hospitals are among the activities she has carried out. As private sector experience, she held administrative manager positions in the hospital management of Academic Hospital and Istanbul Aydın University Faculty of Dentistry. Her fields of interest are total quality in health, logistics and procurement management in hospitals, management ethics, business management, management organization, strategic management in health institutions, human resources management, and organizational behavior. She completed her master's degrees in nursing management at Marmara University Institute of Health Sciences and in Health Management at Bahçeşehir University Institute of Social Sciences. She earned her Ph.D. in Business Administration from İstanbul Aydın University and is currently a lecturer at İstanbul Kent University.

Antoaneta Stoyanova studied Commodity Science at the Univesity of Economics - Varna. Since 2002 she is an auditor on food quality and safety standards among which ISO 9001, ISO 22000 and HACCP. In 2006 Stoyanova received her PhD in Integrated Food Quality and Safety Management Systems from the University of Economics - Varna, Bulgaria. Since 2012 she has been working as a lecturer at the Department of Commodity Science of the University of Economics – Varna. Together with his teaching activities, he worked as a consultant in the development and implementation of Management Systems and Internal Auditor in Business.

Gözde Gülseven Ubay is an undergraduate student of Economics and Finance Department in Istanbul Medipol University. Energy economics, wind energy and renewable energy projects are among her research interests.

Gülsüm Sena Uluer is an undergraduate student of Business Administration department in İstanbul Medipol University. Her research interests lie in energy economics and macroeconomics.

Serhat Yüksel is associate professor of finance in İstanbul Medipol University. Before this position, he worked as a senior internal auditor for seven years in Finansbank, Istanbul-Turkey and 1 year in Konya Food and Agriculture University as an assistant professor. Dr. Yüksel has a BS in Business Administration (in English) from Yeditepe University (2006) with full scholarship. He got his master degree from the Economics Department in Boğaziçi University (2008). He also has a PhD in Banking from Marmara University (2015). His research interests lie in banking, finance and financial crisis. He has more than 70 publications (books, book chapters, scientific articles, etc.).

Index

N

O

P

R

S

T

U

V

W

Y

www.ingramcontent.com/pod-product-compliance
Lightning Source LLC
LaVergne TN
LVHW062113300926
849161LV00010B/2453
* 9 7 8 1 7 9 9 8 4 6 0 1 7 *